Birding
Texas

Roland H. Wauer
and Mark A. Elwonger

FALCON®

HELENA, MONTANA

A FALCON GUIDE ®

Falcon® is continually expanding its list of recreational guidebooks. All books include detailed descriptions, accurate maps, and all the information necessary for enjoyable trips. You can order extra copies of this book and get information and prices for other Falcon guidebooks by writing Falcon, P.O. Box 1718, Helena, MT 59624 or calling toll-free 1-800-582-2665. Also, please ask for a free copy of our current catalog. Visit our website at http://www.falconguide.com.

Printed in the United States of America.

Cover photo: Altamira Oriole, South Texas, by Steve Bentsen.

Back cover photo: Great Kiskadee, by Steve Bentsen.

All black-and-white photos by Roland H. Wauer, except where noted.

Library of Congress Cataloging-in-Publication Data

Wauer, Roland H.
    Birding Texas / by Ro Wauer & Mark Elwonger.
        p.   cm.
    ISBN 1-56044-617-X (paperback)
    1. Bird watching—Texas—Guidebooks. 2. Birding sites—Texas—Guidebooks.
    3. Texas—Guidebooks.   I. Elwonger, Mark, 1956-   II. Title.
    QL684.T4W376 1998
    598' .07'234764—dc21   97-43351
                                                               CIP

CAUTION

Outdoor recreational activities are by their very nature potentially hazardous. All participants in such activities must assume the responsibility for their own actions and safety. The information contained in this guidebook cannot replace sound judgment and good decision-making skills, which help reduce risk exposure, nor does the scope of this book allow for disclosure of all the potential hazards and risks involved in such activities.

Learn as much as possible about the outdoor recreational activities in which you participate, prepare for the unexpected; and be cautious. The reward will be a safer and more enjoyable experience.

 Text pages printed on recycled paper.

We dedicate this book to Greg Lasley, friend and colleague, who, through his constant efforts and kind but firm personality, has made Texas ornithology and the hobby of birding a legitimate and highly respected pursuit.

Contents

Panhandle and Western Plains Region

Edwards Plateau Region

Northern Plains Region

Central Plains Region

Upper Coast Region

Coastal Bend Region

Texas Birding Regions

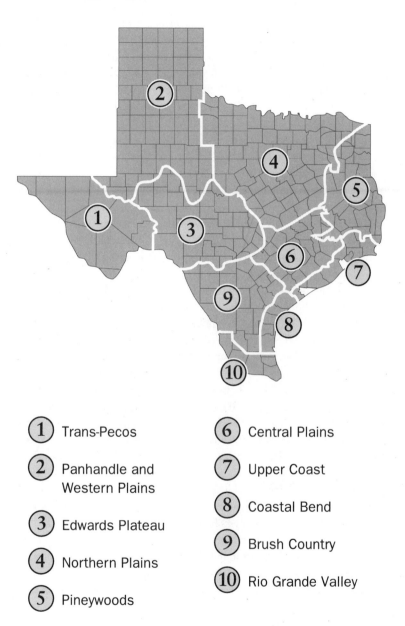

1. Trans-Pecos
2. Panhandle and Western Plains
3. Edwards Plateau
4. Northern Plains
5. Pineywoods
6. Central Plains
7. Upper Coast
8. Coastal Bend
9. Brush Country
10. Rio Grande Valley

Foreword

Birds are one of Texas's greatest natural assets and helping bird watchers find these wonderful creatures will certainly benefit their conservation. Long overdue, Ro Wauer's *Birding Texas* fully meets the needs of traveling bird watchers as it includes a broad spectrum of the birds that one is likely to see at all the top Texas birding sites year-round, in summer and in winter. Until now, many Texas bird books have dealt with bird identification, for example Roger Tory Peterson's classic *A Field Guide to the Birds of Texas,* completed in 1960 for the Texas Game and Fish Commission and the National Audubon Society. Other great books on status and distribution include Harry C. Oberholser's two-volume thesis, *The Bird Life of Texas,* completed posthumously by Edgar Kincaid, or the two American Birding Association guidebooks and Ed Kutac's *Birder's Guide to Texas.*

I am most excited that 67 of the 210 sites in *Birding Texas* are state parks. Although some of the state parks, such as Bentsen–Rio Grande Valley, Lost Maples, Choke Canyon, and Davis Mountains, have long been recognized as choice birding sites, many of our other state parks and wildlife management areas also offer worthwhile birding experiences. Some of these are new and have not yet received adequate birding to establish their reputation; this book will undoubtedly provide the necessary incentive.

Birding Texas also includes a special section on nonpublic birding sites, such as the King and Kenedy ranches and several Nature Conservancy of Texas sites, areas that require preliminary contacts. Too often these nonpublic sites are ignored. Yet, the numerous private ranches and sanctuaries and Nature Conservancy preserves often contain magnificent habitats and significant bird life. These sites also offer the birder opportunities not often available in the more public areas.

The timing of this publication fits well with the 75th anniversary of the Texas Parks System and the opening of our Great Texas Coastal Birding Trail. We hope to take advantage of this excellent book as we extend our efforts at environmental education opportunities within all the Texas state parks and wildlife management areas.

Birding Texas comes at a time when the entire state, from legislators to local chambers of commerce, has begun to recognize the value of nature tourism, which is the fastest growing segment of the travel business worldwide. Texas is uniquely positioned to provide some of the best outdoor experiences anywhere. Birding, in fact, now contributes roughly as much each year to the Texas economy as both hunting and fishing combined.

I am pleased that Ro Wauer asked me to write the foreword to this book. Ro has been one of the most respected naturalists in the state for many years. I have used his books on Big Bend National Park—*Naturalist's Big Bend* and *A Field Guide to Birds of the Big Bend*— time and again. They are true classics that provide concise and up-to-date information on that great national park. *A Field Guide to Birds of the Big Bend* was revised for the third time in 1996, and Ro tells me that his *Naturalist's Big Bend* is currently being revised and expanded, as well.

Whatever your outdoor pursuit, be it hunting, fishing, camping, hiking, canoeing, or birding, I think you will be glad to have a copy of *Birding Texas* in your gear.

—*Andrew Sansom*
Executive Director, Texas Parks and Wildlife Department

Acknowledgments

This book would not have been possible without considerable help from dozens of friends and colleagues. First and foremost, we thank Greg Lasley for providing us with up-to-date information on the status of Texas's many rare birds, advice about various sites, and his continuous support for this project.

We also thank Andy Sansom, Executive Director of the Texas Parks and Wildlife Department, for writing the foreword for this book. His interest in Texas birds and in this project is much appreciated.

In addition, numerous other individuals have helped at various stages, either by providing help in the field or by reviewing a Status and Distribution Checklist for their area or for one or more of the 120 site descriptions. Their counsel was essential and is very much appreciated. To the few individuals who provided on-site assistance, going out of their way to show us their areas, we owe a great deal. These individuals include Lorie Black for Abilene; Kelly Bryan for Big Bend Ranch; Mary Bush for the Waco area; Andy Donnelly for Austin East; Bill Graber for Big Thicket and Beaumont; Lily Engels and James Reveley for San Antonio; Greg Kiernan and J. W. Sifford for the Fort Worth area; Bonnie McKinney for Black Gap; Jim Peterson for the Dallas area; Joel Rease for Buffalo Lake, Palo Duro Canyon, and Caprock Canyons; Chuck Sexton for Balcones-Canyonlands; Ken Steigman for the Heard Museum; and Jim and Lynne Weber for Austin and Alcoa/Granger.

In addition, a select few individuals reviewed pertinent sections of the Status and Distribution Checklist. We thank Kelly Bryan and John Sproul for Trans-Pecos, Ken Seyffert for Panhandle and Western Plains, Ross Dawkins for Edwards Plateau, Mike Patterson and Ross Rassmussen for Northern Plains, Bill Graber for Pineywoods, Brush Freeman for Central Plains, David Bradford for Upper Coast, Arlie and Mel Cooksey for Coastal Bend, Paul Palmer for Brush Country, and Brad McKinney for Rio Grande Valley.

Finally, the following individuals (listed alphabetically) helped with initial area contacts and/or chapter reviews: Mark Abolafia-Rosenzweig for Palmetto; Ron Alton for Big Spring; Jeanne Ansley for Daingerfield; Richard Antonette for Brazoria; Mike Austin for Armand Bayou; Billy Baker for Dinosaur Valley; David Baker for Big Thicket; Ken Benab for Monahans Sandhills; Steve Benn for Boca Chica; Marvin Berry for Atlanta; Steve Best for Davy Crockett; Betty Biggs for Meridian; Nancy Bird for Angelina; Ann Birny for Armand Bayou; Lorie Black for Abilene and Lake Colorado City; David Blankenship for Santa Ana; Mike Bransford for Wright Patman Lake; David Brotherton for Daingerfield and Lake O' The Pines; Ellen Bucham for Martin Dies; Mike Buchanan for Lake Texoma; Mary Bush for Mother Neff and Waco; Dawn Carrie for Sam Houston and W. G. Jones; Ross Carrie for Sabine; Don Clapp for Muleshoe; Charlie Clark for

Rockport-Fulton; Julia Coleman for Forth Worth Nature Center; Rob Comstock for Sheldon Lake; Arlie and Mel Cooksey for Corpus Christi and Padre Island; Tim Cooper for Laguna Atascosa; Peggy Corder for Tyler; Shirley Cravens for Copper Breaks; Bud and Mary Cummings for Lake Arrowhead; David Dauphin for Armand Bayou, Houston East, and Houston West; James Davis for W. G. Jones; Ed Day for Lake Meredith; Angela Deaton for Galveston Island; Shirley Dent for Lake Somerville; Rudy Dominguez for Casa Blanca; Andy Donnally for Austin East; Charles Easley for Cleburne, Mineral Wells, and Lake Whitney; Carolyn Eddy for Dinosaur Valley; James Edwards for Mineral Wells; John Ellisor for Lake Somerville; Lily Engles for San Antonio; Lee Escamilla for Lake Texana; Delores Fenton for Pedernales Falls; Ross Ferguson for Enchanted Rock; Diana Finley for Colorado City; Tom Fisher for Fort Parker; Mark Flippo for Big Bend; Brush Freeman for Chapter 2 and Alcoa/Granger, Attwater, Bastrop, Martin Dies, Red Bluff, and Lake Tawakoni; John Freeman for Seminole Canyon; Marsha Freeman for Cedar Hill; Jim Gallagher for Chaparral; Brent Giezentanner for Aransas; Bill Graber for Big Thicket, High Island/Bolivar, and Sea Rim; Michael Griswold for Fort Worth Nature Center; Susan Grubb for Palo Duro Canyon; Wayne Haley for South Llano River; Carl Haller for Hagerman; Don Hathorn for Alexander Deussen; Steve Hawkins for San Antonio and Friedrich; Roy Heideman for Lost Maples; David Heinicke for Brazos Bend; Dick Heller for Falcon Dam; Petra Hockey for Choke Canyon, Goose Island, Lake Texana, Matagorda Island, Port Lavaca, and Port O'Connor; Buddy Hollis for Village Creek; Scott Holt for Mustang Island and Port Aransas; Bob Hopkins for Copper Breaks; Eric Hopson for Santa Ana; Karen Howard for Hagerman; Bill Hughes for Abilene; Rick Hughes for Caddo Lake; Geoffrey Hulse for Caprock Canyons; Harold Ives for Lake O' The Pines; Bob Johnson for Hueco Tanks; Debbie Johnson for Jones State Forest; Al Jones for San Bernard; Greg Keiran for Lake Benbrook, Fort Worth Nature Center, and Village Creek; Paula Kennedy for Armand Bayou; Richard Kinney for Lake Tawakoni; Paul Kisel for Inks Lake; Mike Krahn for Brownwood; Mike Lange for Brazoria and San Bernard; Martha Laskoskie for B. A. Steinhagen; Henry Leal, Jr., for Casa Blanca; Chris Lena for Martin Dies; Mark Lockwood for Big Bend Ranch and Meridian; David Maple for Hagerman; Wayne McAlister for Aransas and Matagorda Island; Richard McCamant for Guadalupe Mountains (photo); Katherin McCoy for Kerrville; Kelly McDowell for Anahuac; Debbie and Terry McKee for Lake Arrowhead; Bonnie McKinney for Black Gap and Marathon; Brad McKinney for Brownsville, Falcon Dam, and San Ygnacio; Dorothy Metzler for Caddo Lake; Charles Mills for Wright Patman Lake; Linda Mitchell for Fossil Rim; Mike Moncus for Bastrop/Buescher; Michael Morrow for Attwater; Kenneth Nanney for Possum Kingdom; Orvaline Okerstrom for Abilene; Brent Ortego for Chaparral, Guadalupe Delta, Palacios, and Martin Dies; Rey Ortiz for Bentsen–Rio Grande; David Owens for Cleburne; Jay and Laura Packer for Abilene; Paul Palmer for Kingsville and Cayo del Grullo; David Parsons for Sabine River Authority; James

Paton for El Paso; Dwight Peake for Galveston; Jim Petersen for Cedar Hill, Lewisville, Plano, Southside, and White Rock Lake; Wes Phillips for Lake Meredith; Jerald Rashall for Village Creek; Joel Rease for Buffalo Lake, Palo Duro Canyon, and Caprock Canyons; Debbie Reid for Friedrich; Pat Reinken for High Island; James Reveley for San Antonio; David Riskind for Big Bend Ranch; Frank Roberts for Garner; Bob Rogers for Lake Marvin; Terry Rossignol for Attwater; Steve Runnels for Heard Museum; Susan Rust for Friedrich; Chip Ruthven for Chaparral; Rod Rylander for Rockport-Fulton; Lynne Salmon for Lake Arrowhead; Monica Sanders for Cleburne; Tom Schneider for Brazoria; Larry Scruggs for Palo Duro Canyon; Laverne Scruggs for Mustang Island; Willie Sekula for San Antonio; Ken Seyffert for Copper Breaks, Lake Marvin, Rita Blanca, and Palo Duro Canyon; Chuck Sexton for Austin and Balcones-Canyonlands; Cliff Shackleford for Angelina; Reynaldo Sierra for Hueco Tanks; Rick Smith for Tyler; Rick Speer for Big Boggy, Brazoria, and San Bernard; John Sproul for El Paso, Franklin Mountains, and Hueco Tanks; Carmine Stahl for Jesse H. Jones; Cliff Stogner for Muleshoe and Lubbock; Lee Stone for Wild Basin; Murt Sullivan for Village Creek; Glen and Jimmie Swartz for Lake Corpus Christi; Scott Tackett for Benbrook Lake; Susie Taylor for Brazos Bend; David Towers for Lake Whitney; Erik Tschanz for Sea Rim; David Turner for Copper Breaks; Bob Valen for Big Thicket; Christie Vogel for Franklin Mountains; Gary Waggerman for Boca Chica; Fred and Gwen Wallace for Chalk Bluff; Dennis Walsh for Fairfield Lake; Jim and Lynne Weber for Marathon; Steve West for Guadalupe Mountains; Hugh Carter Whatley for Corpus Christi; Karen White for Plano; Matt White for Cooper Lake and Lake Tawakoni; John Whittle for Sea Rim; Sue Wiedenfeld for Kerrville; Jimmie Willhelm for Longhorn Caverns; Frances Williams for Monahans Sandhills; Rebecca Williams for Dallas Nature Center; and Betty Joy With for Big Thicket.

Last, but certainly not of lesser importance, I want to thank my wife, Betty, for her constant support and for putting up with my many trips away from home during the 18 months that it took to complete the site visits for this book.

—*Ro Wauer*

Introduction

Texas has long been recognized as America's number one birding state. More bird species have been recorded in Texas—605 as of October 1997—than in any other state; this represents approximately 75 percent of all bird species that have been recorded in the continental United States. Almost 3 dozen of the 605 Texas species cannot normally be found elsewhere north of the Texas-Mexico border.

Because of this large number of Texas specialties, the state has become a magnet for birders from all across North America and throughout the world. In fact, a comprehensive survey of birders in 1991 showed that Texas is the most popular birding destination worldwide. It therefore is only logical that this book was prepared. *Birding Texas* gives birders the best guidance possible for finding all of the Texas specialties, as well as additional "key birds"—those other species that birders most want to see.

Because of Texas's popularity bird-wise, the state also leads the world in the number of birding events, each designed to commemorate a specific bird species or to provide the visiting birder with special, birding-related activities. Annual Texas celebrations include the Eagle Fest at Emory every January; the Crane Fest at Big Spring in February; the Whooping Crane Winter Bird Festival at Rockport and Fulton every other February; the Attwater Prairie-Chicken Festival in Eagle Lake each March; in April the Bluebird Festival at Wills Point and the Migration Celebration at Clute; the Hummer/Bird Celebration in Rockport-Fulton each September; and the Rio Grande Valley Birding Festival, held in Harlingen in November.

Texans also invented the concept of the "birding trail." Established in 1995, the Great Texas Coastal Birding Trail links about 200 sites along its 600-mile route from the Louisiana border to the lower Rio Grande Valley. Further details about this trail are available in Chapter 5. The Great Texas Birding Classic, founded in 1997, is an annual week-long competition in which teams of birders travel the Texas coast, vying to identify as many bird species as they can. This birding tournament, held in mid-April, is designed to raise money to support bird conservation projects statewide. All birding teams are invited to compete. Further information on both the trail and the competition can be obtained from the Outreach and Promotions Program of the Texas Parks and Wildlife Department, 4200 Smith School Road, Austin, TX 78744-3292; phone, 512-389-4772; fax, 512-389-4388.

Because Texas is a birding paradise, the names of many Texas locations have become imprinted on birders—High Island, Aransas, Santa Ana, and the Chisos Mountains are all part of the Texas birding mystique. Other popular areas include Laguna Atascosa, Bentsen–Rio Grande Valley State Park, Falcon Dam, the Texas Hill Country, the Davis Mountains, and the Guadalupe Mountains. These sites are all included in this guide, as are many additional sites that offer potential though they may not often be birded by keen birders.

HOW TO USE THIS GUIDE

The purpose of this guide is to help birders locate all the birds in Texas. *Birding Texas* helps the birder zero in on the most productive birding sites.

All bird names used in this book were derived from *The A.O.U. Check-list of North American Birds—Sixth Edition* (1983), and 1985, 1987, 1989, 1991, 1993, 1996, and 1997 supplements.

Birding Texas is divided into six chapters and three appendices as follows:

Chapter 1, "Planning a Texas Birding Trip," tells you when to bird, what to wear, and how to go about finding a place to stay, and warns you of possible hazards. The chapter also provides a checklist of essential supplies to bring with you, and a list of state birding contacts, including internet addresses and where to find rare bird alerts.

Chapter 2, "Texas Landscapes," orients the reader to the state's varied biogeographic regions, including its key environmental communities, and provides a discussion of bird migration and seasonal patterns.

Chapter 3, "Gallery of Texas Specialties," is a portfolio of 32 species that normally occur only in Texas. Each of these is illustrated with a pen-and-ink sketch by artist Mimi Hoppe Wolf. Each is captioned with information on the bird's preferred habitat, season, and the "best bet" birding sites for finding that particular species.

The Texas specialty birds include only those that can dependably be found in the state. Several other birds were excluded from this list because they are less dependable, such as Yellow-green Vireo and Blue Bunting, or because they also occur and nest elsewhere in the United States. Examples of the latter include Groove-billed Ani and Cave Swallow, species that usually appear on a birder's want list for Texas.

Chapter 4, "Texas's Best Birding Areas," details Texas's 120 best birding areas. This chapter is the heart of *Birding Texas*. It is divided into 10 regions: Trans-Pecos, Panhandle and Western Plains, Edwards Plateau, Northern Plains, Pineywoods, Central Plains, Upper Coast, Coastal Bend, Brush Country, and Rio Grande Valley. Each regional section is introduced by a map of the region, and each regional map is in turn keyed to maps of the individual sites.

The individual site maps, which accompany each description, are meant to show the route to the birding sites described. Letters of the alphabet, tied to specific locations described in the birding strategies, are used on the site maps to help pinpoint these places. The maps have been drawn to show as much detail as is possible in a book of this size and scope, but we are limited, for the most part, to showing major features. We strongly recommend that the reader travel with a comprehensive Texas map or state atlas, to provide further detail during a trip to any of the sites. Texas is a huge state and a single complete map or collection of maps will provide a better perspective on the locations and distances involved in a particular trip. The Texas Department of Transportation has prepared an Official

Travel Map, available at any of the state's 12 Travel Information Centers or by writing to the Texas Department of Transportation, Travel and Information Division, P.O. Box 5064, Austin, TX 78763, or calling 800-452-9292.

Each site description is divided into nine categories, as follows:

The **Site name** and, in many cases, the names of a few subsites are given.

The **Habitats** category includes all the habitats within and adjacent to the site. In naming the habitats, we have tried to select names which describe the habitat in simple, descriptive terms, for example Gulf (of Mexico), estuary, beach, dune, wetland, salt marsh, mud flat, playa, coastal prairie, coastal scrub, lake, pond, river, creek, floodplain, riparian, pinyon-juniper woodland, juniper-oak woodland, deciduous forest, Tamaulipan scrub, desert scrub, pasture, cropland, cliff, and park. To help the user better understand a particular unique environment, habitat names will sometimes be more specific. For example, perennial stream, sotol grassland, and pine-cypress woodland in the Chisos Mountains; rice fields along the Gulf Coast; and wooded scarps in the Panhandle.

A Glossary of Habitats and Habitat Terms

biogeography geography based on biological components (flora and fauna)

break steep (usually) wooded canyon along the edge of an escarpment

climax mature vegetation, usually reached through successional stages

cropland agricultural land of various kinds

desert scrub brushy, rather dense vegetation found in the Chihuahuan Desert

mud flat muddy place, often seasonal, occurring along lakes, rivers, and streams or along bays or estuaries

oak motte a fairly small and dense stand of oak trees; usually isolated on an open prairie

prairie usually short, natural grasslands that may occur along the coast or inland

riparian vegetation (often dense) that occurs along rivers and streams

savannah a distinct community composed of grasses with scattered trees and/or shrubs

spoil bank pile of dredged materials deposited along a man-made channel

stock tank depression dug by ranchers to catch rainfall for watering stock

Tamaulipan scrub a distinct brushy community named for the state of Tamaulipas in northeastern Mexico

The Anhinga is commonly found on Texas rivers and ponds.

The **Key birds** section includes only those species that a birder might most want to see; these do not necessarily include the birds that are most representative of the site. The key birds are divided into three groups: (1) year-round, those that are present during all 12 months; (2) summer, nesting species, and post-nesting birds that can occur from April through the summer months, and (3) winter, those residents and visitors that can be expected during the winter. All of the specialty birds, those most sought-after of Texas species included in our Gallery (Chapter 3), show up in boldface when mentioned. Closely related species, such as Lesser and Common Nighthawks or Northern Cardinal and Pyrrhuloxia, are mentioned to point out that both are present, even though one of the birds may not be as interesting as the other.

Best times to bird. The best time to bird in Texas is usually the spring, when neotropical migrants pass through and (at least in the south) when nesting activities are most obvious. However, many of the key birds may also occur at other times of year; examples include Colima Warbler in the Chisos Mountains during summer, migrating raptors along the central Gulf Coast in late September, or Whooping Crane at Aransas National Wildlife Refuge in winter. This section highlights the activity you can expect to find, whatever the season.

Birding strategies is the meat and potatoes of the site descriptions. This section includes the details of how best to bird a site to find all the key birds and other representative species. All the locations are keyed to pertinent locator maps with numbers. This section does not take into consideration, however, unexpected birds that may suddenly appear in the area. It therefore behooves the birder to check the Texas or local birders' Rare Bird Alert (RBA) early on (phone numbers and internet addresses are listed in Chapter 1). If you find a bird that is far out of range, or a "review" species, you can use the same RBA number to place your finding on the hotline for other birders. See Appendix B for details on how to report unexpected species.

A number of terms related to status and distribution are used throughout the site descriptions (Chapter 4) and in the Status and Distribution Checklist (Chapter 6). Definitions of these terms are included in the introductory paragraphs of both chapters. A few other terms are listed below.

Some Terms Used in *Birding Texas*

cluster term sometimes used to describe several red-cockaded woodpecker nesting sites near one another

endangered an official designation of the U.S. Fish and Wildlife Service, to provide protection for a species at risk of extinction

fallout a phenomenon in which migrating birds literally fall out of the sky after a long, tiring (usually overnight) flight; occurs regularly in spring along the Gulf Coast

guzzler an above-ground watering device, designed to catch rainfall or connected to a spring; wildlife drink from guzzlers

hacking method of introducing wildlife (usually young of endangered species) to their environment; includes feeding of caged individuals until they are able to forage on their own

lek display site used by a courting prairie-chicken

life list a list, kept by birders, of the species of birds they have seen in their lives

lifer refers to a bird seen for the first time by a birder and placed on that birder's life list

passerine any of the perching songbirds

peeps small sandpipers, such as Semipalmated, Western, and Least

playa an undrained basin that becomes a shallow lake during rainy seasons

post-nesting after nesting; refers to birds that wander to new locations when their nesting is completed

resaca a pond left by a meandering river

review species term used by the Texas Bird Records Committee for birds that need further documentation, usually vagrants

waders water birds with long legs, such herons and egrets

Birders scope a flooded rice field in Calhoun County.

Records of review species. Where appropriate, a section listing species that have been recorded in the area only once or a few times has been included. This section helps clarify the status of the various oddities that have occurred within the area.

Directions are given to guide you to each site from a key nearby landmark. When you use these in conjunction with the regional maps and the more detailed site maps we've provided, you should have no problem finding the site. In addition to interstate, U.S., and state highways, a variety of secondary roads must be used to reach the birding sites in this book. These roads are referred to in the text with abbreviations. They include farm-to-market roads (FM) and, to a lesser extent, ranch roads (R). Roads built and maintained in the state parks are referred to as park roads (PR). The roads to birding sites in the national forests are forest roads (FR). In the text, state highways are preceded with the letters SH.

As mentioned above, take along a state road map to help you find your way between sites.

General information contains details about the site, suggestions that may be helpful in getting around or enjoying other facets of the area, or suggestions with your comfort in mind. For instance, Gulf Coast sites may include a warning about the abundance of mosquitoes and the need for repellent.

Additional help includes four categories: the location (keyed to the Texas Official Travel Map grid); the nearest food, gas, and lodging and camping facilities; and places you can contact for more information.

Chapter 5 includes a discussion of the Great Texas Coastal Birding Trail, including a map of the entire coastal route.

Chapter 6, the Status and Distribution Checklist, includes most of the 605 Texas birds. The reader can use this list as both a personal checklist and as an aid in trip planning.

A list of selected references includes the principal books and articles that might be useful on a Texas birding trip or for reading about the various sites visited.

Appendix A, "Pelagic Birding in Texas Waters," provides an update on what species and times of the year pelagic birds can be expected offshore, and how interested birders can get out to see them. Appendix B, "Texas Bird Records Committee," includes lists of the "review" species for which the committee requests sighting reports. Appendix C, "Contacts," lists the addresses and the telephone and fax numbers of the information sources listed at the end of each site description.

A complete index to all the birds is included to help the user identify preferred birds and birding sites.

BIRDING ETHICS

Birders sometimes forget their manners when chasing a new or rare bird. They may trespass onto private property, risk their well-being for the sake of another lifer, or, worst of all, threaten the bird and even its nesting site.

Everyone who enjoys birds and birding must always respect wildlife, its environment, and the rights of others. In any conflict of interest between birds and birders, the welfare of the birds and their environment comes first.

The American Birding Association has developed this set of Birding Ethics. Read it before birding Texas.

CODE OF BIRDING ETHICS

1   Promote the welfare of birds and their environment.

1(a) Support the protection of important bird habitat.

1(b) To avoid stressing birds or exposing them to danger, exercise restraint and caution during observation, photography, sound recording, or filming.

Limit the use of recordings and other methods of attracting birds, and never use such methods in heavily birded areas or for attracting any species that is Threatened, Endangered, or of Special Concern, or is rare in your local area.

Keep well back from nests and nesting colonies, roosts, display areas, and important feeding sites. In such sensitive areas, if there is a need for extended observation, photography, filming, or recording, try to use a blind or hide, and take advantage of natural cover.

Use artificial light sparingly for filming or photography, especially for close-ups.

1(c) Before advertising the presence of a rare bird, evaluate the potential for disturbance to the bird, its surroundings, and other people in the area, and proceed only if access can be controlled, disturbance can be minimized, and permission has been obtained from private landowners. The sites of rare nesting birds should be divulged only to the proper conservation authorities.

1(d) Stay on roads, trails, and paths where they exist; otherwise keep habitat disturbance to a minimum.

2 Respect the law and the rights of others.

2(a) Do not enter private property without the owner's explicit permission.

2(b) Follow all laws, rules, and regulations governing use of roads and public areas, both at home and abroad.

2(c) Practice common courtesy in contacts with other people. Your exemplary behavior will generate goodwill with birders and nonbirders alike.

3 Ensure that feeders, nest structures, and other artificial bird environments are safe.

3(a) Keep dispensers, water, and food clean and free of decay or disease. It is important to feed birds continually during harsh weather.

3(b) Maintain and clean nest structures regularly.

3(c) If you are attracting birds to an area, ensure the birds are not exposed to predation from cats and other domestic animals, or dangers posed by artificial hazards.

4 Group birding, whether organized or impromptu, requires special care.
Each individual in the group, in addition to the obligations spelled out in Items #1 and #2, has responsibilities as a Group Member.

4(a) Respect the interests, rights, and skills of fellow birders, as well as those of people participating in other legitimate outdoor activities. Freely share your knowledge and experience except where code 1(c) applies. Be especially helpful to beginning birders.

4(b) If you witness unethical birding behavior, assess the situation and intervene if you think it prudent. When interceding, inform the person(s) of the inappropriate action and attempt, within reason, to have it stopped. If the behavior continues, document it and notify the appropriate individuals or organizations.

Group Leader Responsibilities (amateur and professional trips and tours).

4(c) Be an exemplary ethical role model for the group. Teach through word and example.

4(d) Keep groups to a size that limits impact on the environment and does not interfere with others using the same area.

4(e) Ensure everyone in the group knows of and practices this code.

4(f) Learn and inform the group of any special circumstances applicable to the areas being visited (e.g., no tape recording allowed).

4(g) Acknowledge that professional tour companies bear a special responsibility to place the welfare of birds and the benefits of public knowledge ahead of the company's commercial interests. Ideally, leaders should keep track of tour sightings, document unusual occurrences, and submit records to appropriate organizations.

The Code of Birding Ethics is a product of the American Birding Association, P.O. Box 6599, Colorado Springs, CO 80934-6599; 800-859-2473 or 719-578-1614; fax, 800-246-3329 or 719-578-1480; e-mail, member@aba.org.

1. Planning a Texas Birding Trip

Birding is excellent in Texas year-round, but it is important to time your Texas birding trip to find the species you most want to see. You will not find Whooping Crane in late spring or summer, or Colima or Golden-cheeked Warblers in winter. Although the majority of the Rio Grande Valley specialties are year-round residents, the greatest number of bird species is present in the state during the spring migration, especially from mid-April to early May.

The best time to bird Texas, therefore, is April through early May, once the neotropical specialties, such as the Black-capped Vireo and Colima and Golden-cheeked Warblers, have arrived, usually by early to mid-April. It's also a good time for migrants. The best birding sites for finding large numbers of species in spring are along the Gulf Coast, where one can easily find 75 to 125 species in a day; one could possibly find 150 to 200 species or more during a well-planned 24-hour marathon.

Birders often neglect summertime opportunities because of the heat, the humidity, and the mosquitoes. But lingering northbound peeps and other shorebirds nearly collide with southbound post-breeders; therefore, birders who venture out to mud flats in summer will be rewarded with shorebird sightings in all parts of the state.

Summer and early fall offshore in the Gulf of Mexico are good times for birders—seas are calmest and storm-petrels, shearwaters, boobies, and pelagic terns frequent the deep blue waters off the continental shelf. The best way to see these birds is to join other birders on a chartered boat that goes to deeper waters. Although Leach's Storm-Petrel is still regarded by the Texas Bird Record Committee as a "review" species, Band-rumped Storm-Petrel, Audubon's Shearwater, Brown Booby, and Bridled Tern (all considered review species until recently) are regularly seen on most deep-water pelagic trips organized from Port O'Connor. In fact, between May and early September, Band-rumped Storm-Petrels are hard to miss in these waters. The pelagic trips are also fun because lots of surprises, including sperm whales, tropicbirds, and petrels, await birders offshore. For more information on Texas pelagic trips, see Appendix A. For weather information, internet users can visit:

http://www.rap.ucar.edu/weather/satellite/latest_AUS.jpg for satellite images of Texas

http://www.rap.ucar.edu/weather/radar.html for real-time weather data

http://www.intellicast.com/weather/intl/cbsat/ for timely weather information on the Gulf of Mexico.

Late winter (February through March) is a good time for a birding trip. Whooping Crane are still present on their wintering grounds at Aransas National Wildlife Refuge, waterfowl are abundant in the bays, tens of thousands of geese and Sandhill Crane are still present on the coastal plains, and the resident Rio

Grande Valley birds are beginning to sing. This also is when some of the "unexpected" Mexican birds, such as Roadside Hawk, Collared Forest-Falcon, Ruddy Ground-Dove, Ruddy Quail-Dove, Rose-throated Becard, Masked Tityra, White-throated Robin, and Blue Bunting, can appear. In winter several warm-water reservoirs, used for cooling power plants, are worth checking. These newly developed habitats attract an amazing variety of water birds, including pelagics and other species not normally expected so far inland.

A fall visit offers most of the same Rio Grande Valley resident specialties, as well as post-nesting Mexican birds, although they are less active and may be more difficult to find. A few "unexpected" Mexican birds recorded in the region in the fall include Jabiru, Roadside and Short-tailed Hawks, Elegant Trogon, and Gray Silky-flycatcher.

The numbers of migrating raptors that can be seen from a few key sites in the fall can truly be spectacular. Texas's hawkwatch sites include Devil's Backbone near Wimberly in the Hill Country, Daingerfield in northeast Texas, Smith Point near Anahuac, Hazel Bazemore County Park west of Corpus Christi, and Santa Ana National Wildlife Refuge and Bentsen–Rio Grande Valley State Park in the Rio Grande Valley.

Hazel Bazemore Park is undoubtedly the best of these, with peak flights from September 22 to 25. It is estimated that 95 percent of North America's Broad-winged Hawk population funnels through this area each fall. More than 100,000 raptors have been counted at this chokepoint during a single day. Sometimes continuous flights more than 40 miles long are observed. Recorded regularly in moderate numbers are Swainson's, Red-tailed, Cooper's, and Sharp-shinned Hawks; Mississippi Kite; American Kestrel; Peregrine Falcon; and smaller numbers of Ferruginous, Harris's, Red-shouldered, and Zone-tailed Hawks; Bald and Golden Eagles; Osprey; Merlin; and White-tailed and Swallow-tailed Kites.

ADDITIONAL BIRDING INFORMATION

A great deal of information on Texas birds has been documented. Harry C. Oberholser's two-volume book, *The Bird Life of Texas*, summarized all that was known about Texas's birds to the time of its publication (1974). There have been innumerable publications on Texas birds since then. The reference section of this book includes the most worthwhile publications, some of which you will want to purchase. Also check the Texas Rare Bird Alert (RBA), by phone or through the internet, to find out if any truly unexpected species have been reported. The following RBA numbers and/or internet addresses are available:

Statewide: RBA, 713-964-5867; internet address: http://www.birdware.com/lists/rba/_us/tx/statewide/rba.htm

additional web site: http://www.io.com/-pdhulce/txrba

Abilene (Big Country Audubon Society): 915-691-8981

Austin area: RBA, 512-926-8751; internet address: Birding in Central Texas web site: http://www.onr/user/andyd/Birding.html.

Travis Audubon Society web site: http://www.onr.com/user/audubon/

Beaumont area: RBA, 409-769-4029

Corpus Christi area: RBA, 512-265-0377

Lubbock area: RBA, 806-797-6690

Heart of Texas (Central Brazos Valley) area: RBA, 409-694-9850; internet address: bert@bafrenz.com

North-central (Dallas/Fort Worth): RBA, 817-329-1270; internet address: North Texas Birding Connection: http://www.why.net/users/stclark/

Northeast: RBA, 903-234-2473

Panhandle: internet only: jwhall@am.net

Rio Grande Valley: RBA, 956-969-2731

San Antonio area: RBA, 210-308-6788

West Texas: internet only: dsarkozi@infocom.net

Bird checklists are available for almost all federal and state areas. Most of these checklists are very good. Those checklists reviewed and/or published by the Department of Natural Resources of the Texas Parks and Wildlife Department (TPWD) and updated regularly are excellent. Those published or copied locally, especially those developed by perusing state bird guides and those arranged in alphabetical order, are poor or useless.

Texas also has an active Texas Ornithological Society (TOS). The society maintains a Texas Bird Records Committee, which is responsible for documenting the state's rare birds. Details about this program are available in Appendix B. For TOS membership and newsletter, contact Texas Ornithological Society, c/o Jolene Boyd, 411 Fitch, Kerrville, TX 78028.

WHAT TO WEAR

A birder in Texas can encounter a full range of temperature and humidity extremes, depending upon the location and season. Spring on the Gulf Coast can be uncomfortably hot and humid, while the Trans-Pecos can experience an occasional cold front that can drop temperatures 20 degrees in less than an hour's time. It is, therefore, important to plan ahead.

In South Texas, you can expect daily temperature highs in the 60s (F) in winter, 70s and 80s in late winter/early spring and fall, and 80s and 90s in late spring and summer; in desert areas the high can reach 100 degrees or slightly more. In West Texas, May and June are the hottest months; temperatures drop once the summer rains begin, usually by mid-July.

Daily low temperatures vary most in the west, where they can differ by as much as 30 degrees. There is less variation closer to the Gulf. But even along the coast, winter northers can drop temperatures 20 degrees in an hour or so.

In North Texas, winters can be extremely cold and windy, producing severe windchill; spring and fall can be very pleasant; summers can be hot. Humidity is normally very low in the western half of the state, increases measurably in the center of the state, and becomes even higher near the coast.

Birding apparel, therefore, should vary with the seasons. Lightweight clothes are important during spring and summer, and layers of warmer clothes are recommended in fall and winter, especially in the north. Consider short pants for hiking in open areas, long pants when birding brushy and desert areas. Long pants protect legs from pesky insects and thorns. Always wear clothing that blends into the environment; bright colors are more obvious to many wildlife species and frighten some species away altogether.

Rain gear may be necessary in some areas. A small umbrella that fits into your pocket or pack will protect you against surprise showers.

Never spend any time in the field, especially on bright sunny days, without adequate body cover. Long-sleeved shirts and long pants are recommended to protect against both sun and mosquitoes. Hats with a wide brim and sunscreen are advised in all parts of the state.

Footwear is also important. Although tennis shoes may be comfortable and practical when walking about the oak mottes at High Island or on the trails at Santa Ana, a sturdy boot or hiking shoe is recommended in most areas. These are essential when birding the coastal prairies, where snakes and thorns occur, and also for the rocky trails of the Chisos and Guadalupe mountains.

ESSENTIALS FOR A SUCCESSFUL BIRDING TRIP

The following is a checklist of items essential for a successful birding trip:

For birding

- ❏ binoculars and spotting scope
- ❏ field identification guides
- ❏ tape player and bird sound tapes
- ❏ additional field guides (see reference section)
- ❏ Texas maps. The Texas Official Travel Map does not include some of the essential county roads. So if you plan to bird other than the most popular birding sites, consider one of the following: *Texas Atlas & Gazetteer,* DeLorme Mapping, Freeport, Maine, 1995; *The Roads of Texas,* Shearer Publishing, Fredericksburg, Texas, 1996; *County Roads of Texas,* Texas Department of Transportation, 1994.
- ❏ For internet users, county maps (not yet complete at the time this book goes to press) are available at http://www.lib.utexas.edu/Libs/PCL/txdot/ TXDOTCounty.html.
- ❏ field journal and pen
- ❏ camera and film (in case you find a new state or U.S. bird)

For your comfort and convenience

- ❑ drinking water; don't overlook an adequate supply of water anywhere in the state
- ❑ food, either snacks or groceries to eat in the field
- ❑ cooler for food and drinks
- ❑ insect repellent is recommended along the coast most of the year
- ❑ sunscreen should be used year-round
- ❑ toilet paper
- ❑ funds adequate for food, gas, and lodging costs

WHERE TO STAY

Decide if you will be camping out or will need lodging. Because many of the best birding sites can be very busy, plan accordingly. For instance, Big Bend National Park can be overrun with people at Easter and Thanksgiving, and many state park and other campgrounds—especially those near large cities—are often filled on spring and summer weekends.

If you plan to camp in state parks, make reservations by calling 512-389-8900 (for general information, call 800-792-1112; web site: http://www.tpwd.state.tx.us). National parks and other sites usually can be reached by calling the contact number listed at each birding site in this guide (see Appendix C).

If you have internet access, information on accommodations, campgrounds, area attractions, gas, food, mileages and maps, and yellow pages is available at http://www.city.net/countries/united_states/texas/.

Texas has an active tourism program operated by the Texas Department of Transportation. The Texas Travel Counselors program can be reached by calling 800-452-9292; web site: http://www.traveltex.com. These folks will gladly send you a Texas Official Travel Map, the Great Texas Coastal Birding Trail brochure, Texas State Travel Guide, Texas Events Calendar, and Texas Accommodations Guide. You can also get road closure information from them in the event of stormy weather.

FIELD HAZARDS

Like most outdoor activities, birding in unfamiliar places requires the use of good old horse sense. Problems can easily be kept to a minimum by planning wisely, respecting property rights, and not overtaxing your physical ability. Birding in Texas does, however, pose a few hazards. First and foremost is the climate. The aridity of the western desert must be respected; it is imperative that you carry water whenever you leave your vehicle. Dehydration can easily sneak up on the active birder, so drink water throughout the day. Although this is especially true in spring and summer, it also applies to the cooler days in fall and winter. This rule applies even in the more humid eastern portion of the state.

Texas has a reputation for poisonous snakes and alligators. Although poisonous snakes normally are few and far between and it is unlikely that you will even see one, be aware of their presence. Snakes are not limited to the desert; they are found throughout the state, including on the coastal prairie and, to a lesser extent, on the northern plains. To protect yourself from snakes, wear high boots, which are effective against smaller snakes. Most important, watch where you walk. Snakes will avoid you whenever possible.

Alligators reside throughout the coastal plains and several of the warm-water reservoirs; be wary whenever you are birding such wetland sites.

In the desert, there is an old adage that almost everything either stings, sticks, or bites. Although this is an exaggeration, when camping out, especially if you sleep on the ground, be aware that scorpions and spiders are present in almost every habitat. Although the vast majority of these creatures are harmless—except to those who are allergic to their toxins—brown recluse and black widow spiders may be attracted to sleeping bags, duffel bags, clothing, boots, and other dark hiding places. In some areas of the state, especially pastures and areas with pitted limestone bedrock, ticks can be common during the warmer months. Be aware and pick them off when found; shower nightly and do a tick check. And watch out for fire ants; they build low mounds (some as high as 10 inches) that may seem to offer slightly higher platforms for better bird viewing, but using them can lead to serious consequences! Although the native ants can bite when provoked, the exotic fire ants will crawl onto you without warning and several hundred can bite all at the same time. A real ordeal!

In our experiences throughout the state, however, we have suffered more from chiggers, the tiny mites that lurk in grassy areas throughout the eastern third of the state, than all the other pests together. Along the coast, especially on calm, warm days and nights, mosquitoes can be almost unbearable.

Protect yourself from mosquitoes, chiggers, ticks, and fire ants by spraying your boots, pants, and upper body with a good brand of insect repellent.

Also watch out for poison ivy and poison oak—these toxic, three-leafed plants show up in nearly every Texas canyon. Here in Texas, the plants referred to as poison ivy and poison oak are actually varieties of the same plant, *Rhus toxicodendron*. The variety most often found in the eastern part of the state is called poison ivy. Poison oak is the variety found most often in the western part of the state.

The accompanying illustration shows the plant, the leaves of which can change according to its environment.

Poison oak

2. Texas Landscapes

Texas is a vast area of mixed landscapes, ranging from the Gulf Coast with its low coastal plains to West Texas with its forested mountain peaks and mesas surrounded by arid Chihuahuan Desert. An area of 267,000 square miles, Texas extends for more than 900 miles between the northwestern corner of its Panhandle to the mouth of the Rio Grande, and more than 800 miles east to west between the Sabine River, which forms the border between Texas and Louisiana, to El Paso in far West Texas. Elevations vary from sea level to 8,749 feet above, at the summit of Guadalupe Peak. The majority of the state, however, lies between 2,000 and 3,500 feet of elevation.

BIOGEOGRAPHIC REGIONS

Three major regions are evident when examining a topographic map of Texas: (1) the coastal lowlands that stretch from the Gulf of Mexico inland for 50 to 70 miles, (2) the rolling prairies that form a broad band from the northeastern corner of the state southwest to the Rio Grande and west to the Balcones and Caprock escarpments, and (3) the mountainous region that runs from the eastern edge of the Balcones and Caprock escarpments west to the New Mexico and Mexico borders.

These three major regions can further be divided by average amount of rainfall, and by their differing soils and vegetation. This book divides the state into ten regions on the basis of the state's biogeography.

Trans-Pecos

The Trans-Pecos region includes all of Texas west of the Pecos River. This area is characterized by moderately to extremely arid lowlands, dominated by Chihuahuan Desert flora and fauna with scattered mountain peaks and ranges. The more extensive highlands of the Guadalupe, Davis, and Chisos mountains are extensions of the Rocky Mountain/Sierra Madre Oriental of North America. Middle elevations are usually sparsely clad with a juniper woodland in the south and a pinyon-juniper woodland at higher elevations. The upper highlands found in the Guadalupe, Davis, and Chisos mountains support a moist coniferous forest. The Rio Grande, with moderate to deep canyons and open floodplains of cottonwoods, willows, mesquite, and nonnative salt cedar, forms the southern border of the region.

The bird life of Trans-Pecos Texas includes many desert species and a few species that prefer mountain grasslands, juniper, pinyon-juniper, or pine-fir woodlands. Representative desert species include Scaled and Gambel's Quails, Greater Roadrunner, **Lucifer Hummingbird** (Big Bend area), Black-chinned Hummingbird, Black and Say's Phoebes, Chihuahuan and Common Ravens, Verdin, Cactus Wren, Black-tailed Gnatcatcher, Northern Mockingbird, Crissal Thrasher, Pyrrhuloxia, and Black-throated Sparrow. Representative highland birds include

Golden Eagle; Band-tailed Pigeon; White-throated Swift; Blue-throated, Magnificent, and Broad-tailed Hummingbirds; Acorn Woodpecker; Western Wood-Pewee; Cordilleran Flycatcher; Cassin's Kingbird; Violet-green Swallow; Steller's Jay (Guadalupe and Davis mountains); Western Scrub-Jay (Guadalupe and Davis mountains); Mexican Jay (Chisos Mountains); Mountain Chickadee (Guadalupe Mountains); Juniper (Plain) Titmouse (Guadalupe Mountains); Bushtit; Pygmy (Guadalupe and Davis mountains) and White-breasted (all Trans-Pecos mountains) Nuthatches; Bewick's Wren; Gray and Hutton's Vireos; Virginia's and Grace's Warblers (Guadalupe and Davis mountains); **Colima Warbler** (Chisos Mountains); Hepatic Tanager; Black-headed Grosbeak; Varied Bunting (Chisos Mountains); Spotted and Canyon Towhees; Rufous-crowned and Black-chinned Sparrows; Dark-eyed (Gray-headed) Junco (Guadalupe Mountains); and Scott's Oriole.

Panhandle and Western Plains

The Panhandle and Western Plains region is bordered by New Mexico to the west, by Oklahoma to the north and east, and by the Trans-Pecos and Edwards Plateau regions to the south. This area is part of the Great Plains of the central United States and south-central Canada, with elevations between 1,000 to 4,500 feet, with scattered stream valleys and playa lakes. Major features include the Caprock Escarpment and the Canadian River breaks. Though the Panhandle and Western Plains were once dominated by mixed prairie habitats with scattered sand sage and scrub oaks, mesquite and yucca have invaded the region with the introduction of livestock and are now dominant in nonagricultural areas.

Bird life varies from prairie to wetland species. Representative birds include Mississippi Kite, Lesser Prairie-Chicken, Killdeer, Mountain Plover (rare), Long-billed Curlew, Mourning Dove, Burrowing Owl, Common Nighthawk, Red-bellied and Downy Woodpeckers, Western Kingbird, Scissor-tailed Flycatcher, Horned Lark, Carolina Chickadee, Tufted Titmouse, Loggerhead Shrike, Canyon Towhee, Rufous-crowned Sparrow, Eastern and Western Meadowlarks, Common Grackle, and Lesser Goldfinch. A few additional species occur in the more arid southern portion: Scaled Quail, Common Poorwill, Black-tailed Gnatcatcher, Cactus Wren, and Black-throated Sparrow.

Winter specialties, often hard to find elsewhere in Texas, include Tundra Swan, Rough-legged Hawk, Long-eared Owl, Northern Shrike, American Tree Sparrow, and Lapland Longspur.

Edwards Plateau

The Edwards Plateau, often called the Hill Country, comprises about 37,500 square miles in central Texas. The Balcones Escarpment forms a distinct boundary on the southeast and south, while the northern and northeastern borders blend gradually into the Northern Plains and Brush Country regions. Natural vegetation of the Edwards Plateau includes climax grasses on the open slopes and valley bottoms; the rocky slopes and breaks areas support live and shinnery oaks, junipers, and mesquite. Brush and juniper species have invaded much of the region's grasslands and open savannahs.

Bird life on the Edwards Plateau includes one notable species—**Golden-cheeked Warbler**—which occurs nowhere else during the nesting season, and the **Black-capped Vireo,** which does occur elsewhere but is easiest to find in this region. Other representative birds include Wood Duck; Red-shouldered Hawk; Crested Caracara; Northern Bobwhite; Mourning and Inca Doves; Common Ground-Dove; Greater Roadrunner; Common Poorwill; Black-chinned Hummingbird; **Green Kingfisher; Golden-fronted Woodpecker;** Ladder-backed Woodpecker; Eastern and Black Phoebes; Scissor-tailed Flycatcher; Western Scrub-Jay; Carolina Chickadee; Tufted Titmouse; Bushtit; Canyon, Carolina, and Bewick's Wrens; Eastern Blue-bird; Northern Mockingbird; Northern Cardinal; Canyon Towhee; Rufous-crowned and Field Sparrows; Eastern Meadowlark; Great-tailed and Common Grackles; House Finch; and Lesser Goldfinch.

Northern Plains

The Northern Plains cover a huge area of north-central Texas, from the Okla-homa border southward to the Edwards Plateau and Central Plains regions, and bordered on the east by the Pineywoods region. The Northern Plains region is composed of three vegetational zones: cross timbers and prairies on the west, blackland prairies in the center, and post oak savannah on the east. Topography varies from nearly level to gentle rolling hills and to deeply cut stream valleys, all between approximately 300 and 1,000 feet elevation.

Bird life includes many western and eastern species. The most representative birds include Wood Duck, Red-shouldered and Broad-winged Hawks, Ruby-throated Hummingbird, Eastern Screech-Owl, Barred Owl, Common Nighthawk, Chuck-will's-widow, Red-bellied Woodpecker, Eastern Phoebe, Acadian and Great Crested Flycatchers, Eastern and Western Kingbirds, Blue Jay, Carolina Chicka-dee, Tufted Titmouse, Carolina and Bewick's Wrens, White-eyed and Red-eyed Vireos, Summer Tanager, Northern Cardinal, Indigo Bunting, Grasshopper and Lark Sparrows, Eastern Meadowlark, and Common Grackle.

Pineywoods

The Pineywoods region, or the Texas "timber belt," extends along the state's east-ern border with Arkansas and Louisiana south to the Upper Coast region. This region is dominated by gently rolling to hilly forested land, with numerous streams that feed into several large rivers: Angelina, Sabine, Neches, and Trinity. The val-leys and floodplains possess dense stands of hardwood trees, while the upper, drier slopes and ridges are dominated by conifers, including loblolly, shortleaf, longleaf, and slash pines. Elevations vary from 200 to 500 feet.

Bird life within the Pineywoods includes a few exclusives—Red-cockaded Woodpecker, Fish Crow, Brown-headed Nuthatch, Prairie Warbler, and Bachman's Sparrow. Other representative species include Wood Duck; Red-shouldered and

Broad-winged Hawks; Barred Owl; Chuck-will's-widow; Red-headed, Red-bellied, Downy, and Pileated Woodpeckers; Eastern Wood-Pewee; Acadian and Great Crested Flycatchers; White-breasted Nuthatch; Wood Thrush; White-eyed, Yellow-throated, and Red-eyed Vireos; Northern Parula; Yellow-throated, Pine, Black-and-white, Prothonotary, Swainson's, Kentucky, and Hooded Warblers; American Redstart; Louisiana Waterthrush; Yellow-breasted Chat; Summer Tanager; Northern Cardinal; Painted and Indigo Buntings; Blue Grosbeak; Chipping Sparrow; and Eastern Meadowlark. Rusty Blackbird occurs here in winter.

Central Plains

The Central Plains region is bordered (clockwise) by the Northern Plains, Pineywoods, Upper Coast, Brush Country, and Edwards Plateau regions. Topography is nearly level to gently rolling with numerous river valleys, many of which form broad floodplains with hardwood bottomlands, all between 300 and 800 feet elevation. Vegetation in the open areas is dominated by southern extensions of the post oak savannah and blackland prairie zones. The prairie that once dominated the drier hills has largely been replaced by mesquite and yucca.

Bird life in this region is similar to that in the Northern Plains, with the addition of more southern species: Black-bellied Whistling-Duck; White-tailed Kite; Crested Caracara; Inca Dove; Common Ground-Dove; Greater Roadrunner; Ruby-throated Hummingbird; Red-bellied and Ladder-backed Woodpeckers; Bewick's Wren; Northern Mockingbird; Yellow-throated, Pine, Prothonotary, and Hooded Warblers; Louisiana Waterthrush; Blue Grosbeak; Painted Bunting; Dickcissel; and House Finch. Longspur occurs in winter.

Upper Coast

The Upper Coast region extends from the Louisiana border south to the San Antonio River, a significant biogeographic dividing line for many eastern and southern plants and animals. Eastern birds, such as Blue Jay, American Crow, and Carolina Chickadee rarely occur south of the San Antonio River, and **Pauraque, Golden-fronted Woodpecker, Long-billed Thrasher,** and **Olive Sparrow** rarely occur to the northeast. A significant portion of the Upper Coast is protected by barrier islands, Galveston Island in the north and Matagorda Island in the south. This coastal region extends inland only so far as coastal plains are a significant part of the environment.

Additional representative birds of the Upper Coast include Neotropic Cormorant; White and White-faced Ibis; Fulvous and Black-bellied Whistling-Ducks; Greater White-fronted, Snow, and Ross's Geese in winter; Mottled Duck; Wilson's Plover; White-tailed Kite; Bald Eagle; **White-tailed Hawk;** Northern Bobwhite; Black and Clapper Rails; Sandhill Crane in winter; Gull-billed, Royal, Sandwich, Forster's, and Least Terns; Black Skimmer; Common Nighthawk; Eastern Kingbird; Scissor-tailed Flycatcher; Horned Lark; Northern Mockingbird; White-eyed Vireo; Common Yellowthroat; Northern Cardinal; Painted Bunting; Nelson's

Sharp-tailed (winter) and Seaside Sparrows; Eastern Meadowlark; and Great-tailed and Boat-tailed Grackles.

Coastal Bend

The Coastal Bend region lies below the San Antonio River and runs south to the Rio Grande Valley. Like the Upper Coast, this region is dominated by the coastal plains. The entire area is protected by a chain of barrier islands: San Jose, Mustang, and Padre Islands. Both coastal regions are cut by rivers and streams, and estuaries and saltwater wetlands are numerous.

Bird life in the Coastal Bend is similar to that of the Upper Coast with a few additions. Representative species include **Least Grebe,** Magnificent Frigatebird, Reddish Egret, Roseate Spoonbill, Wood Stork, Masked Duck (irregular), **White-tailed Hawk,** Purple Gallinule, **Whooping Crane** (winter), Piping Plover (winter), Common Ground-Dove, Groove-billed Ani, **Ferruginous Pygmy-Owl,** Lesser Nighthawk, **Pauraque, Golden-fronted Woodpecker, Buff-bellied Hummingbird, Green Kingfisher, Great Kiskadee, Couch's Kingbird,** Cave Swallow, **Long-billed Thrasher, Tropical Parula,** Bronzed Cowbird, Botteri's Sparrow, Hooded Oriole, **Audubon's Oriole,** and Lesser Goldfinch.

Brush Country

The Brush Country, or South Texas Plains, runs from the Edwards Plateau region south to the Rio Grande Valley and east to the Coastal Bend region. The topography is level to rolling, with numerous streams, and with elevations from sea level to about 1,000 feet above. Once dominated by grassland and savannah, extensive grazing has altered the vegetation to a dense Tamaulipan scrub, mixed with mesquite, live oaks, several acacias, and cacti.

Bird life in the region includes numerous exclusives that cannot be expected to the north, although a few also occur in the Coastal Bend and southern Edwards Plateau regions. These include **White-tipped Dove** (rare), Groove-billed Ani, **Pauraque, Buff-bellied Hummingbird,** Northern Beardless-Tyrannnulet, **Great Kiskadee, Green Jay, Long-billed Thrasher, Olive Sparrow,** Botteri's Sparrow, and **Audubon's Oriole.** Other representative birds include Harris's Hawk, **White-tailed Hawk,** Crested Caracara, **Golden-fronted Woodpecker,** Brown-crested Flycatcher, **Couch's Kingbird,** Cave Swallow, Chihuahuan Raven, Verdin, Cactus Wren, Curve-billed Thrasher, Pyrrhuloxia, Cassin's Sparrow, Eastern Meadowlark, Bronzed and Brown-headed Cowbirds, and Lesser Goldfinch.

Rio Grande Valley

The Rio Grande Valley region extends upriver for about 165 miles and 20 to 30 miles to the north. The region is dominated by the Rio Grande floodplain, with its tropical flora, such as Texas ebony, tepeguaje, and Sabal palm, and fauna. The adjacent eroded terrain contains a dense, dry Tamaulipan scrub habitat. Rainfall varies considerably and decreases with the distance from the Gulf; the upper region near Falcon Dam is arid, while much of the lower valley has been developed for agriculture. Large natural areas can be found only in protected places, such as the federal refuges and state parks.

Bird life in the region includes more Texas specialties than in any other region of the state. These include **Least Grebe, Muscovy Duck, Hook-billed Kite, White-tailed Hawk, Plain Chachalaca, Red-billed Pigeon, White-tipped Dove, Red-crowned Parrot, Green Parakeet, Ferruginous Pygmy-Owl, Pauraque, Buff-bellied Hummingbird, Ringed Kingfisher, Green Kingfisher, Golden-fronted Woodpecker, Great Kiskadee, Green Jay, Brown Jay, Tamaulipas (Mexican) Crow, Clay-colored Robin, Long-billed Thrasher, Tropical Parula, Olive Sparrow, White-collared Seedeater, Altamira Oriole,** and **Audubon's Oriole.**

Other representative birds in the Rio Grande Valley region include Neotropic Cormorant, Anhinga, Fulvous and Black-bellied Whistling-Ducks, Masked Duck (irregular), White-tailed Kite, Harris's Hawk, Crested Caracara, Aplomado Falcon (reintroduced), Groove-billed Ani, Elf Owl, Lesser Nighthawk, Rose-throated Becard (irregular), Brown-crested Flycatcher, Cave Swallow, Curve-billed Thrasher, Pyrrhuloxia, Painted Bunting, Botteri's and Cassin's Sparrows, Bronzed Cowbird, and Lesser Goldfinch.

TOPOGRAPHY AND MIGRATION

Four major migration routes, or flyways, are recognized in North America. From west to east, these are the Pacific, Central, Mississippi, and Atlantic. The Central Flyway passes through Texas, and is utilized by millions of birds that either follow the Mexico-Texas coastline or cross the Gulf of Mexico between Mexico's Yucatan Peninsula and the Texas coast. Places like High Island, on the Upper Texas Coast, have gained reputations as landing and resting sites for the spring Gulf migrants that can "fall out" of the sky into oak mottes and other vegetative thickets along the Texas coast. These birds, often exhausted from their trans-Gulf flights, will spend a few to several hours, or even a few days, resting and feeding amid the vegetation before they continue northward toward their breeding grounds. At such times it is possible to find 50 to 100 species in one small area.

Although the Central Flyway is most important and receives the greatest attention from birders, several secondary migration routes are recognized throughout the state. Most of the major river valleys, especially those flowing north-south, are important. The Rio Grande, which follows a northwest-southeast direction, also provides an important route where water and food are available.

Farther west in Texas, the long north-south valleys and mountain ranges also influence migrating birds. For instance, Mexico's Sierra Madre Oriental forms a sufficiently high barrier that funnels inland migrants to the east or west of this range. And high-flying raptors take advantage of the high ridges and plateaus in passing.

3. Gallery of Texas Specialties

Thirty-two of the more than 600 birds that have been recorded in the state are Texas specialties, species that occur in Texas but nowhere else or rarely anywhere else in the United States. These 32 birds, therefore, are the state's "most wanted" species, those that birders travel all across the continent or from other continents to find. To help highlight their truly unique status, drawings of the 32 species by Mimi Hoppe Wolf, one of America's most outstanding bird artists, are included in this chapter.

Each of the 32 illustrations also includes a brief biographic sketch to help birders plan their Texas birding trip. Each includes the bird's common and scientific names, habitat preference, seasonal occurrence, and a few of the "best bets," the sites where it is most likely to be found.

LEAST GREBE *Tachybaptus dominicus*
Habitat: shallow ponds and marshes
Season: usually year-round
Best bets: Santa Ana, Sabal Palm, and below Falcon Dam

22

MUSCOVY DUCK *Cairina mochata*
Habitat: river
Season: spring and summer; irregular at other times
Best bets: Salineño, Chapeño

HOOK-BILLED KITE *Chondrohierax uncinatus*
Habitat: thorn forest
Season: year-round; most active in spring
Best bets: Santa Ana, Bentsen, Anzalduas, and Salineño

WHITE-TAILED HAWK *Buteo albicaudatus*
Habitat: coastal prairie
Season: year-round
Best bets: Port O'Connor, Matagorda Island, Kingsville,
Mustang Island, and Laguna Atascosa

PLAIN CHACHALACA *Ortalis vetula*
Habitat: thorn forest
Season: year-round
Best bets: Bentsen and Santa Ana

WHOOPING CRANE *Grus americanus*
Habitat: coastal prairie
Season: winter (October to mid-April)
Best bet: Aransas.

RED-BILLED PIGEON *Columba flavirostris*
Habitat: riparian
Season: spring and summer
Best bets: Saliñeno, Chapeño, below Falcon Dam

WHITE-TIPPED DOVE *Leptotila verreauxi*
Habitat: thorn forest and riparian
Season: year-round
Best bets: Bentsen, Santa Ana, Sabal Palm, Salineño, and King Ranch

RED-CROWNED PARROT *Amazona viridigenalis*
Habitat: fruiting tropical vegetation
Season: year-round
Best bet: Brownsville

GREEN PARAKEET *Aratinga holochroa*
Habitat: fruiting tropical vegetation
Season: year-round
Best bets: Brownsville and McAllen

FERRUGINOUS PYGMY-OWL *Glaucidium brasilianum*
Habitat: thorn forest and oak mottes
Season: year-round, but most active in spring and summer
Best bets: King Ranch and Kenedy Ranch

PAURAQUE *Nyctidromus albicollis*
Habitat: thorn forest and Tamaulipan scrub
Season: year-round, but most active in spring and summer
Best bets: Bentsen, King Ranch, Kenedy Ranch, Kingsville,
Goose Island, and Choke Canyon

33

BUFF-BELLIED HUMMINGBIRD *Amazilia yucatanensis*
Habitat: thorn forest and oak mottes
Season: year-round in south; spring and summer in north
Best bets: Sabal Palm, Santa Ana, King Ranch, and Kenedy Ranch

LUCIFER HUMMINGBIRD *Calothorax lucifer*
Habitat: desert scrub
Season: spring and summer
Best bets: Big Bend National Park and Big Bend Ranch

RINGED KINGFISHER *Ceryle torquata*
Habitat: river and large ponds
Season: year-round
Best bets: Santa Ana, Bentsen, Salineño, and Chapeño

GREEN KINGFISHER *Chloroceryle americana*
Habitat: river and ponds
Season: year-round
Best bets: Santa Ana, Bentsen, Lost Maples, Guadalupe River, Chalk Bluff

GOLDEN-FRONTED WOODPECKER *Melanerpes aurifrons*
Habitat: thorn forest, Tamaulipan scrub, mesquite woodland, cottonwood grove
Season: year-round
Best bets: many sites from Brownsville to Big Bend and north to Austin

GREAT KISKADEE *Pitangus sulphuratus*
Habitat: riparian
Season: year-round
Best bets: Bentsen, Santa Ana, Salineño, Chapeño, Kingsville,
King Ranch, and Choke Canyon

COUCH'S KINGBIRD *Tyrannus couchii*
Habitat: Tamaulipan scrub and riparian
Season: spring and summer
Best bets: Brownsville, Chaparral, Corpus Christi, Goliad, Aransas,
Kingsville, and Lake Casa Blanca

GREEN JAY *Cyanocorax yncas*
Habitat: thorn forest, Tamaulipan scrub, and riparian
Season: year-round
Best bets: Bentsen, Santa Ana, Choke Canyon, Kingsville, Salineño

41

BROWN JAY *Cyanocorax morio*
Habitat: thorn forest
Season: winter
Best bets: Salineño and Chapeño

TAMAULIPAS (MEXICAN) CROW *Corvus imperatus*
Habitat: landfill
Season: winter
Best bet: Brownsville

CLAY-COLORED ROBIN *Turdus grayi*
Habitat: thorn forest
Season: irregular
Best bets: Santa Ana, and Bentsen

LONG-BILLED THRASHER *Toxostoma longirostre*
Habitat: Tamaulipan scrub
Season: year-round
Best bets: Chaparral, Falcon, Lake Corpus Christi, Kingsville,
Santa Ana, and Bentsen

BLACK-CAPPED VIREO *Vireo atricapillus*
Habitat: oak scrub
Season: spring and summer
Best bets: Balcones Canyonlands, Lost Maples,
and Big Bend National Park

COLIMA WARBLER *Vermivora crissalis*
Habitat: oak-pinyon-juniper woodland
Season: spring and summer
Best bet: Big Bend National Park

TROPICAL PARULA *Parula pitiayumi*
Habitat: Tamaulipan scrub
Season: year-round; most active in spring and summer
Best bets: Kenedy Ranch and King Ranch

GOLDEN-CHEEKED WARBLER *Dendroica chrysoparia*
Habitat: juniper-oak woodland
Season: spring/early summer
Best bets: Lost Maples, Balcones Canyonlands, Pedernales Falls, Enchanted Rock, and Austin

OLIVE SPARROW *Arremonops rufivirgatus*
Habitat: Tamaulipan scrub
Season: year-round; most active in spring and summer
Best bets: Bentsen, Santa Ana, Laguna Atascosa, King Ranch,
Kenedy Ranch, Kingsville, and Lake Corpus Christi

WHITE-COLLARED SEEDEATER *Sporophila torqueola*
Habitat: weedy fields
Season: year-round; most active in spring
Best bets: San Ygnacio and Zapata

ALTAMIRA ORIOLE *Icterus gularis*
Habitat: thorn forest
Season: year-round
Best bets: Bentsen, Salineño, Santa Ana, and Brownsville

AUDUBON'S ORIOLE *Icterus graduacauda*
Habitat: Tamaulipan scrub and thorn forest
Season: year-round
Best bets: Salineño, Bentsen, Santa Ana, Chaparral,
Kenedy Ranch, and King Ranch

OTHER HIGH-PROFILE TEXAS BIRDS

NEOTROPIC CORMORANT Widespread at rivers and ponds on coastal plain year-round

ANHINGA Widespread at rivers and ponds on coastal plain and inland year-round; less numerous in winter

REDDISH EGRET Common along southern coast year-round

ROSEATE SPOONBILL Locally common along coast year-round; wanders after nesting

WOOD STORK Summer visitor at coastal wetlands and at ponds; less numerous inland

FULVOUS WHISTLING-DUCK Common spring and summer resident along coast; less numerous inland

BLACK-BELLIED WHISTLING-DUCK Locally common year-round in coastal wetlands and in southern third of state; less numerous in winter

MOTTLED DUCK Locally common along the coast; less numerous inland

SWALLOW-TAILED KITE Very local nester in Pineywoods, rare migrant

MISSISSIPPI KITE Common summer resident in Panhandle and Northern Plains

COMMON BLACK-HAWK Local spring and summer resident in Trans-Pecos

HARRIS'S HAWK Fairly common in South Texas year-round

GRAY HAWK Local resident in Rio Grande Valley and Big Bend National Park

ZONE-TAILED HAWK Spring and summer resident in canyons of western Trans-Pecos

CRESTED CARACARA Common resident in South Texas; less numerous in Edwards Plateau and Plains

APLOMADO FALCON Occasional records in Trans-Pecos; restoration program is under way at Laguna Atascosa and Matagorda Island

ATTWATER'S PRAIRIE-CHICKEN Close to extinction in the wild

LESSER PRAIRIE-CHICKEN Rare, local, year-round resident in Northern Plains

MONTEZUMA QUAIL Local resident in Davis Mountains

YELLOW RAIL Local winter resident in upper coastal prairies

BLACK RAIL Local resident in coastal wetlands year-round

MONK PARAKEET Locally common (introduced) in Austin, Dallas, El Paso, and Houston

GROOVE-BILLED ANI Local spring and summer resident in South Texas, north to San Antonio

ELF OWL Locally common in spring and summer from Santa Ana to Big Bend and north to Davis Mountains

MAGNIFICENT HUMMINGBIRD Local in spring and summer in the Chisos, Davis, and Guadalupe mountains

RED-COCKADED WOODPECKER Local year-round resident in Pineywoods

NORTHERN BEARDLESS-TYRANNULET Local year-round resident in lower Rio Grande Valley

VERMILION FLYCATCHER Local year-round resident in South Texas from the coast to Big Bend National Park; less numerous spring and summer resident elsewhere

TROPICAL KINGBIRD Local year-round resident in Brownsville area

SCISSOR-TAILED FLYCATCHER Widespread in all but Panhandle in spring and summer

ROSE-THROATED BECARD Irregular visitor in lower Rio Grande Valley

MEXICAN JAY Common in Chisos Mountains year-round

CHIHUAHUAN RAVEN Fairly common in Trans-Pecos year-round; less numerous to southern coast

BLACK-TAILED GNATCATCHER Common year-round in desert scrub in Trans-Pecos and east to Falcon Dam; less obvious in winter

CRISSAL THRASHER Local resident in Trans-Pecos

SPRAGUE'S PIPIT Local winter resident along coast; less numerous inland

GRAY VIREO Fairly common spring and summer resident in mountain areas of Trans-Pecos; very rare in winter

GRACE'S WARBLER Local spring and summer resident in Davis and Guadalupe mountains

SWAINSON'S WARBLER Locally common in spring and summer in central Pineywoods

PAINTED REDSTART Irregular spring and summer resident in Chisos Mountains

HEPATIC TANAGER Fairly common in spring and summer in the Chisos, Davis, and Guadalupe mountains

PYRRHULOXIA Widespread and common in desert scrub from El Paso to Falcon Dam

BLUE BUNTING Irregular winter visitor in lower Rio Grande Valley

PAINTED BUNTING Widespread and common in spring and summer throughout the state, except in Panhandle

DICKCISSEL Locally common in spring and summer in all but Trans-Pecos

BACHMAN'S SPARROW Local year-round resident in Pineywoods; most active in spring

BOTTERI'S SPARROW Local resident on lower coastal plain; most active in spring

RUFOUS-CROWNED SPARROW Locally common in foothills of Trans-Pecos and Edwards Plateau

BLACK-CHINNED SPARROW Locally common in mountains of Trans-Pecos

BRONZED COWBIRD Common summer resident in South Texas; locally common in winter

4. Texas's Best Birding Areas

More than 200 sites—national, state, county, and city parks; forests; lakes; and 45 private sites—within 120 chapters, grouped in ten biogeographic regions, are included in the following pages. Each of the 120 chapters is designed to be utilized independently; therefore, many species will be included repeatedly to provide the user a comprehensive perspective of the bird life present at each site. Although the principal target audience is the traveling birder who visits the various sites to find specific birds, it is hoped that each chapter will also provide the novice birder all the information necessary to find the more common species.

The following terms are used to describe the status of the bird species mentioned.

STATUS

Resident = full-time; present year-round

Summer = present at least from early May through July; usually nests

Winter = may arrive as early as mid-October and remain as late as mid-May; many northern birds wintering in the Panhandle may be present only from December through February, while seedeaters in the southern portion of the state may arrive in October and move on as soon as their food supply is depleted, often by early January

Migrant = passing through in spring or fall

Post-nesting Dispersal = visitor or resident only after nesting elsewhere

ABUNDANCE

Common = always present in significant numbers in the proper habitat(s)

Fairly Common = a few are always present in the proper habitat(s)

Uncommon = sometimes present in small numbers in the proper habitat(s)

Rare = occurs regularly in small numbers in the proper habitat(s); a good search can usually find one

Irregular = definitely not expected, but a few occur occasionally in the proper habitat(s)

Sporadic = not expected every year, but can occur in significant numbers

Vagrant = scattered records; well out of the bird's normal range (extralimital)

Map legend

Interstate	(10)	Gate	●—●
US Highway	87 377	Power Line	●—●—●
State or County Road	36 CR 3808	City or Town	○ Laredo or Laredo
State Loop Road	⟨375⟩	Campground	⛺
Park Route	⟨PR 33⟩	One-Way Road	→
Farm to Market Road/ Ranch Road	2871 R 271	Picnic Area	⊤
Forest Service Road	FR 224	Pass	‿
Interstate Highway	⟹	Cabin or Building	■
Paved Road	⟹	Elevation	5,281 ft. X
Secondary Paved Road	⟹	Peak	▲
Minor Streets or Roads	⟹	Hill	▬
Gravel or Unimproved Road	======⟹	Observation Platform or Blind	⋔
Birding Site	17 A	Information/Visitor Center or Ranger Station	◇?
Parking Area	Ⓟ	State/County/ International Boundary	MEXICO
Lake, Dam, River/Creek, Waterfall		Park/Refuge/Forest Boundary	
Mud Flat		Map Orientation	N
Bridge			
Marsh or Wetland		Scale	0 0.5 1 Miles
Levee			
Trail			

Trans-Pecos Region

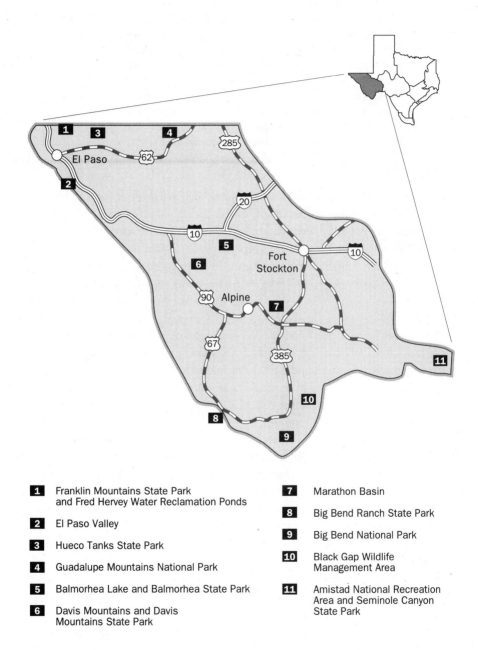

1 Franklin Mountains State Park
and Fred Hervey Water Reclamation Ponds

2 El Paso Valley

3 Hueco Tanks State Park

4 Guadalupe Mountains National Park

5 Balmorhea Lake and Balmorhea State Park

6 Davis Mountains and Davis
Mountains State Park

7 Marathon Basin

8 Big Bend Ranch State Park

9 Big Bend National Park

10 Black Gap Wildlife
Management Area

11 Amistad National Recreation
Area and Seminole Canyon
State Park

1 Franklin Mountains State Park and Fred Hervey Water Reclamation Ponds

Habitats: Desert scrub, desert grassland, sewage pond, marsh

Key birds: "Mexican Duck" (Mallard); Golden Eagle; Harris's Hawk; Scaled and Gambel's Quails; Greater Roadrunner; Chihuahuan Raven; Verdin; Cactus, Rock, and Canyon Wrens; Curve-billed and Crissal Thrashers; Pyrrhuloxia; Rufous-crowned, Black-chinned, and Black-throated Sparrows; Canyon Towhee; and Lesser Goldfinch are present year-round. Swainson's Hawk, Lesser Nighthawk, Common Poorwill, Black-chinned Hummingbird, Violet-green Swallow, Indigo Bunting, and Scott's Oriole occur in summer. Western and Mountain Bluebirds, Townsend's Solitaire, Green-tailed Towhee, Brewer's Sparrow, and Lark Bunting can usually be found in winter.

Best times to bird: April and May for spring migrants and nesting activities; August and September for fall migrants

Birding strategies: The open desert scrub habitat, such as that along the park entrance road (**A**), offers a number of species year-round: Scaled and Gambel's Quails; Greater Roadrunner; Ladder-backed Woodpecker; Say's Phoebe; Verdin; Cactus and Rock Wrens; Curve-billed and Crissal Thrashers; Loggerhead Shrike; Pyrrhuloxia; Rufous-crowned, Black-chinned (more numerous in winter), and Black-throated Sparrows; House Finch; and Lesser Goldfinch. Canyon Wrens prefer the rocky canyons. In summer, Lesser Nighthawk, Common Poorwill, Ash-throated Flycatcher, Northern Mockingbird, Blue Grosbeak, Brown-headed Cowbird, and Scott's Oriole also are present. Post-nesting hummingbirds, including Calliope, Broad-tailed, and Rufous, often are present at flowering shrubs from July through September. A few birds, such as Red-naped Sapsucker, Western Scrub-Jay, Western and Mountain Bluebirds, and Townsend's Solitaire are sporadic winter visitors. Watch overhead year-round for Red-tailed Hawk, Golden Eagle, American Kestrel, and Prairie Falcon. Turkey Vulture, White-throated Swift, and Violet-green Swallow occur in summer.

West Cottonwood Springs (**B**), accessible by trail (1.6 miles) from the picnic area, provides nesting habitat for Black-chinned Hummingbird and Bewick's Wren. The brushy arroyos provide preferred habitat for Crissal Thrasher year-round, and various sparrows in winter. The cottonwoods also attract passing migrants in spring and fall. In fall (mid-August to early October), a variety of neotropical migrants, including western hummingbirds, songbirds, and 15 species of warblers, have been recorded here.

On the eastern slope are three trails that offer additional access routes into the mountains. The trail up Whispering Springs Canyon (**C**) is the best for birds, especially during migration. Resident species are much the same as those on the western slope. Indigo Bunting occasionally is present in summer. And the canyon bottoms, especially after late summer rains, may offer weedy patches for a variety of seedeaters, including Lazuli Bunting; Green-tailed and Spotted Towhees; Chipping, Clay-colored, Brewer's, Vesper, Lark, Lincoln's, and White-crowned Sparrows; Lark Bunting; and Dark-eyed Junco; several may remain through the winter.

1 Franklin Mountains State Park and Fred Hervey Water Reclamation Ponds

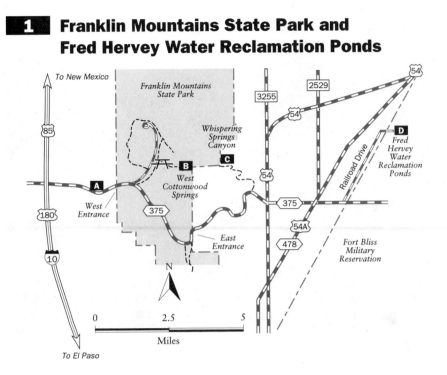

The Fred Hervey Water Reclamation Ponds (**D**) may be the best birding area in the Greater El Paso area. The sewage ponds, heavy growth of surrounding vegetation, and adjacent desert offer a wide diversity of birding habitats year-round. The ponds are most productive during migration, when waterfowl and shorebirds can be abundant; 35 species of shorebirds have been recorded here. The surrounding salt cedars, willows, and other shrubs can also support large numbers of neotropical migrants. Year-round water birds include Pied-billed and Eared Grebes, "Mexican Duck" (Mallard), Ruddy Duck, Common Moorhen, American Coot, and Killdeer.

Records of Review Species: Reddish Egret, July 1986. Glossy Ibis, April–May 1992. White-winged Scoter, Oct 1991. Masked Duck, July 1976. Gray Hawk, April 1984. Red-necked Stint, July 1996. Ruff, Sept 1993. Red Phalarope, Sept–Oct 1991, Oct 1992. Western Gull, May 1985. Groove-billed Ani, July–Dec 1995. Yellow-throated Vireo, May 1996. Blackburnian Warbler, Sept 1995 and Sept 1996. Palm Warbler, April, Oct 1992, Oct–Dec 1993, and April 1994. Varied Bunting, May 1995. White-collared Seedeater, Aug 1989. Lapland Longspur, Nov–Dec 1989 and Nov 1993. Bobolink, May 1976, May 1977. Lawrence's Goldfinch, Feb–Oct 1996.

Directions: To Franklin Mountains State Park, turn off I-10 at Exit 6 onto the Trans-Mountain Road (Loop 375) and proceed east 3.3 miles to the park entrance; or, from the east, take US 54 to the Trans-Mountain Road (Exit 9). To Fred Hervey Water Reclamation Ponds, take Loop 375 east from US 54 for 3 miles to Railroad Drive, and go north for 3.6 miles to the entrance road on the right; cross the tracks and proceed on the paved road to the blue buildings; turn right at the gate on an unpaved (good driving conditions except after rain) road to trees and the first pond; walk from there.

Franklin Mountains from along the state park entrance road.

General information: The Franklin Mountains form a rugged backdrop to the city of El Paso and extend north-south for 23 miles, 8 miles within New Mexico. North Franklin Peak reaches an elevation of 7,192 feet. The state park of 24,000 acres is the largest urban (totally located within a city) park in the nation. Dominated by Chihuahuan Desert vegetation, the park contains an extensive trail system (14 miles). The park's trails can also be accessed through McKellgon Canyon, a city/county facility in the southern portion of the state park.

The Wilderness Park Museum, located just west of US 54, contains a number of exhibits on the area's natural and historical resources, as well as a nature trail. Some of the common desert bird species can be seen here.

Fort Bliss, a U.S. Army post that lies along the eastern flanks of the Franklin Mountains and valley, covers 1.12 million acres, 90 percent of which is in New Mexico. The Fred Hervey Water Reclamation Ponds are an El Paso facility on land along the west edge of the military reservation.

ADDITIONAL HELP

Location: Texas Official Travel Map grid L x 1; El Paso County

Nearest food, gas, and lodging: Food and gas are at Canutillo (3 miles); lodging is off I-10 at Mesa Exit (10 miles).

Nearest camping: Primitive camping on-site; nearest campgrounds in Canutillo (6 miles) and Hueco Tanks State Park (27 miles east of El Paso)

Contact: Superintendent, Franklin Mountains State Park, and city of El Paso (see Appendix C)

2 El Paso Valley

**Feather Lake Wildlife Sanctuary, Tornillo Lakes, Fort Hancock
Reservoir, and McNary Reservoir**

Habitats: River, reservoir, pond, ditch, riparian, marsh, desert scrub,
field, pasture, cropland

Key birds: Clark's Grebe, Neotropic Cormorant, "Mexican Duck"
(Mallard), Harris's Hawk, Scaled and Gambel's Quail, Greater
Roadrunner, Burrowing Owl, Black and Say's Phoebes, Chihuahuan
Raven, Verdin, Cactus Wren, Curve-billed and Crissal Thrashers,
Phainopepla, Pyrrhuloxia, and Black-throated and Cassin's Sparrows
are present year-round. Swainson's Hawk, Lesser Nighthawk,
Common Poorwill, Cave Swallow, Bell's Vireo, and Painted Bunting
occur in summer. Western Grebe, American White Pelican, Least
Bittern, Snow and Ross's Geese, Hooded and Common Mergansers,
Ferruginous Hawk, Prairie Falcon, Vermilion Flycatcher, Brewer's
Sparrow, and Chestnut-collared Longspur can usually be found in
winter.

Best times to bird: April and May for spring migrants and nesting
activities; November to March for winter birds

Birding strategies: Feather Lake Wildlife Sanctuary (A) is located at 9500 North
Loop Drive, off I-10 via Americas Avenue (Loop 375), in southeast El Paso. A
blind is available near the entrance for viewing the water birds, but the greatest
variety of birds usually can be found by walking the levee (about 1 mile) that
circles the 40-acre pond. The pond and marsh are most productive in winter when
Great Blue Heron, Green-winged Teal, Mallard, Northern Pintail, Northern Shoveler, Gadwall, American Wigeon, American Coot, Killdeer, Mourning Dove, Song
Sparrow, Great-tailed Grackle, and House Finch are numerous. Smaller numbers
of Black-crowned Night-Heron, Canada Goose, Cinnamon Teal, Canvasback, Redhead, Ring-necked Duck, Bufflehead, Ruddy Duck, Common Moorhen, Greater
Yellowlegs, Least Sandpiper, Ring-billed Gull, Gambel's Quail, Belted Kingfisher,
Marsh Wren, and Pyrrhuloxia can often be found. Great and Snowy Egrets, Northern Harrier, Red-tailed Hawk, American Kestrel, Burrowing Owl, American Crow,
and Chihuahuan Raven are irregular visitors.

The sanctuary attracts numerous water birds and other species during migra-
tion. Fall is the best time to see large flocks of roosting Cattle Egrets and Red-
winged and Yellow-headed Blackbirds. In spring, up to 6,000 White-faced Ibis
roost here. Visiting shorebirds can include Black-necked Stilt; American Avocet;
Greater and Lesser Yellowlegs; Solitary, Spotted, Western, and Least Sandpipers;
Willet; Long-billed Dowitcher; and Wilson's Phalarope. Northern Rough-winged,
Bank, Cliff, and Barn Swallows are usually common; Tree, Violet-green, and Cave
Swallows are less numerous. A few species nest: Pied-billed Grebe, Green Heron,
"Mexican Duck" (Mallard), Cinnamon Teal, Ruddy Duck, Gambel's Quail, Com-
mon Moorhen, American Coot, Black-necked Stilt and American Avocet (some

years), Common Yellowthroat, and Red-winged Blackbird. Least Bittern, present some years, also nests here sporadically.

To continue south, take either SH 20 or I-10 southeast to Fabens (along SH 20 or off I-10 via FM 793). Southeast of Fabens, SH 20 passes through numerous croplands and past pastures and ponds, with occasional cottonwoods and patches of mesquite (**B**). In general, birding improves along this road as you move southeast toward its terminus at McNary. Year-round residents to be expected along SH 20 include Harris's and Red-tailed Hawks; American Kestrel; Scaled and Gambel's Quail; Killdeer; Rock, White-winged, Mourning, and Inca Doves; Greater Roadrunner; Ladder-backed Woodpecker; Chihuahuan Raven; Cactus Wren; Northern Mockingbird; Curve-billed Thrasher; Loggerhead Shrike; European Starling; Pyrrhuloxia; Great-tailed Grackle; House Finch; and House Sparrow. Check the patches of mesquite for Verdin and Crissal Thrasher, and the desert scrub sites for Black-throated Sparrow; Cassin's Sparrow occurs during wet years. A few additional species can be found in summer: Turkey Vulture; Swainson's Hawk; Common Poorwill; Lesser Nighthawk; Black-chinned Hummingbird; Ash-throated Flycatcher; Western Kingbird; Northern Rough-winged, Cliff, Cave, and Barn Swallows; Summer Tanager; Blue Grosbeak; Painted Bunting; Bronzed and Brown-headed Cowbirds; and Orchard and Bullock's Orioles. Riparian areas along the ditches and reservoirs attract a few other nesting birds, including Yellow-billed Cuckoo, Bell's Vireo, and Yellow-breasted Chat. In summer and fall watch for vagrants such as Mississippi Kite and Groove-billed Ani, and out-of-range songbirds. In winter the fields support a few additional birds: Northern Harrier; Horned Lark; American Pipit; numerous sparrows, including Clay-colored and Brewer's; Eastern and Western Meadowlarks; flocks of blackbirds; and Chestnut-collared Longspur (irregular). And during migration, this area can be extremely busy with all types of birds utilizing the Rio Grande Valley as a flyway.

Tornillo Lakes (**C**), 5 miles below Tornillo (along SH 20), offer all the same water birds that can normally be found at Feather Lake. But because these are larger, a few additional species can often be found. Eared and Western Grebes, Double-crested Cormorant, and Snow and Canada Geese can be expected in winter, while Common Loon, Horned and Clark's Grebes, American White Pelican, Ross's Goose, Greater Scaup, Hooded and Common Mergansers, and Bonaparte's and Herring Gulls are less numerous.

Farther southeast on SH 20 (8.9 miles from the east end of Tornillo Lakes) is **Fort Hancock Reservoir** (**D**); walk up onto the dike to scope the reservoir, so that the sun is behind you (southeast side in the morning and northwest side in the afternoon). Although this reservoir usually supports about the same species as Feather Lake and Tornillo Lakes, migrating shorebirds can be more numerous, especially at the outlet canal in the northwest corner. Both Double-crested and Neotropic Cormorants have nested at this reservoir in recent years.

McNary Reservoir (**E**) is located even farther southeast, below McNary between I-10 and FM 192. Scope this large reservoir, which offers all the same birds

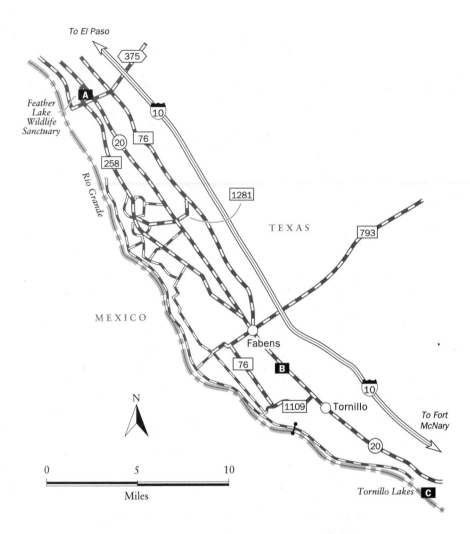

as the earlier lakes and ponds, from the 1.2-mile-long dike that parallels FM 192. However, Snow, Ross's, and Canada Geese, as well as Common Merganser and Western and Clark's Grebes, are usually more numerous here. And in migration, several species of swallows can be seen; Cave Swallows nest under the bridges along the irrigation canal across FM 192 from the reservoir and also under the McNary exit (78) off-ramp on I-10. This reservoir is surrounded by desert scrub on three sides, where all the typical desert birds can usually be found. In recent years, an impressive mix of water birds has nested along the far shore, including

2 El Paso Valley Southeast

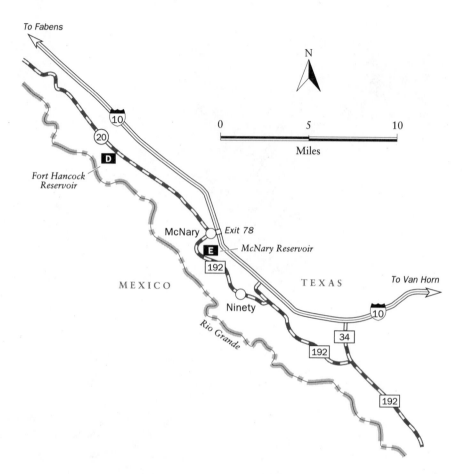

Clark's Grebe; Double-crested and Neotropic Cormorants; Great, Snowy, and Cattle Egrets; and Black-crowned Night-Heron.

Records of Review Species: Pacific Loon, Dec 1988, Dec 1994. White Ibis, April 1991. Eurasian Wigeon, approximately 10 records between Nov and April, 1996/97. Oldsquaw, Dec 1976. Black Scoter, Oct 1990. Surf Scoter, April 1995. Long-tailed Jaeger, June 1996. Laughing Gull, July 1979. Heermann's Gull, April 1997. Mew Gull, Jan–Feb 1988, Jan 1993. Thayer's Gull, Nov 1984, Jan 1997. Sabine's Gull, July 1995, July 1996. Arctic Tern, June 1979. Barrow's Goldeneye, Dec 1995. Sabine's Gull, May 1995. Crested Caracara, March 1992, Jan 1993. Broad-billed Hummingbird, Sept 1985. Red-headed Woodpecker, May–July 1992. Prairie Warbler, Nov 1987. Lapland Longspur, Feb 1986.

Directions: To enter the Rio Grande Valley corridor (SH 20) from I-10, take either Americas Avenue (Loop 375) at the north end, or the McNary exit (78) at the south end.

General information: Spring, fall, and winter are the busiest seasons in this area. Midsummer is quieter and can be very hot and dry, but it also produces its share of avian surprises. Feather Lake is managed as an environmental education and nature preserve by the El Paso/Trans-Pecos Audubon Society and has been leased (since 1976) from the city of El Paso. A nature trail, with a 20-stop brochure, is available on-site. The sanctuary is open to the public at various times throughout the week; as of July 1997 hours are in flux.

Tornillo Lakes and Fort Hancock and McNary reservoirs, farther down the valley, are surrounded by private lands, although birders are allowed to walk onto the dikes. Be sure to respect all private land.

ADDITIONAL HELP

Location: Texas Official Travel Map grid L/M/N x 1/2/3; El Paso and Hudspeth counties
Nearest food, gas, and lodging: Food and gas are available at numerous locations along SH 20; lodging is in El Paso.
Nearest camping: Several sites along I-10 and Americas Avenue
Contact: El Paso/Trans-Pecos Audubon Society (see Appendix C)

3 Hueco Tanks State Park

Habitats: Desert scrub, desert grassland, juniper woodland, cliff, pond, wetland
Key birds: Golden Eagle; Prairie Falcon; Scaled and Gambel's Quail; Greater Roadrunner; White-throated Swift; Say's Phoebe; Chihuahuan Raven; Verdin; Cactus, Rock, and Canyon Wrens; Black-tailed Gnatcatcher; Curve-billed and Crissal Thrashers; Pyrrhuloxia; Canyon Towhee; and Black-throated Sparrow are present year-round. Swainson's Hawk, Burrowing Owl, Lesser Nighthawk, Common Poorwill, Cassin's Sparrow, and Scott's Oriole occur in summer. Ferruginous Hawk; Merlin; Long-eared Owl; Black Phoebe; Eastern, Western, and Mountain Bluebirds; Townsend's Solitaire; Sage Thrasher; Phainopepla; Green-tailed Towhee; and Brewer's, Black-chinned, Sage, and Swamp Sparrows can usually be found in winter.
Best times to bird: Late March to early May for migrants and nesting activities, and November to March for winter visitors

Birding strategies: Winter birding in the park usually produces Scaled and Gambel's Quail; Mourning Dove; Greater Roadrunner; White-throated Swift; Ladder-backed Woodpecker; Northern Flicker; Say's Phoebe; Verdin; Cactus, Rock, Canyon, Bewick's, and House Wrens; Northern Mockingbird; Curve-billed and Crissal

3 **Hueco Tanks State Park**

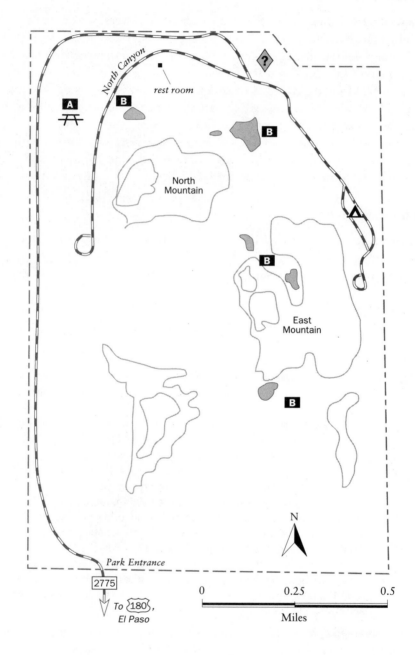

The East Mountain area in Hueco Tanks State Park.

Thrashers; Phainopepla; Loggerhead Shrike; Yellow-rumped Warbler; Pyrrhuloxia; Green-tailed, Spotted, and Canyon Towhees; Rufous-crowned, Chipping, Brewer's, Black-chinned, Vesper, Black-throated, Sage, Savannah, Song, Lincoln's, and White-crowned Sparrows; Dark-eyed Junco (both Oregon and Gray-headed); Eastern and Western Meadowlarks; House Finch; and Lesser Goldfinch. A number of other species are less numerous or irregular: Barn and Long-eared Owls; Steller's Jay; Western Scrub-Jay; Chihuahuan Raven; Eastern, Western, and Mountain Bluebirds; Townsend's Solitaire; American Robin; Sage Thrasher; Field, Swamp, and White-throated Sparrows; Pine Siskin; and American Goldfinch. Check the log at park headquarters for reports. This park also can be good during migration, when a wide variety of neotropical migrants can be expected.

The North Mountain area (**A**) is the best area for summer residents. Common nesters include Turkey Vulture; Red-tailed Hawk; Scaled and Gambel's Quail; Mourning Dove; Greater Roadrunner; Common Poorwill; Lesser Nighthawk; White-throated Swift; Black-chinned Hummingbird; Ladder-backed Woodpecker; Say's Phoebe; Ash-throated Flycatcher; Western Kingbird; Cliff and Barn Swallows; Verdin; Cactus, Rock, and Canyon Wrens; Northern Mockingbird; Crissal Thrasher; Pyrrhuloxia; Blue Grosbeak; Canyon Towhee; Cassin's and Black-throated Sparrows; Eastern Meadowlark; Scott's Oriole; and House Finch. Watch also for less numerous birds, including Barn and Great Horned Owls, Curve-billed Thrasher, Loggerhead Shrike, Rufous-crowned Sparrow, Bullock's Oriole, and Lesser Goldfinch. And overhead, watch for raptors, including Swainson's Hawk in summer and during migration; Ferruginous Hawk and Merlin in winter; and Sharp-shinned and Cooper's Hawks, Golden Eagle, American Kestrel, and Prairie Falcon year-round except midsummer. Chihuahuan Raven and Black-tailed Gnatcatcher occur along FM 2775, leading to the park.

At least four ponds (**B**), or old stock tanks, are worth birding during migration and after summer or fall rains; the small pond in North Canyon, across from the first restroom, has been best of late. Although no water birds nest, a variety of waders, ducks, and shorebirds, as well as Belted Kingfisher, Black Phoebe, and American Pipit, can often be seen there in spring and fall. In winter, after rains, the grassy areas can harbor numerous seedeaters, such as sparrows and goldfinches.

Records of Review Species: Golden-crowned Sparrow, Dec–May 1993/94, Oct–April 1994/95, Nov–April 1995/96. American Tree Sparrow, March 1997. Lawrence's Goldfinch, Dec 1984, Oct–March 1996/97.

Directions: From El Paso, take US 62/180 for 22 miles, then go north on FM 2775 for 8 miles to the park entrance.

General information: This 860-acre park is dominated by Chihuahuan Desert vegetation encircled by granitic cliffs 100 to 400 feet high, a half-mile wide, and extending about a mile in length. The cliffs form three natural amphitheaters that contain shallow water most of the time; hence the name "hueco," Spanish for "tank." Scattered rock paintings, some believed to date back about 6,000 years, occur at about 20 sites. In addition, the massive cliffs are extremely popular with rock climbers, who can dominate the park during weekends and holidays.

ADDITIONAL HELP

Location: Texas Official Travel Map grid L x 1; El Paso County.
Nearest food, gas, and lodging: Food and gas can be found at Montana Vista and Papagayo family store (15 miles); there is lodging in El Paso (30 miles).
Nearest camping: On-site (20 sites)
Contact: Superintendent, Hueco Tanks State Park (see Appendix C)

4 Guadalupe Mountains National Park

Pine and Frijoles Springs, Williams Ranch Road, the Bowl, McKittrick Canyon, and Dog Canyon

Habitats: Desert scrub, sotol grassland, oak-maple woodland, pinyon-juniper-oak woodland, ponderosa pine woodland, creek

Key birds: Golden Eagle; Wild Turkey; Scaled and Montezuma Quail; Spotted Owl; Acorn Woodpecker; Steller's Jay; Western Scrub-Jay; Common Raven; Mountain Chickadee; Juniper (Plain) Titmouse; Pygmy Nuthatch; Cactus, Rock, and Canyon Wrens; Western Bluebird; Crissal and Curve-billed Thrashers; Pyrrhuloxia; Canyon Towhee; Rufous-crowned and Black-chinned Sparrows; and Lesser Goldfinch are present year-round. Zone-tailed Hawk; Peregrine Falcon; Common Poorwill; Band-tailed Pigeon; Elf, Flammulated, and Northern Saw-whet Owls; Common Poorwill; Whip-poor-will; White-throated Swift; Blue-throated, Magnificent, and Broad-tailed Hummingbirds; Black Phoebe; Cordilleran Flycatcher; Cassin's Kingbird; Violet-green Swallow; Hutton's and Gray Vireos; Virginia's and Grace's Warblers; Hepatic and Western Tanagers; Black-headed Grosbeak; Green-tailed Towhee; Cassin's Sparrow; and Scott's Oriole occur in summer. Red-naped and Williamson's Sapsuckers, Townsend's Solitaire, Sage Sparrow, Cassin's Finch (sporadic), and Evening Grosbeak (sporadic) can usually be found in winter.

Best times to bird: April and May for spring migrants and nesting activities; November to March for winter birds

Birding strategies: Pine and Frijoles springs (A) offer a good representation of midelevation species; walk the loop trail to Frijoles Spring. Spring and summer birds here include Scaled Quail; Elf Owl; Common Poorwill; Black-chinned and Broad-tailed Hummingbirds; Acorn and Ladder-backed Woodpeckers; Ash-throated Flycatcher; Cassin's Kingbird; Western Scrub-Jay; Common Raven; Juniper Titmouse; Bushtit; Cactus, Bewick's, Canyon, and Rock Wrens; Curve-billed Thrasher; Blue-gray Gnatcatcher; Hepatic Tanager; Cassin's, Rufous-crowned, and Black-chinned Sparrows; Canyon Towhee; Scott's Oriole; House Finch; and Lesser Goldfinch. Townsend's Solitaire is usually present in winter.

Also in winter, the **Williams Ranch Road (B)** is worth driving to find Curve-billed and Crissal Thrashers, Sage Sparrow, Eastern and Western Meadowlarks, and Scott's Oriole.

The **Bowl (C)**, situated at about 8,000 feet elevation, requires a rather strenuous 2.5-mile hike from Pine Springs Campground. This forested depression offers a variety of high-country birds not known to nest elsewhere in the state: Northern Saw-whet Owl, Brown Creeper, House Wren, and Dark-eyed Junco. Here, too, can be found Sharp-shinned Hawk; Band-tailed Pigeon; Flammulated Owl; Whip-poor-will; Broad-tailed Hummingbird; Acorn and Hairy Woodpeckers; Northern Flicker; Olive-sided Flycatcher; Western Wood-Pewee; Violet-green Swallow; Steller's Jay; Mountain Chickadee; White-breasted and Pygmy Nuthatches; Hermit

4 Guadalupe Mountains National Park

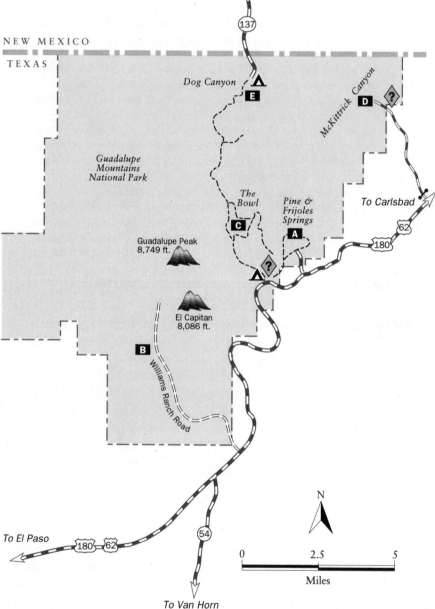

Stream in South McKittrick Canyon, Guadalupe Mountains National Park.
NATIONAL PARK SERVICE PHOTO

Thrush; Western Bluebird; Plumbeous and Warbling Vireos; Orange-crowned, Virginia's, Yellow-rumped, and Grace's Warblers; Western Tanager; Spotted Towhee; and Pine Siskin. Spotted Owls utilize slot canyons in the area during the nesting season. And in winter, a few additional birds occasionally are found in the highlands: Red-naped and Williamson's Sapsuckers, Cassin's Finch, Red Crossbill, and Evening Grosbeak.

McKittrick Canyon (D), a deep canyon in the Guadalupe Escarpment to the north, offers both desert and highland birds from the canyon mouth to the upper canyon and slopes. Lowland birds include Elf Owl, Common Poorwill, Ladder-backed Woodpecker, Say's Phoebe, Ash-throated Flycatcher, Cactus and Rock Wrens, Gray Vireo, Canyon Towhee, Pyrrhuloxia, Rufous-crowned Sparrow, Scott's Oriole, and Lesser Goldfinch. Canyon birds include White-throated Swift; Blue-throated, Magnificent, Black-chinned, and Broad-tailed Hummingbirds; Black Phoebe; Cordilleran Flycatcher; Canyon Wren; Hutton's and Cassin's Vireos; Virginia's Warbler; Black-headed Grosbeak; and Spotted Towhee. Watch also for Golden Eagle, Zone-tailed Hawk, and Peregrine and Prairie Falcons.

Dog Canyon (E), on the northern side of the park and accessible only from New Mexico, offers very different habitats where one is more likely to find Wild Turkey, Common Nighthawk, Common Poorwill, Broad-tailed Hummingbird, Ladder-backed Woodpecker, Cassin's Kingbird, Western Scrub-Jay, Juniper Titmouse, Bushtit, Bewick's Wren, Blue-gray Gnatcatcher, Western Bluebird, Gray Vireo, Hepatic Tanager, Black-headed and Blue Grosbeaks, Canyon Towhee, Scott's Oriole, and Lesser Goldfinch. Montezuma Quail is a rare resident in this area.

Records of Review Species: Northern Saw-whet Owl, June 1973, May 1988, June 1989, May–July 1993, Sept 1993, May 1994. White-eared Hummingbird, June 1991. Clark's Nutcracker, June 1969, Nov 1987. American Dipper, Oct–March 1987/88, Oct–Jan 1988/89. Varied Thrush, Oct 1989. Golden-crowned Sparrow, Nov 1991. Yellow-eyed Junco, Nov 1987, March–April 1988.

Directions: Park headquarters is located at Pine Spring, off US 62/180, 110 miles northeast of El Paso and 55 miles southwest of Carlsbad, New Mexico; Frijoles Spring and the trailhead to the Bowl are located here. McKittrick Canyon entrance road is located off US 62/180, 5 miles north of Pine Spring. Vehicular access to Dog Canyon is possible from Carlsbad, New Mexico, via SH 137.

General information: The park encompasses 86,416 acres of Guadalupe Peak (the highest point in Texas at 8,749 feet) and its adjacent ridges, canyons, and desertscape. Visitor centers are located at Pine Springs and McKittrick Canyon. Approximately 90 miles of trails provide access to the high peaks, deep canyons, and various springs. The Guadalupe Mountains are a section of the Capitan Reef, the most extensive fossil reef of Permian age on record.

ADDITIONAL HELP

Location: Texas Official Travel Map grid L x 4; Hudspeth and Culbertson counties
Nearest food, gas, and lodging: Food and gas can be found at Pine Springs, lodging at White City, 35 miles north of Pine Springs.
Nearest camping: On-site at Pine Springs (39 sites) and Dog Canyon (15 sites)
Contact: Superintendent, Guadalupe Mountains National Park (see Appendix C)

■5■ Balmorhea Lake and Balmorhea State Park

Habitats: Lake, pond, marsh, mud flat, desert scrub, sotol grassland, pasture, cropland

Key birds: "Mexican Duck" (Mallard); Wild Turkey; Scaled Quail; Greater Roadrunner; Burrowing Owl; Black and Say's Phoebes; Vermilion Flycatcher; Common Raven; Verdin; Cactus Wren; Curve-billed Thrasher; Pyrrhuloxia; Canyon Towhee; Rufous-crowned, Cassin's, and Black-throated Sparrows; and Lesser Goldfinch are present year-round. King and Virginia Rails, Sora, Common Ground-Dove, Common Poorwill, Lesser and Common Nighthawks, Scissor-tailed Flycatcher, Chihuahuan Raven, Bell's Vireo, and Painted Bunting occur in summer. Common and Red-throated Loons; American White Pelican; Rough-legged and Ferruginous Hawks; Bald Eagle; Sandhill Crane; Eastern, Mountain, and Western Bluebirds; American and Sprague's Pipits; Green-tailed and Spotted Towhees; Brewer's, Grasshopper, Baird's, and Sage Sparrows; and McCown's and Chestnut-collared Longspurs can usually be found in winter.

Best times to bird: November to January for vagrant water birds; late July and August for migrating shorebirds

Birding strategies: In winter, scope Balmorhea Lake (**A**) and the surrounding flats (from the north levee and from the dam) for Common Loon; Pied-billed, Eared, Western, and Clark's Grebes; American White Pelican; Great Blue and Green Herons; Great, Snowy, and Cattle Egrets; numerous ducks and shorebirds; Ring-billed and Bonaparte's Gulls; and Forster's and Black Terns. Watch for unusual species like Red-throated Loon, Horned Grebe, Brown Pelican, and rare divers and shorebirds.

The shallow pond on the north side of the levee road is a good place to find waders and shorebirds. Most common are Great Blue and Green Herons, White-faced Ibis, Sora, American Coot, Snowy Plover, American Avocet, Black-necked Stilt, Greater and Lesser Yellowlegs, Spotted and Least Sandpipers, and Common Snipe. During migration, also check the mud flats for shorebirds along the western side of the lake, beyond the dam. Watch for the resident "Mexican Duck," currently classified as a subspecies of Mallard, in the irrigation ditches.

The surrounding weedy fields can be very productive during years of normal rainfall. Thousands of migrating and wintering grassland birds utilize these fields, including such rarities as Baird's Sparrow and Smith's Longspur. Both Eastern and Western Meadowlarks occur here. The resident "Lillian's" Meadowlark is likely to receive specific status soon.

Balmorhea State Park (**B**) is less productive but worth birding in winter and spring. Typical birds include Green Heron; White-winged, Mourning, and Inca Doves; Black-chinned Hummingbird; Ladder-backed Woodpecker; Scissor-tailed and Vermilion Flycatchers; Verdin; Cactus Wren; Northern Mockingbird; Curve-billed Thrasher; Loggerhead Shrike; Northern Cardinal; Pyrrhuloxia; Canyon

5 **Balmorhea Lake and Balmorhea State Park**

Towhee; Black-throated Sparrow; meadowlarks; House Finch; and Lesser Goldfinch year-round.

During migration the park cottonwoods and other trees provide good habitat for an amazing variety of neotropical migrants, such as flycatchers, vireos, warblers, and other songbirds. The new (1995) 2- to 3-acre San Solomon Springs Cienega marsh habitat is likely to attract an additional variety of birds. White Ibis, Wood Duck, Greater Scaup, Red-breasted Merganser, and Sedge Wren already were found here.

Records of Review Species: Red-throated Loon, Oct 1983, Jan–Feb 1988, Nov–April 1993/94, winter 1996/97, Dec–Feb 1996/97. Pacific Loon, Oct 1988, Dec–April 1994/95. Yellow-billed Loon, Nov–Dec 1993, Dec–Jan 1996/97. Lesser Black-backed Gull, Nov–Dec 1990. Black-legged Kittiwake, Nov 1991. Sabine's Gull, Oct 1988, Sept 1991. Elegant Tern, Dec 1985. Varied Thrush, Feb 1996. Snow Bunting, Nov 1993.

Directions: The town of Balmorhea is accessible from I-10, or by SH 17 from Fort Davis; Balmorhea Lake is south of town, via Houston Street. The state park is 4 miles west of town along SH 17, adjacent to the small town of Toyahvale.

General information: The state park and lake are near San Solomon Springs, a group of artesian and gravity springs that produce 80 million gallons of water daily; they are known as the Oasis of West Texas. The area has been an important camping area for Indians, pioneers, and ranchers for hundreds of years. The springs were once known as Mescalero Springs, after the Mescalero Apaches who utilized them. The restored San Solomon Cienega provides habitat for two endangered fish—Comanche Springs pupfish and Pecos gambusia—and numerous wetland bird species.

Balmorhea Lake (approximately 600 acres), dammed on the southwestern edge, serves as a reservoir for the surrounding agricultural lands. The dam is a containment dike. The state park contains a huge (1.75-acre) swimming pool that is fed by springs at the rate of 22 to 26 million gallons daily.

ADDITIONAL HELP

Location: Texas Official Travel Map grid O x 6; Reeves County
Nearest food, gas, and lodging: Food and gas are available at Balmorhea; lodging is available at the state park and Balmorhea.
Nearest camping: On-site at state park (68 sites)
Contact: Superintendent, Balmorhea State Park (see Appendix C)

6 Davis Mountains and Davis Mountains State Park

Habitats: Creek, riparian, desert scrub, sotol grassland, oak savannah, pinyon-juniper-oak woodland, ponderosa pine stand, pasture

Key birds: "Mexican Duck" (Mallard), Golden Eagle, Prairie Falcon, Scaled and Montezuma Quail, Band-tailed Pigeon, Greater Roadrunner, White-throated Swift, Acorn Woodpecker, Black and Say's Phoebes, Western Scrub-Jay, Mountain Chickadee, Pygmy Nuthatch, Canyon and Rock Wrens, Curve-billed Thrasher, Phainopepla, Pyrrhuloxia, Canyon Towhee, Rufous-crowned and Black-chinned Sparrows, and Lesser Goldfinch are present year-round. Swainson's and Zone-tailed Hawks; Common Black-Hawk; Common Poorwill; Lesser and Common Nighthawks; Blue-throated, Black-chinned, and Broad-tailed Hummingbirds; Ash-throated Flycatcher; Cassin's Kingbird; Violet-green Swallow; Chihuahuan Raven; Bell's and Plumbeous (Solitary) Vireos; Virginia's and Grace's Warblers; Hepatic and Western Tanagers; Painted Bunting; and Bronzed Cowbird occur in summer. Rough-legged, Ferruginous, and Harris's Hawks; Merlin; Red-naped and Williamson's Sapsuckers; Pinyon Jay; Sage Thrasher; Mountain and Eastern Bluebirds; Townsend's Solitaire; Green-tailed Towhee; Chestnut-collared and McCown's Longspurs; Cassin's Finch; Red Crossbill; and Evening Grosbeak can usually be found in winter.

Best times to bird: April and early May for spring migrants and nesting activities; July and August for fall migrants

6 Davis Mountains and Davis Mountains State Park

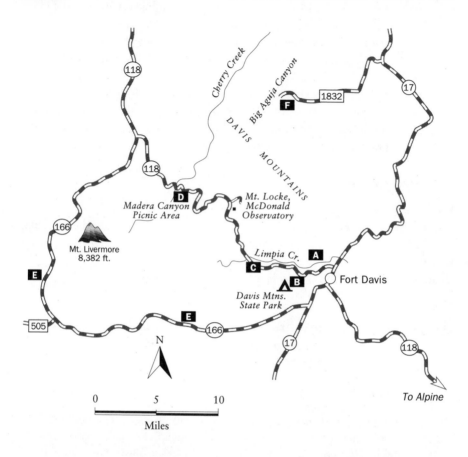

Birding strategies: Limpia Creek (**A**), just beyond the town of Fort Davis, is dominated by huge cottonwood trees. Drive slowly along SH 118, stopping at various places to bird the lush riparian habitat (stay on the roadway). This area has supported two or three pairs of Common Black-Hawks for many years; the most likely place to see this bird is below the state park along SH 118, 1.8 miles below the park entrance. (Park near the "35 mph" sign; bird from the highway edge; sometimes the birds perch on the pinnacles to the south; do not walk into the creekbed; that would disturb the birds, and the land is private property.) Another nesting pair can often be seen along SH 17, across a small pasture, 2.5 miles north of the SH 118/17 intersection.

Other summer birds found along the creek include Western Wood-Pewee, Black Phoebe, Ash-throated Flycatcher, Western and Cassin's Kingbirds, Summer Tanager, Painted Bunting, Orchard and Bullock's Orioles, House Finch, and Lesser Goldfinch. At the palisade-like cliffs opposite Limpia Creek, look for Canyon and Rock Wrens. During the winter months, several additional birds can be expected along Limpia Creek: Vermilion Flycatcher; Eastern, Mountain, and Western Blue-birds; Green-tailed and Spotted Towhees; and several sparrows, including Lincoln's, Swamp, and Song.

Davis Mountains State Park (B), in the heart of the Davis Mountains, is the best place to find Montezuma Quail. This lovely bird usually can be found along the edge of the campground, along the entrance road at the campground host campsite, or at the Interpretive Center. Summer residents of interest here include Greater Roadrunner; Common Poorwill; Acorn and Ladder-backed Woodpeck-ers; Black and Say's Phoebes; Ash-throated Flycatcher; Cassin's Kingbird; Western Scrub-Jay; Tufted Titmouse; Bushtit; Cactus, Bewick's, Canyon, and Rock Wrens; Curve-billed Thrasher; Phainopepla; Black-headed and Blue Grosbeaks; Painted Bunting; Northern Cardinal; Pyrrhuloxia; Canyon Towhee; Rufous-crowned, Black-chinned, Black-throated, and Lark Sparrows; House Finch; and Scott's Oriole.

The scenic road beyond the state park (SH 118) to Mount Locke and McDonald Observatory passes through extensive ranchland (C). You'll probably see the same species as those in the park; watch for Montezuma Quail along the road. Addi-tional possible species include Prairie Falcon and Western Bluebird. And if century plants are in bloom, watch for Black-chinned and Broad-tailed Hummingbirds at the flowers.

Continue beyond the side road to McDonald Observatory to the Madera Can-yon Picnic Area (D). This is the best chance to find some of the high-country birds

Davis Mountains from Davis Mountains State Park.

that are more numerous on private lands at higher elevations. Band-tailed Pigeon, White-throated Swift, Acorn Woodpecker, Violet-green Swallow, Bushtit, Hepatic and Western Tanagers, and Black-headed Grosbeak nest in the area, and occasionally, Gray Flycatcher, Steller's Jay, Mountain Chickadee, Pygmy Nuthatch, and Plumbeous and Hutton's Vireos are present. And after dark, Common Poorwill, Western Screech-Owl, and Elf Owl may be heard.

The scenic drive soon drops into lower, more open country, and it is possible to make a loop drive back to Fort Davis. These lower ranchlands (E) offer good habitat for Golden Eagle, Prairie Falcon, Say's Phoebe, Cassin's Sparrow, and Eastern ("Lillian's") Meadowlark year-round. In summer, watch for Mountain Plover along SH 166 near the Point of Rock Picnic Area. And in winter, watch for McCown's and Chestnut-collared Longspurs.

Aguja Canyon (F), to the Buffalo Trail Boy Scout Ranch, is also worth birding. Watch for Scaled Quail, Greater Roadrunner, Ash-throated Flycatcher, Western Kingbird, Verdin, Cactus Wren, Curve-billed and Sage Thrashers, Pyrrhuloxia, and Black-throated and Brewer's Sparrows in the brushy foothills. Where the road crosses the creek, look for White-winged Dove, Black Phoebe, Bell's Vireo, Summer Tanager, Painted and Varied Buntings, and Black-chinned Sparrow. The cliffs near the entrance to the Boy Scout ranch usually offer White-throated Swift and Canyon Wren.

Records of Review Species: Brown Pelican, June 1992. Tundra Swan, Dec 1986. Gray Hawk, Sept 1976. Northern Saw-whet Owl, June 1991, June 1992. Broad-billed Hummingbird, May 1993. White-eared Hummingbird, June–Aug 1993, July–Aug 1994, July–Aug 1996. Greater Pewee, May 1992. Dusky-capped Flycatcher, June 1991, June 1992. Clark's Nutcracker, Jan 1973. Black-billed Magpie, fall 1995, fall 1996. Rufous-backed Robin, Feb 1992. Varied Thrush, March 1992. Olive Warbler, May 1992. Golden-crowned Sparrow, Nov 1992. Common Redpoll, Nov–Dec 1996.

Directions: Fort Davis is located 25 miles northwest of Alpine via SH 118. Davis Mountains State Park is 4 miles west of Fort Davis; the 74-mile scenic drive circles the southern half of the mountains via SH 118, SH 166, and SH 17; Aguja Canyon and the Boy Scout ranch can be reached via a 6-mile side road (FM 1832) off SH 17, 25 miles north of Fort Davis.

General information: The Davis Mountains represent the most extensive mountain range in Texas (675 square miles above 5,500 feet elevation). The great majority of the Davis Mountains is private property, and birders must not trespass. Public access is extremely limited; none of the forested highlands are currently available to birders. Most of the area ranchers zealously protect their land, and birders who do not heed "no trespassing" signs make it even more difficult for those who do.

Davis Mountains State Park encompasses 2,777 acres within the pinyon-juniper-oak-grassland environment. The park offers extensive hiking trails, interpretive activities, and bird banding seminars in spring and fall.

Fort Davis National Historic Site (at Fort Davis) is a superb example of a frontier fort, including a parade grounds, ruins, and reconstructed barracks. It was established in 1854 and deserted during the Civil War; troops returned to the fort in 1867 and remained until 1891. A special feature of Fort Davis is the aural re-creation of a nineteenth-century military parade. The Chihuahuan Desert Research Institute, with botanical gardens and nature trails, is located on SH 118, 4 miles southeast of Fort Davis.

The McDonald Observatory, located atop 6,791-foot Mount Locke and operated by the University of Texas, houses one of the country's most outstanding telescopes. A visitor center, open daily from 9 A.M. to 5 P.M., offers summer viewing and guided tours.

ADDITIONAL HELP

Location: Texas Official Travel Map grid O x 5; Jeff Davis County
Nearest food, gas, and lodging: Fort Davis and Indian Lodge in Davis Mountains State Park have facilities for all three.
Nearest camping: On-site at Davis Mountains State Park (100 sites)
Contact: Superintendent, Davis Mountains State Park (see Appendix C)

7 Marathon Basin

The Post and Prairie Dog Colony

Habitats: Pond, creek, riparian, cottonwood grove, desert scrub, grassland
Key birds: "Mexican Duck" (Mallard), Harris's Hawk, Scaled Quail, Greater Roadrunner, **Golden-fronted Woodpecker,** Black and Say's Phoebes, Vermilion Flycatcher, Common Raven, Verdin, Cactus Wren, Black-tailed Gnatcatcher, Curve-billed Thrasher, Phainopepla, Pyrrhuloxia, Black-throated Sparrow, House Finch, and Lesser Goldfinch are present year-round. Swainson's Hawk, **Lucifer Hummingbird,** Elf and Burrowing Owls, Lesser and Common Nighthawks, Black-chinned Hummingbird, Scissor-tailed Flycatcher, Cassin's and Western Kingbirds, Chihuahuan Raven, Varied and Painted Buntings, Cassin's Sparrow, Bronzed Cowbird, and Orchard, Hooded, Bullock's, and Scott's Orioles occur in summer. Ferruginous Hawk; Eastern, Western, and Mountain Bluebirds; Sage and Crissal Thrashers; Green-tailed Towhee; Clay-colored, Brewer's, and Vesper Sparrows; and Lark Bunting can usually be found in winter.
Best times to bird: April and early May for spring migrants and nesting activities

Birding strategies: The Post (A), a spring-fed riparian area south of Marathon, offers the area's best birding year-round: Mexican Duck, Harris's and Red-tailed Hawks, Scaled Quail, American Coot, Killdeer, White-winged and Mourning Doves, Greater Roadrunner, Barn and Great Horned Owls, Belted Kingfisher, **Golden-fronted Woodpecker,** Ladder-backed Woodpecker, Black and Say's Phoebes,

7 Marathon Basin

Vermilion Flycatcher, Bewick's Wren, Northern Mockingbird, Curve-billed Thrasher, Phainopepla, European Starling, Northern Cardinal, Lark Sparrow, Red-winged Blackbird, House Finch, and Lesser Goldfinch. Several additional species occur in summer: Green Heron; Inca Dove; Yellow-billed Cuckoo; Elf Owl; Lesser and Common Nighthawks; Black-chinned Hummingbird; Ash-throated and Scissor-tailed Flycatchers; Cassin's and Western Kingbirds; Northern Rough-winged, Cliff, and Barn Swallows; Chihuahuan Raven; Bell's Vireo; Yellow-breasted Chat; Summer Tanager; Blue Grosbeak; Varied and Painted Buntings; Bronzed and Brown-headed Cowbirds; Orchard, Hooded, and Bullock's Orioles. In addition, this site can act as a migrant trap in spring and fall, attracting an amazing number of migrants.

A number of desert scrub species are more likely along the entrance road (**B**): Common Raven, Verdin, Cactus Wren, Black-tailed Gnatcatcher, Crissal Thrasher, Pyrrhuloxia, Rufous-crowned and Black-throated Sparrows, and Western Meadowlark occur year-round. Look for Swainson's Hawk, Chihuahuan Raven, Cassin's

Sparrow, and Scott's Oriole in summer. In late fall and winter the brushy areas and grasslands (especially after summer rains) often harbor additional birds, including Eastern, Western, and Mountain Bluebirds; Sage and Crissal Thrashers; Green-tailed and Spotted Towhees; Chipping, Clay-colored, Brewer's, Field, Vesper, Savannah, Song, Lincoln's, and White-crowned Sparrows; Lark Bunting; Eastern Meadowlark; Brewer's Blackbird; and American Goldfinch.

The town of Marathon (**C**) also supports a number of birds. During spring and fall, migrants often linger around the wooded areas. Hummingbirds, including Black-chinned, Broad-tailed, occasionally **Lucifer Hummingbird,** and Rufous (in late summer and fall), can sometimes be seen at feeders maintained by local residents.

There is an extensive prairie dog colony (**D**) on US 385, 7 miles north of US 90, where Burrowing Owls reside during spring and summer. Also look here and in the immediate grassland area for Swainson's and Red-tailed Hawks, Scaled Quail, Killdeer, Mourning Dove, Scissor-tailed Flycatcher, Western Kingbird, Horned Lark, Chihuahuan Raven, Northern Mockingbird, Curve-billed Thrasher, Loggerhead Shrike, Lark Sparrow, Lark Bunting, and Eastern Meadowlark. Ferruginous Hawk often occurs here in winter.

Records of Review Species: Northern Jacana, Oct 1982. Broad-billed Hummingbird, Aug 1994. Red Crossbill, Oct–March 1996/97. Lawrence's Goldfinch, Nov–Jan 1996/97.

Directions: Marathon lies along US 90, 22 miles east of Alpine and 54 miles west of Sanderson. The Post is located 5.2 miles south of Marathon via an undesignated road; it begins directly south of the railroad tracks, across the highway from the Gage Hotel. The prairie dog colony is located along the east side of US 385, 7 miles north of US 90.

General information: The Marathon Basin is a natural bowl between the Glass Mountains on the north and east and Santiago Mountains on the south and southwest. The Post contains the remains of old Fort Pena Colorado, established in 1879 to protect settlers from hostile Indians; it was abandoned in 1893. Today The Post is a popular picnicking site that can be busy on weekends.

The historic Gage Hotel, in the center of Marathon, was built by Alfred Gage in 1927 as headquarters for his extensive ranch. It has since been renovated for a popular hotel and restaurant. Marathon also contains a number of craft shops and the James Evans Gallery.

ADDITIONAL HELP

Location: Texas Official Travel Map grid P x 7; Brewster County
Nearest food, gas, and lodging: All are available in Marathon.
Nearest camping: Marathon
Contact: Marathon Chamber of Commerce; most of the area is privately owned (see Appendix C)

8 Big Bend Ranch State Park

Habitats: Desert scrub, riparian, stock tank, river, floodplain
Key birds: "Mexican Duck" (Mallard), Scaled Quail, Greater Roadrunner, **Golden-fronted Woodpecker,** Verdin, Cactus and Rock Wrens, Black-tailed Gnatcatcher, Curve-billed and Crissal Thrashers, Phainopepla, Pyrrhuloxia, Canyon Towhee, Rufous-crowned and Black-throated Sparrows, and Lesser Goldfinch are present year-round. Zone-tailed Hawk, Peregrine Falcon, Elf Owl, Lesser and Common Nighthawks, Common Poorwill, **Lucifer Hummingbird,** Cassin's and Western Kingbirds, Chihuahuan Raven, Bell's Vireo, Lucy's Warbler, Summer Tanager, Varied and Painted Buntings, Bronzed Cowbird, and Hooded and Scott's Orioles occur in summer. Golden Eagle; Prairie Falcon; Anna's Hummingbird; Dusky and Gray Flycatchers; Mountain Bluebird; Sage Thrasher; Townsend's Warbler; Gray Vireo; Green-tailed Towhee; Clay-colored, Brewer's, and Sage Sparrows; and McCown's and Chestnut-colored Longspurs can usually be found in winter.
Best times to bird: April and May for spring migrants and nesting activities; September and October for fall migrants; November to March for winter birds

Birding strategies: Fort Leaton State Park (**A**) is a logical place to begin a birding tour of Big Bend Ranch, because the necessary permit for access to Big Bend Ranch's Solitario Viewpoint Road can be obtained there. The picnic grounds at the entrance to the fort offer a good variety of desert species. Scaled Quail; White-winged, Mourning, and Inca Doves; Greater Roadrunner; **Golden-fronted Woodpecker;** Ladder-backed Woodpecker; Say's Phoebe; Western Kingbird; Common Raven; Verdin; Cactus Wren; Northern Mockingbird; Curve-billed Thrasher; Northern Cardinal; Pyrrhuloxia; Canyon Towhee; Black-throated Sparrow; Great-tailed Grackle; House Finch; and Lesser Goldfinch can be expected year-round. Yellow-billed Cuckoo, Elf Owl, Lesser Nighthawk, Ash-throated Flycatcher, Cliff and Barn Swallows, Chihuahuan Raven, Bell's Vireo, Yellow-breasted Chat, Summer Tanager, Blue Grosbeak, Painted Bunting, Bronzed Cowbird, and Orchard and Hooded Orioles occur in summer. And in winter, Northern Flicker; Eastern Phoebe; House Wren; Ruby-crowned Kinglet; Orange-crowned and Yellow-rumped Warblers; Green-tailed and Spotted Towhees; and Clay-colored, Chipping, Brewer's, Vesper, Lincoln's, and White-crowned Sparrows can usually be found.

In the park's heartlands, the riparian and adjacent desert scrub habitats along Bofecillos Creek offer the park's most unique birding sites. The cottonwood-willow–dominated Ojito Adentro (**B**), located 18.3 miles from FM 170 and a 0.7-mile-long trail, supports a wide variety of birds throughout the year. Expected nesting species include White-winged and Mourning Doves, Yellow-billed Cuckoo, Black-chinned Hummingbird, Ladder-backed Woodpecker, Western Wood-Pewee, Black Phoebe, Ash-throated Flycatcher, Cassin's Kingbird, Bell's Vireo, Yellow-

8   Big Bend Ranch State Park

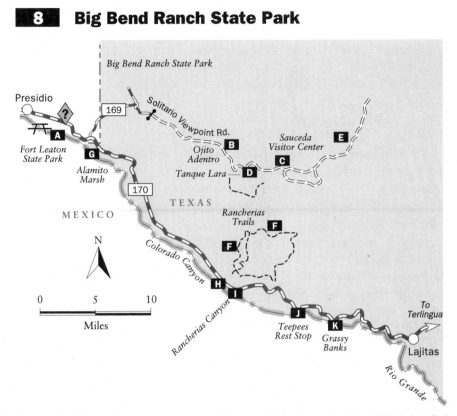

breasted Chat, Summer Tanager, Varied Bunting, Northern Cardinal, Black-headed and Blue Grosbeaks, Brown-headed Cowbird, Orchard Oriole, and Lesser Goldfinch. Less numerous/obvious species are Eastern and Western Screech-Owls and **Golden-fronted Woodpecker.** Spring and fall migration can be superb; flycatchers, thrushes, vireos, warblers, and orioles can be abundant.

Desert birds can be found year-round at numerous places along the park roadway (C), especially in the vicinity of windmills and stock tanks. Common year-round species include Red-tailed Hawk, Scaled Quail, Mourning Dove, Greater Roadrunner, Ladder-backed Woodpecker, Say's Phoebe, Common Raven, Verdin, Cactus and Rock Wrens, Black-tailed Gnatcatcher, Northern Mockingbird, Curve-billed Thrasher, Loggerhead Shrike, Pyrrhuloxia, Rufous-crowned and Black-throated Sparrows, and House Finch. A few additional birds occur in summer: Elf Owl, Lesser and Common Nighthawks, Common Poorwill, **Lucifer Humming-bird,** Ash-throated Flycatcher, Chihuahuan Raven, Painted Bunting, and Bronzed Cowbird. A few other species prefer brushy areas: Bewick's Wren, Crissal Thrasher, Phainopepla, Varied and Painted Buntings, and Hooded Oriole.

Although numerous stock tanks contain water in wet seasons, only Tanque Lara (D) is dependable in all but the driest years. This site attracts all the resident species as well as passing migrants. Also, after summer rains have produced grass crops, the desert arroyos and surrounding grasslands, such as the area just north of the La Posta turnoff (**E**), can harbor numerous wintering seedeaters. Typical species include Mountain Bluebird; Sage Thrasher; Green-tailed and Spotted Towhees; Cassin's, Chipping, Clay-colored, Brewer's, Field, Vesper, Lark, Black-throated, Sage, Savannah, Grasshopper, Fox, Song, Lincoln's, Swamp, and White-crowned Sparrows; Dark-eyed Junco; McCown's and Chestnut-collared Longspurs; Eastern and Western Meadowlarks; Brewer's Blackbird; and Lesser and American Goldfinches.

Also keep watch overhead: Common Raven, Golden Eagle, Red-tailed Hawk, and Peregrine and Prairie Falcons can appear.

In addition, the Rancherias Trails (**F**), accessible off FM 170 (17.5 miles west of Lajitas), offer the hiker many of the same birds that can be found along the Solitario Viewpoint Road.

Good birding sites along the Rio Grande include Alamito Marsh (**G**) (view only from the highway), just east of Fort Leaton State Park; Colorado Canyon (**H**); the riparian areas north of the mouth of Rancherias Canyon (**I**); the Teepees Rest Stop (**J**); and Grassy Banks (**K**). The floodplain and cliff habitats support a number of birds that may not normally be found elsewhere. Great Blue Heron, Mexican Duck, Peregrine Falcon, and White-throated Swift can occur year-round. Watch for Green Heron, Zone-tailed Hawk, Cliff and Cave Swallows, and Lucy's Warbler in summer. And during the winter months, numerous waterfowl, a few shorebirds, Belted Kingfisher, and Northern Rough-winged Swallow occur at choice areas. Other winter species possible along the Rio Grande corridor include Anna's Hummingbird, Dusky and Gray Flycatchers, Gray Vireo, Townsend's Warbler, Varied Bunting, and Blue Grosbeak.

Directions: Fort Leaton is located along FM 170 on the east side of Presidio, 60 miles west of Lajitas. To access the Solitario Viewpoint Road, take Casa Piedra Road (FM 169), 3 miles east of Fort Leaton, for 6.9 miles to the Solitario Viewpoint Road; the entry gate is 2.4 miles beyond, and the Sauceda Visitor Center is 11.5 miles beyond the entry gate.

General information: The 300,000-acre Big Bend Ranch State Park extends along the Rio Grande for 60 miles between Presidio and Lajitas and encompasses the geologically unique Solitario and scenic Bofecillos Creek. Park information and interpretation are available at the Barton Warnock Environmental Center at Lajitas and at Fort Leaton and Sauceda. The Warnock Center also offers a self-guided botanical garden, featuring characteristic Chihuahuan Desert plants. Fort Leaton was built in 1848 on the site of an earlier fort established during the U.S.-Mexican War by Benjamin Leaton, a scalp hunter.

Entry to the park's heartlands is by permit only, available at either the Warnock Center or Fort Leaton. Bus tours into the interior, including a guide, scheduled stops, and a chuck wagon lunch, are also available ($30) by reservations.

ADDITIONAL HELP

Location: Texas Official Travel Map grid R x 5; Presidio County

Nearest food, gas, and lodging: All are available at Lajitas and Presidio; lodging is also available on-site at Sauceda (reservations only).

Nearest camping: Primitive camping on-site; RV hookups at Presidio and Lajitas

Contact: Superintendent, Big Bend Ranch State Park (see Appendix C)

9 Big Bend National Park

Rio Grande Village, Chisos Mountains, Blue Creek Canyon, and Cottonwood Campground/Santa Elena Canyon

Habitats: River, creek, pond, marsh, riparian, cottonwood grove, cliff, desert scrub, sotol grassland, oak-maple woodland, pinyon-juniper-oak woodland, pine-cypress woodland

Key birds: "Mexican Duck" (Mallard), Golden Eagle, Peregrine and Prairie Falcons, Scaled Quail, Greater Roadrunner, White-throated Swift, Eastern and Western Screech-Owls, Acorn Woodpecker, **Golden-fronted Woodpecker,** Black and Say's Phoebes, Vermilion Flycatcher, Mexican Jay, Verdin, Black-tailed Gnatcatcher, Rock and Canyon Wrens, Curve-billed and Crissal Thrashers, Hutton's Vireo, Pyrrhuloxia, Canyon Towhee, Rufous-crowned and Black-chinned Sparrows, and Lesser Goldfinch are present year-round. Common Black-Hawk; Zone-tailed and Gray Hawks; Lesser Nighthawk; Common Poorwill; Whip-poor-will; Band-tailed Pigeon; Elf and Flammulated Owls; **Lucifer Hummingbird;** Blue-throated, Magnificent, Broad-tailed, and Rufous (by July) Hummingbirds; Cordilleran Flycatcher; Violet-green and Cave Swallows; Phainopepla; **Black-capped Vireo;** Gray Vireo; **Colima Warbler;** Lucy's Warbler; Hepatic Tanager; Varied and Painted Buntings; Bronzed Cowbird; and Hooded and Scott's Orioles occur in summer. Anna's Hummingbird, Yellow-bellied and Red-naped Sapsuckers, Townsend's Solitaire, Mountain and Western Bluebirds, Sage Thrasher, Green-tailed Towhee, and Cassin's, Clay-colored, Brewer's, Sage, and Baird's Sparrows can usually be found in winter.

Best times to bird: April and May for spring migrants and nesting activities; mid-August to mid-October for fall migrants and post-nesting visitors; November to March for winter birds

Birding strategies: Start at Rio Grande Village on the nature trail (**A**) in the southeastern corner of the campground, where various water birds and spring migrants are possible. The trail provides an overall view of the area. Watch for Peregrine Falcon along the river in the early morning. Then check the campground proper (**B**), especially along the eastern edge, where spring migrants often forage in the mesquites and cottonwoods. Eastern and Western Screech-Owls can sometimes be found here after dark. Elf Owl utilizes woodpecker cavities in utility poles for nesting. Vermilion Flycatcher is common within the campground, as are

⬛ 9 ⬛ Big Bend National Park Southeast

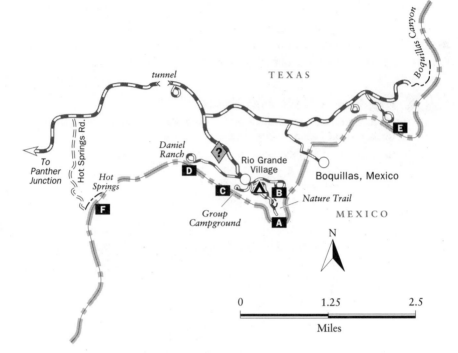

White-winged Dove, Yellow-billed Cuckoo, **Golden-fronted Woodpecker,** Ladder-backed Woodpecker, Summer Tanager, Painted Bunting, Pyrrhuloxia, and Orchard Oriole. Watch also for Bronzed Cowbird in summer.

The group campground and picnic area (**C**) behind the store often harbors spring migrants and is a good area for various roosting raptors in spring and summer. Walk upriver along the road, checking the mesquite thickets and open fields for Verdin, Curve-billed and Crissal Thrashers, sparrows, and migrants in spring. Common Black-Hawk is an irregular visitor.

Next, drive to the end of the road west of the store and bird Daniel Ranch (**D**). Check the river beyond the old ranch house for water birds, Black Phoebe, and swallows, including Northern Rough-winged, year-round; and Cliff and Cave Swallows in summer. Then walk through the cottonwood grove, looking for migrants and Gray Hawk (nested there since 1988; do not disturb!). Walk up the closed road (west of the cottonwood grove at the base of the open slope) to the silt ponds, which offer a variety of water birds at all seasons. The adjacent mesquites, willows, and cottonwoods can be alive with spring migrants. The rocky slopes often harbor Rock and Canyon Wrens; watch overhead for soaring Zone-tailed Hawk.

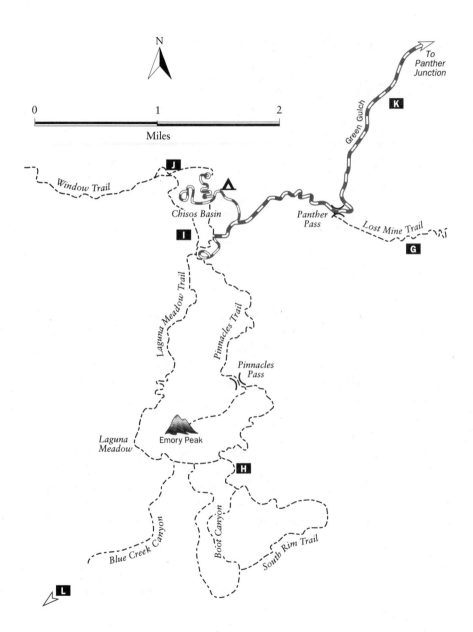

N

0   1   2
Miles

To
Panther
Junction

K

Green Gulch

Window Trail

J

Chisos Basin

Panther
Pass

Lost Mine Trail

G

I

Laguna Meadow Trail

Pinnacles Trail

Pinnacles
Pass

Emory Peak

Laguna
Meadow

H

Blue Creek Canyon

Boot Canyon

South Rim Trail

L

9 Big Bend National Park West

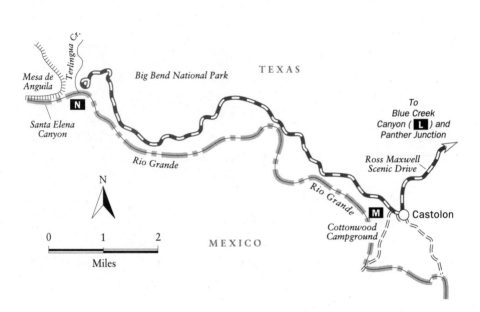

After birding Rio Grande Village, drive to Boquillas Canyon (**E**), checking various overlooks along the Rio Grande en route. Spring migrants frequent vegetation along the entire floodplain. In late fall and winter, walk through the open flats in front of Boquillas Canyon, looking for Sage Thrasher and various sparrows. At the canyon mouth, watch for Peregrine Falcon, which hunts the floodplain and soars overhead year-round. This road is an excellent place to find Common Poorwill in spring and summer.

Check Hot Springs (**F**), located on the Rio Grande at the mouth of Tornillo Creek, in spring (for migrants) and during the evening hours in spring and summer. Lesser Nighthawk feeds over the water at dusk.

The **Chisos Mountains** dominate the center of the park, and should also be birded year-round. The Lost Mine Trail (**G**), starting at Panther Pass, provides the easiest access into the highlands, where all the characteristic woodland species—Mexican Jay, Tufted Titmouse, Bushtit, Bewick's Wren, and Hutton's Vireo—can usually be found. However, you must hike either the Pinnacles Trail or Laguna Meadow Trail toward Boot Canyon (9 miles round-trip either route) to see the **Colima Warbler**. It normally is present along the upper portions of these trails and in Boot Canyon from late March to early September. Colimas also can be found most years in Pine Canyon and the upper Green Gulch canyons.

Boot Canyon (**H**) is the only sure place for finding the Flammulated Owl; overnight camping is necessary. Eastern and Western Screech-Owls, as well as

The Chisos Mountains from Green Gulch in Big Bend National Park.

Whip-poor-will, can also be found along the canyon after dark. Key daylight species here include **Lucifer Hummingbird,** Blue-throated, Magnificent (rare), and Broad-tailed Hummingbirds; Acorn Woodpecker; Cordilleran Flycatcher; White-breasted Nuthatch; Rock and Canyon Wrens; and Painted Redstart (irregular). In winter, Mountain and Western Bluebirds frequent the open slopes, such as along the Emory Peak Trail; Williamson's Sapsucker, Red Crossbill, and Cassin's Finch are sporadic.

The Chisos Basin proper (**I**), including the area just above the park cottages, usually supports White-winged Dove, Say's Phoebe, Barn Swallow, Mexican Jay, Hepatic Tanager, Canyon Towhee, Black-chinned Sparrow, and Scott's Oriole.

In spring and summer, bird the upper half of the Window Trail (**J**), starting in Basin Campground. Expected birds include Gray Vireo, Varied Bunting, Black-chinned Sparrow, Scott's Oriole, and Lesser Goldfinch. Watch also for Crissal Thrasher and **Black-capped Vireo.** Band-tailed Pigeon frequents oak groves along the lower portion of this trail. Check around the sewage lagoons for most of the above birds plus Violet-green Swallow, Phainopepla, Yellow-breasted Chat, and Pyrrhuloxia. Also, watch for Zone-tailed Hawk anywhere in the Basin. And in winter, this area is a good place to find Townsend's Solitaire.

Green Gulch (**K**) offers many key birds from along the road, including Hepatic Tanager, Rufous-crowned and Black-chinned Sparrows, and Scott's Oriole. In upper

Green Gulch one can usually find Whip-poor-will (at dusk and dawn), Mexican Jay, Bushtit, and Hutton's Vireo.

Mid- to late summer can produce numerous post-nesting visitors and early fall migrants in the highlands, including Rufous Hummingbird and an assortment of warblers: Black-throated Gray, Townsend's, Hermit, Black-throated Green, Grace's, and Black-and-white.

Cottonwood Campground and Santa Elena Canyon are accessible via the Ross Maxwell Scenic Drive. In spring walk up Blue Creek Canyon (**L**) about a mile to find Scaled Quail, **Lucifer Hummingbird,** Black-tailed Gnatcatcher, Crissal Thrasher, Phainopepla, Gray Vireo, and Varied Bunting. Continue to **Cottonwood Campground** (**M**), just beyond Castolon. This small cottonwood grove, with its dense mesquite-dominated border adjacent to the Rio Grande, provides nesting habitats for several western birds: Black-chinned Hummingbird, Western Kingbird, Thick-billed Kingbird (nested here from 1988 to 1991), Lucy's Warbler (has nested since 1986), as well as three orioles (Orchard, Hooded, and Bullock's). The area also attracts numerous birds in spring; eastern and western neotropical migrants are equally abundant from mid-April to early June. Greater Roadrunner, (**Golden-fronted Woodpecker,**) and Vermilion Flycatcher are common here year-round. Check the river for Mexican Duck year-round and various ducks and shorebirds in spring, fall, and winter. And both Yellow-bellied and Red-naped Sapsuckers occur in winter.

It is worthwhile to bird up and down the river from the campground in spring. Also drive upriver to Santa Elena Canyon, stopping to check each thicket of willows and salt cedar along the way. At **Santa Elena Canyon** (**N**) the vegetation surrounding the parking area can be alive with birds in spring. Watch overhead at the canyon mouth for Golden Eagle, Zone-tailed Hawk, and Peregrine and Prairie Falcons, all of which nest or roost on the high cliffs.

In late fall and winter, especially after a rainy summer when the floodplain is crowded with seed plants, one often can find a large variety of seedeaters: buntings; Dickcissel; Green-tailed Towhee; numerous sparrows, including Clay-colored, Brewer's, Baird's (rare), Grasshopper, Lincoln's, Swamp, Golden-crowned (irregular), and White-crowned; and Lark Bunting. Watch also in winter for Anna's Hummingbird and Gray Flycatcher.

Records of Review Species: *Chisos Mountains*—Northern Pygmy-Owl, Aug 1982, April 1993. Northern Saw-whet Owl, Feb 1968. Broad-billed Hummingbird, May 1991. White-eared Hummingbird, Aug 1974, June 1980. Elegant Trogon, April 1993. Greater Pewee, Aug 1991. Dusky-capped Flycatcher, May 1991, Sept 1991, May 1997. Thick-billed Kingbird, June 1967. Clark's Nutcracker, Jan 1993. American Dipper, March 1986. Varied Thrush, Dec–Jan 1981/82. Aztec Thrush, Aug 1977, July–Aug 1982. Crescent-chested Warbler, June 1993. Red-faced Warbler, Aug 1982, Aug 1988, May 1990, Aug 1991, April–Aug 1993. Rufous-capped Warbler, Sept–June 1973/74, March 1986, May 1993. Olive Warbler, May 1991. Yellow-eyed Junco, June 1980, April–May 1990. Snow Bunting, May 1988. Flame-colored Tanager, April 1996.

Rio Grande Village/Boquillas area—Swallow-tailed Kite, Aug 1969. Yellow Rail, Jan 1976. Ruddy Ground-Dove, Dec–May 1987/88. Violet-crowned Hummingbird, April 1996. Tufted Flycatcher, Nov–Jan 1991/92. Sulphur-bellied Flycatcher, May 1969. Tropical Parula, May 1992. Black-vented Oriole, Sept 1968, April–Sept 1969, June–Oct 1970. *Cottonwood Campground–Santa Elena Canyon area*—Swallow-tailed Kite, Aug 1990. Ruddy Ground-Dove, Dec–May 1991/92. Tropical Kingbird, Aug 1996. Varied Thrush, April 1989. Yellow-green Vireo, July 1972. Rufous-capped Warbler, March–June 1979. Evening Grosbeak, April 1993.

Directions: From I-90, take US 385 south from Marathon for 69 miles or SH 118 south from Alpine for 100 miles to Panther Junction, park headquarters. **Rio Grande Village** is 30 miles beyond to the southeast; the **Chisos Basin** is 10 miles above Panther Junction, via Green Gulch; **Cottonwood Campground** is 35 miles west of Panther Junction. It is 13 miles to **Santa Elena Junction** with an additional 22 miles to Castolon.

General information: Big Bend National Park, encompassing more than 800,000 acres and with elevations that vary from 1,850 to 7,835 feet, contains a wide variety of habitats, from river and desert in the lowlands to coniferous forest in the mountains. It is one of the nation's primary birding sites, and more bird species have been recorded (more than 450) here than in any other national park.

The Chisos Mountains, the southernmost mountain range in the United States, contain vegetation and wildlife typical of that found in the mountains of north-eastern Mexico. The Chisos Basin (5,400 feet elevation) forms the heart of the Chisos Mountains, where most of the mountain trails begin. These trails range from short and easy to longer and more difficult. The 9-mile round-trip hike to Boot Canyon is rough. The Lost Mine Trail and the Window Trail are moderate 5-mile round-trips.

Birders should check the birder's log at the Panther Junction Visitor Center when they first arrive in the park for any extraordinary sightings. The visitor center also contains an excellent bookstore.

ADDITIONAL HELP

Location: Texas Official Travel Map grid R/S x 6/7; Brewster County

Nearest food, gas, and lodging: Food and gas are available at Panther Junction and Rio Grande Village. There is food at Castolon and lodging (cottages) is available on-site in the Chisos Basin. Reservations for accommodations, especially in spring and summer, should be made early, by calling the National Park Concessions, Inc.: 915-477-2291.

Nearest camping: Available on-site at Rio Grande Village, Chisos Basin, and Cottonwood Campground. The only hookups are available at the Rio Grande Village store. There also are numerous primitive campsites (permit only) scattered throughout the mountains.

Contact: Superintendent, Big Bend National Park (see Appendix C)

10 Black Gap Wildlife Management Area

Habitats: Desert scrub, sotol grassland, river, riparian, stock tank

Key birds: "Mexican Duck" (Mallard); Peregrine Falcon; Scaled and Gambel's Quail; Greater Roadrunner; Common Raven; Cactus Wren; Black-tailed Gnatcatcher; Curve-billed and Crissal Thrashers; Gray Vireo; Phainopepla; Pyrrhuloxia; Rufous-crowned, Black-throated, and Black-chinned Sparrows; and Lesser Goldfinch are present year-round. Swainson's and Zone-tailed Hawks; Elf Owl; Lesser and Common Nighthawks; **Lucifer Hummingbird;** Cassin's and Western Kingbirds; Bell's Vireo; Varied and Painted Buntings; Bronzed Cowbird; and Orchard, Hooded, Bullock's, and Scott's Orioles occur in summer. Osprey; Golden Eagle; Prairie Falcon; Sage Thrasher; and Clay-colored, Brewer's, and Baird's (irregular) Sparrows can usually be found in winter.

Best times to bird: April and May for spring migrants and nesting activities; mid-September through January for southbound migrants and winter birds

Birding strategies: FM 2627 runs northwest to southeast through the area; the lower 10 miles have been established as an interpretive driving tour (**A**), providing access to some excellent habitats to find desert birds. Expected year-round species include Red-tailed Hawk; Scaled Quail; White-winged and Mourning Doves; Greater Roadrunner; Great Horned Owl; Ladder-backed Woodpecker; Say's Phoebe; Common Raven; Verdin; Cactus, Rock, Canyon, and Bewick's Wrens; Black-tailed Gnatcatcher; Northern Mockingbird; Curve-billed Thrasher; Phainopepla; Loggerhead Shrike; Pyrrhuloxia; Canyon Towhee; Rufous-crowned and Black-throated Sparrows; House Finch; and Lesser Goldfinch. Less numerous are Wild Turkey, Crissal Thrasher, Gray Vireo, and Black-chinned Sparrow. In winter watch for Northern Harrier, Harris's and Ferruginous Hawks, Golden Eagle, American Kestrel, Merlin, and Prairie Falcon.

The Rio Grande floodplain offers several additional birds throughout the year. It is accessible at the southeastern end (**B**) of the driving tour, as well as downriver via boat/raft or the graveled roads (**C**) that lead away from Area headquarters. Obtain a permit at the headquarters. Expected year-round species include Mexican Duck, Black Vulture, Black Phoebe, Northern Rough-winged Swallow, Common Yellowthroat, and Northern Cardinal. Less numerous are Great Blue Heron, Wild Turkey, Gambel's Quail, Belted Kingfisher, **Golden-fronted Woodpecker,** and Red-winged Blackbird. In winter watch for various waterfowl, Northern Harrier, American Coot, occasional shorebirds, Yellow-bellied and Red-naped Sapsuckers, Eastern Phoebe, Marsh Wren, Hermit Thrush, American Robin, American Pipit, Cedar Waxwing, Orange-crowned and Yellow-rumped Warblers, Spotted Towhee, and (in weedy areas) a variety of sparrows.

The high cliffs of the river canyons support a few additional birds that can be seen almost anywhere along the Rio Grande. These include Peregrine Falcon and White-throated Swift year-round and Zone-tailed Hawk and Cliff Swallow in summer.

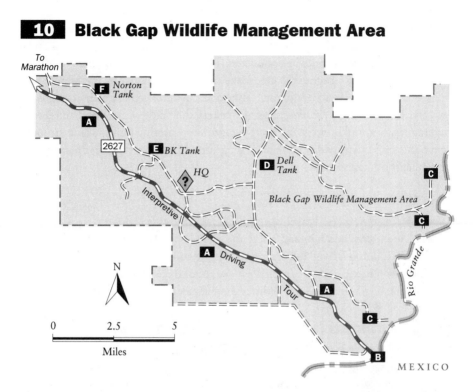

During winters following rainy summer or fall seasons, grasses can be abundant on the open floodplain as well as within various drainages. At such times, numerous seedeaters can be present: Northern Cardinal; Pyrrhuloxia; Blue Grosbeak; Indigo, Varied, and Painted Buntings; Green-tailed, Spotted, and Canyon Towhees; Cassin's, Rufous-crowned, Chipping, Clay-colored, Brewer's, Field, Vesper, Lark, Savannah, Baird's, Fox, Song, Lincoln's, Swamp, White-throated, White-crowned, and Harris's Sparrows; and McCown's Longspur.

Dell Tank (**D**) holds water in all but the driest years and is a magnet for many resident and migrating birds. Nesting species include Mexican Duck and Killdeer. Many of the desert birds drink there; waterfowl, shorebirds, and a host of other species stop in migration; and winter visitors can include a wide variety of unexpected species, ranging from geese and ducks to raptors and sparrows. Two additional tanks—BK (**E**) and Norton (**F**)—are also worth visiting after rainy periods.

Records of Review Species: Reddish Egret, Aug 1982. Wood Stork, July 1994. Yellow Rail, Aug 1984. Purple Gallinule, June 1983. Spotted Owl, June 1982. Mountain Chickadee, Jan 1982. Red Crossbill, Dec 1996. Altamira Oriole, March 1982.

Directions: Black Gap Wildlife Management Area, 58 miles south of Marathon, lies along the eastern edge of Big Bend National Park, and can be accessed via FM 2627 off US 385. Dell Tank is accessible via a gravel road running east from the refuge headquarters. BK and Norton tanks are accessible via a gravel road running north from the refuge headquarters.

General information: This 106,000-acre state-managed refuge was purchased from 1947 to 1969 to provide a large area where long-term wildlife research and range management practices could be conducted. The refuge is bounded on the south for 25 miles by the Rio Grande; the landscape there is dominated by impressive canyons and narrow, green floodplains. Although the management area contains no live creeks or springs, *tinajas* (natural pockets that hold water) and numerous manmade stock tanks and guzzlers (above-ground watering tanks) occur throughout. Some of these provide excellent birding sites. Contact refuge headquarters for scheduled birding events.

ADDITIONAL HELP

Location: Texas Official Travel Map grid R x 7; Brewster County
Nearest food, gas, and lodging: Food and gas are available at Stillwell Store (on FM 2627); lodging is available in Marathon (38 miles).
Nearest camping: Primitive camping on-site; hookups at Stillwell Store
Contact: Manager, Black Gap Wildlife Management Area (see Appendix C)

11 Amistad National Recreation Area and Seminole Canyon State Park

Habitats: Lake, river, pond, riparian, Tamaulipan scrub, cliff
Key birds: Least Grebe; Neotropic Cormorant; Anhinga; Harris's Hawk; Wild Turkey; Scaled Quail; Greater Roadrunner; White-throated Swift; **Ringed Kingfisher; Green Kingfisher; Golden-fronted Woodpecker;** Black and Say's Phoebes; Vermilion Flycatcher; Chihuahuan and Common Ravens; Cactus, Rock, and Canyon Wrens; Black-tailed Gnatcatcher; Curve-billed Thrasher; Pyrrhuloxia; **Olive Sparrow;** and Lesser Goldfinch are present year-round. Black-bellied Whistling-Duck, Swainson's and Zone-tailed Hawks, Groove-billed Ani, Lesser Nighthawk, Brown-crested and Scissor-tailed Flycatchers, **Great Kiskadee, Couch's Kingbird, Long-billed Thrasher,** Bell's Vireo, Painted Bunting, Cassin's Sparrow, Dickcissel, and Hooded and Bullock's Orioles occur in summer. Osprey, Golden Eagle, Sandhill Crane, Sage Thrasher, Green-tailed Towhee, and Lark Bunting can usually be found in winter.
Best times to bird: April and May for spring migrants and nesting activities

Birding strategies: The riparian sites in the side canyons to the Amistad Reservoir offer the best birding; the campground (**A**) on Spur 406 is one example. In spring all the summer and full-time residents can usually be found there: Brown-crested Flycatcher, **Long-billed Thrasher,** and **Olive Sparrow** (typical birds of the Tamaulipan scrub habitat), as well as Scaled Quail, **Golden-fronted Woodpecker,** Black Phoebe, Vermilion Flycatcher, Bewick's Wren, Bell's Vireo, Yellow-breasted Chat, Northern Cardinal, Pyrrhuloxia, Orchard and Bullock's Orioles, and Lesser Goldfinch.

11 Amistad National Recreation Area and Seminole Canyon State Park

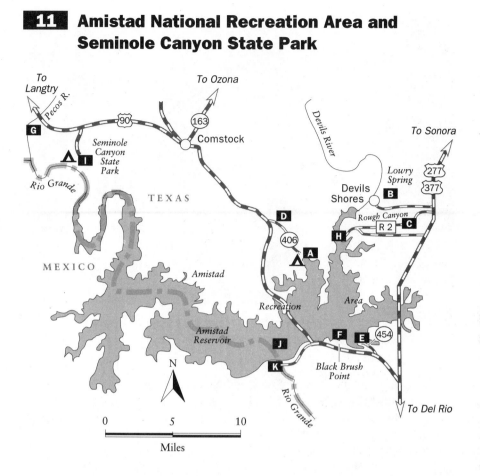

At Lowry Spring (**B**), located along a paved road northeast of Rough Canyon, a few additional birds can usually be found: Tufted Titmouse, Blue-gray Gnatcatcher, White-eyed Vireo, Summer Tanager, and Painted Bunting.

The drier habitats above the reservoir, such as along the entrance roads to Rough Canyon (**C**), Spur Roads 406 (**D**) and 454 (San Pedro Flat, **E**), and Black Brush Point (**F**), support all the desert species: Scaled Quail, Lesser Nighthawk, Chihuahuan and Common Ravens, Verdin, Cactus Wren, Black-tailed Gnatcatcher, Curve-billed Thrasher, Pyrrhuloxia, and Cassin's and Black-throated Sparrows. In winter Sage Thrasher and Green-tailed Towhee occur in these same areas.

High cliffs, including those at the mouth of the Pecos River (**G**) and Rough Canyon (**H**), offer nesting sites for Great Blue Heron, White-throated Swift, Common Raven, and Canyon and Rock Wrens.

Seminole Canyon State Park (**I**), 9 miles west of Comstock, provides easy access to canyon and desert birds. All the year-round residents can usually be found here, and a spring or summer walk into the canyon will surely produce a variety of species. Most obvious are Turkey Vulture, White-throated Swift, Cliff and Cave

View from the visitor center toward the Fate Bell Rockshelter in Seminole Canyon State Park.

Swallows, Cactus and Canyon Wrens, and Northern Mockingbird. Also possible are Zone-tailed Hawk, Say's Phoebe, Common Raven, Rock Wren, Curve-billed Thrasher, Pyrrhuloxia, Canyon Towhee, Rufous-crowned Sparrow, and Lesser Goldfinch.

The park's weedy roadsides support a number of seed-eating birds after summer or fall rains: Northern Cardinal; Pyrrhuloxia; Painted Bunting; Green-tailed, Spotted, and Canyon Towhees; Cassin's, Rufous-crowned, Chipping, Clay-colored, Brewer's, Field, Vesper, Black-throated, Lincoln's, and White-crowned Sparrows; and Lark Bunting.

Amistad Reservoir (**J**) is reasonably sterile in midsummer, but in winter thousands of water birds take advantage of the open water. Most abundant are Eared Grebe, Double-crested Cormorant, Northern Pintail, Blue-winged Teal, Northern Shoveler, American Wigeon, and Bufflehead. Less numerous are American White Pelican, Green-winged and Cinnamon Teal, Mallard, Gadwall, Canvasback, Redhead, Lesser Scaup, and Common Goldeneye. These birds are best viewed by boat, but they also can be seen from shore at many places. The Rio Grande below Amistad Dam (**K**) often offers a number of water birds and swallows; this is also a good place to find **Ringed Kingfisher**.

Nearby Del Rio contains another choice birding site—Moore Park—which lies along San Felipe Creek and is readily accessible off US 90. This park can be crowded on weekends and holidays, but an early morning walk can usually produce **Green Kingfisher, Golden-fronted Woodpecker,** Black Phoebe, Vermilion Flycatcher, **Great Kiskadee,** and Lesser Goldfinch. Watch also for **Least Grebe,** Neotropic Cormorant, and Black-bellied Whistling-Duck.

Directions: Access lies along US 90: Moore Park and San Felipe Spring Road are east of Del Rio; Rough Canyon is accessible off US 277, at the end of 7.2-mile FM R2. Spur Roads 454 and 406 and Black Brush Road are located west of Del Rio and north of US 90, and Amistad Dam is south. Seminole Canyon State Park is 9 miles west of Comstock; the Pecos River cliffs are located across from the Pecos River picnic site, 2 miles west of the Seminole Canyon turnoff.

General information: Amistad, meaning "friendship" in Spanish, is an international recreation area with facilities on both sides of the border. Amistad Reservoir was created in 1966, with the completion of the 6-mile-long Amistad Dam on the Rio Grande. Water was backed up for 74 miles along the Rio Grande, 14 miles up the Pecos, and 25 miles up Devils River. The 67,000-acre reservoir includes 850 miles of shoreline.

The region lies at the confluence of three major biogeographic regions: Trans-Pecos to the west, Edwards Plateau to the north, and Tamaulipan to the southeast.

The national recreation area is primarily a boating, fishing, and water sports impoundment, but the region also contains numerous archeological sites, including a rich assortment of Indian rock art. One site near the mouth of Seminole Canyon contains a pictograph of a mountain lion, believed to be more than 10,000 years old. Seminole Canyon State Park, 2,173 acres of rough canyonlands, offers guided tours into the canyon for viewing the abundant Indian pictographs.

ADDITIONAL HELP

Location: Texas Official Travel Map grid Q/R x 10/11; Val Verde County
Nearest food, gas, and lodging: Food and gas at Lake Amistad Resort and Marina, Rough Canyon Marina, and Pecos River Junction; all three are available in Del Rio
Nearest camping: On-site primitive camping (free) at four designated locations in the recreation area, as well as numerous full-service facilities in and about Del Rio and at Seminole Canyon State Park
Contact: Superintendent, Amistad National Recreation Area; Superintendent, Seminole Canyon State Park (see Appendix C)

Panhandle and Western Plains Region

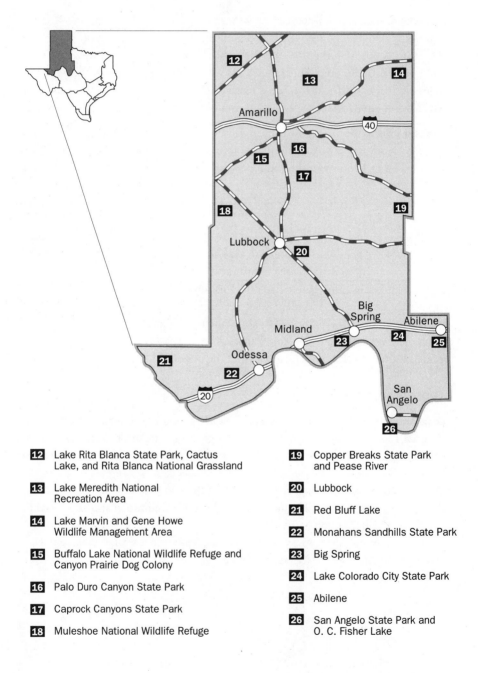

12 Lake Rita Blanca State Park, Cactus Lake, and Rita Blanca National Grassland

13 Lake Meredith National Recreation Area

14 Lake Marvin and Gene Howe Wildlife Management Area

15 Buffalo Lake National Wildlife Refuge and Canyon Prairie Dog Colony

16 Palo Duro Canyon State Park

17 Caprock Canyons State Park

18 Muleshoe National Wildlife Refuge

19 Copper Breaks State Park and Pease River

20 Lubbock

21 Red Bluff Lake

22 Monahans Sandhills State Park

23 Big Spring

24 Lake Colorado City State Park

25 Abilene

26 San Angelo State Park and O. C. Fisher Lake

12 Lake Rita Blanca State Park, Cactus Lake, and Rita Blanca National Grassland

Habitats: Lake, playa, creek, riparian, marsh, prairie

Key birds: Ferruginous Hawk, Golden Eagle, Ring-necked Pheasant, Scaled Quail, Greater Roadrunner, and Chihuahuan Raven are present year-round. Mississippi Kite, Swainson's Hawk, Mountain Plover, Long-billed Curlew, Burrowing Owl, Say's Phoebe, Cassin's and Grasshopper Sparrows, Lark Bunting, and Yellow-headed Blackbird occur in summer. Hooded and Common Mergansers; Bald Eagle; Rough-legged Hawk; Prairie Falcon; Long-eared Owl; Mountain Bluebird; Northern Shrike; American Tree, Fox, and Harris's Sparrows; and McCown's, Lapland, and Chestnut-collared Longspurs can usually be found in winter.

Best times to bird: May and June for prairie nesters and December to mid-February for winter birds

Birding strategies: Scope Lake Rita Blanca, located on the southwestern edge of Dalhart, from either Rita Blanca Park (**A**) or from the dam (**B**) on the southeast side. Common resident water birds include Pied-billed Grebe, Great Blue Heron, Canada Goose, Mallard, Northern Pintail, Northern Shoveler, Redhead, Ruddy Duck, American Coot, Killdeer, and Ring-billed Gull. Less numerous are Black-crowned and Yellow-crowned Night-Herons; Wood Duck; Green-winged, Blue-winged, and Cinnamon Teal; Gadwall; American Wigeon; Canvasback; Lesser Scaup; Hooded and Common Mergansers; Virginia Rail; Sora; Common Moorhen; and Franklin's Gull. A few additional birds can be expected in summer: Great and Cattle Egrets; Green Heron; Black-necked Stilt; Greater and Lesser Yellowlegs; Solitary, Spotted, Upland, Western, Least, Baird's, and Stilt Sandpipers; Long-billed Dowitcher; Wilson's Phalarope; and Black Tern. Snowy Plover, Semipalmated and Pectoral Sandpipers, Red-necked Phalarope, Forster's Tern, and Belted Kingfisher occur in smaller numbers. Additional winter birds include Snow and Ross' Geese, Ring-necked Duck, Common Goldeneye, and Bufflehead. Watch overhead for Bald Eagle around the lake and for Northern Harrier; Red-tailed, Ferruginous, and Rough-legged Hawks; Golden Eagle; American Kestrel; Merlin; and Prairie Falcon over the adjacent grasslands.

Numerous narrow and open rocky canyons occur along the edge of the lake, several of which contain shrubs and trees. Check these areas for migrants in spring and fall and for resident species in summer and winter. Mourning Dove, Ladder-backed Woodpecker, Rock and Bewick's Wrens, Northern Mockingbird, Curve-billed Thrasher, American Robin, Northern Cardinal, Canyon Towhee, Rufous-crowned Sparrow, and House Finch can be expected year-round. In winter these sites may contain Yellow-bellied and Red-naped Sapsuckers; Bushtit; Winter Wren; Golden-crowned and Ruby-crowned Kinglets; Townsend's Solitaire; Hermit Thrush; Cedar Waxwing; Spotted Towhee; American Tree, Field, Fox, Song, Lincoln's, White-throated, White-crowned, and Harris's Sparrows; Dark-eyed Junco; Pine

12 Lake Rita Blanca State Park, Cactus Lake, and Rita Blanca National Grassland

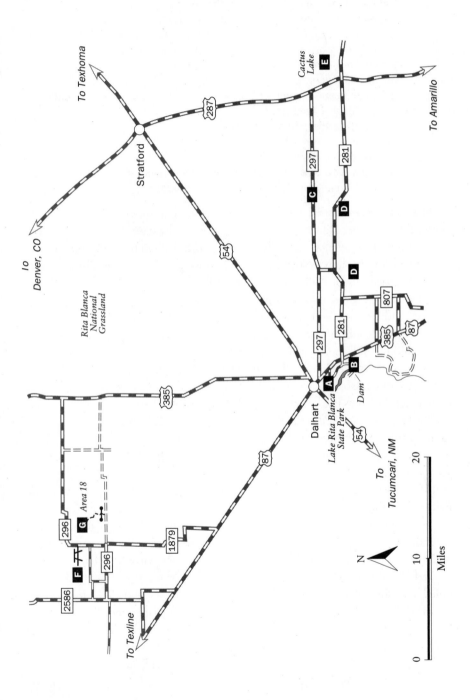

Siskin; and American Goldfinch. Watch also for irregular winter visitors, such as Northern Shrike and Purple Finch. Although many of the same birds can be found in the riparian habitat below the dam, a wide variety of neotropical songbirds can be expected during migration. A few of these remain and nest: Yellow-billed Cuckoo, Ash-throated and Scissor-tailed Flycatchers, Western Kingbird, Blue Grosbeak, Painted Bunting, and Orchard and Bullock's Orioles. In winter look here for Long-eared Owl.

FM 297 (**C**) and FM 281 (**D**), highways that run east-west between US 385 and US 287, pass by scattered prairie dog colonies, good places to see Burrowing Owl in all seasons but midwinter. McCown's, Lapland, and Chestnut-collared Longspurs utilize these areas in winter. Also check these sites for Ferruginous Hawk, Golden Eagle, and other predators.

Cactus Lake (**E**) lies 1.5 miles east of US 287 on FM 281, and can be superb in winter and during migration. Thousands of waterfowl, including Snow, Ross's, and Canada Geese, along with various raptors, such as Ferruginous Hawk and Bald and Golden Eagles, can be expected in winter. And during spring migration, concentrations of waterfowl and shorebirds can be truly spectacular. As many as 10,000 Wilson's Phalarope have been observed on the playa at one time. Thousands of swallows feed over the lake and adjacent fields in late summer, large flocks of Yellow-headed Blackbird pass through, and countless Sandhill Crane may be seen overhead. The surrounding grasslands are excellent for Ring-necked Pheasant during all seasons.

Rita Blanca National Grassland (**F, G**) lies 18 miles north of Dalhart, via US 87 and FM 1879. In summer drive the numerous roads (many unpaved), paying particular attention to the scattered groves of trees, to find the most birds. Nesting species include Swainson's, Red-tailed, and Ferruginous Hawks; American Kestrel; Prairie Falcon; Ring-necked Pheasant; Killdeer; Long-billed Curlew; Mourning Dove; Burrowing Owl; Common Nighthawk; Say's Phoebe; Western Kingbird; Horned Lark; Barn Swallow; Chihuahuan Raven; Northern Mockingbird; Curve-billed Thrasher; Loggerhead Shrike; Blue Grosbeak; Cassin's, Lark, and Grasshopper Sparrows; Lark Bunting; Common Grackle; and Bullock's Oriole. Also in summer are Prairie Falcon, Mountain Plover, Cassin's Kingbird, and Brewer's Sparrow.

At least two grassland locations should be birded year-round, Thompson Grove picnic and camping site (**F**) and Area 18 (**G**). Both contain trees that serve as important resting and feeding sites for numerous migrants, nesting sites for a few species, and roosting sites for a handful of winter residents. At Thompson Grove, check the surrounding vegetation in winter for American Tree Sparrow. In Area 18, the scattered groves of trees may harbor roosting Long-eared Owl. You are permitted to drive into this area, but be sure to close any gates you encounter. Watch also for Merlin.

Records of Review Species: Williamson's Sapsucker, April 1996. Black-billed Magpie, Dec 1993. Mountain Chickadee, Dec 1982, Oct 1989. Bohemian Waxwing, Jan 1997. Snow Bunting, Dec 1993. Red Crossbill, Feb 1997.

Directions: Lake Rita Blanca State Park lies directly south of Dalhart via US 385; take FM 281 west to a parking area and walk to the dam. Cactus Lake is located to the east; take FM 281 or 297 east, passing several prairie dog colonies, to Cactus Lake, just east of US 287. Rita Blanca National Grassland lies north of Dalhart, via US 87 and FM 1879, or east of Texline via FM 296; see map for details.

General information: Lake Rita Blanca (at the time of this writing under development as a state park) was once part of the XIT Ranch, the world's largest (3,050,000 acres) under fence in the 1880s. The XIT Ranch has since been divided into numerous smaller ranches.

Rita Blanca National Grassland includes 77,463 acres in Texas and an additional 15,860 acres in nearby Oklahoma. The area contains 35 separate units, divided by private ranchlands. FM 296 and 1879 are paved, but the majority of the roads are unpaved, and care must be used during rainy weather.

ADDITIONAL HELP

Location: Texas Official Travel Map grid A/B x 8/9; Dallam, Hartley, and Hutchinson counties

Nearest food, gas, and lodging: Food and gas are available at numerous locations; lodging is available only in Dalhart.

Nearest camping: On-site at Lake Rita Blanca State Park (31 sites)

Contact: Superintendent, Lake Rita Blanca State Park; Manager, Rita Blanca National Grassland (see Appendix C)

13 Lake Meredith National Recreation Area

Habitats: Reservoir, river, stream, pond, riparian, marsh, mud flat, mesquite grassland, juniper woodland

Key birds: Golden Eagle, Scaled Quail, Chukar, Greater Roadrunner, Rock and Canyon Wrens, Curve-billed Thrasher, and Rufous-crowned Sparrow are present year-round. Mississippi Kite, Swainson's Hawk, Virginia Rail, Burrowing Owl, Red-headed Woodpecker, Scissor-tailed Flycatcher, and Cassin's Sparrow occur in summer. Common Goldeneye; Common Merganser; Ferruginous and Rough-legged Hawks; Bald Eagle; Long-eared Owl; Mountain Bluebird; Townsend's Solitaire; American Tree, Fox, and Harris's Sparrows; and Lapland Longspur can usually be found in winter.

Best times to bird: May and June for spring migrants and nesting activities, and November to March for winter birds

Birding strategies: The best birding area year-round is Spring Canyon (**A**), below Sanford Dam (off FM 1319), an area with open ponds, extensive marsh, and an

13 Lake Meredith National Recreation Area

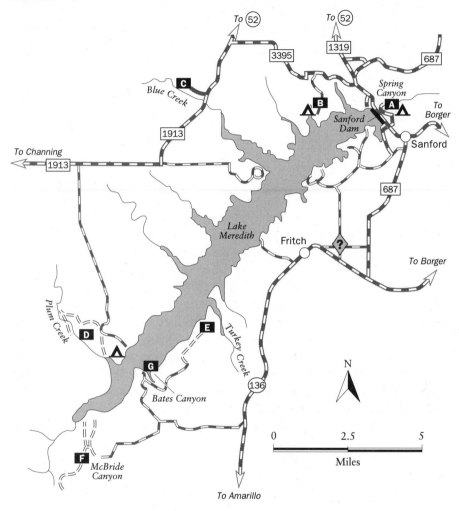

adjacent wooded canyon. Although a few diving ducks may be more numerous on the deeper reservoir, many more water and marsh birds can be found at Spring Canyon. Expected year-round residents include Pied-billed Grebe, Great Blue Heron, Green-winged Teal, Mallard, Northern Pintail, Northern Shoveler, Gadwall, American Wigeon, Virginia Rail, American Coot, and Red-winged Blackbird. In summer expect Blue-winged and Cinnamon Teal, Redhead, Common Moorhen, American Avocet, and Spotted Sandpiper. Less numerous are Little Blue Heron, Least Bittern, Greater and Lesser Yellowlegs, and Wilson's Phalarope. And in winter Horned, Eared, and Western Grebes; Snow and Canada Geese; Canvasback; Ring-necked Duck; Lesser Scaup; Common Goldeneye; Bufflehead; Hooded, Common, and Red-breasted Mergansers; Ruddy Duck; Sora; Common Snipe; Bonaparte's, Ring-billed, and Herring Gulls; and Marsh Wren may be found.

At Spring Canyon, the open drainage to the north, full-time residents include Red-tailed Hawk; American Kestrel; Wild Turkey; Northern Bobwhite; Scaled Quail; Mourning Dove; Greater Roadrunner; Great Horned Owl; Ladder-backed Woodpecker; Northern Flicker; Carolina Chickadee; Rock, Canyon, and Bewick's Wrens; Northern Mockingbird; Curve-billed Thrasher; Loggerhead Shrike; Rufous-crowned Sparrow; Northern Cardinal; Western Meadowlark; and House Finch. A few additional species occur here in summer: Ash-throated and Scissor-tailed Flycatchers, Western Kingbird, Cliff Swallow, Blue Grosbeak, Painted Bunting, and Bullock's Oriole.

Bugbee (**B**), Blue Creek (**C**), and Plum Creek (**D**), all on the north side of the reservoir, and Turkey Creek (**E**) and McBride Canyon (**F**) on the south side, offer extensive cottonwood groves that attract a wide variety of passing migrants in spring and fall and also offer nesting sites for breeding birds. Nesting birds in the cottonwoods and in the brushy surroundings include Mississippi Kite; American Kestrel; Mourning Dove; Yellow-billed Cuckoo; Great Horned Owl; Red-headed, Red-bellied, and Ladder-backed Woodpeckers; Ash-throated and Scissor-tailed Flycatchers; Western Kingbird; Blue Jay; Carolina Chickadee; Bewick's Wren; Eastern Bluebird; European Starling; Northern Cardinal; Blue Grosbeak; Painted Bunting; and Bullock's Oriole. Other summer residents that often can be found soaring overhead at all of the above locations include Turkey Vulture, Swainson's and Red-tailed Hawks, Golden Eagle, and Common Nighthawk.

In winter the cottonwood groves and brushy areas in all the canyons harbor a number of additional birds: Hairy and Downy Woodpeckers; Western Scrub-Jay; Brown Creeper; Winter Wren; Golden-crowned and Ruby-crowned Kinglets; Cedar Waxwing; American Tree, Field, Fox, Song, Lincoln's, White-crowned, White-throated, and Harris's Sparrows; Spotted Towhee; Pine Siskin; and American Goldfinch. Densely wooded sites may contain Long-eared Owl.

Bald Eagles winter at Lake Meredith, but usually stay in less accessible areas in the upper portion of the lake. Some of the best sites for observing these magnificent birds fishing over the lake include the overlooks at Plum Creek (**D**) and Bates Canyon (**G**). Views upriver may also produce American White Pelican.

The extensive floodplain and marshes at Plum Creek and McBride Canyon offer many of the same birds as Spring Canyon. The Canadian River floodplain, evident at McBride, is dominated by salt cedar, a nonnative tree that is used by very few birds.

Mesquite grasslands and/or juniper woodlands, which occur on the flatlands above the reservoir, are readily accessible along many of the entrance roads to the various areas. The Turkey Creek and Plum Creek roads pass through good examples of these habitats. Year-round birds here include Horned Lark, Curve-billed Thrasher, and Eastern Meadowlark. In summer watch for Swainson's Hawk; Common Nighthawk; Burrowing Owl; and Cassin's, Chipping, and Lark Sparrows.

Plum Creek in winter at Lake Meredith National Recreation Area.

And in winter these areas may harbor Northern Harrier, Ferruginous and Rough-legged Hawks, Townsend's Solitaire, Mountain Bluebird, Northern Shrike, Canyon Towhee, Lapland Longspur (look in stubble fields), and Brewer's Blackbird.

Directions: Lake Meredith is situated along the Canadian River west of Borger; take SH 136 to FM 1319 and north to Sanford (10 miles). Sanford Dam and Spring Canyon are just beyond. Bugbee, Blue Creek, and Plum Creek are located across the dam and west on FM 3395 and FM 1913; Turkey Creek, Bates Canyon, and McBride Canyon are located off SH 136, south of Fritch (see map for details).

General information: Lake Meredith is in the geographic center of the Texas Panhandle. The 45,000-acre national recreation area offers extensive recreational opportunities, from boating and fishing to birding and backcountry hiking. Alibates Flint Quarries National Monument, situated along the south-central edge of the recreation area, contains extensive quarries that were worked by prehistoric peoples, perhaps 11,500 years ago. Several associated ruins are found throughout the dual areas and range in age from historic cabins to a few paleosites.

ADDITIONAL HELP

Location: Texas Official Travel Map grid C x 10; Moore, Hutchinson, Potter, and Carson counties

Nearest food, gas, and lodging: Food and gas are at Sanford (on-site) and Fritch (3 miles); lodging is in Fritch, Borger (15 miles), Amarillo (20 miles), and Dumas (25 miles).

Nearest camping: On-site in recreation area (no hookups) and in Fritch or Borger (with hookups)

Contact: Superintendent, Lake Meredith National Recreation Area (see Appendix C)

14 Lake Marvin and Gene Howe Wildlife Management Area

Habitats: River, lake, riparian, cottonwood grove, prairie, field, pasture, cropland

Key birds: Wild Turkey is present year-round. Mississippi Kite, Least Tern, Chuck-will's-widow, Red-headed Woodpecker, Scissor-tailed Flycatcher, Warbling Vireo, Indigo and Painted Buntings, and Dickcissel occur in summer. Tundra Swan; Hooded and Common Mergansers; Bald Eagle; Ferruginous Hawk; Northern Shrike; and American Tree, Fox, and Harris's Sparrows can usually be found in winter.

Best times to bird: Mid-April through May for spring migrants and nesting activities; December through February for winter birds

Birding strategies: The huge cottonwood trees and other riparian vegetation along the entrance road (FM 2266) (A) can be alive with migrants in spring. This habitat also provides nesting sites for several full-time and summer residents: Red-tailed Hawk; American Kestrel; Mourning Dove; Yellow-billed Cuckoo; Great Horned Owl; Red-bellied, Downy, and Hairy Woodpeckers; Great Crested Flycatcher; Blue-gray Gnatcatcher; Warbling Vireo; Bullock's Oriole; and American Goldfinch.

The more open areas, brushy fields, and river bottomland (B) along FM 2266, including those within the Gene Howe Wildlife Management Area, support an additional group of birds in spring and summer. Watch for Turkey Vulture, Wild Turkey, Northern Bobwhite, Common Nighthawk (at dawn and dusk), Chimney Swift, Red-headed and Ladder-backed Woodpeckers, Ash-throated Flycatcher, Northern Rough-winged and Barn Swallows, American Crow, Northern Mockingbird, Loggerhead Shrike, Dickcissel, Field Sparrow, Eastern Meadowlark, and Red-winged Blackbird. Adjacent thickets harbor Bewick's and House Wrens, Yellow-breasted Chat, Northern Cardinal, Blue Grosbeak, and Indigo and Painted Buntings. Least Terns nest on sandbars on the river, and Chuck-will's-widow may be heard calling along the river bottom at night. Check marshy areas for Great Blue and Green Herons and Common Yellowthroat.

In winter, the fields contain a very different bird life. This includes Canada Goose, Northern Harrier, Red-tailed and Ferruginous Hawks, Eastern and Western Meadowlarks, Common Grackle, and Brown-headed Cowbird. And the brushy

14 Lake Marvin and Gene Howe Wildlife Management Area

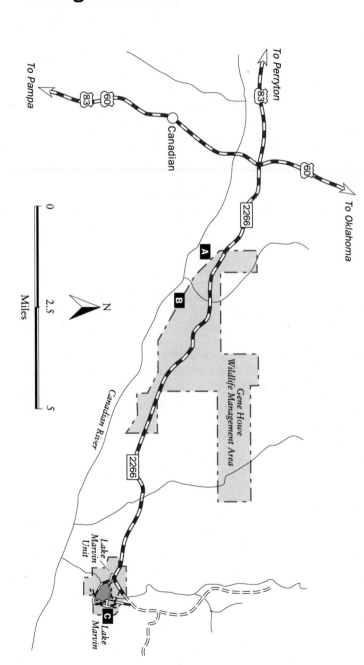

edges often harbor some of the more interesting winter birds: Eastern and Spotted Towhees; American Tree, Field, Song, Lincoln's, Swamp, White-throated, White-crowned, and Harris's Sparrows; Dark-eyed Junco; and American Goldfinch.

The Lake Marvin area contains a few additional habitats. The lake itself and surrounding marsh are worth birding year-round; the A. S. Jackson Birding Trail (C) skirts the lake on the eastern and northern sides. Summer birds may include Pied-billed Grebe; Wood Duck; Mississippi Kite; American Coot; Barred Owl; Belted Kingfisher; Red-bellied, Downy, and Hairy Woodpeckers; Great Crested Flycatcher; Carolina Chickadee; Carolina, Bewick's, and House Wrens; Warbling Vireo; Common Grackle; and both Bullock's and Baltimore Orioles. In winter several additional birds can usually be found: Canada Goose; a wide variety of diving and dabbling ducks, including Common Goldeneye and Hooded and Common Mergansers; Brown Creeper; Red-breasted and White-breasted Nuthatches; Marsh Wren; Golden-crowned and Ruby-crowned Kinglets; Spotted Towhee; American Tree, Song, Lincoln's, Fox, White-throated, White-crowned, and Harris's Sparrows; and Dark-eyed Junco. The lake sometimes hosts Tundra Swan in late fall and winter; watch also for Bald Eagle.

Records of Review Species: Trumpeter Swan, Dec 1993. Eurasian Wigeon, Oct–Nov 1995, winter 1995/96.

Directions: From the junction of US 83 and US 60, just north of Canadian, take FM 2266 east for 13 miles, along the river floodplain, to Lake Marvin.

General information: The 576-acre Lake Marvin Unit, including a 63-acre lake, is part of the 31,399-acre Black Kettle National Grasslands; an additional 30,724 acres are located in nearby Oklahoma. Birding, hiking, fishing, picnicking, and camping are available. No hunting is allowed in the wildlife management area.

ADDITIONAL HELP

Location: Texas Official Travel Map grid B x 12; Hemphill County
Nearest food, gas, and lodging: All can be found in Canadian (13 miles).
Nearest camping: On-site (23 sites)
Contact: Supervisor, Black Kettle Ranger District (see Appendix C)

15 Buffalo Lake National Wildlife Refuge and Canyon Prairie Dog Colony

Habitats: Lake, creek, riparian, marsh, mud flat, prairie, pasture, cropland

Key birds: Wild Turkey, Scaled Quail, Greater Roadrunner, Curve-billed Thrasher, and Rufous-crowned Sparrow are present year-round. Swainson's Hawk, Snowy Plover, Burrowing Owl, Scissor-tailed Flycatcher, Horned Lark, Rock Wren, Dickcissel, Lark Bunting, and Grasshopper Sparrow occur in summer. Tundra Swan; Greater White-fronted, Snow, Ross's, and Canada Geese; Common Goldeneye; Hooded and Common Mergansers; Bald Eagle; Ferruginous and Rough-legged Hawks; Merlin; Peregrine Falcon; Long-eared and Short-eared Owls; Townsend's Solitaire; American Tree, Fox, and Harris's Sparrows; and McCown's, Lapland, Chestnut-collared, and Smith's Longspurs can usually be found in winter.

Best times to bird: Mid-April to mid-June for spring migrants and nesting activities; October to mid-February for winter birds

Birding strategies: The interpretive auto tour drive, between the refuge entrance and observation deck site, includes a number of worthwhile stops. Cottonwood Canyon Birding Trail (**A**) offers a 0.5-mile loop route that can be superb for neotropical migrants during spring migration. A few remain and nest: Mississippi Kite, Yellow-billed Cuckoo, Ash-throated and Scissor-tailed Flycatchers, Western and Eastern Kingbirds, Barn Swallow, Blue Grosbeak, and Orchard and Bullock's Orioles. Additional residents include Red-tailed Hawk, American Kestrel, Mourning Dove, Great Horned Owl, Ladder-backed Woodpecker, Northern Mockingbird, American Robin, Curve-billed Thrasher, European Starling, Northern Cardinal, Lark Sparrow, Common Grackle, and House Finch. Most of the same birds can also be found among the cottonwoods in the picnic and camping areas (**B**) beyond.

The rocky, wooded slopes at the Cottonwood Canyon Birding Trail and near the picnic and camping areas offer a few additional birds: Greater Roadrunner, Bewick's Wren, and Rufous-crowned Sparrow year-round; Say's Phoebe, Blue-gray Gnatcatcher, and Rock Wren in summer; and Western Scrub-Jay, Western Bluebird, and Townsend's Solitaire in winter.

At the prairie habitat (**C**) beyond the camping area, year-round species include Ring-necked Pheasant, Wild Turkey, Northern Bobwhite, Scaled Quail, Horned Lark, Loggerhead Shrike, and Western Meadowlark. In summer Turkey Vulture, Swainson's Hawk, Prairie Falcon, Burrowing Owl, Common Nighthawk, Dickcissel, Lark Bunting, and Grasshopper Sparrow occur. And in winter watch for Northern Harrier, Ferruginous and Rough-legged Hawks, Golden Eagle, Merlin, Sandhill Crane, and Short-eared Owl. The brushy edges often support several additional winter birds: Spotted Towhee; American Tree, Chipping, Vesper, Fox, Song, White-crowned, and Harris's Sparrows; and Dark-eyed Junco. There also are several records of Long-eared Owl and Northern Shrike.

15 Buffalo Lake National Wildlife Refuge and Canyon Prairie Dog Colony

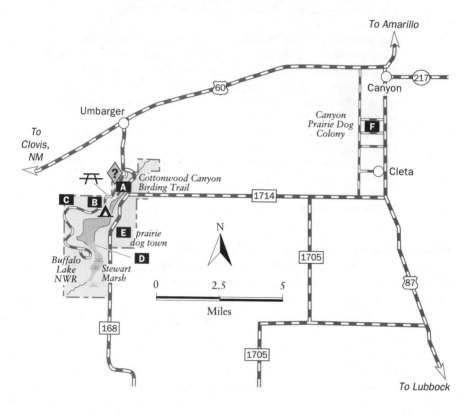

Stewart Marsh (**D**), at the end of the tour drive, can be viewed from the observation deck (blind), from the woods beyond, or from the dike a short distance to the north. Since the lake waters have drastically declined in recent years, the number of geese and ducks utilizing the area also has been reduced. But the increase of mud flats attracts greater numbers of shorebirds. Typical water birds include Pied-billed Grebe, Great Blue Heron, Mallard, Northern Pintail, Blue-winged and Cinnamon Teal, Northern Shoveler, Gadwall, American Coot, Killdeer, and Ring-billed Gull year-round. Eared Grebe; Green Heron; Black-crowned and Yellow-crowned Night-Herons; White-faced Ibis; Common Moorhen; Snowy Plover; American Avocet; Greater and Lesser Yellowlegs; Spotted, Upland, Semipalmated, Western, Least, Baird's, and Pectoral Sandpipers; Long-billed Dowitcher; Wilson's Phalarope; and Black Tern usually are present in summer. In winter, Greater White-fronted, Snow, Ross's, and Canada Geese; Green-winged Teal; American Wigeon; Bufflehead; and Common Merganser usually are present. Double-crested Cormorant, Tundra Swan, Wood Duck, Common Goldeneye, Hooded Merganser, and Marsh Wren are less numerous. Watch also for Bald Eagle and Peregrine Falcon.

The prairie dog town (**E**) along FM 168, 1.7 miles south of FM 1714, includes an interpretive trail into the prairie. In spring/summer this area offers most of the same birds listed for the prairie habitat (site **C** above). Burrowing Owl and Horned Lark are residents.

There is a larger prairie dog colony (**F**) near Canyon, along Pandeseta Road, behind the roadside park on US 87, south of town. The various roads between the refuge and US 87 pass through extensive pasture and croplands, where a few additional birds can occur. In winter, the stubble fields often contain longspurs. McCown's, Lapland, and Chestnut-collared Longspurs can be expected most years; Smith's Longspur is rare.

Records of Review Species: Trumpeter Swan, Dec 1993. Northern Saw-whet Owl, May 1979. Lewis's Woodpecker, Sept 1989. Common Redpoll, Nov–Jan 1965/66.

Directions: The refuge lies west of Canyon 11.5 miles, via US 60 to Umbarger and 1.5 miles south on FM 168, or 10 miles from Canyon via US 87 south and west on FM 1714.

General information: The 7,664-acre Buffalo Lake National Wildlife Refuge was established in 1958 to protect habitat utilized by migrating and wintering water-fowl and other birds. Although more than 800,000 ducks and 40,000 Canada Geese wintered on the refuge in the mid-1960s, the numbers have declined due to decreased inflows of water. The 300-acre Stewart Marsh, where the majority of the waterfowl now occur, was developed to catch smaller water inflows. Refuge hours run from 8 A.M. to 6 P.M. daily from October 1 through March 31, and from 8 A.M. until 8 P.M. daily from April 1 through September 30.

ADDITIONAL HELP

Location: Texas Official Travel Map grid D x 9; Randall County
Nearest food, gas, and lodging: Food and gas are available at Umbarger (1.5 miles); lodging can be found in Canyon (11.5 miles).
Nearest camping: On-site in refuge (15 sites without hookups) and in Canyon
Contact: Manager, Buffalo Lake National Wildlife Refuge; Canyon Chamber of Commerce (see Appendix C)

16 Palo Duro Canyon State Park

Habitats: Juniper woodland, mesquite grassland, river, creek, riparian, field

Key birds: Golden Eagle, Wild Turkey, Scaled Quail, Greater Roadrunner, **Golden-fronted Woodpecker,** Western Scrub-Jay, Bushtit, Rock and Canyon Wrens, Curve-billed Thrasher, Canyon Towhee, and Rufous-crowned Sparrow are present year-round. Mississippi Kite, Red-headed Woodpecker, Say's Phoebe, Scissor-tailed Flycatcher, and Painted Bunting occur in summer. Bald Eagle, Prairie Falcon, Mountain Bluebird, Townsend's Solitaire, Northern Shrike, and American Tree and Fox Sparrows can usually be found in winter.

Best times to bird: Mid-April through May for spring migrants and nesting activities; December and January for winter birds

Birding strategies: The loop road in the canyon provides the best birding, especially in and about (counterclockwise) Hackberry camp area (**A**), Juniper camp area (**B**), Cottonwood picnic area (**C**), and Sunflower camp area (**D**). Also check Chinaberry day use area, near Hackberry. Visitors and park hosts feed birds in these areas, particularly in winter. Expected year-round species along this loop include Wild Turkey, Northern Bobwhite, Scaled Quail, Mourning Dove, Greater Roadrunner, **Golden-fronted Woodpecker,** Ladder-backed Woodpecker, Northern Flicker, Western Scrub-Jay, Tufted Titmouse, Bewick's Wren, Northern Mockingbird, Northern Cardinal, and House Finch. Less numerous birds include Eastern Screech-Owl, Red-headed Woodpecker, Blue Jay, Carolina Chickadee, American Crow, Curve-billed Thrasher, and Canyon Towhee. In summer Yellow-billed Cuckoo, Ash-throated and Scissor-tailed Flycatchers, Blue-gray Gnatcatcher, Blue Grosbeak, Painted Bunting, and Bullock's Oriole can usually be found as well. Watch overhead for Turkey Vulture, Mississippi Kite, Red-tailed Hawk, Golden Eagle, American Kestrel, Common Nighthawk at dawn and dusk, and Northern Rough-winged, Cliff, and Barn Swallows.

In winter Inca Dove; Downy Woodpecker; Golden-crowned and Ruby-crowned Kinglets; Townsend's Solitaire; American Robin; Brown Thrasher; Cedar Waxwing; Spotted Towhee; Lincoln's, White-throated, and White-crowned Sparrows; Dark-eyed Junco; House Finch; Pine Siskin; and American Goldfinch can usually be found in the canyon. Less numerous species include Red-naped and Yellow-bellied Sapsuckers, Brown Creeper, Red-breasted and White-breasted Nuthatches, Hermit Thrush, and American Tree, Fox, and Harris's Sparrows. And occasionally, Gray Catbird, Northern Shrike, Eastern Towhee, LeConte's Sparrow, Purple Finch, Red Crossbill, and Evening Grosbeak are recorded.

The juniper woodland habitat is also available along the Red Star Ridge Trail (**E**), accessible from Hackberry. Year-round residents include Ladder-backed Woodpecker, Western Scrub-Jay, Tufted Titmouse, Bewick's Wren, Northern Mockingbird, Canyon Towhee, Rufous-crowned Sparrow, and House Finch. At

16 Palo Duro Canyon State Park

rocky canyons and cliff sites, watch for Rock and Canyon Wrens. In summer Say's Phoebe, Blue-gray Gnatcatcher, and Lark Sparrow can be expected. Common Poorwill is possible along the rocky slopes. In winter Mountain Bluebird, Townsend's Solitaire, American Robin, Cedar Waxwing, and Northern (irregular) and Loggerhead Shrikes utilize this area.

The more open woodlands, such as near the park entrance (F), offer a slightly different bird life. Horned Lark and Western Meadowlark occur year-round; Scissor-tailed Flycatcher can be found in spring and summer; Sage Thrasher and Northern Shrike may be present in winter.

Records of Review Species: Northern Goshawk, Sept 1973, Dec 1992. American Woodcock, Feb 1987. Williamson's Sapsucker, April 1964, Dec 1967, Nov 1990. Bohemian Waxwing, Jan 1969, Jan 1973, Jan 1993. Golden-crowned Sparrow, Dec 1964, Dec 1981, March 1985, Dec 1985. Bronzed Cowbird, May 1995. Hooded Oriole, May 1991. Pine Grosbeak, Jan 1970.

Directions: From I-27 in Canyon, take SH 217 east for 12 miles to the park entrance.

General information: The 16,402-acre Palo Duro Canyon State Park, located on the eastern edge of the Texas High Plains (Llano Estacado), was carved by the Prairie Dog Town Fork of the Red River. The park boasts a visitor center with excellent exhibits and book sales, a variety of trails (4.6-mile hiking and horse-back, 3-level mountain-bike trail, and 9-mile running trail), the historic Goodnight Trading Post, and the Pioneer Amphitheater for summer performances of historical musical drama.

ADDITIONAL HELP

Location: Texas Official Travel Map grid D x 10; Armstrong and Randall counties
Nearest food, gas, and lodging: All facilities are available on-site.
Nearest camping: On-site (116 sites)
Contact: Superintendent, Palo Duro Canyon State Park (see Appendix C)

17 Caprock Canyons State Park

Habitats: Prairie, mesquite grassland, juniper woodland, cliff, pond, creek, riparian, wetland, field, cropland
Key birds: Golden Eagle, Scaled Quail, Greater Roadrunner, **Golden-fronted Woodpecker**, Western Scrub-Jay, Verdin, Rock and Canyon Wrens, Curve-billed Thrasher, Rufous-crowned Sparrow, Canyon Towhee, and Lark Bunting are present year-round. Least Bittern, Mississippi Kite, Swainson's Hawk, Common Poorwill, White-throated Swift, Scissor-tailed Flycatcher, Painted Bunting, and Cassin's Sparrow occur in summer. Hooded and Common Mergansers; Ferruginous and Rough-legged Hawks; Prairie Falcon; Chihuahuan Raven; Western and Mountain Bluebirds; Townsend's Solitaire; Northern Shrike; American Tree, Brewer's, Fox, and Harris's Sparrows; and McCown's and Chestnut-collared Longspurs can usually be found in winter.
Best times to bird: May for spring migrants and nesting activities; November to mid-February for winter birds

Birding strategies: Lake Theo (A) and nearby Dry Creek Lake (B), accessible via the dirt road on the south side of Lake Theo, support a number of water birds. Four species—Pied-billed Grebe, Mallard, Killdeer, and Ring-billed Gull—occur year-round. In summer Least Bittern, Green Heron, and Spotted Sandpiper occur as well. Expected winter residents and visitors include Green-winged Teal, Northern Pintail, Northern Shoveler, Gadwall, American Wigeon, Canvasback, Ring-necked Duck, Lesser Scaup, and Bufflehead. Fewer numbers of Snow and Canada Geese, Redhead, Greater Scaup, Common Goldeneye, and Hooded and Common Mergansers may be present.

The adjacent cattails and cottonwoods attract a variety of migrant songbirds in spring and fall. A few remain and nest: Yellow-billed Cuckoo, Western Kingbird, Scissor-tailed Flycatcher, Yellow Warbler, Blue Grosbeak, and Orchard and

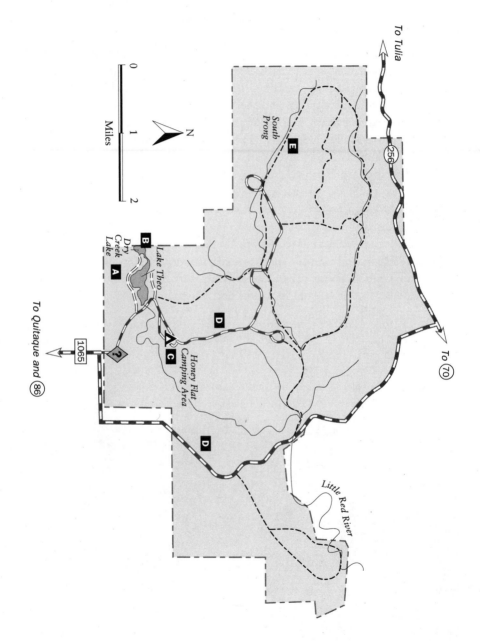

Bullock's Orioles. **Golden-fronted Woodpecker,** Ladder-backed Woodpecker, Northern Flicker, Northern Cardinal, and Red-winged Blackbird can be found here, too. In winter the wetlands and adjacent brushy areas often harbor Spotted Towhee; American Tree, Brewer's, Field, Vesper, Savannah, Grasshopper, Fox, Song, Lincoln's, Swamp, White-throated, White-crowned, and Harris's Sparrows; and Dark-eyed Junco.

Honey Flat Camping Area and surroundings (**C**) are dominated by juniper woodlands. Year-round species include Scaled Quail, Mourning Dove, Greater Roadrunner, Western Scrub-Jay, Tufted Titmouse, Bushtit, Bewick's Wren, Northern Mockingbird, Curve-billed Thrasher, Loggerhead Shrike, Canyon Towhee, Rufous-crowned Sparrow, Chipping Sparrow, Western Meadowlark, and House Finch. Ash-throated Flycatcher, Blue-gray Gnatcatcher, and Lark Sparrow can be found here in summer. Watch overhead for Turkey Vulture, Swainson's and Red-tailed Hawks, and Common Nighthawk at dawn and dusk.

Mesquite grasslands (**D**) occur along the park road as well as along some highways outside the park. Year-round resident prairie birds include Northern Bobwhite, Scaled Quail, Greater Roadrunner, Northern Mockingbird, Loggerhead Shrike, and Western Meadowlark. In summer this habitat is utilized by Swainson's Hawk and Cassin's Sparrow. Lark Buntings prefer the old fields and agricultural lands. In winter watch for Northern Harrier, Ferruginous and Rough-legged Hawks, Prairie Falcon, Horned Lark, Chihuahuan Raven, Western and

Juniper woodland habitat in Caprock Canyons State Park.

116

Mountain Bluebirds, Savannah Sparrow, and McCown's and Chestnut-collared Longspurs.

South Prong (E) offers many of the same birds mentioned above, but cliffs, a stream, and more extensive cottonwood groves in the upper portion of the canyon support a greater diversity of birds year-round. The cliffs provide yet another habitat for Rock Dove year-round, and nesting Turkey Vulture, Golden Eagle, American Kestrel, Great Horned Owl, Common Poorwill, White-throated Swift, Cliff and Barn Swallows, and Rock and Canyon Wrens in summer.

The large, more isolated cottonwoods in the upper canyon should be birded throughout the year. Look here for Mississippi Kite, Red-tailed Hawk, Western Kingbird, American Crow, and Bullock's Oriole in summer; and Downy Woodpecker, Yellow-bellied Sapsucker, and Orange-crowned and Yellow-rumped Warblers in winter. Watch also for the occasional, sporadic Northern Shrike in winter.

Directions: The park is located just north of Quitaque. Take FM 1065 for 3 miles north of Quitaque (pronounced *kitty*-quay) to the park entrance.

General information: Caprock Canyons is one of the state's most underrated parks. This 13,906-acre park is a smorgasbord of grand scenery, wildlife, geology, and history. The exposed red sandstones and siltstones are some of the most colorful found anywhere. The park also includes a portion of the Caprock Canyons State Park Trail, a 65-mile hiking, biking, and horseback trail that runs from South Plains northeast to Estelline.

ADDITIONAL HELP

Location: Texas Official Travel Map grid F x 11; Briscoe County
Nearest food, gas, and lodging: All are available in Quitaque, 3 miles from the park entrance.
Nearest camping: On-site (55 sites)
Contact: Superintendent, Caprock Canyons State Park (see Appendix C)

18 Muleshoe National Wildlife Refuge

Habitats: Lake, creek, honey locust–hackberry woodland, mesquite grassland, prairie
Key birds: Lesser Prairie-Chicken, Scaled Quail, Greater Roadrunner, Cactus Wren, Curve-billed Thrasher, Canyon Towhee, and Rufous-crowned Sparrow are present year-round. Swainson's Hawk, Snowy Plover, Burrowing Owl, Scissor-tailed Flycatcher, and Grasshopper Sparrow occur in summer. Bald Eagle; Ferruginous and Rough-legged Hawks; Golden Eagle; Prairie Falcon; Sandhill Crane; Eastern, Western, and Mountain Bluebirds; Lark Bunting; and McCown's and Chestnut-collared Longspurs can usually be found in winter.
Best times to bird: April to June for spring migrants and nesting activities; November to mid-February for winter birds

18 Muleshoe National Wildlife Refuge

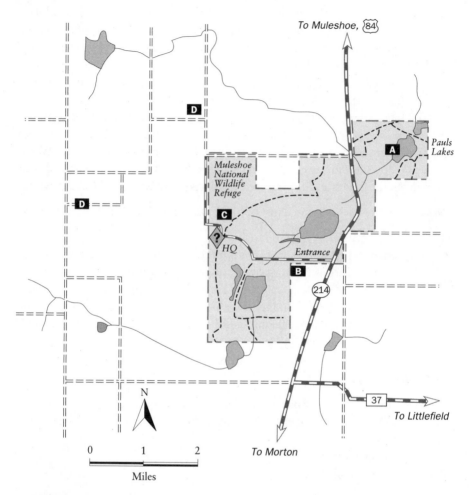

Birding strategies: Upper and Lower Pauls lakes (**A**) are the best sites for finding migrating and wintering water birds. Sandhill Cranes (as many as 250,000 in 1981, but only 2,000 by the 1990s) winter, usually roosting on Lower Pauls Lake at night and flying in and out of the refuge throughout the day. Waterfowl prefer Upper Pauls Lake. Most numerous there are Green-winged Teal, Mallard, Northern Pintail, Northern Shoveler, Gadwall, and American Wigeon. Fewer numbers of Horned, Eared, and Western Grebes; Greater White-fronted, Snow, and Ross's Geese; Wood Duck; Canvasback; Redhead; Ring-necked Duck; Lesser Scaup; Bufflehead; Hooded and Common Mergansers; and Ruddy Duck occur.

The wetlands and mud flats surrounding Pauls Lakes harbor a few additional species in summer: Pied-billed Grebe, Black-crowned Night-Heron, Snowy Plover, Killdeer, Black-necked Stilt, American Avocet, and Red-winged and Yellow-headed Blackbirds.

All the land birds can be found along the main entrance road (B) and in the vicinity of the refuge headquarters (C), where there is a 1-mile nature trail. Expected summer residents include Red-tailed Hawk; Northern Bobwhite; Scaled Quail; Greater Roadrunner; Common Nighthawk at dawn and dusk; Scissor-tailed Flycatcher; Cliff and Barn Swallows; Northern Mockingbird; Loggerhead Shrike; Cassin's, Lark, and Grasshopper Sparrows; and Eastern and Western Meadowlarks. Ring-necked Pheasant, Canyon Towhee, and Rufous-crowned Sparrow are less numerous.

At headquarters the prairie dog colony has a resident population of Burrowing Owls (rare in winter). The nature trail circles a wooded drainage that acts as a migrant trap in spring and fall. A wide variety of flycatchers, vireos, warblers, and orioles have been found here. Nesting birds include Mourning Dove, Yellow-billed Cuckoo, Greater Roadrunner, Great Horned Owl, Ladder-backed Woodpecker, Ash-throated and Scissor-tailed Flycatchers, Western Kingbird, Northern Mockingbird, Curve-billed Thrasher, Loggerhead Shrike, Blue Grosbeak, Bullock's Oriole, and House Sparrow. Occasionally, Black-chinned Hummingbird, Red-headed Woodpecker, Northern Flicker, Western Wood-Pewee, Brown Thrasher, and Painted Bunting can be found here in summer. Several other birds may occur here in winter: Sharp-shinned and Cooper's Hawks; Long-eared Owl; Yellow-bellied Sapsucker; Downy and Hairy Woodpeckers; Say's Phoebe; Mountain Chickadee; Brown Creeper; Golden-crowned and Ruby-crowned Kinglets; Eastern Bluebird; Townsend's Solitaire; American Robin; Cedar Waxwing; Orange-crowned and Yellow-rumped Warblers; Northern Cardinal; Pyrrhuloxia; Spotted Towhee; American Tree, Field, Sage, Fox, Song, Lincoln's, Swamp, and White-crowned Sparrows; Dark-eyed Junco; McCown's and Chestnut-collared Longspurs; Brewer's Blackbird; Common Grackle; Pine Siskin; American Goldfinch; and Evening Grosbeak.

Watch for predators: Bald Eagle, Ferruginous and Rough-legged Hawks, Golden Eagle, American Kestrel, and Peregrine and Prairie Falcons.

Lesser Prairie-Chicken populations have declined dramatically in recent years, and can no longer be seen on the refuge. However, a few birds still occasionally are found on their springtime leks just northwest of the refuge (D); see map for details.

Records of Review Species: Red Phalarope, Sept 1982. Lewis's Woodpecker, May 1989.

Directions: From US 84, take SH 214 south from Muleshoe for 20 miles; or from Littlefield, take FM 54 and FM 37 west for 30 miles to SH 214, then north on 214 about 2.5 miles to the refuge.

General information: The oldest national wildlife refuge in Texas, Muleshoe was established as a wintering area for migratory waterfowl and Sandhill Crane. The refuge includes 5,809 acres of prairie and sink-type lakes with no outlets. Refuge roads are open from dawn to dusk, but the refuge headquarters (2.25 miles west of SH 214) is open Monday through Friday from 8 A.M. to 4:30 P.M.

ADDITIONAL HELP

Location: Texas Official Travel Map grid G x 8; Bailey County
Nearest food, gas, and lodging: Muleshoe has facilities for gas, food, and lodging (20 miles).
Nearest camping: On-site, primitive sites only; full hookups in Littlefield (30 miles)
Contact: Manager, Muleshoe National Wildlife Refuge (see Appendix C)

19 Copper Breaks State Park and Pease River

Habitats: Lake, pond, river, marsh, riparian, mesquite grassland, prairie, pasture
Key birds: Virginia Rail, Greater Roadrunner, **Golden-fronted Woodpecker**, Canyon Towhee, and Rufous-crowned and Black-chinned Sparrows occur year-round. Mississippi Kite, Swainson's Hawk, Scissor-tailed Flycatcher, Chihuahuan Raven, and Blue Grosbeak reside here in spring and summer. Rough-legged Hawk, Winter Wren, Mountain Bluebird, Townsend's Solitaire, and American Tree Sparrow occur in winter.
Best times to bird: Mid-April through June for spring migrants and nesting activities

Birding strategies: Lake Copper Breaks (**A**) offers easy access to a variety of water birds: Pied-billed Grebe, Great Blue Heron, Mallard, Ruddy Duck, Virginia Rail, American Coot, Belted Kingfisher, and Red-winged Blackbird can be expected year-round. In summer watch for Green Heron and Black-crowned Night-Heron, and in winter Eared Grebe, Canada Goose, Northern Pintail, Blue-winged and Cinnamon Teal, Northern Shoveler, Gadwall, American Wigeon, Ring-necked Duck, Lesser Scaup, Bufflehead, Hooded Merganser, Marsh Wren, and Song and Swamp Sparrows can usually be found.

Big Pond (**B**), best viewed from behind campsite 44, usually contains about the same water birds that can be found in the lake. However, because this pond is more isolated and surrounded by marsh habitat, there is greater probability for finding some of the more secretive birds, such as rails and visiting migrants.

Bird the mesquite grassland and juniper woodland habitats along the 2-mile Bull Canyon Hiking Trail (**C**) and Juniper Ridge Nature Trail (**D**). Expected full-time resident birds in both areas include Red-tailed Hawk, American Kestrel, Northern Bobwhite, Mourning Dove, Greater Roadrunner, **Golden-fronted Woodpecker**, Ladder-backed Woodpecker, American Crow, Blue Jay, Bewick's Wren, Northern Mockingbird, Loggerhead Shrike, Canyon Towhee, Rufous-crowned Sparrow, and Western Meadowlark. In summer expect Turkey Vulture, Mississippi Kite, Swainson's Hawk, Chihuahuan Raven, Scissor-tailed Flycatcher, Western King-bird, Cliff and Barn Swallows, Eastern Bluebird, American Robin, Blue Grosbeak, and Black-chinned and Lark Sparrows. In winter the woodlands and weedy fields

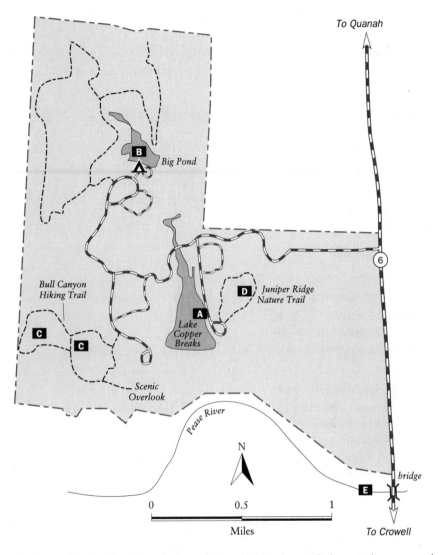

and edges often harbor Rough-legged Hawk; Northern Flicker; Ruby-crowned Kinglet; Winter Wren; Mountain Bluebird; Townsend's Solitaire; Cedar Waxwing; Spotted Towhee; Chipping, Field, Vesper, and White-crowned Sparrows; and Dark-eyed Junco. In addition, the Scenic Overlook offers a good view of the surrounding area and Pease River valley; the fall raptor migration can best be observed from this site.

The Pease River (E), just south of the park along SH 6, is readily accessible at the bridge on SH 6 (see map). This area offers dense riparian habitat, riverway, and mud flats that can be superb during migration. The riparian zone also supports a few additional nesting and wintering birds. Look for Blue Jay, Carolina Wren, and Northern Cardinal year-round; Eastern Phoebe and Cliff Swallow in summer; and Brown Thrasher and various seedeaters, including American Tree Sparrow, in winter.

Directions: The park lies along SH 6 between Quanah and Crowell. From Quanah, take SH 6 for 13 miles south; from Crowell, take SH 6 for 8 miles north to the park entrance.

General information: This 1,933-acre state park offers camping, picnicking, and hiking and equestrian trails year-round. Fishing is allowed on the 60-acre Lake Copper Breaks, an impoundment on Devil's Creek. The park, whose name was derived from the copper deposits scattered throughout the area and the rugged, broken terrain, contains a visitor center with exhibits on bison and the Comanche Indians. The park is also home to a Texas longhorn herd. The Pease River is a tributary of the Red River.

ADDITIONAL HELP

Location: Texas Official Travel Map grid F x 13; Hardeman County
Nearest food, gas, and lodging: Food and gas can be found in Crowell (8 miles); lodging is in Quanah (13 miles).
Nearest camping: On-site (40 sites)
Contact: Superintendent, Copper Breaks State Park (see Appendix C)

20 Lubbock

Buffalo Springs Lake, Lake Ransom, Twin Ponds, Boles Lake, and Mackenzie Park

Habitats: Lake, pond, river, creek, wetland, mud flat, riparian, prairie, mesquite grassland, lawn, field, pasture, cropland
Key birds: Greater Roadrunner, Burrowing Owl, **Golden-fronted Woodpecker,** Chihuahuan Raven, Rock Wren, Curve-billed Thrasher, Canyon Towhee, and Rufous-crowned Sparrow are present year-round. Mississippi Kite, Swainson's Hawk, Snowy Plover, Red-headed Woodpecker, Scissor-tailed Flycatcher, Bell's Vireo, Painted Bunting, Dickcissel, and Cassin's Sparrow occur in summer. Hooded and Common Mergansers; Ferruginous and Rough-legged Hawks; Golden Eagle; Prairie Falcon; Long-eared and Short-eared Owls; Eastern and Mountain Bluebirds; Townsend's Solitaire; Sage Thrasher; and American Tree, Fox, and Swamp Sparrows can usually be found in winter.
Best times to bird: April to June for spring migrants and nesting activities; November to mid-February for winter birds

Birding strategies: The Double Mountain Fork of the Brazos River runs through the northeastern half of Lubbock, providing a series of birding sites within the city

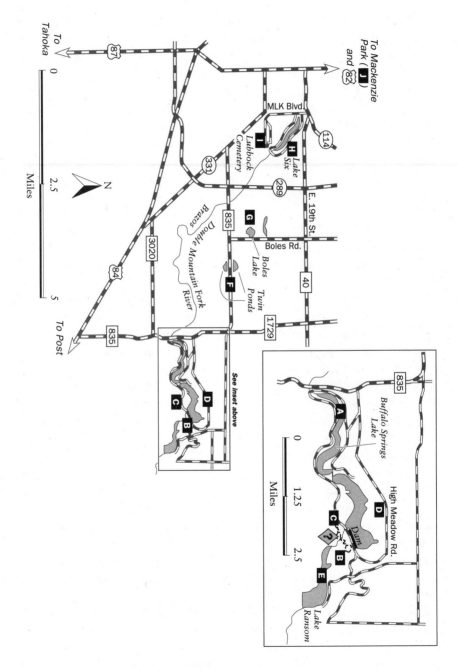

limits and to the southeast. Although the majority of the Lubbock sites are within an urban setting, migratory birds and wintering waterfowl can be exceptional.

The greatest habitat diversity is present at **Buffalo Springs Lake (A)**, a private area that can be crowded on weekends and holidays. The lake and scattered patches of marsh support a few birds year-round: Pied-billed Grebe, Great Blue Heron, Black-crowned Night-Heron, Canada Goose, Mallard, Northern Pintail, Northern Shoveler, Cinnamon Teal, Redhead, Ruddy Duck, Common Moorhen, American Coot, Belted Kingfisher, and Red-winged Blackbird. Additional water birds can be expected in winter, including Horned and Eared Grebes, Double-crested Cormorant, Snow Goose, Green-winged and Blue-winged Teal, Gadwall, Canvasback, Ring-necked Duck, Lesser Scaup, Common Goldeneye, Bufflehead, Hooded and Common Mergansers, Greater Yellowlegs, Common Snipe, Ring-billed Gull, Marsh Wren, and Song and Swamp Sparrows. Occasionally Common Loon, Western Grebe, Greater Scaup, and Red-breasted Merganser are also found.

The Audubon Society wetland below the dam **(B)** supports additional water birds at various times of year; the nature trail offers easy access. This area can be very good during spring and fall, when neotropical migrants are passing through. A few remain and nest: Green Heron, Yellow-billed Cuckoo, Black-chinned Hummingbird, Blue Grosbeak, and Yellow-headed Blackbird. The drier mesquite-grassland and woodland habitats **(C)** along the trail support several additional breeding birds in summer: Mourning and Inca Doves; Greater Roadrunner; **Golden-fronted Woodpecker;** Ladder-backed Woodpecker; Ash-throated and Scissor-tailed Flycatchers; Western Kingbird; Tufted Titmouse; Verdin; Carolina and Bewick's Wrens; Blue-gray Gnatcatcher; Northern Mockingbird; Curve-billed Thrasher; Loggerhead Shrike; Painted Bunting; Canyon Towhee; Cassin's, Rufous-crowned, and Lark Sparrows; Eastern and Western Meadowlarks; Orchard and Bullock's Orioles; and House Finch. Watch also for Rock and Canyon Wrens about the rocky breaks.

Walk through this area at dawn or dusk and you might find Great Horned Owl (year-round), Eastern Screech-Owl (winter), and Common Nighthawk and Common Poorwill (summer). A number of diurnal raptors are probable: Red-tailed Hawk and American Kestrel year-round; Turkey Vulture, Mississippi Kite, and Swainson's Hawk in spring and summer; Northern Harrier; Sharp-shinned, Cooper's, Ferruginous, and Rough-legged Hawks; Merlin; and Prairie Falcon in winter. Many of these are also likely along the High Meadow Road **(D)**, which circles the north side of the area. Watch in the open mesquite grasslands for Cassin's Sparrow.

Lake Ransom (E) lies downriver from Buffalo Springs Lake. This urban area supports most of the same water birds mentioned above, including significant numbers of Canada Geese in winter.

Return to town via FM 835 and check **Twin Ponds (F)** and **Boles Lake (G)**, along Boles Road, for water birds. Both sites can be very good during migration, and Boles Lake offers mud flats that attract shorebirds. Snowy Plover, Black-necked Stilt, and American Avocet nest.

Bird Lake Six (**H**) and the adjacent Lubbock Cemetery (**I**). Drive the loop road around Lake Six, stopping at various locations, such as at the dam site. Year-round residents include **Golden-fronted Woodpecker**, Blue Jay, Carolina Wren, American Robin, and Great-tailed and Common Grackles. This site can be very productive during migration. And in summer, watch for Eastern Phoebe; Purple Martin; Northern Rough-winged, Cliff, and Barn Swallows; and Brown Thrasher.

The Lubbock Cemetery is a good spot for migrating warblers in spring. And in winter flocks of Cedar Waxwing, Pine Siskin, and American Goldfinch occur with regularity. Clark's Nutcracker, Bohemian Waxwing, and Evening Grosbeak are irregular winter visitors.

Mackenzie Park (**J**) contains a prairie dog colony that supports several Burrowing Owls. Although they may not be readily apparent in winter, good close-up views are possible most of the year.

Records of Review Species: Yellow-billed Loon, Dec–Jan 1981/82. Red-necked Grebe, Jan 1989. Brant, Nov 1994, April 1997. Little Gull, April 1983. Black-legged Kittiwake, Aug 1993. Varied Thrush, Dec 1990, Dec 1991. Bohemian Waxwing, Dec–March 1977/78, Nov 1996. Pine Grosbeak, May 1988. White-winged Crossbill, Dec–March 1975/76.

Directions: Buffalo Springs Lake and Lake Ransom lie east of Loop 289, off FM 835. Lake Six and the Lubbock Cemetery are located off Martin Luther King, Jr., Boulevard between East 19th and East 21st streets; Mackenzie Park is located on US 87, northeast of its junction with US 82.

General information: Buffalo Springs Lake is a county-owned recreation area ($2 entry fee) that offers camping, picnicking, fishing, water sports, and hiking. The Llano Estacado Audubon Society maintains a 55-acre portion of the area, where a 1.7-mile nature trail is available for birding.

The 542-acre Mackenzie Park, named for General Ranald Mackenzie and operated by the city of Lubbock, is primarily a recreational area, with playgrounds and a swimming pool.

ADDITIONAL HELP

Location: Texas Official Travel Map grid G x 9; Lubbock County
Nearest food, gas, and lodging: All are available throughout the area.
Nearest camping: On-site at Buffalo Springs Lake and elsewhere in Lubbock
Contact: Lubbock Parks and Recreation Department; Buffalo Springs Lake; Llano Estacado Audubon Society (see Appendix C)

21 Red Bluff Lake

Habitats: Lake, river, riparian, rock dam, desert scrub
Key birds: Golden Eagle, Prairie Falcon, Scaled Quail, Greater
Roadrunner, Say's Phoebe, Chihuahuan Raven, Verdin, Cactus Wren,
Curve-billed Thrasher, Pyrrhuloxia, Black-throated Sparrow, and
Lesser Goldfinch are present year-round. Swainson's Hawk, Lesser
and Common Nighthawks, Common Poorwill, Cave Swallow, Bell's
Vireo, Cassin's Sparrow, and Scott's Orioles occur in summer.
Horned, Eared, Western, and Clark's Grebes; American White
Pelican; Common Goldeneye; Common and Red-breasted
Mergansers; Rock Wren; Sage and Crissal Thrashers; and Sage
Sparrow can usually be found in winter.
Best times to bird: November to early February for water birds and
various desert dwellers

Birding strategies: The small park (**A**) northwest of the little town of Red Bluff
offers good views of the southwest corner of the lake. In winter water birds can be
abundant: Horned, Eared, Western, and Clark's Grebes; Great Blue Heron; Northern Pintail; Northern Shoveler; Gadwall; American Wigeon; Lesser Scaup; Bufflehead; Ruddy Duck; American Coot; and Ring-billed Gull are the most common.
Less numerous are Green-winged Teal, Mallard, Ring-necked Duck, Common
Goldeneye, Common and Red-breasted Mergansers, and Forster's Tern. American Pipit and Vesper, Black-throated, and Savannah Sparrows utilize the grassy
areas above the rocky shoreline.

The opposite side of the lake, an area known as Sandy Beach (**B**), usually offers
the same assortment of water birds. Access is by a gravel road that skirts the
runoff area below the dam. More extensive views of the lake, including an extensive shoreline, are possible from this east side. American White Pelicans and Double-crested Cormorants are more obvious here, as are various soaring birds: Northern
Harrier, Red-tailed and Rough-legged Hawks, and American Kestrel.

Red Bluff Lake has received little attention from birders, so there is much to
learn about this area. In January 1997, a Black-legged Kittiwake was recorded.

The salt cedar thickets along both sides of the dam at the lake's southeast
corner usually harbor a number of wintering birds, including Bewick's Wren; Rock
Wrens can often be found on the rocky dam proper.

The lake runoff below the dam (**C**) offers an open pool edged with salt cedars.
Check this site in passing for ducks, shorebirds, and land birds. Scaled Quail;
Ladder-backed Woodpecker; Verdin; Bewick's Wren; Orange-crowned and Yellow-rumped Warblers; Green-tailed Towhee; Pyrrhuloxia; various sparrows, including
Golden-crowned; and House Finch can be found here in winter. Bell's Vireo and
Orchard Oriole utilize this area in summer.

In winter bird the open creosote bush–dominated desert habitat, such as that
along paved CR 447 (**D**), the entrance to Red Bluff. This area usually contains
Cactus Wren, Northern Mockingbird, Sage and Crissal Thrashers, Black-throated

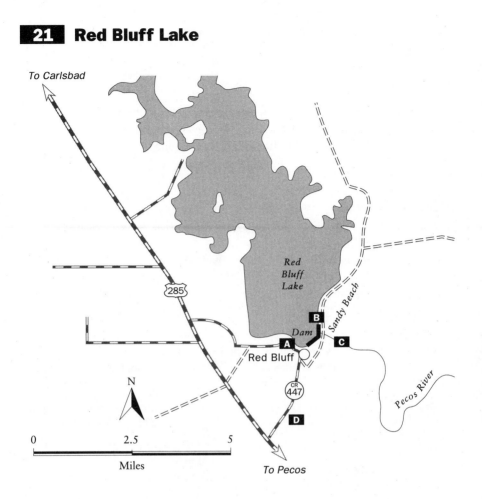

To Carlsbad

285

Red Bluff Lake

Sandy Beach

B

Dam

A

C

Red Bluff

Pecos River

N

CR 447

D

0   2.5   5

Miles

To Pecos

and Sage Sparrows, and Western Meadowlark. Other possible residents include Golden Eagle, Prairie Falcon, Greater Roadrunner, Say's Phoebe, Curve-billed Thrasher, and Loggerhead Shrike. Turkey Vulture, Swainson's Hawk, Lesser and Common Nighthawks, Common Poorwill, Cliff and Cave Swallows, Cassin's Sparrow, and Scott's Oriole occur in summer.

Directions: Turn off US 285 (5 miles north of Orla or 43 miles north of Pecos) onto CR 447 and drive 3 miles to Red Bluff; Sandy Beach is 3 miles beyond Red Bluff. Turn south on a dirt oil field road just before reaching town and follow the road across the Pecos River. Veer left where signs direct you to Sandy Beach and the east side of the dam.

General information: Red Bluff Lake is located on the Pecos River just below the Texas–New Mexico border. The 11,700-acre (when full) reservoir is a water irrigation project that provides a variety of water sports year-round, including excellent fishing. Do not drive on the beach; the sand is deceptive and getting stuck here is a real possibility.

ADDITIONAL HELP

Location: Texas Official Travel Map grid L x 6; Loving County
Nearest food, gas, and lodging: Pecos (43 miles) has food, gas, and lodging.
Nearest camping: Pecos (43 miles); primitive camping is allowed on the beach
Contact: Pecos Chamber of Commerce (see Appendix C)

22 Monahans Sandhills State Park

Habitats: Dune, mesquite grassland, desert scrub, willow thicket, field
Key birds: Harris's Hawk, Scaled Quail, Greater Roadrunner, Chihuahuan Raven, Verdin, Cactus Wren, Curve-billed Thrasher, Pyrrhuloxia, Canyon Towhee, and Black-throated Sparrow are present year-round. Swainson's Hawk, Common Poorwill, Ash-throated and Scissor-tailed Flycatchers, and Lesser Goldfinch occur in summer. Ferruginous Hawk, Prairie Falcon, Say's Phoebe, Lark Bunting, and Brewer's Blackbird can usually be found in winter.
Best times to bird: April and May for spring migrants and nesting activities

Birding strategies: Bird the nature trail behind the visitor center (**A**) for year-round residents: Scaled Quail, Mourning Dove, Ladder-backed Woodpecker, Cactus and Bewick's Wrens, Northern Mockingbird, Curve-billed Thrasher, Pyrrhuloxia, Canyon Towhee, Black-throated Sparrow, Brown-headed Cowbird, and House Finch. In summer Ash-throated and Scissor-tailed Flycatchers, Barn Swallow, Blue Grosbeak, Great-tailed Grackle, and Bullock's Oriole can also be expected. In winter Say's Phoebe; Yellow-rumped Warbler; Spotted Towhee; Chipping, Lark, and White-crowned Sparrows; and American Goldfinch can usually be seen. Lark Bunting and Brewer's Blackbird often are present in and adjacent to the parking lot.

Most of these same birds can usually be found in the mesquite grasslands (**B**) along the utility right-of-way west and east of the visitor center parking lot. Additional summer birds to watch for here include Western Kingbird, Chihuahuan Raven, Verdin, Loggerhead Shrike, and Lark Sparrow. Great Horned Owl, Common Nighthawk, and Common Poorwill can usually be seen and/or heard, as well. This area also supports a few additional wintering birds: American Kestrel, Northern Flicker, and Brewer's, Field, and Lincoln's Sparrows.

Several willow thickets (**C**) occur along the gated road, accessible at the end of the paved road (next to an oil well pump). Birds nesting in this habitat include Mourning Dove, Yellow-billed Cuckoo, Black-chinned Hummingbird, Ladder-backed Woodpecker, Ash-throated and Scissor-tailed Flycatchers, Western Kingbird,

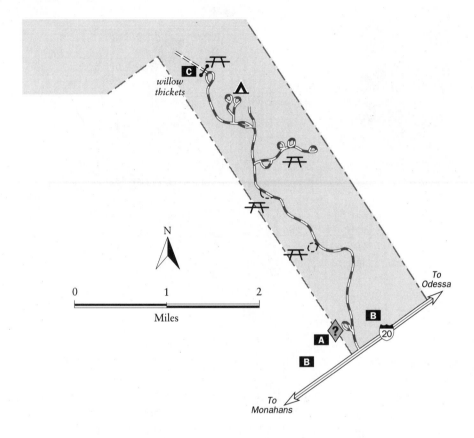

Bewick's Wren, Blue Grosbeak, and Bullock's Oriole. In years when the area has had plenty of rainfall and ponds fill the depressions, Great Blue and Green Herons and a few shorebirds are occasional visitors. These thickets also can act as migrant traps, especially in spring. And in winter, Yellow-rumped Warbler; Spotted Towhee; Song, Lincoln's, and White-crowned Sparrows; and Dark-eyed Juncos are most numerous. Watch also for Northern Harrier, Sharp-shinned and Cooper's Hawks, and Prairie Falcon at these sites.

Additional raptors are more often seen in the surrounding area. Harris's Hawk and Great Horned Owl can usually be found year-round; Turkey Vulture and Swainson's Hawk are most numerous in summer; and Red-tailed and Ferruginous Hawks, Golden Eagle, and Burrowing Owl are more often found in winter.

Directions: The park is located off I-20, 5 miles east of Monahans or 25 miles west of Odessa.

General information: The 3,840-acre park is dominated by shining white sand dunes, many of which are 70 feet high. The Monahans dunes are only a small

Sand dunes in Monahans Sandhills State Park.

portion of a dune field that extends for about 200 miles from south of Monahans west and north into New Mexico. Havard shin oak and pockets of willows occur throughout.

A watering station, maintained behind the visitor center, attracts a variety of birds and mammals that can be viewed through large glass windows. The building also contains a number of wildlife, history, and archeology exhibits.

ADDITIONAL HELP

Location: Texas Official Travel Map grid M x 7; Ward County
Nearest food, gas, and lodging: Monahans, 5 miles from the state park, has food, gas, and lodging.
Nearest camping: On-site (24 sites)
Contact: Superintendent, Monahans Sandhills State Park (see Appendix C)

23 Big Spring

Big Spring State Park, Comanche Trail Park, Perimeter Road, and Sandhill Crane Sanctuary

Habitats: Juniper-oak woodland, pond, wetland, playa, field, cropland

Key birds: Scaled Quail, Greater Roadrunner, **Golden-fronted Woodpecker,** Vermilion Flycatcher, Western Scrub-Jay, Chihuahuan Raven, Cactus and Rock Wrens, Curve-billed Thrasher, Pyrrhuloxia, Canyon Towhee, and Lesser Goldfinch are present year-round. Mississippi Kite, Swainson's Hawk, Snowy Plover, American Avocet, Burrowing Owl, Common Poorwill, Scissor-tailed Flycatcher, Painted Bunting, Dickcissel, Cassin's Sparrow, and Lark Bunting occur in summer. Ferruginous Hawk; Prairie Falcon; Sandhill Crane; Short-eared Owl; Say's Phoebe; Sage Thrasher; Eastern, Western, and Mountain Bluebirds; Townsend's Solitaire; Phainopepla; and Green-tailed Towhee can usually be found in winter.

Best times to bird: April and May for spring migrants and nesting activities; late October for migrating Sandhill Crane

Birding strategies: At **Big Spring State Park (A)**, the pinyon-juniper woodlands harbor year-round Mourning Dove, Ladder-backed Woodpecker, Western Scrub-Jay, Tufted Titmouse, Bewick's Wren, Canyon Towhee, Rufous-crowned and Lark Sparrows, House Finch, and Lesser Goldfinch. In summer expect Ash-throated and Scissor-tailed Flycatchers, Western Kingbird, Painted Bunting, and Cassin's Sparrow (irregular). Check the water stations for Scaled Quail and Inca Dove and the open rocky slopes for Greater Roadrunner and Rock Wren. After dark, Common Poorwill can usually be heard.

In winter the woodlands support a number of other birds, including Say's Phoebe, Ruby-crowned Kinglet, Townsend's Solitaire, Phainopepla, and Orange-crowned and Yellow-rumped Warblers. And after summer and fall rains have produced a good grassy cover, several seedeaters can usually be found: Green-tailed and Spotted Towhees; Field, Vesper, Lincoln's, and White-crowned Sparrows; Dark-eyed Junco; and American Goldfinch are common. Chipping, Clay-colored, Brewer's, Song, Lincoln's, and White-throated Sparrows are less numerous. Watch also for the occasional Prairie Falcon.

Nearby **Comanche Trail Park (B)** can be good for migrants, including a variety of songbirds, as well as gulls and terns. In summer this area is the best place to find Mississippi Kite, **Golden-fronted Woodpecker,** Vermilion Flycatcher, Painted Bunting, and Orchard and Bullock's Orioles.

Perimeter Road (C) circles Big Spring's McMahonwrinkle Airport west of town, and offers a prairie dog town with Swainson's Hawk, Burrowing Owl, Chihuahuan Raven, Scissor-tailed Flycatcher, Horned Lark, Dickcissel, and Lark Bunting in summer; in winter, watch for Ferruginous Hawk; Eastern, Western, and Mountain Bluebirds; and Brewer's Blackbird, as well as the occasional Short-eared Owl and Sage Thrasher. Other year-round resident birds along Perimeter Road include Verdin, Cactus Wren, Curve-billed Thrasher, and Pyrrhuloxia.

 **Big Spring**

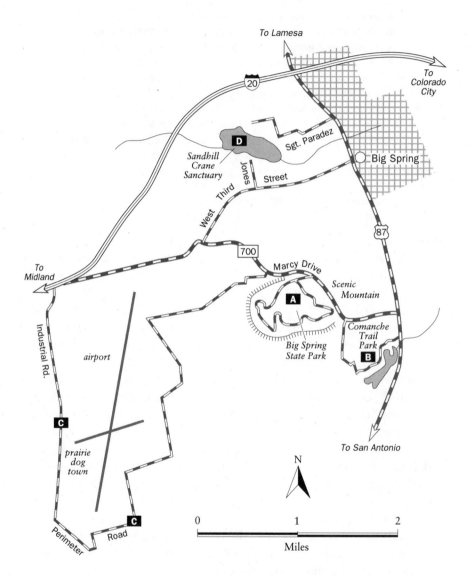

From late October to April, Sandhill Crane, along with geese and an occasional Whooping Crane, can be seen at the **Sandhill Crane Sanctuary (D)**, north of the state park. This area and other playas in the area also support nesting Snowy Plover, Black-necked Stilt, and American Avocet.

Records of Review Species: Greater Pewee, Oct–Nov 1984. Varied Thrush, Dec–Feb 1979/ 80. Golden-crowned Sparrow, Dec 1983.

Directions: From Big Spring, take US 87 south to FM 700, which leads to both the state park entrance and adjacent Comanche Trail Park. Perimeter Road, accessed off FM 700 or, from the north, I-20 (via Industrial Road) or from Marcy Drive (from the east), circles the Big Spring McMahonwrinkle Airport. The Sandhill Crane Sanctuary lies north of the state park; take FM 700 north to West 3rd Street, go east to Jones Street, then turn north to the sanctuary.

General information: Scenic Mountain dominates the state park (382 acres). It is an erosional limestone-capped remnant of the northern edge of the Edwards Plateau. The Llano Estacado (pronounced *yawn*-o esta-*ka*-do), or Staked Plains, lies to the west, and the Rolling Plains lie to the north and east. A Scenic Mountain (self-guided) trail booklet provides information on the area's flora and fauna. Historic, turn-of-the-century carvings, left by cattle drovers and immigrants, can be found along the caprock.

The park was developed by the Civilian Conservation Corps in 1934. Limestone blocks, some weighing as much as 2 tons, were quarried on-site for construction of the retaining walls for the 3-mile scenic drive.

The adjacent Comanche Trail Park (400 acres) contains the historic Big Spring and freshwater ponds, unique features in an otherwise arid terrain. The spring served as the only watering place for herds of bison, pronghorn, and wild horses within a 60-mile radius. Comanches regularly used the spring as a campsite on their raids to the south.

ADDITIONAL HELP

Location: Texas Official Travel Map grid L x 10; Howard County
Nearest food, gas, and lodging: Food, gas, and lodging can be found in Big Spring.
Nearest camping: On-site at state park (10 sites)
Contact: Superintendent, Big Spring State Park; city of Big Spring (see Appendix C)

▉24▉ Lake Colorado City State Park

Habitats: Lake, wetland, mesquite grassland, juniper woodland, pasture, cropland

Key birds: Scaled Quail, Wild Turkey, Greater Roadrunner, **Golden-fronted Woodpecker,** Western Scrub-Jay, Chihuahuan Raven, Verdin, Cactus Wren, Curve-billed Thrasher, Pyrrhuloxia, Canyon Towhee, Rufous-crowned Sparrow, and Lesser Goldfinch are present year-round. Mississippi Kite, Swainson's Hawk, Lesser and Common Nighthawks, Common Poorwill, Black-chinned Hummingbird, Scissor-tailed Flycatcher, Canyon Wren, Bell's Vireo, and Painted Bunting occur in summer. Western Grebe, Osprey, Sandhill Crane, Western and Mountain Bluebirds, Townsend's Solitaire, Sage Thrasher, Green-tailed and Spotted Towhees, and Lark Bunting can usually be found in winter.

Best times to bird: April and May for spring migrants and nesting activities; November to March for winter birds

Birding strategies: Lake Colorado City can best be viewed from the Mesquite Circle (**A**) and Lakeview (**B**) camping areas as well as from the end of the road (day use area) (**C**). Year-round water birds include Great Blue Heron, Mallard, and Greater Yellowlegs. Several additional species can be expected in winter: Pied-billed, Horned, and Eared Grebes; American White Pelican; Double-crested Cormorant; Green-winged and Blue-winged Teal; Northern Pintail; Northern Shoveler; Gadwall; American Wigeon; Lesser Scaup; Bufflehead; Ring-billed Gull; American Coot; and Belted Kingfisher. Pied-billed Grebe and Black-crowned Night-Heron are less numerous. Killdeer, Spotted Sandpiper, and American Pipit occur along the shoreline, and Sandhill Cranes often roost in wetlands on the far side of the lake. A few additional water birds usually occur in summer: Little Blue and Green Herons, Yellow-crowned Night-Heron, Black-necked Stilt, and American Avocet.

The juniper woodland habitat can best be birded along the Craig Hiking Trail (**D**) between the Mesquite Circle and Lakeview camping areas. Full-time resident birds here include Scaled Quail, Mourning Dove, Greater Roadrunner, Ladder-backed Woodpecker, Western Scrub-Jay, Carolina Chickadee, Tufted Titmouse, Cactus and Bewick's Wrens, Northern Mockingbird, Curve-billed Thrasher, Loggerhead Shrike, Pyrrhuloxia, Canyon Towhee, Rufous-crowned Sparrow, House Finch, and Lesser Goldfinch. In summer Black-chinned Hummingbird, Ash-throated and Scissor-tailed Flycatchers, Canyon Wren, Blue-gray Gnatcatcher, Blue Grosbeak, Painted Bunting, Lark Sparrow, and Bullock's Oriole are also present. In winter, watch for Bushtit, Western and Mountain Bluebirds, Townsend's Solitaire, and American Robin. **Golden-fronted Woodpecker,** Inca Dove, Common Ground-Dove, and Eastern Bluebird prefer the more open mesquite grasslands, such as that within the camping areas.

The open fields, utility poles, and wires (**E**) surrounding the park offer a number of other birds at various times of year. Red-tailed Hawk, American Kestrel,

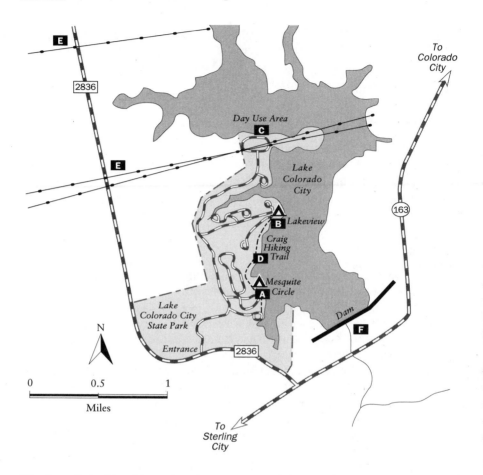

Northern Bobwhite, Horned Lark, European Starling, and Eastern Meadowlark can be found year-round. Scissor-tailed Flycatchers are common in summer. And in winter, watch for Black Vulture, Northern Harrier, Ferruginous Hawk, American Kestrel, American Crow, Vesper and Savannah Sparrows, Lark Bunting, Brewer's Blackbird, and Western Meadowlark. Brushy edges often harbor wintering Green-tailed and Spotted Towhees, and Field, Fox, Lincoln's, White-throated, White-crowned, and Harris's Sparrows.

An additional site, outside the state park, is also worth birding. The stream below the dam (F) along SH 163 offers riparian vegetation and a rocky area in the juniper woodland. This is a good place for Canyon Towhee and Northern Cardinal year-round; Green Heron, Yellow-billed Cuckoo, Common Poorwill, Cliff Swallow, Canyon Wren, and Bell's Vireo in spring and summer; and Rock Wren and Song Sparrow in winter.

Directions: Take SH 163 for 7 miles west of Colorado City (on I-20) to FM 2836 and the park entrance.

General information: This 500-acre park is located along the southwest shore of the 1,612-acre Lake Colorado City. The lake is a reservoir containing warm-water outlets from the Texas Utility Morgan Creek Power Plant. Fishing and other water sports are available year-round.

ADDITIONAL HELP

Location: Texas Official Travel Map grid K x 11; Mitchell County
Nearest food, gas, and lodging: Food and gas are available at the park entrance; lodging is available in Colorado City (7 miles).
Nearest camping: On-site (132 sites)
Contact: Superintendent, Lake Colorado City State Park (see Appendix C)

25 Abilene

Abilene State Park, Lake Abilene, Kirby Lake, Seabee Park, and Abilene Waste Water Treatment Plant

Habitats: Lake, pond, mud flat, creek, riparian, juniper-oak woodland, oak-hackberry woodland, pecan woodland, field, pasture, cropland
Key birds: Greater Roadrunner, **Golden-fronted Woodpecker,** Ladder-backed Woodpecker, Western Scrub-Jay, Chihuahuan Raven, Cactus Wren, Pyrrhuloxia, Canyon Towhee, and Rufous-crowned Sparrow are present year-round. Mississippi Kite, Scissor-tailed Flycatcher, and Bell's Vireo occur in summer. Winter Wren, Western and Mountain Bluebirds, Lark Bunting, Fox and Harris's Sparrows, and Lesser and American Goldfinches can usually be found in winter.
Best times to bird: April and May for spring migrants and nesting activities

Birding strategies: Abilene State Park (**A**) contains extensive oak, juniper, and pecan woodlands, creek and riparian vegetation, open lawn edged with brush, and old fields, all evident along the Elm Creek Nature Trail. Year-round residents likely to be found along the trail include Mallard, Mourning and Inca Doves, Belted Kingfisher, **Golden-fronted Woodpecker,** Ladder-backed Woodpecker, Eastern Phoebe, Blue Jay, Western Scrub-Jay, Carolina Chickadee, Tufted Titmouse, Carolina and Bewick's Wrens, Eastern Bluebird, American Robin, Northern Mockingbird, Curve-billed Thrasher, Northern Cardinal, Eastern Meadowlark, and Brown-headed Cowbird. Less obvious full-time residents are Cooper's and Red-shouldered Hawks, Eastern Screech-Owl, and Great Horned Owl.

Several other species occur along the trail in summer: Mississippi Kite, Yellow-billed Cuckoo, Ash-throated and Scissor-tailed Flycatchers, Western Kingbird, Marsh Wren, Bell's Vireo, Summer Tanager, Blue Grosbeak, Painted Bunting, Lark

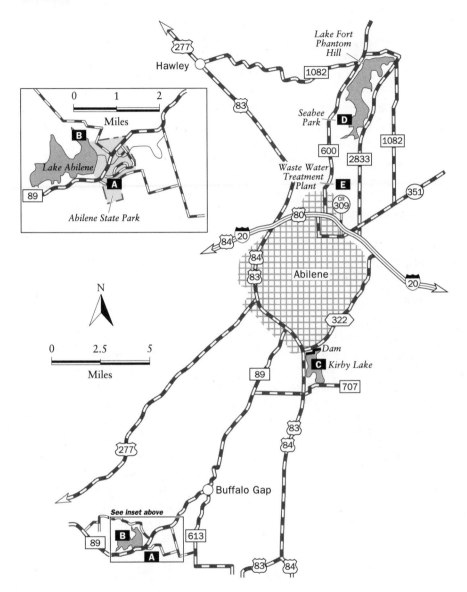

Sparrow, and Orchard and Bullock's Orioles. In winter Golden-crowned and Ruby-crowned Kinglets, Red-breasted Nuthatch, Winter Wren, Hermit Thrush, Brown Thrasher, Cedar Waxwing, Orange-crowned and Yellow-rumped Warblers, Spotted and Canyon Towhees, Dark-eyed Junco, Pine Siskin, and Lesser and American Goldfinches can often be found. Brown Creeper and Cassin's Finch are sporadic in winter.

The old fields adjacent to FM 89 offer a drier habitat where Northern Bob-white, Cactus Wren, Loggerhead Shrike, and Pyrrhuloxia reside. And a few additional species can often be found overhead: Turkey Vulture, Red-tailed Hawk, and American Kestrel year-round; Swainson's Hawk, Common Nighthawk, Chimney Swift, Purple Martin, and Cliff and Barn Swallows in summer; Black Vulture, Osprey, Merlin, and Peregrine and Prairie Falcons in winter.

Lake Abilene (B), 0.5 mile west of the park along FM 89, offers a totally different habitat and assortment of birds. Year-round water birds include Great Blue Heron and Belted Kingfisher. Winter birding here usually produces Pied-billed and Eared Grebes, Double-crested Cormorant, Green-winged and Blue-winged Teal, Northern Pintail, Northern Shoveler, Gadwall, American Wigeon, Lesser Scaup, Bufflehead, Ruddy Duck, and American Coot; while Horned Grebe, Wood Duck, Canvasback, Common Goldeneye, and Hooded and Common Mergansers are less numerous. Also, the dirt roads around the western and northern ends of the lake provide access to a juniper woodland that offers many of the same woodland birds that occur in the state park.

Kirby Lake (C), closer to town at the junction of US 83 and Loop 322, is considered the area's best birding site. The lake, as well as an isolated pond in the southwest corner, usually contains the same water birds to be expected at Abilene Lake and many more. In winter look for American White Pelican; Great, Snowy, and Cattle Egrets; and Ring-billed Gull. Also, Kirby Lake and pond usually possess excellent mud flats that attract shorebirds during migration. Expected species include Killdeer, Greater and Lesser Yellowlegs, Least and White-rumped Sandpipers, Long-billed Dowitcher, and Common Snipe. Less numerous are Black-bellied, Snowy, and Semipalmated Plovers; American Golden-Plover; Black-necked Stilt; American Avocet; Long-billed Curlew; Whimbrel; Hudsonian Godwit; Western, Baird's, Stilt, and Pectoral Sandpipers; and Wilson's Phalarope. Also watch for Franklin's Gull and Common, Forster's, Least, and Black Terns.

The weedy areas below the dam (north end) and along the edges often harbor brush-loving birds in winter. These include Bewick's Wren; Northern Cardinal; Spotted Towhee; Field, Vesper, Savannah, Fox, Song, Swamp, Lincoln's, White-throated, White-crowned, and Harris's Sparrows; and Brewer's Blackbird.

Seabee Park (D), at the south end of Lake Fort Phantom Hill, also is worth birding year-round. The open water, weedy shore, and mud flats offer about the same birds that occur at Kirby Lake, but this area can also harbor Sandhill Crane. The willow thickets on the park's western edge can be good for neotropical migrants in spring and fall. Look there also for Barred Owl.

Abilene Waste Water Treatment Plant (E), at the north end of CR 309, contains a very different habitat that can include numerous waterfowl, shorebirds, gulls, and terns during migration and in winter. Three of the four large basins usually hold water, and it is possible to walk the levees surrounding the basins. The northeastern basin often contains the least common species, such as White-faced Ibis, Cinnamon Teal, and Black-bellied and Semipalmated Plovers.

Records of Review Species: Clark's Grebe, Dec 1993. Neotropic Cormorant, April 1995. Swallow-tailed Kite, Aug 1994. Long-tailed Jaeger, Sept 1993.

Directions: Abilene State Park and Lake Abilene are located 16 miles southwest of Abilene, via US 83 and FM 89. Kirby Lake lies at the southern edge of town, southeast of the junction of US 83 and Loop 322. Seabee Park is situated off FM 600, 6 miles north of I-20; Abilene Waste Water Treatment Plant is located at the end of CR 309, 2 miles north of SH 351.

General information: The city of Abilene, established by cattlemen in 1821 as a shipping point for cattle, is today an oil town with a U.S. Air Force base and three universities: Abilene Christian, Hardin-Simmons, and McMurry. The 489-acre Abilene State Park is located at the northern edge of the Edwards Plateau and southern edge of the Rolling Plains. Fort Phantom Hill, 10 miles north of town via FM 600, was established in 1851 to protect the frontier from Indians; it is today administered by the state.

Notice: Although visitors are welcome at the Abilene Waste Water Treatment Plant, birders should call first: 915-548-2237.

ADDITIONAL HELP

Location: Texas Official Travel Map grid K x 13; Taylor and Jones counties
Nearest food, gas, and lodging: All are available in Abilene. From Abilene State Park, food and gas are available in Buffalo Gap (5 miles), and the nearest lodging is in Abilene (16 miles).
Nearest camping: Numerous sites in Abilene, and also at Abilene State Park (95 sites)
Contact: Superintendent, Abilene State Park; City of Abilene (see Appendix C)

26 San Angelo State Park and O. C. Fisher Lake

Habitats: Lake, seasonal mud flat and sandbar, river, riparian, juniper-oak woodland, mesquite grassland, field, cropland
Key birds: American White Pelican, Wood Duck, Harris's Hawk, Wild Turkey, Scaled Quail, Greater Roadrunner, **Golden-fronted Woodpecker,** Vermilion Flycatcher, Western Scrub-Jay, Cactus Wren, Curve-billed Thrasher, Pyrrhuloxia, Canyon Towhee, Rufous-crowned and Black-throated Sparrows, and Lesser Goldfinch are present year-round. Neotropic Cormorant; Mississippi Kite; Zone-tailed and Swainson's Hawks; Groove-billed Ani; Common Poorwill; Black-chinned Hummingbird; Scissor-tailed Flycatcher; Cave Swallow; **Black-capped Vireo;** Bell's and Gray Vireos; Cassin's and Grasshopper Sparrows; and Orchard, Bullock's, and Scott's Orioles occur in summer. Ferruginous Hawk; Say's Phoebe; Sage Thrasher; American and Sprague's Pipits; and McCown's, Smith's (casual), and Chestnut-collared Longspurs can often be found in winter.
Best times to bird: April and May for spring migrants and nesting activities; November to March for longspurs

Birding strategies: Water birds, including waders (two Great Blue Heron rookeries), ducks, and shorebirds, can best be seen from the Isabel Harte Camping and Day Use Area (**A**). Birds of the riparian habitat, such as Wood Duck, Mississippi Kite, Red-shouldered Hawk, Yellow-billed Cuckoo, Eastern and Western Screech-Owls, Black-chinned Hummingbird, Eastern Wood-Pewee, Great Crested Flycatcher, Western Kingbird, Bell's Vireo, Yellow-breasted Chat, Blue Grosbeak, Painted Bunting, and Orchard and Bullock's Orioles, are most accessible in the North Concho Camping Area (**B**). The campground itself is good habitat for **Golden-fronted Woodpecker,** Vermilion Flycatcher, and Eastern Bluebird.

Also bird the Wilderness Trail (**C**), especially between River Bend Camping Area and the Highland Range Scenic Lookout, for mesquite-grassland birds: Harris's and Swainson's Hawks; Scaled Quail; Greater Roadrunner; Groove-billed Ani; Lesser and Common Nighthawks; **Golden-fronted Woodpecker** and Ladder-backed Woodpecker; Ash-throated and Scissor-tailed Flycatchers; Verdin; Cactus and Bewick's Wrens; Curve-billed Thrasher; Pyrrhuloxia; Canyon Towhee; Cassin's, Rufous-crowned, Lark, and Black-throated Sparrows; Scott's Oriole; and Lesser Goldfinch. Watch for Grasshopper Sparrow in the old fields. Western Scrub-Jay, **Black-capped Vireo,** and Gray Vireo frequent the juniper-oak woodlands at the breaks.

In winter look for Rock Wren on the dam proper (**D**), a variety of sparrows in the weedy fields, and Short-eared Owls flying at dawn and dusk. Also, McCown's and Chestnut-collared Longspurs can usually be found (Smith's Longspur is irregular) in fallow fields 10 miles east of San Angelo along US 87 and various side roads.

Records of Review Species: Lewis's Woodpecker, Dec–April 1971/72. Elf Owl (1996 nesting).

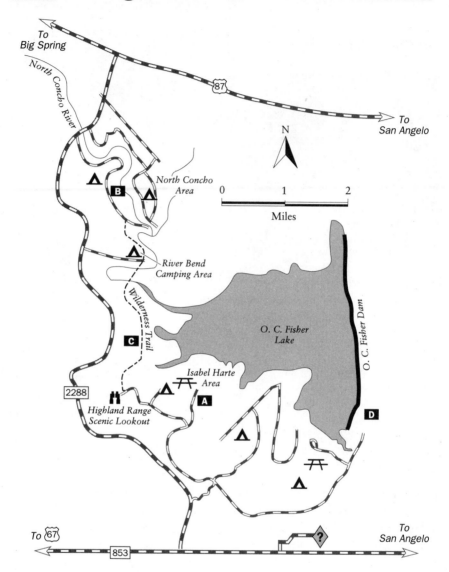

Directions: From San Angelo, take SH 87 north or FM 853 west to FM 2288, which skirts the western side of O. C. Fisher Lake and offers access to the park (see map).

General information: The 12,500-acre state park (established in November 1994) includes the 5,440-acre O. C. Fisher Lake, on the Concho River. The lake was named for a U.S. representative from Texas. The U.S. Army Corps of Engineers manages the dam and spillway. Boating, fishing, and swimming are popular pastimes.

O. C. Fisher Lake from dam at San Angelo State Park.

The general area is situated where four biogeographic zones converge: Trans-Pecos to the west, High Plains to the north, Rolling Plains to the east, and Texas Hill Country to the south. The area also has a significant history, extending from the time of the paleo-Indian hunters of ice age mammals to the establishment of Spanish missions in the sixteenth and seventeenth centuries and the establishment of Fort Concho in 1867 (restored).

ADDITIONAL HELP

Location: Texas Official Travel Map grid M x 12; Tom Green County
Nearest food, gas, and lodging: All can be found in San Angelo.
Nearest camping: On-site (72 sites)
Contact: Superintendent, San Angelo State Park (see Appendix C)

Edwards Plateau Region

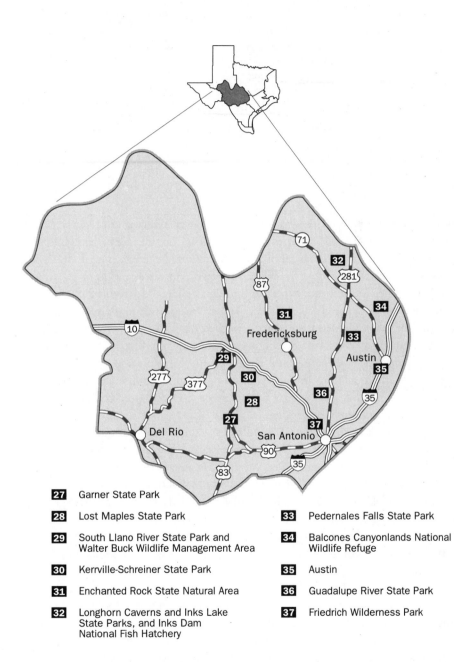

27	Garner State Park
28	Lost Maples State Park
29	South Llano River State Park and Walter Buck Wildlife Management Area
30	Kerrville-Schreiner State Park
31	Enchanted Rock State Natural Area
32	Longhorn Caverns and Inks Lake State Parks, and Inks Dam National Fish Hatchery
33	Pedernales Falls State Park
34	Balcones Canyonlands National Wildlife Refuge
35	Austin
36	Guadalupe River State Park
37	Friedrich Wilderness Park

27 Garner State Park

Habitats: River, creek, riparian, juniper-hackberry woodland, oak savannah, oak motte, mesquite grassland, prairie, field

Key birds: Wood Duck; Wild Turkey; Greater Roadrunner; **Green Kingfisher; Golden-fronted Woodpecker;** Ladder-backed Woodpecker; Black Phoebe; Western Scrub-Jay; Common Raven; Cactus, Rock, and Canyon Wrens; Pyrrhuloxia; Canyon Towhee; Rufous-crowned Sparrow; and Lesser Goldfinch are present year-round. Common Poorwill, Chuck-will's-widow, Black-chinned Hummingbird, Scissor-tailed Flycatcher, Bell's Vireo, **Golden-cheeked Warbler,** Summer Tanager, Painted Bunting,Dickcissel, Bronzed Cowbird, and Hooded and Scott's Orioles occur in summer. Golden-crowned Kinglet and Pine Siskin can usually be found in winter.

Best times to bird: April and May for spring migrants and nesting activities

Birding strategies: The riverway, especially between the pavilion (**A**) and Pecan Grove Camping Area (**B**), can provide excellent birding during migration and in spring and summer. Neotropical migrants following the river can include a wide variety of flycatchers, vireos, warblers, tanagers, and orioles; a number of these remain and nest. In summer expect to find Great Blue and Green Herons; Wood Duck; Red-shouldered Hawk; Killdeer; Yellow-billed Cuckoo; Belted Kingfisher; **Green Kingfisher; Golden-fronted Woodpecker;** Black Phoebe; Great Crested Fly-catcher; Carolina Wren; Tufted Titmouse; Carolina Wren; Blue-gray Gnatcatcher; White-eyed, Yellow-throated, and Red-eyed Vireos; Northern Parula; Yellow-throated Warbler; Summer Tanager; Northern Cardinal; House Finch; and Lesser Goldfinch. Less numerous here are Eastern Screech-Owl, Barred Owl, Bell's Vireo, and Orchard and Bullock's Orioles.

The adjacent open fields and woodlands, including the camping area (**B**), at-tract an additional group of birds in summer: Rock, White-winged, and Inca Doves; Greater Roadrunner; Ladder-backed Woodpecker; Eastern Phoebe; Vermilion, Ash-throated, and Scissor-tailed Flycatchers; Western Kingbird; Bewick's Wren; East-ern Bluebird; Northern Mockingbird; Loggerhead Shrike; Painted Bunting; Dick-cissel; Chipping and Lark Sparrows; Bronzed and Brown-headed Cowbirds; and House Sparrow. The drier sites, including the open fields (**C**) along FM 1050, attract Common Ground-Dove, Verdin, Cactus Wren, Pyrrhuloxia, and Black-throated Sparrow.

The open areas also offer the best views of birds soaring or passing overhead. These include Black and Turkey Vultures, Red-shouldered and Red-tailed Hawks, and Common Raven year-round; Common Nighthawk, Chimney Swift, Purple Martin, and Northern Rough-winged, Cliff, and Barn Swallows in summer; and Northern Harrier and American Kestrel in winter. Three additional species occur irregularly in summer: Zone-tailed Hawk, Lesser Nighthawk, and Chihuahuan Raven.

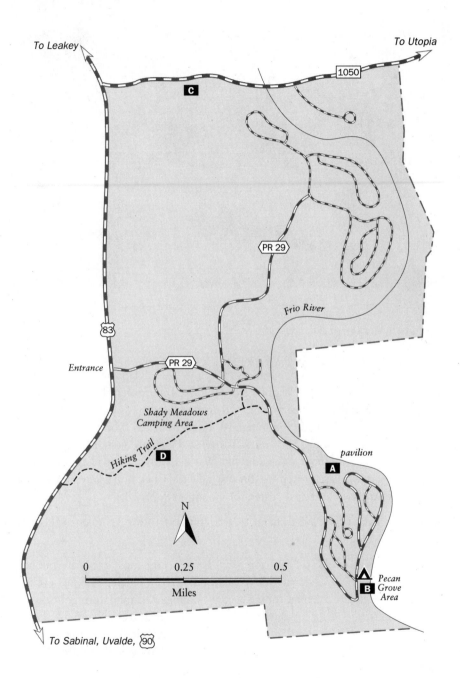

Frio River from the Pecan Grove Camping Area in Garner State Park.

Juniper-hackberry woodlands can best be birded from the hiking trail (**D**), starting just below the Shady Meadows Camping Area. This area is the best bet for finding **Golden-cheeked Warbler** from mid-March through July. Listen for its very distinct three-part, wheezy song. Other woodland birds expected along this trail include Black-chinned Hummingbird, Ladder-backed Woodpecker, Western Scrub-Jay, Carolina Chickadee, Tufted Titmouse, Bewick's Wren, Blue-gray Gnatcatcher, White-eyed Vireo, Black-and-white Warbler, Canyon Towhee, and Rufous-crowned Sparrow. Also watch for Bushtit and for Rock and Canyon Wrens at rocky sites. At dawn and dusk, listen for Common Poorwill songs.

Directions: Take US 83 north from Uvalde (on US 90) for 31 miles to the park entrance (PR 29).

General information: This 1,420-acre park is one of the most attractive but also one of the busiest in the state. Park recreational activities include hiking, cycling, fishing, swimming, canoeing, tubing, pedal boating, and miniature golf; do not bird here on weekends or holidays. The Frio River, a crystal clear, spring-fed river, crowded with a gallery woodland of bald cypress trees, winds through hills dominated by juniper-hackberry woodlands, where the endangered **Golden-cheeked Warbler** occurs during the nesting season.

ADDITIONAL HELP

Location: Texas Official Travel Map grid R x 13; Uvalde County
Nearest food, gas, and lodging: There are grocery stores on-site and in Leakey (9 miles); lodging is available on-site (17 cabins) or at Leakey. Gas at Leakey.
Nearest camping: On-site (357 sites)
Contact: Superintendent, Garner State Park (see Appendix C)

28 Lost Maples State Park

Habitats: Juniper woodland, oak-juniper woodland, river, creek, pond, riparian
Key birds: Wild Turkey, Greater Roadrunner, **Green Kingfisher, Golden-fronted Woodpecker,** Western Scrub-Jay, Canyon Wren, Canyon Towhee, Rufous-crowned Sparrow, and Lesser Goldfinch are present year-round. Zone-tailed Hawk; Chuck-will's-widow; Vermilion and Scissor-tailed Flycatchers; Cave Swallow; **Black-capped Vireo; Golden-cheeked Warbler;** Indigo and Painted Buntings; Dickcissel; Bronzed Cowbird; and Orchard, Hooded, and Scott's Orioles occur in summer. Bald Eagle, Ferruginous Hawk, and Mountain Bluebird can often be found in winter.
Best times to bird: Mid-March through June for **Green Kingfisher, Black-capped Vireo,** and **Golden-cheeked Warbler**

Birding strategies: The best place to find **Green Kingfisher, Black-capped Vireo,** and **Golden-cheeked Warbler** is along the first mile of the East Trail (**A**), along Can Creek. The same three species also occur along the lower portion (0.4 mile) of the Maple Trail (**B**), starting at the picnic area (1 mile from the park entrance) and following the Sabinal River.

Additional summer birds expected along these trails include Black and Turkey Vultures; Red-tailed Hawk; Killdeer; Mourning Dove; Yellow-billed Cuckoo; Black-chinned Hummingbird; Ladder-backed Woodpecker; Eastern Wood-Pewee; Acadian, Ash-throated, and Scissor-tailed Flycatchers; Cliff Swallow; Western Scrub-Jay; Carolina Chickadee; Tufted Titmouse; Bushtit; Canyon, Carolina, and Bewick's Wrens; Blue-gray Gnatcatcher; White-eyed, Yellow-throated, and Red-eyed Vireos; Black-and-white Warbler; Summer Tanager; Northern Cardinal; Indigo Bunting; Canyon Towhee; Rufous-crowned and Chipping Sparrows; House Finch; and Lesser Goldfinch. Several other species are less numerous: Red-shouldered Hawk, Wild Turkey, Eastern Screech-Owl, Common Poorwill, Chuck-will's-widow, Bell's Vireo, Kentucky Warbler, and Hooded and Scott's Orioles.

The picnic area (**C**) offers a different habitat with lawns and open space. It is a good place to watch soaring birds such as vultures, Red-tailed and Zone-tailed Hawks, and Common Raven; various flycatchers; and seedeaters attracted to grasses. It also is a good place to find **Golden-fronted Woodpecker.**

28 Lost Maples State Park

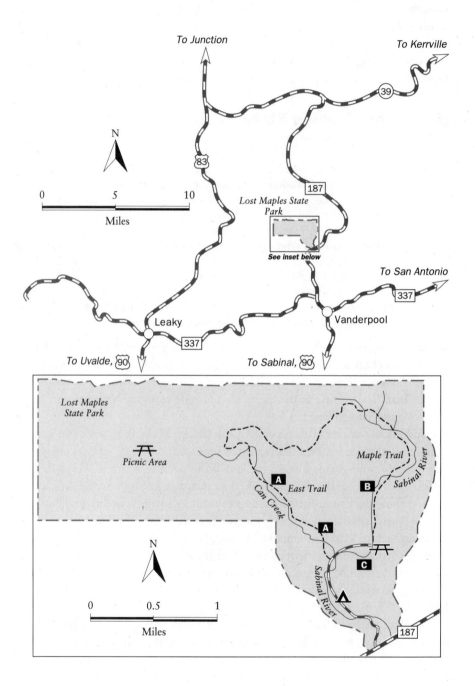

Records of Review Species: Short-tailed Hawk, May–June 1995. Green Violet-ear, July 1995.

Directions: From US 90, take FM 187 north 30 miles to Vanderpool. Lost Maples State Park is located 5 miles north of Vanderpool off FM 187.

General information: This 2,208-acre park is named for the abundant bigtooth maples that annually provide brilliant red, yellow, and orange colors from late October to mid-November. Lost Maples is a hiking park with 11 miles of trails and only 1 mile of roadway; parking is limited to 250 spaces, which can be filled on weekends, especially at the height of the fall color season. Maple, West, and East trails provide access to a number of spectacular canyons and overviews. The park operates an interpretive center and a store, where books and gifts are available.

ADDITIONAL HELP

Location: Texas Official Travel Map grid Q x 13; Bandera County
Nearest food, gas, and lodging: All are available at Vanderpool (4 miles).
Nearest camping: On-site (40 sites)
Contact: Superintendent, Lost Maples State Park (see Appendix C)

29 South Llano River State Park and Walter Buck Wildlife Management Area

Habitats: Pecan floodplain, riparian, juniper-oak woodland, field
Key birds: Wood Duck, Wild Turkey, Greater Roadrunner, **Green Kingfisher, Golden-fronted Woodpecker,** Western Scrub-Jay, Curve-billed Thrasher, Pyrrhuloxia, Canyon Towhee, and Black-throated Sparrow are present year-round. Common Poorwill, Chuck-will's-widow, Vermilion and Scissor-tailed Flycatchers, Cave Swallow, **Black-capped Vireo,** Bell's Vireo, Indigo and Painted Buntings, Cassin's Sparrow, and Lesser Goldfinch occur in summer. Bald Eagle, Red-headed Woodpecker, Sage and Brown Thrashers, Green-tailed Towhee, and Lark Bunting can often be found in winter.
Best times to bird: April and May for spring migrants and nesting activities; winter to watch Wild Turkeys from a distance

Birding strategies: Wild Turkeys are common on the floodplain, although the heart of this area is closed from October 1 through March to protect the roosting sites of up to 800 turkeys. Turkeys roost on the huge pecan trees and often wander through the campground into the drier woodlands.

Walk the woodland and river trails (**A**) in spring and summer for passing neotropical migrants and breeding flycatchers, swallows, Eastern Bluebird, vireos, Summer Tanager, and Orchard Oriole in the riparian and floodplain habitats; waders and ducks; and **Green Kingfisher,** which frequent the ponds and river.

29 South Llano River State Park and Walter Buck Wildlife Management Area

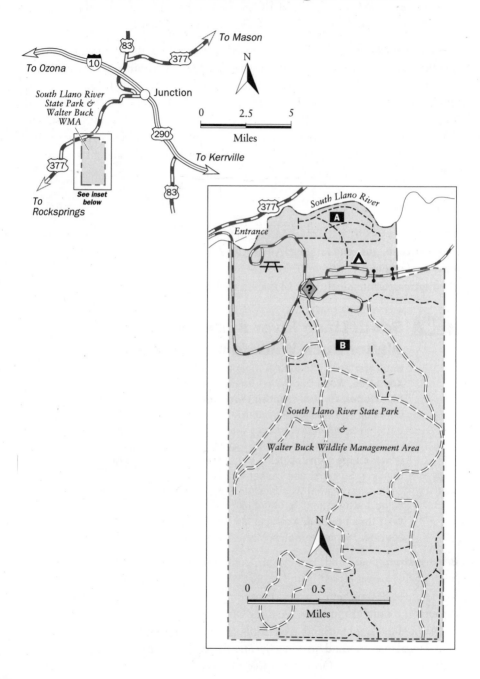

Many of the nesting birds, including Golden-fronted Woodpecker, can be found within the campground. Other nesting birds of the riparian and floodplain habitats include Red-shouldered Hawk, Ladder-backed and Downy Woodpeckers, Eastern Wood-Pewee, Acadian and Great Crested Flycatchers, Carolina Chickadee, Tufted Titmouse, Carolina Wren, Blue-gray Gnatcatcher, Yellow-throated and Red-eyed Vireos, Summer Tanager, Northern Cardinal, and Orchard Oriole. Red-headed Woodpeckers occasionally occur in winter.

After dark in summer, listen for Eastern Screech-Owl and Great Horned Owl throughout the area; Chuck-will's-widow in the riparian habitat; and Common Poorwill along the drier slopes. Watch overhead for Black (rare) and Turkey Vultures; Red-tailed Hawk; Common Nighthawk at dawn and dusk; Chimney Swift; Purple Martin; and Northern Rough-winged, Cliff, Cave, and Barn Swallows.

The fields within and adjacent to the floodplain offer a few additional birds, such as Greater Roadrunner, Scissor-tailed Flycatcher, Northern Mockingbird, and Painted Bunting, in summer. In winter, these areas usually harbor a number of seedeaters: Green-tailed and Spotted Towhees; Chipping, Field, Fox, White-throated, and White-crowned Sparrows; Dark-eyed Junco; and American Goldfinch.

The drier upland trails within the Walter Buck Wildlife Management Area (**B**) offer a slightly different group of birds in summer: Verdin, Cactus and Bewick's Wrens, Northern Mockingbird, Canyon Towhee, Black-throated Sparrow, and Scott's Oriole. **Black-capped Vireo** resides in the dry arroyos.

Directions: Turn off I-10 at Junction and take US 377 south 5 miles to the park entrance. The Walter Buck Wildlife Management Area is situated on the brushy hills south of the park.

General information: The clear, cool waters of the South Llano (*yawn*-oh) River wind through a floodplain dominated by stately pecan trees. The state park (507 acres) contains 1.5 miles of river frontage on its northern border, and the Walter Buck Wildlife Management Area (2,123 acres) is noted for an abundance of wildlife. Hunting blinds in the management area can be used for wildlife observation and photography when hunts are not in progress. The park roads and trails, including a 2-mile trail that circles the oxbow lakes, provide easy hiking access throughout.

The river is popular for swimming, canoeing, and tubing. Fishing is best in the oxbow lakes. Weekends and holidays can be crowded, so birding along the river and in the floodplain is recommended during the early morning hours.

ADDITIONAL HELP

Location: Texas Official Travel Map grid P x 13; Kimble County
Nearest food, gas, and lodging: Junction has facilities for food, gas, and lodging.
Nearest camping: On-site (56 sites)
Contact: Superintendent, South Llano River State Park (see Appendix C)

30 Kerrville-Schreiner State Park

Habitats: River, riparian, juniper-oak woodland, mesquite grassland, field

Key birds: Wild Turkey, Greater Roadrunner, **Golden-fronted Woodpecker,** Ladder-backed Woodpecker, Western Scrub-Jay, Canyon Towhee, and Rufous-crowned Sparrow are present year-round. Neotropic Cormorant, Common Poorwill, Chuck-will's-widow, Black-chinned Hummingbird, Scissor-tailed Flycatcher, Bell's and Yellow-throated Vireos, Yellow-throated Warbler, Painted Bunting, Dickcissel, Bronzed Cowbird, and Lesser Goldfinch occur in summer. Spotted Towhee, Fox and Harris's Sparrows, and Purple Finch can usually be found in winter.

Best times to bird: April and May for spring migrants and nesting activities

Birding strategies: Of the two key birding areas in the park, the riverside area (**A**) northeast of SH 173 and the juniper woodland area (**B**) southwest of SH 173, the riverside area offers the greatest diversity of birds throughout the year. This area can be especially good during migration, when various flycatchers, vireos, warblers, tanagers, and orioles pass through. A few water birds can usually be found year-round: Pied-billed Grebe, Great Blue Heron, Double-crested Cormorant, Killdeer, and Belted Kingfisher. Neotropic Cormorant and Green Heron occur in summer. Several additional species frequent the river and shoreline in winter: Eared Grebe, Great Egret, Green-winged Teal, Northern Pintail, Northern Shoveler, Gadwall, American Wigeon, Canvasback, Ring-necked Duck, Lesser Scaup, Ruddy Duck, American Coot, Spotted Sandpiper, and Common Snipe.

In summer the riparian habitat comes alive with songbirds. Nesting species include Yellow-billed Cuckoo; Acadian, Great Crested, and Scissor-tailed Flycatchers; Eastern Phoebe; Western Kingbird; Carolina Chickadee; Tufted Titmouse; Carolina Wren; Blue-gray Gnatcatcher; White-eyed, Yellow-throated, and Red-eyed Vireos; Yellow-throated Warbler; Yellow-breasted Chat; Summer Tanager; Northern Cardinal; Great-tailed Grackle; Orchard Oriole; House Finch; and Lesser Goldfinch. Watch also in dense areas along the river for Red-shouldered Hawk, Barred Owl, and Eastern Screech-Owl.

The parklike environment in the riverside camping area usually attracts White-winged and Inca Doves, Great Horned Owl, **Golden-fronted Woodpecker,** Purple Martin, Vermilion Flycatcher, Blue Jay, Eastern Bluebird, American Robin, and

30 Kerrville-Schreiner State Park

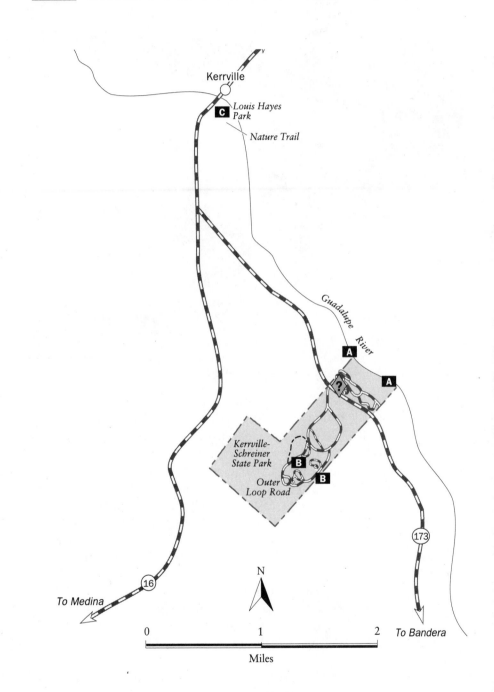

Black-chinned Hummingbird. DON McIVOR PHOTO

Eastern Meadowlark in summer. In winter watch for Wild Turkey, Yellow-bellied Sapsucker, Purple Finch, Pine Siskin, and American Goldfinch.

Although many of these same birds also frequent the juniper woodlands, by walking the Outer Loop Road (B), you are likely to find Greater Roadrunner, Western Scrub-Jay, Bewick's Wren, and Rufous-crowned Sparrow year-round. Common Poorwill, Chuck-will's-widow, Eastern Wood-Pewee, Ash-throated Flycatcher, Bushtit, Canyon Wren, White-eyed Vireo, Black-and-white Warbler, and Lesser Goldfinch occur here in summer. And Red-breasted Nuthatch, Brown Creeper, Golden-crowned and Ruby-crowned Kinglets, and Hermit Thrush often are found in winter.

The park's weedy roadsides and old fields also support a number of additional birds. Check these areas for Indigo and Painted Buntings and Dickcissel in summer, and in winter, for Spotted Towhee; Chipping, Field, Vesper, Grasshopper, Fox, Song, Lincoln's, White-throated, White-crowned, and Harris's Sparrows; and Dark-eyed Junco.

Black and Turkey Vultures and Cooper's and Red-tailed Hawks can be expected year-round, and Sharp-shinned Hawk and American Kestrel occur in winter.

In addition, Louis Hayes Park (C), located along the river to the north of the state park (via SH 173 and SH 16) where SH 16 crosses the Guadalupe River, contains a nature trail that can provide good birding during migration.

Directions: From I-10, take SH 16 south for 0.5 mile to Loop 534, then go south on Loop 534 for 4 miles to SH 173; the state park entrance is just beyond.

General information: The 517-acre state park, situated along the upper Guadalupe River, is primarily a recreational area, featuring hiking, fishing, swimming, and nature study. A riverside trail has been developed as a self-guiding interpretive trail, where various plants are identified. The park was named for Charles A. Schreiner, a prominent Kerrville resident and philanthropist.

ADDITIONAL HELP

Location: Texas Official Travel Map grid Q x 14; Kerr County
Nearest food, gas, and lodging: Food and gas are available near the junction of SH 173 and Loop 534 (1 mile), and lodging can be found in Kerrville (4 miles).
Nearest camping: On-site (120 sites)
Contact: Superintendent, Kerrville-Schreiner State Park (see Appendix C)

31 **Enchanted Rock State Natural Area**

Habitats: Creek, riparian, oak savannah, mesquite grassland, pond, rock
Key birds: Wild Turkey, Greater Roadrunner, **Golden-fronted Woodpecker,** Western Scrub-Jay, Pyrrhuloxia, Canyon Towhee, Rufous-crowned and Black-throated Sparrows, and Lesser Goldfinch are present year-round. Common Poorwill, Chuck-will's-widow, Black-chinned Hummingbird, Vermilion and Scissor-tailed Flycatchers, Bell's and Yellow-throated Vireos, Blue Grosbeak, Painted Bunting, and Orchard Oriole occur in summer. Vesper, Fox, and Harris's Sparrows can usually be found in winter.
Best times to bird: April and May for spring migrants and nesting activities

Birding strategies: In summer the Sandy Creek floodplain (A), directly behind the natural area entrance station, supports a variety of birds. Expect Eastern Phoebe, Barn Swallow, Northern Mockingbird, and House Finch at the entrance station; Bell's Vireo, Blue Grosbeak, Painted Bunting, and Red-winged Blackbird along the floodplain; and Mourning Dove, Yellow-billed Cuckoo, Black-chinned Hummingbird, **Golden-fronted Woodpecker,** Ladder-backed Woodpecker, Carolina Chickadee, Tufted Titmouse, Carolina and Bewick's Wrens, Blue-gray Gnatcatcher, White-eyed Vireo, Northern Cardinal, Brown-headed Cowbird, and Orchard Oriole in the surrounding vegetation. The taller riparian habitat farther up Sandy Creek

31 **Enchanted Rock State Natural Area**

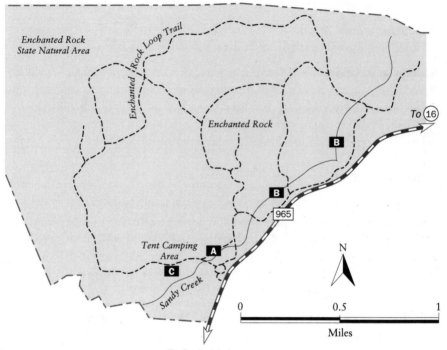

Enchanted Rock State Natural Area

Enchanted Rock Loop Trail

Enchanted Rock

To (16)

B

B

965

Tent Camping Area **A**

C

Sandy Creek

N

0   0.5   1

Miles

To Fredericksburg

(**B**), beyond the Enchanted Rock Trailhead, also supports Barred Owl, Chuck-will's-widow, Eastern Wood-Pewee, Great Crested Flycatcher, Yellow-throated and Red-eyed Vireos, and Summer Tanager.

Several additional birds reside in the drier oak savannah habitat, such as that along the Loop Trail in the vicinity of the Tent Camping Area (**C**). Although there is considerable overlap with species occurring near the natural area's entrance, Wild Turkey; Northern Bobwhite; Greater Roadrunner; Common Ground-Dove; Ash-throated and Scissor-tailed Flycatchers; Western Kingbird; Western Scrub-Jay; Bushtit; Eastern Bluebird; Dickcissel; Chipping, Field, and Lark Sparrows; and Lesser Goldfinch are more likely here. Canyon Towhee and Rufous-crowned Sparrow prefer the adjacent rocky slopes.

The songs of Canyon Wren can be heard along the trail. Both the Canyon and Rock Wrens reside on Enchanted Rock; Rock Wren is most common near the summit. Cliff Swallow is common overhead. Other expected high-flying species include Black and Turkey Vultures; Red-tailed Hawk; Common Nighthawk at dawn and dusk; Chimney Swift; Purple Martin; and Common Raven. After dark, Eastern Screech-Owl and Great Horned Owl can often be heard in late winter and spring.

The 4-mile Loop Trail that circles Enchanted Rock passes through all the possible habitats and provides the hiking birder with all the representative species, including Belted Kingfisher at Moss Pond on the north side.

Migration offers an additional assortment of birds that usually are most numerous along the floodplain. Occasionally a few ducks and shorebirds appear; only Spotted Sandpiper is dependable. And in winter the weedy fields attract a variety of seedeaters, such as Spotted Towhee; Vesper, Savannah, Fox, Song, Lincoln's, White-throated, White-crowned, and Harris's Sparrows; Dark-eyed Junco; and American Goldfinch.

General information: Enchanted Rock State Natural Area is one of the true gems of the Texas state park system, with an interesting diversity of birds and 5 miles of hiking trails, all within 1,643 acres. Weekends and holidays can be extremely busy. The rock rises more than 400 feet above the surrounding landscape and consists of pink granite about 1 billion years old, some of the oldest exposed rock in North America. Enchanted Rock is a dome-shaped mass formed by intrusive magma with the top materials eroded away. Only the top of the greater Enchanted Rock batholith, which covers an area of over 90 square miles, is present within the park. Enchanted Rock is a designated National Natural Landmark.

ADDITIONAL HELP

Location: Texas Official Travel Map grid P x 15; Gillespie County
Nearest food, gas, and lodging: Fredericksburg, 18 miles from the state natural area, has food, gas, and lodging.
Nearest camping: Crabapple Crossing (4 miles); tent sites only in state natural area
Contact: Superintendent, Enchanted Rock State Natural Area (see Appendix C)

32 Longhorn Caverns and Inks Lake State Parks, and Inks Dam National Fish Hatchery

Habitats: Lake, pond, river, creek, riparian, oak-juniper woodland, mesquite grassland, field
Key birds: Wild Turkey, Greater Roadrunner, **Golden-fronted Woodpecker,** Western Scrub-Jay, Cactus and Canyon Wrens, Canyon Towhee, Rufous-crowned and Black-throated Sparrows, and Lesser Goldfinch are present year-round. Scissor-tailed Flycatcher, Bell's Vireo, **Golden-cheeked Warbler,** Painted Bunting, and Orchard Oriole occur in summer. Osprey, Bald Eagle, and Fox and Harris's Sparrows can usually be found in winter.
Best times to bird: Mid-March to July for **Golden-cheeked Warbler** at Longhorn Caverns; April and May for spring migrants and nesting activities

32 Longhorn Caverns and Inks Lake State Parks, and Inks Dam National Fish Hatchery

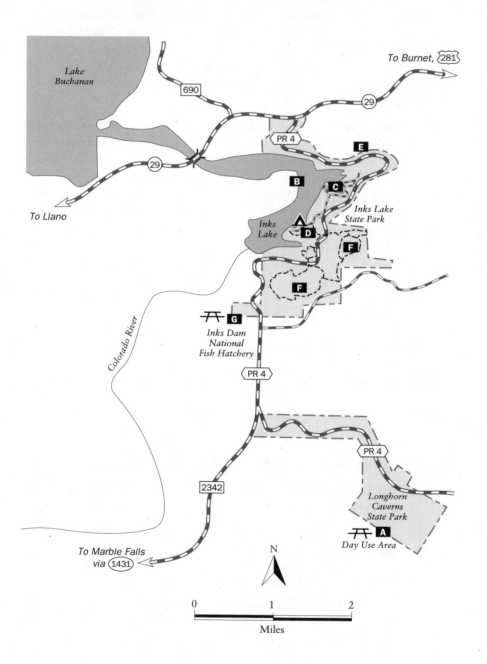

Birding strategies: The oak-juniper woodlands at the day use area and immediate trails at Longhorn Caverns State Park (**A**) offer easy access to Golden-cheeked Warbler habitat. These birds can best be detected by their three-part, wheezy songs, which are sung from the treetops. Other summer woodland birds include Mourning Dove, Yellow-billed Cuckoo, Black-chinned Hummingbird, Ladder-backed Woodpecker, Western Scrub-Jay, Carolina Chickadee, Tufted Titmouse, Bewick's Wren, Blue-gray Gnatcatcher, White-eyed Vireo, Canyon Towhee, and Rufous-crowned and Lark Sparrows. Less numerous birds include Eastern Screech-Owl, Barred Owl, Ash-throated Flycatcher, and Lesser Goldfinch.

The open area around the picnic area offers a few additional species: Inca Dove, Greater Roadrunner, **Golden-fronted Woodpecker,** Eastern Phoebe, Blue Jay, Eastern Bluebird, Northern Mockingbird, and Northern Cardinal. Black and Turkey Vultures, Red-tailed Hawk, Common Nighthawk at dawn and dusk, Chimney Swift, Purple Martin, and Cliff and Barn Swallows usually can be seen in flight overhead. Watch also for Common Raven.

Inks Lake State Park, with its lake and associated habitats, offers a very different assortment of birds. The lake and wetlands (**B**) attract Great Blue Heron, Mallard, Killdeer, and Belted Kingfisher year-round; as many as 40 pairs of Great Blue Herons nest in sycamore trees across the cove from the store and boat ramp (**C**). Additional water birds utilize the area in winter: Pied-billed Grebe, Double-crested Cormorant, Green-winged Teal, Gadwall, Lesser Scaup, Bufflehead, Red-breasted Merganser, American Coot, Ring-billed Gull, and Forster's Tern. Common Loon; Horned, Eared, and Western (rarely) Grebes; Northern Shoveler; American Wigeon; Ring-necked Duck; Common Goldeneye; Hooded Merganser; Osprey; Bald Eagle; and Bonaparte's and Herring Gulls are less numerous. Watch also for the occasional Oldsquaw.

The vegetation around the campground (**D**) is utilized by Carolina Wren, Red-winged Blackbird, Great-tailed and Common Grackles, Brown-headed Cowbird, House Finch, and House Sparrow year-round; add Scissor-tailed Flycatcher, Bell's Vireo, Summer Tanager, Painted Bunting, and Orchard Oriole in summer.

Inks Lake State Park also contains mesquite grasslands along the northern edge, accessible along PR 4 (**E**), and in the southeastern corner (**F**), which is accessible by a series of trails. These open, rocky sites support several additional birds, although there is considerable overlap with those found in the oak-juniper woodland. Also watch here in summer for Wild Turkey, Greater Roadrunner, Verdin, Cactus and Canyon Wrens, White-eyed Vireo, and Lark and Black-throated Sparrows.

The riparian zones along the Colorado River, which can best be birded at the Inks Dam National Fish Hatchery picnic area (**G**), are best during spring migration, when large numbers of neotropical migrants are moving northward. The river itself is utilized by a variety of migrating waterfowl and other water birds in spring and fall and by all the same birds that winter at Inks Lake.

The fish hatchery ponds and surrounding fields also attract a variety of migrants and post-nesting birds. In winter the weedy fields attract numerous seedeaters. Spotted Towhee; Field, Vesper, Savannah, Song, White-crowned, and Harris's Sparrows; Dark-eyed Junco; and American Goldfinch are commonplace. Chipping, Fox, Lincoln's, and White-throated Sparrows are less numerous.

Directions: The three sites are located along PR 4, which runs for 12 miles between SH 29 and US 281. From Burnet, take US 281 south for 6 miles to PR 4, and go west 6 miles to Longhorn Caverns; also from Burnet, take SH 29 west 9 miles to PR 4, and go 3 miles south to Inks Lake. Inks Dam National Fish Hatchery is halfway between the two state parks on PR 4.

General information: Inks Lake, located between Lake Buchanan and Lake LBJ, is the smallest of a series of six lakes along the Colorado River. The 2,000-acre park is dominated by the 1,200-acre lake, which is heavily used for boating, fishing, and swimming; birding should be limited to early mornings. From early July to early September, the park offers canoe tours, with special emphasis on bird life, to Devils Waterhole.

Longhorn Caverns State Park, located on Backbone Ridge, a huge piece of limestone, was established in 1932 to provide protection to the cave. It is a Registered National Landmark. The park also contains a network of hiking trails that offer easy access to good **Golden-cheeked Warbler** habitat.

The 85-acre Inks Dam National Fish Hatchery, located on a narrow bench along the Colorado River, contains 25 acres of ponds. Established in 1938 to supply fish to the lakes along the Colorado River, the hatchery produces nearly a million catfish and numerous striped and largemouth bass and rainbow trout annually. The 27 ponds, which are maintained on a rotating basis, and the adjacent fields, woods, and river are popular birding sites year-round. Visiting hours are limited to weekdays, 8 A.M. to 4 P.M.

ADDITIONAL HELP

Location: Texas Official Travel Map grid O x 15/16; Burnet County
Nearest food, gas, and lodging: Food is available at Inks Lake State Park; gas and lodging are available in Hoover Valley (3 miles).
Nearest camping: On-site at Inks Lake State Park (228 sites)
Contact: Superintendents, Longhorn Caverns and Inks Lake State Parks; Manager, Inks Dam National Fish Hatchery (see Appendix C)

33   Pedernales Falls State Park

Habitats: River, riparian, oak-juniper woodland, oak savannah, mesquite grassland, field

Key birds: Wood Duck, Wild Turkey, Greater Roadrunner, **Green Kingfisher, Golden-fronted Woodpecker,** Western Scrub-Jay, Canyon Wren, Canyon Towhee, Rufous-crowned and Black-throated Sparrows, and Lesser Goldfinch are present year-round. Common Poorwill, Chuck-will's-widow, Vermilion and Scissor-tailed Flycatchers, Bell's Vireo, **Golden-cheeked Warbler,** Indigo and Painted Buntings, Dickcissel, and Cassin's Sparrow occur in summer. Grasshopper, Fox, and Harris's Sparrows can often be found in winter.

Best times to bird: Mid-March to July for **Golden-cheeked Warbler;** April and May for spring migrants and nesting activities

Birding strategies: Golden-cheeked Warbler is most easily found from mid-March through June at the overlook (**A**), just beyond the entrance station; along the Wolf Mountain Trail (**B**), which begins at the overlook and runs southeastward to the Primitive Camping Area; and along the Hill Country Nature Trail (**C**), accessible from the southeast corner of the campground. Listen for the warbler's high-pitched, wheezy songs; males sing from conspicuous perches atop oaks and junipers. They disperse in July and August and are rarely recorded by September.

Other oak-juniper woodland birds to be expected along these trails include Mourning Dove, Ladder-backed Woodpecker, Eastern Phoebe, Carolina Chickadee, Tufted Titmouse, Canyon and Bewick's Wrens, Northern Mockingbird, White-eyed Vireo, Northern Cardinal, Field Sparrow, and House Finch year-round. Less numerous are Wild Turkey, Common Ground-Dove, Greater Roadrunner, Eastern Screech-Owl, Great Horned Owl, **Golden-fronted Woodpecker,** Western Scrub-Jay, American Crow, Verdin, Bushtit, Carolina Wren, Canyon Wren at rocky outcrops, Canyon Towhee, Rufous-crowned and Lark Sparrows, and Lesser Goldfinch. In summer, Yellow-billed Cuckoo, Common Nighthawk, Black-chinned Hummingbird, Ash-throated and Scissor-tailed Flycatchers, Blue-gray Gnatcatcher, and Black-and-white Warbler also utilize this habitat.

In the more open mesquite grasslands, scattered within the woodlands, Northern Bobwhite; Greater Roadrunner; Painted Bunting; Dickcissel; Cassin's, Field, Lark, and occasionally Black-throated Sparrows; and Eastern Meadowlark occur. Common Poorwills call at dawn and dusk from rocky outcrops. Watch overhead for soaring Black and Turkey Vultures and Red-shouldered and Red-tailed Hawks year-round. Chimney Swift, Purple Martin, and Northern Rough-winged and Barn Swallows are present in summer.

The riparian zones along the Pedernales River, such as at Pedernales Falls and Cypress Pool (**D**), offer an additional assortment of birds, although there is some overlap with the woodland birds. Additional summer birds here include Great Blue and Green Herons; Belted and **Green Kingfishers;** Red-bellied Woodpecker; Great Crested Flycatcher; Bell's, Yellow-throated, and Red-eyed Vireos; and Summer

33 **Pedernales Falls State Park**

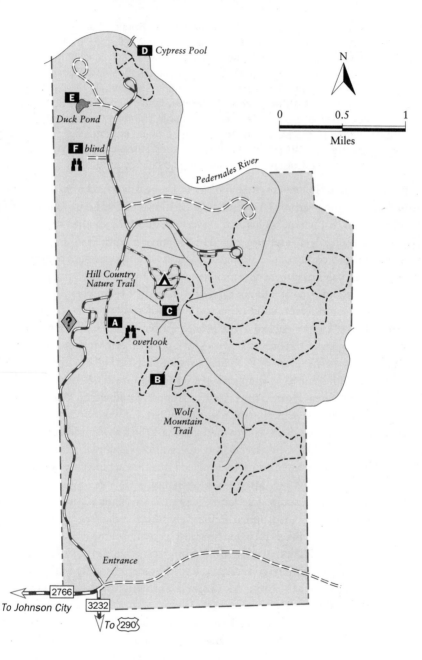

N

0   0.5   1
Miles

D *Cypress Pool*

E
Duck Pond

F *blind*

Pedernales River

*Hill Country
Nature Trail*

C

A
overlook

B

*Wolf
Mountain
Trail*

Entrance

2766
To Johnson City
3232
To 290

Tanager. Chuck-will's-widows call at dawn and dusk. Blue Grosbeaks occur in moist, weedy sites. Waterfowl and shorebirds are only infrequent visitors along the river.

The Duck Pond (E), at the end of a short graveled road to the west, south of the Pedernales Falls parking area, is the best site for Wood Duck and Vermilion Flycatcher in summer and good for migrants of all types in both spring and fall. And 1 mile south of this site is another short graveled road to the corral area (F), which offers open fields and a blind. Winter seedeaters and other brush-living birds can be common here. Expect House Wren; Spotted Towhee; Chipping, Field, Vesper, Savannah, Grasshopper, Fox, Song, Lincoln's, White-throated, White-crowned, and Harris's Sparrows; Dark-eyed Junco; Eastern and Western Meadowlarks; and American Goldfinch. Also watch for the occasional Winter Wren, Lark Bunting, and LeConte's Sparrow. Winter songbirds usually attract a few raptors, such as Northern Harrier, Sharp-shinned and Cooper's Hawks, and American Kestrel.

Directions: This park is 32 miles west of Austin. Take US 290 to FM 3232, beyond Dripping Spring, then head north on FM 3232 for 6 miles to the park entrance. From Johnson City on US 281, take FM 2766 east 9 miles to the park entrance.

General information: This 4,860-acre park, bisected by the Pedernales River, is a hiker's park with more than 20 miles of meandering trails, including the 8.2-mile Wolf Mountain Trail. Pedernales Falls extends for about 3 miles through a rugged and picturesque gorge at the northern edge of the park. Swimming and tubing are permitted only below the falls. The park can be busy on weekends and holidays.

ADDITIONAL HELP

Location: Texas Official Travel Map grid P x 16; Blanco County
Nearest food, gas, and lodging: Johnson City, 12 miles, has food, gas, and lodging.
Nearest camping: On-site (69 sites)
Contact: Superintendent, Pedernales Falls State Park (see Appendix C)

34 Balcones Canyonlands National Wildlife Refuge

Habitats: Oak-juniper woodland, oak savannah, oak scrub, pond, creek, riparian, prairie

Key birds: Wild Turkey, Greater Roadrunner, **Golden-fronted Woodpecker,** Canyon Towhee, Rufous-crowned and Grasshopper Sparrows, and Lesser Goldfinch are present year-round. Common Poorwill, Chuck-will's-widow, Vermilion and Scissor-tailed Flycatchers, Bell's Vireo, **Black-capped Vireo, Golden-cheeked Warbler,** and Painted Bunting occur in summer. LeConte's, Fox, and Harris's Sparrows and Chestnut-collared Longspur can usually be found in winter.

Best times to bird: Mid-March through June for **Black-capped Vireo** and **Golden-cheeked Warbler**

Birding strategies: The Eckhardt Tract (**A**), on the north side of the refuge, harbors as many as 20 pairs of Black-capped Vireo within one 200-acre area in spring and summer. The entrance, parking area, and a short trail to a viewing platform are on FM 1869, east of FM 1174. This site is the most accessible and reliable site near Austin to find this endangered bird. Other nesting birds in the shinnery and adjacent oaks include Mourning Dove; Yellow-billed Cuckoo; Black-chinned Hummingbird; White-eyed Vireo; Yellow-breasted Chat; Summer Tanager; Northern Cardinal; Painted Bunting; and Rufous-crowned, Field, and Black-throated Sparrows.

The Nagel Tract (**B**) offers the greatest habitat diversity and largest variety of birds throughout the year. This site is located along FM 1174, 2.3 miles south of FM 1869 or 4.3 miles north of FM 1431. A 2-mile loop trail provides access to prairie, creek and riparian, and oak and juniper woodland habitats. Expected year-round residents along the trail include Black and Turkey Vultures; Red-tailed Hawk; Wild Turkey; Northern Bobwhite; Mourning Dove; Greater Roadrunner; Ladder-backed Woodpecker; Western Scrub-Jay; Carolina Chickadee; Tufted Titmouse; Carolina and Bewick's Wrens; Eastern Bluebird; Northern Mockingbird; Northern Cardinal; Canyon Towhee; Rufous-crowned, Field, and Lark Sparrows; Eastern Meadowlark; House Finch; and Lesser Goldfinch. Several less numerous or obvious birds also occur here year-round: Cooper's and Red-shouldered Hawks, Eastern Screech-Owl, Great Horned Owl, **Golden-fronted Woodpecker,** Bushtit, Canyon Wren, Loggerhead Shrike, and Black-throated and Grasshopper Sparrows.

In spring and summer the most prized species in this area is the Golden-cheeked Warbler, which frequents the dense oak-juniper woodland along the ridgetop and north slope. Other neotropical migrants that nest along the trail include Yellow-billed Cuckoo; Common Nighthawk; Common Poorwill; Black-chinned Hummingbird; Eastern Wood-Pewee; Vermilion, Ash-throated, Great Crested, and Scissor-tailed Flycatchers; Cliff and Barn Swallows; Blue-gray Gnatcatcher; White-eyed and Red-eyed Vireos; Black-and-white Warbler; Yellow-breasted Chat; Summer Tanager; Blue Grosbeak; Painted Bunting; and Orchard Oriole.

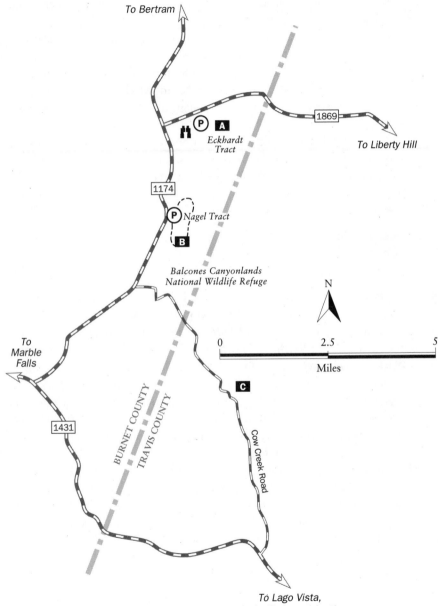

To Bertram

1869

To Liberty Hill

A

Eckhardt Tract

1174

P *Nagel Tract*

B

Balcones Canyonlands National Wildlife Refuge

N

To Marble Falls

0   2.5   5

Miles

C

1431

BURNET COUNTY

TRAVIS COUNTY

Cow Creek Road

To Lago Vista, Cedar Park, and Austin

The ridgetop is also a good site for observing migrating raptors in the fall. Swainson's Hawks can be numerous during the first week of October. Other expected southbound raptors, usually during September, include Mississippi Kite; Northern Harrier; Sharp-shinned, Cooper's, Broad-winged, Red-shouldered, and Red-tailed Hawks; and American Kestrel.

In winter the native grasslands and brush in the area can attract a wide variety of seedeaters. These include Spotted Towhee; Chipping, Vesper, Savannah, LeConte's, Fox, Song, Lincoln's, Swamp, White-throated, White-crowned, and Harris's Sparrows; Dark-eyed Junco; Western Meadowlark; and American Goldfinch. Chestnut-collared Longspurs are irregular visitors, and may be more numerous on grazed pastures elsewhere in the refuge area.

Cow Creek Road (C) connects FM 1174 and FM 1431, providing another good birding area. However, all lands along Cow Creek Road, including areas at low water crossings, are private, even those that are not fenced; bird only from the roadway! Groves of oak, elm, pecan, mesquite, and sycamore along the road provide cover for migrants in both spring and fall.

Directions: Take FM 1869 for 8.9 miles west of Liberty Hill to the refuge entrance. Cow Creek Road can be reached along FM 1174, 1.3 miles south of the Nagel Tract or along FM 1431, 6.5 miles west of Lago Vista.

General information: Only two tracts—Eckhardt and Nagel—within this 46,000-acre refuge are now open to general visitation. Additional tracts will likely be opened at a later time. Established in 1992, Balcones Canyonlands National Wildlife Refuge is intended principally to conserve the nesting habitats of the endangered **Black-capped Vireo** and **Golden-cheeked Warbler.** Both species are monitored annually, and various habitat management activities are under way to restore additional habitat, especially for Black-caps. These activities include trapping of Brown-headed Cowbirds during the nesting season, cutting some encroaching trees, and prescribed burning. Fire is being applied to restore native prairies and savannahs in parts of the refuge.

The refuge encompasses scenic terrain typical of the Balcones region of the larger Edwards Plateau. It is composed of deeply dissected, heavily wooded limestone hills with topographic relief exceeding 500 feet in some areas. The northern portion of the refuge consists of gently rolling upland plateaus and ridges capped by the resistant Edwards limestone.

ADDITIONAL HELP

Location: Texas Official Travel Map grid P x 16; Travis, Burnet, and Williamson counties

Nearest food, gas, and lodging: Food and gas are available in Lago Vista, Bertram, and Liberty Hill; lodging available at Lago Vista, 14 miles from the Eckhardt Tract.

Nearest camping: Several campgrounds along US 183 and around Lake Travis

Contact: Manager, Balcones Canyonlands National Wildlife Refuge (see Appendix C)

35 Austin

State Capitol Grounds; Eastwoods, Emma Long, and Zilker Metropolitan Parks; Barton Creek Greenbelt; Krieg Field; Town Lake and Longhorn Dam; Wild Basin Wilderness Preserve; and Forest Ridge Preserve

Habitats: Lake, creek, riparian, bottomland hardwood forest, oak-juniper woodland, mesquite grassland, field

Key birds: Wood Duck, Monk Parakeet, Greater Roadrunner, **Green Kingfisher, Golden-fronted Woodpecker,** Western Scrub-Jay, Canyon Wren, Rufous-crowned Sparrow, and Lesser Goldfinch are present year-round. Neotropic Cormorant, Black-bellied Whistling-Duck, Common Poorwill, Chuck-will's-widow, Black-chinned Hummingbird, Scissor-tailed Flycatcher, **Golden-cheeked Warbler,** Indigo and Painted Buntings, and Dickcissel occur in summer. Common Loon; Osprey; Bald Eagle; LeConte's, Fox, and Harris's Sparrows; and Rusty Blackbird can usually be found in winter.

Best times to bird: Mid-March to July for **Golden-cheeked Warbler;** April and May for spring migrants and nesting activities; November to March for winter birds

Birding strategies: Golden-cheeked Warbler occurs from mid-March to July along Barton Creek Greenbelt and at Forest Ridge Preserve and Emma Long Metropolitan Park; it no longer nests at Wild Basin Wilderness Preserve. The most likely place to see this endangered species is at **Emma Long Metropolitan Park (A)**, only 45 minutes from downtown Austin, via Loop 360 to the northwest. The juniper-oak woodland along Turkey Creek Trail, at the base of the long hill just before the park entrance station, supports several pairs. This species can also be found along City Park Road, the entrance road to Emma Long Park off FM 2222. Golden-cheeks can best be found by their distinct, three-part, wheezy songs in spring.

Beyond Turkey Creek in Emma Long Park are open lawns, scattered trees, and fields that border Lake Austin. This area is a good place to find Northern Bob-white, Rock and Inca Doves, Scissor-tailed Flycatcher, Blue Jay, American Crow, Loggerhead Shrike, Blue Grosbeak, Great-tailed Grackle, Eastern Meadowlark, and Orchard Oriole in summer. The riparian areas along the lakeshore at both ends of the visitor use areas also harbor Red-bellied Woodpecker, Red-eyed Vireo, and Summer Tanager. And in winter, the brushy fields are likely to attract House Wren; Spotted Towhee; Chipping, Song, Lincoln's, White-throated, and White-crowned Sparrows; Dark-eyed Junco; and American Goldfinch.

Lake Austin acts as a migratory route for both spring and fall migrants. Water birds and terrestrial species can be found along the waterway and on the adjacent vegetation, respectively. Water birds frequent the open lake during quiet periods. Pied-billed Grebe, Great Blue Heron, Wood Duck, Mallard, and Belted Kingfisher are present year-round. Neotropic Cormorant; Great, Snowy, and Cattle Egrets; Green Heron; Yellow-crowned Night-Heron; Black-bellied Whistling-Duck; American Coot; and Black Tern are often present in summer. In winter the lake can be crowded with waterfowl and several other less numerous species, including Common Loon, Eared Grebe, Double-crested Cormorant, Osprey, Bald Eagle, Bonaparte's and Ring-billed Gulls, and Forster's Tern. Occasionally, **Green Kingfisher** also appears along the margins of Lake Austin.

Wild Basin Wilderness Preserve (B), located off Loop 360, just north of Bee Caves Road (FM 2244), is nearest to downtown Austin. The preserve's 1.5-mile loop trail to Laurel Falls and along Possum Creek offers a wide variety of birds in summer. The rather dense oak-juniper woodland here supports Mourning Dove, Black-chinned Hummingbird, Ladder-backed Woodpecker, Ash-throated Fly-catcher, Western Scrub-Jay, Carolina Chickadee, Tufted Titmouse, Bewick's Wren, Northern Cardinal, Rufous-crowned Sparrow, Brown-headed Cowbird, House Finch, and Lesser Goldfinch. Less numerous or obvious breeders include Yellow-billed Cuckoo, Eastern Screech-Owl, Common Poorwill, Chuck-will's-widow, Blue-gray Gnatcatcher, Black-and-white Warbler, Indigo Bunting, and Chipping Sparrow. The open areas along the trail are more likely to contain Greater Roadrunner, Northern Mockingbird, Painted Bunting, and Field Sparrow.

Forest Ridge Preserve (C) is located along Loop 360 just south of Spicewood Springs Road. A small parking area is available adjacent to the highway at the trailhead. This area also is dominated by an oak-juniper woodland where most of the same birds mentioned above for Wild Basin Preserve can be found.

In Central Austin, at least five sites are worth birding at various times of year. These include the **State Capitol Grounds (D)**; **Eastwoods Metropolitan Park (E)**, including Waller Creek Greenbelt; **Zilker Metropolitan Park (F)**, including the Austin Nature Center; **Barton Creek Greenbelt (G)**, which runs from Barton Springs in Zilker Park westward for 7.5 miles to the Gus Fruh Access Point; and **Town Lake and Longhorn Dam (H)**, east of downtown.

All of these sites are best during the spring migration, when great numbers of neotropical migrants are passing through the area. Flycatchers, vireos, warblers, tanagers, orioles, and various other birds can usually be found. The **State Capitol Grounds (D)** and **Eastwoods Metropolitan Park (E)**, near the University of Texas campus, between 26th and 31st streets, act as migrant traps. Eastwoods Park, in particular, contains huge old hardwood trees that provide feeding and resting sites

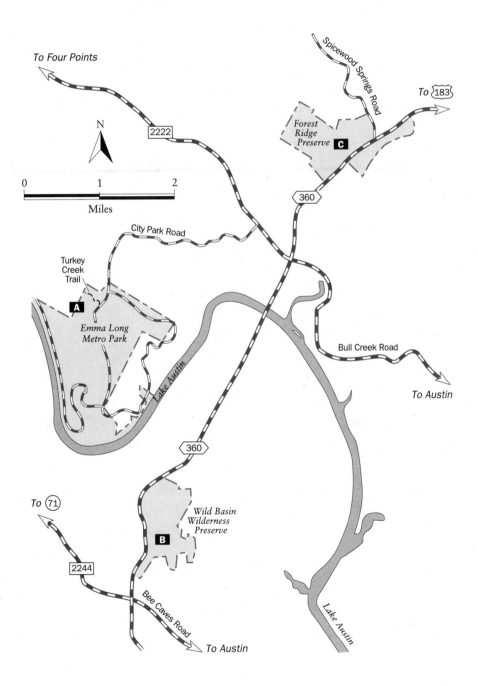

To Four Points

N

2222

0   1   2
Miles

Spicewood Springs Road

To 183

Forest Ridge Preserve **C**

360

City Park Road

Turkey Creek Trail

A

Emma Long Metro Park

Lake Austin

Bull Creek Road

To Austin

360

To 71

Wild Basin Wilderness Preserve

B

2244

Bee Caves Road

Lake Austin

To Austin

35 Austin Central

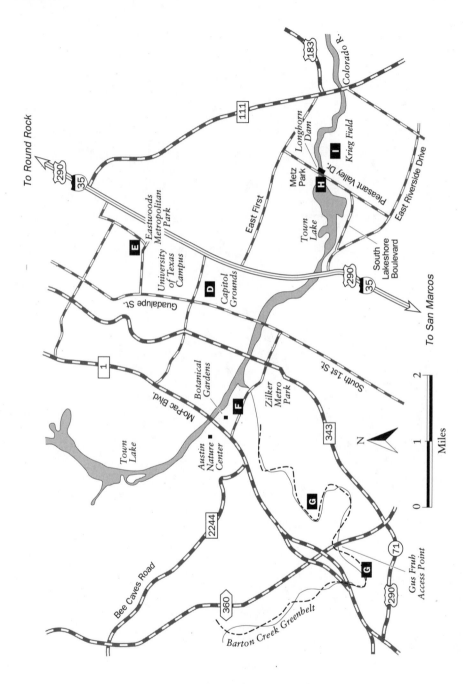

for the exhausted travelers. Several of the neotropical migrants remain and nest with the full-time residents. This combined bird life includes Green Heron; White-winged, Mourning, and Inca Doves; Yellow-billed Cuckoo; Eastern Screech-Owl; Barred Owl; Chimney Swift; Black-chinned Hummingbird; Red-bellied and Downy Woodpeckers; Great Crested Flycatcher; Blue Jay; American Crow; Carolina Chickadee; Tufted Titmouse; Carolina Wren; Blue-gray Gnatcatcher; American Robin; White-eyed, Yellow-throated, and Red-eyed Vireos; Summer Tanager; Northern Cardinal; Common and Great-tailed Grackles; Brown-headed Cowbird; and House Finch.

Zilker Metropolitan Park (F) is a sprawling area of lawns and scattered trees and shrubs. Trails along the river offer access to some good riparian habitat where most of the same birds mentioned for the Wild Basin preserve can be found. The Botanical Gardens, situated on a wooded ridge, can be good during migration and, in late summer and fall, hummingbirds can be abundant around the flowering plants. Also in Zilker Park, the Austin Nature Center contains a series of short trails along Dry Creek, through oak-juniper woodlands, and across fields. The more interesting birds here in summer include Brown Thrasher, Blue Grosbeak, Painted Bunting, Dickcissel, Red-winged Blackbird, and Orchard Oriole. In nearby Town Lake, Mute Swans have taken up residence.

Barton Creek Greenbelt (G) is one of the city's most popular running trails, but it offers a wide range of habitats, from dense riparian vegetation to open fields along the route. This area also supports **Golden-cheeked Warbler** from mid-March to July. This endangered species can best be found along the trail near the Gus Fruh Access Point or at the MoPac Trailhead.

The fields and mesquite grassland areas along Barton Creek Greenbelt attract a variety of birds year-round. In summer Northern Bobwhite, **Golden-fronted Woodpecker,** Ladder-backed Woodpecker, Western Kingbird, Scissor-tailed Flycatcher, Purple Martin, Cliff and Barn Swallows, Bewick's Wren, Northern Mockingbird, Loggerhead Shrike, Painted Bunting, Field and Lark Sparrows, and Eastern Meadowlark can be expected. Also listen at rocky bluffs along the greenbelt for the descending and decelerating songs of Canyon Wrens. In winter, brushy areas may harbor House and Sedge Wrens; Common Yellowthroat; Spotted Towhee; Vesper, Savannah, Grasshopper, LeConte's, Fox, Song, Lincoln's, Swamp, White-throated, White-crowned, and Harris's Sparrows; Dark-eyed Junco; Western Meadowlark; and American Goldfinch.

The surrounding woodland edges usually contain Northern Flicker, Ruby-crowned Kinglet, American Robin, Hermit Thrush, Cedar Waxwing, and Orange-crowned and Yellow-rumped Warblers. Watch also for the less numerous Yellow-bellied Sapsucker, Red-breasted Nuthatch, Brown Creeper, Golden-crowned Kinglet, Gray Catbird, White-eyed Vireo, Rusty Blackbird, and Purple Finch. Sharp-shinned and Cooper's Hawks and American Kestrel can usually be found where there is an adequate prey base.

East of downtown is lower **Town Lake and Longhorn Dam (H)**, accessible from East Riverside Drive, South Lakeshore Boulevard, and Pleasant Valley Drive. The basin of Town Lake, behind the dam and easily viewed from Metz Park and Festival Beach, is the best bet for migrating and wintering waterfowl. **Krieg Field (I)**, a recreation complex on the east side of Pleasant Valley Drive (west of the dam), contains a number of tall light posts on which Monk Parakeets have constructed bulky nests; they can be seen here year-round.

Directions: Three sites are located off Loop 360, between Bee Caves Road (FM 2244) on the south and US 183 to the north. **Wild Basin Preserve** is only 1.5 miles north of Bee Caves Road; **Emma Long Park** is 6.2 miles off FM 2222, north of 360, at the end of City Park Road. **Forest Ridge Preserve** is located just off 360 to the north, below Spicewood Springs Road.

The **State Capitol Grounds** are situated in downtown Austin, at the intersection of Congress Avenue and East 11th Street; the entrance to **Eastwoods Park** is located along Harris Park Avenue, off East 26th Street; **Zilker Metropolitan Park** is located along upper **Town Lake** on the west side of the city, and is bisected by Barton Springs Road. **Barton Creek Greenbelt** runs from Barton Springs (within Zilker Park) westward, between MoPac Expressway and Lamar Boulevard; lower **Town Lake and Longhorn Dam** are located east of I-35, and can best be reached on the south side by taking East Riverside Drive, South Lakeshore Boulevard, and Pleasant Valley Road, which crosses Longhorn Dam, or from the north side by taking East First Street to Pleasant Valley Road. **Krieg Field** is located along Pleasant Valley Road, east of Longhorn Dam.

General information: The city of Austin, with a population in excess of 500,000, contains numerous city parks and greenbelts and several surrounding parks and preserves. Since most of this area is located at the southeastern edge of the Edwards Plateau, this site has been placed in the Edwards Plateau region; however, Austin East (site 74), which lies immediately to the east, includes Hornsby Bend Wastewater Treatment Plant, probably the single best birding site in the Greater Austin area.

Lake Austin and Town Lake are 2 of 6 lakes (including Inks Lake; site 32) along the Colorado River, all managed by the Lower Colorado River Authority. Emma Long Park contains 1,150 acres, 70 of which are developed, along Lake Travis. A similar developed park, with 10 miles of hike-and-bike trails, exists both above and below Longhorn Dam. These areas can be extremely busy on weekends and holidays a good part of the year; birding is best during the early morning hours.

Wild Basin Wilderness, a private, nonprofit organization, is dedicated to environmental education programs. Its 227-acre preserve contains 2.5 miles of trails. Visitor use at the 360-acre Forest Ridge Preserve is pretty well limited to hikers and nature lovers, so birding is more relaxed.

ADDITIONAL HELP

Location: Texas Official Travel Map grid P x 17; Travis County

Nearest food, gas, and lodging: All can be found at numerous sites in and around Austin.

Nearest camping: Available on-site at Emma Long Park, and at numerous other sites throughout the Austin area.

Contact: For Emma Long, Forest Ridge, and city parks: Director, Austin Parks and Recreation; Director, Wild Basin Wilderness Preserve; Manager, Lower Colorado River Authority (see Appendix C)

36 Guadalupe River State Park

Habitats: River, creek, riparian, oak-juniper woodland, field

Key birds: Wild Turkey, Greater Roadrunner, **Green Kingfisher,** Western Scrub-Jay, Canyon Wren, Rufous-crowned Sparrow, and Lesser Goldfinch are present year-round. Common Poorwill, Chuck-will's-widow, Scissor-tailed Flycatcher, Yellow-throated Vireo, **Golden-cheeked Warbler,** and Painted Bunting occur in spring and summer. **Golden-fronted Woodpecker,** Winter Wren, and Harris's Sparrow can usually be found in winter.

Best times to bird: April and May for spring migrants and nesting activities

Birding strategies: Golden-cheeked Warbler is concentrated in isolated canyons along the Guadalupe River and in adjacent Honey Creek State Natural Area (**A**), from mid-March to July. Weekly interpretive tours of the state natural area are offered each Saturday at 9 A.M.; the area is otherwise closed.

All of the oak-juniper woodland birds can usually be found in the Old Cedar Area (**B**), located past the entrance station and accessible from the first road to the left beyond the entrance station. Full-time residents to be expected in this area include Wild Turkey; Northern Bobwhite; Mourning Dove; Greater Roadrunner; Ladder-backed Woodpecker; Western Scrub-Jay; Carolina Chickadee; Tufted Titmouse; Bewick's Wren; Eastern Bluebird; Northern Mockingbird; Northern Cardinal; Rufous-crowned, Chipping, and Field Sparrows; Eastern Meadowlark; Brown-headed Cowbird; House Finch; and Lesser Goldfinch.

The park's best birding is found at the end of the road at the day use area and along a 2-mile loop trail (**C**) that runs from the day use area upriver through riparian and oak-juniper woodlands and old fields. Good views of the river are available from the day use area and along the trail. This is the most likely area to find **Green Kingfisher,** which often sits on bare branches just above the water; it can often be detected first by sharp *"tick tick"* notes. Watch also for the larger Belted Kingfisher. Cliff Swallow nests on the cliff face across the river, Canyon Wren can often be heard singing in the daytime and Common Poorwill after dark, and Great Blue Heron sometimes flies by.

36 Guadalupe River State Park

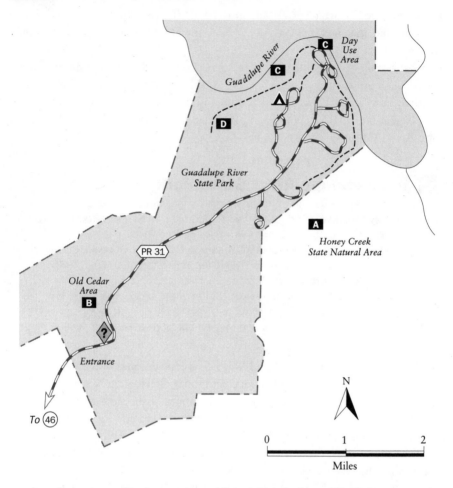

A walk upriver offers numerous additional birds. In spring and summer, the riparian habitat along the river can be alive with birds. This area is good for migrants, including various vireos and warblers. Several of the neotropical migrants remain and nest with the year-round residents. The combined species include Green Heron; Red-shouldered Hawk; Mourning Dove; Yellow-billed Cuckoo; Black-chinned Hummingbird; Ladder-backed Woodpecker; Eastern Wood-Pewee; Acadian and Great Crested Flycatchers; Eastern Phoebe; Carolina Chickadee; Tufted Titmouse; Blue-gray Gnatcatcher; Carolina Wren; White-eyed, Yellow-throated, and Red-eyed Vireos; Northern Parula; Summer Tanager; Northern Cardinal; Painted Bunting; and Lesser Goldfinch.

The drier oak-juniper woodland (**D**) has most of the same birds mentioned for the Old Cedar Area. However, this area attracts a wider variety of migrants, and it can provide good birding in winter. The open woodlands attract numerous northern

Guadalupe River and cliff at the day use area in Guadalupe River State Park.

species such as Northern Flicker, Golden-crowned and Ruby-crowned Kinglets, American Robin, Cedar Waxwing, and Yellow-rumped Warbler. The weedy fields and edges often harbor House and Winter Wrens; Spotted Towhee; Field, Vesper, Song, Lincoln's, White-throated, White-crowned, and Harris's Sparrows; Dark-eyed Junco; and American Goldfinch.

In winter, be sure to bird the day use area. The savannah-like environment attracts several of the birds mentioned above as well as American Kestrel, Yellow-bellied Sapsucker, and **Golden-fronted Woodpecker.**

Directions: From San Antonio, take US 281 north for 22 miles to SH 46; then take SH 46 west for 8 miles to PR 31. The park entrance is 3 miles ahead. From Boerne, pronounced *burn*-ay (on I-10), take SH 46 for 17 miles to PR 31.

General information: The 1,900-acre park is bisected by the clear waters of the Guadalupe River, which cuts through the rugged, scenic landscape of the Hill Country. The huge bald cypress trees that edge the river form a majestic cathedral in spring and summer. The river is heavily used for canoeing and tubing, so the area can be extremely busy on weekends. Almost 2,300 additional acres are included in the adjacent Honey Creek State Natural Area, which is closed to general visitation; Saturday morning interpretive tours are available at $5 per family or $2 per adult.

ADDITIONAL HELP

Location: Texas Official Travel Map grid Q x 16; Kendall County

Nearest food, gas, and lodging: Food is available at Bergheim (3 miles); gas is available at the junction of US 281 and SH 46 (8 miles); lodging is available at Boerne (17 miles).

Nearest camping: On-site (105 sites, including 20 walk-in tent sites)

Contact: Superintendent, Guadalupe River State Park (see Appendix C)

37 Friedrich Wilderness Park

Habitats: Oak-juniper woodland, juniper woodland, field

Key birds: Greater Roadrunner, **Golden-fronted Woodpecker,** Western Scrub-Jay, Rufous-crowned Sparrow, and Lesser Goldfinch are present year-round. Chuck-will's-widow, Scissor-tailed Flycatcher, **Black-capped Vireo,** and **Golden-cheeked Warbler** occur in summer. There are no key birds in winter.

Best times to bird: Late March through July for **Black-capped Vireo** and **Golden-cheeked Warbler**

Birding strategies: The Main Loop Trail (**A**) provides a 1.5-mile route through oak-juniper woodlands where **Golden-cheeked Warbler,** best detected by its high-pitched, wheezy song, resides in spring and early summer. Other birds present here in summer include Eastern Screech-Owl, Ladder-backed Woodpecker, Western Scrub-Jay, Carolina Chickadee, Tufted Titmouse, Bewick's Wren, Blue-gray Gnatcatcher, Black-and-white Warbler, Northern Cardinal, and Spotted Towhee.

The longer (2 miles) Vista Loop Trail (**B**) passes through drier uplands preferred by **Black-capped Vireo,** which can best be located by its distinct call (a rapid series of grating and squeaking notes). This upper area also harbors White-eyed Vireo, Rufous-crowned Sparrow, and Spotted Towhee in summer. And the open views offer passing raptors and other soaring birds, including Black and Turkey Vultures, Red-tailed Hawk, Chimney Swift, Purple Martin, and Cliff and Barn Swallows.

The grassy fields around the parking area and administration buildings (**C**) provide a habitat that is utilized by several other species. Expected year-round birds include Rock, Mourning, and Inca Doves; **Golden-fronted Woodpecker;** Eastern Phoebe; Western Scrub-Jay; Carolina Chickadee; Tufted Titmouse; Carolina and Bewick's Wrens; Northern Mockingbird; European Starling; Northern Cardinal; Chipping and Field Sparrows; Brown-headed Cowbird; House Finch; and Lesser Goldfinch. A few other birds are found here in summer: Black-chinned Hummingbird, Ash-throated and Scissor-tailed Flycatchers, Western Kingbird, Purple Martin, Cliff and Barn Swallows, Lark Sparrow, and Red-winged Blackbird. And White-winged Dove, Great Crested Flycatcher, Blue Jay, Summer Tanager, Painted Bunting, and Great-tailed Grackle have been recorded on a few occasions.

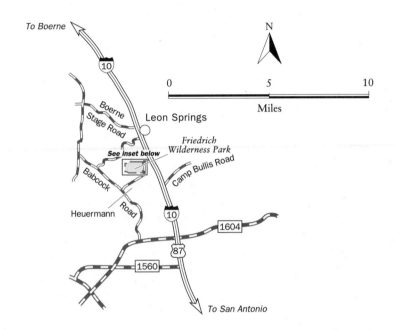

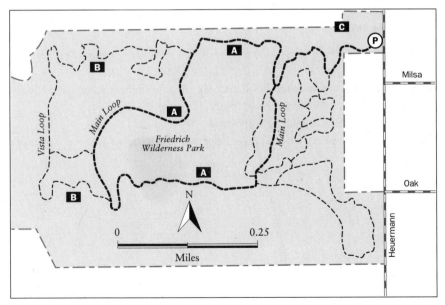

In winter Sharp-shinned Hawk, American Kestrel, Northern Flicker, Ruby-crowned Kinglet, Hermit Thrush, American Robin, Cedar Waxwing, Orange-crowned and Yellow-rumped Warblers, Dark-eyed Junco, Common Grackle, and American Goldfinch are found regularly. Golden-crowned Kinglet, Red-breasted Nuthatch, and Pine Siskin occur sporadically.

Records of Review Species: Greater Pewee, April 1991.

Directions: From San Antonio, take I-10 north to Camp Bullis Road. Exit and turn under the highway to the access road and follow the signs to the park entrance. From the north, take I-10 and exit at Boerne Stage Road onto the access road. Follow the signs to the park entrance.

General information: Located at the northern edge of San Antonio, Friedrich Wilderness Park offers easy access to two specialty birds of the Texas Hill Country: **Black-capped Vireo** and **Golden-cheeked Warbler.** The vireo is rare, but an active habitat restoration program is under way to enhance its essential habitat.

The 232-acre park contains nearly 5 miles of trails, some of which pass through a relatively undisturbed juniper-oak community. Many of the trails are rocky; hiking boots are recommended. The park (smoke- and pet-free) is open from 8 A.M. to 5 P.M. October to March and 8 A.M. to 8 P.M. April to September, Wednesday through Sunday. Guided nature walks (free) and numerous educational opportunities (minimum fee) are scheduled year-round, including talks on the second Saturday of each month.

ADDITIONAL HELP

Location: Texas Official Travel Map grid R x 15; Bexar (pronounced "Bear") County
Nearest food, gas, and lodging: Food and gas are at Leon Springs (2 miles); lodging is available along the access road south (1.5 miles).
Nearest camping: Several San Antonio sites
Contact: Nature Preserve Coordinator, Friedrich Wilderness Park (see Appendix C)

Northern Plains Region

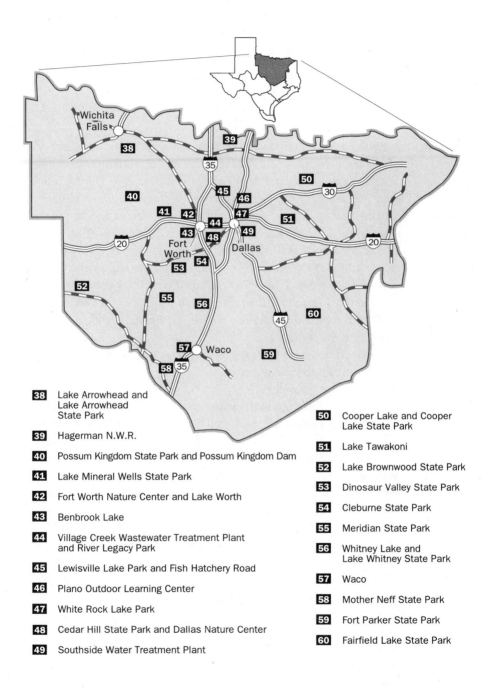

38 Lake Arrowhead and Lake Arrowhead State Park

39 Hagerman N.W.R.

40 Possum Kingdom State Park and Possum Kingdom Dam

41 Lake Mineral Wells State Park

42 Fort Worth Nature Center and Lake Worth

43 Benbrook Lake

44 Village Creek Wastewater Treatment Plant and River Legacy Park

45 Lewisville Lake Park and Fish Hatchery Road

46 Plano Outdoor Learning Center

47 White Rock Lake Park

48 Cedar Hill State Park and Dallas Nature Center

49 Southside Water Treatment Plant

50 Cooper Lake and Cooper Lake State Park

51 Lake Tawakoni

52 Lake Brownwood State Park

53 Dinosaur Valley State Park

54 Cleburne State Park

55 Meridian State Park

56 Whitney Lake and Lake Whitney State Park

57 Waco

58 Mother Neff State Park

59 Fort Parker State Park

60 Fairfield Lake State Park

38 Lake Arrowhead and Lake Arrowhead State Park

Habitats: Lake, pond, riparian, mesquite grassland, prairie
Key birds: Red-headed Woodpecker and **Golden-fronted
Woodpecker** are present year-round. Neotropic Cormorant,
Swainson's Hawk, Scissor-tailed Flycatcher, Bell's Vireo, Painted
Bunting, Dickcissel, and Grasshopper Sparrow occur in summer.
American White Pelican; Bald Eagle; Merlin; Hooded, Common, and
Red-breasted Mergansers; Sandhill Crane; and Fox and Harris's
Sparrows can usually be found in winter.
Best times to bird: April to late May for spring migrants and nesting
activities

Birding strategies: The best birding in spring and summer is within the state park, especially in the mesquite grassland along the hiking and equestrian trails (**A**), just beyond the entrance station to the right. Expected species include Northern Bobwhite, Killdeer, Mourning Dove, **Golden-fronted Woodpecker,** Ladder-backed Woodpecker, Western Kingbird, Scissor-tailed Flycatcher, American Crow, Carolina Chickadee, Bewick's Wren, Blue-gray Gnatcatcher, Eastern Bluebird, Northern Mockingbird, Northern Cardinal, Painted Bunting, Dickcissel, Lark Sparrow, Eastern Meadowlark, Great-tailed and Common Grackles, and Brown-headed Cowbird. Less numerous birds include Yellow-billed Cuckoo, Greater Roadrunner, Great Horned Owl, Carolina Wren, Brown Thrasher, Bell's Vireo, and Orchard Oriole. Watch overhead for Turkey Vulture, Red-tailed Hawk, and Common Nighthawk at dawn and dusk.

The spillway (**B**) is an excellent place to observe waterfowl and shorebirds; the lower water level attracts feeding water birds. Rarities sometimes appear here. Cliff Swallow nests under the spillway.

The lake (**C**) supports only a few birds in summer: Double-crested and Neotropic Cormorants; Great Blue, Little Blue, and Green Herons; Great and Snowy Egrets; Canada Goose; Mallard; and Belted Kingfisher. During migration and in winter, however, water birds can be numerous. Most abundant are Pied-billed and Horned Grebes, American White Pelican, Double-crested Cormorant, Canada Goose, Green-winged Teal, Mallard, Northern Pintail, Northern Shoveler, Gadwall, American Wigeon, Ring-necked Duck, and American Coot. Watch also for Blue-winged Teal; Canvasback; Redhead; Common Goldeneye; Ruddy Duck; Hooded, Common, and Red-breasted Mergansers; Bonaparte's and Herring Gulls; and Forster's Tern. Check along the lake shoreline and overhead in winter for Bald Eagles.

In summer the adjacent fields, fences, and wires, such as those along West Arrowhead Drive (**D**), offer Swainson's Hawk, Western Kingbird, Scissor-tailed Flycatcher, Horned Lark, Eastern Bluebird, Loggerhead Shrike, European Starling, Field Sparrow, and Eastern Meadowlark. In winter these fields sometimes contain Greater White-fronted, Snow, and Canada Geese and Sandhill Crane. Weedy areas often harbor wintering seedeaters, such as Spotted Towhee; Field, Vesper, Fox, Song, Lincoln's, White-crowned, and Harris's Sparrows; Dark-eyed Junco;

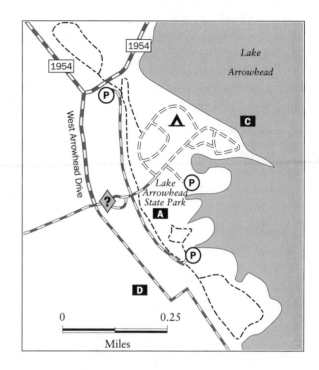

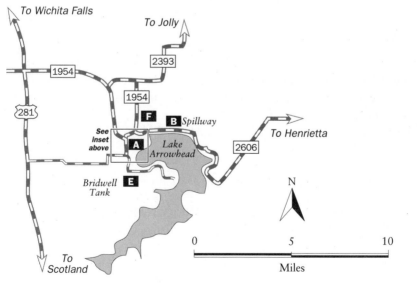

and American Goldfinch. A few raptors, including Northern Harrier, American Kestrel, and Merlin, may also be present.

Stop at Bridwell Tank (**E**), along West Arrowhead Drive south of the park; the trees and shrubs are utilized by Double-crested and Neotropic Cormorants, Great Blue Heron, and Great Horned Owl for nest sites, and the pond can attract an abundance of migrants in spring and fall.

Also visit Sloop Creek (**F**), located beyond the entrance to the north. Take the equestrian tunnel and follow the trail along the creek. This area is good for woodland birds, including Red-headed Woodpecker.

Records of Review Species: Brown Pelican, Aug–Oct 1994. Roseate Spoonbill, Aug 1976, Sept 1995. Tundra Swan, Dec 1989. Caspian Tern, June 1994.

Directions: The park is located south of Wichita Falls. Take either US 281 to FM 1954 and go 8 miles east, or US 287 to FM 2393 and go south for 8 miles to the park entrance.

General information: The Little Wichita River was dammed to form Lake Arrowhead in 1965, primarily as a water supply for the city of Wichita Falls. The 13,500-acre lake offers a number of recreational activities, including fishing, boating, and swimming. The area is located on the eastern edge of the Rolling Plains, characterized by rolling grasslands that have since been invaded by mesquite and other woody plants. The vast majority of the area is privately owned.

The state park is located at the northwest portion of the lake and features a number of hiking and equestrian trails, as well as a Bluebird Trail, where several nest boxes have been installed to attract Eastern Bluebirds.

ADDITIONAL HELP

Location: Texas Official Travel Map grid G x 15; Archer and Clay counties
Nearest food, gas, and lodging: Food and gas are available along FM 1954 (3 miles); the nearest lodging is in Wichita Falls (18 miles).
Nearest camping: On-site (68 sites)
Contact: Superintendent, Lake Arrowhead State Park (see Appendix C)

39 **Hagerman National Wildlife Refuge**

Habitats: Lake, pond, river, riparian, mud flat, bottomland hardwood forest, mesquite grassland, prairie, field, pasture, cropland
Key birds: Wood Duck, Wild Turkey, Greater Roadrunner, and Red-headed Woodpecker are present year-round. Neotropic Cormorant, Least Bittern, Roseate Spoonbill, Mississippi Kite, Swainson's Hawk, Chuck-will's-widow, Scissor-tailed Flycatcher, Prothonotary and Kentucky Warblers, Indigo and Painted Buntings, and Dickcissel occur in summer. Ross's Goose; Bald Eagle; Short-eared Owl; LeConte's, Fox, and Harris's Sparrows; McCown's, Lapland, Smith's, and Chestnut-collared Longspurs; and Purple Finch can usually be found in winter.
Best times to bird: April and May for spring migrants and nesting activities; November through mid-February for winter birds

Birding strategies: Meadow Pond Road (**A**), a gated extension of Wildlife Drive, can be superb during spring migration. Watch for Bobolink and Yellow-headed Blackbird in late April and early May. The dense vegetation along the roadsides, fields, and pond offers a variety of birds. A few of the neotropical migrants nest here: Yellow-billed Cuckoo; Chuck-will's-widow (rare); Ruby-throated Hummingbird; Eastern Wood-Pewee; Great-crested and Scissor-tailed Flycatchers; Western and Eastern Kingbird; White-eyed and Red-eyed Vireos; Black-and-white, Prothonotary, and Kentucky Warblers; Yellow-breasted Chat (rare); Summer Tanager; Blue Grosbeak; Indigo and Painted Buntings; and Dickcissel. Also expect several of the year-round residents: Wood Duck; Red-tailed Hawk; Wild Turkey; Northern Bobwhite; Mourning Dove; Great Horned and Barred Owls; Red-headed, Red-bellied, Downy, and Hairy Woodpeckers; Blue Jay; American Crow; Carolina Chickadee; Tufted Titmouse; Carolina and Bewick's Wrens; Northern Mockingbird; Brown Thrasher; Northern Cardinal; Field and Lark Sparrows; Red-winged Blackbird; Eastern Meadowlark; Common Grackle; and Brown-headed Cowbird.

Goode Picnic Area (**B**), located north of refuge headquarters, supports many of the same birds in summer. However, this area contains more grassland- and prairie-associated bird species. Look for Swainson's Hawk and Bewick's Wren in summer, and LeConte's Sparrow in grassy fields in winter.

The open waters and shoreline of Lake Texoma (**C**) visible from the Wildlife Drive contain a rather sparse bird population in summer. Pied-billed Grebe; Great Blue, Little Blue, and Green Herons; Great and Snowy Egrets; Wood Duck; Mallard; American Coot; and Killdeer can be expected. Watch also for Neotropic Cormorant; Anhinga; Black-crowned and Yellow-crowned Night-Herons; Roseate Spoonbill; and Caspian, Forster's, and Least Terns.

In winter water birds are more abundant: Common Loon (most likely on Lake Texoma); American White Pelican; Greater White-fronted, Snow, and Ross's Geese; an occasional shorebird and gull (2,500 to 5,000 Ring-billed Gulls in January and

39   Hagerman National Wildlife Refuge

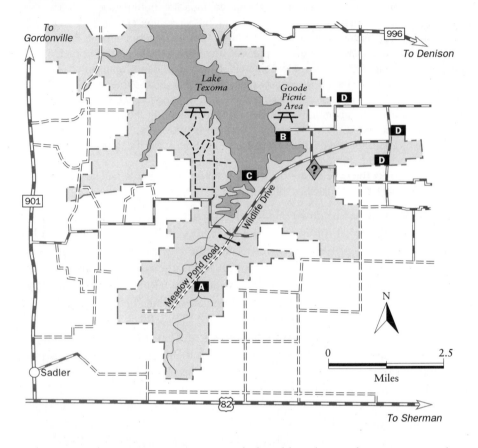

February), and Forster's Tern. Raptors include Bald Eagle, Northern Harrier, Red-tailed Hawk, American Kestrel, and Merlin; Rough-legged Hawk occurs irregularly. Bald Eagle is best observed at the dam site area near Denison. In winter the various fields surrounding the refuge (**D**) often harbor seedeaters such as Field, Savannah, White-throated, White-crowned, and Harris's Sparrows and American Goldfinch; watch also for the less numerous birds such as Eastern and Spotted Towhees and Vesper, LeConte's, Fox, Song, Lincoln's, and Swamp Sparrows. Horned Larks and (rarely) all four longspurs prefer stubble fields.

Records of Review Species: Reddish Egret, March–April 1997. Brant, Nov–Dec 1987. Red Phalarope, Nov 1991. Sabine's Gull, Sept–Oct 1990. Black Skimmer, May 1996.

General information: The 11,320-acre refuge was established to provide food and protected nesting habitat for waterfowl during the winter and migration seasons. The shallow marshes and ponds are usually full most of the year because of elevated lake levels. Only during very dry summers are the ponds and marshes partially empty. Located at the south end of the Big Mineral Arm of Lake Texoma, on the

Red River, refuge uplands are managed and restored by periodic burning, controlled grazing, and replanting of native grasses and forbs. The Red River serves as the border between Texas and Oklahoma.

Lake Texoma, an 89,000-acre impoundment, is managed by the U.S. Army Corps of Engineers. The 457-acre Eisenhower State Park is located in the southeastern corner. The dam site is near Denison.

ADDITIONAL HELP

Location: Texas Official Travel Map grid G x 18; Grayson County
Nearest food, gas, and lodging: Food and gas are available on FM 1417 (7 miles); lodging is in Denison (14 miles) or Sherman (15 miles).
Nearest camping: Sixteen Corps and state sites along the Texas lakeshore
Contact: Manager, Hagerman National Wildlife Refuge (see Appendix C)

40 Possum Kingdom State Park and Possum Kingdom Dam

Habitats: Lake, river, riparian, juniper woodland, oak savannah, mesquite grassland, field
Key birds: Wood Duck, Wild Turkey, Greater Roadrunner, **Golden-fronted Woodpecker,** Canyon Wren, Canyon Towhee, and Rufous-crowned Sparrow are present year-round. Mississippi Kite, Common Poorwill, Scissor-tailed Flycatcher, **Black-capped Vireo, Golden-cheeked Warbler,** Painted Bunting, Dickcissel, Cassin's and Grasshopper Sparrows, and Lesser Goldfinch occur in summer. Common Loon, Osprey, Bald Eagle, Ferruginous and Rough-legged Hawks, Rock Wren, and LeConte's and Fox Sparrows can usually be found in winter.
Best times to bird: Black-capped Vireo and **Golden-cheeked Warbler** are present during April through July; November to March for winter birds

Birding strategies: Six pairs of **Golden-cheeked Warbler** were recorded for the state park in 1996; **Black-capped Vireo** is found only outside the park. The best bet for finding Golden-cheeks in the park is along the Longhorn Trail (**A**), which runs west from the campground. From mid-March through May, males sing distinct three-part wheezy songs, often from treetops. Other expected summer residents in this oak-juniper habitat include Mourning Dove, Yellow-billed Cuckoo, Black-chinned Hummingbird, Ladder-backed Woodpecker, Carolina Chickadee, Tufted Titmouse, Bushtit, Carolina Wren, Blue-gray Gnatcatcher, White-eyed Vireo, Northern Cardinal, and Field Sparrow. A few additional birds prefer more open areas, including the mesquite grasslands, in the same general areas: Mississippi Kite, Wild Turkey, Northern Bobwhite, Greater Roadrunner, **Golden-fronted Woodpecker,** Eastern Phoebe, Ash-throated and Scissor-tailed Flycatchers, Barn

40 **Possum Kingdom State Park and Possum Kingdom Dam**

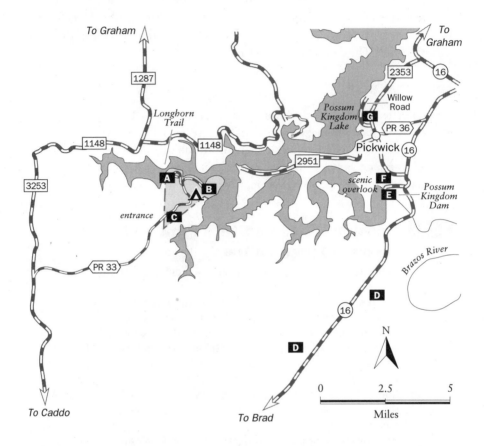

Swallow, Eastern Bluebird, Northern Mockingbird, American Robin, Loggerhead Shrike, Painted Bunting, Canyon Towhee, Rufous-crowned and Lark Sparrows, Eastern Meadowlark, Brown-headed Cowbird, Bullock's Oriole, and House Finch. Common Poorwill, Verdin, and Lesser Goldfinch are less numerous.

The scenic overlook along the Longhorn Trail, as well as numerous sites in the campground (B), provide good views of Possum Kingdom Lake. Water birds on the lake and along the shoreline are limited to only a few summer species, such as Great Blue, Little Blue, and Green Herons; Great and Snowy Egrets; Killdeer; and Belted Kingfisher. Winter birds can be far more numerous: expect Green-winged Teal, Mallard, Northern Pintail, Gadwall, American Wigeon, Northern Shoveler, Canvasback, Redhead, Lesser Scaup, Bufflehead, American Coot, Common Snipe, Bonaparte's and Ring-billed Gulls, and Forster's Tern. Watch also for Ring-necked Duck, Common Goldeneye, Hooded Merganser, and Ruddy Duck. Common Loon, Horned and Eared Grebes, Osprey, and Bald Eagle occur in variable numbers.

The mesquite grasslands and open fields, such as those along the park entrance road (C), attract a variety of winter birds. Especially after summer and fall rains have produced a good seed crop, weedy areas can attract House Wren; Spotted Towhee; Field, Vesper, Lark, Savannah, Fox, Song, Lincoln's, Swamp, White-throated, and White-crowned Sparrows; Dark-eyed Junco; House Finch; and American Goldfinch. Several other birds can usually be found in winter within the woodlands or along the edges: Yellow-bellied Sapsucker, Northern Flicker, Golden-crowned and Ruby-crowned Kinglets, Hermit Thrush, and Orange-crowned and Yellow-rumped Warblers. Raptors, such as Northern Harrier; Sharp-shinned, Cooper's, and Red-tailed Hawks; and American Kestrel, utilize these same areas, taking advantage of unsuspecting prey.

The woodlands and fields outside the park, especially along SH 16 (D), between Brad and the Brazos River, attract various birds. Bird only from the roadsides as this area is all private property. In summer all the land birds mentioned above can usually be found here, as well as **Golden-fronted Woodpecker,** Ladder-backed Woodpecker, Ash-throated Flycatcher, White-eyed and Bell's Vireos, Yellow-breasted Chat, Lark Sparrow, and Bullock's Oriole; the area also supports a small population of **Black-capped Vireo;** and some years Dickcissel and Cassin's and Grasshopper Sparrows are reasonably common. In winter watch for the occasional Ferruginous and Rough-legged Hawks and Golden Eagle along this route.

The high cliffs and riparian areas below Possum Kingdom Dam (E), only 0.6 mile from SH 16, offer the birder different birds. Black and Turkey Vultures and Cliff Swallows can number in the hundreds. And the descending and decelerating songs of Canyon Wren are commonplace. Below the dam, the river is accessible from the parking area. Be careful on the steep, rocky trails! Great Blue and Green Herons, Great and Snowy Egrets, Wood Duck, Killdeer, Belted Kingfisher, and Northern Rough-winged Swallow can usually be found along the waterway in summer; Yellow-billed Cuckoo, Red-bellied and Downy Woodpeckers, Great Crested Flycatcher, Carolina and Bewick's Wrens, Bell's and Red-eyed Vireos, Summer Tanager, Blue Grosbeak, Painted Bunting, and Common Grackle frequent the riparian areas. A Rock Wren winters in the riprap below the dam. Walk through the marshy area in winter to find Marsh Wren; Common Yellowthroat; and LeConte's, Song, Lincoln's, and Swamp Sparrows.

The scenic overlook (F) near the Brazos River Authority Headquarters, off FM 2353, offers a marvelous view of the lake and passing birds. Although the overlook is too high above the lake for good close-up views, occasional Osprey, Bald Eagle, and other species can sometimes be seen in winter. Willow Road (G) (off FM 2353 north of Pickwick) skirts the lake and provides good riparian habitat that attracts migrants and all the same nesting birds mentioned for the riparian habitat above.

Directions: From US 180 at Caddo, take PR 33 north for 17 miles to the state park. SH 16 is east of Caddo, between US 180 and SH 337. Possum Kingdom

Dam and the overlook and Willow Road are situated off SH 16, north of the Brazos River.

General information: The 1,615-acre Possum Kingdom State Park is situated on the southeastern corner of Possum Kingdom Lake, a 19,800-acre freshwater lake, 65 miles long and with more than 300 miles of shoreline, administered by the Brazos River Authority. The lake and park are managed primarily for water recreation; visitation can be heavy on weekends and holidays. Before venturing into the riverbed below the dam, read the warning signs at the parking area; get out of the riverbed immediately when the siren sounds, as the water can rise very quickly when releases from the dam begin.

Possum Kingdom lies within the Texas Rolling Plains, at the eastern edge of the Northern Plains, although the area also contains considerable characteristics of the Texas Hill Country, such as ashe juniper. Therefore, it is ideal habitat for the endangered **Golden-cheeked Warbler.**

ADDITIONAL HELP

Location: Texas Official Travel Map grid J x 15; Palo Pinto County

Nearest food, gas, and lodging: Food and gas are available at Pickwick, above the dam; lodging is available at Graham (32 miles).

Nearest camping: On-site in the state park (116 sites); primitive camping is also permitted below the dam (no fee)

Contact: Superintendent, Possum Kingdom State Park; Manager, Brazos River Authority (see Appendix C)

41 Lake Mineral Wells State Park

Habitats: Lake, spillway, wetland, creek, riparian, oak savannah, mesquite grassland, field

Key birds: Wood Duck, Wild Turkey, Greater Roadrunner, Canyon Wren, and Rufous-crowned Sparrow are present year-round. Mississippi Kite, Common Poorwill, Chuck-will's-widow, Black-chinned Hummingbird, Scissor-tailed Flycatcher, and Indigo and Painted Buntings occur in summer. American White Pelican, Hooded Merganser, Bald Eagle, Sora, Red-headed Woodpecker, Winter Wren, and Fox and Harris's Sparrows can usually be found in winter.

Best times to bird: April and May for spring migrants and nesting activities; November to March for winter birds

Birding strategies: Much of the park's landscape is dominated by oak savannah (A). Expected year-round birds in this habitat include Red-shouldered Hawk; Northern Bobwhite; Mourning Dove; Red-bellied, Ladder-backed, and Downy Woodpeckers; Blue Jay; American Crow; Carolina Chickadee; Tufted Titmouse; Carolina and Bewick's Wrens; Northern Mockingbird; Northern Cardinal; and Field

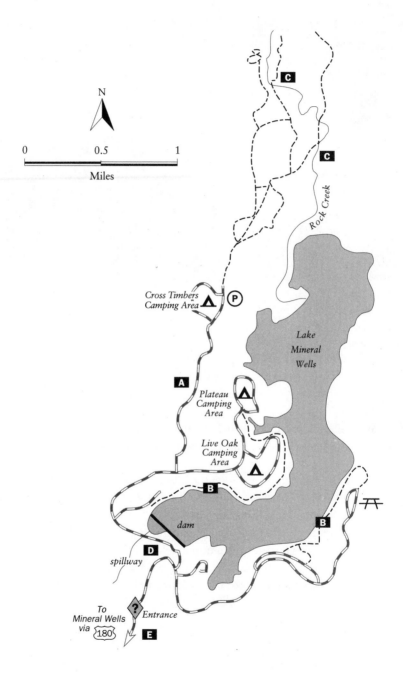

N

0   0.5   1

Miles

C

C

Rock Creek

Cross Timbers Camping Area ▲ Ⓟ

Lake Mineral Wells

A

Plateau Camping Area ▲

Live Oak Camping Area ▲

B

B

dam

D

spillway

To Mineral Wells via ⑱⓪ ? *Entrance*

E

Looking northeast at Lake Mineral Wells in Lake Mineral Wells State Park.

and Lark Sparrows. Wild Turkey, Greater Roadrunner, Great Horned Owl, Canyon Wren, Eastern Bluebird, Brown Thrasher, Rufous-crowned Sparrow, and Eastern Meadowlark are less numerous. In summer look for Mississippi Kite, Black-chinned Hummingbird, Scissor-tailed Flycatcher, White-eyed Vireo, Blue Grosbeak, Indigo and Painted Buntings, Common Grackle, and Brown-headed Cowbird. Turkey Vulture, Red-tailed Hawk, Common Nighthawk at dawn and dusk, Chimney Swift, Purple Martin, and Cliff and Barn Swallows can be commonplace.

In summer the riparian areas along the lakeshore (**B**) and along Rock Creek (**C**) attract Yellow-billed Cuckoo, Chuck-will's-widow, Great Crested Flycatcher, Red-eyed Vireo, and Summer Tanager.

The open water and wetlands along Rock Creek offer the park's best birding. Much of this area can be birded from a trail overlook 0.25 mile north of the Cross Timbers Camping Area. In the summer water birds to be expected include Great Blue, Little Blue, and Green Herons; Great Egret; Yellow-crowned Night-Heron; Wood Duck; American Coot; and Killdeer. Watch also for Black-crowned Night-Heron and White-faced Ibis. In winter, Pied-billed Grebe, Double-crested Cormorant, Green-winged Teal, Mallard, Northern Pintail, Gadwall, American Wigeon, Ring-necked Duck, Lesser Scaup, Bufflehead, and Hooded Merganser can be expected. Eared and Horned Grebes, Ruddy Duck, and Sora are irregular. Watch for Red-headed Woodpecker, Bald Eagle in February, and American White Pelican in March.

Rock Creek and the lake can also be very productive during spring migration. The open spillway (**D**), actually a low-water crossing, attracts northbound and southbound shorebirds.

Open fields and forest edges, such as those along the entrance road (**E**), attract Scissor-tailed Flycatcher, Purple Martin, Cliff and Barn Swallows, American Crow, Eastern Bluebird, Northern Mockingbird, Loggerhead Shrike, Blue Grosbeak, Painted Bunting, Lark Sparrow, Red-winged Blackbird, Eastern Meadowlark, and Common Grackle in summer. In winter brushy areas often harbor House and Winter Wrens; Common Yellowthroat; Spotted Towhee; Field, Vesper, Savannah, Fox, Song, Lincoln's, Swamp, White-throated, White-crowned, and Harris's Sparrows; Dark-eyed Junco; and American Goldfinch.

Directions: From Mineral Wells, take US 180 east for 3 miles to the park entrance. From Weatherford, take US 180 west for 14 miles.

General information: This 2,809-acre park, including the 646-acre Lake Mineral Wells, incorporates lands donated by the city of Mineral Wells and the transfer of a portion of Fort Wolters army post by the federal government. The park contains 16 miles of trails: 6 miles of hiking-only trails and 10 miles of multi-use trail, available for horseback riding and bicycling.

ADDITIONAL HELP

Location: Texas Official Travel Map grid J x 16; Parker County
Nearest food, gas, and lodging: All are available in Mineral Wells (3 miles).
Nearest camping: On-site (90 sites)
Contact: Superintendent, Lake Mineral Wells State Park (see Appendix C)

42 Fort Worth Nature Center and Lake Worth

Habitats: Lake, marsh, riparian, bottomland hardwood forest, oak savannah, prairie
Key birds: Wood Duck, Wild Turkey, and Greater Roadrunner are present year-round. Neotropic Cormorant, Mississippi Kite, Chuck-will's-widow, Scissor-tailed Flycatcher, Prothonotary Warbler, Indigo and Painted Buntings, and Dickcissel occur in summer. Hooded Merganser, Osprey, Bald Eagle, Fox and Harris's Sparrows, and Rusty Blackbird can usually be found in winter.
Best times to bird: April and May for spring migrants and nesting activities; November through February for winter birds

Birding strategies: Stop first at Hardwicke Interpretive Center (**A**) for a map and orientation, and also to check the feeders for whatever might be present. Black-chinned and Ruby-throated Hummingbirds feed here in summer. Winter visitors can include several northern species such as Yellow-bellied Sapsucker; Red-breasted Nuthatch; Field, Fox, Lincoln's, White-throated, White-crowned, and Harris's Sparrows; Dark-eyed Junco; Purple Finch; Pine Siskin; and American Goldfinch.

42 Fort Worth Nature Center and Lake Worth

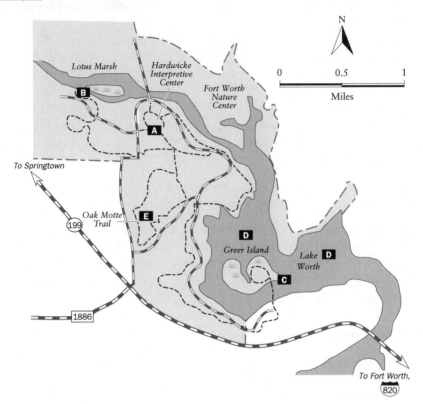

The 900-foot-long Lotus Marsh Boardwalk (**B**) offers a good perspective on the area's wetland birds. Year-round species include Pied-billed Grebe, Great Blue Heron, Great Egret, Wood Duck, American Coot, and Belted Kingfisher. In summer also expect Snowy Egret, Little Blue and Green Herons, Black-crowned and Yellow-crowned Night-Herons, Prothonotary Warbler, and Common Yellowthroat. Neotropic Cormorant, Anhinga, Least Bittern, Tricolored Heron, White Ibis, Roseate Spoonbill, Wood Stork, Black-bellied Whistling-Duck, Purple Gallinule, and Common Moorhen are irregular summer visitors.

Bottomland hardwood forest occurs all along the lakeshore, but can best be sampled on Greer Island and causeway (**C**). This dense forest vegetation attracts a wide variety of spring and fall migrants, including numerous neotropical migrants, such as flycatchers, vireos, warblers, tanagers, and orioles. A few of these remain and nest with the full-time residents. Expected species (both resident and migrant) include Red-shouldered Hawk, Yellow-billed Cuckoo, Red-bellied and Downy Woodpeckers, Great Crested Flycatcher, Blue Jay, Carolina Chickadee, Tufted Titmouse, Carolina Wren, White-eyed and Red-eyed Vireos, and Summer Tanager. Less numerous summer birds here include Eastern Screech-Owl, Barred Owl, Chuck-will's-widow, Eastern Wood-Pewee, Blue-gray Gnatcatcher, Warbling Vireo,

Northern Parula, and Yellow-throated Warbler. Yellow-bellied Sapsucker, Hairy Woodpecker, Northern Flicker, Red-breasted Nuthatch, Brown Creeper, Winter Wren, Golden-crowned and Ruby-crowned Kinglets, Hermit Thrush, Orange-crowned and Yellow-rumped Warblers, Rusty Blackbird, Purple Finch, and Pine Siskin occur here in winter.

Lake Worth (D) can also be birded from along the Greer Island trails. Although lake birds are rather sparse in summer, fall and winter birding can be more productive. Waterfowl can be common during the fall migration and through much of the winter. Most numerous are Green-winged and Blue-winged Teal, Mallard, Northern Pintail, Northern Shoveler, Gadwall, American Wigeon, Ring-necked Duck, Lesser Scaup, Bufflehead, Hooded Merganser, and Ruddy Duck. Fewer numbers of Greater White-fronted and Canada Geese, Cinnamon Teal, Canvasback, Redhead, Common Goldeneye, and Red-breasted and Common Mergansers are recorded. Watch also in winter for Osprey and Bald Eagle.

The 3.2-mile Oak Motte Trail (E) offers a drier environment through oak savannah and prairie habitats with a very different bird life. Year-round residents include Red-tailed Hawk; Wild Turkey; Northern Bobwhite; Mourning Dove; Greater Roadrunner; Great Horned Owl; Ladder-backed Woodpecker; American Crow; Bewick's Wren; Eastern Bluebird; Northern Mockingbird; Brown Thrasher; Loggerhead Shrike; Northern Cardinal; Lark Sparrow; Eastern Meadowlark; Great-tailed and Common Grackles; and Brown-headed Cowbird. In summer look for Black-chinned Hummingbird; Western and Eastern Kingbirds; Scissor-tailed Fly-catcher; White-eyed Vireo; Blue Grosbeak; Indigo and Painted Buntings; Dickcis-sel; and Orchard, Baltimore, and Bullock's Orioles. Watch overhead for Black and Turkey Vultures; Mississippi Kite; Red-tailed Hawk; Common Nighthawk at dawn and dusk; Chimney Swift; Purple Martin; and Northern Rough-winged, Cliff, and Barn Swallows.

In winter the prairie and brushy sites attract a variety of northern seedeaters, including Spotted and Eastern Towhees; Field, Vesper, Fox, Song, Lincoln's, Swamp, White-throated, White-crowned, and Harris's Sparrows; Dark-eyed Junco; Western Meadowlark; and American Goldfinch. American Woodcock is also found occasionally. All these in turn attract winter raptors: Northern Harrier and American Kestrel are common; Sharp-shinned and Cooper's Hawks are uncommon; Merlin and Peregrine and Prairie Falcons are irregular visitors.

Directions: Ten miles from downtown Fort Worth, the center entrance is situated along SH 199, 4 miles west of Loop 820.

General information: This 3,500-acre urban refuge is the largest in North America. It contains more than 25 miles of hiking trails with easy access to a wide variety of habitats. Although closed on Mondays, the refuge is open from 9 A.M. to 5 P.M. Tuesday through Saturday, and noon to 5 P.M. on Sunday. The Hardwicke Interpretive Center, which has exhibits and a gift shop, hosts interpretive activities year-round.

193

Lake Worth covers an area of 3,560 acres. Boating, waterskiing, and sailing are permitted. The area is noted for scenic vistas along Meandering Drive.

ADDITIONAL HELP

Location: Texas Official Travel Map grid J x 17; Tarrant County
Nearest food, gas, and lodging: Food and gas are available at the entrance; several overnight accommodations are located nearby.
Nearest camping: Several areas in northwest Fort Worth
Contact: Manager, Fort Worth Nature Center (see Appendix C)

43 Benbrook Lake

Habitats: Lake, river, creek, riparian, oak-hackberry woodland, prairie, field, golf course
Key birds: Wood Duck, Greater Roadrunner, and Red-headed Woodpecker are present year-round. Neotropic Cormorant, Swainson's Hawk, Least and Black Terns, Chuck-will's-widow, Scissor-tailed Flycatcher, Prothonotary Warbler, Indigo and Painted Buntings, Dickcissel, and Grasshopper Sparrow occur in summer. Common Loon; Common Goldeneye; Hooded, Common, and Red-breasted Mergansers; Osprey; Bald Eagle; Ferruginous and Rough-legged Hawks; Merlin; Prairie Falcon; Mountain Bluebird; Lark Bunting; LeConte's, Fox, and Harris's Sparrows; and Rusty Blackbird can usually be found in winter.
Best times to bird: April and May for spring migrants and nesting activities; late summer for post-nesting shorebirds, gulls, and terns; November to February for winter water birds and sparrows

Birding strategies: Although the entire Benbrook Lake area is a magnet for migrants, the riparian vegetation along the Trinity River and various creeks is best. During late summer and fall, scope the lake and shoreline for a good variety of water birds.

The boat ramp area (**A**) at Benbrook Marina, on the north shore, is one of the best places to scope the lake for water birds. Year-round, expect only Double-crested Cormorant, Great Blue Heron, Great Egret, and Killdeer. However, summer visitors (usually post-nesting birds by early to late July) include Neotropic Cormorant; Snowy and Cattle Egrets; Little Blue and Green Herons; Black-crowned Night-Heron; American Coot; American Avocet; Spotted, Upland, Semipalmated, Western, and Least Sandpipers; and Black Tern. Less numerous are American White Pelican; Greater and Lesser Yellowlegs; Solitary, Baird's, Pectoral, and Stilt Sandpipers; Willet; Long-billed Dowitcher; Wilson's Phalarope; and Forster's and Least Terns. Watch also for the occasional Roseate Spoonbill, Osprey, Bald Eagle, Piping Plover, Marbled Godwit, Red-necked Phalarope, and Dunlin. Some of these same birds, such as Bald Eagle, remain through the winter. Other birds of interest

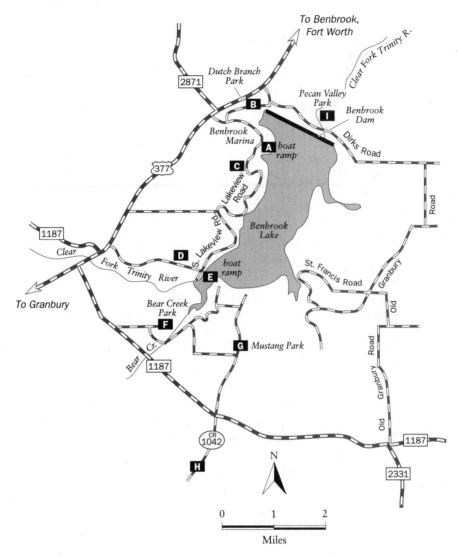

include Common Loon; Common Goldeneye; and Hooded, Common, and Red-breasted Mergansers.

Dutch Branch Park (**B**), across the bay to the northwest, includes a nature trail and campground. The wooded areas support numerous migrants in spring and fall and a variety of breeding birds in summer. Most evident are Red-shouldered Hawk, Yellow-billed Cuckoo, Black-chinned Hummingbird, Red-bellied and Downy Woodpeckers, Great Crested Flycatcher, Western and Eastern Kingbirds, Blue Jay, American Crow, Carolina Chickadee, Tufted Titmouse, Carolina Wren, Blue-gray Gnatcatcher, White-eyed and Red-eyed Vireos, Summer Tanager,

Northern Cardinal, Common Grackle, and Brown-headed Cowbird. Also watch for Green Heron, Wood Duck, Chuck-will's-widow, and Prothonotary Warbler. In winter this is a good area for Rusty Blackbirds.

In summer the open grasslands (C) along Lakeview Road, as well as those (D) along South Lakeview Road, offer Northern Bobwhite; Common Nighthawk at dawn and dusk; Northern Rough-winged, Cliff, and Barn Swallows; Indigo and Painted Buntings; Dickcissel; Cassin's (irregular) and Lark Sparrows; Red-winged Blackbird; and Eastern Meadowlark. Swainson's Hawk, Greater Roadrunner, Loggerhead Shrike, and Grasshopper Sparrow are less numerous. In winter watch for Northern Harrier; Golden Eagle; American Kestrel; Horned Lark; and Field, Vesper, Savannah, Song, Lincoln's, White-throated, and White-crowned Sparrows. LeConte's, Fox, and Harris's Sparrows are less numerous. The boat ramp (E) at the end of South Lakeview Road in Holiday Park is another good area for viewing the lake.

Bear Creek Park (F), including the area on the south side of Bear Creek, is a good place to look for Red-headed Woodpeckers, while Mustang Park (G) offers most of the grassland and woodland birds mentioned above.

One of the area's most productive grasslands (H) occurs along CR 1042, south of FM 1187. All the grassland birds mentioned above can usually be found along this route. Grasshopper Sparrows nest here, and raptors, even Ferruginous and Rough-legged Hawks, Crested Caracara, Merlin, and Prairie Falcon, occur some winters. Also watch for Mountain Bluebirds and Lark Buntings, which occur irregularly.

Continue around the lake to the east and north, following Old Granbury Road to Dirks Road and Pecan Valley Park (I), the area of the U.S. Army Corps of Engineers office, golf course, Memorial Oak Park, and Benbrook Dam. Memorial Oak Park has extensive grassland habitat for various grassland shorebirds, which can appear in spring, late summer, and fall on the golf course. Check the soccer fields in winter for longspurs; scope the lake from the dam overview for water birds in fall and winter.

Records of Review Species: Western Grebe, March 1985. Sabine's Gull, Oct 1986. Palm Warbler, Jan 1985.

Directions: The park is located southwest of Fort Worth. Take US 377 to Benbrook and continue through town for 2 miles to the Benbrook Marina entrance.

General information: This 3,770-acre U.S. Army Corps of Engineers impoundment, situated on the Clear Fork of the Trinity River, can be extremely busy on weekends and holidays, when many of the entrance roads are closed to anyone but paying campers and fishermen. The area offers a wide variety of recreational opportunities, ranging from boating and fishing to horseback riding and hiking. It is worth your while in winter to check with the Corps office about road closures; however, closed roads make for good birding, even if it has to be done on foot!

ADDITIONAL HELP

Location: Texas Official Travel Map grid K x 17; Tarrant County
Nearest food, gas, and lodging: Benbrook (2 miles) has all three.
Nearest camping: On-site at six areas scattered around the lake
Contact: Reservoir Manager, Benbrook Project Office (see Appendix C)

44 Village Creek Wastewater Treatment Plant and River Legacy Park

Habitats: River, pond, marsh, riparian, bottomland hardwood forest, field
Key birds: Wood Duck can be found year-round. White-faced Ibis, Black-bellied Whistling-Duck, Common Moorhen, King Rail, Hairy Woodpecker, Scissor-tailed Flycatcher, Prothonotary Warbler, Indigo and Painted Buntings, and Dickcissel occur in summer. Virginia Rail, Fox and Harris's Sparrows, and Rusty and Brewer's Blackbirds can usually be found in winter.
Best times to bird: March, April, and mid-July through September are best for seeing migrating shorebirds.

Birding strategies: Village Creek Wastewater Treatment Plant (**A**) contains numerous drying basins within an area of approximately one square mile. To find the greatest number of birds drive or walk the 2.5-mile-long outer levee or any of the connecting levees. Expected year-round residents about the ponds and adjacent fields include Pied-billed Grebe, Great Blue Heron, Great Egret, Wood Duck, Mallard, Northern Bobwhite, American Coot, Killdeer, Rock and Mourning Doves, American Crow, Northern Mockingbird, Loggerhead Shrike, European Starling, Northern Cardinal, Red-winged Blackbird, Eastern Meadowlark, Great-tailed and Common Grackle, and House Sparrow. Additional birds utilize the area in summer: Snowy and Cattle Egrets, Little Blue and Green Herons, Black-crowned and Yellow-crowned Night-Herons, White-faced Ibis, and Common Moorhen frequent the wetlands; watch also for Neotropic Cormorant, Anhinga, American and Least Bitterns, Tricolored Heron, King Rail, and Purple Gallinule. Expect Western and Eastern Kingbirds, Scissor-tailed Flycatcher, Painted Bunting, and Dickcissel in the adjacent fields. Overhead, look for Black and Turkey Vultures; Red-tailed Hawk; Common Nighthawk at dawn and dusk; Purple Martin; and Northern Rough-winged, Cliff, and Barn Swallows.

In winter, the ponds and fields attract numerous waterfowl and other birds. Most common are Horned and Eared Grebes, Double-crested Cormorant, numerous ducks, Northern Harrier, American Kestrel, Least Sandpiper, Common Snipe, Bonaparte's and Ring-billed Gulls, Forster's Tern, Eastern Phoebe, Horned Lark, Marsh Wren, American Pipit, Savannah Sparrow, Eastern and Western Meadowlarks, and Rusty and Brewer's Blackbirds. Watch also for Virginia Rails.

44 Village Creek Wastewater Treatment Plant and River Legacy Park

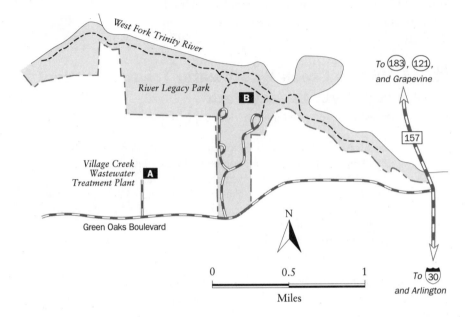

Migration time is quite exciting, as a wide variety of shorebirds, gulls, and terns are likely to appear. Typical migrants include American Avocet; Greater and Lesser Yellowlegs; Solitary, Spotted, Upland, Semipalmated, Western, Least, Baird's, Pectoral, and Stilt Sandpipers; Long-billed Curlew; Long-billed Dowitcher; Wilson's Phalarope; Franklin's Gull; and Black Tern. In spring, also watch for Black-bellied and Semipalmated Plovers, American Golden-Plover, Black-necked Stilt, Whimbrel, Hudsonian Godwit, and White-rumped Sandpiper. Other spring migrants include Swainson's Hawk, Peregrine Falcon, Tree and Bank Swallows, and Yellow-headed Blackbird. In fall, look for Short-billed Dowitcher. In good years, even Snowy, Piping, and Mountain Plovers; Marbled Godwit; Ruddy Turnstone; Sanderling; Dunlin; and Red-necked Phalarope have appeared.

The tall vegetation on the far side of the ponds is part of adjacent River Legacy Park (**B**), an area of private acreage along the Trinity River. The entrance lies along Green Oaks Boulevard, just east of the Village Creek plant. Trails provide access to the riverway and a bottomland hardwood forest habitat that supports very different bird life than is found at Village Creek Wastewater Treatment Plant. These woods harbor Red-shouldered and Red-tailed Hawks, Eastern Screech Owl, Great Horned and Barred Owls, Red-bellied and Downy Woodpeckers, Blue Jay, American Crow, Carolina Chickadee, Tufted Titmouse, Carolina Wren, Northern Cardinal, and Common Grackle year-round.

In spring, thousands of neotropical migrants, including flycatchers, vireos, warblers, tanagers, and orioles, stop to feed and rest along the riverway. Several remain to nest: Black-chinned Hummingbird; Eastern Wood-Pewee; Great Crested Flycatcher; Western and Eastern Kingbirds; Purple Martin; Northern Rough-winged, Cliff, and Barn Swallows; Blue-gray Gnatcatcher; White-eyed, Warbling, and Red-eyed Vireos; Prothonotary Warbler; Summer Tanager; Blue Grosbeak; Indigo and Painted Buntings; and Orchard, Bullock's, and Baltimore Orioles.

In winter, an additional group of birds frequents the same area: Northern Flicker, Red-breasted Nuthatch, Brown Creeper, Winter Wren, Golden-crowned and Ruby-crowned Kinglets, Hermit Thrush, Cedar Waxwing, Orange-crowned and Yellow-rumped Warblers, Purple Finch, Pine Siskin, and American Goldfinch. The fields and woodland edges usually support a variety of wintering seedeaters, including Spotted and Eastern Towhees; Field, Vesper, Savannah, Fox, Song, Lincoln's, Swamp, White-throated, White-crowned, and Harris's Sparrows; and Dark-eyed Junco.

Records of Review Species: Wood Stork, Aug 1989. Roseate Spoonbill, Sept 1989. Fulvous Whistling-Duck, April 1997. Sharp-tailed Sandpiper, May 1991. Red Knot, Aug 1989. Ruff, April 1995. Red Phalarope, Sept 1991. Little Gull, March 1992. Crested Caracara, May 1997.

Directions: Both sites are located in northern Arlington. From I-30, take SH 157 north for 2.3 miles and turn west on Green Oaks Boulevard. Follow Green Oaks Boulevard for 1.8 miles to the entrance of River Legacy Park, or continue on Green Oaks the short distance to Village Creek Wastewater Treatment Plant.

General information: The Village Creek Wastewater Treatment Plant has outlived its usefulness to the city and nutrients are no longer being pumped into the drying beds. Therefore, because the only water in the ponds is rainwater, the mud flats will no longer continue to contain as rich a food supply as they have in the past. However, biosolids are now being removed from the drying beds, so the plant will remain open at least through 1999. Gates will be locked daily at 5:30 P.M., and birders are asked to park well off the edge of the road so that the trucks will have a clear route. Birders also may be asked to sign a liability release. Be sure to exercise caution in driving the levees and roads, especially after rains.

River Legacy Park, containing 200 acres and more than 4 miles of trails, was donated to the City of Arlington in 1976. It is managed by the River Legacy Foundation, whose mission is "to preserve and enhance the forest floodplain . . . as an extraordinary natural, educational and recreational amenity." Eventually the park will be part of a continuous greenbelt along the Trinity River. The interpretive center offers an indoor nature exhibit tour for a fee of $3 for adults and $2 for children aged 2 to 18. Children under age two are free.

ADDITIONAL HELP

Location: Texas Official Highway Map grid J x 17; Tarrant County
Nearest food, gas, and lodging: All are available along Green Oaks Boulevard.
Nearest camping: Numerous sites in Arlington–Fort Worth.
Contact: Manager, Village Creek Wastewater Treatment Plant; River Legacy Foundation (See Appendix C).

45 Lewisville Lake Park and Fish Hatchery Road

Habitats: Lake, pond, mud flat, riparian, oak grove, pine grove, field, golf course
Key birds: Wood Duck is present year-round. Scissor-tailed Flycatcher, Indigo and Painted Buntings, Dickcissel, and Baltimore Oriole occur in summer. Common Loon, Horned and Eared Grebes, Osprey, Winter Wren, and Fox and Harris's Sparrows can usually be found in winter.
Best times to bird: April and May for spring migrants and nesting activities; November to March for winter birds

Birding strategies: The scattered groves of oaks and riparian habitat and fields along Sandy Beach Road (**A**) and Trout Line Road (**B**), within Lewisville Lake Park, can harbor a variety of migrants in spring and fall. A few of the neotropical migrants remain and nest: Yellow-billed Cuckoo, Great Crested and Scissor-tailed Flycatchers, Western and Eastern Kingbirds, Dickcissel, and Baltimore Oriole. Year-round residents to be expected along these routes include Northern Bobwhite, Mourning Dove, Downy Woodpecker, Eastern Phoebe, Blue Jay, American Crow, Carolina Chickadee, Tufted Titmouse, Carolina Wren, American Robin, Northern Mockingbird, Loggerhead Shrike, Northern Cardinal, and Common and Great-tailed Grackles. Black and Turkey Vultures, Red-tailed Hawk, Chimney Swift, Purple Martin, and Cliff and Barn Swallows usually can be found overhead.

Several water birds can be expected along the lakeshore or flying overhead in summer: Great Blue Heron, Great and Snowy Egrets, Yellow-crowned Night-Heron, Mallard, Killdeer, and an occasional gull (including Franklin's) or tern.

Mud flats are often present in the shallow bay (**C**) south of Sailboard Point. This area attracts numerous shorebirds during migration. Most numerous are Lesser Yellowlegs and Solitary, Spotted, Semipalmated, Western, Least, and Pectoral Sandpipers. Also watch for American Golden-Plover; Semipalmated Plover; American Avocet; Greater Yellowlegs; White-rumped, Baird's, and Stilt Sandpipers; Long-billed Dowitcher; and Common Snipe.

The lake supports a very different bird life in winter. Scope the lake from Sand Bass (**D**) or Hobie (**E**) points for Horned and Eared Grebes, American White Pelican, Double-crested Cormorant, Green-winged and Blue-winged Teal, Mallard, Northern Pintail, Northern Shoveler, Gadwall, American Wigeon, Ring-necked Duck, Lesser Scaup, Bufflehead, Ruddy Duck, and American Coot. Less numerous

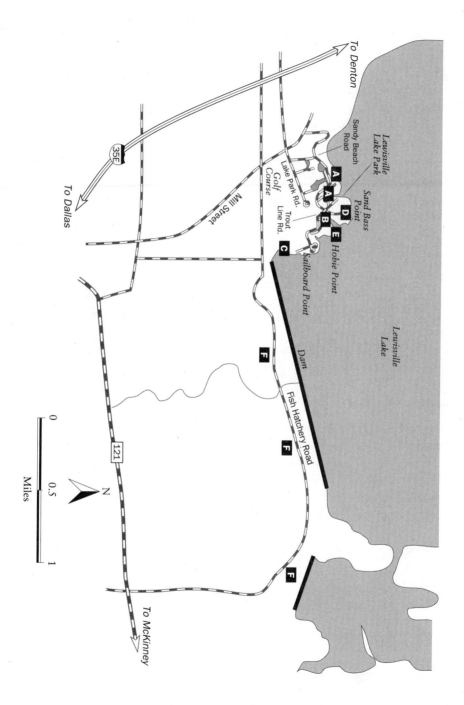

are Northern Pintail, Canvasback, Redhead, Greater Scaup, Common Goldeneye, and Hooded Merganser.

The Fish Hatchery Road (**F**), situated below the dam, contains a different environment. In summer look for Green Heron, Ruby-throated Hummingbird, Red-bellied Woodpecker, Northern Rough-winged Swallow, Blue-gray Gnatcatcher, Brown Thrasher, White-eyed Vireo, Northern Cardinal, and Indigo Bunting. In winter the brushy roadsides can harbor several other birds, including House and Winter Wrens; Eastern Towhee; Chipping, Field, Savannah, Fox, Song, Lincoln's, Swamp, White-throated, White-crowned, and Harris's Sparrows; Dark-eyed Junco; and American Goldfinch. Also in winter, check the ponds for ducks, Pied-billed Grebe, and Black-crowned Night-Heron. Sharp-shinned and Cooper's Hawks and American Kestrel can be seen as well.

Directions: Take the Valley Ridge Boulevard exit off I-35 to Mill Street and go north to Lake Park Road into Lewisville Lake Park. To get to Fish Hatchery Road, take North Mill Street south past the golf course and dam, then turn left onto Jones Road (Fish Hatchery Road).

General information: Lewisville Lake Park (a fee area open daily from 8 A.M. to 9 P.M.) can be extremely busy on weekends. This park is primarily a recreational area with baseball, soccer, and football fields and the Lake Park Golf Course. The adjacent Fish Hatchery Road, which runs below the dam for about a mile, offers excellent birding year-round. This area contains dense riparian woodlands, brushy roadsides, wetlands, and drier fields.

ADDITIONAL HELP

Location: Texas Official Travel Map grid H x 18; Denton County
Nearest food, gas, and lodging: Food and gas can be found along the entrance road; lodging can be found in Lewisville (2 miles).
Nearest camping: On-site (78 sites)
Contact: Lewisville Lake Park is operated by Lewisville Parks and Leisure Services (see Appendix C)

46 Plano Outdoor Learning Center

Habitats: Creek, riparian, bottomland hardwood forest, prairie, field
Key birds: Wood Duck and Barred Owl are present year-round. Indigo and Painted Bunting occur in spring and summer. Fox and Harris's Sparrows can usually be found in winter.
Best times to bird: April and May for spring migrants and nesting activities

Birding strategies: A loop route (from the learning center and mowed meadow, across the prairie into the woods, and along Rowlett Creek to where the trail loops back to the learning center) offers the widest variety of birds throughout the

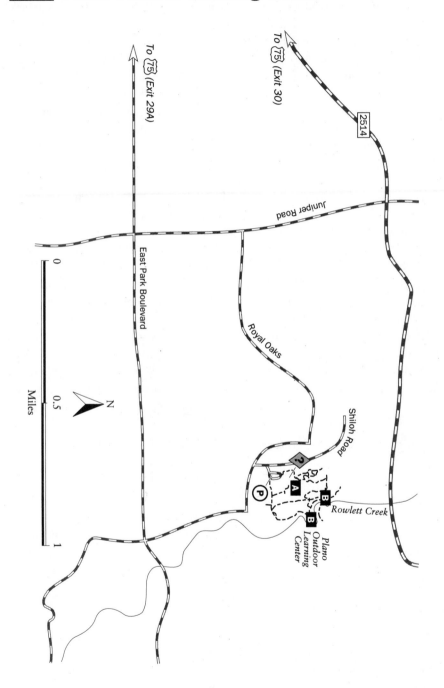

year. The mowed meadow and open prairie (**A**) are best in spring and summer for breeding birds such as Mourning Dove, Common Nighthawk at dawn and dusk, Eastern Phoebe, Scissor-tailed Flycatcher, Purple Martin, Barn Swallow, Blue Jay, American Crow, Eastern Bluebird, American Robin, Northern Mockingbird, Brown Thrasher, European Starling, Northern Cardinal, Painted Bunting, Eastern Meadowlark, Brown-headed Cowbird, Common Grackle, and House Finch. Indigo Bunting and Dickcissel are less numerous. In winter the brushy edges attract a number of seedeaters: Eastern Towhee; Chipping, Field, Vesper, Fox, Song, Lincoln's, Swamp, White-throated, White-crowned, and Harris's Sparrows; Dark-eyed Junco; and American Goldfinch.

The forest beyond, especially along Rowlett Creek (**B**), supports the widest variety of birds. This area can be exceptional during the spring migration, when large numbers of flycatchers, vireos, warblers, tanagers, grosbeaks, and orioles are moving northward. A number of the neotropical migrants remain and nest with the resident birds. This combined nesting fauna includes Green Heron; Red-shouldered, Broad-winged, and Red-tailed Hawks; Yellow-billed Cuckoo; Eastern Screech-Owl; Barred Owl; Ruby-throated Hummingbird; Red-headed, Red-bellied, Downy, and Hairy Woodpeckers; Eastern Wood-Pewee; Acadian and Great Crested Flycatchers; Carolina Chickadee; Tufted Titmouse; Carolina Wren; Blue-gray Gnatcatcher; Wood Thrush; Gray Catbird; White-eyed, Yellow-throated, Warbling, and Red-eyed Vireos; Northern Parula; Yellow-throated Warbler; and Summer Tanager. A few additional birds utilize these woods in winter: Yellow-bellied Sapsucker, Northern Flicker, Red-breasted and White-breasted Nuthatches, Winter Wren, Golden-crowned and Ruby-crowned Kinglets, Brown Creeper, Hermit Thrush, Cedar Waxwing, Orange-crowned and Yellow-rumped Warblers, Rusty Blackbird, Purple Finch, and Pine Siskin.

Directions: The center is located in the northeast section of the Dallas metroplex. Take exit 30 off US 75 in Plano. Follow Parker Road east to Juniper Road south to Royal Oaks, then east to Shiloh Road and north one block.

General information: The Plano Outdoor Learning Center, operated by the Plano Independent School District, is part of the city's larger Bob Woodruff Park in east Plano. Because it is a teaching center, the trails are heavily used by schoolchildren after 9 A.M.; therefore, birding should be done in the early mornings when school is in session. The relatively undisturbed condition of this bottomland hardwood forest habitat in the midst of an extremely fast-growing area makes the area unique.

ADDITIONAL HELP

Location: Texas Official Travel Map grid J x 18; Collin County
Nearest food, gas, and lodging: Plano has facilities for all three.
Nearest camping: Collin Park–Lavon Lake, at the end of Parker Road
Contact: Plano Outdoor Learning Center (see Appendix C)

47 White Rock Lake Park

Habitats: Lake, pond, creek, riparian, bottomland hardwood forest, spillway, lawn

Key birds: Wood Duck and Monk Parakeet are present year-round. Least Bittern, Scissor-tailed Flycatcher, Prothonotary Warbler, and Warbling Vireo occur in summer. American White Pelican, Fox and Harris's Sparrows, and Rusty Blackbird are found in winter.

Best times to bird: April and May for migrants and nesting activities; November to March for winter birds

Birding strategies: The mature bottomland hardwoods (**A**) to the north of the spillway are readily accessible by a series of trails and attract a wide range of neotropical migrants in both spring and fall; the spillway attracts waders and shorebirds year-round. A number of neotropical migrants remain and nest with the full-time residents in the woods. These include Red-shouldered Hawk, Yellow-billed Cuckoo, Eastern Screech-Owl, Barred Owl, Ruby-throated Hummingbird, Red-bellied and Downy Woodpeckers, Great Crested Flycatcher, Blue Jay, American Crow, Carolina Chickadee, Tufted Titmouse, Carolina Wren, Blue-gray Gnatcatcher, American Robin, European Starling, Warbling Vireo, Northern Cardinal, and Great-tailed and Common Grackles. The several ponds (old settling tanks) within the wooded tract attract a few additional birds in spring and summer: Least Bittern (irregular), Green Heron, Black-crowned and Yellow-crowned Night-Herons, Wood Duck, and Prothonotary Warbler (irregular). The spillway attracts all the resident swallows—Purple Martin and Northern Rough-winged, Cliff, and Barn—and Killdeer.

In winter the woods usually harbor Yellow-bellied Sapsucker, Northern Flicker, Brown Creeper, Winter Wren, Golden-crowned and Ruby-crowned Kinglets, Hermit Thrush, Orange-crowned and Yellow-rumped Warblers, Rusty Blackbird, and Pine Siskin. Winter seedeaters, including Spotted and Eastern Towhees; Chipping, Field, Fox, Song, Lincoln's, Swamp, White-throated, White-crowned, and Harris's Sparrows; and Dark-eyed Junco, prefer the brushy edges.

Beyond the woods is the old pump house (Dallas Water Works) and an open area (**B**), where Mourning Dove, Western and Eastern Kingbirds, Scissor-tailed Flycatcher, American Robin, Northern Mockingbird, Loggerhead Shrike, and House Finch can be expected. Monk Parakeet nests on the power poles. A similar open park area—Teepee Hill (**C**)—is worth checking across the lake on the north shore.

White Rock Lake (**D**) supports only a minimal number of water birds in spring and summer; scoping the lake from the dam is best, but there are numerous other possible viewing sites. Great Blue and Little Blue Herons, Great and Snowy Egrets, and Mallard are common, while Black-crowned and Yellow-crowned Night-Herons are less obvious. In winter, however, the lake attracts a much wider variety of water birds. Most numerous are Pied-billed Grebe, Double-crested Cormorant, Green-winged Teal, Mallard, Gadwall, American Wigeon, Ring-necked Duck,

47 White Rock Lake Park

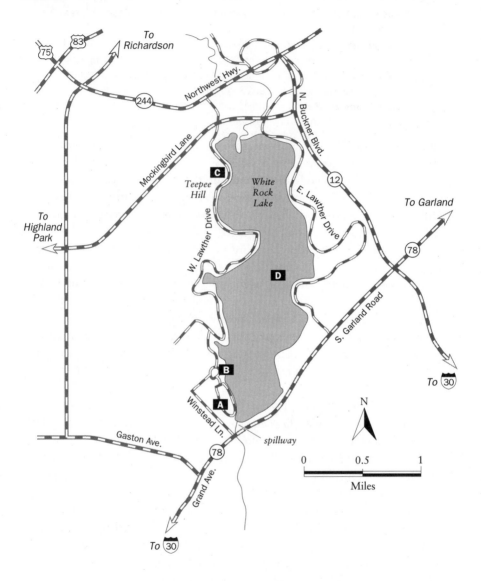

Lesser Scaup, and Ruddy Duck. Fewer numbers of Common Loon, Horned and Eared Grebe, American White Pelican, Northern Pintail, Northern Shoveler, Canvasback, Redhead, Greater Scaup, Common Goldeneye, Bufflehead, Hooded and Red-breasted Mergansers, American Coot, Bonaparte's and Ring-billed Gulls, and Forster's Tern can be expected. Watch also for Franklin's and Herring Gulls.

Records of Review Species: Trumpeter Swan, Dec–Jan 1989/90. Little Gull, Feb 1993. Black-legged Kittiwake, Nov 1990. Western Tanager, Dec 1995.

General information: The 1,119-acre lake, situated in White Rock Lake Park in northeast Dallas, is a popular boating (no motorized craft) lake. Although the wooded portion of the park still supports a good variety of birds, the general area has become a popular walking-biking-picnicking spot. Weekends can be especially busy! But the gradual spillway offers an excellent feeding site for shorebirds, waders, and occasional waterfowl throughout the year. The spillway area lies along South Garland Road, with parking off Winsted Lane. East and West Lawther drives are the two roads around the lake.

ADDITIONAL HELP

Location: Texas Official Travel Map grid J x 18; Dallas County
Nearest food, gas, and lodging: All are available at numerous sites in the immediate area.
Nearest camping: Numerous sites in northeast Dallas
Contact: Dallas Park and Recreation Department (see Appendix C).

48 Cedar Hill State Park and Dallas Nature Center

Habitats: Lake, pond, creek, juniper-hackberry woodland, mesquite grassland, prairie, field, cropland
Key birds: Greater Roadrunner and Eastern Bluebird are present year-round. Swainson's Hawk, Chuck-will's-widow, Ruby-throated and Black-chinned Hummingbirds, Scissor-tailed Flycatcher, Indigo and Painted Buntings, and Dickcissel occur in summer. Vesper, Fox, and Harris's Sparrows; Lapland Longspur; Rusty Blackbird (irregular); and Purple Finch can usually be found in winter.
Best times to bird: April and May for spring migrants and nesting activities; November to February for winter birds

Birding strategies: The Dallas Nature Center's 1.5-mile round-trip Cattail Pond Trail (**A**) and Cedar Hill State Park's 0.5-mile Pond Trail (**B**) offer similar birds year-round. Spring migrants, including a variety of flycatchers, vireos, warblers, tanagers, and orioles, can usually be found from early April to late May; many of these remain and nest with the year-round residents. Expected nesters along these trails include Red-tailed Hawk; Mourning Dove; Yellow-billed Cuckoo; Black-chinned Hummingbird; Red-bellied, Ladder-backed, and Downy Woodpeckers; Western and Eastern Kingbirds; Blue Jay; American Crow; Carolina Chickadee; Tufted Titmouse; Carolina and Bewick's Wrens; Blue-gray Gnatcatcher; Northern Mockingbird; White-eyed Vireo; Northern Cardinal; Indigo and Painted Buntings; Common Grackle; Brown-headed Cowbird; and Baltimore Oriole. Less numerous are Eastern Screech-Owl, Great Horned Owl, and Chuck-will's-widow. In riparian areas, watch for Green Heron, Great Crested Flycatcher, Warbling Vireo, and Summer Tanager.

48 Cedar Hill State Park and Dallas Nature Center

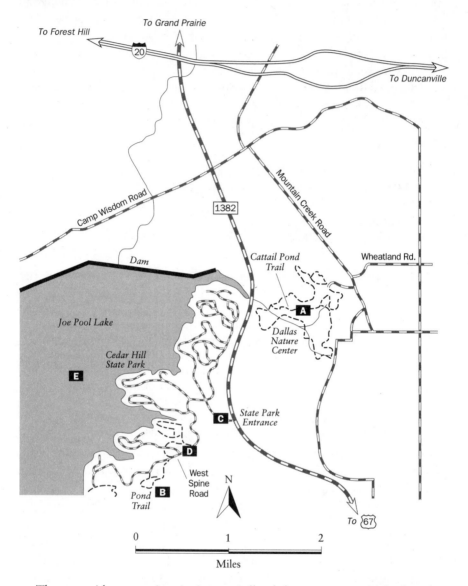

The open ridges contain a juniper woodland that once supported a breeding population of **Black-capped Vireo.** Although an individual is occasionally reported, a viable breeding population is now unlikely.

A few additional birds, though there is considerable species overlap, utilize open fields and edges such as those found along the park's entrance road (**C**) and West Spine Road (**D**). Summer residents here include Black and Turkey Vultures, Swainson's Hawk (irregular), Northern Bobwhite, Rock Dove, Greater Roadrunner, Common Nighthawk, Eastern Phoebe (especially at structures), Scissor-tailed

Flycatcher, Purple Martin, Cliff and Barn Swallows, Eastern Bluebird, Brown Thrasher, Loggerhead Shrike, Dickcissel, Lark Sparrow, Eastern Meadowlark, and Great-tailed Grackle.

These same areas can also harbor a variety of winter birds, especially when summer and fall rains have produced a weedy habitat. Expected species include Northern Harrier; American Kestrel; Horned Lark; Vesper, Savannah, Fox, Song, Lincoln's, White-throated, White-crowned, and Harris's Sparrows; and Dark-eyed Junco. Other less numerous winter birds include Sharp-shinned and Cooper's Hawks, House and Winter Wrens, Common Yellowthroat, Spotted Towhee, Swamp Sparrow, Lapland Longspur, and Rusty and Brewer's Blackbirds. Other winter birds that frequent the wooded areas include Northern Flicker, Brown Creeper, Golden-crowned and Ruby-crowned Kinglets, Hermit Thrush, Cedar Waxwing, Orange-crowned and Yellow-rumped Warblers, Purple Finch, and Pine Siskin.

An additional group of birds occurs along or over adjacent Joe Pool Lake (E). Only a few species occur year-round: Great Blue Heron, Great Egret, Wood Duck, Mallard, American Coot, Killdeer, and Belted Kingfisher. By midsummer post-nesting birds appear. Occasional mud flats attract shorebirds. A few ducks; Franklin's, Bonaparte's, Ring-billed, and Herring Gulls; and Caspian, Forster's, and Black Terns occur on or over the lake. Many of these remain throughout the winter. Bald Eagles also occur irregularly along the lake in winter.

Directions: From I-20 or US 67, take FM 1382 south or north, respectively, to Cedar Hill State Park. The adjacent Dallas Nature Center can be reached from the state park via FM 1382 north and Camp Wisdom Road to the entrance on Mountain Creek Parkway. From I-20, take the Cedar Ridge Road exit south to Wheatland Road. Turn west (right) and go to the entrance.

General information: The 1,810-acre state park, which lies along the northeastern edge of Joe Pool Lake, opened in 1992. The park lies in the rugged chain of wooded hills known as the Cedar Mountains, and is less than an hour from either Dallas or Fort Worth. The 630-acre Dallas Nature Center is a nonprofit organization, funded by donations and grants, designed to foster a greater appreciation and understanding of the natural environment through conservation, education, recreation, and research. The center provides regularly scheduled guided walks, weekend outdoor education programs, and school/youth group field trips.

ADDITIONAL HELP

Location: Texas Official Travel Map grid K x 18; Dallas County
Nearest food, gas, and lodging: All are available along FM 1382 and Mountain Creek Parkway (1 to 2 miles).
Nearest camping: On-site at Cedar Hills State Park (355 sites)
Contact: Superintendent, Cedar Hills State Park; Director, Dallas Nature Center (see Appendix C)

49 Southside Water Treatment Plant

Habitats: Pond, mud flat, field, cropland
Key birds: Wood Duck and Greater Roadrunner are present year-round. Wood Stork, Black-bellied Whistling-Duck, Common Moorhen, Least Tern, Scissor-tailed Flycatcher, and Dickcissel occur in summer. American White Pelican, Cinnamon Teal, Redhead, and Hooded Merganser can usually be found in winter.
Best times to bird: mid-March to May for spring migrants, July through October for fall migrants, and November to February for winter birds

Birding strategies: Dallas's Southside Water Treatment Plant offers the birder a wide array of birds year-round, in spite of the small size of this area. Only slightly more than a mile square, it is possible to drive or walk the circumference levee as well as several inner levees. A few birds, including Pied-billed Grebe, Great Blue Heron, Cattle Egret, Wood Duck, American Coot, Killdeer, Rock Dove, American Crow, European Starling, Great-tailed and Common Grackles, and Red-winged Blackbird, can be expected around the ponds at all seasons. Red-tailed Hawk, Northern Bobwhite, Northern Mockingbird, and Eastern Meadowlark can usually be found in the adjacent fields year-round.

The mud flats attract shorebirds in both spring and fall. Lesser Yellowlegs and Solitary, Spotted, Semipalmated, Western, Least, and Pectoral Sandpipers can be

Pond at Southside Water Treatment Plant in the Greater Dallas area.

49 Southside Water Treatment Plant

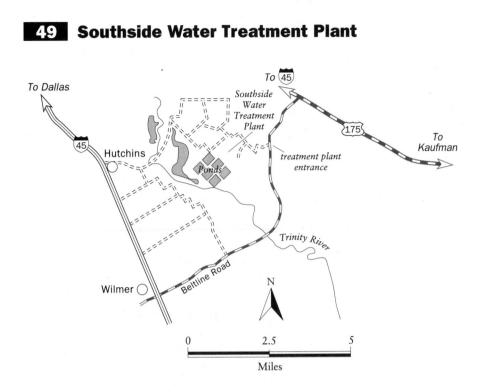

expected. Less abundant are American Golden-Plover; Semipalmated Plover; American Avocet; Greater Yellowlegs; White-rumped, Baird's, Stilt, and Buff-breasted Sandpipers; Long-billed Dowitcher; Common Snipe; and Wilson's Phalarope.

Summer resident birds can include Great, Snowy, and Cattle Egrets; a number of lingering ducks; Black-bellied Whistling-Duck; Common Moorhen; Black-necked Stilt; Least Tern (nests on levee); Eastern Kingbird; Scissor-tailed Flycatcher; Barn Swallow; and Dickcissel.

In winter, typical birds at the ponds include Pied-billed and Eared Grebes; American White Pelican; Double-crested Cormorant; Great Blue Heron; Great Egret; Canada Goose; Wood Duck; Green-winged Teal; Mallard; Northern Pintail; Northern Shoveler; Gadwall; American Wigeon; Canvasback; Ring-necked Duck; Lesser Scaup; Common Goldeneye; Bufflehead; Hooded Merganser; Ruddy Duck; American Coot; Killdeer; Spotted Sandpiper; Least Sandpiper; Common Snipe; Bonaparte's and Ring-billed Gulls; Forster's Tern; and Belted Kingfisher. In adjacent fields expect Rock and Mourning Doves, American Crow, Northern Mockingbird, European Starling, Yellow-rumped Warbler, Northern Cardinal, Red-winged Blackbird, Great-tailed and Common Grackles, Brown-headed Cowbird, House Finch, and American Goldfinch. Also, watch in winter for the occasional Bald Eagle around the ponds and for Lapland Longspur during harsh winters in the fields.

Records of Review Species: Eurasian Wigeon, Oct 1993.

Directions: From I-30, take I-45 south to US 175; go south until you pass under I-20; then take the third exit onto Beltline Road west. Follow Beltline for about 2 miles to the water treatment plant entrance gates.

General information: Birders are welcome so long as they act responsibly. The area consists of multiple ponds at various stages of operation. Some ponds contain open water (at various depths), while others are little more than sludge. Weekdays are better for visits, as the gates are often closed on weekends.

ADDITIONAL HELP

Location: Texas Official Travel Map grid K x 18; Dallas County
Nearest food, gas, and lodging: All are available in the vicinity.
Nearest camping: Several sites along I-20 and I-45
Contact: City of Dallas (see Appendix C)

50 Cooper Lake and Cooper Lake State Park

Habitats: Lake, pond, river, creek, riparian, marsh, oak woodland, grassland, field, pasture, cropland
Key birds: Wood and Mottled Ducks, Red-headed and Pileated Woodpeckers, and Brown-headed Nuthatch are present year-round. Neotropic Cormorant; Anhinga; Least Bittern; White and White-faced Ibis; Wood Stork; Chuck-will's-widow; Scissor-tailed Flycatcher; Bell's Vireo; Yellow-throated, Black-and-white, Prothonotary, and Kentucky Warblers; Indigo and Painted Buntings; and Dickcissel occur in summer. Hooded and Red-breasted Mergansers; Osprey; Bald Eagle; LeConte's, Fox, and Harris's Sparrows; McCown's, Lapland, Smith's, and Chestnut-collared Longspurs; and Rusty Blackbird can usually be found in winter.
Best times to bird: April and May for spring migrants and nesting activities; November to March for winter birds

Birding strategies: In summer the woodland and old field habitats of the Doctor's Creek (**A**) and South Sulphur Park (**B**) units of the state park support a variety of birds. Common species include Mississippi Kite; Red-shouldered and Broad-winged Hawks; Northern Bobwhite; Mourning Dove; Ruby-throated Hummingbird; Red-headed, Red-bellied, Downy, and Pileated Woodpeckers; Eastern Wood-Pewee; Acadian and Great Crested Flycatchers; Eastern Kingbird; Blue Jay; American and Fish Crows; Carolina Chickadee; Tufted Titmouse; White-breasted Nuthatch; Carolina Wren; Blue-gray Gnatcatcher; American Robin; Northern Mockingbird; Red-eyed Vireo; Northern Parula; Yellow-throated, Pine, Black-and-white, and Kentucky Warblers; Summer Tanager; Northern Cardinal; Blue Grosbeak; Indigo and Painted Buntings; Field, Lark, and Grasshopper Sparrows; Eastern Meadowlark; Common Grackle; and Brown-headed Cowbird. Less numerous are Eastern

50 Cooper Lake and Cooper Lake State Park

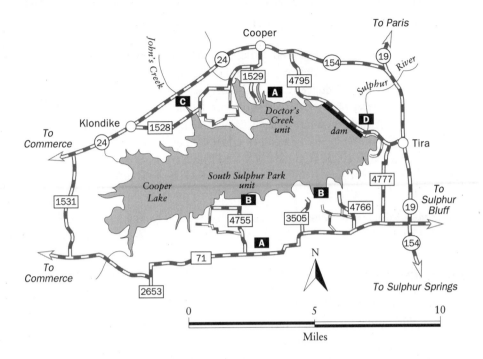

Screech-Owl, Great Horned and Barred Owls, Chuck-will's-widow, and Prairie Warbler.

John's Creek (**C**), including the adjacent areas on SH 24 and FM 1528 and the boat ramp area, and the Cooper Lake Dam area (**D**), including the lake, Sulphur River wetlands, adjacent field, and juniper woodlands, support several additional species in summer. These include Anhinga; Great Blue, Little Blue, and Green Herons; Great and Snowy Egrets; Yellow-crowned Night-Heron; White and White-faced Ibis; Wood and Mottled Ducks; Common Moorhen; Killdeer; Yellow-billed Cuckoo; Belted Kingfisher; Prothonotary Warbler; Louisiana Waterthrush; and Red-winged Blackbird.

John's Creek (**C**) and Game Preserve is a tiny strip of land along the John's Creek inlet, but it has a rich diversity of habitats. It can be exceptional during migration; the oak mottes serve as an effective migrant trap for Gray-cheeked Thrush; Bell's Vireo; Blue-winged, Golden-winged, Blackpoll, and Bay-breasted Warblers; and Bullock's Oriole. In summer look for Eastern Wood-Pewee, White-breasted Nuthatch, and Summer Tanager in the oaks; White-eyed Vireo and Painted Bunting in brushy sites; and Prothonotary Warbler near the water.

Check John's Creek just above the FM 1528 causeway. Waders can be common here year-round, and Neotropic Cormorant in summer and fall; Tricolored Heron, White Ibis, Roseate Spoonbill, and Wood Stork in late summer; and geese, ducks, and shorebirds during migration and in winter, depending on the water level. The nearby fields (to the east) sometimes contain hundreds of ducks, and may support Mountain Plover in March and Horned Lark, American Pipit, and Lapland Longspur in winter.

Watch overhead for Black and Turkey Vultures; Red-tailed Hawk; American Kestrel; Common Nighthawk at dawn and dusk; Chimney Swift; Purple Martin; and Northern Rough-winged, Cliff, and Barn Swallows.

The open water of Cooper Lake is almost devoid of birds in summer. Exceptions include American White Pelican; Ring-billed Gull; and Caspian, Forster's, Least, and Black Terns. By September and October, however, Common Loon, Horned and Eared Grebes, American White Pelican, Surf Scoter, and Bald Eagle appear. One of the best viewing areas is from the dam, although parking is available only below the dam.

Records of Review Species: Little Gull, Feb 1993, Dec 1996. Black-headed Gull, Feb–March 1996, Oct 1996. Thayer's Gull, Dec–Feb 1994/95. Sooty Tern, Aug 1995. Red Phalarope, May 1996.

Directions: From Sulphur Springs, take SH 154 north for 14 miles to FM 4795, which crosses the dam. (Do not park on the dam; use the adjacent Tira Boat Ramp parking.) The Doctor's Creek unit is 4.5 miles beyond (or 10 miles north of Sulphur Springs). Turn west onto FM 71 to FM 3505 and the South Sulphur Park unit. From Commerce, take FM 24 east to Cooper, then go 1 mile east on SH 154 to FM 1529. Drive south for 2 miles on FM 1529 to the Doctor's Creek Park unit.

General information: The 19,280-acre Cooper Lake (impoundment began in fall 1991) was built for flood control, water supply, and recreation, and is managed by the U.S. Army Corps of Engineers. Cooper Lake State Park (opened in 1996) contains two units: the 466-acre Doctor's Creek unit, with 6.2 miles of shoreline, and the 2,560-acre South Sulphur Park unit, with 25.5 miles of shoreline. Both sites provide boat ramps, a swimming beach, playgrounds, and hiking trails.

ADDITIONAL HELP

Location: Texas Official Travel Map grid H x 20; Delta and Hopkins counties

Nearest food, gas, and lodging: Food and gas are at Birthright (junction of FM 71 and FM 19, 5 miles from Cooper Lake Dam). The nearest lodging is in Sulphur Springs (15 miles from the dam) or Commerce (24 miles from the dam).

Nearest camping: On-site in both state park units: Doctor's Creek with 42 and South Sulphur with 87 sites

Contact: Lake Manager, Cooper Dam Project; Superintendent, Cooper Lake State Park (see Appendix C)

Habitats: Lake, river, creek, riparian, mud flat, bottomland hardwood forest, oak savannah, field, pasture, cropland, rock dam face, spillway

Key birds: Wood and Mottled Ducks, Crested Caracara, Greater Roadrunner, and Pileated Woodpecker are present year-round. Wood Stork, Chuck-will's-widow, Scissor-tailed Flycatcher, Prothonotary and Kentucky Warblers, Louisiana Waterthrush, Grasshopper Sparrow, and Indigo and Painted Buntings occur in summer. Pacific and Common Loons; Bald Eagle; American Woodcock; Sprague's Pipit; Sedge Wren; Fox, LeConte's, and Harris's Sparrows; and Lapland and Smith's Longspurs can usually be found in winter.

Best times to bird: Late April and May for migrants, late summer for post-nesting wanderers, and late November to early February for Smith's Longspur and vagrants

Birding strategies: To find the most species, circle the southern half of the lake, starting below Iron Bridge Dam at the outflow along FM 47 (**A**). Park in the paved lot south of the highway and walk the track along the south bank of the Sabine River. This route offers wetland and brush-loving birds along the river and forest birds to the south. Summer species include Great Blue, Little Blue, and Green Herons; Great and Cattle Egrets; Wood and Mottled Ducks; Red-shouldered Hawk; Northern Bobwhite; Mourning Dove; Yellow-billed Cuckoo; Chuck-will's-widow; Ruby-throated Hummingbird; Red-bellied, Downy, and Pileated Woodpeckers; Eastern Wood-Pewee; Acadian, Great Crested, and Scissor-tailed Flycatchers; Eastern Phoebe; Eastern Kingbird; Cliff and Barn Swallows; Carolina Chickadee; Tufted Titmouse; Carolina Wren; Blue-gray Gnatcatcher; American Robin; Northern Mockingbird; Brown Thrasher; White-eyed and Red-eyed Vireos; Black-and-white, Prothonotary, and Kentucky Warblers; Louisiana Waterthrush; and Indigo and Painted Buntings.

Look for water birds from atop the dam (**B**), accessible through the fenced Sabine River Authority compound at the north end of the dam (open from 8 A.M. to 4:30 P.M. on weekdays; stop at the office for entry permission). Waders and a few shorebirds can usually be found year-round. Spring and fall migration can be exceptional if water levels allow for mud flats; 30 species of shorebirds have been reported. Also seen are American White Pelican, Double-crested Cormorant, White and White-faced Ibis, Roseate Spoonbill, numerous ducks, King Rail, and Sora.

Some of the most interesting birds occur here in winter. Watch for Bald Eagle over and along the lakeshore, and water birds on the lake, including Pacific and Common Loons, Horned Grebe, Red-breasted Merganser, and Common Goldeneye. A scope and warm clothing are essential in winter.

Bird the open grasslands east of the dam and in and around the compound (**C**). Smith's Longspur is occasional in winter, while American Kestrel; Loggerhead Shrike; Vesper, Savannah, and LeConte's Sparrows; and Eastern and Western

51 Lake Tawakoni

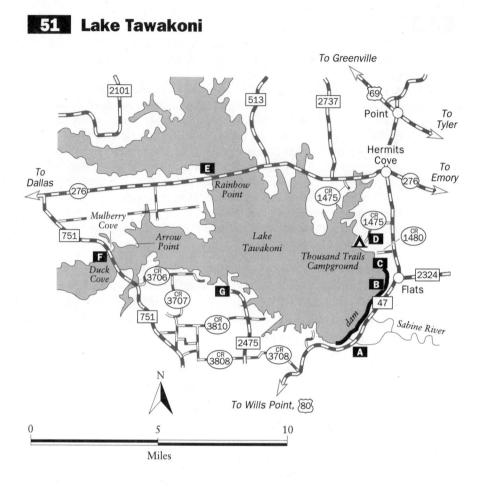

To Greenville

2101

513

2737

69

Point

To Tyler

Hermits Cove

E

To Dallas

276

Rainbow Point

CR 1475

To Emory

276

Mulberry Cove

CR 1475

CR 1480

751

Arrow Point

Lake Tawakoni

D

Thousand Trails Campground

C

2324

F

Duck Cove

CR 3706

B

Flats

CR 3707

G

47

Sabine River

751

CR 3810

dam

2475

CR 3708

A

CR 3808

N

To Wills Point, 80

0   5   10

Miles

Meadowlarks are common. The best bet for Smith's Longspur is a short distance north; turn off SH 47 onto CR 1475 and continue to where it dead-ends at a small turnaround at the entrance of the Thousand Trails Campground. Park and cross the fence into the open field (**D**) to the left; birders have permission to walk into the field (owned by the Dallas County Audubon Society). The little wooded cove on the far eastern side contains a small patch of bluestem grasses, good for wintering Sedge Wren and LeConte's Sparrow.

Continue counterclockwise via FM 47, SH 276, and FM 751 around the lake back to FM 47. This route offers numerous open fields and woodlands and several additional lake views. Field and wire birds in summer may include American Kestrel; Mourning Dove; Greater Roadrunner (rare); Common Nighthawk; Eastern Phoebe; Western and Eastern Kingbirds; Scissor-tailed Flycatcher; Purple Martin; Northern Rough-winged, Cliff, and Barn Swallows; American Crow; Eastern Bluebird; Loggerhead Shrike; Indigo Bunting; Dickcissel; Field and Grasshopper Sparrows; Red-winged Blackbird; Eastern Meadowlark; Great-tailed and Common Grackles;

Lake Tawakoni from atop Iron Bridge Dam.

and Brown-headed Cowbird. House Finch is often present in fall and winter. Great White-fronted, Snow, Ross's, and Canada Geese; Northern Harrier; House and Sedge Wrens; American and Sprague's Pipits; Eastern and Spotted Towhees; Vesper, LeConte's, Fox, Song, Lincoln's, Swamp, White-throated, White-crowned, and Harris's Sparrows; and Brewer's Blackbird can be seen in winter.

Stop and check the water birds at Rainbow Point (**E**), at the west side of the Tawakoni Causeway (along SH 276), and also Mulberry and Duck coves (**F**), both along FM 751 near Arrow Point. When the lake level is low, these sites offer good mud flats for shorebirds.

Records of Review Species: Red-throated Loon, Nov–March 1993/94, Dec–Jan 1994/95. Pacific Loon, April–May 1990, Dec–Feb 1992/93, Nov 1994. Red-necked Grebe, Nov–March 1992/93. Harlequin Duck, Jan 1995. Parasitic Jaeger, Aug 1996. Long-tailed Jaeger, Nov 1996. Common Black-headed Gull, Dec 1995. Black-legged Kittiwake, Dec 1995. Sabine's Gull, Dec 1994, Aug 1996.

Directions: From Wills Point (on US 80), take FM 47 northeast for 10 miles to the dam. From Greenville (on I-30), take US 69 southeast for 18 miles to Point, then go south on FM 47 for 7 miles to the dam.

General information: The 36,700-acre Lake Tawakoni, one of the state's larger manmade reservoirs, is one of the two Sabine River Authority impoundments on the main stem of the Sabine River. The river begins in north-central Texas and eventually flows into the Gulf of Mexico near Orange. Iron Bridge Dam, including the spillway, is 5.5 miles long; access is available on weekdays from 8 A.M. to 4:30 P.M.

Lake Tawakoni State Park, located on the south shore off SH 2475, is in the development stage. Nearby Wills Point, advertised as the bluebird capital of America, sponsors an annual Bluebird Festival the second weekend of April.

ADDITIONAL HELP

Location: Texas Official Travel Map grid J x 19; Van Zandt, Hunt, and Rains counties

Nearest food, gas, and lodging: Food and gas are available at Stephen's Corner (intersection of FM 47 and SH 276), 2 miles north of the dam; lodging is available in Wills Point and Greenville.

Nearest camping: On-site at Arm Point, Que Pasa, and Wind Point parks (159 sites total)

Contact: Sabine River Authority, Lake Tawakoni (see Appendix C)

52 Lake Brownwood State Park

Habitats: Lake, oak savannah, mesquite grassland, field, pasture, cropland

Key birds: Wild Turkey, Greater Roadrunner, Cactus Wren, Canyon Towhee, and Rufous-crowned Sparrow are present year-round. Mississippi Kite, Black-chinned Hummingbird, Scissor-tailed Flycatcher, and Painted Bunting occur in summer. Common Loon, Osprey, Sandhill Crane, **Golden-fronted Woodpecker,** Lark Bunting, and Harris's Sparrow can usually be found in winter.

Best times to bird: Mid-April through May for spring migrants and nesting activities

Birding strategies: The park entrance and adjacent Texas Oak Trail (**A**) offer a mixture of mesquite grassland and oak savannah habitats, where full-time residents include Wild Turkey; Northern Bobwhite; Mourning and Inca Doves; Greater Roadrunner; Eastern Screech-Owl; Great Horned Owl; Black-chinned Hummingbird; Ladder-backed Woodpecker; Eastern Phoebe; Blue Jay; Carolina Chickadee; Tufted Titmouse; Cactus, Carolina, and Bewick's Wrens; Eastern Bluebird; Loggerhead Shrike; European Starling; Northern Cardinal; Canyon Towhee; Rufous-crowned Sparrow; and Eastern Meadowlark. In summer look for Mississippi Kite, Common Nighthawk, Chimney Swift, Ash-throated and Scissor-tailed Flycatchers, Western Kingbird, Purple Martin, Barn Swallow, Blue-gray Gnatcatcher, Painted Bunting, and Common Grackle. And in winter expect

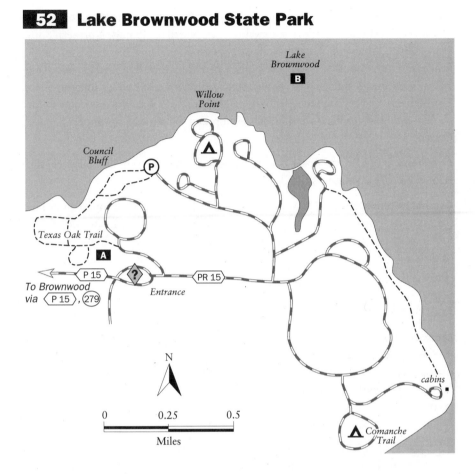

Red-tailed Hawk, American Kestrel, Yellow-bellied Sapsucker, Northern Flicker, American Crow, Ruby-crowned Kinglet, American Robin, Cedar Waxwing, Orange-crowned and Yellow-rumped Warblers, and American Goldfinch.

The brushy fields and edges also support wintering Spotted Towhee; Chipping, Field, Vesper, Song, White-crowned, and Harris's Sparrows; and Dark-eyed Junco. Sharp-shinned and Cooper's Hawks, **Golden-fronted Woodpecker,** Brown Creeper, Golden-crowned Kinglet, Hermit Thrush, Pyrrhuloxia, Lark Bunting, Western Meadowlark, and Pine Siskin are less numerous.

Scan the lake (**B**) from the boat ramps at Council Bluff, Willow Point, behind Beach Lodge, and Comanche Trail. Only Pied-billed Grebe, Double-crested Cormorant, Great Blue Heron, Mallard, and Killdeer can be expected year-round.

Great and Snowy Egrets and Green Heron usually are present in summer. In winter Horned and Eared Grebes, Canada Goose, Northern Pintail, Northern Shoveler, Gadwall, American Wigeon, Redhead, Ring-necked Duck, Lesser Scaup, Bufflehead, American Coot, Spotted Sandpiper, Common Snipe, Bonaparte's and Ring-billed Gulls, and Forster's Tern frequent the area. Common Loon, Cinnamon Teal, Canvasback, Osprey, Greater Yellowlegs, and Forster's Tern are less dependable.

In winter the croplands and fields surrounding the park often support Sandhill Crane.

Directions: From Brownwood, take SH 279 northwest for 16 miles to PR 15; turn right. The park entrance is 6 miles ahead.

General information: This 568-acre state park is located on a hilltop, overlooking the lake and surrounding hills, on the western edge of Lake Brownwood. The 8,000-acre reservoir contains impounded waters from two of the main tributaries of the Colorado River. The park offers 2.75 miles of hiking trails, boating, water sports, and fishing. There is a lighted fishing pier.

ADDITIONAL HELP

Location: Texas Official Travel Map grid M x 14; Brown County
Nearest food, gas, and lodging: The nearest food is at Park's Place (7 miles). Gas is available at Cross Roads (1 mile); cabins are available on-site.
Nearest camping: On-site (87 sites)
Contact: Superintendent, Lake Brownwood State Park (see Appendix C)

53 Dinosaur Valley State Park

Habitats: River, riparian, bottomland hardwood forest, juniper woodland, field
Key birds: Wild Turkey, Greater Roadrunner, Canyon Wren, Rufous-crowned Sparrow, and Lesser Goldfinch are present year-round. Common Poorwill, Chuck-will's-widow, Black-chinned Hummingbird, Scissor-tailed Flycatcher, **Black-capped Vireo, Golden-cheeked Warbler,** Painted Bunting, and Dickcissel occur in summer. LeConte's, Fox, and Harris's Sparrows can usually be found in winter.
Best times to bird: Mid-March through June for finding **Black-capped Vireo** and **Golden-cheeked Warbler.**

Birding strategies: Both the **Black-capped Vireo** and **Golden-cheeked Warbler** occur on the wooded plateau across the Paluxy River; wading is necessary during high water. Longhorn Pasture (**A**), across the river from Dinosaur Track Site 3, is best for finding **Black-capped Vireo**, while the Denio Creek Trail (**B**), most accessible from the Cedar Brake Trail, is best for **Golden-cheeked Warbler.** Other summer birds to be expected in this juniper woodland include Mourning Dove; Black-chinned Hummingbird; Ladder-backed Woodpecker; Scissor-tailed Flycatcher; Blue

53 Dinosaur Valley State Park

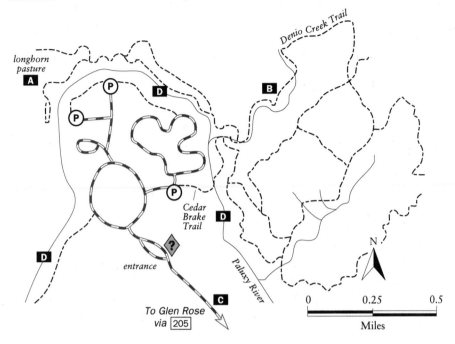

Jay; American Crow; Carolina Chickadee; Tufted Titmouse; Bewick's Wren; Blue-gray Gnatcatcher; Northern Mockingbird; Loggerhead Shrike; Black-and-white Warbler; Northern Cardinal; Painted Bunting; Rufous-crowned, Field, and Lark Sparrows; and Brown-headed Cowbird. Less numerous birds here include Wild Turkey, Eastern Screech-Owl, Great Horned Owl, Canyon Wren (at rocky outcrops), Brown Thrasher, Cassin's Sparrow (irregular), Orchard Oriole, and Lesser Goldfinch.

The old fields, such as those along the entrance road (**C**), harbor a few additional birds in summer, although there is some overlap with the woodlands. Northern Bobwhite, Killdeer, Greater Roadrunner, Dickcissel, and Eastern Meadowlark prefer the open fields. Black and Turkey Vultures, Red-tailed Hawk, Common Nighthawk at dusk and dawn, Chimney Swift, and Northern Rough-winged, Cliff, and Barn Swallows can often be seen overhead.

The riparian habitat along the river (**D**) supports a number of additional birds in summer: Great Blue and Green Herons, Yellow-billed Cuckoo, Chuck-will's-widow, Belted Kingfisher, Red-bellied Woodpecker, Great Crested Flycatcher, Eastern Kingbird, Carolina Wren, White-eyed and Bell's Vireos, Yellow-breasted Chat, Summer Tanager, and Bullock's Oriole. Common Poorwills can often be heard calling at dusk and dawn from the riverbanks or from along CR 1007, on the park's western border, accessible from FM 205. The river, especially when mud flats are present after heavy rains, can attract shorebirds in migration.

In winter, an occasional water bird, such as Mallard, Green-winged Teal, or Gadwall, can be found. Northern Harrier and Sharp-shinned and Cooper's Hawks occur regularly. Look in the riparian habitat or along the weedy edges for Winter Wren; Golden-crowned and Ruby-crowned Kinglets; Hermit Thrush; American Robin; Cedar Waxwing; Yellow-rumped Warbler; Spotted Towhee; Vesper, Savannah, LeConte's, Fox, Song, Lincoln's, White-throated, White-crowned, and Harris's Sparrows; Dark-eyed Junco; and American Goldfinch.

Directions: The park entrance is 4 miles west of Glen Rose via US 67 west and FM 205.

General information: This 1,523-acre park, a designated National Natural Landmark, was established primarily to protect the abundance of dinosaur tracks exposed in the riverbed of the Paluxy River, a tributary of the Brazos River. The bedrock consists of eastward-dipping limestones, sandstones, and mudstones deposited from 110 to 105 million years ago along the shorelines of an ancient sea.

Black-capped Vireo and **Golden-cheeked Warbler** are monitored annually, and the park staff can provide up-to-date information on the best sites to see these two endangered species. Take care not to disturb them!

ADDITIONAL HELP

Location: Texas Highway Map L x 16; Somervell County
Nearest food, gas, and lodging: All three can be found at Glen Rose (5 miles).
Nearest camping: On-site (46 sites)
Contact: Superintendent, Dinosaur Valley State Park (see Appendix C)

54 Cleburne State Park

Habitats: Lake, creek, riparian, juniper-oak woodland, oak savannah, field

Key birds: Wild Turkey, Greater Roadrunner, and Rufous-crowned Sparrow are present year-round. Wood Duck, Common Poorwill, Scissor-tailed Flycatcher, and Indigo and Painted Buntings occur in summer. Osprey, Mountain Bluebird, and Fox and Harris's Sparrows can usually be found in winter.

Best times to bird: April and May for spring migrants and nesting activities

Birding strategies: The north end (A) of Cedar Lake supports the park's greatest bird diversity. This area is good for migrating songbirds, a number of which remain and nest with the year-round residents. Migrants and residents include Red-shouldered Hawk; Yellow-billed Cuckoo; Chuck-will's-widow; Black-chinned Hummingbird; Red-bellied and Downy Woodpeckers; Great Crested Flycatcher;

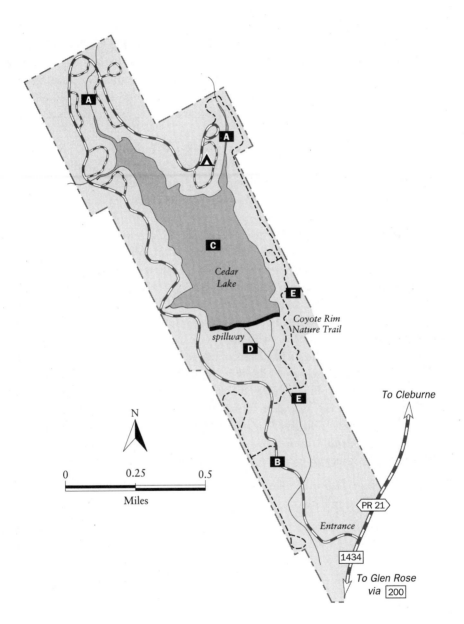

Blue Jay; Carolina Chickadee; Tufted Titmouse; Carolina Wren; Blue-gray Gnat-catcher; White-eyed, Yellow-throated, and Red-eyed Vireos; Summer Tanager; Northern Cardinal; and Red-winged Blackbird.

The oak savannah, fields, and edges, such as those along the entrance road (**B**), also attract a variety of summer birds: Northern Bobwhite; Rock, Mourning, and Inca Doves; Greater Roadrunner; Great Horned Owl; Ladder-backed Woodpecker; Eastern Phoebe, especially near buildings; Scissor-tailed Flycatcher; American Crow; Northern Mockingbird; Eastern Bluebird; American Robin; Loggerhead Shrike; Field and Lark Sparrows; Eastern Meadowlark; and Brown-headed Cowbird. Look for Common Poorwills on the roads at night.

The open areas are good for observing Black and Turkey Vultures; Red-tailed Hawk; Common Nighthawk; Chimney Swift; Purple Martin; and Northern Rough-winged, Cliff, and Barn Swallows in summer. Broad-winged Hawks can be numerous in September and October. Watch for Northern Harrier, American Kestrel, and Mountain Bluebird in winter.

The lake (**C**) and creeks (**D**) attract a few migrating water birds in spring and fall, but only a handful of species can be expected at other times with any certainty. Great Blue, Little Blue, and Green Herons; Great and Snowy Egrets; Mallard; and Wood Duck occur in summer. Watch for Eared Grebe, Canada Goose, Green-winged and Blue-winged Teal, Northern Pintail, Gadwall, Ring-necked Duck, Lesser Scaup, Hooded Merganser, Bufflehead, Ruddy Duck, Osprey, American Coot, and Spotted Sandpiper in winter.

A major portion of the park consists of juniper woodland, which also supports a variety of birds. In summer hike the Coyote Rim Nature Trail (**E**) from the campground to the spillway for Black-chinned Hummingbird; Ladder-backed Woodpecker; Carolina Chickadee; Tufted Titmouse; Bewick's and Canyon Wrens; Blue-gray Gnatcatcher; Black-and-white Warbler; Northern Cardinal; Indigo and Painted Buntings; and Rufous-crowned, Field, and Lark Sparrows. In winter, numerous sparrows, including Fox and Harris's, can usually be found.

Directions: From Cleburne, take US 67 west for 4 miles to PR 21. The park entrance is another 6 miles to the southwest.

General information: The 528-acre park, located in the White Rock Hills, contains a 116-acre lake of clear, clean water, flowing from 3 natural springs beneath the lake. It is a quiet park, good for early morning walks. Named for Confederate general Pat Cleburne, the park was built by the Civilian Conservation Corps in the late 1930s.

ADDITIONAL HELP

Location: Texas Official Travel Map grid L x 17; Johnson County
Nearest food, gas, and lodging: Facilities for all three can be found in Cleburne (10 miles).
Nearest camping: On-site (58 sites)
Contact: Superintendent, Cleburne State Park (see Appendix C)

55 Meridian State Park

Habitats: Lake, pond, riparian, juniper woodland, field
Key birds: Wood Duck, Wild Turkey, Greater Roadrunner, and Rufous-crowned Sparrow are present year-round. Chuck-will's-widow, Black-chinned Hummingbird, Scissor-tailed Flycatcher, **Golden-cheeked Warbler,** Painted Bunting, and Dickcissel occur in summer. Fox and Harris's Sparrows can usually be found in winter.
Best times to bird: Mid-March to early July for **Golden-cheeked Warbler**

Birding strategies: Golden-cheeked Warbler can most readily be seen on Shinnery Ridge (**A**). Take the paved trail for about half a mile beyond the parking area to a bench on the left, marking the territory of a pair of breeding birds. Additional Golden-cheeks occur along this 1.6-mile loop trail, as well as across the lake along the Little Springs Nature Trail (**B**), Little Forest Junior Trail (**C**), and the Bosque Hiking Trail (**D**). The endangered warblers are monitored by the park, so up-to-date information on the best sites to find these birds can be obtained at park headquarters.

In summer the prevailing juniper woodland harbors Mourning Dove; Black-chinned Hummingbird; Ladder-backed Woodpecker; Western Kingbird; Scissor-tailed Flycatcher; Blue Jay; American Crow; Carolina Chickadee; Tufted Titmouse; Bewick's Wren; Blue-gray Gnatcatcher; Northern Mockingbird; Northern Cardinal; Painted Bunting; Chipping and Lark Sparrows; and Brown-headed Cowbird. Other less numerous birds include Wild Turkey, Northern Bobwhite, Greater Roadrunner, Great Horned Owl, Loggerhead Shrike, Black-and-white Warbler, Blue Grosbeak, Dickcissel, Rufous-crowned Sparrow, and Orchard Oriole.

The open water areas, including the lake (**E**) and Bee Creek below the dam (**F**), offer only a few additional summer birds: Great Blue and Green Herons, Double-crested Cormorant, Wood Duck, and Belted Kingfisher. But the riparian habitat along the lakeshore and creek support a richer bird life, including Yellow-billed Cuckoo, Eastern Screech-Owl, Chuck-will's-widow, Ruby-throated Hummingbird, Red-bellied and Downy Woodpeckers, Great Crested Flycatcher, Carolina Wren, White-eyed Vireo, and Summer Tanager.

Open fields and brushy edges and roadsides, such as along adjacent SH 22 (**G**), also provide good birding. Common field and wire birds to be expected in summer

Meridian State Park

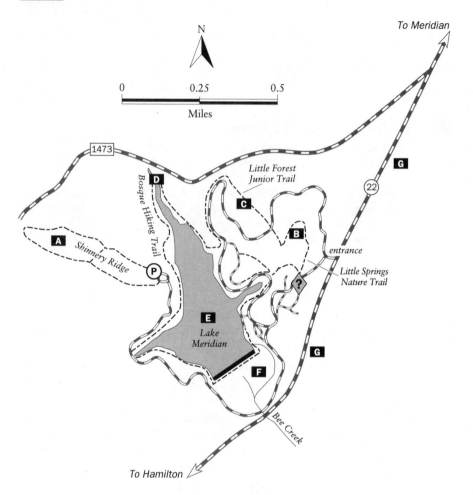

include Northern Bobwhite, Scissor-tailed Flycatcher, American Crow, Eastern Bluebird, Northern Mockingbird, Loggerhead Shrike, European Starling, Northern Cardinal, Painted Bunting, Dickcissel, Lark Sparrow, Red-winged Blackbird, Eastern Meadowlark, and Brown-headed Cowbird. Watch overhead for Black and Turkey Vultures; Red-tailed Hawk; Common Nighthawk at dawn and dusk; Chimney Swift; Purple Martin; and Northern Rough-winged, Cliff, and Barn Swallows.

In winter the wires, fields, and brushy edges usually harbor Northern Harrier; American Kestrel; Northern Flicker; American Robin; Cedar Waxwing; Orange-crowned and Yellow-rumped Warblers; Spotted Towhee; Lincoln's, White-throated, White-crowned, and Harris's Sparrows; and Dark-eyed Junco. Less numerous winter birds may include Sharp-shinned and Cooper's Hawks; Field, Vesper, Lark, Savannah, Fox, Song, and Lincoln's Sparrows; Western Meadowlark; Pine Siskin; and American Goldfinch.

Betty Wauer listening to Golden-cheeked Warblers along Shinnery Ridge, Meridian State Park.

Winter water birds occasionally are found on Lake Meridian and/or along the lakeshore and nearby creeks: Pied-billed Grebe, Green-winged and Blue-winged Teal, Mallard, Northern Pintail, Northern Shoveler, Gadwall, American Wigeon, Canvasback, Redhead, Ring-necked Duck, Lesser Scaup, Ruddy Duck, American Coot, Spotted Sandpiper, and Ring-billed Gull.

Directions: From Meridian (junction of SH 6, 22, 144, and 174), take SH 22 west for 3 miles to the park entrance.

General information: This 503-acre park, with the 70-acre Lake Meridian and ashe juniper–dominated uplands, lies near the northern edge of the range of the endangered **Golden-cheeked Warbler;** 13 pairs were recorded here in 1997.

The park, acquired in the 1930s, also has the distinction of being one of the oldest in the state; the earthen dam, roads, and trail were constructed by the Civilian Conservation Corps. There are 5 miles of walking and 5 miles of bicycling trails around the lake.

ADDITIONAL HELP

Location: Texas Official Travel Map grid L x 16; Bosque County
Nearest food, gas, and lodging: Meridian, 4 miles, has facilities for all three.
Nearest camping: On-site (15 sites)
Contact: Superintendent, Meridian State Park (see Appendix C)

56 Whitney Lake and Lake Whitney State Park

Habitats: Lake, river, creek, riparian, marsh, oak woodland, mesquite grassland, prairie, field, cropland

Key birds: Greater Roadrunner is present year-round. Wood Duck, Chuck-will's-widow, Black-chinned Hummingbird, Scissor-tailed Flycatcher, Bell's Vireo, Painted Bunting, and Dickcissel occur in summer. Common Loon; Bald Eagle; Horned Lark; Fox and Harris's Sparrows; and McCown's, Lapland, and Chestnut-collared Longspurs can usually be found in winter.

Best times to bird: April and May for spring migrants and nesting activities; November to February for Bald Eagle, sparrows, and longspurs

Birding strategies: Lake Whitney State Park's 0.9-mile nature trail loop (**A**), across from the plane tiedown area, offers habitats from woodlands to wetlands. In summer woodland birds include Mourning Dove; Yellow-billed Cuckoo; Red-bellied, Hairy, and Downy Woodpeckers; Great Crested Flycatcher; Blue Jay; American Crow; Carolina Chickadee; Tufted Titmouse; Bewick's and Carolina Wrens; Blue-gray Gnatcatcher; White-eyed Vireo; Summer Tanager; and Northern Cardinal. Less numerous birds here include Eastern Screech-Owl, Barred Owl, Chuck-will's-widow, Hairy Woodpecker, and Bell's Vireo. Wetland species include Great Blue,

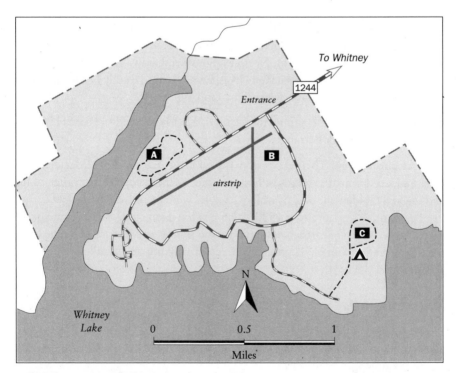

Lake Whitney State Park. (See map, page 229)

56 Whitney Lake and Lake Whitney State Park

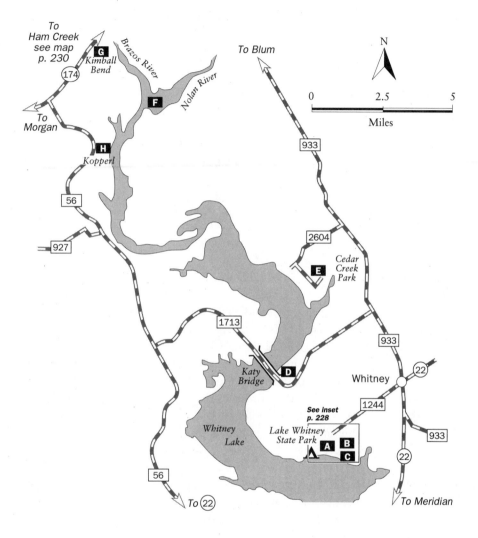

To Ham Creek see map p. 230

Kimball Bend

174

Brazos River

G

To Morgan

F

Nolan River

To Blum

N

0   2.5   5

Miles

933

H

Kopperl

56

927

2604

Cedar Creek Park

E

933

1713

22

Katy Bridge

D

Whitney

See inset p. 228

1244

Whitney Lake

Lake Whitney State Park

A   B
C

933

22

56

To 22

To Meridian

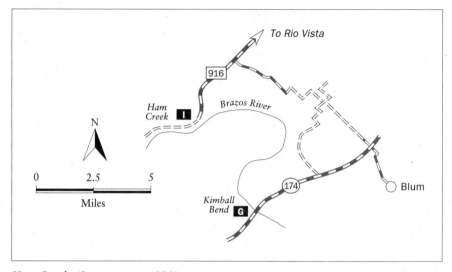

Ham Creek. (See map, page 229)

Little Blue, and Green Herons; Wood Duck; Belted Kingfisher; and Red-winged Blackbird.

Check the abundant fields surrounding the runways (B) and adjacent mesquite grasslands in summer for Killdeer, Northern Bobwhite, Greater Roadrunner, Ladder-backed Woodpecker, Western and Eastern Kingbirds, Scissor-tailed Flycatcher, Eastern Phoebe (especially near structures), Northern Mockingbird, Brown Thrasher (along the edges), Eastern Bluebird, Loggerhead Shrike, Blue Grosbeak, Painted Bunting, Dickcissel, Lark Sparrow, and Eastern Meadowlark. Great Horned Owl and Orchard and Bullock's Orioles are less numerous. Overhead, watch for Black and Turkey Vultures, Red-tailed Hawk, Common Nighthawk at dawn and dusk, Chimney Swift, Purple Martin, and Northern Rough-winged, Cliff, and Barn Swallows.

The open fields and runways also attract migrating raptors and shorebirds. Early southbound shorebirds can appear by July. During the winter, Northern Harrier, American Kestrel, and Horned Lark can be commonplace. Watch for Fox and Harris's Sparrows in brushy areas. McCown's, Lapland, and Chestnut-collared Longspurs may be found along the airstrip or in fallow fields along the adjacent roadways.

Look for wintering Bald Eagle in the state park from the short loop trail (C) beyond campsites 124 to 130. Other wintering water birds include Double-crested Cormorant, Mallard, Gadwall, Northern Pintail, Blue-winged Teal, American Wigeon, Northern Shoveler, Redhead, Ring-necked Duck, Canvasback, Lesser Scaup, Bufflehead, American Coot, and Ring-billed Gull. Also watch for Common Loon; Horned and Eared Grebes; American White Pelican; Greater White-fronted,

Snow, and Canada Geese; Common Goldeneye; Bufflehead; Hooded and Red-breasted Mergansers; and Bonaparte's and Herring Gulls.

Many of these same birds can be found around Whitney Lake. Good Bald Eagle viewing sites are located near the Katy Bridge (**D**), at Cedar Creek Park (**E**), and at the confluence of the Brazos and Nolan rivers (**F**). Access to this last area is by boat from Kimball Bend (**G**) or Kopperl (**H**). Some of the best riparian habitat can be found at Ham Creek (**I**), along the Brazos River in Johnson County.

Directions: From I-35, take SH 22 west at Hillsboro to Whitney (10 miles) and continue west on FM 1244 for 3 miles to the park entrance.

General information: The 955-acre Lake Whitney State Park lies along the east shore of Whitney Lake, a U.S. Army Corps of Engineers–managed lake on the Brazos River that covers 23,550 acres, with a shoreline of 225 miles. The area is located in the Grand Prairie subregion of the Blackland Prairie Natural Region. A 2,000-foot airstrip, along with accommodations for small airplanes, is available within the park, as are nature and bike trails, boating, fishing, and swimming.

ADDITIONAL HELP

Location: Texas Official Travel Map grid L x 17; Comanche County
Nearest food, gas, and lodging: Food and gas are available in Whitney (3 miles); lodging is available in Laguna Park (8 miles).
Nearest camping: On-site within the park (137 sites), and at 14 campgrounds within Corps lands around the lake
Contact: Reservoir Manager, Whitney Lake; Superintendent, Lake Whitney State Park (see Appendix C)

57 Waco

Cameron Park, Waco Lake, Waco Water Treatment Plant, and Tradinghouse Creek Reservoir

Habitats: Lake, pond, river, creek, mud flat, marsh, riparian, bottomland hardwood forest, juniper-oak woodland, oak savannah, mesquite grassland, field, pasture, cropland
Key birds: Neotropic Cormorant, Wild Turkey, and Greater Roadrunner are present year-round. Anhinga, White-faced Ibis, Black-bellied Whistling-Duck, Mississippi Kite, Swainson's Hawk, Chuck-will's-widow, Scissor-tailed Flycatcher, Wood Thrush, Indigo and Painted Buntings, Grasshopper Sparrow, and Dickcissel occur in summer. Common Loon; American White Pelican; Hooded Merganser; Osprey; Bald Eagle; Virginia Rail; Clay-colored, Vesper, LeConte's, Fox, and Harris's Sparrows; McCown's, Lapland, and Chestnut-colored Longspurs; and Rusty and Brewer's Blackbirds can usually be found in winter.
Best times to bird: April and May for spring migrants and nesting activities; November to February for winter birds

The Brazos River in Waco's Cameron Park.

Birding strategies: Cameron Park (A), Waco's best-known birding site, lies along the western bank of the Brazos River; it is located along North University Parks Drive, north of US 84. The riparian vegetation here provides the best birding for migrating flycatchers, vireos, warblers, tanagers, and orioles. Several of the neotropical migrants remain and nest along with the year-round residents. Common breeders in the park's wooded areas include Mourning Dove, Yellow-billed Cuckoo, Red-bellied and Downy Woodpeckers, Great Crested Flycatcher, Blue Jay, American Crow, Carolina Chickadee, Tufted Titmouse, Carolina Wren, Blue-gray Gnatcatcher, White-eyed Vireo, Northern Cardinal, and Common Grackle. Less numerous are Red-shouldered and Broad-winged Hawks, Chuck-will's-widow, Barred Owl, Eastern Screech-Owl, Ruby-throated and Black-chinned Humming-birds, Eastern Wood-Pewee, Wood Thrush, Yellow-throated and Red-eyed Vireos, and Black-and-white Warbler. Look in the open areas for Mississippi Kite, Swainson's and Red-tailed Hawks, Rock and Inca Doves, Common Nighthawk, Chimney Swift, Eastern Phoebe, Western Kingbird, Scissor-tailed Flycatcher, Purple Martin, Cliff and Barn Swallows, Eastern Bluebird, American Robin, Northern Mockingbird, Loggerhead Shrike, Indigo Bunting, Brown-headed Cowbird, and Bullock's Oriole.

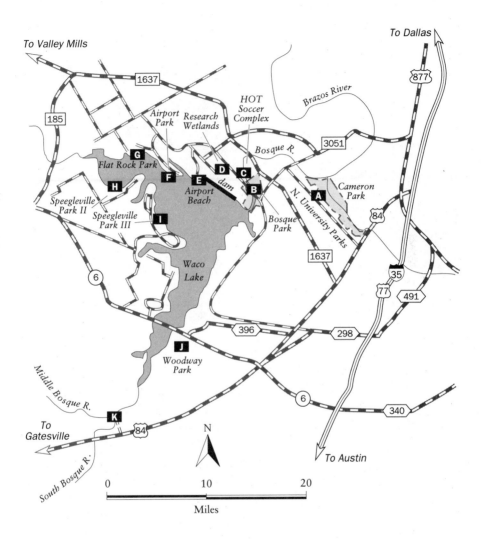

Most of these birds can also be found at wooded areas surrounding **Waco Lake**, to the west of Cameron Park. Several streets connect the park with FM 1637 (parallels the park to the west), which connects with all the Waco Lake north shore sites. Key sites around the lake include (counterclockwise) Bosque Park (**B**), at the spillway, which can be busy with gulls and terns in winter; the HOT (Heart of Texas) Soccer Complex (**C**), for an abundance of spring and fall migrants along

57 Waco Southeast

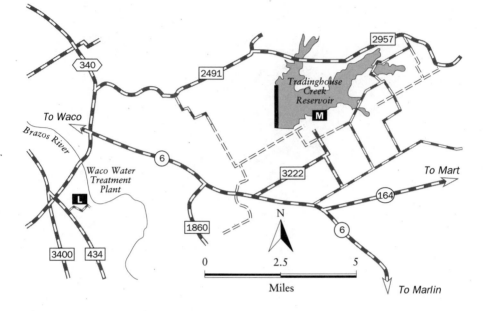

the wooded edge; and the research wetlands (**D**), worth general birding year-round and for water birds during migration and in winter, plus Carolina Wren, Common Yellowthroat, Painted Bunting, and Bullock's Oriole in summer. Airport Beach (**E**) offers lake views where waterfowl and gulls can usually be seen in winter; the adjacent riparian areas support numerous songbirds, including Warbling Vireo and Bullock's Oriole in summer.

At Airport Park (**F**), look in the bay for wintering Common Loon, grebes, waterfowl, gulls, and terns, including Black Tern, during late summer and migration. The vegetation is dominated by drier juniper woodland and oak savannah habitats. Typical birds here include Wild Turkey, Greater Roadrunner, Bewick's Wren, Eastern Bluebird, and Painted Bunting. Just beyond is one of the best birding sites along the lake, Flat Rock Park (**G**). American White Pelican; numerous waders, including Black-crowned and Yellow-crowned Night-Herons; waterfowl; gulls, especially Bonaparte's, Ring-billed, and Herring; Osprey; Bald Eagle; and even Peregrine Falcon are found here in winter. In summer watch for both Double-crested and Neotropic Cormorants, Anhinga, White-faced Ibis, and Black-bellied Whistling-Duck. When the river is low, mud flats often attract passing shorebirds. Check here for Cinnamon Teal in spring.

Flat Rock Park is an excellent area for migrating songbirds as well. In winter the fields and weedy edges can harbor House and Winter Wrens; Brown Thrasher; Northern Cardinal; Eastern and Spotted Towhees; Chipping, Clay-colored, Field, Vesper, Lark, Savannah, Grasshopper, LeConte's (irregular), Fox, Song, Lincoln's, Swamp, White-throated, White-crowned, and Harris's Sparrows; Dark-eyed Junco; and Lesser and American Goldfinches.

Across the lake, via FM 185, Speegleville Park II (H) and Speegleville Park III (I) offer good riparian woodlands, oak groves, mesquite grasslands, and fields, with plenty of easy access. In summer most of the typical mesquite grassland birds can usually be found here, including Ladder-backed Woodpecker; Western King-bird; Scissor-tailed Flycatcher; Bewick's Wren; Eastern Bluebird; Northern Mock-ingbird; Loggerhead Shrike; Blue Grosbeak; Painted Bunting; Dickcissel; Field, Lark, and Grasshopper Sparrows; Red-winged Blackbird; Eastern Meadowlark; Brown-headed Cowbird; and Orchard and Bullock's Orioles.

Continue south, cross the Highway 6 bridge, and turn off into Woodway Park (J), another good migrant viewing area at the far end of the roadway. The narrow bays of Middle Bosque River and Hog Creek are good for wintering waterfowl. At the southwestern corner of Waco Lake is the confluence of South Bosque and Middle Bosque rivers (K), another good area for migrating songbirds, accessible by a 0.3-mile graveled road off US 84.

The **Waco Water Treatment Plant** (L) is located southeast of town along FM 434, less than a mile south of SH 6 via Loop 340; turn left into the complex, follow the main road past the buildings, and turn left at the first side road; drive the levees for the best birding. The ponds and drying beds attract a huge variety of birds year-round, especially during migration. This area is the best bet for finding unexpected water birds.

Tradinghouse Creek Reservoir (M), located between FM 3222 and FM 2957, off SH 6, is a reasonably new power plant lake that has only begun to attract birders. The surrounding cattails, riparian woodlands, and adjacent fields and pastures hold great promise. In winter watch for Hooded Merganser on the lake, Virginia Rail and Rusty Blackbird in the wetlands, and Osprey and Bald Eagle overhead.

In winter the fallow fields along FM 3222 and FM 2957 are worth checking for Horned Lark, American Pipit, and longspurs; McCown's, Lapland, and Chest-nut-collared occur regularly. Watch also for Sprague's Pipit and Smith's Longspur.

Records of Review Species: Pacific Loon, Dec 1987. Western Grebe, 1996. Brown Peli-can, 1988, 1996. Roseate Spoonbill, 1996. Wood Stork, 1983. Little Gull, Dec–Jan 1989/90, Dec–Jan 1993/94. Black-headed Gull, Dec–Feb 1989/90, Dec–Feb 1990/91. Thayer's Gull, Dec 1991. Sabine's Gull, Oct 1990, 1991. Varied Thrush, 1983. Pyrrhuloxia, Dec 1994, Dec 1995, Dec 1996.

General information: Waco is a modern city with a population of more than 106,000 situated along the banks of the Brazos River. The area contains several well-known landmarks: Baylor University, the world's largest Baptist university; Strecker Museum, the state's oldest natural and cultural history museum; the Texas Ranger Hall of Fame and Museum; and the original (1906) Dr Pepper bottling plant, now a museum. The city also contains a network of 36 spacious municipal parks, including 416-acre Cameron Park.

Waco Lake, also within the city limits, is a 7,270-acre U.S. Army Corps of Engineers impoundment with 60 miles of shoreline. Boating, fishing, swimming, camping, and picnicking are available.

ADDITIONAL HELP

Location: Texas Official Travel Map grid M x 17/18; McLennan County
Nearest food, gas, and lodging: All are plentiful in the Greater Waco area.
Nearest camping: On-site at Waco Lake sites and in and around Waco
Contact: Cameron Park, city of Waco; Reservoir Manager, Waco Lake; Treatment Plant and Tradinghouse Creek Reservoir; Brazos River Authority (see Appendix C)

58 Mother Neff State Park

Habitats: River, creek, riparian, oak motte, juniper woodland, prairie, field
Key birds: Wood Duck and Greater Roadrunner are present year-round. Swainson's Hawk, Chuck-will's-widow, Ruby-throated and Black-chinned Hummingbirds, Scissor-tailed Flycatcher, Painted Bunting, and Dickcissel occur in summer. Lark Bunting, Fox and Harris's Sparrows, and McCown's and Lapland Longspurs can usually be found in winter.
Best times to bird: April and May for spring migrants and nesting activities; November to February for sparrows and longspurs

Birding strategies: The riparian habitat along the Leon River (A) provides the best birding year-round. During migration this area can harbor a variety of flycatchers, vireos, warblers, tanagers, and orioles. Several of the neotropical migrants remain and nest with the full-time residents. The combined species include Red-shouldered and Broad-winged Hawks; Mourning Dove; Yellow-billed Cuckoo; Eastern Screech-Owl; Barred Owl; Chuck-will's-widow; Black-chinned Hummingbird; Red-bellied, Downy, and Ladder-backed Woodpeckers; Great Crested Flycatcher; Blue Jay; American Crow; Carolina Chickadee; Tufted Titmouse; Carolina Wren; Brown Thrasher; Blue-gray Gnatcatcher; White-eyed, Yellow-throated, and Red-eyed Vireos; Summer Tanager; Northern Cardinal; and Common Grackle.

In winter this same area can harbor Northern Flicker, Brown Creeper, House and Winter Wrens, American Robin, Hermit Thrush, Ruby-crowned Kinglet, Cedar Waxwing, Yellow-rumped Warbler, Purple Finch, and Pine Siskin. Chipping, Field, Fox, Song, Lincoln's, White-throated, White-crowned, and Harris's Sparrows and Dark-eyed Juncos prefer brushy areas.

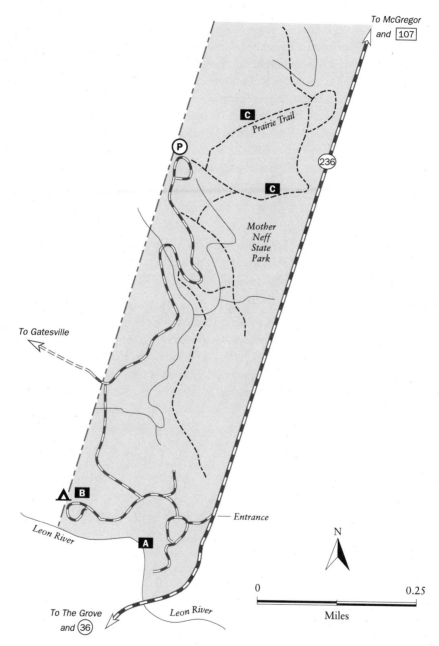

The interior park complex, including the campground (**B**), supports many of the same birds throughout the year. But Inca Dove, Eastern Phoebe, Barn Swallow, Northern Mockingbird, Eastern Bluebird, and Great-tailed Grackle can also be expected.

237

The Prairie Trail (**C**) offers more open habitats and a different bird life most of the year. In summer expect Black and Turkey Vultures, Red-tailed Hawk, Northern Bobwhite, Greater Roadrunner, Common Nighthawk, Chimney Swift, Eastern and Western Kingbirds, Scissor-tailed Flycatcher, Purple Martin, Cliff Swallow, Bewick's Wren, Loggerhead Shrike, Painted Bunting, Dickcissel, Field and Lark Sparrows, Eastern Meadowlark, and Orchard Oriole. Less numerous birds include Swainson's Hawk, Great Horned Owl, and Grasshopper Sparrow. In winter Sharp-shinned Hawk, American Kestrel, Horned Lark, Lark Bunting, Vesper Sparrow, McCown's and Lapland Longspurs, and Western Meadowlark may be present.

Look for a few water birds at Wash and Prairie ponds along the trail or at open areas along the Leon River. Year-round residents include only Great Blue Heron, Wood Duck, and Belted Kingfisher. Yellow-crowned Night-Herons frequent these sites in summer; and waterfowl and shorebirds are occasional visitors during migration and in winter.

Directions: From Waco, take US 84 west to McGregor; then go south on SH 317 to FM 2671 and SH 236; follow SH 236 to the park entrance. From Moody, take SH 107 west about 6 miles to SH 236, and proceed south on SH 236 to park entrance.

General information: The 259-acre Mother Neff State Park was named for Mrs. Isabelle Eleanor (Mother) Neff, mother of Governor Pat M. Neff (1921–25), who donated 6 acres of land in 1916 for the first park site. Governor Neff created the park in honor of his mother in 1921. The state's oldest park, it was developed by the Civilian Conservation Corps during the mid-1930s. It contains 2.75 miles of hiking trails through prairie, limestone hills, and river/creek bottomlands. Additional features include the national champion Texas oak and a cave used by Tonkawa Indians. In addition to the park, nearby County Road 1995, below Oglesby, is a favorite place to see birds and wildflowers, along with interesting geologic strata.

ADDITIONAL HELP

Location: Texas Official Travel Map grid N x 17; Coryell County
Nearest food, gas, and lodging: Food and gas are available in Moody (8 miles); lodging is available in Gatesville (22 miles).
Nearest camping: On-site (21 sites)
Contact: Superintendent, Mother Neff State Park (see Appendix C)

59 Fort Parker State Park

Habitats: River, lake, riparian, oak savannah, field, pasture
Key birds: Wood Duck, Wild Turkey, and Red-headed Woodpecker are present year-round. Anhinga, Chuck-will's-widow, Scissor-tailed Flycatcher, Prothonotary Warbler, and Indigo Bunting occur in summer. Hooded Merganser; Bald Eagle; American Woodcock; and Grasshopper, Fox, and Harris's Sparrows can usually be found in winter.
Best times to bird: April and May for spring migrants and nesting activities.

Birding strategies: The dam and spillway (**A**), along with the trails on both sides of the river, offer the greatest diversity of bird life throughout the year; during migration, vireos, warblers, tanagers, and orioles can be encountered. Many of these neotropical migrants remain and nest with the full-time resident birds. These include Red-shouldered Hawk, Yellow-billed Cuckoo, Chuck-will's-widow, Ruby-throated Hummingbird, Red-bellied and Downy Woodpeckers, Eastern Wood-Pewee, Great Crested Flycatcher, Blue Jay, American Crow, Carolina Chickadee, Tufted Titmouse, Carolina Wren, White-eyed and Red-eyed Vireos, Prothonotary Warbler, Northern Cardinal, and Blue Grosbeak. In spring and summer look around the dam and lake for Pied-billed Grebe; Double-crested Cormorant; Anhinga; Great Blue, Little Blue, and Green Herons; Great and Snowy Egrets; Black-crowned and Yellow-crowned Night-Herons; Wood Duck; American Coot; Killdeer; and Belted Kingfisher.

In fall and winter the lake (**B**) normally contains many more water birds: Canada Goose, Mallard, Northern Pintail, Green-winged and Cinnamon Teal, Northern Shoveler, Gadwall, American Wigeon, Canvasback, Redhead, Ring-necked Duck, Lesser Scaup, Bufflehead, Hooded Merganser, and Ruddy Duck are common. Bonaparte's and Ring-billed Gulls and Forster's Tern are irregular visitors.

The open fields, such as the Springfield Cemetery and Group Barracks area (**C**), as well as the park entrance, are good places to find Wild Turkey, Eastern Phoebe, Carolina Wren, Eastern Bluebird, and Loggerhead Shrike year-round and Cattle Egret in summer. Watch for Black and Turkey Vultures, Red-tailed Hawk, Common Nighthawk, Chimney Swift, and Cliff and Barn Swallows overhead. In winter the fields and brushy edges often harbor American Woodcock; Winter Wren; various sparrows, such as Chipping, Field, Grasshopper, Fox, White-throated, White-crowned, and Harris's; and Dark-eyed Junco.

The picnic area (**D**), just beyond the Activity Center, is also worth birding year-round for Red-headed Woodpecker. Look for soaring Bald Eagle in winter and spring. This open oak savannah area can harbor passing migrants or winter residents, such as Pine Warbler.

The Scout Camping Wilderness Area (**E**), at the far end of River Road, is also a good birding area year-round. The dense woods along the road and on the peninsula attract wintering Brown Creeper, House and Winter Wrens, Golden-crowned and Ruby-crowned Kinglets, various sparrows, Dark-eyed Junco, and Purple Finch.

Directions: Take either US 84 or SH 164 east of Waco (on I-35) for 40 miles to Mexia or 38 miles to Groesbeck, respectively. The park entrance is located along SH 14, 6 miles north of Groesbeck or 6 miles south of Mexia.

General information: The 1,485-acre Fort Parker State Park contains 735 acres of rolling hills and the 750-acre Lake Fort Parker (also known as Springfield Lake), created by a dam on the Navasota River. The reservoir has over a mile of shoreline, two lighted fishing piers, and a concrete boat ramp.

The nearby Old Fort Parker State Historic Site is a reconstructed fort complex, representing a private fort established in 1834 by Silas and James Parker. Comanches

59 Fort Parker State Park

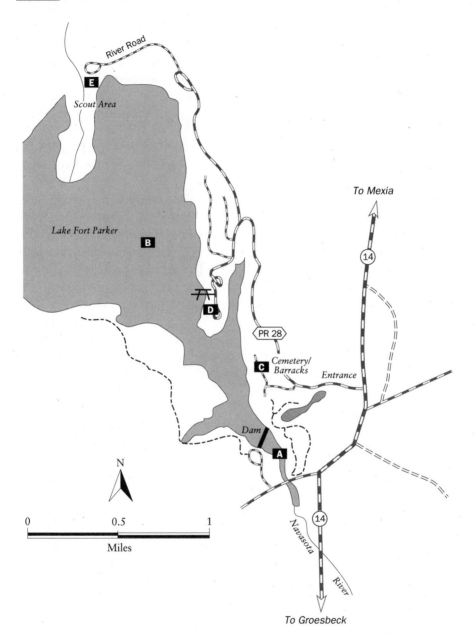

overran the fort in 1836, killing five Parker family members and capturing another five individuals, including Cynthia Ann Parker, who grew up as a Comanche. She was the mother of Quanah Parker, the last great Comanche chief.

ADDITIONAL HELP

Location: Texas Official Travel Map grid M x 19; Limestone County
Nearest food, gas, and lodging: All available in Groesbeck and Mexia (both 6 miles).
Nearest camping: On-site (25 sites)
Contact: Superintendent, Fort Parker State Park (see Appendix C)

60 Fairfield Lake State Park

Habitats: Lake, pond, marsh, creek, riparian, bottomland hardwood
forest, juniper-oak woodland, oak savannah, field, cropland
Key birds: Wood Duck, Wild Turkey, and Pileated Woodpecker are
present year-round. Anhinga, Least Tern, Red-headed Woodpecker,
Scissor-tailed Flycatcher, Prothonotary Warbler, and Painted Bunting
occur in summer. American White Pelican and Bald Eagle can usually
be found in winter.
Best times to bird: May and June for nesting activities; winter for
Bald Eagle and sparrows

Birding strategies: The greatest diversity of birds can be expected along the 1-mile Bird
Watching Trail (**A**), which passes through oak-juniper woodlands and old fields and
skirts an arm of the lake that is dominated by cattails. Expected summer birds here
include Red-bellied Woodpecker, Scissor-tailed Flycatcher, Blue Jay, American Crow,
Carolina Chickadee, Tufted Titmouse, White-breasted Nuthatch, Carolina Wren, Eastern Bluebird, American Robin, Painted Bunting, and Northern Cardinal in the woods
and fields; and Pied-billed Grebe, Anhinga, Great Blue and Little Blue Herons, Great
and Snowy Egrets, Wood Duck, American Coot, Least Tern, and Belted Kingfisher in
the marsh or on the lake. Watch also for Prothonotary Warbler in the partially flooded
wetlands and along the creeks.

Hike the 6-mile Big Brown Creek Trail (**B**), which also passes through a variety of
habitats, including riparian areas with beaver ponds, for many of the same birds in
summer. This is especially good during migration and in winter. Barred Owl and Pileated
Woodpecker may be found year-round and Red-headed Woodpecker in summer.

In winter American White Pelican and Bald Eagle frequent the warm-water outlet
at the Texas Utility Company, located across the lake; the highest numbers (15 to 20)
occur in December. For the best observations, take the Bald Eagle Boat Tours, offered
four to six times monthly (fee) from November through February; ask the park staff for
details. Eagles can also be observed from the boat ramp beyond the Post Oak Camping
Area (**C**) and from the Day Use Area (**D**). These two sites are also good for viewing
wintering ducks.

Directions: From US 84, take FM 488 east to FM 2570, then follow FM 2570
north to FM 3285 and FM 3285 east to PR 64 and the park entrance.

General information: This area, including the 1,460-acre state park, the 2,400-
acre lake, and surrounding fields and pastures, is one of the state's least-known
birding sites. Yet, because of the constant warm water produced by Texas Utilities

60 Fairfield Lake State Park

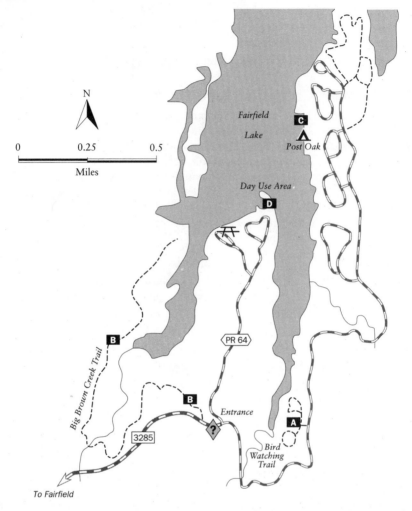

Big Brown Steam Electric Power Plant on the north shore, the area has considerable potential.

Besides the numerous Bald Eagle tours, the park also sponsors an annual Bird House Day on the first Saturday in February to encourage visitors to participate in hands-on habitat improvements. An outreach version of this program is also available.

ADDITIONAL HELP

Location: Texas Official Travel Map grid M x 19; Freestone County

Nearest food, gas, and lodging: Food and gas are available 4 miles away, at the junction of PR 64 and FM 488. Lodging can be found in Fairfield (9 miles).

Nearest camping: On-site (135 sites)

Contact: Superintendent, Fairfield Lake State Park (see Appendix C)

242

Pineywoods Region

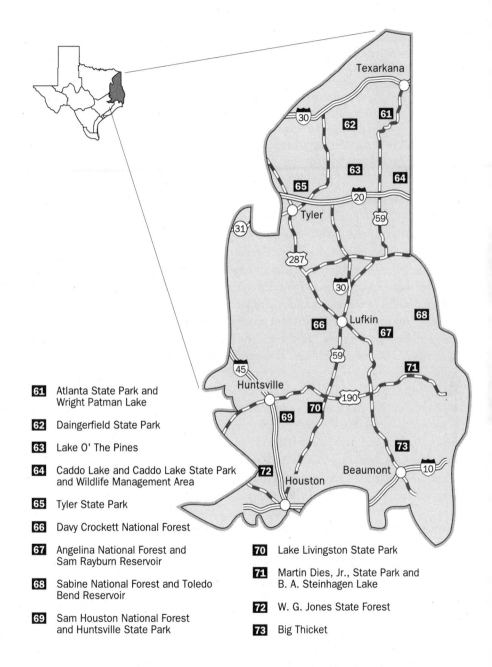

61 Atlanta State Park and Wright Patman Lake

62 Daingerfield State Park

63 Lake O' The Pines

64 Caddo Lake and Caddo Lake State Park and Wildlife Management Area

65 Tyler State Park

66 Davy Crockett National Forest

67 Angelina National Forest and Sam Rayburn Reservoir

68 Sabine National Forest and Toledo Bend Reservoir

69 Sam Houston National Forest and Huntsville State Park

70 Lake Livingston State Park

71 Martin Dies, Jr., State Park and B. A. Steinhagen Lake

72 W. G. Jones State Forest

73 Big Thicket

61 Atlanta State Park and Wright Patman Lake

Habitats: Lake, pond, river, creek, riparian, mud flat, bottomland hardwood forest, pine forest, field, pasture, cropland
Key birds: Wood and Mottled Ducks, Red-headed and Pileated Woodpeckers, Fish Crow, and Brown-headed Nuthatch are present year-round. Anhinga; White Ibis; Mississippi Kite; Chuck-will's-widow; Scissor-tailed Flycatcher; Wood Thrush; Yellow-throated, Prothonotary, Kentucky, and Hooded Warblers; Louisiana Waterthrush; Painted Bunting; and Dickcissel occur in summer. Surf and White-winged Scoters, Hooded and Red-breasted Mergansers, Osprey, Bald Eagle, American Woodcock, LeConte's and Harris's Sparrows, and Lapland Longspur can usually be found in winter.
Best times to bird: April and May for spring migrants and nesting activities; October for vagrants; November to March for winter birds

Birding strategies: Atlanta State Park (**A**), located along the south shore of Wright Patman Lake, offers the birder a variety of terrestrial habitats. In summer the woodlands along the Arrowhead and Hickory Hollow nature trails are likely to contain Mississippi Kite; Red-shouldered Hawk; Yellow-billed Cuckoo; Chuck-will's-widow; Ruby-throated Hummingbird; Red-bellied, Downy, and Pileated Woodpeckers; Eastern Wood-Pewee; Acadian and Great Crested Flycatchers; Eastern Kingbird; Carolina Chickadee; Tufted Titmouse; White-breasted and Brown-headed Nuthatches; Carolina Wren; Blue-gray Gnatcatcher; Wood Thrush; White-eyed and Red-eyed Vireos; Northern Parula; Pine, Black-and-white, Prothonotary, and Hooded Warblers; Summer Tanager; and Northern Cardinal. Northern Bobwhite, Eastern Phoebe, American Crow, Eastern Bluebird, Northern Mockingbird, Painted Bunting, Dickcissel, and Lark Sparrow prefer the savannah habitat.

Many of the woodland species mentioned above can be found at Rocky and Piney points, Paradise Cove, North Shore, Clear Springs, and along the Sulphur River. Rocky and Piney points (**B**) and the grassy fields adjacent to the U.S. Army Corps of Engineers Project Office (**C**) offer other species as well: Fish Crow and Eastern Meadowlark year-round; Cattle Egret; Killdeer; Scissor-tailed Flycatcher; Purple Martin; and Northern Rough-winged, Cliff, and Barn Swallows in summer. In winter the fields and weedy areas attract Northern Harrier; American Kestrel; American Pipit; Eastern Towhee; numerous sparrows, including LeConte's (irregular) and Harris's; Lapland Longspur; Brewer's Blackbird; and American Goldfinch. Watch also for American Woodcock.

The best view of the lake is from Rocky and Piney points and Elliott Bluff (**D**). Typical full-time resident water birds include Pied-billed Grebe, Double-crested Cormorant, Great Blue Heron, Great Egret, Wood and Mottled Ducks, American Coot, Ring-billed Gull, and Forster's Tern. Anhinga and White Ibis occur in summer. In winter the lake can be busy with ducks, gulls, and terns. Most numerous are Green-winged Teal, Mallard, Northern Shoveler, Gadwall, American Wigeon, Ring-necked and Ruddy Ducks, Lesser Scaup, Common Goldeneye, Bufflehead,

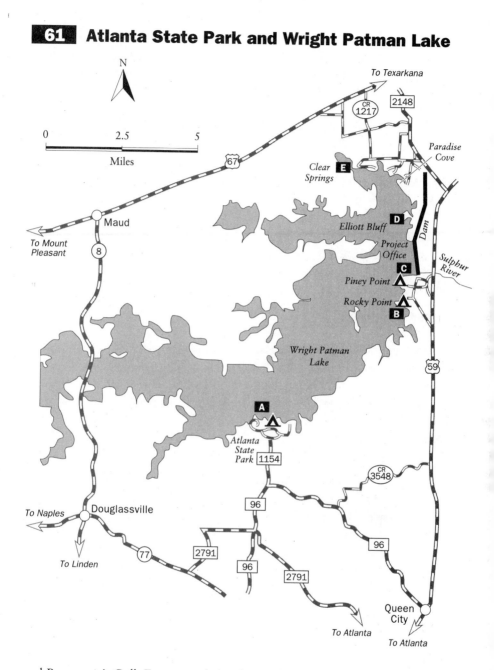

and Bonaparte's Gull. Fewer numbers of Canada Goose, Northern Pintail, Canvasback, Greater Scaup, Surf and White-winged Scoters, and Hooded and Red-breasted Mergansers can be found. Watch also for Oldsquaw, Black Scoter, and Common Merganser.

Clear Springs (E), especially the mouth of Elliott Creek (viewed from near the boat ramp), can also be good year-round. This site offers all the waders in summer and all the dabbling ducks in winter. Scope the mud flats for shorebirds, especially in spring and fall. And in summer this area also harbors a full complement of neotropical songbirds, including Yellow-throated Vireo; Northern Parula; Yellow-throated, Prothonotary, Kentucky, and Hooded Warblers; Northern Parula; and Louisiana Waterthrush.

Bald Eagle counts of 8 to 12 individuals are taken at the lake each January by the Texarkana Audubon Society. Watch for eagles from various sites next to the dam.

Records of Review Species: Red-necked Grebe, Dec–March 1993/94. Little Gull, Jan 1992, Dec–Feb 1993/94. Black-headed Gull, Jan 1993, Dec–Feb 1993/94, Dec–Jan 1996/97. Black-legged Kittiwake, Nov 1996.

Directions: To reach Atlanta State Park, take US 59 north from Atlanta to FM 96, west for 8 miles to FM 1154, then north for 2 miles to PR 42 and the park entrance. Wright Patman Dam is located off SH 59, 17 miles north of Atlanta or 9 miles south of Texarkana.

General information: The 1,474-acre state park is the largest of the many parks surrounding the reservoir. The 20,300-acre Wright Patman Lake (a conservation pool) and most of the surrounding lands are administered by the U.S. Army Corps of Engineers. The earthfill dam is 18,500 feet long, with a maximum height of 100 feet, and was designed to retain floodwaters of the Sulphur River. Wright Patman Dam and Lake are named for Congressman Wright Patman.

ADDITIONAL HELP

Location: Texas Official Travel Map grid H x 22/23; Bowie County

Nearest food, gas, and lodging: Food and gas are 3 miles from the state park entrance, and lodging is available in Texarkana and Atlanta.

Nearest camping: On-site, including 59 sites in the state park and 15 on Corps lands

Contact: Project Manager, Wright Patman Project Office; Superintendent, Atlanta State Park (see Appendix C)

62 Daingerfield State Park

Habitats: Lake, creek, riparian, bottomland hardwood forest, pine forest, field, pasture, cropland

Key birds: Wood Duck, Wild Turkey, Red-headed and Pileated Woodpeckers, White-breasted and Brown-headed Nuthatches, Pine Warbler, and Bachman's Sparrow are present year-round. Anhinga; Chuck-will's-widow; Scissor-tailed Flycatcher; Wood Thrush; Yellow-throated, Prothonotary, Kentucky, and Hooded Warblers; Louisiana Waterthrush; Indigo and Painted Buntings; and Dickcissel occur in summer. American White Pelican; Osprey; Bald Eagle; LeConte's, Fox, and Harris's Sparrows; Rusty Blackbird; and Purple and House Finches can usually be found in winter.

Best times to bird: April and May for spring migrants and nesting activities

Birding strategies: The hiking trail that circles the lake, especially above the Dogwood Camping Area (**A**) and along the southeastern corner of the lake to the bridge (**B**) in spring and early summer, supports the greatest variety of resident and neotropical migrants. Among them are Red-shouldered and Broad-winged Hawks; Chuck-will's-widow; Red-bellied, Downy, Hairy, and Pileated Woodpeckers; Eastern Wood-Pewee; Acadian and Great Crested Flycatchers; Eastern Kingbird; Carolina Chickadee; Tufted Titmouse; White-breasted and Brown-headed Nuthatches; Carolina Wren; Blue-gray Gnatcatcher; Wood Thrush; American Robin; Brown Thrasher; White-eyed, Yellow-throated, and Red-eyed Vireos; Yellow-throated, Pine, Black-and-white, and Prothonotary Warblers; Louisiana Waterthrush; Summer Tanager; Northern Cardinal; Common Grackle; and Orchard Oriole. Check the open woodlands with moderate undergrowth in spring and summer for Bachman's Sparrow.

The lawns and edges near the Overflow Camping Area (**C**) and along the roadsides support Northern Bobwhite, Killdeer, Mourning Dove, Eastern Phoebe, Eastern Bluebird, Northern Mockingbird, Indigo Bunting, Chipping and Field Sparrows, and Eastern Meadowlark. Watch overhead for Black and Turkey Vultures, Red-tailed Hawk, Common Nighthawk, Chimney Swift, Purple Martin, and Barn Swallow.

Lake Daingerfield (**D**) is too small to attract a large number of birds, but Pied-billed Grebe, Great Blue Heron, Great Egret, and Wood Duck can be expected year-round; Anhinga and Green Heron can be found in summer; and American White Pelican, Double-crested Cormorant, Green-winged and Blue-winged Teal, Mallard, Northern Shoveler, Gadwall, Bald Eagle, Osprey, and Belted Kingfisher are irregular in winter.

The park also serves as a hawkwatch site during the last two weeks in September, when as many as 3,500 Broad-winged Hawks have been reported in a single day. Other common raptors include Mississippi Kite; Osprey; Sharp-shinned, Cooper's, Red-shouldered, and Red-tailed Hawks; and American Kestrel. Merlin and Peregrine Falcon are less numerous.

62 Daingerfield State Park

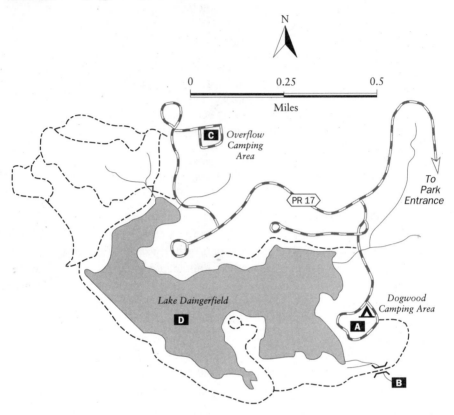

N

| 0 | 0.25 | 0.5 |

Miles

C Overflow
Camping
Area

PR 17

To
Park
Entrance

Lake Daingerfield

D

Dogwood
Camping Area

A

B

In spring and summer check the open fields and utility poles and wires outside the park for American Kestrel, Wild Turkey, Scissor-tailed Flycatcher, Eastern King-bird, Tree and Northern Rough-winged Swallows, Loggerhead Shrike, Blue Gros-beak, Painted Bunting, Dickcissel, and Lark Sparrow. In winter the open and weedy fields support Greater White-fronted, Snow, and Canada Geese; Northern Har-rier; Bewick's, House, and Sedge Wrens; Eastern and Spotted Towhees; several sparrows, including Savannah, LeConte's, Fox, Song, Lincoln's, Swamp, White-throated, White-crowned, and Harris's; Dark-eyed Junco; Rusty and Brewer's Black-birds; Great-tailed Grackle; and American Goldfinch.

Directions: From Daingerfield, take SH 49 for 3 miles to PR 17 and the park entrance. From Linden, take SH 49 for 2 miles to PR 17 and the entrance.

General information: The 551-acre state park, with the 88-acre Lake Daingerfield, was established in the early 1930s as a Civilian Conservation Corps project. The park landscape is noted for its blooming dogwoods in spring and its quiet, serene beauty. A 2.5-mile hiking trail circles the lake.

Lake Daingerfield from the hiking trail in Daingerfield State Park.

ADDITIONAL HELP

Location: Texas Official Travel Map grid J x 22; Cass County

Nearest food, gas, and lodging: Food and gas are available at Hughes Spring (3 miles) or Daingerfield (3 miles); lodging is available at Mount Pleasant (25 miles).

Nearest camping: On-site (40 sites)

Contact: Superintendent, Daingerfield State Park (see Appendix C)

63 Lake O' The Pines

Habitats: Lake, pond, creek, riparian, bottomland hardwood forest, pine forest, field, pasture, cropland

Key birds: Wood Duck, Pileated Woodpecker, Brown-headed Nuthatch, Pine Warbler, and Bachman's Sparrow are present year-round. Anhinga; Purple Gallinule; Chuck-will's-widow; Scissor-tailed Flycatcher; Wood Thrush; Yellow-throated, Prairie, Black-and-white, Prothonotary, Swainson's, Kentucky, and Hooded Warblers; Louisiana Waterthrush; Indigo and Painted Buntings; and Dickcissel occur in summer. Common Loon; American White Pelican; American Woodcock; American and Sprague's Pipits; Spotted and Eastern Towhees; and Henslow's, LeConte's, Vesper, and Fox Sparrows can usually be found in winter.

Best times to bird: April and May for spring migrants and nesting activities; November to March for vagrants and winter birds

63 **Lake O' The Pines**

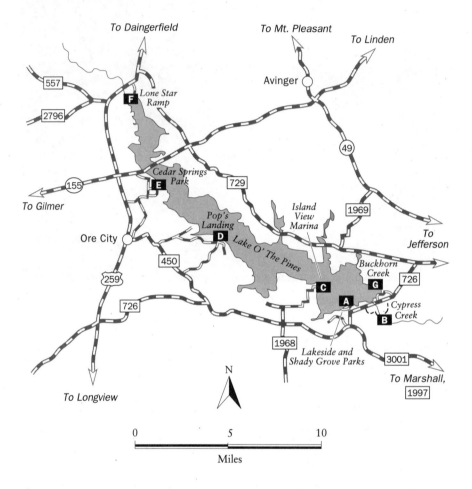

To Daingerfield

To Mt. Pleasant

To Linden

557

2796

Lone Star
Ramp **F**

Avinger

49

155

Cedar Springs
Park **E**

729

To Gilmer

Island
View
Marina

1969

Pop's
Landing

To
Jefferson

Ore City

D

Lake O' The Pines

450

Buckhorn
Creek

259

C

G

726

726

A

Cypress
Creek

B

1968

*Lakeside and
Shady Grove Parks*

3001

N

To Marshall,

1997

To Longview

0   5   10

Miles

Birding strategies: The best birding area is below the Ferrells Bridge Dam at Lakeside and Shady Grove parks (**A**). These combined sites contain open water, wetlands, dense brush, fields, and a bottomland hardwood forest. The riparian areas (**B**) along Cypress Creek below the dam (reached via trail, see map) can also be good in spring and early summer. Good views of the lake are available at Island View Marina (**C**), Pop's Landing (**D**), Cedar Springs Park (**E**), and near Lone Star Ramp (**F**). Walk 0.25 mile south on an old road from the Lone Star Ramp parking lot to where it intersects another old road; turn right and go downhill to where there are good views of the upper portion of the lake (especially good in winter).

A winter or early spring visit is likely to produce Pied-billed Grebe; American White Pelican; Double-crested Cormorant; Great Blue Heron; Great Egret; Yellow-crowned and Black-crowned Night-Herons; Wood, Mottled, Ring-necked, and Ruddy Ducks; Green-winged and Blue-winged Teal; Mallard; Northern Pintail;

Northern Shoveler; Gadwall; American Wigeon; Canvasback; Redhead; Lesser Scaup; Sora; American Coot; Killdeer; Solitary and Spotted Sandpipers; Common Snipe; Ring-billed, Franklin's, and Bonaparte's Gulls; and Black Tern. When mud flats are available, Black-bellied and Semipalmated Plovers; Greater Yellowlegs; and Pectoral, Baird's, Least, Semipalmated, and Western Sandpipers can be expected. Common Loon; Horned and Eared Grebes; Greater Scaup; Oldsquaw; and Black, Surf, and White-winged Scoters occur irregularly. Fish Crows are irregular year-round. In summer Anhinga, Little Blue and Green Herons, and Purple Gallinule are usually present.

Bald Eagles occur along the lake in winter; 38 sightings (23 adults and 8 immatures) were recorded in January 1997. The dam overlook at Buckhorn Creek (**G**) is one of the better viewing areas.

Look for woodland birds at Shady Grove (**A**) and Cedar Springs (**E**) parks and near Lone Star Ramp (**F**). These areas can be very good in migration. Nesting birds here include Red-shouldered Hawk; Yellow-billed Cuckoo; Eastern Screech-Owl; Barred Owl; Chuck-will's-widow; Northern Flicker; Red-headed, Red-bellied, Downy, and Pileated Woodpeckers; Eastern Wood-Pewee; Acadian and Great Crested Flycatchers; Blue Jay; American Crow; Carolina Chickadee; Tufted Titmouse; White-breasted and Brown-headed Nuthatches; Carolina Wren; Blue-gray Gnatcatcher; Wood Thrush; American Robin; Brown Thrasher; White-eyed, Yellow-throated, and Red-eyed Vireos; Northern Parula; Yellow-throated, Pine, Black-and-white, Prothonotary, Kentucky, and Hooded Warblers; American Redstart; Louisiana Waterthrush; Yellow-breasted Chat; Summer Tanager; Northern Cardinal; Bachman's and Chipping Sparrows; and Common Grackle.

Scan the open fields and utility poles for American Kestrel, Wild Turkey, Northern Bobwhite, Greater Roadrunner, Great Horned Owl, Scissor-tailed Flycatcher, Eastern Kingbird, Horned Lark, Eastern Bluebird, Loggerhead Shrike, Blue Grosbeak, Indigo Bunting, Dickcissel, Lark and Grasshopper Sparrows, and Eastern Meadowlark in summer. Watch overhead for Common Nighthawk; Chimney Swift; Purple Martin; and Tree, Northern Rough-winged, Cliff, and Barn Swallows. In winter the open fields attract Horned Lark and Sprague's Pipit, whereas the weedy fields can be filled with seedeaters. Most numerous are Lark, Chipping, Field, White-throated, Swamp, and Song Sparrows; Dark-eyed Junco; and American Goldfinch. Less frequent are Eastern and Spotted Towhees; Henslow's, LeConte's, Vesper, White-crowned, and Fox Sparrows; Purple Finch; and Pine Siskin.

Records of Review Species: Red-throated Loon, Jan–Feb 1991. Pacific Loon, Nov 1993, March 1994, Jan 1996. Yellow-billed Loon, Jan 1992. Red-necked Grebe, Jan 1995. Barrow's Goldeneye, Nov 1993. Thayer's Gull, Dec 1996. Black-legged Kittiwake, Dec 1990.

Directions: Lake O' The Pines lies between I-20 and I-30, 26 miles north of Marshall via FM 1997 and 3001; 34 miles northeast of Longview via US 259; or 50 miles southeast of Mount Pleasant via SH 49 and US 259. Ferrells Bridge Dam is 9 miles west of Jefferson via FM 729 and 726.

General information: This 18-mile-long lake, which covers 38,200 acres, evolved in the 1950s when Cypress Creek was dammed for flood control by the U.S. Army Corps of Engineers. Principally a recreation lake, it is surrounded by numerous hidden bays and a variety of good birding habitats.

ADDITIONAL HELP

Location: Texas Official Travel Map grid J x 22; Harrison County
Nearest food, gas, and lodging: All can be found at numerous sites surrounding the lake.
Nearest camping: On-site at Buckhorn Creek Park (62 sites) and Brushy Creek Park (71 sites), both near the dam and open year-round
Contact: Reservoir Manager, Lake O' The Pines (see Appendix C)

64 Caddo Lake and Caddo Lake State Park and Wildlife Management Area

Habitats: Lake, pond, river, riparian, cypress swamp, marsh, bottomland hardwood forest, mixed conifer-deciduous forest, pine forest, field, pasture, cropland
Key birds: Wood Duck, Wild Turkey, Greater Roadrunner, Red-headed and Pileated Woodpeckers, Fish Crow, and Brown-headed Nuthatch are present year-round. Anhinga; White Ibis; Wood Stork; Mississippi Kite; King Rail; Purple Gallinule; Chuck-will's-widow; Scissor-tailed Flycatcher; Wood Thrush; Yellow-throated, Prairie, Prothonotary, Swainson's, Kentucky, and Hooded Warblers; American Redstart; Louisiana Waterthrush; Indigo and Painted Buntings; and Dickcissel occur in summer. Bald Eagle, American Woodcock, Winter and Sedge Wrens, Eastern and Spotted Towhees, LeConte's and Fox Sparrows, and Rusty Blackbird can usually be found in winter.
Best times to bird: April and May for spring migrants and nesting activities; November to March for winter birds

Birding strategies: Saw Mill Pond (**A**) is the most representative birding site in this area, with wetlands and surrounding forest habitats. Typical summer birds include Pied-billed Grebe; Anhinga; Great Blue, Little Blue, and Green Herons; Yellow-crowned Night-Heron; Wood Duck; Mallard; Red-shouldered Hawk; Yellow-billed Cuckoo; Belted Kingfisher; Red-headed, Red-bellied, Downy, and Pileated Woodpeckers; Eastern Wood-Pewee; Acadian and Great Crested Flycatchers; Eastern Kingbird; Blue Jay; American and Fish Crows; Carolina Chickadee; Tufted Titmouse; Carolina Wren; Blue-gray Gnatcatcher; White-eyed, Yellow-throated, and Red-eyed Vireos; Northern Parula; Yellow-throated, Pine, Black-and-white, Prothonotary, and Hooded Warblers; Louisiana Waterthrush; Yellow-breasted Chat; Common Yellowthroat; Summer Tanager; Northern Cardinal; Blue Grosbeak; Painted Bunting; Red-winged Blackbird; and Common Grackle. Less

64 Caddo Lake and Caddo Lake State Park and Wildlife Management Area

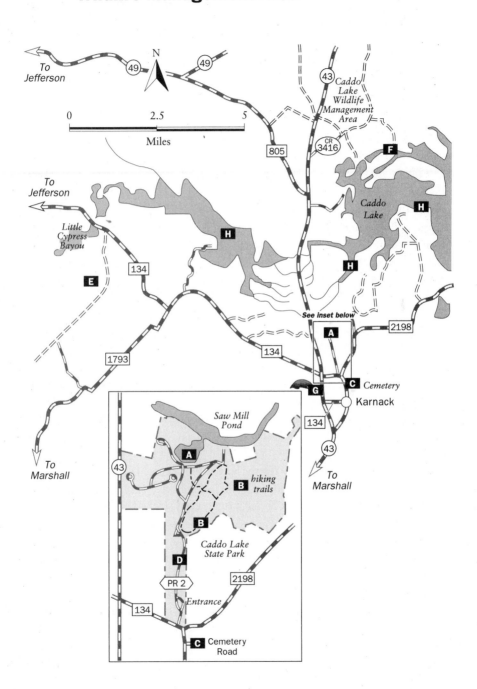

numerous are Snowy Egret, Black-crowned Night-Heron, White Ibis, Wild Turkey, Purple Gallinule, Eastern Screech-Owl, Barred Owl, Chuck-will's-widow, White-breasted Nuthatch, and Swainson's and Kentucky Warblers. Wood Storks usually appear in midsummer.

The hiking and Caddo Forest trails (**B**) offer Hairy Woodpecker, Northern Flicker, Brown-headed Nuthatch, Wood Thrush, American Robin, and American Redstart. Look along Cemetery Road (**C**), east of FM 134 (south of FM 2198) for pine forest birds, particularly Brown-headed Nuthatch.

The grassy roadsides, and cabin areas along PR 2 (**D**) offer a few additional spring and summer birds, including Northern Bobwhite, Killdeer, Mourning Dove, Greater Roadrunner, Ruby-throated Hummingbird, Eastern Phoebe, Eastern Bluebird, Northern Mockingbird, Indigo Bunting, Chipping and Lark Sparrows, Eastern Meadowlark, and House Finch. Dickcissels can usually be found in summer along an unnamed dirt road (**E**) that runs south toward Woodlawn (7.5 miles beyond the junction of SH 43 and FM 2198 and just before crossing Little Cypress Bayou). Check the fields in about 1 to 2 miles; all this area is private property.

Swainson's Warbler has been found in **Caddo Lake Wildlife Management Area** along Johnson Road (CR 3416) (**F**). The area is swampy but usually accessible by a fairly well-maintained dirt road. Watch too for Northern Parula; Yellow-throated, Prothonotary, Kentucky, and Hooded Warblers; American Redstart; Louisiana Waterthrush; and Yellow-breasted Chat in summer. Look in stands of young pines for Prairie Warblers. In winter this area usually supports American Woodcock, Eastern and Spotted Towhees, and Rusty Blackbird.

In summer look overhead throughout the area for Black and Turkey Vultures, Mississippi Kite, Red-tailed Hawk, Chimney Swift, Scissor-tailed Flycatcher, Purple Martin, and Barn Swallow. Watch for migrating raptors from a hill (**G**) 0.75 mile west of the park entrance, at the southwest corner of the SH 43/FM 134 junction. Fall migrants include Osprey, Bald Eagle, various hawks and falcons, White Ibis, and Wood Stork.

In winter Caddo Lake, especially the backwater areas (**H**) away from the busier channels, attracts Common Loon; Horned and Eared Grebes; Double-crested Cormorant; and a number of ducks, including Green-winged Teal, Northern Shoveler, Gadwall, American Wigeon, Canvasback, Redhead, Ring-necked and Ruddy Ducks, Greater and Lesser Scaup, Common Goldeneye, Bufflehead, and Hooded and Red-breasted Mergansers; Virginia Rail; Common Snipe; Bonaparte's, Ring-billed, and Herring Gulls; and Forster's Tern. Bald Eagle overwinters around the lake, as well.

The numerous open fields and brushy edges outside the park also attract a variety of birds in winter: Greater White-fronted and Canada Geese; Northern Harrier; American Kestrel; House, Winter, and Sedge Wrens; American Pipit; Eastern and Spotted Towhees; numerous sparrows, including Vesper, LeConte's, and Fox; Brewer's Blackbird; Purple Finch; and American Goldfinch.

Directions: From Marshall, take SH 43 northeast for 15 miles to the second junction with FM 134 (north of Karnack). Follow FM 134 east for 1 mile to the state park entrance. Johnson Road and the wildlife management area are 5.5 miles north of the SH 43/FM 2198 junction.

General information: The 32,000-acre lake, including the 478-acre state park, contains some of the finest cypress swamp in Texas. It is one of only 15 U.S. sites recognized by the Ramsar Convention on Wetlands of International Importance, dedicated to worldwide protection of wetland ecosystems. The overall area encompasses a sprawling maze of bayous, sloughs, and channels through pine and hardwood forest, bald cypress swamp, and open lake. In warmer months, one can rent canoes in the state park and elsewhere around the lake. Boaters should carry a map of the lake and a compass; the densely wooded, confusing channels make it easy to get lost. Boats with motors are also available for rent, and guides can be hired.

The Caddo Lake ecosystem predates that of any other large lake in Texas. It contains many stands of bald cypress trees 250 to 400 years old.

ADDITIONAL HELP

Location: Texas Official Travel Map grid J x 23; Harrison and Marion counties
Nearest food, gas, and lodging: All are available near the park entrance, and cabins are available on-site.
Nearest camping: On-site (48 sites)
Contact: Superintendent, Caddo Lake State Park (see Appendix C)

65 Tyler State Park

Habitats: Lake, creek, riparian, oak-pine woodland, bottomland hardwood forest, field, pasture
Key birds: Wood Duck, Greater Roadrunner, Pileated Woodpecker, and White-breasted and Brown-headed Nuthatches are present year-round. Chuck-will's-widow, Scissor-tailed Flycatcher, Wood Thrush, Louisiana Waterthrush, and Indigo and Painted Buntings occur in summer. Fox and Harris's Sparrows usually can be found in winter.
Best times to bird: April and May for spring migration and nesting activities

Birding strategies: The hiking trail, especially the area between Big Pine Camping Area and Dogwood Ridge (**A**), should be birded year-round. Summer birds to be expected here include Red-shouldered Hawk; Mourning Dove; Chuck-will's-widow; Ruby-throated Hummingbird; Belted Kingfisher; Red-bellied, Downy, and Pileated Woodpeckers; Northern Flicker; Blue Jay; American Crow; Carolina Chickadee; Tufted Titmouse; White-breasted and Brown-headed Nuthatches; Carolina Wren; Blue-gray Gnatcatcher; Gray Catbird; Brown Thrasher; Pine and Black-and-white Warblers; Northern Cardinal; Indigo Bunting; and Common Grackle.

65 Tyler State Park

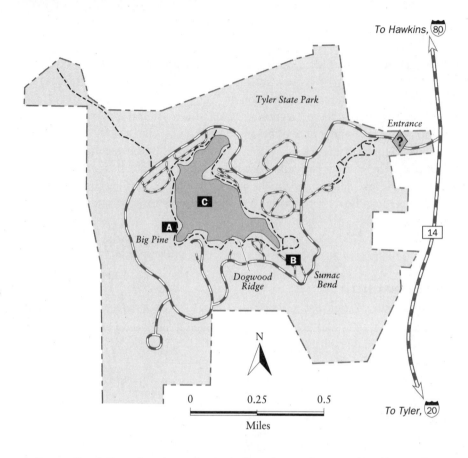

To Hawkins, 80

Tyler State Park

Entrance

?

14

C

A

Big Pine

B

Dogwood
Ridge

Sumac
Bend

N

0   0.25   0.5

To Tyler, 20

Miles

Sumac Bend Camping Area (**B**), including the outflow creek, offers Yellow-billed Cuckoo, Great Crested Flycatcher, Wood Thrush, Red-eyed Vireo, Louisiana Waterthrush, Summer Tanager, Painted Bunting, and Red-winged Blackbird.

Watch overhead for Black and Turkey Vultures, Chimney Swift, Purple Martin, and Barn Swallow. After dark listen for Eastern Screech-Owl. In winter look in the forest and weedy habitats for Yellow-bellied Sapsucker; Red-breasted Nuthatch; Brown Creeper; Golden-crowned and Ruby-crowned Kinglets; Hermit Thrush; Cedar Waxwing; Orange-crowned and Yellow-rumped Warblers; Eastern Towhee; Chipping, Field, Fox, Song, Lincoln's, and White-throated Sparrows; Dark-eyed Junco; Purple Finch; Pine Siskin; and American Goldfinch.

The lake (**C**) supports only a few birds. Great Blue Heron, Wood Duck, and Mallard can be found year-round. Gadwall, American Wigeon, Redhead, Ring-necked Duck, Lesser Scaup, Spotted Sandpiper, and Ring-billed Gull are occasional visitors during migration. Pied-billed and Horned Grebes, Double-crested Cormorant, and American Coot can occur in winter.

Bird the open fields outside the park, such as north of the park entrance along FM 14, for summer residents: Northern Bobwhite, Greater Roadrunner, Eastern Phoebe, Scissor-tailed Flycatcher, and Eastern Bluebird. In winter watch for Greater White-fronted, Snow, and Canada Geese; and Sharp-shinned, Cooper's, and Red-tailed Hawks.

Directions: From Tyler, take FM 14 north and cross I-20. The park entrance is 2 miles beyond.

General information: This 994-acre park, with a 64-acre spring-fed lake, was established in 1934. The park is primarily a recreation area with fishing (3 piers), swimming, boating, hiking, and a 12-mile mountain bike trail.

The city of Tyler maintains Brookshire's World of Wildlife Museum, which features more than 250 specimens of mammals, reptiles, and fish from Africa and North America; the 35-acre, free Caldwell Zoo; and the 22-acre Municipal Rose Garden and Museum.

ADDITIONAL HELP

Location: Texas Official Travel Map grid K x 21; Smith County

Nearest food, gas, and lodging: Food is available at the park entrance; gas is available in 4 miles on FM 14 or 6 miles on I-20. Lodging is available in Tyler (8 miles).

Nearest camping: On-site; 117 sites

Contact: Superintendent, Tyler State Park (see Appendix C)

66 Davy Crockett National Forest

Habitats: River, creek, pond, riparian, swamp, bottomland hardwood forest, mixed pine-hardwood forest, pine forest, field, pasture, cropland

Key birds: Wood Duck, Wild Turkey, Red-cockaded and Pileated Woodpeckers, Brown-headed Nuthatch, and Bachman's Sparrow are present year-round. Wood Stork; Broad-winged Hawk; American Woodcock; Chuck-will's-widow; Scissor-tailed Flycatcher; Wood Thrush; Yellow-throated, Prairie, Prothonotary, Worm-eating, Swainson's, Kentucky, and Hooded Warblers; Louisiana Waterthrush; American Redstart; and Indigo and Painted Buntings occur in summer. Eastern and Spotted Towhees; Vesper, Grasshopper, LeConte's, Fox, and Harris's Sparrows; and Rusty Blackbird can usually be found in winter.

Best times to bird: April and May for spring migrants and nesting activities; April and September for huge kettles of migrating Broad-winged Hawks

Birding strategies: The most productive birding occurs in the Alabama Creek Wildlife Management Area. The best bet for finding endangered Red-cockaded

66 Davy Crockett National Forest

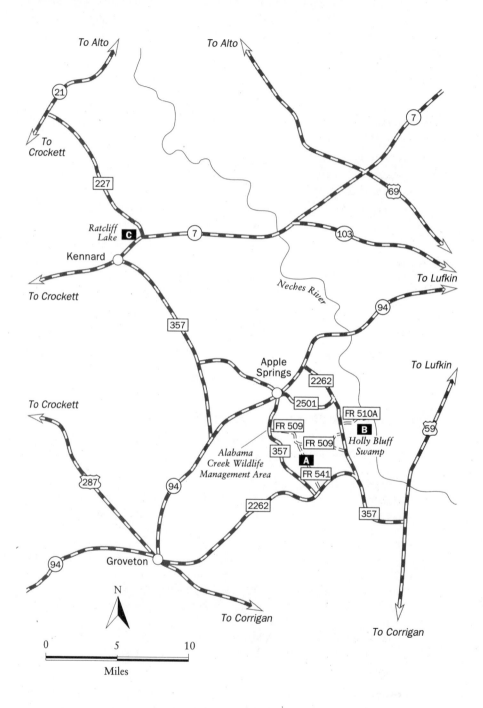

Woodpeckers is along FR 541 (**A**), off FM 2262 0.75 mile north of FM 357; cavity trees are marked with a green band. Brown-headed Nuthatch and Bachman's Sparrow also occur in this area; the sparrow's preferred habitat includes a grassy understory with scattered shrubs.

Other summer birds in this area include Red-shouldered Hawk, Mourning Dove, Ruby-throated Hummingbird, Barred Owl, Red-bellied and Pileated Woodpeckers, Eastern Wood-Pewee, Acadian and Great Crested Flycatchers, White-eyed and Red-eyed Vireos, Pine and Black-and-white Warblers, American Redstart, Northern Cardinal, Painted Bunting, Lark Sparrow, Eastern Meadowlark, Common Grackle, and Brown-headed Cowbird. Look in second-growth pine forests that have been cut in the past few years for Prairie Warbler, Yellow-breasted Chat, Indigo Bunting, and Blue Grosbeak.

Holly Bluff Swamp (**B**), located on FR 510A, 1.5 miles east of FM 2262, offers the greatest variety of birds year-round. Summer birds include Great Blue, Little Blue, and Green Herons; Great and Cattle Egrets; Wood Duck; Broad-winged Hawk; Yellow-billed Cuckoo; Chuck-will's-widow; Belted Kingfisher; Red-headed and Downy Woodpeckers; Scissor-tailed Flycatcher; Eastern Kingbird; Purple Martin; Barn Swallow; Blue Jay; American Crow; Carolina Chickadee; Tufted Titmouse; Carolina Wren; Wood Thrush; Eastern Bluebird; Gray Catbird; Northern Mockingbird; Brown Thrasher; White-eyed, Yellow-throated, and Red-eyed Vireos; Northern Parula; Prothonotary, Worm-eating, Swainson's, Kentucky, and Hooded Warblers; Louisiana Waterthrush; Common Yellowthroat; Summer Tanager; Red-winged Blackbird; Common Grackle; Brown-headed Cowbird; and Orchard Oriole.

In winter this area is the best bet for Rusty Blackbird, as well as Mallard, Blue-winged Teal, Common Snipe, and Yellow-bellied Sapsucker.

Continue on FR 510A to the Neches River and Holly Bluff Campground. The riparian corridor is an excellent place to find passing migrants in spring and fall: waterfowl, flycatchers, swallows, thrushes, vireos, warblers, tanagers, and orioles. And in winter, Brown Creeper, Red-breasted Nuthatch, Golden-crowned and Ruby-crowned Kinglets, Hermit Thrush, Cedar Waxwing, Orange-crowned and Yellow-rumped Warblers, Purple Finch, Pine Siskin, and American Goldfinch frequent this area.

Also in winter, the open fields along the numerous roadways support House, Winter, and Sedge Wrens; Brown Thrasher; Orange-crowned Warbler; Common Yellowthroat; Eastern and Spotted Towhees; Field, Vesper, Savannah, Grasshopper, LeConte's, Fox, Song, Lincoln's, Swamp, White-throated, White-crowned, and Harris's Sparrows; and Dark-eyed Junco.

Ratcliff Lake (**C**) (along SH 7 in the northern half of the forest) provides easy access to water birds. Expect Pied-billed Grebe, waders, and Wood Duck year-round, and a much greater number of waterfowl in winter. In summer check along SH 7 for areas of second-growth pine for Prairie Warbler, as well as American Woodcock, Yellow-breasted Chat, Blue Grosbeak, and Indigo Bunting.

Directions: Alabama Creek Wildlife Management Area is 8 miles north of Corrigan, via US 59, FM 2262, and SH 357. Ratcliff Lake lies along SH 7, 20 miles east of Crockett or 25 miles west of Lufkin.

General information: The 161,497-acre Davy Crockett National Forest is managed under the multiple-use concept with logging, hunting, and other recreational activities. The forest contains a 20-mile hiking trail, the 45-acre Ratcliff Lake (once a log pond and a source of water for the 4C Lumber Mill) and the 3,639-acre Big Slough Wilderness Area.

ADDITIONAL HELP

Location: Texas Official Travel Map grid M/N x 21; Houston and Trinity counties
Nearest food, gas, and lodging: Food and gas are available at Apple Springs, Groveton, and Kennard. Lodging is available at Groveton, Crockett, and Lufkin.
Nearest camping: On-site at Holly Bluff and at Ratcliff Lake (75 sites total)
Contact: District Ranger, Davy Crockett National Forest (see Appendix C)

67 Angelina National Forest and Sam Rayburn Reservoir

Habitats: Lake, river, creek, riparian, bottomland hardwood forest, mixed pine-hardwood forest, longleaf pine savannah, field, pasture, cropland

Key birds: Wood Duck; Red-headed, Red-cockaded, and Pileated Woodpeckers; Brown-headed Nuthatch; and Bachman's Sparrow are present year-round. Neotropic Cormorant; Anhinga; Roseate Spoonbill; Wood Stork; White Ibis; Chuck-will's-widow; Scissor-tailed Flycatcher; Wood Thrush; Prothonotary, Kentucky, Swainson's, and Hooded Warblers; Louisiana Waterthrush; and Indigo and Painted Buntings occur in summer. American White Pelican; Bald Eagle; American Woodcock; Sedge Wren; Grasshopper, Henslow's, and LeConte's Sparrows; and Rusty Blackbird can usually be found in winter.

Best times to bird: April and May for spring migrants and nesting activities; November to March for winter birds

Birding strategies: Saint's Rest Road (A), south of FM 1275, is actually an old railroad bed. Its year-round accessibility and good bottomland habitats make it an ideal spot during spring migration. In summer expected woodland birds include Red-shouldered Hawk; Mourning Dove; Yellow-billed Cuckoo; Red-bellied, Downy, and Pileated Woodpeckers; Eastern Wood-Pewee; Acadian and Great Crested Flycatchers; Blue Jay; American Crow; Carolina Chickadee; Tufted Titmouse; Brown-headed Nuthatch; Carolina Wren; Blue-gray Gnatcatcher; White-eyed and Red-eyed Vireos; Northern Parula; Yellow-throated, Pine, Black-and-white, Swainson's, and Hooded Warblers; Northern Cardinal; and Brown-headed

67 Angelina National Forest and Sam Rayburn Reservoir

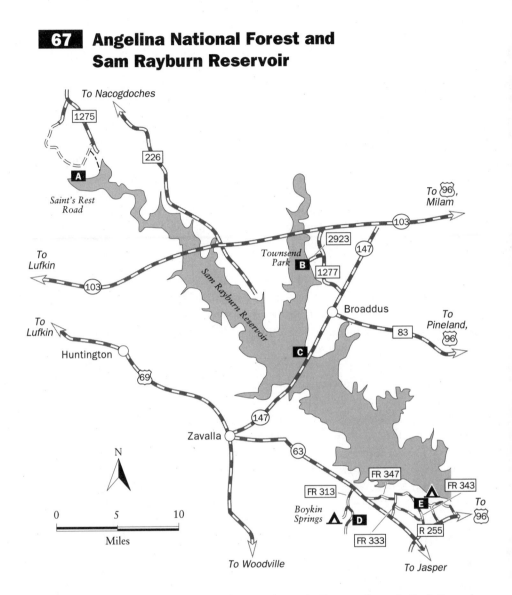

Cowbird. Less numerous are Broad-winged Hawk, Eastern Screech-Owl, Barred Owl, Chuck-will's-widow, Ruby-throated Hummingbird, Hairy Woodpecker, Wood Thrush, Kentucky Warbler, and Blue Grosbeak.

Townsend Park (**B**) and area, at the end of FM 2923, contains both woodland and wetland habitats, as well as good views of the lake. The majority of the woodland species mentioned above can be found here. In summer look also for Pied-billed Grebe; Anhinga; Great Blue, Little Blue, and Green Herons; Great and Snowy Egrets; Wood Duck; Belted Kingfisher; Red-headed Woodpecker; Eastern Kingbird; Yellow-throated Vireo; Prothonotary Warbler; Summer Tanager; and Red-winged Blackbird.

The SH 147 bridge (C) across Sam Rayburn Reservoir is one of the better sites for finding water birds. Park along the Broaddus side (north) of the bridge and walk along the road shoulder to bird the lake. Pied-billed Grebe, Great Blue and Little Blue Herons, and Great and Snowy Egrets can be found year-round. In summer watch for Neotropic Cormorant, Tricolored Heron, Yellow-crowned Night-Heron, and White Ibis. Black-crowned Night-Heron, Roseate Spoonbill, and Wood Stork occur as post-nesting visitors. In winter watch for Common Loon, Horned Grebe, American White Pelican, Green-winged Teal, Mallard, Northern Pintail, Northern Shoveler, Gadwall, American Wigeon, Canvasback (sometimes abundant), Redhead, Ring-necked Duck, Lesser Scaup, Bufflehead, Hooded Merganser, Ruddy Duck, Bald Eagle, and Bonaparte's and Ring-billed Gulls. Blue-winged Teal, Greater Scaup, and Common Goldeneye are less numerous.

The forest sites lack a weedy understory due to prescribed fires and therefore offer the best locations for Red-cockaded Woodpecker. Twenty-six clusters were recorded in the Angelina National Forest in 1996. Nesting trees are painted with a green band at chest height. Areas with a grass/forb understory and very few woody shrubs are utilized by Bachman's Sparrow, which is most easily found from March to August. These same areas may support Sedge Wren and Grasshopper and Henslow's Sparrows in winter.

The Boykin Springs area (D), accessible via FR 313 and FR 326 (south of SH 63), offers good woodpecker and sparrow habitats, as well as most of the other woodland birds mentioned above; Louisiana Waterthrush occurs here in summer. Similar habitats can be found near Pluma Ridge Road north of SH 63, along FR 343 and FR 306 (E), accessible off the Sandy Creek Road (FM 333).

Drive the area in winter and watch for grassy fields; those with bluestem often support LeConte's Sparrow. Several winter birds can be expected in brushy edges: House and Sedge Wrens; Common Yellowthroat; Eastern Towhee; Dark-eyed Junco; and Field, Vesper, Savannah, Song, Lincoln's, Swamp, and White-throated Sparrows. Henslow's Sparrow is less numerous. These same areas support Scissor-tailed Flycatcher and Indigo and Painted Buntings in summer.

Records of Review Species: Pacific Loon, March 1991. Eurasian Wigeon, Feb 1990.

Directions: From Lufkin, take SH 103 east to the key forest access roads. From Jasper, take SH 63 north (see map for additional directions).

General information: Although the Angelina is the smallest national forest in Texas (154,307 acres), Sam Rayburn Reservoir is one of the largest inland lakes (114,500 acres), 50 miles long with approximately 560 miles of shoreline. Only 100 miles northeast of Houston, the reservoir is a popular recreation area.

The forest contains a scattering of bogs with pitcher plants, sundews, and sphagnum moss, which occur in hillside seeps, in places where prescribed fires occur frequently, and in a few mowed areas in road right-of-ways.

ADDITIONAL HELP

Location: Texas Official Travel Map grid N/M x 22; Angelina, Jasper, Nacogdoches, and San Augustine counties

Nearest food, gas, and lodging: Food and gas are available at numerous sites, including Zavalla and Broaddus. Lodging is in Lufkin, Jasper, and Nacogdoches.

Nearest camping: Numerous on-site areas, including Bouton Lake, Boykin Springs, Caney Creek, Harvey Creek, Letney, Rayburn Park, Sandy Creek, and Townsend

Contact: District Manager, Angelina National Forest; Project Engineer, Sam Rayburn Dam and Reservoir (see Appendix C)

68 Sabine National Forest and Toledo Bend Reservoir

Habitats: Reservoir, river, pond, marsh, mud flat, riparian, mixed pine-hardwood forest, pine forest, field, pasture, cropland

Key birds: Wood Duck, Red-cockaded and Pileated Woodpeckers, Brown-headed Nuthatch, and Bachman's Sparrow are present year-round. Red-headed Woodpecker; Chuck-will's-widow; Wood Thrush; Yellow-throated, Prairie, Prothonotary, Worm-eating, Swainson's, Kentucky, and Hooded Warblers; American Redstart; Louisiana Waterthrush; Indigo and Painted Buntings; and Eastern Towhee occur in summer. Bald Eagle; American Woodcock; and Grasshopper, Henslow's, and LeConte's Sparrows can usually be found in winter.

Best times to bird: April and May for spring migrants and nesting activities; November to March for winter birds

Birding strategies: Foxhunter's Hill (**A**), near the southern boundary of the forest, offers the opportunity to see several rare species unique to the southern pine forest. Five clusters of Red-cockaded Woodpeckers reside along FR 113; cavity trees are marked with a green band. The woodpeckers can best be seen in the mornings and evenings. Do not disturb! Brown-headed Nuthatch is common here as well, and Bachman's Sparrow occurs in areas with a grassy understory. In spring and summer check any of the large young pine plantations for Prairie Warbler.

Other full-time resident birds of the Foxhunter's Hill area include American Kestrel; Mourning Dove; Red-bellied, Downy, and Pileated Woodpeckers; Blue Jay; Carolina Chickadee; Tufted Titmouse; Carolina Wren; Eastern Bluebird; and Pine Warbler. Several additional species can usually be found in summer: Chuck-will's-widow; Eastern Wood-Pewee; Great Crested Flycatcher; Wood Thrush; White-eyed Vireo; Hooded Warbler; Blue Grosbeak; and Indigo Bunting. And in winter, Red-breasted Nuthatch, Brown Creeper, Henslow's Sparrow, Red Crossbill, and Pine Siskin may be present.

The old fields and brushy edges in the area contain resident Red-tailed Hawk, Northern Bobwhite, Northern Mockingbird, Brown Thrasher, Loggerhead Shrike, Northern Cardinal, Lark Sparrow, Eastern Meadowlark, Common Grackle, and

68 Sabine National Forest and Toledo Bend Reservoir

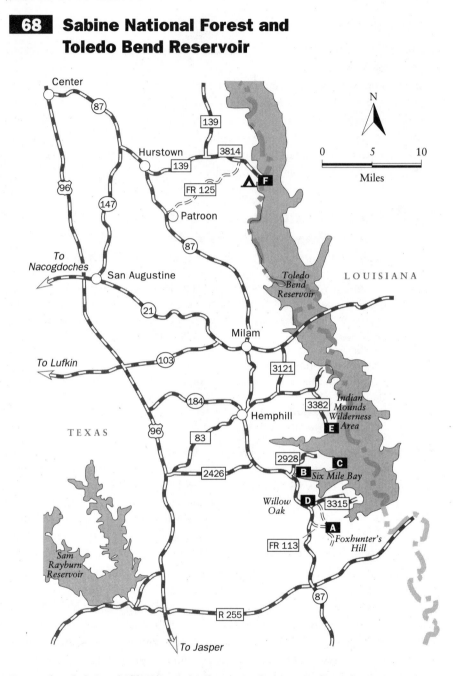

Brown-headed Cowbird. Winter birds can include several northern sparrows—Grasshopper, LeConte's, Fox, Swamp, White-crowned, and Harris's—as well as American Woodcock.

Six Mile Bay (**B**), an area dominated by bottomland hardwoods along FM 2928, offers in summer Red-shouldered Hawk; Barred Owl; Broad-winged Hawk;

Yellow-billed Cuckoo; Common Nighthawk; Acadian Flycatcher; Gray Catbird; Red-eyed Vireo; Northern Parula; Yellow-throated, Black-and-white, Prothonotary, Worm-eating, Swainson's, and Kentucky Warblers; American Redstart; Summer Tanager; Painted Bunting; and Orchard Oriole. This area also is usually very good during migration.

Lakeview (C), Willow Oak (D), and Indian Mounds Wilderness Area (E) also support a variety of forest birds. These areas offer extensive trail systems for experiencing the bird life.

The Ragtown area (F), to the north, also contains a few Red-cockaded Woodpecker clusters; banded trees can be found along FM 3814, where it intersects FR 125. The brushy field edges near the intersection support nesting Eastern Towhee. Bald Eagles nest along the reservoir near the campground and may be seen from the Ragtown boat ramp. Watch also for Wood Duck.

The Toledo Bend Reservoir, which can be viewed from the end of most of the above-mentioned roads, offers additional species during the year. Year-round water birds include Pied-billed Grebe, Great Blue and Little Blue Herons, Cattle, Great, and Snowy Egrets, Yellow-crowned Night-Heron, Forster's Tern, and Belted Kingfisher. Green Herons can be found here in summer, as can an abundance of waterfowl in winter.

Directions: Foxhunter's Hill and Six Mile Bay are located south of Hemphill via SH 87 and FR 113 or FM 3315 and FM 2928, respectively. The Ragtown area is north of Milam via SH 87 to Hurstown, then east on FM 139 and FM 3814.

General information: Sabine National Forest encompasses 157,951 acres along the western side of the Toledo Bend Reservoir. Trail Between the Lakes provides a 28-mile route between Lakeview Recreation Area north to US 96, within sight of the easternmost point of Sam Rayburn Reservoir. Toledo Bend Reservoir, covering an area of 185,000 acres with 1,200 miles of shoreline, was developed for water supply, hydroelectric power generation, and recreation.

ADDITIONAL HELP

Location: Texas Official Travel Map grid M/N x 23; Jasper, Sabine, San Augustine, Newton, and Shelby counties

Nearest food, gas, and lodging: Food and gas can be found in Hemphill and Milam; lodging in Center, San Augustine, and Hemphill.

Nearest camping: On-site at Indian Mounds, Lakeview, Ragtown, Red Hills Lake, and Willow Oak (129 sites total)

Contacts: Supervisor, Sabine National Forest; Manager, Toledo Bend Reservoir (see Appendix C)

69 Sam Houston National Forest and Huntsville State Park

Habitats: Lake, pond, creek, riparian, pine woodland, hardwood forest, field, pasture, cropland

Key birds: Wood Duck; American Woodcock; Red-headed, Red-cockaded, and Pileated Woodpeckers; White-breasted and Brown-headed Nuthatches; and Bachman's Sparrow are present year-round. Mississippi Kite; Chuck-will's-widow; Scissor-tailed Flycatcher; Wood Thrush; Yellow-throated, Prothonotary, Worm-eating, Swainson's, Kentucky, and Hooded Warblers; American Redstart; Louisiana Waterthrush; and Indigo and Painted Buntings occur in summer. Osprey; Bald Eagle; Grasshopper, LeConte's, and Fox Sparrows; and Rusty and Brewer's Blackbirds can usually be found in winter.

Best times to bird: April and May for spring migrants and nesting activities; April and late September for huge kettles of migrating Broad-winged Hawks

Birding strategies: The national forest contains 156 breeding clusters of Red-cockaded Woodpeckers, the state's largest concentration and one of the easiest places anywhere to see this endangered species. Although these woodpeckers are widely scattered, easily accessible clusters occur near the junction of FM 1375 and FR 233 (**A**), 3.5 miles west of I-45 (in the Raven District), and also at the interpretive site (**B**), just below the San Jacinto Work Center on FM 2025 (in the eastern San Jacinto District), west of Shepherd. Be especially careful not to disturb the birds when they are nesting, from mid-April to mid-June.

The forest and beaver pond at Cagle Campground (**C**), on FR 205 (south of FM 1375), support most of the forest and pond birds, including Wood Duck, Red-headed and Pileated Woodpeckers, Eastern Kingbird, Brown-headed Nuthatch, Red-eyed Vireo, Northern Parula, Prothonotary Warbler, Summer Tanager, and Indigo Bunting. Wintering waterfowl and Osprey are readily visible from the causeway across Lake Conroe (**D**). Watch too for Bald Eagle; a nesting pair can often be seen from the causeway through April; these birds also winter here. Continue west of the causeway on FM 1375 for 8.75 miles to FM 149; bear right onto 149 and drive 1.5 miles, then turn right onto FM 1791; drive 3 miles to the open forest habitat (**E**), where Bachman's Sparrow is most likely. Also watch for American Woodcock, which frequents brushy areas in winter and grassy sites in spring and summer.

In the eastern portion of the forest, the Big Creek Scenic Area (**F**) can be very good in spring for northbound migrants. The Winters Bayou area (**G**), north of FM 1725 via FR 241 or FR 274, contains good bottomland hardwood, pine, and palmetto habitats. In summer look here for Red-shouldered Hawk; Barred Owl; Chuck-will's-widow; Red-headed, Downy, and Pileated Woodpeckers; Acadian Flycatcher; Wood Thrush; Yellow-throated and Red-eyed Vireos; Northern Parula; Yellow-throated and Black-and-white Warblers; and Louisiana Waterthrush.

Swainson's Warbler is more numerous along FR 201 (**H**), a short distance to the southwest.

During winter the old fields along gated FR 2112 (**I**), off FM 2025, 6.5 miles north of Cleveland, can produce a different assortment of birds. Expected species include Eastern Phoebe; House, Winter, and Sedge Wrens; Eastern and Spotted Towhees; and Field, Vesper, Savannah, Grasshopper, LeConte's, Fox, Song, Lincoln's, Swamp, White-throated, White-crowned, and Harris's Sparrows.

Huntsville State Park, 6 miles south of Huntsville off I-45, offers many of the same water and woodland birds. Lake Raven (**J**), especially the area below the dam and along Little Chinquapin Creek (most easily accessed from the Coloneh Camping Area), can be filled with migrants in spring. Red-bellied, Downy, and Pileated Woodpeckers; Blue Jay; American Crow; Carolina Chickadee; Tufted Titmouse; White-breasted and Brown-headed Nuthatches; Carolina Wren; Pine Warbler; Northern Cardinal; and Chipping Sparrow are common in the campground year-round. In summer check the lakeshore for Prothonotary and Swainson's Warblers, and Scissor-tailed Flycatcher and Indigo and Painted Buntings in the open fields. Watch overhead for Mississippi Kite.

Directions: Take I-45 north of Conroe for 17 miles to the New Waverly exit and FM 1375 west into the Raven District; or take FM 2025 north of Cleveland for 10 miles to the Red-cockaded Woodpecker interpretive site (near the San Jacinto Work Center); or take FM 2025, FM 945, and FR 274 to the Winters Bayou area; or take US 59 north of Cleveland 10 miles to Shepherd, west on SH 150 for 2.5 miles to FR 2666, then turn left and continue to the Big Creek Scenic Area. Huntsville State Park is located along the northern boundary of the forest. Turn off I-45 at exit 109, and follow PR 40 to the park entrance.

General Information: The 158,411-acre Sam Houston National Forest, about 50 miles north of Houston, offers ready access to numerous clusters of the endangered Red-cockaded Woodpecker. The forest also contains some of the best remaining examples of native pineywood forest.

The forest is crisscrossed by approximately 150 miles of hiking trails, including the Lone Star (national recreation) Hiking Trail. This 140-mile-long trail stretches from its eastern trailhead near Cleveland north through the Big Creek Scenic Area to Double Lake, then northwest to Huntsville State Park and southwest to the Little Lake Creek Wilderness Area. Since much of this route crosses private land, it is important that hikers do not trespass. Hiking is not recommended from November 15 to December 31, during deer hunting season.

The 2,083-acre state park is dominated by Lake Raven, a 210-acre impoundment of Prairie Branch, Alligator Branch, and Chinquapin Creek. The park contains 8 miles of hiking and biking trails that circle the lake, providing easy access to birding sites year-round. The park can be extremely busy on weekends.

69 Sam Houston National Forest Northwest of Conroe and Huntsville State Park

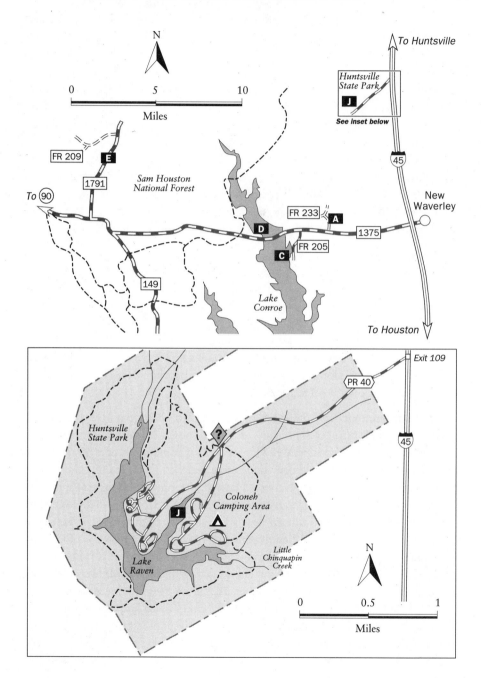

69 Sam Houston National Forest North of Cleveland

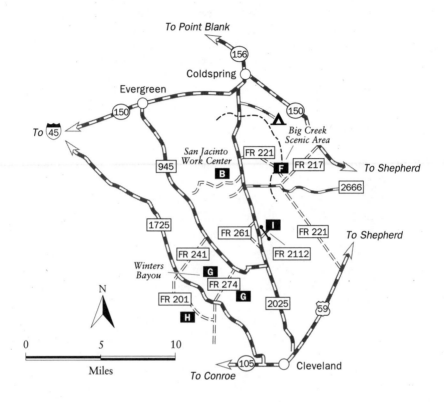

ADDITIONAL HELP

Location: Texas Official Travel Map grid O/P x 20/21; Walker, San Jacinto, and Montgomery counties

Nearest food, gas, and lodging: Food and gas are available in New Waverly, Cleveland, and Coldspring, as well as at a concession stand at Double Lake. Lodging is available in Cleveland, Coldspring, Huntsville, and Conroe.

Nearest camping: On-site at Double Lake (59 sites), Stubblefield (28 sites), and Huntsville State Park (191 sites)

Contact: District Ranger, Sam Houston National Forest; Superintendent, Huntsville State Park (see Appendix C)

70 Lake Livingston State Park

Habitats: Lake, pond, wetland, pine woodland, bottomland hardwood forest, field

Key birds: Wood Duck, Pileated Woodpecker, and Brown-headed Nuthatch are present year-round. American White Pelican, Chuck-will's-widow, Scissor-tailed Flycatcher, and Painted Bunting occur in summer. Osprey, Bald Eagle, and LeConte's Sparrow can usually be found in winter.

Best times to bird: April and May for spring migrants and nesting activities; November to February for Bald Eagle and waterfowl

Birding strategies: Migrants can best be found in vegetation along the lakeshore and by walking the various hiking trails. The trail south of the southern campground (behind sites 92 through 94), which loops through upland pine forest habitat (**A**), and the trail that continues north of the Oak Flats Nature Trail (**B**) to the Duck Pond are likely to provide the widest variety of resident birds. Woodland birds, such as Red-shouldered Hawk; Red-bellied, Downy, and Pileated Woodpeckers; Eastern Wood-Pewee; Acadian and Great Crested Flycatchers; Carolina Chickadee; Tufted Titmouse; Brown-headed Nuthatch; and Pine Warbler, are more likely along the south loop. Wood Duck, Yellow-billed Cuckoo, Barred Owl, Chuck-will's-widow, Eastern Kingbird, Summer Tanager, and Orchard Oriole are more likely along the Duck Pond Trail.

Visit the restored prairie (**C**) along FM 3126, where you are likely to find Scissor-tailed Flycatcher, Eastern Bluebird, Loggerhead Shrike, Painted Bunting, and Eastern Meadowlark. In winter look here for Savannah, LeConte's, White-throated, and Song Sparrows, and for Eastern Meadowlark.

The lake attracts numerous waterfowl during migration and in winter. Birding can be extremely productive off the 2-mile causeway on US 190 (**D**); watch for American White Pelican, gulls, terns, and cormorants. Flights of more than 10,000 Double-crested Cormorants, flying between their feeding and roosting sites, are possible. The spillway below the dam (**E**), at the south end of the lake, is worth a visit during most of the year; pelicans, cormorants, various waders, and American Coot can be expected. This area also attracts Osprey and Bald Eagle in winter.

Records of Review Species: Pacific Loon, May 1994. *Lake Livingston Dam*—Black-headed Gull, Jan–Feb 1982. Black-legged Kittiwake, Dec 1981, Jan 1982. *Lake Livingston*—Black-legged Kittiwake, March 1992. Snow Bunting, Dec 1977.

Directions: Take US 59 south of Livingston for 1 mile, or north of Houston for 75 miles, to FM 1988. Go 4 miles west to FM 3126 and the park entrance. The dam and spillway are 1 mile south of the park entrance along FM 1988.

General information: The 635-acre state park is primarily a recreation area used by Houston residents and local communities. The park's 2.5 miles of shoreline provide an excellent base for fishing, boating, and swimming. Picnicking, bicycling,

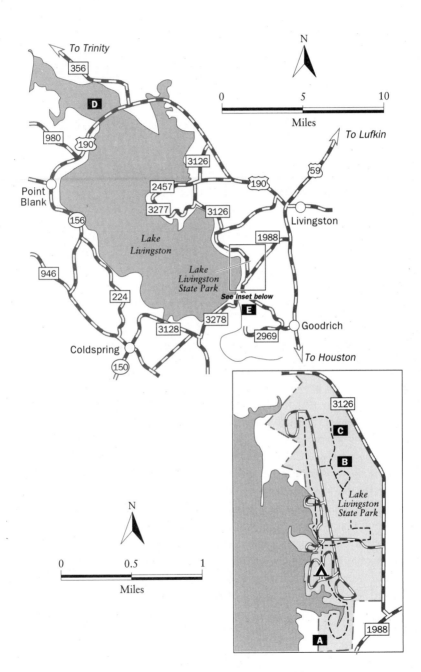

horseback riding, and wildlife observation and photography are also encouraged. The 84,000-acre reservoir, a project of the Trinity River Authority, is especially busy on weekends and holidays.

ADDITIONAL HELP

Location: Texas Official Travel Map grid O x 21; Polk County
Nearest food, gas, and lodging: Livingston has all three.
Nearest camping: On-site (152 sites)
Contact: Superintendent, Lake Livingston State Park (see Appendix C)

71 Martin Dies, Jr., State Park and B. A. Steinhagen Lake

Habitats: River, reservoir, wetland, riparian, hardwood forest, mixed pine-hardwood forest, field, pasture
Key birds: Wood Duck, Wild Turkey, Red-headed and Pileated Woodpeckers, and Brown-headed Nuthatch are present year-round. Anhinga; White Ibis; Chuck-will's-widow; Wood Thrush; Yellow-throated, Prairie, Prothonotary, Swainson's, Kentucky, and Hooded Warblers; Louisiana Waterthrush; and Indigo and Painted Buntings occur in summer. Bald Eagle, American Woodcock, and Rusty and Brewer's Blackbirds can usually be found in winter.
Best times to bird: April and May for spring migrants and nesting activities

Birding strategies: In spring and early summer, start birding in the Cherokee Unit of the state park (**A**), especially the south side, which serves as a migrant trap for songbirds. This area also provides good views of the lake and a heronry utilized by Little Blue and Tricolored Herons, Snowy and Cattle Egrets, and Yellow-crowned Night-Herons, as well as Anhinga and White Ibis; also watch for Wood Duck. Migrating and wintering waterfowl are usually numerous in season, and shorebirds can be abundant when the lake level is low.

Magnolia Ridge Park and the Walnut Ridge and Hen House Ridge units also provide good lake views. Magnolia Ridge Park (**B**) usually contains the greatest avian diversity; bird along the entrance road for songbirds and near the three boat ramps for water birds. In summer, expected woodland birds include Red-shouldered and Broad-winged Hawks; Yellow-billed Cuckoo; Red-headed, Red-bellied, Downy, Hairy, and Pileated Woodpeckers; Eastern Wood-Pewee; Acadian and Great Crested Flycatchers; Eastern Kingbird; Blue Jay; Carolina Chickadee; Tufted Titmouse; Brown-headed Nuthatch; Carolina Wren; Blue-gray Gnatcatcher; Eastern Bluebird; Wood Thrush; Brown Thrasher; White-eyed, Yellow-throated, and Red-eyed Vireos; Northern Parula; Yellow-throated, Pine, Black-and-white, Swainson's, Kentucky, and Hooded Warblers; Summer Tanager; Northern Cardinal; Blue Grosbeak; Indigo and Painted Bunting; and Orchard Oriole. Less numerous here are Wild Turkey,

71 Martin Dies, Jr., State Park and B. A. Steinhagen Lake

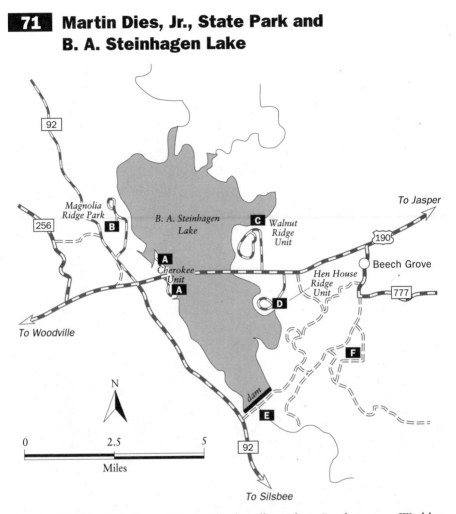

Eastern Screech-Owl, Barred Owl, Chuck-will's-widow, Prothonotary Warbler, and Louisiana Waterthrush.

The Walnut Ridge and Hen House Ridge units are dominated by pines with adjacent mixed forest habitats. Although many of the same birds mentioned above occur in these areas, the 1-mile loop trail in the Walnut Ridge Unit (**C**) is well worth the time and effort in summer. The nature trail in the Hen House Ridge Unit (**D**) is also worth birding. The slough and bottom hardwoods offer easy access to a variety of wetland and forest birds. Northern Parula and Yellow-throated, Prothonotary, Kentucky, and Hooded Warblers can be numerous. In winter watch for Rusty Blackbird.

Visit the Town Bluff Dam area (**E**), at the south end of the lake off SH 92, where you can walk down the service road to the dam. Follow the fishing trails below the dam. Bald Eagle and American Woodcock can often be found here in winter.

Cove of B. A. Steinhagen Lake in the Cherokee Unit of Martin Dies, Jr., State Park.

Explore the county roads (F) south of Beech Grove and east of Town Bluff Dam in late spring and early summer for Prairie Warbler. Watch for large clearcuts with a thick growth of young pines between 6 and 12 feet high. The birds are easier to find if you can hear them singing.

Directions: The principal birding sites lie north and south of US 190, on the west and east shorelines of B. A. Steinhagen Lake, 8 miles west of Jasper or 10 miles east of Woodville. Town Bluff Dam is at the south end of the lake; FM 777 and adjacent roads are located to the east.

General information: The shoreline of B. A. Steinhagen Lake includes a 705-acre state park and land managed by the U.S. Army Corps of Engineers. Weekends and holidays can be very busy, so bird on weekdays and on early mornings.

The state park was named for Martin Dies, Jr., a former Texas senator, Texas secretary of state, and chief justice of the Ninth U.S. Circuit Court of Appeals.

The Angelina River from Bevilport to the Walnut Ridge Unit of the Angelina-Neches Wildlife Management Area offers the canoe enthusiast the opportunity to see beautiful scenery as well as a wide variety of wildlife.

ADDITIONAL HELP

Location: Texas Official Travel Map grid N x 23; Tyler County
Nearest food, gas, and lodging: Food and gas are available on-site at Tidelands along US 190. The nearest lodging is in Jasper (13 miles) or Woodville (17 miles).
Nearest camping: On-site in the state park (181 sites)
Contact: Superintendent, Martin Dies, Jr., State Park; Project Engineer, B. A. Steinhagen Lake (see Appendix C)

72 W. G. Jones State Forest

Habitats: Mixed pine-hardwood forest, creek, riparian, field, pasture, cropland
Key birds: Wood Duck; Red-headed, Red-bellied, Downy, Hairy, Red-cockaded, and Pileated Woodpeckers; and Brown-headed Nuthatch are present year-round. Chuck-will's-widow; Wood Thrush; Worm-eating, Swainson's, Kentucky, and Hooded Warblers; Louisiana Waterthrush; and Indigo and Painted Buntings occur in summer. American Woodcock; Sedge Wren; and Henslow's, LeConte's, Fox, and Harris's Sparrows can usually be found in winter.
Best times to bird: April and May for spring migrants and nesting activity

Birding strategies: The forest supports 17 groups (clusters) of Red-cockaded Woodpecker, many readily accessible by vehicle or a short walk. Cavity trees are painted with a green band. Clusters directly behind the headquarters (**A**) on FM 1488 and within a quarter-mile north and south along People's Road (west edge) (**B**) are most accessible.

Most of the other year-round residents can be found at these same sites. These include American Kestrel; Mourning Dove; Eastern Screech-Owl; Great Horned Owl; Red-headed, Red-bellied, Downy, Hairy, and Pileated Woodpeckers; Blue Jay; American Crow; Carolina Chickadee; Tufted Titmouse; Brown-headed Nuthatch; Carolina Wren; Blue-gray Gnatcatcher; Pine Warbler; Northern Cardinal; and Common Grackle. Summer species include Broad-winged Hawk; Chuck-will's-widow; Ruby-throated Hummingbird; Eastern Wood-Pewee; Acadian and

72 W. G. Jones State Forest

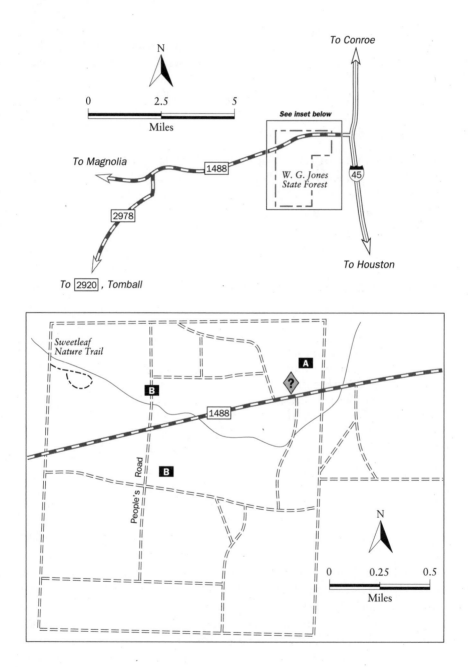

Great Crested Flycatchers; Wood Thrush; Red-eyed Vireo; Black-and-white, Worm-eating, Kentucky, and Hooded Warblers; Louisiana Waterthrush; Yellow-breasted Chat; and Summer Tanager. American Woodcock frequents these areas in winter; a few remain and nest. The few ponds in the forest attract migrants and occasional visitors only.

Various small creeks and riparian habitat in and adjacent to the forest support Red-shouldered Hawk, Wood Duck, and Barred Owl year-round. In summer Yellow-billed Cuckoo; Yellow-throated Vireo; Yellow-throated (rare), Prothonotary (rare), and Swainson's Warblers; Louisiana Waterthrush; and Common Yellowthroat utilize this habitat.

The area's fields and pastures and their brushy edges support Black and Turkey Vultures, Red-tailed Hawk, American Kestrel, Northern Bobwhite, Eastern Bluebird, Northern Mockingbird, Loggerhead Shrike, Red-winged Blackbird, and Eastern Meadowlark year-round. Common Nighthawk, Chimney Swift, Scissor-tailed Flycatcher, Purple Martin, Barn Swallow, Blue Grosbeak, Indigo and Painted Buntings, and Orchard Oriole are usually present only in summer. Eastern Phoebe; House, Winter, and Sedge Wrens; Brown Thrasher; Common Yellowthroat; Eastern and Spotted (rare) Towhees; Chipping, Field, Vesper, Savannah, Henslow's (irregular), LeConte's, Fox, Song, Lincoln's, Swamp, White-throated, White-crowned, and Harris's Sparrows; Dark-eyed Junco; Pine Siskin; and American Goldfinch can be expected in winter.

Directions: The forest is situated along FM 1488, 5 miles south of Conroe (30 miles north of Houston) via I-45.

General information: This 1,725-acre state forest was named for W. Goodrich Jones, the "Father of Forestry" in Texas. Primarily a native loblolly pine forest, it is managed as a "demonstration forest" to test various forest management techniques, forest genetics, and forest product utilization. Prescribed fires are set annually, and the mature pine areas are burned once every three to five years.

The self-guided Sweetleaf Nature Trail is located in the northwest corner of the forest; it serves as an ideal classroom for learning about typical flora and fauna of southeast Texas.

ADDITIONAL HELP

Location: Texas Official Travel Map grid P x 21; Montgomery County
Nearest food, gas, and lodging: Food and gas can be found east on FM 1488 (1.5 miles); lodging is in Conroe or Woodlands (5 miles).
Nearest camping: Conroe and Woodlands
Contact: Texas Forest Service (see Appendix C)

73 Big Thicket

Big Thicket National Preserve, Village Creek State Park, Roy E. Larsen Sandyland Sanctuary and Tyrrell Park

Habitats: River, creek, pond, marsh, riparian, bottomland hardwood forest, mixed pine-hardwood forest, pine forest, pine-oak savannah, prairie, field, pasture, cropland

Key birds: Wood Duck, Greater Roadrunner, Red-headed and Pileated Woodpeckers, Brown-headed Nuthatch, Fish Crow, Brown-headed Nuthatch, and Bachman's Sparrow are present year-round. **Least Grebe;** Anhinga; Chuck-will's-widow; Wood Thrush; Yellow-throated, Prairie, Black-and-white, Prothonotary, Swainson's, and Kentucky Warblers; Louisiana Waterthrush; and Indigo and Painted Buntings occur in summer. Hooded Merganser; Osprey; Bald Eagle; American Woodcock; Henslow's, LeConte's, and Fox Sparrows; and Rusty Blackbird can usually be found in winter.

Best times to bird: April and May for migrants and nesting activities; November to February for winter birds

Birding strategies: Big Thicket National Preserve contains 12 units that are scattered over an extensive area 45 miles long and 50 miles wide. Sites along the Neches River, such as Cooks Lake (**A**) in the Beaumont Unit and Lakeview Sand Bar (**B**) in the Lower Neches River Corridor Unit, offer the greatest number of neotropical migrants, including flycatchers, thrushes, vireos, warblers, tanagers, and orioles, in April and May. Both sites are accessible off FM 1131 via I-10 east of Beaumont and north on FM 105. These sites also provide good views of the river, where many of the resident water birds can be expected. In summer Pied-billed Grebe; Anhinga; Great Blue, Little Blue, and Green Herons; Great and Snowy Egrets; Wood Duck; and Fish Crow are likely. Tricolored Heron, Yellow-crowned Night-Heron, White Ibis, Black-bellied Whistling-Duck, Ruddy Duck, Black Tern, and American Coot are less numerous.

The Kirby Nature Trail (**C**), behind the Turkey Creek Visitor Information Station (located north of Kountze on FM 420, 2.9 miles east of US 69), may offer the best general introduction to Big Thicket's terrestrial bird life. Expected full-time residents here include Red-shouldered Hawk; Eastern Screech-Owl; Barred Owl; Red-bellied, Downy, and Pileated Woodpeckers; Blue Jay; American Crow; Carolina Chickadee; Tufted Titmouse; Carolina Wren; and Northern Cardinal. In summer Yellow-billed Cuckoo; Ruby-throated Hummingbird; Eastern Wood-Pewee; Acadian and Great Crested Flycatchers; Wood Thrush; Yellow-throated and Red-eyed Vireos; Northern Parula; Yellow-throated, Pine, Black-and-white, Prothonotary, and Kentucky Warblers; American Redstart; Louisiana Waterthrush; and Summer Tanager can usually be found, as well.

The Turkey Creek Trail (**D**) is located 3.7 miles east of US 69, along the unmarked road known locally as either Gore Store or R&B Road, and 3.6 miles north of FM 420. It is the best bet for finding Swainson's Warbler in summer. Most of the birds mentioned above can be found here as well. The open pine habitat (**E**), approximately 9 miles farther east on Gore Store Road (1 to 2 miles west of FM 92), is a good place to find

Bachman's Sparrow, as well as Brown-headed Nuthatch and Pine Warbler. Check for Yellow-throated and Prothonotary Warblers at the bridge on Beech Creek. Camp Waluka Road (F), south off Gore Store Road, contained singing Prairie Warblers in cut-over sites in 1997.

The Sundew Trail (G), in the Hickory Creek Savannah Unit, contains open longleaf pine forest that supports populations of Brown-headed Nuthatch and Pine Warbler. This area is burned regularly by the National Park Service in an attempt to restore the habitat for Red-cockaded Woodpecker. The only active area colony, however, is located in the Alabama-Coushatta Indian Reservation, near Livingston.

The Woodlands Trail (H), in the north end of the Big Sandy Creek Unit (north of SH 943, 20 miles northwest of US 69), is also worth birding in summer. This much longer trail provides access to a diversity of habitats where all the same birds mentioned for Kirby Nature Trail can usually be found. Additional possibilities here include Red-headed Woodpecker in the old-growth stand at the end of the trail; Prairie Warbler in young pine stands; and Yellow-breasted Chat, Blue Grosbeak, and Indigo and Painted Buntings in old fields.

The **Roy E. Larsen Sandyland Sanctuary** (I), 3.4 miles west of Silsbee off SH 327, contains a trail system through one of the last remaining undisturbed longleaf pine communities in Texas. Hairy Woodpecker, Brown-headed Nuthatch, Wood Thrush, Warbling Vireo, Worm-eating Warbler, American Redstart, Yellow-breasted Chat, Blue Grosbeak, Indigo Bunting, and Bachman's Sparrow can usually be found here in summer.

Village Creek State Park, on the east side of Lumberton, supports a diversity of birds, but in a different setting. This area can be superb during spring migration. Village Creek Trail (J) offers the best birding during migration, and the Water Oak Trail (K), especially along the pipeline right-of-way, is worth checking out. Look here for Sharp-shinned, Broad-winged, Red-tailed, and Swainson's Hawks; American Kestrel; and Painted Bunting. The wetlands along Tupelo Trail (L) often support Least Bittern, Wood Stork, Eastern Kingbird, and Common Yellowthroat in summer.

The park's Village Slough Loop Trail (M) offers access to habitat along a smaller waterway and drier woodland, including several acres of dead pines, killed by a southern pine beetle infestation. These habitats are especially good in summer for Chuck-will's-widow; Red-headed, Red-bellied, and Pileated Woodpeckers; Eastern Wood-Pewee; Acadian and Great Crested Flycatchers; Wood Thrush; Northern Parula; Black-and-white, Swainson's, and Kentucky Warblers; and American Redstart.

Near Beaumont, bird **Tyrrell Park** (N), southwest of town off I-10. It contains woodlands, brushy areas, and Cattail Marsh, the city's water reclamation system. In spring, migrants can be abundant. In summer, look for resident Red-headed Woodpecker and Fish Crow. And in winter, Cattail Marsh can offer **Least Grebe** and Horned and Eared Grebes, Cinnamon Teal, and Oldsquaw.

In summer scattered pastures and fields throughout the Big Thicket area support Northern Bobwhite, Mourning and Rock Doves, American Crow, Northern Mockingbird, American Robin, Eastern Bluebird, Indigo Bunting, Eastern Bluebird, Red-winged Blackbird, and Common Grackle. Watch overhead for Black and Turkey

73 Big Thicket

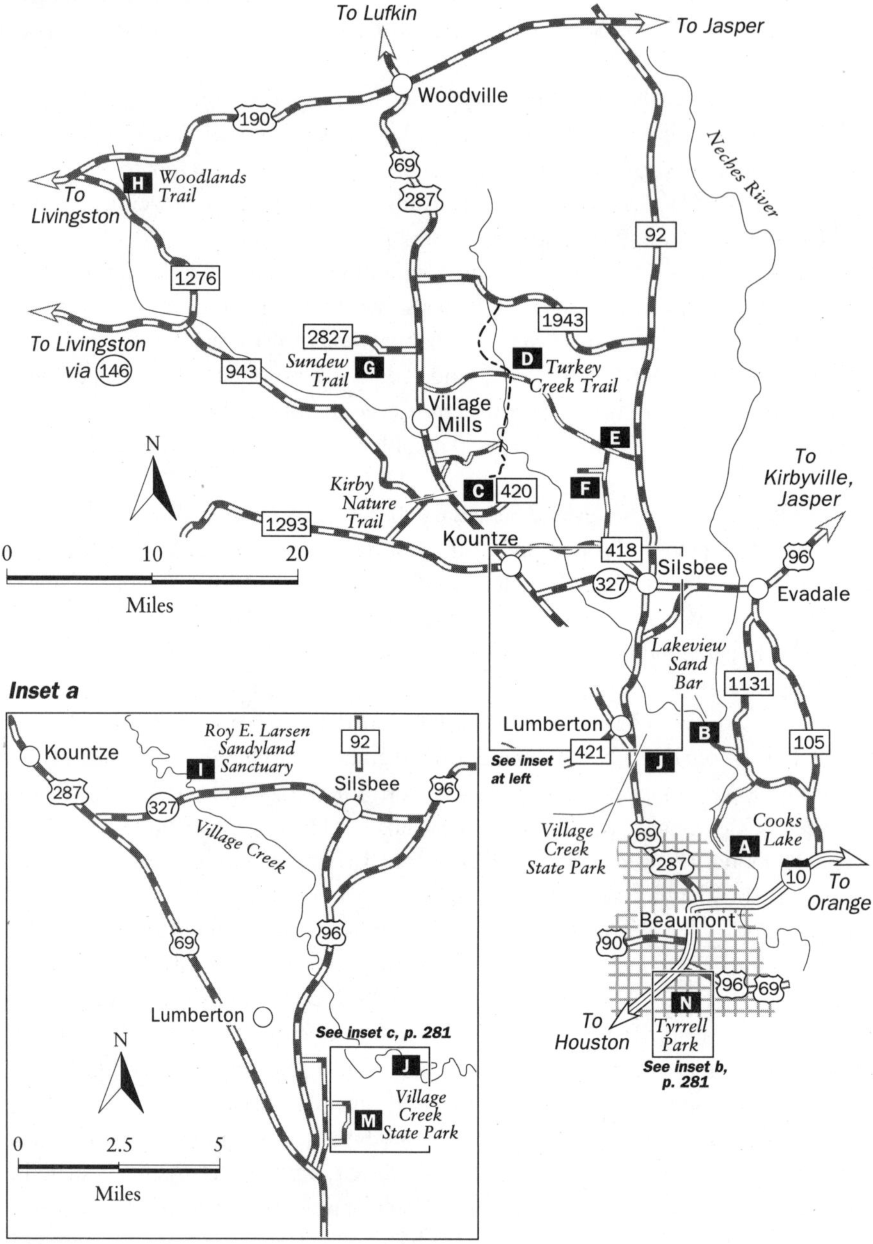

To Lufkin

To Jasper

190 Woodville

To Livingston

H Woodlands Trail

1276

69
287

Neches River

92

To Livingston via 146

943

2827

Sundew Trail **G**

1943

D *Turkey Creek Trail*

Village Mills

N

Kirby Nature Trail

1293

C 420

E

F

Kountze

418

327 Silsbee

96

To Kirbyville, Jasper

Evadale

0   10   20

Miles

Lakeview Sand Bar

1131

105

Inset a

Lumberton

See inset at left

421

J

B

Kountze

287

Roy E. Larsen Sandyland Sanctuary **I**

92

327

Silsbee

96

Village Creek

96

69

Lumberton

N

0   2.5   5

Miles

See inset c, p. 281

J

M

Village Creek State Park

Village Creek State Park

69
287

Cooks Lake **A**

10 To Orange

Beaumont

90

N *Tyrrell Park*

96 69

To Houston

See inset b, p. 281

Vultures, Red-tailed Hawk, Common Nighthawk, Chimney Swift, Purple Martin, and Barn Swallow. The brushy fields usually house wintering American Kestrel; Eastern Phoebe; House and Sedge Wrens; Eastern Towhee; Field, Henslow's, Fox, Swamp, and White-throated Sparrows; and American Goldfinch.

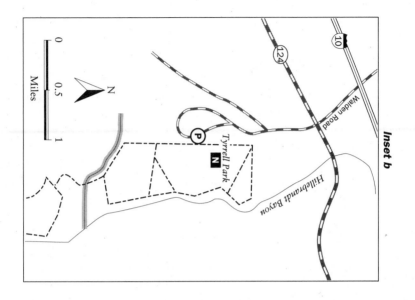

Inset b

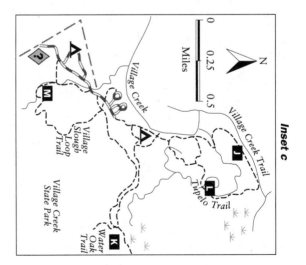

Inset c

Directions: Aside from Cooks Lake and Lakeview, for which directions are given in "Birding Strategies," the principal national preserve units are located north of Beaumont along FM 92 and US 69/287 (see map). Village Creek State Park is east of Lumberton off South Village Creek Parkway (FM 3513). Sandyland Sanctuary is located 20 minutes north of Lumberton: take US 69 and Spur 498 north to Silsbee and go 3.4 miles west on SH 327 to the entrance. Beaumont's Tyrrell Park lies south of I-10: take Walden Road south from I-10, cross the railroad tracks to Tyrrell Park, and follow the park loop road to Cattail Marsh at the far end.

General information: The original Big Thicket covered about 3.5 million acres from Louisiana west to what is now Houston, and from the coastal plains north to the upper watersheds of the Trinity, Neches, and Sabine rivers. Only about 300,000 acres of the thicket remain today, with just 96,757 acres protected in the national preserve.

According to the park brochure, the national preserve contains "85 tree species, more than 60 shrubs, and nearly 1,000 flowering plants, including 26 ferns and allies, 28 orchids, and four of North America's five types of insect-eating plants." In addition, the region has produced 56 state and 15 national champion trees, the largest known specimens of each species.

Village Creek (63 miles long) is a major tributary of the Neches River. The 1,020-acre state park lies along the west bank, 4 miles above the Neches River. With over 50 inches of annual rainfall, the park is often flooded. The 2,400-acre Roy E. Larsen Sandyland Sanctuary, owned and operated by The Nature Conservancy of Texas, is open to the public during daylight hours year-round. The sanctuary has 6 miles of nature trails and offers a beautiful canoe trip on 8 miles of Village Creek; guided tours are available.

Beaumont's Tyrrell Park contains a golf course, public garden, stables, picnic area, woodlands, and an extensive (900-acre) marsh ecosystem. Constructed in 1993, this wetland habitat has something to offer birders year-round. The outer levees of the marsh feature a 5-mile graveled outer loop route, but shorter circuits of 4.7, 3.2, and 2.8 miles cover most of the marsh. Although you cannot drive into the fenced area, birders are welcome to walk the levees.

ADDITIONAL HELP

Location: Texas Official Travel Map grid N/P x 23; Polk, Tyler, Jasper, Hardin, and Orange counties

Nearest food, gas, and lodging: Food and gas are scattered throughout; lodging is available in Beaumont, Kountze, Silsbee, and Woodville.

Nearest camping: Available at numerous sites, including Village Creek State Park, Tyrrell Park in Beaumont, and on the Alabama-Coushatta Indian Reservation, near Livingston.

Contact: Superintendent, Big Thicket National Preserve; Superintendent, Village Creek State Park; Sandyland Sanctuary; Tyrrell Park, owned and operated by the city of Beaumont (see Appendix C)

Central Plains Region

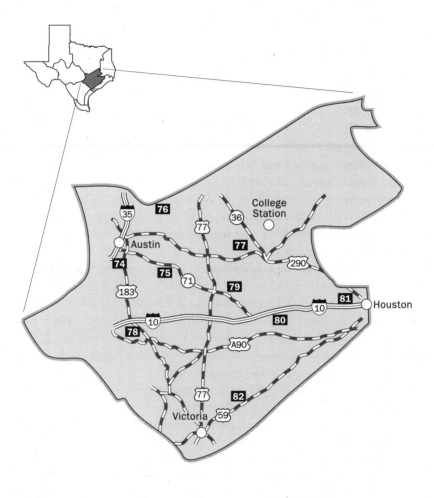

74 Austin East

75 Bastrop, Buescher, and Lake Bastrop State Parks

76 Alcoa Lake and Granger Lake

77 Lake Somerville State Park

78 Palmetto State Park

79 Fayette Lake

80 Attwater Prairie Chicken National Wildlife Refuge

81 Houston West

82 Lake Texana and Lake Texana State Park

74   Austin East

Hornsby Bend and Walnut Creek Wastewater Treatment Plants and McKinney Falls State Park

Habitats: River, stream, pond, mud flat, riparian, juniper-hackberry woodland, mesquite grassland, cropland

Key birds: Least Grebe, Wood and Mottled Ducks, and **Green Kingfisher** are present year-round. Chuck-will's-widow, Black-chinned Hummingbird, Scissor-tailed Flycatcher, and Indigo and Painted Buntings occur in summer. American Woodcock and Fox and Harris's Sparrows can usually be found in winter.

Best times to bird: April to mid-May for spring migrants and nesting activities; late fall and winter for vagrants and waterfowl at Hornsby Bend

Birding strategies: Hornsby Bend Wastewater Treatment Plant (A), located in a bend of the Colorado River off FM 973, is Austin's best birding area year-round (open daily from dawn to dusk). Check the drying basins on the right just past the entrance first; Buff-breasted Sandpiper and other shorebirds occur here in spring. Then drive or walk around the sewage ponds counterclockwise and scope them for Pied-billed Grebe, Great Blue Heron, Great Egret, Mallard, Ruddy Duck, and American Coot. In summer expect Snowy and Cattle Egrets, Little Blue and Green Herons, Yellow-crowned Night-Heron, White and White-faced Ibis, Black-bellied Whistling-Duck, Black-necked Stilt, and American Avocet. Watch also for Neotropic Cormorant, Anhinga, Wood Stork, and Mottled Duck. In winter you should find grebes, Double-crested Cormorant, geese, ducks, gulls, and terns. The adjacent grassy fields to the west can produce a variety of grassland migrants, including American Golden-Plover and Upland Sandpiper.

Walk the road along the river to check the riparian vegetation for songbirds. This area can be especially good in spring, when neotropical migrants may be present. In winter look for a variety of sparrows, including Fox and Harris's, and other brush-loving species.

Stop at **Walnut Creek Wastewater Treatment Plant (B)**, along Martin Luther King, Jr., Boulevard en route back to town. **Least Grebe** is seen regularly in the one accessible pond near the entrance; Hooded Merganser often occurs in winter.

At **McKinney Falls State Park,** located to the west off US 183, start at the Smith Visitor Center and walk the park trails along Onion Creek (C), especially between the lower and upper falls. Look for resident and migratory birds along the waterway, as well as in the adjacent fields. Expected breeding birds include Green Heron, Wood Duck, Red-shouldered Hawk, Killdeer, Mourning Dove, Black-chinned Hummingbird, Belted Kingfisher, Red-bellied and Downy Woodpeckers, Eastern Phoebe, Great Crested Flycatcher, Northern Rough-winged and Cliff Swallows, Carolina Chickadee, Tufted Titmouse, Canyon and Carolina Wrens, White-eyed Vireo, Northern Cardinal, Blue Grosbeak, Indigo and Painted Buntings, Red-winged Blackbird, Brown-headed Cowbird, and House Finch. **Green Kingfisher** is

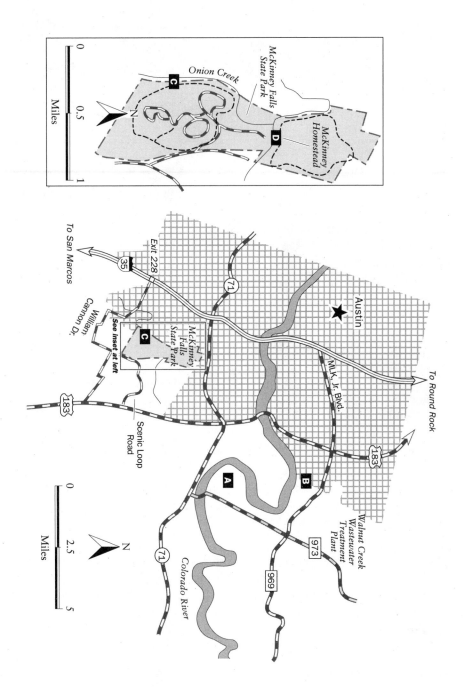

Low-water trickle on Onion Creek in McKinney Falls State Park.

irregular year-round. Twenty-eight species of warbler have been seen here during spring migration.

Walk the trails behind the McKinney Homestead (**D**), including the Homestead Mountain Bike Trail (watch for bikers). Expected breeding birds include Northern Bobwhite, Inca Dove, Common Ground-Dove, Ladder-backed Woodpecker, Scissor-tailed Flycatcher, Bewick's Wren, Blue-gray Gnatcatcher, Northern Mockingbird, Loggerhead Shrike, Lark Sparrow, and House Finch.

Records of Review Species: Pacific Loon, Jan 1982. Oldsquaw, Dec 1996. Northern Jacana, Nov–Dec 1989. Curlew Sandpiper, Sept 1989. Ruff, Oct 1982, Aug 1988, July–Aug 1992. Long-tailed Jaeger, Aug 1975. Lesser Black-backed Gull, March 1995. Glaucous Gull, April–May 1988, Dec 1990. Sabine's Gull, Oct 1978, Sept 1985. Fork-tailed Flycatcher, May 1981, May 1997.

Directions: From Austin, take Martin Luther King, Jr., Boulevard east, past Walnut Creek and across US 183, to FM 973. Turn right and drive 3.3 miles to the entrance of Hornsby Bend Wastewater Treatment Plant. McKinney Falls State Park lies to the west. From US 183, take the Scenic Loop Road and drive 2 miles to the park entrance, or exit 228 from I-35 via East William Cannon Drive and the Scenic Loop Road.

General information: The three sites are located within the Austin city limits. The state park, only 13 miles from the state capitol, can be extremely crowded on weekends and holidays; birding is best in the early morning. Environmental education programs, centered around the Smith Visitor Center, are popular in summer. Significant park resources include two small waterfalls on Onion Creek, an Indian rock shelter, and a variety of trails: short interpretive trails; a paved, 3.7-mile hike-and-bike trail; and a more rugged 3-mile-long trail ideal for mountain biking.

Hornsby Bend is an active wastewater treatment plant, so you must be careful not to interfere with activities; birders are welcome. Only the front pond of the Walnut Creek plant is accessible.

ADDITIONAL HELP

Location: Texas Official Travel Map grid P x 17; Travis County
Nearest food, gas, and lodging: Food and gas are available in Austin and along US 183, 5 miles from the park. Lodging is available in Austin.
Nearest camping: On-site at McKinney Falls State Park (98 sites) and numerous other sites in nearby Austin
Contact: City of Austin; Superintendent, McKinney Falls State Park (see Appendix C)

75 Bastrop, Buescher, and Lake Bastrop State Parks

Habitats: Lake, creek, riparian, loblolly pine forest, juniper woodland, oak-yaupon woodland, post oak savannah, field
Key birds: Wood Duck, White-tailed Kite, Crested Caracara, Wild Turkey, Greater Roadrunner, and Red-headed and Pileated Woodpeckers are present year-round. Chuck-will's-widow; Wood Thrush; Black-and-white, Swainson's, Kentucky, and Hooded Warblers; and Indigo and Painted Buntings occur in summer. Bald Eagle, American Woodcock, and Purple Finch can usually be found in winter.
Best times to bird: April and early May for spring migrants and nesting activities

Birding strategies: Copperas Creek (A) in Bastrop State Park; Alum Creek (B), which crosses PR 1 halfway between the two parks; and Hunt Branch (C) in Buescher (pronounced *bish*-er) State Park usually provide the birder with the greatest number and variety of migrants in spring. Expect flycatchers, vireos, warblers, tanagers, sparrows, and orioles. Also watch for migrating raptors, including Osprey; Mississippi Kite; Cooper's, Broad-winged, and Swainson's Hawks; American Kestrel; Merlin; and Peregrine Falcon, in the power line and gas line right-of-ways (D). These sites also are the best locations to find Wild Turkey, Northern Bob-white, Greater Roadrunner, Eastern Bluebird, and Painted Bunting.

Lake Bastrop (E) supports Great Blue and Little Blue Herons and Great Egret year-round. Green-winged and Blue-winged Teal, Gadwall, American Wigeon, Redhead, Ring-necked and Ruddy Ducks, and Lesser Scaup are common in winter,

75 Bastrop, Buescher, and Lake Bastrop State Parks

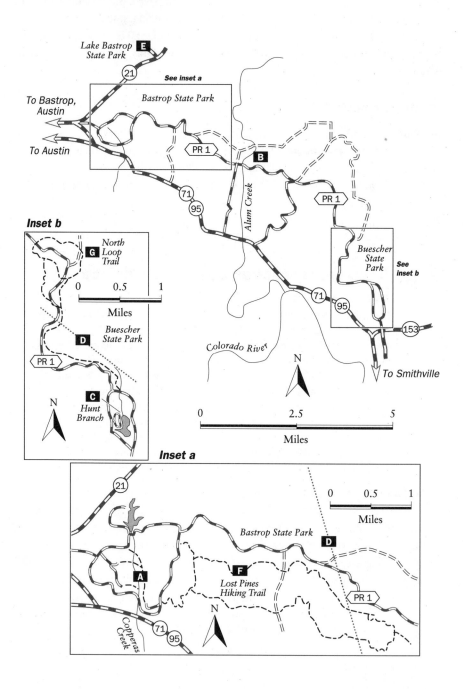

Lake Bastrop State Park **E**

21

See inset a

To Bastrop, Austin

Bastrop State Park

To Austin

PR 1

B

71

95

Alum Creek

PR 1

Inset b

North Loop Trail **G**

0   0.5   1

Miles

Buescher State Park

Buescher State Park

See inset b

PR 1

D

C

Hunt Branch

N

Colorado River

71

95

153

N

To Smithville

0   2.5   5

Miles

Inset a

21

Bastrop State Park

0   0.5   1

Miles

D

A

F

Lost Pines Hiking Trail

PR 1

N

Copperas Creek

71   95

and Northern Pintail, Northern Shoveler, Canvasback, Bufflehead, and Hooded Merganser are less numerous then. Post-nesting vagrants, such as Roseate Spoonbill and Wood Stork, and irregular winter visitors, such as Common Loon, Greater Scaup, and Oldsquaw, occur occasionally.

The parks' pine-oak woodlands support a good variety of breeding birds: the Lost Pines Hiking Trail (**F**) at Bastrop and the North Loop Trail (**G**) at Buescher are the best places to look for Red-shouldered Hawk; Barred Owl; Chuck-will's-widow; Red-headed (at Bastrop) and Pileated Woodpeckers; Eastern Wood-Pewee; Wood Thrush; Northern Parula; Pine, Black-and-white, Swainson's, Hooded, and Kentucky Warblers; and Summer Tanager. In winter a number of northern, sporadic species, including Red-breasted Nuthatch, Red Crossbill, and Pine Siskin, are sometimes present.

Records of Review Species: Blue-footed Booby, Dec–April 1994/95. Green Violet-ear, May–July 1996. Ringed Kingfisher, May 1996. Red-faced Warbler, May 1982.

Directions: The three parks are east of Austin. Bastrop State Park is located off SH 21, 1 mile east of Bastrop, and Buescher lies 2 miles north of Smithville, off SH 153. Lake Bastrop State Park is located off US 21, 10 miles north of Bastrop. The parks are connected by a 13-mile scenic drive (PR 1).

General information: The parks are located in the Lost Pines of Texas, a scenic remnant of a more extensive pine-oak forest that once covered much of central Texas. This isolated loblolly pine woodland lies approximately 100 miles west of the pineywoods of East Texas. Hiking trails (8.5 miles at Bastrop and 7.7 miles at Buescher) provide easy access to this unique environment.

The 3,503-acre Bastrop State Park contains a 10-acre lake, the 1,730-acre Buescher State Park includes a 15-acre lake, and Lake Bastrop State Park (900 acres) includes a 750-acre lake.

Bastrop County marks the western edge of the range of the endangered Houston toad, a 2-inch amphibian found only in Texas's more isolated pine forests and sandy-ridged prairies. Do not disturb this toad, whose color can vary from green or brown to gray or purplish gray, with dark mottling that can form vague zigzag lines on its back.

ADDITIONAL HELP

Location: Texas Official Travel Map grid P/Q x 17/18; Bastrop County

Nearest food, gas, and lodging: The towns of Bastrop and Smithville have food and gas. Bastrop State Park has cabins and Buescher State Park has screened shelters.

Nearest camping: On-site at Bastrop (72 sites), Lake Bastrop (38 sites), and Buescher (65 sites)

Contact: Superintendents, Bastrop and Lake Bastrop state parks and Buescher State Park (see Appendix C)

76 **Alcoa Lake and Granger Lake**

Habitats: Lake, pond, river, creek, marsh, riparian, oak woodland, mesquite grassland, field, cropland

Key birds: Neotropic Cormorant, Wood Duck, Wild Turkey, and Greater Roadrunner are present year-round. Anhinga, Least Bittern, Black-bellied Whistling-Duck, Chuck-will's-widow, Scissor-tailed Flycatcher, Painted Bunting, and Dickcissel occur in spring and summer. Western Grebe, American White Pelican, American Bittern, Bald Eagle, Mountain Plover, Burrowing Owl, McCown's and Chestnut-collared Longspurs, and Rusty Blackbird can sometimes be found in winter.

Best times to bird: April and May for spring migrants and nesting activities; November to mid-February for Bald Eagle and winter gulls, terns, and field birds

Birding strategies: Alcoa Lake is the better of the two areas, primarily because of the warm water from Alcoa's aluminum plant. The entrance road (**A**), FM 1766 off US 79, extends for 5 miles through an oak-dominated woodland with stretches of fields along the roadside; railroad tracks are present on the east side. This area can harbor a variety of migrants in spring and fall, and several of the neotropical migrants remain and nest with the full-time residents. This

76 **Alcoa Lake**

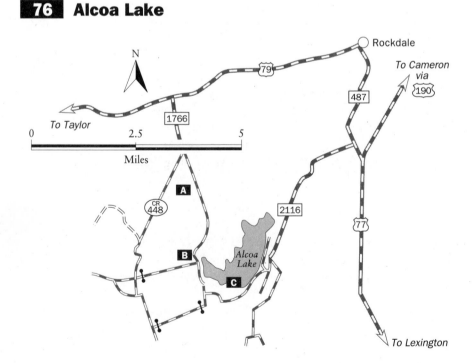

combined bird life includes Red-shouldered Hawk, Yellow-billed Cuckoo, Chuck-will's-widow, Ruby-throated Hummingbird, Red-bellied and Downy Woodpeckers, Eastern Wood-Pewee, Acadian and Great Crested Flycatchers, Carolina Chickadee, Tufted Titmouse, Carolina Wren, Blue-gray Gnatcatcher, White-eyed Vireo, Northern Cardinal, and Common Grackle. Scan the roadside fields and mesquite savannah areas for Wild Turkey, Northern Bobwhite, Greater Roadrunner, Scissor-tailed Flycatcher, American Crow, Bewick's Wren, Northern Mockingbird, Brown Thrasher, Loggerhead Shrike, Blue Grosbeak, Painted Bunting, Dickcissel, Lark Sparrow, and Eastern Meadowlark.

About 4 miles from the entrance (from US 79), you will see a pond on the right and the corner of Alcoa Lake on the left. This area of lake and wetlands (**B**) is extremely productive year-round. Expected summer residents include Pied-billed Grebe; Double-crested and Neotropic Cormorants; Great Blue, Little Blue, and Green Herons; Great, Snowy, and Cattle Egrets; Yellow-crowned Night-Heron; Wood Duck; Black-bellied Whistling-Duck; Mallard; American Coot; and Killdeer. Anhinga, Tricolored Heron, Yellow-crowned Night-Heron, Common Moorhen, Franklin's Gull, and Black Tern are less numerous. The cattail marsh, along the edges of both bodies of water, attracts Red-winged Blackbird year-round; Least Bittern in summer; American Bittern, Virginia Rail,

76 Granger Lake

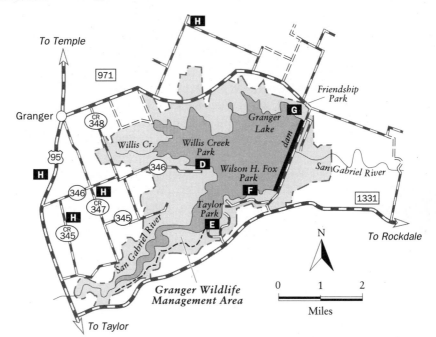

Sora, Marsh Wren, Common Yellowthroat, and Song and Swamp Sparrows in winter. Watch also in winter for Red-headed Woodpecker on the snags and Rusty Blackbird among the cattails. Note: there is at least one huge alligator here.

There is a warmer pond (C), the result of hot water outflow from the aluminum plant, to the left of the roadway a mile ahead. This pond attracts White and White-faced Ibis, Roseate Spoonbill, and Wood Stork in summer. In winter American White Pelican can be numerous, and Bonaparte's and Ring-billed Gulls can number in the hundreds. Common Loon, Western and Clark's Grebes, Brown Pelican, Surf and White-winged Scoters, and Bald Eagle are irregular visitors.

Granger Lake (managed by the U.S. Army Corps of Engineers) and its surroundings also offer worthwhile birding. Spring and summer woodland birds are similar to those mentioned above for the Alcoa area, but spring and fall migrants, wintering waterfowl, and field birds can be different. The Willis Creek Wildlife Area (D) is best birded during migration. Where CR 348 crosses Willis Creek and at Willis Creek Park (at the end of CR 346), migrants can be especially numerous in April and May. These areas act as migrant traps, where flycatchers, thrushes, vireos, warblers, tanagers, and orioles can be commonplace. In winter up to 14 sparrow species can be found along Willis Creek. Taylor Park (E), on the south shore off FM 1331, contains a 1.5-mile nature trail that provides easy access along the south side of the San Gabriel River. These woodland and mesquite grassland habitats support a variety of birds in summer: Yellow-billed Cuckoo, Greater Roadrunner, Common Nighthawk, Ladder-backed Woodpecker, Western Kingbird, Scissor-tailed Flycatcher, Bewick's Wren, Eastern Bluebird, Painted Bunting, Dickcissel, Field and Lark Sparrows, and Orchard Oriole.

Granger Lake is not as warm as Alcoa, but water birds can be abundant during migration and during winter; huge flocks of 14,000 to 16,000 Franklin's Gulls have been reported in late October. The best viewing sites include Wilson H. Fox Park (F), south of the dam, and Friendship Park (G), north of the dam.

The surrounding fields (H) can also be very productive in winter. County Roads 345, 346, and 347, as well as CR 338 on the west side of US 95, are good sites for finding Mountain Plover, LeConte's Sparrow, and McCown's and Chestnut-collared Longspurs in winter.

Records of Review Species: *Granger Lake*—Little Gull, Jan 1987. *Alcoa Lake*—Sabine's Gull, Nov 1993.

Directions: Alcoa Lake is located southwest of Rockdale. Take either FM 1766 off US 79 on the west or FM 2116 off FM 487 on the south (these roads connect within the plant). Granger Lake is located northwest of Taylor. Take SH 95 north to FM 1331 or FM 971 to the principal sites (see map).

General information: Alcoa Lake is a private warm-water lake (cooling pond) owned by the Aluminum Company of America. It is bordered on two sides by the processing plant and open-pit coal mines. Birders must check in immediately upon arrival at the security office, located near the administration building; watch for signs directing visitors to security. All visitors must remain on the roadways, and photography is absolutely prohibited! A loop route between US 79 and FM 487, via FM 1766 and 2116, is suggested.

The 4,400-acre Granger Lake, managed by the U.S. Army Corps of Engineers (headquarters at the dam), was opened in 1981. The area lies in the center of the Blackland Prairie, halfway up the San Gabriel River from its confluence with the Little River.

ADDITIONAL HELP

Location: Texas Official Travel Map grid O x 17/18; Milam and Williamson counties
Nearest food, gas, and lodging: All are available at Rockdale and Taylor. Granger (7 miles) has food and gas.
Nearest camping: On-site at Granger Lake (156 sites) and Rockdale
Contact: Alcoa Aluminum Company; U.S. Army Corps of Engineers, Granger Lake (see Appendix C)

77 Lake Somerville State Park

Habitats: Lake, pond, creek, mud flat, wetland, riparian, oak-hickory woodland, oak motte, oak savannah, juniper woodland, field, pasture, cropland
Key birds: Neotropic Cormorant, Wood Duck, and Greater Roadrunner are present year-round. Roseate Spoonbill, Wood Stork, Black-bellied Whistling-Duck, Scissor-tailed Flycatcher, Wood Thrush, Prothonotary and Swainson's Warblers, and Painted Bunting occur in summer. American White Pelican, Bald Eagle, and Fox and Harris's Sparrows can usually be found in winter.
Best times to bird: April and May for spring migrants and nesting activities; November to March for winter waterfowl and Bald Eagle

Birding strategies: Observe wintering waterfowl, Osprey, and Bald Eagle by boat or from the shore at sites with the least amount of boat traffic. Expected open-water species include Green-winged Teal, Mallard, Northern Shoveler, Gadwall,

77 Lake Somerville State Park

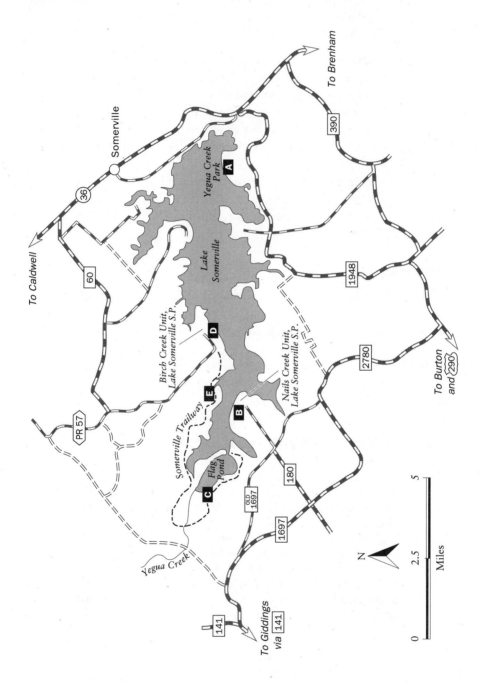

American Wigeon, Canvasback, and Lesser Scaup. Fewer numbers of Northern Pintail, Blue-winged and Cinnamon Teal, Redhead, Ring-necked Duck, and Bufflehead occur. Wood Ducks prefer more protected sites, such as Yegua (pronounced *yah*-wha) Creek Park and the Nails Creek Unit (**A** and **B**, respectively) and Flag Pond (**C**). Also watch for American White Pelican, Double-crested and Neotropic Cormorants, and Forster's Tern over the lake. Roseate Spoonbills and Wood Storks often are present in summer.

During periods of low water in spring and fall, shorebirds can be numerous; 24 species have been reported. Songbirds can best be found in the riparian vegetation along Yegua Creek and at heavily wooded sites, such as the Yaupon and Post Oak camping areas in Lake Somerville State Park's Birch Creek Unit (**D**), the Nature Trail in the Nails Creek Unit, and along the Somerville Trailway (**E**).

Many of the neotropical migrants remain and nest with the full-time residents. Migrants and residents include: Yellow-billed Cuckoo, Ruby-throated Hummingbird, Red-bellied Woodpecker, Great Crested Flycatcher, Eastern Kingbird, Blue Jay, American Crow, Carolina Chickadee, Tufted Titmouse, Wood Thrush, White-eyed Vireo, Northern Parula, Prothonotary and Swainson's Warblers, Summer Tanager, Northern Cardinal, and Common Grackle. Less numerous are Red-shouldered Hawk, Eastern Screech-Owl, and Barred Owl.

Summer residents such as Scissor-tailed Flycatcher, Northern Mockingbird, Loggerhead Shrike, Painted Bunting, and Eastern Meadowlark utilize fields and edges. Watch overhead in summer for Black and Turkey Vultures; Red-tailed Hawk; Common Nighthawk at dawn and dusk; Chimney Swift; Purple Martin; and Northern Rough-winged, Cliff, and Barn Swallows.

In winter the weedy fields harbor a number of seedeaters: Spotted Towhee; Chipping, Field, Vesper, Savannah, Fox, Song, Lincoln's, Swamp, White-throated, White-crowned, and Harris's (irregular) Sparrows; and American Goldfinch.

Directions: The two units of Lake Somerville State Park are about 30 miles west of Bryan–College Station, off SH 36 between Brenham and Caldwell. The park's Birch Creek Unit, on the north shore of the lake, is 15 miles west of the junction of FM 60 and SH 36. Yegua Creek Park, on the south shore, is 4 miles west of SH 36 on FM 1948. The Nails Creek Unit is 15 miles north of US 290 at Burton, off old FM 1697 (see map).

General information: Somerville Lake encompasses 11,460 acres, and its entire 85-mile shoreline is contained within lands managed by either the U.S. Army Corps of Engineers or the Texas Parks and Wildlife Department (TPWD). The principal watershed of Yegua Creek drains approximately 1,320 square miles, and is dammed by a 20,210-foot-long earthfill embankment (20 miles above its confluence with the Brazos River) near Somerville.

The entire area is managed as a recreation area, offering boating, fishing, swimming, and hunting. Two floating marinas and ten boat ramps provide plenty of lake access during normal wet periods. Playgrounds are available at Big Creek,

Yegua Creek, and Overlook Park. And TPWD maintains a 7.5-mile nature trail at Yegua Creek and the 21.6-mile Somerville Trailway between Nails Creek and Birch Creek. All-terrain bicycles and horses are also permitted on the trails.

ADDITIONAL HELP

Location: Texas Official Travel Map grid P x 18; Burleson County

Nearest food, gas, and lodging: Food is available at the Birch Creek Unit and Overlook Park, gasoline is available at the Birch Creek Unit, and lodging can be found at Big Creek and Overlook parks.

Nearest camping: On-site at Overlook Park, Big Creek Park, the Birch Creek Unit, the Nails Creek Unit, Rocky Creek Park, and Yegua Creek Park; primitive camping is allowed in designated areas

Contact: Superintendent, Lake Somerville State Park; Reservoir Manager, U.S. Army Corps of Engineers (see Appendix C)

78 Palmetto State Park

Habitats: Lake, river, wetland, riparian, post oak woodland, pasture, cropland

Key birds: Wood Duck, Crested Caracara, Wild Turkey, Greater Roadrunner, **Green Kingfisher,** Pileated Woodpecker, and Grasshopper Sparrow are present year-round. Anhinga; Black-bellied Whistling Duck; Purple Gallinule; Chuck-will's-widow; Scissor-tailed Flycatcher; Prothonotary, Swainson's, and Kentucky Warblers; Indigo and Painted Buntings; and Dickcissel occur in summer. White-tailed Kite, Ferruginous Hawk, Sandhill Crane, and LeConte's, Fox, and Harris's Sparrows can usually be found in winter.

Best times to bird: April and May for spring migrants and nesting activities; November to March for winter birds

Birding strategies: Look for nesting Prothonotary, Swainson's, and Kentucky Warblers along the Palmetto Trail (0.33 mile, **A**), and for Pileated Woodpecker, Black-chinned Hummingbird, Acadian and Great Crested Flycatchers, Red-eyed Vireo, Northern Parula, Yellow-breasted Chat, Summer Tanager, Blue Grosbeak, and Indigo and Painted Buntings along the River Trail (0.66 mile, **B**) in summer. Watch for Green Heron, Wood Duck, Purple Gallinule, and **Green Kingfisher** along the river. Eastern Screech-Owl, Barred Owl, and Chuck-will's-widow can usually be heard from the campgrounds (**C**) and in the area of Oxbow Lake soon after dark. The somewhat drier woods along the Hiking Trail (1.25 miles, **D**) normally support many of the same nesting species, plus Red-shouldered Hawk, Ash-throated Flycatcher, Bewick's Wren, and Blue-gray Gnatcatcher.

Bird along PR 11 and nearby county roads (**E**) (respect private property) in spring and summer for Black-bellied Whistling-Duck; Crested Caracara; Wild

78 Palmetto State Park

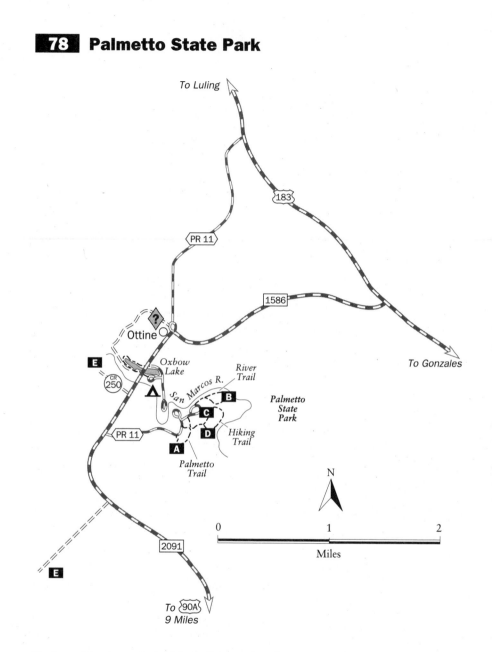

Turkey; Northern Bobwhite; Greater Roadrunner; Scissor-tailed Flycatcher; swallows; Eastern Bluebird; Loggerhead Shrike; buntings; Dickcissel; and Field, Lark, and Grasshopper Sparrows. In winter geese and ducks, White-tailed Kite, and Sandhill Crane are often found. Check weedy areas for seedeaters, including Spotted Towhee; Field, LeConte's, Fox, Swamp, and Harris's Sparrows; Dark-eyed Junco; and American Goldfinch.

Directions: Take US 183 south of Luling to PR 11 (8 miles), or north of Gonzales to FM 1586 (13 miles). Follow either of these roads to Ottine and park headquarters. Continue south on PR 11 to the campground and trails.

General information: The 263-acre Palmetto State Park was named for the dwarf palmetto that occurs along the San Marcos River in the park's Ottine Swamp. The area lies at the point where the blackland prairie, post oak savannah, and coastal plains biogeographic regions converge; it represents the western edge of the dwarf palmetto's range.

The Palmetto and River trails are self-guided, with numbered posts. A booklet provides the user with the identification and description of several common plants.

Of historic interest are the structures built by the Civilian Conservation Corps, including an outdoor pavilion constructed of native sandstone, a large water storage tower, and a hydraulic pump (one of the few operating ram-jet pumps in existence), needed to maintain a water supply to the palmetto wetlands.

Two artesian wells supply warm sulfur-laden water to different sites in the park, but the mud boils and spring are no longer active. Ottine is the site of Warm Springs Hospital, an institution for treating victims of accidents and crippling diseases.

ADDITIONAL HELP

Location: Texas Official Travel Map grid R x 17; Gonzales County
Nearest food, gas, and lodging: Food and lodging are available at Luling (9 miles). Gas is at the intersection of I-10 and US 183 (5 miles).
Nearest camping: On-site (37 sites)
Contact: Superintendent, Palmetto State Park (see Appendix C)

79 Fayette Lake

Habitats: Lake, pond, marsh, oak-hackberry-juniper woodland, field, cropland
Key birds: Neotropic Cormorant and Wood Duck are present year-round. Chuck-will's-widow, Scissor-tailed Flycatcher, Painted Bunting, and Dickcissel occur in summer. Western Grebe, American White Pelican, and Osprey can usually be found in winter.
Best times to bird: November to March for winter water birds

Birding strategies: Oak Thicket Park (**A**), just off SH 159, offers the greatest diversity of habitats and an excellent view of the lake, also known locally as Cedar Creek Reservoir. Scope the lake from the viewing platform at the edge of the campground. Wintering water birds can be abundant! Most numerous are Pied-billed Grebe, Double-crested Cormorant, Great Blue Heron, Green-winged Teal, Mallard, Northern Pintail, Northern Shoveler, Gadwall, American Wigeon, Lesser Scaup, Bufflehead, Ruddy Duck, American Coot, Ring-billed Gull, Belted Kingfisher, and Red-winged Blackbird. Less numerous are Common Loon, Horned

79 Fayette Lake

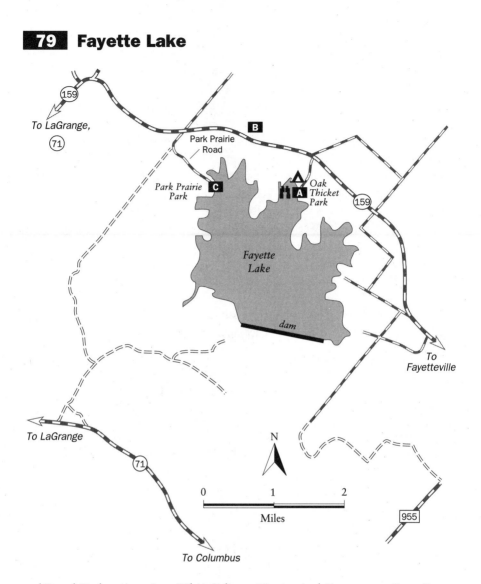

and Eared Grebes, American White Pelican, Neotropical Cormorant, Great Egret, Tricolored Heron, Wood Duck, Blue-winged and Cinnamon Teal, Canvasback, Redhead, Ring-necked Duck, Common Goldeneye, and Hooded and Red-breasted Mergansers. Watch for the occasional Western Grebe, Black-crowned Night-Heron, Greater Scaup, and scoters. Oak Thicket Park has been open only since 1996 and so far has received little attention from birders, but because the lake gets warm water from Fayette Power Plant, winter birding should be good.

The campground at Oak Thicket Park, situated within oak-hackberry-juniper woodlands, offers year-round Mourning and Inca Doves, Red-bellied Woodpecker, Blue Jay, American Crow, Carolina Chickadee, Tufted Titmouse, Carolina Wren, Northern Mockingbird, Northern Cardinal, and Common Grackle. Yellow-billed

Cuckoo, Chuck-will's-widow, Great Crested and Scissor-tailed Flycatchers, White-eyed Vireo, and Painted Bunting occur here in summer. Most of these same birds are also present along the 2.5-mile Rice-Osborne Bird and Nature Trail, which starts to the right of the Oak Thicket Park entrance.

The picturesque countryside along SH 159 (**B**), between Oak Thicket Park and Park Prairie Park (2 miles to the west), contains a few stock ponds and open fields that attract various birds throughout the year. In summer expect Black and Turkey Vultures, Red-tailed Hawk, Common Nighthawk at dawn and dusk, Western and Eastern Kingbirds, Purple Martin, Cliff and Barn Swallows, Eastern Bluebird, Loggerhead Shrike, Dickcissel, and Field and Lark Sparrows. In winter Greater White-fronted, Snow, and Ross's Geese and Sandhill Cranes (irregular) feed in the open fields. Weedy areas usually harbor House Wren, Spotted and Eastern Towhees, a variety of sparrows, American Goldfinch, and Pine Siskin. The land birds attract a number of raptors: Northern Harrier; Sharp-shinned, Cooper's, Red-tailed, and Ferruginous (irregular) Hawks; Crested Caracara; and American Kestrel.

Park Prairie Park (**C**) is primarily a fishing site, but it offers views of the lake and shoreline habitats. It is worth checking, especially in winter.

Directions: This area is located along SH 159 between LaGrange and Fayetteville. Oak Thicket Park is 10 miles north of Fayetteville; Park Prairie Park is 2 miles beyond. From LaGrange, Park Prairie Park is on Park Prairie Road, off SH 159, 7 miles northeast of SH 159's junction with SH 71.

General information: The 2,400-acre Fayette Lake is a cooling basin for the coal-fired Fayette Power Plant, administered by the Lower Colorado River Authority. However, both Oak Thicket and Park Prairie parks are managed as private parks through a cooperative agreement. There is a $5 daily fee.

ADDITIONAL HELP

Location: Texas Official Travel Map grid Q x 18; Fayette County
Nearest food, gas, and lodging: Food and gas can be found in Fayetteville (8 miles); food, gas, and lodging are available in LaGrange (10 miles).
Nearest camping: on-site (19 sites)
Contact: Park concessionaires and Lower Colorado River Authority (see Appendix C)

80 Attwater Prairie Chicken National Wildlife Refuge

Habitats: River, creek, riparian, marsh, prairie, field

Key birds: Least Grebe, White-faced Ibis, Black-bellied Whistling-Duck, Mottled Duck, **White-tailed Hawk,** Crested Caracara, Attwater's Prairie-Chicken, King Rail, and Greater Roadrunner are present year-round. Neotropic Cormorant, Anhinga, Least Bittern, White and Glossy Ibis, Roseate Spoonbill, Fulvous Whistling-Duck, Swainson's Hawk, Purple Gallinule, Scissor-tailed Flycatcher, Painted Bunting, and Dickcissel occur in summer. Ross's Goose; Cinnamon Teal; Bald Eagle; Ferruginous and Rough-legged Hawks; Peregrine Falcon; Sandhill Crane; Short-eared Owl; American and Sprague's Pipits; and Grasshopper, LeConte's, and Harris's Sparrows can usually be found in winter.

Best times to bird: Late February through April for prairie-chicken displays (slim chance due to declining population); April and May for spring migrants and nesting activities; November to March for winter birds

Birding strategies: Tours to the prairie-chicken booming grounds are no longer provided. Bird the 5-mile Auto Tour (loop) Route (**A**), which circles LaFitte Prairie and Pintail Marsh, for the majority of the water birds. Nesting species of interest include **Least Grebe,** American and Least Bitterns, White-faced Ibis, Black-bellied Whistling-Duck, Mottled and Ruddy Ducks, **White-tailed Hawk,** Crested Caracara, King Rail, Purple Gallinule, Common Ground-Dove, Scissor-tailed Flycatcher, Loggerhead Shrike, Painted Bunting, and Dickcissel.

In winter this area can be filled with waterfowl, including as many as 50,000 geese, especially Snow, with smaller numbers of Greater White-fronted, Ross's, and Canada; numerous ducks, including Cinnamon Teal; occasional shorebirds; Sandhill Crane; and sparrows. Watch also for White-tailed Kite, Northern Harrier, Bald Eagle, Ferruginous and Rough-legged (sporadic) Hawks, Crested Caracara, American Kestrel, Merlin, Peregrine and Prairie Falcons, and Burrowing and Short-eared Owls. Rusty Blackbirds occur some years, as well.

During migration shorebirds can be numerous. Of special interest in spring are American Golden-Plover; Mountain Plover (rare); Upland, White-rumped, Stilt, and Buff-breasted Sandpipers; and Hudsonian Godwit.

Bird the two trails in late winter and spring. Sycamore Trail (**B**) offers the greatest diversity of neotropical migrants in spring, whereas the Pipit Trail (**C**) is best in winter, when it often harbors Sedge Wren; American and Sprague's Pipits; numerous sparrows, including Henslow's (irregular), Grasshopper, and LeConte's; and other seedeaters.

Records of Review Species: Masked Duck, Dec 1993, July–Dec 1994.

80 Attwater Prairie Chicken National Wildlife Refuge

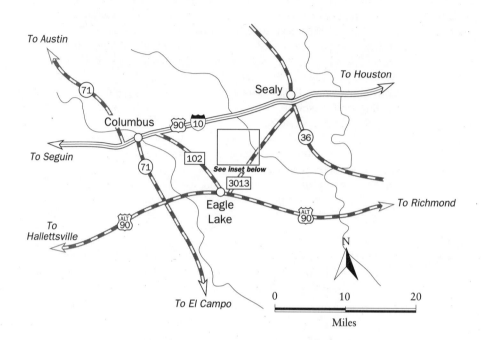

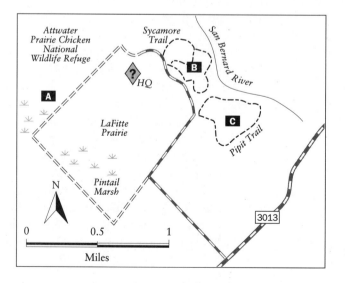

Directions: The refuge is 7 miles northeast of Eagle Lake, via FM 3103, or 10 miles south of Sealy (on I-10) via SH 36 and FM 3103 west. Refuge sites are limited to the loop route and two trails near headquarters, near the entrance.

General information: This 8,000-acre refuge, located on the inland edge of the coastal prairie, is one of the last strongholds of Attwater's Prairie-Chicken, a sub-species of the Greater Prairie-Chicken and the now extinct Heath Hen. Populations of this unique bird have declined dramatically in recent years; fewer than 900 birds were estimated for Texas in 1986, 456 in 1993, and fewer than 50 birds in the wild in 1996.

Although the reason for these declines is not fully understood, it is likely a combination of urbanization, industrial expansion, brush encroachment, conversion of land to crops, overgrazing, adverse weather conditions (especially during the reproductive season), and predation, including fire ants. Refuge personnel are implementing several management techniques designed to improve the habitat: controlled grazing, prescribed burning, strip-row cropping, mowing, pest plant control, and predator control.

Personnel are also working to restore the natural grasslands, and increased numbers of Sedge Wren and winter sparrows, such as Grasshopper and LeConte's, will benefit. A small herd of bison can be seen along the refuge's Auto Tour Route.

ADDITIONAL HELP

Location: Texas Official Travel Map grid Q x 19; Colorado County
Nearest food, gas, and lodging: All are at Eagle Lake (6.5 miles).
Nearest camping: Stephen F. Austin State Park, 2.2 miles north of San Felipe (80 sites)
Contact: Manager, Attwater Prairie Chicken National Wildlife Refuge (see Appendix C)

81 **Houston West**

Bear Creek Park and Addicks Reservoir, Spring Creek Park, Katy Prairie, and Warren Lake

Habitats: Oak and pine stand, reservoir, pond, creek, riparian, wetland, field, pasture, cropland

Key birds: Neotropic Cormorant, Anhinga, White and White-faced Ibis, Roseate Spoonbill, Black-bellied Whistling-Duck, Wood and Mottled Ducks, **White-tailed Hawk,** Crested Caracara, King Rail, Greater Roadrunner, and Red-headed and Pileated Woodpeckers are present year-round. Least Bittern; Wood Stork; Fulvous Whistling-Duck; Swainson's Hawk; Chuck-will's-widow; Scissor-tailed Flycatcher; Swainson's, Kentucky, and Hooded Warblers; Painted Bunting; and Dickcissel occur in summer. American White Pelican; American Bittern; Snow and Ross's Geese; Osprey; Bald Eagle; Ferruginous Hawk; Peregrine Falcon; Sandhill Crane; American Woodcock; Burrowing and Short-eared Owls; Say's Phoebe; Vermilion Flycatcher; American and Sprague's Pipits; Grasshopper, Henslow's, LeConte's, Fox, and Harris's Sparrows; and Rusty Blackbird can usually be found in winter.

Best times to bird: April and May for migrants and nesting activities; November to March for wintering waterfowl and sparrows

Birdng strategies: Bear Creek Park and Addicks Reservoir (A), on SH 6 just north of I-10, offer a wide variety of habitats, including the Bear Creek riparian woodlands and wetlands. Expected year-round birds include Great Blue, Little Blue, and Tricolored Herons; Great, Snowy, and Cattle Egrets; White and White-faced Ibis; Black-bellied Whistling-Duck; Wood and Mottled Ducks; King Rail; Common Moorhen; American Coot; Killdeer; Common Yellowthroat; and Red-winged Blackbird on the reservoir and in the surrounding wetlands. Red-shouldered Hawk; Mourning Dove; Eastern Screech-Owl; Barred Owl; Red-bellied, Downy, and Pileated Woodpeckers; Blue Jay; American Crow; Carolina Chickadee; Tufted Titmouse; Carolina Wren; Blue-gray Gnatcatcher; American Robin; Northern Cardinal; Brown-headed Cowbird; and Great-tailed and Common Grackles occur in the woodlands.

In summer expect Green Heron; Yellow-billed Cuckoo; Chuck-will's-widow; Ruby-throated Hummingbird; Eastern Wood-Pewee; Acadian and Great Crested Flycatchers; Eastern Kingbird; White-eyed, Yellow-throated, and Red-eyed Vireos; Northern Parula; Swainson's, Kentucky, and Hooded Warblers; Summer Tanager; Blue Grosbeak; Painted Bunting; and Orchard Oriole. In midsummer Wood Storks usually appear.

During the winter, a variety of ducks; Sharp-shinned and Cooper's Hawks; Virginia Rail; Sora; American Woodcock; Belted Kingfisher; Red-breasted and White-breasted Nuthatches; Brown Creeper; Bewick's, House, and Winter Wrens; Golden-crowned and Ruby-crowned Kinglets; Hermit Thrush; and Brown Thrasher can be found. Look in the picnic grounds for Vermilion Flycatcher, Golden-crowned

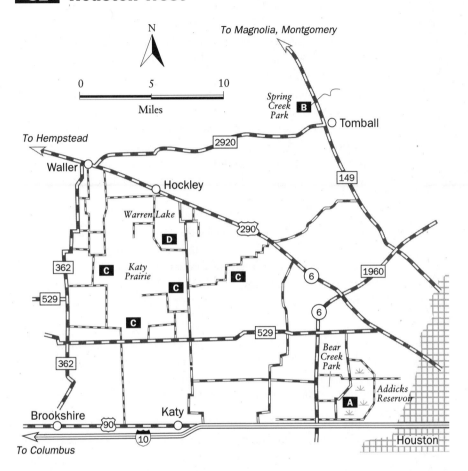

Kinglet, Eastern Bluebird, Chipping and Lark Sparrows, Rusty Blackbird, and Purple Finch.

The old fields and brushy edges in the area also support year-round Red-tailed Hawk, Northern Bobwhite, Inca Dove, Common Ground-Dove, Greater Roadrunner, Great Horned Owl, Northern Mockingbird, Loggerhead Shrike, and Eastern Meadowlark. In winter look for American Kestrel; Eastern Phoebe; Gray Catbird; Brown Thrasher; Eastern Towhee; Field, Vesper, Savannah, Grasshopper, LeConte's, Fox, Song, Lincoln's, Swamp, White-throated, and Harris's Sparrows; Dark-eyed Junco; and American Goldfinch.

Spring Creek Park (B), off FM 149 north of Tomball, contains good riparian, oak, and pine habitats that support many of the same species found at the larger Bear Creek Park. The open pine stands offer habitat for Red-headed Woodpecker and Pine Warbler year-round, and Red-breasted and White-breasted Nuthatches and Brown Creeper in winter.

The **Katy Prairie** area **(C)**, including a series of paved county roads between US 290 and I-10 and east of FM 362, contains superb wintering grounds for water and brush-loving birds. The extensive fields and pastures usually contain thousands of wintering geese, especially Snow Geese, but Greater White-fronted and Ross's Geese and Sandhill Crane can be found as well. In summer these fields and edges can be extremely productive. The rice fields and the occasional sorghum field are also good for geese, cranes, and American and Sprague's Pipits in winter, and Painted Bunting and Dickcissel in summer.

During migration these same fields attract multitudes of shorebirds; raptors can also be numerous. Look for White-tailed Kite, Red-tailed Hawk, and Crested Caracara year-round; Swainson's and **White-tailed Hawks** in summer; and Bald Eagle, Northern Harrier, Ferruginous Hawk, American Kestrel, Peregrine Falcon, and Burrowing and Short-eared Owls in winter.

Warren Lake (D), 3 miles south of US 290 at Hockley, offers the largest number and variety of wintering water birds. Scope this lake from the road for waders and waterfowl, including Pied-billed, Horned, and Eared Grebes; American White Pelican; Double-crested and Neotropic Cormorants; Anhinga; White and White-faced Ibis; Roseate Spoonbill; Osprey; and Bald Eagle. In summer Wood Stork and Fulvous Whistling-Duck are often present. The entire area is private property; stay on the roads!

Directions: Bear Creek Park and Addicks Reservoir are located northeast of the junction of I-10 and SH (Loop) 6. Spring Creek Park is located to the north, 0.8 mile west of FM 149 on the northern edge of Tomball. Warren Lake is located off Warren Ranch Road, 3 miles south of US 290/SH 6 at Hockley (on US 290/SH 6).

General information: Although the two parks and Addicks Reservoir are reasonably safe from development, birding habitats in the remainder of this area are fast disappearing due to expanding human populations. All the Katy Prairie and Warren Lake areas (land west of SH 6) are privately owned, and birders must not trespass.

The 2,168-acre Bear Creek Park, managed by Harris County, contains playgrounds, picnic sites, 3 golf courses, equestrian facilities, and considerable wild acreage with trails. The park is open daily from 7 A.M. to 10 P.M. Addicks Reservoir is managed by the U.S. Army Corps of Engineers. The 114-acre Spring Creek Park, managed by the city of Tomball, contains playgrounds and picnic sites.

ADDITIONAL HELP

Location: Texas Official Travel Map grid P/Q x 20/21; Harris and Waller counties
Nearest food, gas, and lodging: All can be found at numerous locations throughout the area.
Nearest camping: Numerous sites in West Houston, as well as in Tomball
Contact: Bear Creek Park, Harris County Parks; Manager, Addicks Reservoir Project; Spring Creek Park, city of Tomball (see Appendix C)

82 Lake Texana and Lake Texana State Park

Habitats: Lake, wetland, mud flat, riparian, oak savannah, oak motte, coastal scrub, coastal prairie, pasture, cropland

Key birds: Neotropic Cormorant, White and White-faced Ibis, Black-bellied Whistling-Duck, Wood and Mottled Ducks, **White-tailed Hawk,** Crested Caracara, and Pileated Woodpecker are present year-round. Mississippi Kite, Purple Gallinule, Groove-billed Ani, Scissor-tailed Flycatcher, Painted Bunting, and Dickcissel occur in summer. Western Grebe; American White Pelican; Greater White-fronted, Snow, and Ross's Geese; Osprey; Bald Eagle; Merlin; and Sandhill Crane can usually be found in winter.

Best times to bird: April and May for spring migrants and nesting activities; November through March for waterfowl, hawks, Bald Eagle, and Sandhill Crane

Birding strategies: A wintertime loop drive around the entire lake (see map) will produce the largest number of birds. Mottled Duck, Northern Pintail, Blue-winged Teal, Northern Shoveler, Gadwall, and American Wigeon can be abundant. Green-winged and Cinnamon Teal, Canvasback, Common Goldeneye, Bufflehead, and Hooded Merganser are less numerous. Watch for Common Loon and Pied-billed, Eared, and Western Grebes. The boat ramp site at the west end of the bridge on US 59 (**A**) is one of the best viewing areas for water birds and sometimes Bald Eagle.

The winter pastures and fields (**B**), such as those along FM 3131 and FM 1593, can contain thousands of Greater White-fronted, Snow, and (fewer) Ross's Geese, as well as several hundred Sandhill Crane. Watch also in winter for Northern Harrier; Sharp-shinned, Cooper's, and Red-tailed Hawks; **White-tailed Hawk;** Crested Caracara; American Kestrel; Merlin; and Peregrine Falcon. During migration flooded fields attract an abundance of shorebirds. In summer White and White-faced Ibis, Roseate Spoonbill, Wood Stork, Black-bellied and Fulvous Whistling-Ducks, and Mottled Duck frequent the irrigated fields; those (**C**) along SH 111 and SH 172 can be especially good. Also expect Scissor-tailed Flycatcher, Painted Bunting, and Dickcissel here. Later in summer, watch for Groove-billed Ani at fence rows.

Neotropical migrants can best be found in spring and fall in the oaks and thickets within the state park and along the roads. Lake Texana is near enough to the Gulf Coast that occasional fallouts of spring migrants do occur; two dozen or more neotropical migrants are possible. The state park (**D**) is productive year-round, particularly in late spring, fall, and winter. Various water birds, including herons, egrets, Yellow-crowned Night-Heron, White Ibis, Black-bellied Whistling-Duck, Purple Gallinule, Common Moorhen, Killdeer, and Black-necked Stilt, can usually be found along or near the shoreline. Woodland birds of interest include Mississippi Kite, Red-shouldered Hawk, Yellow-billed Cuckoo, Barred Owl, and Great Crested Flycatcher. In winter Pine Warbler frequents the park's pine groves.

82 Lake Texana and Lake Texana State Park

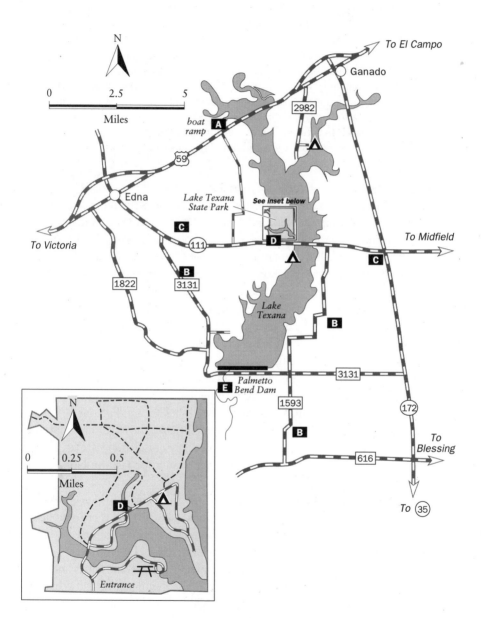

Bald Eagle is an early spring nester, migrating northward after nesting, but returning in early winter. One pair can often be seen in the tall trees below the Palmetto Bend Dam spillway (E). Pileated Woodpecker is a resident in the wooded areas below the dam.

Directions: Lake Texana loop route lies southeast of US 59, in a triangle between the towns of Edna and Ganado and the junction of SH 172 and FM 3131. From the state park entrance, take SH 111 east across the lake to FM 1593 and turn right (south). Continue on FM 1593 to FM 3131. Turn right (west) along the lake, cross the dam (check for birds below the spillway) to SH 111, and turn right (east) to return to the state park.

General information: Lake Texana, named for the historic town of Texana which was drowned by the reservoir, extends approximately 18 miles up the Navidad River valley above Palmetto Bend Dam (completed in 1980). The reservoir, intended as a municipal and industrial water supply, contains a surface area of about 11,000 acres with about 125 miles of shoreline. It has become a popular recreation (especially fishing and boating) site that can be crowded on weekends and holidays. The Brackenridge Plantation (across SH 111 from the park entrance) maintains a campground, nature trail, a marina, and two lighted fishing piers.

Lake Texana State Park (575 acres) is a popular area for wildlife watching; white-tailed deer and eastern fox squirrels are abundant; alligators and numerous other wild creatures are common. The park also has a 1.9-mile nature trail that runs along the northwestern edge of the campground, providing a good perspective on the area's oak-hackberry environment.

ADDITIONAL HELP

Location: Texas Official Travel Map grid S x 19; Jackson County
Nearest food, gas, and lodging: Edna, 6 miles, has all three.
Nearest camping: On-site at Lake Texana State Park (141 sites) and the adjacent Brackenridge Plantation (106 sites)
Contact: Manager, Lavaca-Navidad River Authority; Superintendent, Lake Texana State Park (see Appendix C)

Upper Coast Region

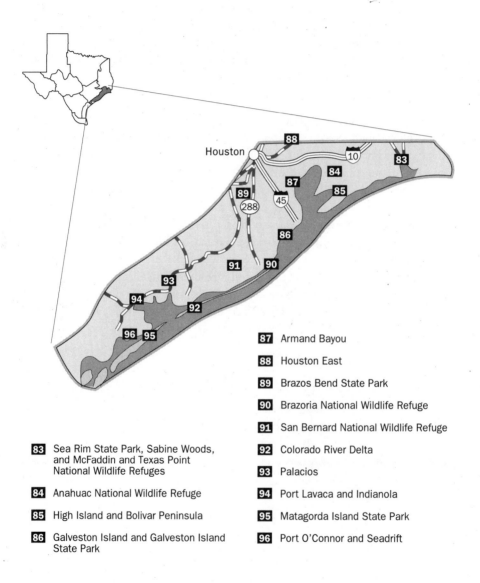

83 Sea Rim State Park, Sabine Woods, and McFaddin and Texas Point National Wildlife Refuges

84 Anahuac National Wildlife Refuge

85 High Island and Bolivar Peninsula

86 Galveston Island and Galveston Island State Park

87 Armand Bayou

88 Houston East

89 Brazos Bend State Park

90 Brazoria National Wildlife Refuge

91 San Bernard National Wildlife Refuge

92 Colorado River Delta

93 Palacios

94 Port Lavaca and Indianola

95 Matagorda Island State Park

96 Port O'Connor and Seadrift

83   Sea Rim State Park, Sabine Woods, and McFaddin and Texas Point National Wildlife Refuges

Habitats: Gulf, bay, lake, river, beach, dune, mud flat, marsh, coastal prairie, oak motte

Key birds: Brown Pelican, White and White-faced Ibis, Roseate Spoonbill, Wood and Mottled Ducks, Fish Crow, Seaside Sparrow, and Great-tailed and Boat-tailed Grackles are present year-round. Neotropic Cormorant; Anhinga; Magnificent Frigatebird; Least Bittern; Wood Stork; Fulvous Whistling-Duck; Purple Gallinule; Wilson's Plover; Sandwich, Least, Common, and Black Terns; Scissor-tailed Flycatcher; Cliff and Cave Swallows; Prothonotary and Swainson's Warblers; Painted Bunting; and Dickcissel occur in summer. Common Loon; Northern Gannet; American White Pelican; American Bittern; Yellow and Black Rails; Snowy and Piping Plovers; Groove-billed Ani; Short-eared Owl; Sprague's Pipit; Palm Warbler; Grasshopper, Henslow's, LeConte's, and Nelson's Sharp-tailed Sparrows; and Rusty Blackbird can usually be found in winter. Cape May Warbler and Bobolink are rare but regular spring migrants.

Best times to bird: April and May for spring migrants and nesting activities; November to March for winter birds

Birding strategies: The Marshland Unit (**A**) of Sea Rim State Park is a good place to begin. Resident wetland birds include Pied-billed Grebe; Great Blue, Little Blue, and Tricolored Herons; Great, Snowy, and Cattle Egrets; Black-crowned and Yellow-crowned Night-Herons; White and White-faced Ibis; Mottled Duck; Clapper and Virginia Rails; Common Moorhen; American Coot; Killdeer; Black-necked Stilt; Willet; Caspian and Forster's Terns; Black Skimmer; Marsh Wren; Common Yellowthroat; Seaside Sparrow; Red-winged Blackbird; Eastern Meadowlark; and Great-tailed and Boat-tailed Grackles.

During spring migration, the wetlands can be swarming with neotropical migrants, especially significant numbers of waterfowl, shorebirds, swallows, and a variety of songbirds. Only a few species stay and nest: Neotropic Cormorant; Anhinga; Least Bittern; Green Heron; Purple Gallinule; Least Tern; Common Nighthawk; Eastern Kingbird; Scissor-tailed Flycatcher; Purple Martin; Cliff, Cave (nests in the boathouse), and Barn Swallows; and Dickcissel. Wood Stork and Fulvous Whistling-Duck occasionally occur.

In winter waterfowl include Greater White-fronted, Snow, and Canada Geese; Green-winged and Blue-winged Teal; Northern Pintail; Gadwall; American Wigeon; Canvasback; Redhead; Ring-necked Duck; Lesser Scaup; Red-breasted Merganser; and Ruddy Duck. American White Pelican; Double-crested Cormorant; Northern Harrier; Red-tailed Hawk; American Kestrel; Sora; Black-bellied, Snowy, Piping, and Semipalmated Plovers; Spotted, Western, and Least Sandpipers; Long-billed Curlew; Dunlin; Short-billed and Long-billed Dowitchers; Common Snipe; Bonaparte's, Ring-billed, and Herring Gulls; Gull-billed Tern; Savannah and

83 Sea Rim State Park, Sabine Woods, and McFaddin and Texas Point National Wildlife Refuges

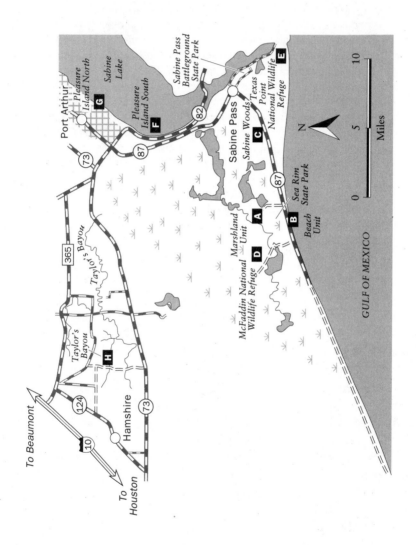

Nelson's Sharp-tailed Sparrows; and all three Grackles can be numerous. In weedy areas, look for Henslow's, LeConte's, Lincoln's, and Swamp Sparrows. Less numerous in winter are American Bittern, Mallard, Cinnamon Teal, Redhead, Common Goldeneye, Hooded Merganser, Yellow and Black Rails, American Avocet, Greater and Lesser Yellowlegs, Fish Crow, Sprague's Pipit, Palm Warbler, and Brewer's Blackbird.

The Beach Unit (B) of Sea Rim State Park has many of the same species throughout the year. Spring migrants can be abundant in the rows of willows and salt cedars. The Gambusia Trail boardwalk provides easy access into the marsh. However, the beach and open Gulf waters offer different species. In summer expect Brown Pelican; Wilson's Plover; Sanderling; Laughing Gull; and Caspian, Royal, Sandwich, Least, Common, and Black Terns. Watch overhead for Magnificent Frigatebird. The Gulf waters usually produce the greatest variety of water birds in winter, including Common Loon, Eared Grebe, and Northern Gannet; look for Snowy and Piping Plovers on the beach. Horned Grebe; Greater Scaup; Oldsquaw; Black, Surf, and White-winged Scoters; and Pomarine and Parasitic Jaegers occur occasionally.

Sabine Woods (C), a sanctuary owned by the Texas Ornithological Society, is 5 miles east of the state park; watch for a "TOS Sanctuary" sign, and park along the highway outside the gate. This area is best in spring, especially after a fallout when the woods can be filled with songbirds. Warblers, vireos, flycatchers, thrushes, tanagers, grosbeaks, sparrows, and orioles are common visitors from late March through early May. Even Green Heron, Yellow-crowned Night-Heron, and various hawks rest here in spring. White-tailed Kite has nested in the oaks near the entrance. Other breeding woodland birds include Mourning Dove, Yellow-billed Cuckoo, Downy Woodpecker, Eastern Kingbird, Common Yellowthroat, and Brown-headed Cowbird. Field birds to be expected in summer include Northern Bobwhite, Painted Bunting, Dickcissel, and Eastern Meadowlark.

Fall migration (August through early November) can be rewarding, although migrants are less concentrated than they are in spring. In fall and winter, look along the brushy edges for Groove-billed Ani (rare), Eastern Phoebe, House and Winter Wrens, Gray Catbird, Northern Mockingbird, Brown Thrasher, White-eyed and Plumbeous (Solitary) Vireos, Orange-crowned and Yellow-rumped Warblers, Eastern and Spotted Towhees, and LeConte's, Song, Lincoln's, Swamp, White-throated, and White-crowned Sparrows. Migrating Mourning Warbler, although difficult to find, occurs here as well.

McFaddin National Wildlife Refuge (D) lies directly west of Sea Rim State Park, and generally contains all the same marsh, beach, and Gulf birds. The refuge contains 8 miles of roads that provide access to the inland wetlands, which can be birded year-round.

Texas Point National Wildlife Refuge (E) is located in the extreme eastern corner of the state, between the Sabine River and the Gulf, and contains most of the same birds mentioned above. However, the refuge is burned off regularly; this burned prairie, best seen from along SH 87, provides good views of small ponds and prairie that are attractive to birds. The east-side Pilot Station Road (accessed by FM 3322) is lined with salt cedars that attract neotropical migrants in both spring and fall. Marshes occur on both sides of the road. Scope the Sabine Pass Channel for passing water birds; the jetty across the channel can also be worth a look. On the Louisiana side is a rookery with Roseate Spoonbills. During migration, bird the Sabine Pass Battleground State Park, which contains a picnic area, edged by marsh on the north and with a small pond near the entrance.

Two additional sites are well worth visiting in winter. Pleasure Island was formed by dredged spoil that provides wonderful resting sites for many birds and nesting sites for a few. Pleasure Island South (**F**) and Pleasure Island North (**G**) are visible from SH 82, but are best birded from the spoil levee roads. The impoundments can contain Canvasback, Bufflehead, Red-breasted and (occasionally) Hooded Mergansers, plus the more usual wintering waterfowl. This is the best place in the area to find Common Loon, usually on the Sabine Lake side of the levee roads.

The North Fork of Taylor's Bayou (**H**) (on Jap Road north of SH 73, 17 miles west of the junction of SH 73 and SH 82—see map) features a cypress swamp, which can be excellent during migration. Nesting birds include Wood Duck, Barred Owl, Red-headed Woodpecker, Fish Crow, Northern Parula, and Prothonotary and Swainson's Warblers. Also watch for the occasional Swallow-tailed Kite.

Records of Review Species: Masked Duck, Feb–May 1993. Glaucous Gull, April 1988. Hooded Oriole, April–June 1995.

Directions: The entire area is located south and west of Port Arthur, accessible via SH 87 and SH 73. SH 87 south is closed beyond McFaddin National Wildlife Refuge due to encroachment by the Gulf (see map).

General information: McFaddin National Wildlife Refuge, Sea Rim State Park, Sabine Woods, and Texas Point National Wildlife Refuge are all on the Gulf side of the Intracoastal Waterway, and include a combined area of more than 67,000 acres and approximately 25 miles of beach. Sea Rim State Park (15,109 acres) is accessible by boat; exceptions include the beach, a 0.7-mile boardwalk over a marsh, and short roads to the boathouse, Gambusia Nature Trail, and beach parking area. Sabine Woods has an amazing diversity of habitats for its 32 acres and is easily birded. There is now an entry fee, and contributions to the Texas Ornithological Society, which owns the property, are welcome.

The 42,955-acre McFaddin National Wildlife Refuge contains 8 miles of roads to extensive wetlands; the area contains the state's largest known population of alligators. The 8,952-acre Texas Point National Wildlife Refuge is not accessible by vehicle, but part of the refuge can be birded from the Texas Point/Pilot Station Road. Both refuges are hunted in early winter.

ADDITIONAL HELP

Location: Texas Official Travel Map grid Q x 23/24; Jefferson County
Nearest food, gas, and lodging: All are available at Sabine Pass, 10 miles from the state park
Nearest camping: On-site at the state park (20 sites)
Contact: Superintendent, Sea Rim State Park; Manager, Golden Triangle Audubon Society; McFaddin and Texas Point national wildlife refuges (see Appendix C)

84 Anahuac National Wildlife Refuge

Habitats: Bay, pond, freshwater and saltwater marsh, riparian, coastal prairie, salt cedar, field, cropland
Key birds: Least Grebe, Brown Pelican, White and White-faced Ibis, Roseate Spoonbill, Fulvous Whistling-Duck, Wood and Mottled Ducks, Clapper and King Rails, Seaside Sparrow, and Boat-tailed Grackle are present year-round. Neotropic Cormorant, Least Bittern, Wood Stork, Purple Gallinule, Least Tern, Scissor-tailed Flycatcher, Painted Bunting, and Dickcissel occur in summer. American White Pelican; Greater White-fronted, Snow, and Ross's Geese; Osprey; White-tailed Kite; Yellow, Black, and Virginia Rails; Short-eared Owl; Sedge Wren; American and Sprague's Pipits; and LeConte's Sparrow can usually be found in winter.
Best times to bird: November to April for waterfowl and rails

Birding strategies: Anahuac is best known to birders for its rails; nine species occur during the year. Clapper and King Rails and Common Moorhen are present year-round; Yellow, Black, Sora, and Virginia Rails and American Coot occur in winter; Purple Gallinule is a summer resident. All these species are present in April.

The refuge's 17 miles of graveled roads provide good viewing of several key habitats. Take the one-way Shoveler Pond Road (**A**) that loops the pond, stopping to check the willows just beyond the entrance and scoping Shoveler Pond from the elevated platform. The willows attract passing migrants like a magnet. In winter Shoveler Pond can be alive with water birds. Common species include Pied-billed Grebe; American White Pelican; Double-crested Cormorant; Great Blue and Tri-colored Herons; Great and Snowy Egrets; White-faced Ibis; Greater White-fronted and Snow Geese; Green-winged Teal; Mottled Duck; Northern Pintail; Northern Shoveler; Gadwall; Canvasback; Lesser Scaup; Ruddy Duck; Common Moorhen; American Coot; Greater and Lesser Yellowlegs; Western Sandpiper; Dunlin; Long-billed Dowitcher; Laughing, Ring-billed, and Herring Gulls; and Forster's Tern. Less numerous are **Least Grebe,** Little Blue Heron, Black-crowned Night-Heron, White Ibis, Roseate Spoonbill, Fulvous Whistling-Duck, Ross's Goose, Wood Duck, Blue-winged and Cinnamon Teal, Ring-necked Duck, Greater Scaup, Common Goldeneye, Hooded and Red-breasted Mergansers, King and Virginia Rails, Sora, and a variety of shorebirds. Watch for the occasional Bald Eagle, Merlin, and Peregrine Falcon.

84 Anahuac National Wildlife Refuge

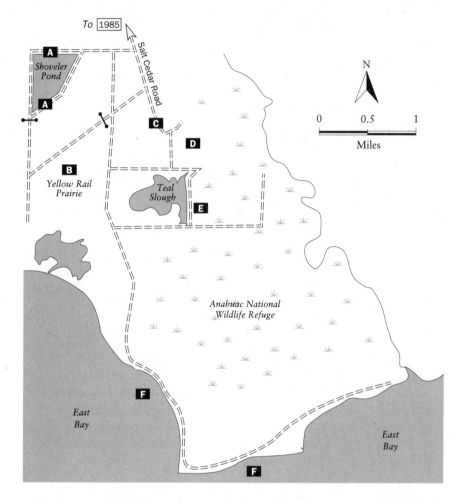

In summer look for Neotropic Cormorant, Anhinga, Least Bittern, Green Heron, Yellow-crowned Night-Heron, Wood Stork, Purple Gallinule, and Least Tern.

The abundant wintering geese normally spend their nights in the refuge and fly out in the early morning to feed in adjacent fields. A flight of several thousand geese is truly spectacular.

The Yellow Rail Prairie (**B**) is the best bet for finding this shy bird. Both Yellow and Black Rails can sometimes be flushed by walking through the area in winter; dragging a rope between two walkers is acceptable.

The coastal prairie habitat along Salt Cedar Road (**C**) offers most of the prairie birds. These include Horned Lark and Eastern Meadowlark year-round, and White-tailed Kite, Northern Harrier, American Kestrel, Long-billed Curlew, Short-eared

Owl, Sedge Wren, Sprague's Pipit, and Savannah and LeConte's Sparrows in winter. During migration the row of salt cedars (**D**) often harbors passerines. In summer expect Scissor-tailed Flycatcher, Painted Bunting, and Dickcissel.

Beyond Salt Cedar Road is Teal Slough Road, which crosses Teal Slough (**E**). Although this area usually harbors many of the same birds that occur in and about Shoveler Pond, a few additional species can be expected, including Clapper and Yellow Rails and Seaside Sparrow.

The open bay (**F**) lies beyond Teal Slough, at the end of the maintained road. In winter look here for Common Loon, Double-crested Cormorant, Brown Pelican, Osprey, Willet, and Caspian and Royal Terns.

Migrating shorebirds can best be seen along FM 1985, where areas are flooded to provide feeding and resting sites in spring, late summer, and fall. Most numerous are Black-bellied and Semipalmated Plovers; Killdeer; Black-necked Stilt; Greater and Lesser Yellowlegs; Semipalmated, Western, Least, Pectoral, and Stilt Sandpipers; Dunlin; and Long-billed Dowitchers. Less numerous are American Avocet; Solitary, Upland, White-rumped, and Buff-breasted Sandpipers; Hudsonian and Marbled Godwits; Ruddy Turnstone; Short-billed Dowitcher; and Wilson's Phalarope.

Nearby Smith Point (20 miles west of the national wildlife refuge via FM 1985 and FM 562) has become a key hawkwatch site each fall, from early September to mid-November. Fifteen raptor species can be expected. A total of 40,977 raptors were recorded in 1997 by Winnie Burkett and others. These included, in descending order of abundance, Broad-winged hawk 30,374, Sharp-shinned Hawk 4,779, Mississippi Kite 2,125, American Kestrel 1,297, Cooper's Hawk 1,136, Northern Harrier 444, Red-tailed Hawk 338, Swainson's Hawk 136, Osprey 90, Merlin 88, Peregrine Falcon 64, Red-shouldered Hawk 44, American Swallow-tailed Kite 40, White-tailed Kite 11, Crested Caracara 6, Golden Eagle 3, Bald Eagle 2.

Records of Review Species: Brant, Jan 1995. Eurasian Wigeon, April 1979. Masked Duck, Dec–Jan 1977/78. Ruff, April 1994.

Directions: From I-10 at Winnie, take SH 124 south for 13 miles to FM 1985 and turn right (west). Shorebird fields lie at 4.3 miles and the refuge entrance road is situated 8 miles west of SH 124.

General information: The more than 34,000-acre Anahuac National Wildlife Refuge was established in 1963 to provide habitat for wintering waterfowl along the Central Flyway. Between October and March, 32 species of waterfowl utilize the refuge; concentrations of Snow Geese sometimes exceed 80,000.

The refuge ponds and prairie habitats are readily accessible by a series of graveled roads with occasional pullouts; trails are at a minimum. Restroom facilities are available at the entrance area; there is no drinking water available in the refuge.

ADDITIONAL HELP

Location: Texas Official Travel Map grid Q/R x 22; Chambers County
Nearest food, gas, lodging: High Island (7 miles) and Winnie (10 miles) both have food, gas, and lodging.
Nearest camping: High Island and Winnie
Contact: Manager, Anahuac National Wildlife Refuge (see Appendix C)

85 High Island and Bolivar Peninsula

Boy Scout Woods, Smith Oaks Sanctuary, Rollover Pass, Bob's Road, Bolivar Flats Shorebird Sanctuary, Fort Travis Seashore Park, and Galveston-Bolivar Channel

Habitats: Gulf, beach, dune, mud flat, creek, freshwater pond and wetland, saltwater wetland, coastal prairie, coastal scrub, oak motte, field, pasture

Key birds: American White and Brown Pelicans; Neotropic Cormorant; Anhinga; Reddish Egret; White, Glossy, and White-faced Ibis; Roseate Spoonbill; Mottled Duck; American Oystercatcher; Black Skimmer; Horned Lark; and Seaside Sparrow are present year-round. Magnificent Frigatebird; Least Bittern; Wood Stork; Fulvous and Black-bellied Whistling-Ducks; Gull-billed, Least, and Black Terns; Scissor-tailed Flycatcher; Painted Bunting; and Dickcissel occur in summer. Common Loon, Northern Gannet, Ross's Goose, Peregrine Falcon, Snowy Plover, **Buff-bellied Hummingbird,** and Nelson's Sharp-tailed Sparrow can usually be found in winter.

Best times to bird: April and May for spring migrants and nesting activities; late summer for post-nesting birds; late September and early October for fall migrants; winter for water birds, including rails

Birding strategies: High Island, especially **Boy Scout Woods (A)** and **Smith Oaks Sanctuary (B)**, is one of the country's best known birding sites during spring migration; it also can be superb in late summer and fall. Totals of 15 species of flycatchers, 8 thrushes, 10 vireos, and 42 warblers have been recorded here. Fallouts can provide birders with literally thousands of songbirds; peaks usually occur during late April and late September. Only a few of these remain and nest with the full-time residents. These combined species include White-tailed Kite, Mourning and Inca Doves, Yellow-billed Cuckoo, Downy Woodpecker, Great Crested and Scissor-tailed Flycatchers, Blue Jay, Carolina Wren, American Robin, Northern Mockingbird, Brown Thrasher, Northern Parula, Northern Cardinal, Painted Bunting, and Orchard Oriole.

Smith Oaks Sanctuary (B) contains a wide diversity of habitats, including woodlands, ponds, wetlands, and fields. Fields and wooded edges along the entrance roads (Old Mexico and Smith Pond roads) can provide good birding much of the year. In spring and summer, expect Northern Bobwhite, Common Nighthawk at dawn and dusk, Eastern Kingbird, Scissor-tailed Flycatcher, Purple Martin, Cliff

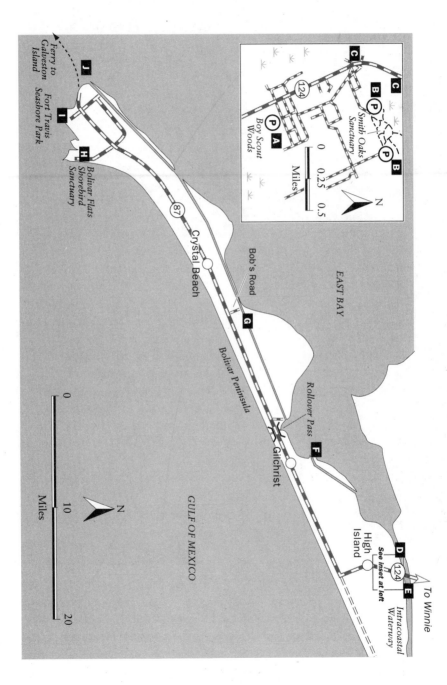

A birder at the Cathedral in Boy Scout Woods, High Island.

and Barn Swallows, Northern Mockingbird, Loggerhead Shrike, Northern Cardinal, Painted Bunting, Dickcissel, Red-winged Blackbird, Eastern Meadowlark, and Great-tailed Grackle.

The ponds usually harbor Pied-billed Grebe; Neotropic Cormorant; Anhinga; Great Blue, Little Blue, and Tricolored Herons; Great and Snowy Egrets; Black-crowned and Yellow-crowned Night-Herons; White and White-faced Ibis; Roseate

Spoonbill; Fulvous and Black-bellied Whistling-Ducks; Mottled Duck; Common Moorhen; Killdeer; Laughing Gull; and Caspian and Forster's Terns year-round. Herons, egrets, and a few spoonbills nest on the island in Claybottom Pond. Least Bittern, Wood Stork, and Purple Gallinule often occur in summer. Numerous ducks and a few shorebirds, such as Black-necked Stilt, American Avocet, Greater and Lesser Yellowlegs, Willet, and Spotted Sandpiper, utilize the ponds in winter and during migration. Occasional **Buff-bellied Hummingbird** frequents flowering herbs and shrubs in late fall and winter.

The roadside park and adjacent fields (**C**), off SH 124 on the north side of town, offer most of the same woodland and field birds mentioned above; it is worth checking this area during migration. The coastal prairie (**D**) to the west of SH 124 to the Intracoastal Waterway can also be productive. This area often contains Greater White-fronted, Snow, and Ross's Geese in winter. The vegetation along the Intracoastal Waterway, as well as the waterway itself, which can be birded from below the bridge (**E**), sometimes produces interesting birds. Least Bitterns have nested here. North of the Intracoastal Waterway is Anahuac National Wildlife Refuge (site 84).

Drive south from High Island on SH 87 toward Galveston to bird **Rollover Pass** (**F**), 7 miles below High Island—a must any time of year. This area can harbor Magnificent Frigatebird in summer and jaeger and kittiwake in winter. Year-round when the tide is out, an oyster bar on the inner bay is usually busy with shorebirds, including Reddish Egret and American Oystercatcher. Watch for Peregrine Falcon here from October through April.

Bob's Road (**G**) near Crystal Beach, 9 miles south of Rollover Pass, offers a brackish pond on the right, which can be busy with waterfowl in winter, and saltwater wetlands to the left. Besides the numerous waders and shorebirds, this is a good place to find White-tailed Kite and Clapper Rail year-round.

Bolivar Flats Shorebird Sanctuary (**H**) is 8 miles beyond, and another excellent birding site year-round. If time does not allow for more than one stop between High Island and the Galveston ferry, spend time here. Turn off SH 87 onto Rettilon Road and drive south along the beach to the vehicular barrier; then walk down the beach to near the tip of land and scope the flats and water. A tower just beyond the barrier to the right is useful for viewing the adjacent wetlands; walk this area for Seaside Sparrow year-round and Nelson's Sharp-tailed Sparrow in winter. Except for a few weeks in June, thousands of shorebirds can normally be found along the flats and shallow waters, and hundreds of waterfowl, gulls, and terns can normally be found offshore. Key species include Common Loon; Northern Gannet; American White and Brown Pelicans; Reddish Egret; Peregrine Falcon; American Oystercatcher; Black Skimmer; Gull-billed, Least, and Black Terns; and Snowy Plover. In spring and fall, more than 100 species are possible from this location.

Fort Travis Seashore Park (**I**), located 2.7 miles beyond Rettilon Road, is another worthwhile stop, especially during spring migration. Check the mulberry

Birders in the protected Bolivar Flats Shorebird Sanctuary; Galveston is visible in the background.

trees along the entrance road. The manicured lawns beyond sometimes harbor American Golden-Plover, Upland and Buff-breasted Sandpipers, and other shorebirds.

The **Galveston-Bolivar Channel (J)** always has passing gulls and terns, and an occasional Magnificent Frigatebird flying overhead or perched on the pilings.

Records of Review Species: White-chinned Petrel, April 1986. Greater Shearwater, April 1980. Sooty Shearwater, July 1976. Brant, Dec 1986. Curlew Sandpiper, April–May 1984, June–July 1994. Ruff, April 1981, May 1984, Sept 1989. Red Phalarope, April 1984. Long-tailed Jaeger, Nov 1971. Thayer's Gull, April 1990, April 1994. Lesser Black-backed Gull, March 1976, Nov 1981, April 1984, April 1990, Oct 1994. Glaucous Gull, April 1978, April 1981, April 1983, April–May 1989, April 1990, April 1991, Nov 1993. Great Black-backed Gull, Feb 1990. Black-legged Kittiwake, March–April 1988, April 1990, April 1991, Dec 1991. Bridled Tern, Sept 1988. Mangrove Cuckoo, Dec–Jan 1981/82. Greenish Elaenia, May 1984. Sulphur-bellied Flycatcher, May 1983. Fork-tailed Flycatcher, April 1991. Yellow-green Vireo, May 1992, April 1996. Black-whiskered Vireo, April 1987, Aug–Oct 1989, Aug 1991. Yucatan Vireo, April–May 1984. Connecticut Warbler, Sept 1978.

Directions: From Winnie (on I-10), take SH 124 south for 20 miles to High Island. From Galveston, take SH 87 north and cross the channel on the free Galveston-Bolivar Ferry. See the map for the numerous sites along the Bolivar Peninsula.

General information: The 27-mile-long Bolivar Peninsula runs from High Island south to Bolivar Flats. The principal birding areas (the two High Island sanctuaries and Bolivar Flats Shorebird Sanctuary) are managed by the Houston Audubon Society, to protect significant migratory bird resting and feeding sites. Bolivar Flats is a member of the Western Hemisphere Shorebird Reserve Network. The High Island sanctuaries are open daily from dawn to dusk. Check in at Boy Scout Woods; a donation is expected!

High Island's oak mottes (locally known as cheniers) offer welcome resting and feeding sites for the millions of birds that cross the Gulf of Mexico each spring. These neotropical migrants leave the Yucatan Peninsula in the evenings and fly for as much as 600 miles, nonstop across the Gulf at night, arriving on the Texas coast the next morning or midday, depending upon weather conditions en route. Often they are so exhausted that they literally fall out of the sky onto the first land available. The oak mottes and other vegetation along the Bolivar Peninsula are essential for their survival.

ADDITIONAL HELP

Location: Texas Official Travel Map grid Q/R x 22/23; Galveston County
Nearest food, gas, and lodging: All three are at High Island, Winnie, and Galveston. Food and gas are also available at Gilchrist and Crystal Beach.
Nearest camping: High Island and Rollover Pass
Contact: Boy Scout Woods, Smith Oaks Sanctuary, and Bolivar Flats Shorebird Sanctuary are managed by the Houston Audubon Society (see Appendix C).

86 Galveston Island and Galveston Island State Park

Habitats: Gulf, bay, estuary, beach, dune, mud flat, marsh, pond, coastal prairie, coastal scrub, field, pasture
Key birds: Brown Pelican, Neotropic Cormorant, Reddish Egret, White and White-faced Ibis, Roseate Spoonbill, Mottled Duck, American Oystercatcher, Black Rail, and Seaside Sparrow are present year-round. Magnificent Frigatebird, Least Bittern, Fulvous and Black-bellied Whistling-Ducks, Purple Gallinule, Wilson's Plover, Least Tern, Scissor-tailed Flycatcher, Painted Bunting, Dickcissel, and Bronzed Cowbird occur in summer. Northern Gannet, American White Pelican, Hooded Merganser, Osprey, Yellow and Virginia Rails, Sandhill Crane, Snowy and Piping Plovers, Short-eared Owl, Sprague's Pipit, and Nelson's Sharp-tailed Sparrow can usually be found in winter.
Best times to bird: April and May for spring migrants and nesting activities; November to March for winter birds

Birding strategies: All of Galveston Island and the offshore waters are worth birding if time allows. Galveston Island State Park provides open Gulf waters as

86 Galveston Island State Park

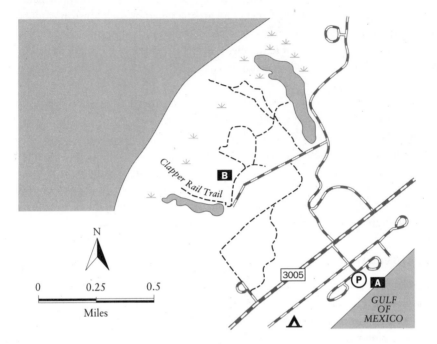

well as a diversity of habitats on the bay side. Typical beach and Gulf (**A**) birds include Brown Pelican; Black-bellied Plover; Willet; Ruddy Turnstone; Sanderling; Laughing Gull; and Caspian, Royal, Sandwich, and Forster's Terns. In winter expect Common Loon, Horned and Eared Grebes, Northern Gannet, Double-crested Cormorant, and Lesser Scaup offshore, and a variety of shorebirds along the beach. Look for Pacific Loon; Greater Scaup; Oldsquaw; and Black, Surf, and White-winged Scoters. In summer watch for Magnificent Frigatebird.

Across FM 3005 to the north is a network of roads. Drive these roads, checking the freshwater ponds, and walk the trails (see map). The Clapper Rail Trail (**B**) can be productive. In summer these wetlands normally contain Pied-billed Grebe; Least Bittern; Great Blue, Little Blue, Tricolored, and Green Herons; Great, Snowy, Reddish, and Cattle Egrets; Black-crowned Night-Heron; White and White-faced Ibis; Roseate Spoonbill; Mottled Duck; Blue-winged Teal; White-tailed Kite; Clapper Rail; Killdeer; Black-necked Stilt; Willet; Laughing Gull; Gull-billed, Caspian, Forster's, and Least Terns; Black Skimmer; Marsh Wren; Common Yellowthroat; Seaside Sparrow; Red-winged Blackbird; and Great-tailed Grackle. Also watch for Purple Gallinule and Common Moorhen. Black Rails nest in the cord grass marsh in June and July, but finding them means tolerating hordes of mosquitoes and watching for poisonous snakes. Check the ponds for Neotropic Cormorant, Anhinga, and Fulvous Whistling-Duck.

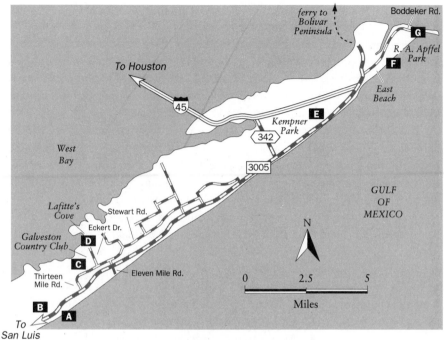

These wetlands are not as busy in winter, but you may find American White Pelican; Osprey; Sandhill Crane; Yellow, Black, and Virginia Rails; American Avocet; Whimbrel; Long-billed Curlew; Marbled Godwit; Common Snipe; and Seaside and Nelson's Sharp-tailed Sparrows. Hooded Merganser is regular in the channels in the marshes near the bay, and Short-eared Owl can usually be found flying at dusk and dawn.

The brush and small trees along the edges can be alive with songbirds during migration. Species totals of 15 flycatchers, 6 thrushes, 6 vireos, and 36 warblers have been recorded. Only Eastern Kingbird, Scissor-tailed Flycatcher, Purple Martin, Barn Swallow, Painted Bunting, Dickcissel, and Bronzed Cowbird remain to nest.

In late fall and winter, the weedy fields and wires often contain Mourning and Inca Doves; Horned Lark; House and Sedge Wrens; Savannah, Lincoln's, Swamp, and White-throated Sparrows; Eastern Meadowlark; Great-tailed Grackle; and American Goldfinch. Occasionally Groove-billed Ani; Short-eared Owl; Palm Warbler; Indigo Bunting; Eastern Towhee; Chipping, Field, Vesper, Grasshopper, LeConte's, and White-crowned Sparrows; and Western Meadowlark can be found.

The Galveston Country Club golf course (**C**) just east of the park, near Thirteen Mile Road and Stewart Road, offers birding year-round. In spring the open greens provide resting and feeding habitats for various neotropical migrants, including American Golden-Plover, Upland Sandpiper, and Buff-breasted Sandpiper. Beyond the golf course along Stewart Road are ponds that are excellent for waders, ducks, and shorebirds at any time of year.

The nature preserve at Lafitte's Cove subdivision (**D**) (locally known as Mitchel's Woods, private property, and open to the public during daylight hours only), is located on Eckert Drive, off Stewart Road, 0.2 mile west of Eleven Mile Road. It includes a cement walkway that traverses an oak motte, a prime spot for migrant flycatchers, thrushes, vireos, and warblers.

The older portion of downtown Galveston, with its tree-lined streets, can be busy with migrants in spring; the best accessible place to bird is Kempner Park (**E**), between Avenue O and 27th and 29th streets. The park and the grounds of the adjacent Sealy Hutchings Mansion are excellent in migration. The park is public, but do not get off the sidewalk onto the private mansion grounds.

Drive north along the Gulf to Seawall Boulevard. Investigate East Beach (**F**), R. A. Apffel Park, and South Jetty (**G**, at the end of Boddeker Road). Scope the flats in the Big Reef Nature Preserve along Boddeker Road and in the park; Laughing, Franklin's, Bonaparte's, Ring-billed, Kelp, California, Herring, Lesser Black-backed, Glaucous, and Great Black-backed Gulls have all been recorded at the same time in fall and winter. Common Terns are present along the Gulf beach at the jetty from March to December. Scope the exposed mud flats for Reddish Egret, Piping and Snowy Plovers, American Oystercatcher, Black-necked Stilt, American Avocet, Long-billed Curlew, and Marbled Godwit.

South Jetty offers exposure to the open Gulf; pelagic birds are sometimes recorded here and along the seawall and Gulf beachfront. Northern Gannets and jaegers can be seen almost daily December through March. Watch for Purple Sandpiper on the jetty and for scoters over the open waters.

If time allows, visit San Luis Pass at the southern end of the island. This is one of the Texas coast's top birding sites. Large numbers of pelicans, cormorants, gulls, and terns feed and rest here. A large Black Skimmer, Least Tern, and Gull-billed Tern colony is located here, allowing close approach from April through June. From late April through September, Magnificent Frigatebird may be seen over the bay; it roosts on the poles and channel markers. In winter the fields along FM 3005 contain flocks of Sandhill Crane.

Records of Review Species: Red-necked Grebe, Dec 1987. Greater Shearwater, Nov 1973. Sooty Shearwater, Dec 1990. Red-footed Booby, Mar 1983. Wandering Tattler, Apr–May 1992. Eskimo Curlew, Mar–Apr 1962. Surfbird, Mar 1988. Ruff, Mar–Apr 1981. Kelp Gull, winter 1995/96. Thayer's Gull, Dec 1993. Glaucous Gull, winter 1995/96. Black-legged Kittiwake, Nov–Dec 1990. Gray Kingbird, Apr 1974. Black-whiskered Vireo, Apr–May 1981.

Directions: Galveston Island is situated on the Gulf Coast along FM 3005 between Bolivar Peninsula to the north and San Luis Pass on the south. From Houston, Galveston is 50 miles via I-45.

General information: Galveston Island extends for 30 miles and is nowhere more than 5 miles wide. It is a wonderful birding area year-round; 100 species can be found any day of the year, and 150 species or more can be recorded on a good day in spring.

The 2,000-acre state park lies 6 miles southwest of the western tip of the Galveston seawall. The city of Galveston, with a population of about 65,000, dominates the northern end of the island. The port of Galveston is the oldest major port in Texas. The city also contains a significant historic district and the 156-acre Moody Gardens, with a rain forest pyramid that houses tropical vegetation and butterflies.

ADDITIONAL HELP

Location: Texas Official Travel Map grid R/S x 22; Galveston County
Nearest food, gas, and lodging: All are on-site in Galveston.
Nearest camping: On-site at the state park (150 sites)
Contact: Galveston Island Convention and Visitors Bureau; Superintendent, Galveston Island State Park (see Appendix C)

87 Armand Bayou

Habitats: Estuarine bayou, oak-hackberry woodland, coastal prairie, farm
Key birds: Mottled Duck, Wild Turkey, and Pileated Woodpecker are present year-round. Neotropic Cormorant, White Ibis, Kentucky and Hooded Warblers, and Indigo and Painted Buntings occur in summer. American White Pelican; Osprey; Clapper Rail; Sandhill Crane; LeConte's and Fox Sparrows; and Rusty Blackbird can usually be found in winter.
Best times to bird: April and May for spring migrants and nesting activities; November to March for winter birds

Birding strategies: Bird both the Armand Bayou Nature Center and adjacent Bay Area Park. Trails at the nature center provide access to a variety of habitats. The woodlands along the 1.4-mile Martyn and 1.4-mile Karankawa trails (**A**) are best in spring and early summer. Migrants can be abundant, especially after a fallout of flycatchers, vireos, and warblers. Full-time residents include Red-shouldered Hawk; Mourning Dove; Red-bellied, Downy, and Pileated Woodpeckers; Blue Jay; Carolina Chickadee; Tufted Titmouse; Carolina Wren; Northern Cardinal; Red-winged Blackbird; and Common Grackle. In summer Green Heron, Yellow-billed Cuckoo, Ruby-throated Hummingbird, Eastern Wood-Pewee, Acadian and Great Crested Flycatchers, White-eyed Vireo, and Hooded Warbler utilize these woodlands for nesting. And in winter, watch for Sharp-shinned and Cooper's Hawks, Yellow-bellied Sapsucker, Ruby-crowned Kinglet, Hermit Thrush, Gray Catbird, Brown Thrasher, Cedar Waxwing, Orange-crowned and Yellow-rumped Warblers, Pine Siskin, and Purple Finch.

87 Armand Bayou

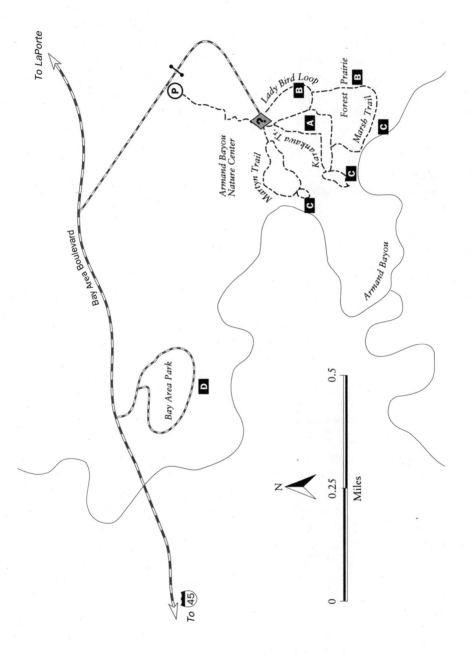

Bird the prairie habitat along the 0.7-mile Lady Bird Loop Trail (**B**) for resident Black and Turkey Vultures, Loggerhead Shrike, Northern Mockingbird, European Starling, and Eastern Meadowlark. White-tailed Kite is less numerous. In spring and summer, Cattle Egret, Common Nighthawk, Chimney Swift, Scissor-tailed Flycatcher, Purple Martin, Barn Swallow, Eastern Bluebird, and Indigo and Painted Buntings can usually be found. And in winter look for Northern Harrier, Red-tailed Hawk, American Kestrel, Eastern Phoebe, American Robin, and American Goldfinch. Several other wintering species are less numerous: Greater White-fronted, Snow, and Canada Geese; Sandhill Crane; House and Sedge Wrens; Rusty and Brewer's Blackbirds; and Purple Finch.

View Armand Bayou (**C**) at the nature center from the end of Martyn or Karankawa trails or from the 1.2-mile Marsh Trail. Year-round, expect Pied-billed Grebe; Great Blue, Little Blue, and Tricolored Herons; Great and Snowy Egrets; American Coot; Laughing Gull; Forster's Tern; Common Yellowthroat; and Red-winged Blackbird. In summer Neotropic Cormorant, Yellow-crowned Night-Heron, and Black-necked Stilt can usually be found. White and White-faced Ibis, Roseate Spoonbill, and Wood and Mottled Ducks are less numerous. In winter American White Pelican, Double-crested Cormorant, Northern Pintail, Blue-winged Teal, Northern Shoveler, Gadwall, American Wigeon, Lesser Scaup, Ruddy Ducks, Osprey, Clapper Rail, Spotted and Least Sandpipers, Ring-billed and Herring Gulls, Caspian Tern, Belted Kingfisher, and Marsh Wren frequent this area. You also may see an occasional Anhinga, Greater and Lesser Yellowlegs, Willet, Western Sandpiper, Common Snipe, and Royal Tern.

The Bay Area Park boardwalk (**D**) allows an even closer view of the wetlands. It offers all of the same birds.

Directions: From Houston, take I-45 south to Bay Area Boulevard (exit 28) and go east 6 miles to the entrance of Bay Area Park and, beyond, the entrance to Armand Bayou Nature Center.

General information: The 1,900-acre Armand Bayou Nature Center is one of the few remaining wild tracts left in the Greater Houston area. Environmental education programs, including bird walks and owl prowls, are scheduled. The center is open daily from 9 A.M. to 5 P.M. The bayou and center are named for naturalist Armand Yramatequi, who dreamed about preserving this area, but was killed in 1970. The adjacent Bay Area Park contains 65 acres along Armand Bayou, offering trails and canoe access (no motorized boats are permitted on Armand Bayou). The picnic areas and jogging trails can be crowded in warm weather.

ADDITIONAL HELP

Location: Texas Official Travel Map grid R x 21; Harris County

Nearest food, gas, and lodging: All can be found along I-45 (6 miles).

Nearest camping: Several areas, at League City, Dickinson, La Marque, and Texas City

Contact: Director, Armand Bayou Nature Center; Bay Area Park, Harris County Parks (see Appendix C)

88 Houston East

Jesse H. Jones Park, Alexander Deussen Park, Sheldon Lake and San Jacinto State Parks, and Baytown Nature Center

Habitats: Bay, bayou, reservoir, creek, riparian, marsh, cypress swamp, mixed hardwood-pine forest, field, pasture, cropland

Key birds: Reddish Egret, White and White-faced Ibis, Wood and Mottled Ducks, Pileated Woodpecker, and Fish Crow are present year-round. Anhinga; Neotropic Cormorant; Least Bittern; Roseate Spoonbill; Wood Stork; Fulvous Whistling-Duck; Least Tern; Red-headed Woodpecker; Wood Thrush; Prothonotary, Swainson's, Kentucky, and Hooded Warblers; Louisiana Waterthrush; Indigo and Painted Buntings; Dickcissel; and Bronzed Cowbird occur in summer. American White Pelican; Osprey; Bald Eagle; Sandhill Crane; American Woodcock, and Field, LeConte's, Fox, and Harris's Sparrows can usually be found in winter.

Best times to bird: April and May for spring migrants and nesting activities

Birding strategies: Jesse H. Jones Park (A), to the north off FM 1960, contains extensive forest and wetland habitats that attract numerous spring migrants and breeding birds. Neotropical migrants can include a wide array of flycatchers, vireos, warblers, tanagers, and other birds. The Canoe Launch Trail is best during migration. Several species remain and nest, most notably Swainson's Warbler, which can best be found along the Cypress Boardwalk and High Banks trails. Other summer birds include Yellow-billed Cuckoo; Ruby-throated and Black-chinned Humming-birds; Eastern Wood-Pewee; Acadian and Great Crested Flycatchers; Eastern King-bird; Wood Thrush; White-eyed and Red-eyed Vireos; Northern Parula; Yellow-throated, Prothonotary, Kentucky, and Hooded Warblers; Louisiana Waterthrush; Yellow-breasted Chat; and Summer Tanager.

Year-round residents at Jesse H. Jones Park include Wood Duck; Red-shouldered Hawk; Eastern Screech-Owl; Barred Owl; Red-bellied, Downy, and Pileated Woodpeckers; Blue Jay; American Crow; Carolina Chickadee; Tufted Titmouse; Carolina Wren; American Robin; European Starling; Pine Warbler; and Northern Cardinal. A few water birds frequent Spring Creek, including various waders, occasional waterfowl and shorebirds, and Belted Kingfisher.

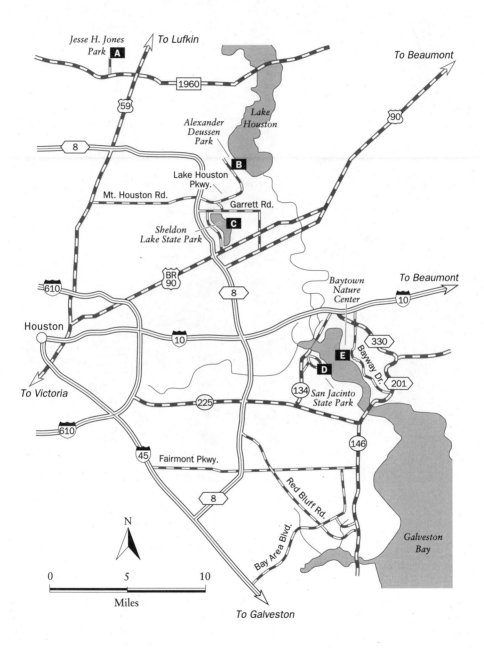

Jesse H. Jones Park **A**

To Lufkin

To Beaumont

1960

59

Lake Houston

Alexander Deussen Park

8

Lake Houston Pkwy.

B

Mt. Houston Rd.

Garrett Rd.

Sheldon Lake State Park

C

BR 90

8

610

Houston

Baytown Nature Center

To Beaumont

10

330

Bayway Dr.

10

E

D

201

To Victoria

225

134

San Jacinto State Park

146

610

45

Fairmont Pkwy.

8

Red Bluff Rd.

Bay Area Blvd.

Galveston Bay

N

0   5   10
Miles

To Galveston

View along the Cypress Boardwalk in Jesse H. Jones Park in the Greater Houston area.

Alexander Deussen Park (B), at the southern end of Lake Houston, harbors some of the same year-round residents, but this park has very little wild habitat. Typical summer birds in the picnic areas include Red-headed, Red-bellied, Downy, and Pileated Woodpeckers; Blue Jay; American Crow; Eastern Bluebird; American Robin; and Pine Warbler. The park also provides access to Lake Houston, where waders, gulls, and terns can be found.

Sheldon Lake State Park (C), located between US 90 and Garrett Road, offers a greater variety and number of water birds. Year-round residents include Pied-billed Grebe; Great Blue, Little Blue, and Tricolored Herons; Great, Snowy, and

Cattle Egrets; Black-crowned and Yellow-crowned Night-Herons; White and White-faced Ibis; Wood and Mottled Ducks; King Rail; Common Moorhen; American Coot; Killdeer; Laughing and Ring-billed Gulls; and Caspian, Royal, and Forster's Terns. In summer look for Neotropic Cormorant, Anhinga, Least Bittern, Green Heron, Roseate Spoonbill, Fulvous Whistling-Duck, and Black Tern. Waterfowl are most numerous here in winter, when geese and ducks can be abundant. Watch for passing Sandhill Crane and the occasional American Woodcock.

San Jacinto State Park (D), south of I-10 off SH 134, offers even larger numbers of waterfowl and better viewing. The extensive bayou behind the San Jacinto Monument usually contains thousands of wintering ducks. Most numerous are Northern Pintail, Northern Shoveler, Gadwall, American Wigeon, Lesser Scaup, and Ruddy Duck. Fewer numbers of Green-winged, Blue-winged, and Cinnamon Teal; Mallard; Mottled and Ring-necked Ducks; Canvasback; Redhead; Common Goldeneye; Bufflehead; and Hooded and Red-breasted Mergansers occur. Pied-billed, Horned, and Eared Grebes; American White Pelican; Double-crested Cormorant; various waders; Common Moorhen; American Coot; and various gulls and terns are present in winter. Large concentrations of Wood Stork occur here in summer and fall.

Bird the park grounds for spring and fall migrants, which can be abundant. Sometimes American Golden-Plover and Upland and Buff-breasted Sandpipers can be found. Summer birds are pretty well limited to the year-round residents, including Red-bellied Woodpecker, Blue Jay, American Crow, Carolina Wren, Tufted Titmouse, Eastern Bluebird, American Robin, Loggerhead Shrike, European Starling, Northern Cardinal, Eastern Meadowlark, Great-tailed and Common Grackles, and House Sparrow.

Baytown Nature Center (E) offers forest, fields, and both freshwater and brackish marshes, attracting a wide variety of migrants and breeding birds. This area is accessible from San Jacinto State Park via the free ferry across the Houston Ship Channel to Baytown. Year-round residents at the nature center include Mottled Duck, Roseate Spoonbill, Eastern Screech-Owl, Downy and Pileated Woodpeckers, Marsh and Carolina Wrens, and American Robin. In summer there is a large colony of Least Tern; Prothonotary, Swainson's, and Hooded Warblers nest. Indigo and Painted Buntings, Dickcissel, and Bronzed Cowbird can also be found in summer. This is the most inland area on the Texas coast for Reddish Egret. Waterfowl, Osprey, and Bald Eagle occur in winter. The brushy fields harbor winter seedeaters such as Eastern Towhee; Chipping, Field, Vesper, Savannah, Grasshopper, LeConte's, Fox, Song, Lincoln's, Swamp, White-throated, White-crowned, and Harris's Sparrows; Dark-eyed Junco; and American Goldfinch.

In central Houston, Memorial Park, Houston Arboretum and Nature Center, Hermann Park, Glenwood Cemetery, Russ Pittman Park, the City Hall reflection pond, and Sam Houston Park can offer surprising opportunities to see migrants during spring fallouts. These sites are islands of green in an otherwise dreary urban landscape.

Directions: Jesse H. Jones Park is located at the end of Kenswick Drive, 1.3 miles north of FM 1960, west of US 59. Sheldon Lake State Park and Alexander Deussen Park are located at the south end of Lake Houston, the state park off Lake Houston Parkway, Alexander Deussen Park off Garrett Road. San Jacinto State Park is south of I-10, via Loop 8, SH 225, and SH 134. Baytown Nature Center is located in Baytown. Take Loop 330 south 1 mile from I-10 to Bayway Drive. Take Bayway Drive south for 1.25 miles past Baker Road, then turn right and follow the bayshore to the nature center.

General information: The 225-acre Jesse H. Jones Park offers 5 miles of paved, all-weather trails, natural white sand beaches along Spring Creek, picnic sites, and a nature center featuring live animals, displays, and dioramas. The park staff offers a wide assortment of environmental education activities. The park is open from dawn to dusk.

Alexander Deussen Park offers duck ponds, picnic sites, and a variety of recreational activities; hours run from daylight to 6 P.M. in winter and 9 P.M. in summer. This area can be crowded on weekends and holidays. Nearby Dwight D. Eisenhower Park is closed due to flooding. The 2,800-acre Sheldon Lake State Park includes a wildlife management area for hunting, and marsh and prairie restoration areas.

The 1,005-acre San Jacinto State Park is managed primarily as the historic site of the 1836 Battle of San Jacinto (war for Texas's independence), but the area also includes picnic sites and the home of the battleship *Texas*.

The 420-acre Baytown Nature Center is a former subdivision reclaimed by subsidence and hurricanes. It is a large peninsula bordered by Burnett, Crystal, and Scott bays, diagonally across the Houston Ship Channel from San Jacinto State Park. The center, open from dawn to dark, offers 3 miles of paved trails and excellent birding.

ADDITIONAL HELP

Location: Texas Official Travel Map grid Q x 21; Harris County
Nearest food, gas, and lodging: All are available at numerous sites in the immediate area.
Nearest camping: Humble, LaPorte, Baytown, Bacliff, and Highlands
Contact: Jesse H. Jones and Alexander Deussen parks are Harris County parks; Superintendents, Sheldon Lake State Park and San Jacinto State Park; Baytown Nature Center (see Appendix C)

89 Brazos Bend State Park

Habitats: Lake, pond, river, creek, swamp, riparian, coastal prairie, oak savannah, oak motte, bottomland hardwood forest, old field, pasture, cropland

Key birds: Anhinga, White and White-faced Ibis, Black-bellied Whistling-Duck, Wood Duck, **White-tailed Hawk,** Crested Caracara, and Pileated Woodpecker are present year-round. Least Bittern, Roseate Spoonbill, Wood Stork, Mississippi Kite, King Rail, Purple Gallinule, Scissor-tailed Flycatcher, Wood Thrush, Prothonotary and Swainson's Warblers, Indigo and Painted Buntings, and Dickcissel occur in summer. American Bittern, Bald Eagle, Merlin, Sandhill Crane, American Woodcock, Sprague's Pipit, and LeConte's and Henslow's Sparrows can usually be found in winter.

Best times to bird: April and May for spring migrants and nesting activities; winter for waterfowl and sparrows

Birding strategies: Look for the majority of the park's bird life at Forty Acre Lake (**A**), with its circle trail and a three-tiered observation tower. Neotropical migrants can be numerous following a spring fallout, when hundreds of flycatchers, thrushes, vireos, warblers, tanagers, and orioles may appear. Only a few remain to nest: Eastern Wood-Pewee; Acadian, Great Crested, and Scissor-tailed Flycatchers; Eastern Kingbird; Wood Thrush; White-eyed, Yellow-throated, and Red-eyed Vireos; Northern Parula; Prothonotary and Swainson's Warblers; Summer Tanager; Indigo and Painted Buntings; and Dickcissel.

Look here or at Pilant Lake (**B**) for nesting Pied-billed Grebe; Anhinga; Least Bittern; Great Blue, Little Blue, Tricolored, and Green Herons; Great, Snowy, and Cattle Egrets; Black-crowned and Yellow-crowned Night-Herons; White Ibis; Roseate Spoonbill; Black-bellied Whistling-Duck; Wood and Mottled Ducks; Mallard; Blue-winged Teal; Purple Gallinule; Common Moorhen; American Coot; Killdeer; and Black-necked Stilt. Don't miss the rookery at the far end of the lake. In winter American Bittern, Bald Eagle, and a wide variety of waterfowl occur.

Full-time resident and summer woodland birds include Red-shouldered Hawk; Barn, Great Horned, and Barred Owls; Eastern Screech-Owl; Ruby-throated Hummingbird; Red-bellied, Downy, and Pileated Woodpeckers; Blue Jay; American Crow; Carolina Chickadee; Tufted Titmouse; Carolina Wren; Northern Mockingbird; Loggerhead Shrike; Northern Cardinal; Common Grackle; and Brown-headed Cowbird. A few other species can usually be found overhead: Black and Turkey Vultures, White-tailed Kite, Red-tailed Hawk, and Common Nighthawk at dawn and dusk.

Bird Horseshoe Lake Trail along Elm Lake to Old and New Horseshoe lakes (**C**), Creekfield Lake (**D**), and the weedy fields (**E**) along the entrance road. Elm Lake offers deeper water where some of the diving ducks are most likely in migration and during winter. Creekfield Lake offers an easy (wheelchair accessible) 0.5-mile walk through varied habitats.

89 Brazos Bend State Park

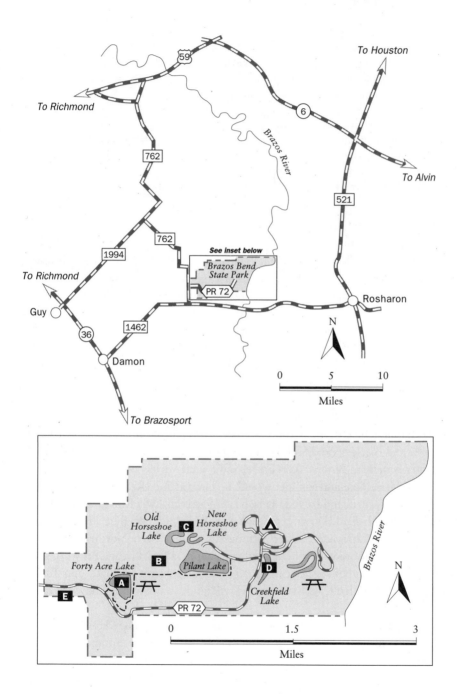

The open fields along the entrance road are the best bet for finding brush-loving birds, especially in fall and winter. Typical species include Eastern Phoebe; American Crow; House, Winter, and Sedge Wrens; Eastern Bluebird; Loggerhead Shrike; Orange-crowned and Yellow-rumped Warblers; Northern Cardinal; Eastern Towhee; Chipping, Field, Vesper, Fox, Song, Lincoln's, Swamp, and White-throated Sparrows; Dark-eyed Junco; Red-winged Blackbird; Eastern Meadowlark; Common Grackle; and American Goldfinch. Look also for Green-tailed Towhee; Savannah, Henslow's, LeConte's, and Harris's Sparrows; and Lapland Longspur. Watch overhead for White-tailed Kite, Crested Caracara, and American Kestrel.

There are several recent park records of Masked Duck, ranging from November to May. Forty Acre Lake is one of the state's best bets for finding this tropical species, although it occurs irregularly.

Directions: The park, which is only 20 miles south of Houston, can be reached by taking FM 521 to Rosharon and continuing 15 miles west on FM 1462, or by following FM 762 south from Richmond 15 miles.

General information: The 4,897-acre park, named for a bend in the Brazos River, has a rich diversity of habitats that attract a wide variety of wildlife, including 270 species of birds, 23 mammals, and 21 reptiles and amphibians. Twelve miles of hiking trails and 9 miles of hiking/bike trails offer good access. The visitor center, containing several exhibits, is open on weekends. Guided nature walks include owl prowls on Saturday evenings in winter and weekend bird walks from October to February.

The park also houses the George Observatory, a facility operated by the Houston Museum of Natural Science. It is open to the public every Saturday from 3 P.M. to 10 P.M. Tickets for observing through the 36-inch research telescope are sold on a first-come, first-served basis. For information, call 409-553-3243.

ADDITIONAL HELP

Location: Texas Official Travel Map grid R x 20; Fort Bend County
Nearest food, gas, and lodging: Food and gas are available at the junction of FM 762 and FM 1462, about 2 miles from the park. The nearest lodging is in Rosenberg, West Columbia, or Alvin, each about 15 miles away.
Nearest camping: On-site (90 sites)
Contact: Superintendent, Brazos Bend State Park (see Appendix C)

90 Brazoria National Wildlife Refuge

Habitats: Gulf, bay, estuary, lake, mud flat, marsh, pond, creek, riparian, saline and nonsaline coastal prairie, field, pasture, rice field
Key birds: Brown Pelican, Reddish Egret, White and White-faced Ibis, Roseate Spoonbill, **White-tailed Hawk,** Crested Caracara, Black Rail, and Seaside Sparrow are present year-round. Magnificent Frigatebird, Least Bittern, Wood Stork, Fulvous and Black-bellied Whistling-Ducks, Purple Gallinule, Least Tern, Scissor-tailed Flycatcher, and Painted Bunting occur in summer. American White Pelican; Greater White-fronted, Snow, and Ross's Geese; Bald Eagle; Peregrine Falcon; Yellow Rail; Short-eared Owl; Vermilion Flycatcher; American and Sprague's Pipits; Sedge Wren; Palm Warbler; and LeConte's and Nelson's Sharp-tailed Sparrows can usually be found in winter.
Best times to bird: April and May for spring migrants and nesting activities; November to March for winter birds

Birding strategies: The 7-mile Big Slough Auto Tour (A) contains both salt- and freshwater wetlands that support a wide variety of birds. Expected year-round species include Pied-billed Grebe; Great Blue, Little Blue, and Tricolored Herons; Great, Snowy, and Cattle Egrets; Black-crowned Night-Heron; White and White-faced Ibis; Roseate Spoonbill; Mottled Duck; Common Moorhen; American Coot; Killdeer; Black-necked Stilt; American Avocet; Laughing Gull; Gull-billed, Caspian, Royal, and Forster's Terns; and Black Skimmer. Less numerous/obvious are Black, Clapper, and King Rails. Year-round terrestrial species include White-tailed Kite; White-tailed Hawk; Crested Caracara; Horned Lark; Northern Mockingbird; Loggerhead Shrike; Common Yellowthroat; Northern Cardinal; Seaside Sparrow; Red-winged Blackbird; Eastern Meadowlark; Great-tailed, Boat-tailed, and Common Grackles; and Brown-headed Cowbird.

In summer look for Least Bittern, Wood Stork, Fulvous and Black-bellied Whistling-Ducks, Purple Gallinule, and Least Tern. Watch also for high-flying Magnificent Frigatebird. In winter this area supports Eared Grebe and thousands of waterfowl, especially Snow Goose. American White Pelican, Double-crested Cormorant, Northern Harrier, American Kestrel, Sandhill Crane, Black-bellied Plover, Greater and Lesser Yellowlegs, Long-billed Curlew, Western and Least Sandpipers, Dunlin, Short-billed and Long-billed Dowitchers, Common Snipe, Belted Kingfisher, Marsh and Sedge Wrens, American Pipit, and Savannah and Swamp Sparrows are common. Less numerous are Common Loon, Horned Grebe, Greater White-fronted and Ross's Geese, Osprey, Bald Eagle, Merlin, Peregrine Falcon, Yellow and Virginia Rails, Sora, Semipalmated Plover, Marbled Godwit, Short-eared Owl, Vermilion Flycatcher, Sprague's Pipit, Sedge Wren, Palm Warbler, and LeConte's and Nelson's Sharp-tailed Sparrows.

In spring the scattered shrub and tree areas along the auto tour route, as well as similar habitats along the entrance road (B), harbor migrant flycatchers, thrushes,

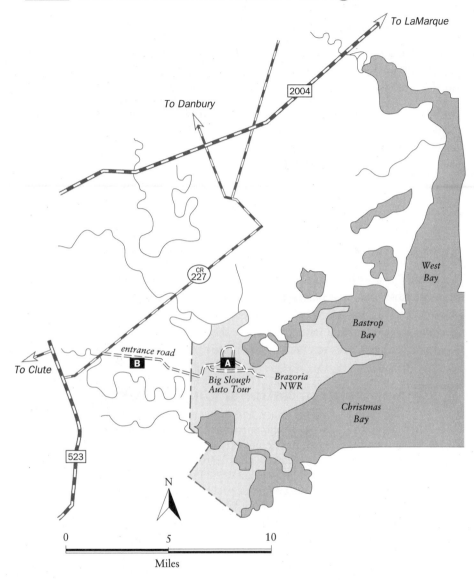

To LaMarque

To Danbury

2004

CR 227

West Bay

Bastrop Bay

entrance road

To Clute

B

A

Big Slough Auto Tour

Brazoria NWR

Christmas Bay

523

N

0   5   10

Miles

vireos, warblers, and sparrows. Only a handful of these remain to nest: Yellow-billed Cuckoo, Common Nighthawk, Eastern Kingbird, Scissor-tailed Flycatcher, Red-eyed Vireo, Northern Parula, Painted Bunting, and Dickcissel. Full-time residents here include Red-shouldered Hawk, Northern Bobwhite, Mourning Dove, Great Horned and Barred Owls, Blue Jay, American Crow, Carolina Chickadee, Tufted Titmouse, Carolina Wren, Northern Mockingbird, Loggerhead Shrike, White-eyed Vireo, Northern Cardinal, Eastern Meadowlark, Great-tailed and Common Grackles, and Brown-headed Cowbird. Watch overhead for Black and

Turkey Vultures, Red-tailed Hawk, Crested Caracara, Common Nighthawk, Chimney Swift, Purple Martin, and Barn Swallow.

Records of Review Species: Glossy Ibis, Dec 1991. Masked Duck, April 1989, April 1994.

Directions: From Lake Jackson (on SH 288), take SH 332 south to FM 523; turn left (north) on FM 523 for 5.5 miles to CR 227; then turn right (east). The refuge entrance road is 1.7 miles ahead.

General information: This 43,388-acre national wildlife refuge is one of several along the upper Texas Gulf Coast established to provide unaltered habitat for migrating and wintering waterfowl and other bird life. More than 425 wildlife species (including 300 birds) use the refuge during all or part of their life cycles.

Public access to the refuge is limited. The Big Slough Auto Tour is available sporadically, usually from 7 A.M. to 4 P.M. weekdays and on the first weekend of each month. Other areas are available only by prior arrangement.

ADDITIONAL HELP

Location: Texas Official Travel Map grid S x 21; Brazoria County
Nearest food, gas, and lodging: Food and gas are available on-site at Bastrop Marina. The nearest lodging is available at Clute (10 miles).
Nearest camping: Several camping areas in the greater Freeport/Lake Jackson area
Contact: Manager, Brazoria National Wildlife Refuge Complex (see Appendix C)

91 San Bernard National Wildlife Refuge

Habitats: Gulf, bay, estuary, beach, dune, mud flat, marsh, lake, river, creek, riparian, saline and freshwater prairie, mesquite grassland, field, pasture, cropland
Key birds: Brown Pelican, Reddish Egret, White and White-faced Ibis, Roseate Spoonbill, Black-bellied Whistling-Duck, **White-tailed Hawk,** Crested Caracara, King and Black Rails, and Seaside Sparrow are present year-round. Magnificent Frigatebird, Least Bittern, Wood Stork, Fulvous Whistling-Duck, Purple Gallinule, Wilson's Plover, Least Tern, Scissor-tailed Flycatcher, and Indigo and Painted Buntings occur in summer. American White Pelican; Bald Eagle; Peregrine Falcon; Yellow and Virginia Rails; Piping Plover; Short-eared Owl; Vermilion Flycatcher; Sprague's Pipit; Palm Warbler; and LeConte's, Nelson's Sharp-tailed, and Fox Sparrows can usually be found in winter.
Best times to bird: April and May for migrants and nesting activities; November to March for winter birds

Birding strategies: Drive the Moccasin Pond Auto Tour (**A**), at the end of the entrance road, for the best birding. Year-round birds include Pied-billed Grebe; Great Blue, Little Blue, and Tricolored Herons; Great, Snowy, and Cattle Egrets;

91 San Bernard National Wildlife Refuge

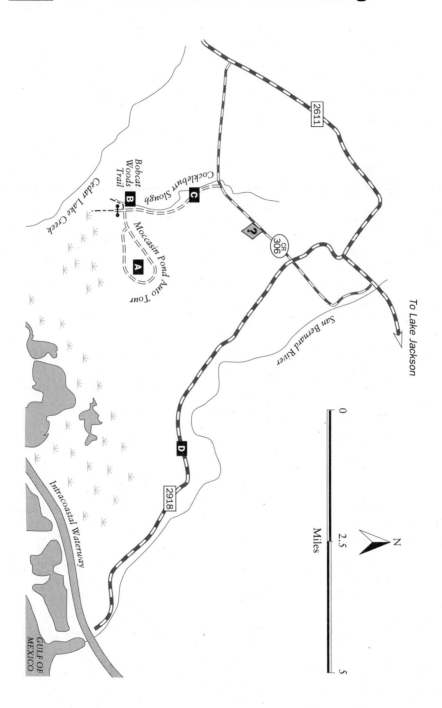

Black-crowned Night-Heron; White and White-faced Ibis; Roseate Spoonbill; Mottled Duck; Common Moorhen; American Coot; Killdeer; Black-necked Stilt; American Avocet; Willet; Laughing Gull; Gull-billed, Caspian, Royal, and Forster's Terns; Black Skimmer; Common Yellowthroat; and Red-winged Blackbird in the wetlands. Full-time terrestrial species include White-tailed Kite; **White-tailed Hawk;** Crested Caracara; Horned Lark; Northern Mockingbird; Loggerhead Shrike; Northern Cardinal; Seaside Sparrow; Eastern Meadowlark; Great-tailed, Boat-tailed, and Common Grackles; and Brown-headed Cowbird. Less obvious full-time residents include Black, Clapper, and King Rails.

In winter this area supports an assortment of water birds: Eared Grebe; thousands of waterfowl, especially Snow Geese; American White Pelican; Double-crested Cormorant; Yellow and Virginia Rails; Sora; Black-bellied and Semipalmated Plovers; Greater and Lesser Yellowlegs; Long-billed Curlew; Western and Least Sandpipers; Dunlin; Short-billed and Long-billed Dowitchers; Common Snipe; and Belted Kingfisher are most numerous. Also watch for Common Loon, Horned Grebe, Osprey, Bald Eagle, Northern Harrier, American Kestrel, Merlin, Sandhill Crane, Short-eared Owl, and Nelson's Sharp-tailed Sparrow.

The trees and shrubs along the auto tour harbor a variety of birds year-round, although spring migration is best, when neotropical migrants pass through. A few species nest here: Black Vulture, Yellow-billed Cuckoo, Great Horned and Barred Owls, Common Nighthawk, Eastern Kingbird, Scissor-tailed Flycatcher, Blue Jay, American Crow, Carolina Chickadee, Tufted Titmouse, Carolina Wren, Eastern Bluebird, Northern Mockingbird, Loggerhead Shrike, White-eyed Vireo, Painted Bunting, and Orchard Oriole.

The Bobcat Woods Trail (**B**) supports the same woodland birds, as well as neotropical migrants in April and early May. Only a few remain and nest here: Eastern Kingbird, Scissor-tailed Flycatcher, Red-eyed Vireo, Northern Parula, and Painted Bunting.

Bird the open fields and Cockleburr Slough (**C**) along the entrance road. Eastern Meadowlark is common year-round. In winter American and Sprague's Pipits and Vesper, Lark, and Savannah Sparrows can be found here. Search the weedy borders for Field, Grasshopper, LeConte's, Song, Lincoln's, Swamp, and White-throated Sparrows.

If time allows, bird along FM 2918 (**D**) southeast of CR 306 to the Gulf. This route passes through open prairie. The San Bernard River is visible to the east in a few places. Although the refuge offers more concentrated flocks and closer views, this area can help add to a day's bird list.

Directions: From Lake Jackson, take SH 332 west for 7 miles to its junction with SH 36. Take SH 36 south for 5 miles, then take FM 2611 south for 4 miles to FM 2918; follow FM 2918 left (south) for 1 mile to CR 306 on the right, and farther along CR 306, the gravel entrance road.

General information: The 24,455-acre national wildlife refuge contains a diversity of habitats that are especially important to wintering waterfowl; up to 100,000 Snow Geese can occur each year. More than 400 wildlife species have been recorded, including 250 bird species. Refuge waters also provide essential feeding and nursery areas for marine life. Water levels are manipulated through a series of dikes and water control structures at strategic marsh locations.

Access to the refuge is limited, although the auto tour is open daily from dawn to dusk, seven days a week. Other areas in the refuge are available only by prior arrangement.

ADDITIONAL HELP

Location: Texas Official Travel Map grid S x 21; Brazoria County
Nearest food, gas, and lodging: Food and gas are available in Churchill (3.5 miles). The nearest lodging is in Brazosport (15 miles) or Brazoria (20 miles).
Nearest camping: Brazoria (20 miles)
Contact: Manager, Brazoria National Wildlife Refuge Complex (see Appendix C)

92 Colorado River Delta

Habitats: River, pond, gulf, estuary, beach, dune, riparian, saltwater marsh, coastal prairie, coastal scrub, field, pasture, cropland
Key birds: Neotropic Cormorant, Reddish Egret, White and White-faced Ibis, Roseate Spoonbill, Mottled Duck, White-tailed Kite, **White-tailed Hawk,** Crested Caracara, Black Rail, and Seaside Sparrow are present year-round. Magnificent Frigatebird; Wood Stork; Fulvous and Black-bellied Whistling-Ducks; Wilson's Plover; Sandwich, Least, and Black Terns; Scissor-tailed Flycatcher; Painted Bunting; and Bronzed Cowbird occur in summer. Northern Gannet, Snow and Ross's Geese, Osprey, Merlin, Peregrine Falcon, Sandhill Crane, Short-eared Owl, **Buff-bellied Hummingbird,** American and Sprague's Pipits, Palm Warbler, and Nelson's Sharp-tailed Sparrow can usually be found in winter.
Best times to bird: April and May for spring migrants; November to March for winter birds

Birding strategies: East Gulf Road (**A**) follows the northern bank of the Intracoastal Waterway eastward from SH 60 for 4.5 miles to a gated oil field lease. This road offers a variety of habitats and can be extremely productive during migration. During migration, numbers of songbirds use the riparian and brushy habitats; American Golden-Plover and Upland and Buff-breasted Sandpipers frequent the pastures and wet croplands; water birds occur along the waterway and in the wetlands.

Several of the migrants remain and nest. These and the resident birds include Pied-billed Grebe; Neotropic Cormorant; all the waders, including Reddish Egret and Roseate Spoonbill; Fulvous and Black-bellied Whistling-Ducks; Mottled Duck;

92 Colorado River Delta

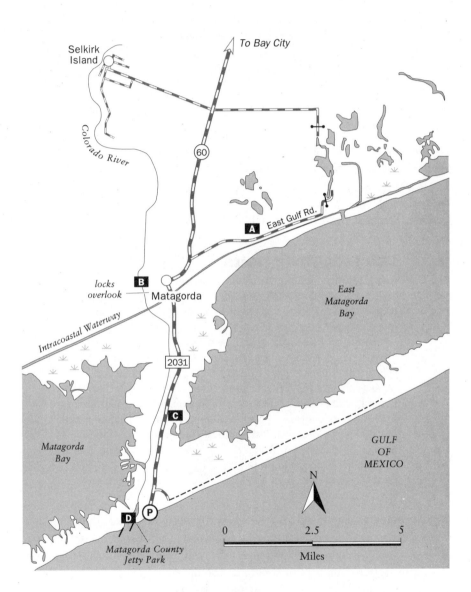

Black, Clapper, and King Rails; Common Moorhen; American Coot; Wilson's Plover; Killdeer; Willet; Laughing Gull; Gull-billed, Caspian, Royal, Sandwich, and Forster's Terns; Black Skimmer; Marsh Wren; Common Yellowthroat; Seaside Sparrow; Red-winged Blackbird; and Boat-tailed Grackle in the wetlands. Wood Storks are post-nesting visitors. Mourning Dove; Common Ground-Dove; Ladder-backed Woodpecker; Scissor-tailed Flycatcher; Horned Lark; American Crow; Carolina Chickadee; Tufted Titmouse; Carolina Wren; Eastern Bluebird; Northern Mockingbird; Loggerhead Shrike; White-eyed Vireo; Common Yellowthroat; Northern Cardinal; Painted Bunting; Dickcissel; Eastern Meadowlark; Great-tailed Grackle; and Brown-headed and Bronzed Cowbirds prefer the drier areas. Watch overhead for **White-tailed Hawk** and Red-tailed Hawk, Common Nighthawk at dawn and dusk, and Crested Caracara, Purple Martin, and Cliff and Barn Swallows.

In winter scan the wetlands for Double-crested Cormorant; Greater White-fronted, Snow, and Ross's Geese; numerous ducks, often numbering in the thousands; Osprey; Northern Harrier; Peregrine Falcon; Yellow and Virginia Rails; Sora; Sandhill Crane; Greater and Lesser Yellowlegs; Spotted, Western, and Least Sandpipers; Dunlin; Long-billed Dowitcher; Common Snipe; Bonaparte's Gull; Short-eared Owl; Belted Kingfisher; and, occasionally, Palm Warbler. The drier fields and edges support Eastern Phoebe; House and Sedge Wrens; Ruby-crowned Kinglet; Blue-gray Gnatcatcher; American Robin; Brown Thrasher; American and Sprague's Pipits; and Orange-crowned and Yellow-rumped Warblers. These woodland birds usually attract Sharp-shinned and Cooper's Hawks and American Kestrel. And weedy fields attract Vesper, Savannah, Lincoln's, Swamp, and White-throated Sparrows and American Goldfinch. Watch also for the less numerous birds such as American Bittern, Cinnamon Teal, Red-breasted Merganser, Yellow Rail, Merlin, Burrowing Owl, Winter Wren, vagrant warblers, Indigo and Painted Buntings, and Field, Lark, Grasshopper, LeConte's, Nelson's Sharp-tailed, Fox, White-crowned, and Harris's Sparrows.

In Matagorda (B) some homeowners maintain hummingbird feeders, where **Buff-bellied Hummingbird** and Ruby-throated and Rufous Hummingbirds can be found. Additional town birds include Inca Dove, Chimney Swift, Blue Jay, European Starling, and House Sparrow. The Colorado River Locks Overlook, at the end of Matagorda Street, offers river views of waders, gulls, and terns. During migration, especially during a spring fallout, the town's trees and shrubs can be swarming with neotropical migrants.

FM 2031 (C), beyond the Intracoastal Waterway, offers extensive coastal marshes to the east and Colorado River views to the west. Although birds along this 6.4-mile route are about the same as those listed above, the marsh habitat is one of the most extensive and least disturbed in the state. Scope the marsh and river from the numerous pullouts along the road. Herons, egrets, ibis, gulls, and terns can be expected year-round.

Matagorda County Jetty Park (**D**), at the end of FM 2031, offers three special habitats: the Colorado River mouth, with its sandbars and mixing of fresh with salt waters; the beach; and the jetty views into the Gulf of Mexico. The extensive sandbar almost always contains significant populations of pelicans, cormorants, shorebirds, gulls, Black Skimmer, and terns. This site is especially good in the late afternoon and evening. Look for Snowy and Piping Plovers and Red Knot during migration. The jetty offers access to the Gulf where passing birds can be seen year-round. Northern Gannet, scoters, and jaegers can be expected in winter, and Magnificent Frigatebird in summer.

In spring and fall, also visit the turf farms along SH 60, just south of Wadsworth. American Golden-Plover, Mountain Plover, Upland and Buff-breasted Sandpipers, and various other shorebirds feed in the short grass during migration.

Records of Review Species: Western Grebe, Dec 1994. Masked Booby, Dec 1995. Brown Booby, March 1989. Oldsquaw, Dec 1996. Glaucous Gull, April 1993. Shiny Cowbird, April 1995.

Directions: From Bay City, take SH 60 south for 28 miles to Matagorda. FM 2031 extends for another 8 miles to the mouth of the Colorado River and Jetty Park.

General information: This entire area is within the 15-mile-diameter circle of the Mad Island Marsh Christmas Bird Count, which since its inception has netted annual totals in excess of 200 species. Matagorda County Jetty Park is included in the Great Texas Coastal Birding Trail. The massive 0.4-mile-long jetty is a popular fishing site, especially on weekends.

ADDITIONAL HELP

Location: Texas Official Travel Map grid S/T x 20; Matagorda County
Nearest food, gas, and lodging: Matagorda has all three.
Nearest camping: Matagorda; primitive camping is allowed on the beach at Matagorda County Jetty Park.
Contact: Bay City Chamber of Commerce. Aside from the county park, most of this area is private (see Appendix C).

93   Palacios

Habitats: Bay, estuary, pond, saltwater marsh, oak motte, mesquite grassland, coastal scrub, coastal prairie

Key birds: Brown Pelican, Neotropic Cormorant, White and White-faced Ibis, Reddish Egret, Roseate Spoonbill, Black-bellied Whistling-Duck, Mottled Duck, **White-tailed Hawk,** Crested Caracara, Black Rail, and Seaside Sparrow are present year-round. Anhinga, Least Bittern, Magnificent Frigatebird, Wood Stork, Fulvous Whistling-Duck, Least and Black Terns, **Buff-bellied Hummingbird, Couch's Kingbird,** Scissor-tailed Flycatcher, Painted Bunting, and Dickcissel occur in summer. American White Pelican, Osprey, Peregrine Falcon, Yellow Rail, Short-eared Owl, and Nelson's Sharp-tailed Sparrow can usually be found in winter.

Best times to bird: April and May for spring migrants and nesting activities; November to March for winter birds

Birding strategies: Tres Palacios Bay (A) is readily accessible along South Bay Boulevard. Although this area offers an array of water birds year-round, winter birding is best. Expect Common Loon; Eared Grebe; Brown Pelican; Double-crested Cormorant; a variety of waterfowl; Osprey; Laughing, Bonaparte's, Ring-billed, and Herring Gulls; and Caspian, Royal, and Forster's Terns. Less common winter birds include Horned Grebe; Greater Scaup; Common Goldeneye; Franklin's Gull; and Sandwich Tern. Add Magnificent Frigatebird and Least and Black Terns in summer.

East Bayshore Drive (B) extends 3 miles to the northeast, passing through the Texas Baptist Encampment and going on to Trull Marsh. Habitats here include open bay with private docks, grassy yards and banks, fresh- and saltwater wetlands, and brush. Although most of the same ducks mentioned above can be expected here in winter, waders, shorebirds, and prairie species can also be found. Year-round, look for Pied-billed Grebe; Neotropic Cormorant; Great Blue, Little Blue, and Tricolored Herons; Great and Snowy Egrets; Black-crowned Night-Heron; White and White-faced Ibis; Roseate Spoonbill; Black-bellied Whistling-Duck; Mottled Duck; Clapper Rail; Common Moorhen; American Coot; Greater Yellowlegs; Willet; Gull-billed Tern; Black Skimmer; Carolina and Marsh Wrens; Common Yellowthroat; Northern Cardinal; Red-winged Blackbird; Eastern Meadowlark; and Great-tailed Grackle.

In summer Fulvous Whistling-Duck, Black-necked Stilt, Common Nighthawk, Scissor-tailed Flycatcher, Purple Martin, Barn Swallow, and Painted Bunting can be expected. Check the wires for the occasional **Couch's Kingbird,** and watch for **Buff-bellied Hummingbird** at feeders and flowering plants. In winter Belted Kingfisher; Sedge Wren; American Pipit; Orange-crowned and Palm Warblers; and Savannah, Nelson's Sharp-tailed, Song, Lincoln's, and Swamp Sparrows can be expected.

The croplands and pastures in the Cash's Creek area (C), along FM 2853 and beyond, offer fields that can be spectacular in winter when thousands of geese,

 **Palacios**

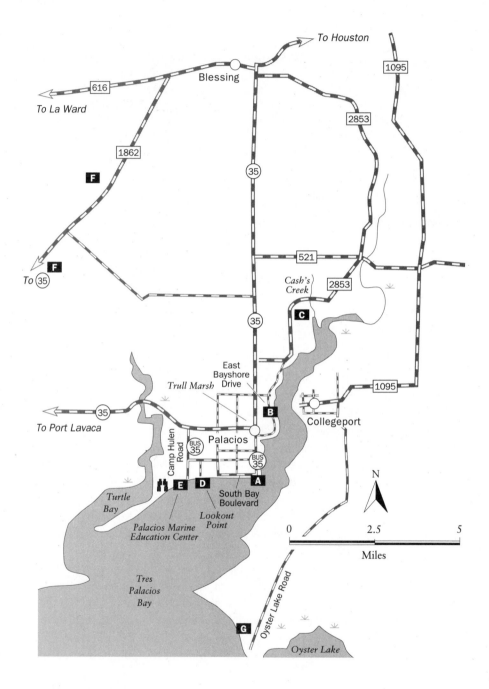

especially Snow Geese, and fewer numbers of Greater White-fronted, Canada, and Ross's, are present. During spring migration these fields can be filled with waterfowl and shorebirds, including American Golden-Plover and Upland and Buff-breasted Sandpipers. In winter the area also supports a good raptor population, including White-tailed Kite, Northern Harrier, **White-tailed Hawk** (year-round), Red-tailed Hawk, Crested Caracara, and American Kestrel. Watch also for Ferruginous Hawk, Merlin, and Peregrine Falcon.

Lookout Point (**D**), at the end of Margerum Boulevard (0.5 mile long), located at the west end of town and accessible via Business SH 35, overlooks the bay and a saltwater marsh to the south. Birds are about the same as those that can be seen along East Bayshore Drive. The Palacios Marine Education Center (**E**), on Camp Hulen Road, west of Margerum Boulevard, includes a short nature trail through brushy vegetation to the bay, and an observation deck. This area can be busy with migrants in spring, especially during a fallout. In winter both Seaside and Nelson's Sharp-tailed Sparrows can be seen near the observation deck.

If time allows, bird the turf farms (**F**) along FM 1862 for shorebirds during spring migration. Oyster Lake Road (**G**), on the east side of Tres Palacios Bay, is good for southbound migrants, geese, shorebirds, and rails, and offers a possible trap for southbound raptors.

Directions: Palacios is situated along SH 35 on Tres Palacios Bay, a finger of Matagorda Bay. East Bayshore Drive runs from FM 2853 to Business SH 35. Margerum Boulevard and Camp Hulen Road are on the west side of town.

General information: Palacios, founded in 1903, maintains an attractive waterfront with picnic tables, lighted fishing piers, public boat ramps, and a 1.5-mile railed walkway that offers good birding. This site is included as six separate sites on the Great Texas Coastal Birding Trail.

ADDITIONAL HELP

Location: Texas Official Travel Map grid S/T x 19/20; Matagorda County
Nearest food, gas, and lodging: All can be found on-site, including accommodations in the historic Luther Hotel.
Nearest camping: On-site along East Bayshore Drive
Contact: Palacios Chamber of Commerce (see Appendix C)

94 Port Lavaca and Indianola

Habitats: Bay, mud flat, brackish marsh, pond, coastal prairie, coastal scrub, pasture, cropland, rice field

Key birds: Brown Pelican, Neotropic Cormorant, Reddish Egret, White and White-faced Ibis, Roseate Spoonbill, Mottled Duck, **White-tailed Hawk,** Crested Caracara, Black and Clapper Rails, American Oystercatcher, Black Skimmer, Curve-billed Thrasher, and Seaside Sparrow are present year-round. Magnificent Frigatebird; Least Bittern; Wood Stork; Fulvous and Black-bellied Whistling-Ducks; Purple Gallinule; Wilson's Plover; Sandwich, Least, and Black Terns; Brown-crested and Scissor-tailed Flycatchers; Painted Bunting; and Dickcissel occur in summer. Ross's Goose, Peregrine Falcon, Yellow Rail, Piping Plover, Sandhill Crane, Short-eared Owl, Sprague's Pipit, and Nelson's Sharp-tailed Sparrow can usually be found in winter.

Best times to bird: April and May for spring migrants and nesting activities; November through March for winter birds

Birding strategies: Begin along Zimmerman Road (**A**), near the eastern end of SH 316, to the left just past the historical marker but before the bridge. You can drive this road, but it is best to walk. Although the brushy roadsides offer good birding year-round, this area can be exceptional in spring, when northbound migrants are funneled between the ridge and the bay. Watch for Brown-crested and Scissor-tailed Flycatchers, Bewick's Wren, Curve-billed Thrasher, and Painted Bunting along the ridge and cemetery; and listen for Black Rail in the adjacent wetland and Cassin's Sparrow in the drier fields.

Continue to the fishing community of Indianola (**B**) by traveling down the bayshore or along the county road. The marsh and ponds along the way are likely to harbor waders, gulls, and terns. Neotropic Cormorant and White and White-faced Ibis can be expected. Least Bittern is less reliable. Watch for Magnificent Frigatebird and Sandwich, Least, and Black Terns over the bay. In winter look for Piping and Snowy Plovers along the beach, scoters on the bay, and Short-eared Owl over the marshes at dusk and dawn. At the end of the road, scope southeast across the mouth of Powderhorn Lake for Brown Pelican; all the waders, including Reddish Egret and Roseate Spoonbill; a variety of shorebirds, including American Oystercatcher; and Black Skimmer.

The croplands along SH 316 (**C**), especially the rice fields, which are often flooded in spring and summer, attract numerous migrating shorebirds; 19 sandpiper species are possible at different times of year. Glossy Ibis is also seen occasionally. Watch for Fulvous and Black-bellied Whistling-Ducks and Mottled Duck. **White-tailed Hawk** and Crested Caracara occur here as well. Dickcissel nests in the sorghum and weedy fields. In winter Greater White-fronted, Snow, and Ross's Geese and Sandhill Crane are usually present. Check stubble fields for Sprague's Pipit, Merlin, and Peregrine Falcon.

At Port Lavaca, the boardwalk at Lighthouse Beach Park (west end of the SH 35 causeway) (**D**) can be good for shorebirds, waders, and Clapper Rail. Scope the

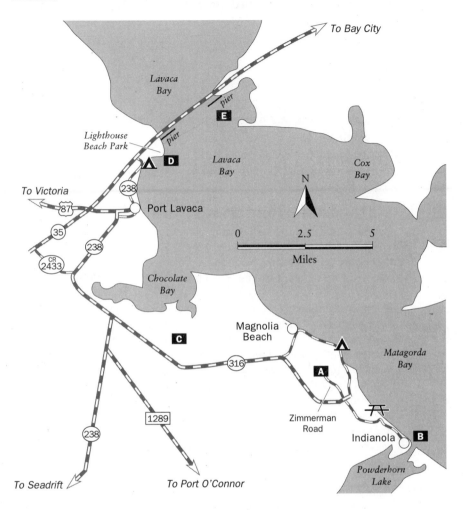

adjacent bay for waterfowl in winter. Also check the pier (**E**) at the east end of the causeway for waterfowl (especially goldeneyes in winter) and shorebirds.

Directions: Port Lavaca is located on the west side of the SH 35 causeway across Lavaca Bay. To reach Zimmerman Road and Indianola, turn south off SH 35 onto SH 238 (north of Port Lavaca) or onto CR 2433 (2 miles west of Port Lavaca), then head south on SH 316 and continue to the end of the road.

General information: This area is the heart of Calhoun County, which has led the nation for the highest number of bird species found on the Annual North American (spring) Migration Counts from 1992 to 1996. The area has a rich assemblage of habitats accessible along the route—enough habitats, in fact, to establish several "ABA Monthly Big Day" records for the state and the nation.

Indianola was once the largest seaport in Texas, but was twice wiped out by major hurricanes in the late nineteenth century. A large granite block on the beach southeast of the LaSalle Monument marks the town's original location, which now lies under Matagorda Bay.

ADDITIONAL HELP

Location: Texas Official Travel Map grid T x 19; Calhoun County

Nearest food, gas, and lodging: All three are available in Port Lavaca; food is also available at Indianola.

Nearest camping: Magnolia Beach County Park (free, no hookups) and Port Lavaca

Contact: Port Lavaca/Calhoun County Chamber of Commerce (see Appendix C)

95 Matagorda Island State Park

Habitats: Gulf, bay, estuary, beach, dune, pond, salt marsh, mud flat, salt cedar thicket, coastal prairie

Key birds: Brown Pelican, Neotropic Cormorant, Reddish Egret, White and White-faced Ibis, Roseate Spoonbill, Mottled Duck, **White-tailed Hawk,** Crested Caracara, Aplomado Falcon, Black Rail, Black Skimmer, and Seaside Sparrow are present year-round. Magnificent Frigatebird; Least Bittern; Wood Stork; Purple Gallinule; Wilson's Plover; Gull-billed, Least, and Black Terns; Scissor-tailed Flycatcher; Painted Bunting; Dickcissel; and Boat-tailed Grackle occur in summer. Northern Gannet; Surf Scoter; Merlin; Peregrine Falcon; Sandhill Crane; Snowy and Piping Plovers; Short-eared Owl; and Grasshopper, LeConte's, and Nelson's Sharp-tailed Sparrows can usually be found in winter.

Best times to bird: April and May for spring migrants and nesting activities; August and September for southbound migrants; November to March for winter birds

Birding strategies: The ferry ride to Matagorda Island offers an array of gulls, terns, waders, and shorebirds. Check the flats around the Army Cut (**A**) for Roseate Spoonbill, Wood Stork (in midsummer), and rafts of Northern Pintail and American Wigeon in winter. The channel markers (**B**) near Matagorda Island often contain perching Peregrine Falcon in winter and Magnificent Frigatebird in summer.

Unless you take a special tour with the Texas Parks and Wildlife Department (TPWD), you must hike or bike on the island. To get the most out of your visit, bird the bayshore, Army Hole Campground on the bay, and the old air base (**C**), all located just beyond the docks. This area should produce all the waders, gulls, and terns, as well as most of the shorebirds present; 37 shorebird species are included on the park checklist. Reddish Egret, White and White-faced Ibis, Gull-billed Tern, and Black Skimmer can be found here as well. Areas on the old runway may be closed due to nesting Least Tern; Wilson's Plover, Common Nighthawk, and Horned Lark nest there as well. In spring the shrubbery around the old buildings can be

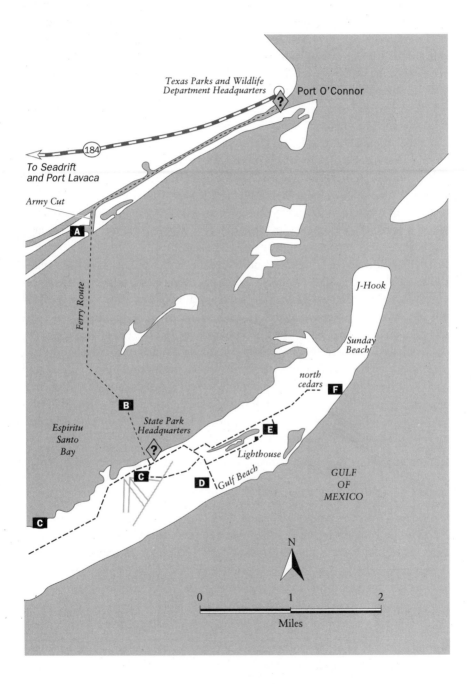

alive with neotropical migrants. The salt marsh along the bay supports Seaside and Nelson's Sharp-tailed Sparrows in winter. Wilson's Plover and Seaside Sparrow nest in May and June. Check the bay markers and pilings in Espiritu Santo Bay for perched Magnificent Frigatebird and heron nests in summer and Brown Pelican and Peregrine Falcon in winter. Also in winter, the grassy edges along the runway offer habitat for seedeaters, including Vesper, Savannah, Grasshopper, LeConte's, Fox, Song, Lincoln's, Swamp, White-throated, and White-crowned Sparrows.

Follow the old road (**D**) south across the island to the Gulf beach, watching for American and Least Bitterns, White-tailed Kite, **White-tailed Hawk,** Crested Caracara, and Aplomado Falcon (six introduced in 1996). Other common birds in summer include Scissor-tailed Flycatcher, Cliff and Barn Swallows, Painted Bunting, Dickcissel, and Boat-tailed Grackle. This is a good area for Merlin, Sandhill Crane, and Short-eared Owl in winter. On the outer beach, winter birds can include Peregrine Falcon, Snowy and Piping Plovers, Ruddy Turnstone, Sanderling, and Royal Tern. Offshore look for Northern Gannet, Surf Scoter, and a variety of pelagic species. Magnificent Frigatebird often can be found here from May through October.

The lighthouse area (**E**) and the north cedars (**F**) beyond are best in spring—fallouts can be spectacular. The north cedars (thickets of salt cedar) serve as traps, providing feeding and resting sites for neotropical migrants after they've crossed the Gulf. Flycatchers, vireos, warblers, tanagers, grosbeaks, buntings, and sparrows can be abundant. Watch for Bobolink in May.

Depressions along the old road, between the road junction and the lighthouse, sometimes hold enough water to attract Neotropic Cormorant, night-herons, and Black Rail. The perfect Black Rail habitat is when bulrushes provide a dense mat of vegetation over just an inch or so of water. Don't be fooled by Northern Mockingbird imitating their *"KEE-KEE-doo"* calls, or Forster's Terns making a *"kgrrr"* call similar to a Black Rail's growl.

Records of Review Species: Oldsquaw, March 1995. Ruff, April 1993. Glaucous Gull, April 1993. Burrowing Owl, Nov 1994. Green Kingfisher, Aug 1992. Red-headed Woodpecker, Oct 1993. Say's Phoebe, March 1991. Hepatic Tanager, Sept 1996.

Directions: TPWD operates a passenger ferry that provides service between Port O'Connor (dock and parking at TPWD headquarters) and Matagorda Island from Thursday to Sunday and holidays (call 512-983-2215 for current schedule, fee, and space availability). On the island, a shuttle vehicle makes round-trips from the ferry dock to the Gulf beach.

General information: This 56,668-acre undeveloped barrier island is 38 miles long and 0.75 to 4.5 miles wide. The entire island is public property: the northern two-thirds is managed as a state park and wildlife management area, while the southern third is part of Aransas National Wildlife Refuge.

Public access is generally limited to ferry passengers and private boats with permission to dock at the ferry. Ferry passengers arrive too late in the day for serious birding, so an overnight stay is recommended. Primitive camping or utilizing the TPWD bunkhouse (reservation required) is possible. Insect repellent is advised year-round; mosquitoes can be horrible! And it is essential that you carry plenty of drinking water.

Matagorda Island has an extensive and fascinating history that includes prehistoric and Karankawa Indians, and visits from Cabeza de Vaca, Rene Robert Sieur de La Salle, and Jean Lafitte. A cast-iron lighthouse was established in 1852 (but moved 2 miles inland in 1872) to help guide ships through Paso Cavallo to the port of Indianola. The island also features Civil War trenches and Fort Esperanza (now submerged); cattle ranching; a World War II air base for training bomber pilots; and a wildlife refuge.

ADDITIONAL HELP

Location: Texas Official Travel Map grid T x 19; Calhoun County
Nearest food, gas, and lodging: Port O'Connor has all three.
Nearest camping: Port O'Connor; on-site camping at Army Hole Campground, located a few yards from the ferry dock, is primitive and best in winter, when cool northers keep the mosquitoes down; beach camping (2.5 miles from the ferry dock and served by island shuttle) is best in summer, due to the fairly constant Gulf breeze
Contact: Superintendent, Matagorda Island State Park (see Appendix C)

96 Port O'Connor and Seadrift

Habitats: Bay, estuary, coastal prairie, coastal scrub, canal, riparian, oak motte, pasture, cropland, rice field
Key birds: Brown Pelican; Neotropic Cormorant; Reddish Egret; Roseate Spoonbill; White and White-faced Ibis; Black-bellied Whistling-Duck; Mottled Duck; **White-tailed Hawk;** Crested Caracara; Black, Clapper, and King Rails; and Seaside Sparrow are present year-round. Magnificent Frigatebird; Wood Stork; Fulvous Whistling-Duck; Purple Gallinule; Sandwich, Least, and Black Terns; Scissor-tailed Flycatcher; Painted Bunting; Dickcissel; and Boat-tailed Grackle occur in summer. American White Pelican, American Bittern, Snow and Ross's Geese, Osprey, Yellow Rail, Sandhill Crane, Short-eared Owl, and Nelson's Sharp-tailed Sparrow can usually be found in winter.
Best times to bird: April and May for spring migrants; May, June, and October for rice field birding; November to March for geese and Sandhill Crane

Birding strategies: Port O'Connor, at the east end of SH 185, and the adjacent bay and estuary contain habitats for all the water birds in season. The Port O'Connor jetty and Intracoastal Waterway area (**A**) is a good place to start. Brown Pelican; waders, including Reddish Egret; shorebirds, including American Oystercatcher; gulls; Black Skimmer; and terns, including Least, usually are present in summer. Magnificent Frigatebirds sometimes soar overhead in late summer and fall. Osprey can be common in winter.

96 Port O'Connor and Seadrift

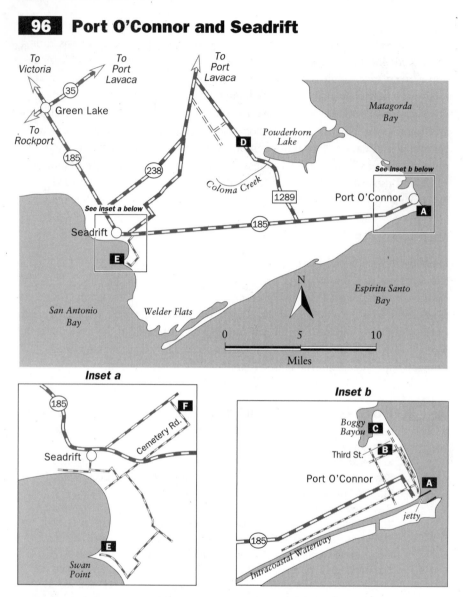

In spring drive along the northern edge of town (**B**); migrants are sometimes among the thickets and vacant lots along Boggy Bayou and at mulberry trees in town. In winter Redheads and other waterfowl, as well as numerous shorebirds, are usually present. In Boggy Bayou (**C**), accessed from the north end of Third Street, White and White-faced Ibis, Roseate Spoonbill, and all the herons and egrets can be found here year-round.

FM 1289 (**D**), the highway between SH 185 and SH 238, is especially productive in late spring, when the rice fields are flooded. Thousands of shorebirds (30 species), all the waders (even Glossy Ibis), and numerous waterfowl are possible then. The flooded fields and canals can be equally busy with Fulvous and Black-bellied Whistling-Ducks,

Mottled Duck, King Rail, Black-necked Stilt, Willet, and gulls and terns, including Gull-billed, all summer. Where rice is being harvested (especially the second crop, in October), watch for Sora, Black, and Yellow Rails flushed by the combines.

Stop at the bridge over Coloma Creek, an excellent place to find Neotropic Cormorant; all the waders, including Roseate Spoonbill year-round; Wood Stork, Clapper Rail, and Seaside Sparrow in summer; and Nelson's Sharp-tailed Sparrow in winter and spring. Also in winter, American White Pelican can be numerous. Watch for Short-eared Owl at dusk and dawn.

White-tailed Hawk perches on the utility poles along FM 1289, as well as along SH 185, year-round. In winter the fields are host to thousands of geese and Sandhill Crane. Scope the flocks of Snow Geese for the smaller and stubby-billed Ross's Goose. In summer Eastern Kingbird, Scissor-tailed Flycatcher, White-eyed Vireo, Painted Bunting, Dickcissel, and Great-tailed and Boat-tailed Grackles can be found.

Seadrift lies at the southwestern corner of the peninsula, facing San Antonio Bay. Bird the bay front and adjacent Swan Point (**E**) in winter and early spring, when waterfowl feed in nearby protected areas. Watch for the occasional scoter. Cemetery Road (**F**), which in 2 miles turns into Old Seadrift Road, can be super in spring and summer. Numerous pastures and fields, some planted in rice, lie along Old Seadrift Road, where all the same birds that occur along FR 1289 can be found. However, this area also is good for Crested Caracara year-round. In early spring, this route is excellent for American Golden-Plover and Upland Sandpiper.

Records of Review Species: *Off Swan Point*—Oldsquaw and Lesser Black-backed Gull, late winter 1995. *At nearby Union Carbide Seadrift Plant*—Masked Duck and Northern Jacana, winter 1992/93. *Port O'Connor*—Great Kiskadee, May 1996.

Directions: Turn off SH 35, either onto SH 316, SH 238, or FM 1289, just south of Port Lavaca, or take SH 185 at Green Lake, south to Seadrift.

General information: Calhoun County consistently leads the nation in the number of birds recorded on the Annual North American (spring) Migration Counts. Port O'Connor also is the gateway to Matagorda Island (see site 95), and a port for pelagic trips (see Appendix A).

Both Port O'Connor and Seadrift are ports for commercial fishing and shrimp boats; Seadrift holds an annual Shrimp Festival each July. Port O'Connor boasts two fishing piers, a long rock jetty, and a lighted pier at the grassy Pier Park. Bay and offshore fishing are excellent. The town annually hosts a number of fishing tournaments between Memorial Day and Labor Day.

ADDITIONAL HELP

Location: Texas Official Travel Map grid T x 19; Calhoun County
Nearest food, gas, and lodging: All of these are available in Port O'Connor and Seadrift.
Nearest camping: Port O'Connor
Contact: Port Lavaca/Calhoun County Chamber of Commerce (see Appendix C)

Coastal Bend Region

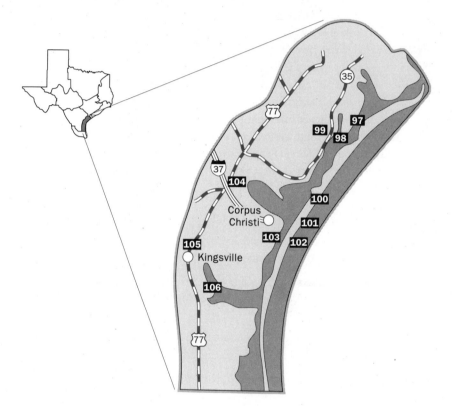

97 Aransas National Wildlife Refuge	**102** Padre Island National Seashore
98 Goose Island State Park	**103** Corpus Christi
99 Rockport and Fulton	**104** West Corpus Christi and Hazel Bazemore County Park
100 Port Aransas	
	105 Kingsville
101 Mustang Island State Park and Packery Channel County Park	**106** Cayo del Grullo

Habitats: Bay, mud flat, pond, freshwater and saltwater marsh, coastal prairie, oak motte, oak savannah, field

Key birds: Least Grebe, Brown Pelican, Reddish Egret, White and White-faced Ibis, Roseate Spoonbill, Mottled Duck, **White-tailed Hawk,** Crested Caracara, Black and Clapper Rails, Black Skimmer, **Pauraque, Golden-fronted Woodpecker,** and Seaside Sparrow are present year-round. Neotropic Cormorant; Magnificent Frigatebird; Least Bittern; Wood Stork; Fulvous and Black-bellied Whistling-Ducks; Wilson's Plover; Gull-billed, Sandwich, and Least Terns; Groove-billed Ani; **Buff-bellied Hummingbird;** Brown-crested and Scissor-tailed Flycatchers; Swainson's Warbler; Painted Bunting; Dickcissel; and Bronzed Cowbird occur in summer. American White Pelican, Ross's Goose, Osprey, Ferruginous and Rough-legged (irregular) Hawks, Peregrine Falcon, Yellow Rail, **Whooping Crane,** Sandhill Crane, Vermilion Flycatcher, **Couch's Kingbird,** and Green-tailed and Eastern Towhees can usually be found in winter.

Best times to bird: November to April for Whooping Crane and wintering water birds; April and early May for spring migrants and nesting activities; August to October for shorebirds

Birding strategies: The Heron Flats Trail (**A**) provides a broad overview of the wetlands and bay. Wading birds, including Roseate Spoonbill in spring and summer, and **Whooping Crane** from mid-November to mid-March, can be expected. Also in winter, watch for the occasional Vermilion Flycatcher. Migrating and wintering shorebirds and waterfowl utilize the shallow ponds and open bay. In summer watch for Groove-billed Ani along the brushy middle ridge, **Buff-bellied Hummingbird** feeding on Turk's-cap and coral bean flowers, and Painted Bunting in semi-open areas.

The Rail Trail (**B**) is especially good during spring migration, when northbound birds are following the north-south line of vegetation. More than 40 species of warblers, 7 vireos, 6 thrushes, and numerous other neotropical migrants have been recorded here. The ponds along this trail and the alligator pond, directly across from the visitor center, occasionally contain interesting birds, including **Least Grebe,** Neotropic Cormorant, and Anhinga. Watch along the trail for **Couch's Kingbird** in fall and winter.

The Picnic Area (**C**), just south of the Heron Flats parking area, is a good place for spring warblers and other migrants. Swainson's Warbler nests behind the picnic area, as well as at four to five other sites in the refuge; these birds sing throughout the summer. **Pauraque** frequent this and other wooded areas, but usually are detected only after dark by their distinct songs. Watch also for **Golden-fronted Woodpecker.** In winter this area often harbors a variety of warblers, vireos, and other songbirds.

Check Jones Lake (**D**) any time of year. This freshwater lake, with its cattail marsh, is good for water birds. Unless the lake is dry, as it is during drought years,

97 Aransas National Wildlife Refuge

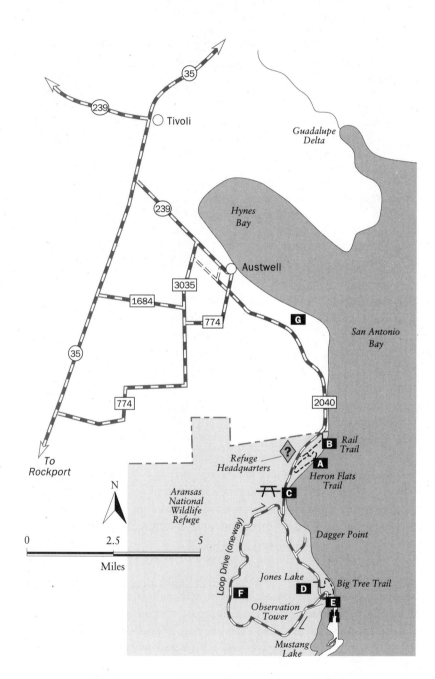

American Bittern, King Rail, Sora, Common Moorhen, American Coot, and Marsh Wren can be expected in winter, and Anhinga, Least Bittern, Black-crowned Night-Heron, Fulvous and Black-bellied Whistling-Ducks, Purple Gallinule, and Common Yellowthroat in summer.

The observation tower (**E**) provides a wonderful view of the entire region, including the open bay, saltwater marsh, mud flats, and oak woodlands. In winter **Whooping Crane** can usually be seen feeding in the saltwater marsh to the south; don't confuse them with the common Great Egret. The mud flats may be filled with dozens of waders and up to 20 species of shorebirds. The oak mottes surrounding the tower can contain a variety of songbirds in winter and summer. Watch also for soaring raptors, especially in spring and fall.

The boardwalk, starting at the base of the tower and running over the salt marsh to the bay, offers closer views of waders and bay birds. Reddish Egrets feed nearby; Brown Pelicans are slightly farther out. An occasional Magnificent Frigatebird and a vast array of gulls and terns, including Laughing Gull and Caspian, Royal, Sandwich, Least, and Black Terns, can be expected in summer. Waterfowl, especially large numbers of Redheads, are numerous in winter. Scope the bay for vagrants.

Take the 16-mile Loop Drive (**F**), stopping at various pullouts to check the ponds, oaks, and prairie for whatever birds might be present. Watch for **White-tailed Hawk** and Crested Caracara year-round, Wood Stork in summer, and both **Whooping Crane** and Sandhill Crane in winter. In spring the fields outside the refuge around Austwell (**G**) often support migrating shorebirds. Watch for American Golden-Plover and Upland and Buff-breasted Sandpipers in April; Brown-crested and Scissor-tailed Flycatchers, Painted Bunting, and Dickcissel in summer; and raptors in winter.

Records of Review Species: Red-throated Loon, April 1976. Red-necked Grebe, Dec 1944. Sooty Shearwater, May 1995. White-tailed Tropicbird, 1937, 1945. Brown Booby, June 1948. Harlequin Duck, Jan 1945. Zone-tailed Hawk, Nov 1992. Red-necked Phalarope, Dec 1965. Pomarine Jaeger, June 1937. Little Gull, March 1988. Band-tailed Pigeon, Dec 1971. White-throated Swift, April 1972. Acorn Woodpecker, Dec 1994. Dusky-capped Flycatcher, June 1972. Fork-tailed Flycatcher, Oct 1958, Dec 1989. Clay-colored Robin, Feb–Nov 1988. Phainopepla, Jan 1973. Crimson-collared Grosbeak, Feb 1988.

Directions: From Rockport, drive north on SH 35 to FM 774. Take FM 774 to Austwell (9 miles), then take FM 774 to FM 2040 and FM 2040 to the refuge headquarters (7 miles). From Tivoli, drive south on SH 35 for 1 mile to SH 239 to Austwell, then follow FM 774 and FM 2040 to the headquarters.

General information: Most of the 115,000-acre refuge is situated on the Blackjack Peninsula, between San Antonio and Mesquite bays on the east and St. Charles Bay on the west; a portion of the refuge is located on nearby Matagorda Island. The refuge is the principal wintering ground for the endangered **Whooping Crane**

Dominic Delaca looking for Whooping Cranes from the observation tower at Aransas National Wildlife Refuge.

(properly pronounced "hooping"), which arrives in mid-October, after a 2,500-mile flight from its northern nesting grounds in Canada's Wood Buffalo National Park. Winter flocks currently number about 150 birds.

Although Whoopers usually can be seen reasonably well from the Heron Flats Trail or the observation tower, closer views can be obtained by tour boats that operate out of Rockport: Captain Ted's Whooping Crane Tours, Star Route 1, Box 2251, Rockport, TX 78382; 512-729-9589 or 800-338-4551; Captain John Howell's Pisces, 1019 North Allen, Rockport, TX 78382; 512-729-7525; New Pelican, 34 Turning Basin, Rockport, TX 78382; 512-729-8448.

Check the wildlife log at the refuge visitor center when arriving to learn if any unexpected birds have been reported. Refuge volunteers maintain a bird checklist year-round that is updated weekly.

The refuge also is one of the easiest places anywhere to see alligators. One of these huge reptiles is almost always present in a little pond directly across the road from the visitor center. The paved Tour Loop Drive usually provides good views of white-tailed deer, javelinas, armadillos, and feral hogs.

ADDITIONAL HELP

Location: Texas Official Travel Map grid U x 18; Aransas County
Nearest food, gas, and lodging: Food and gas are available at Tivoli (15 miles); lodging can be found at Rockport (36 miles) and Port Lavaca (35 miles).
Nearest camping: Austwell RV Park (7 miles); Goose Island State Park (33 miles)
Contact: Manager, Aransas National Wildlife Refuge (see Appendix C)

98 Goose Island State Park

Habitats: Bay, estuary, mud flat, saltwater marsh, pond, oak motte, coastal scrub, cropland
Key birds: Least Grebe, Brown Pelican, Reddish Egret, White Ibis, Black-bellied Whistling-Duck, Mottled Duck, **White-tailed Hawk,** Crested Caracara, Black Skimmer, **Pauraque,** Greater Roadrunner, **Buff-bellied Hummingbird, Golden-fronted Woodpecker, Long-billed Thrasher,** Curve-billed Thrasher, and Seaside Sparrow are present year-round. Magnificent Frigatebird, Roseate Spoonbill, Wood Stork, Fulvous Whistling-Duck, Purple Gallinule, Wilson's Plover, Sandwich and Least Terns, Lesser and Common Nighthawks, Scissor-tailed Flycatcher, Painted Bunting, and Bronzed Cowbird occur in summer. American Bittern, Merlin, Sandhill Crane, **Whooping Crane** (distant), Piping Plover, Short-eared Owl, Pyrrhuloxia, and LeConte's and Nelson's Sharp-tailed Sparrows can usually be found in winter.
Best times to bird: April and May for spring migrants and breeding activities; November to March for winter birds

Birding strategies: The majority of the Texas specialty birds—Pauraque, Buff-bellied Hummingbird, Golden-fronted Woodpecker, and Long-billed Thrasher (more numerous on nearby Newcomb Point; see map)—can be found within or adjacent to the park campground (**A**). This area also supports Red-shouldered Hawk, Yellow-billed Cuckoo, Eastern Screech-Owl, Great Horned and Barred Owls, Ladder-backed Woodpecker, Carolina and Bewick's Wrens, Curve-billed Thrasher, White-eyed Vireo, Northern Cardinal, Painted Bunting, and Bronzed and Brown-headed Cowbirds in summer. In winter Sharp-shinned and Cooper's Hawks, Yellow-bellied Sapsucker, House Wren, Blue-gray Gnatcatcher, Hermit Thrush, Brown Thrasher, Plumbeous (Solitary) Vireo, various warblers (usually Orange-crowned, Yellow-rumped, Pine, and Black-and-white), and numerous sparrows can be found here.

   This same area can be alive with neotropical migrants, especially flycatchers, thrushes, vireos, warblers (36 species), tanagers, and sparrows, during a spring fallout. Irregular migrants include Willow and Ash-throated Flycatchers; Gray-cheeked Thrush; Bell's Vireo; Cape May, Black-throated Blue, Black-throated Gray, Townsend's, Hermit, Palm, Blackpoll, and Mourning Warblers; Western Tanager; and Bobolink.

98 Goose Island State Park

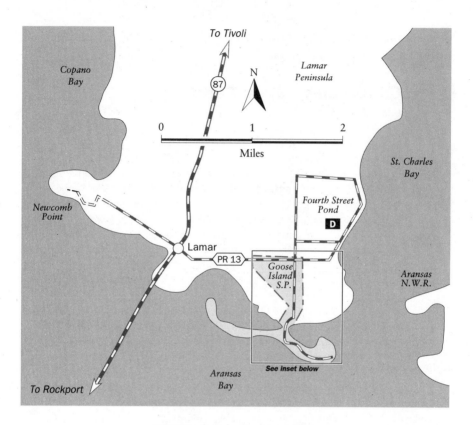

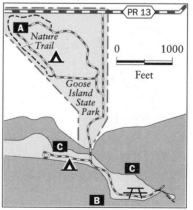

In the fields within and adjacent to the state park, year-round residents include Cattle Egret, White and White-faced Ibis, **White-tailed Hawk,** Crested Caracara, Northern Bobwhite, and Eastern Meadowlark. Both Lesser and Common Night-hawks can be seen at dawn and dusk. Expect Scissor-tailed Flycatcher and Painted Bunting in summer. And in winter, watch for Greater White-fronted, Snow, and Canada Geese; White-tailed Kite; Northern Harrier; Ferruginous Hawk; American Kestrel; Sandhill Crane; House and Sedge Wrens; Loggerhead Shrike; Chipping, Clay-colored, Field, Vesper, Lark, Savannah, Grasshopper, LeConte's, Fox, Song, Lincoln's, Swamp, White-throated, White-crowned, and Harris's Sparrows; Western Meadowlark; and Brewer's Blackbird.

The bay waters and shoreline (**B**) harbor a variety of birds year-round. In winter the most common are Green-winged and Blue-winged Teal, Mottled Duck, Northern Pintail, Northern Shoveler, Gadwall, American Wigeon, Redhead, Lesser Scaup, Common Goldeneye, Bufflehead, and Red-breasted Merganser. Less numerous are Wood Duck, Mallard, Cinnamon Teal, Ring-necked Duck, Greater Scaup, Oldsquaw, Canvasback, Hooded Merganser, and Ruddy Duck.

On the open and marshy shorelines (**C**), accessible along the outer roads and picnic area, waders include Reddish Egret, both night-herons, White and White-faced Ibis, and Roseate Spoonbill, as well Clapper Rail, Killdeer, Willet, and Laughing Gull year-round. Shorebirds are abundant in winter and during migration. Also watch then for American Bittern, King and Virginia Rails, Sora, and Nelson's Sharp-tailed and Seaside Sparrows. **Whooping Crane** occasionally can be seen feeding along the distant shore at the tip of Blackjack Peninsula (see site 97 for details about viewing Whoopers close-up by boat). In winter watch along the shoreline and over the bays for Osprey, Merlin, and Peregrine Falcon.

In summer Magnificent Frigatebird and Sandwich and Least Terns can be seen over the bay. Wood Stork can be expected by June, and several post-nesting shorebirds can appear as early as mid-July.

To visit the Fourth Street Pond (**D**), take the outer loop to the right from the park entrance. This is a good place to find ducks in winter. Night-herons roost here year-round; neotropical migrants can be numerous in spring and fall; and Purple Gallinule is usually present in summer. The **Least Grebe** is occasionally found here.

Records of Review Species: *In Aransas Bay*—Long-tailed Jaeger, June 1987.

Directions: Turn off SH 35, 12 miles north of Rockport, onto PR 13 (Main Street), and continue 1.4 miles to the park entrance on the right. Fourth Street Pond is east on Main Street, toward the bay (0.4 mile), then north along the bay to Fourth Street (0.3 mile). Turn left on Fourth Street for the best views.

General information: Goose Island State Park lies at the southern edge of the Lamar Peninsula, between Aransas and St. Charles bays, across the causeway from the

The live oak–dominated campground at Goose Island State Park.

Fulton and Rockport area, site of the annual Hummer/Bird Celebration each September. Here too, just off 12th Street on the Lamar Peninsula, is the "big tree," the national champion live oak tree, estimated to be 1,000 years old.

The 307-acre state park is a popular fishing and boating area. It offers a 1,620-foot-long lighted fishing pier and boat ramp. There is also a loop hiking trail that provides good access to oak mottes and brush. The park can be crowded on weekends and holidays, so birding is best during early mornings.

ADDITIONAL HELP

Location: Texas Official Travel Map grid U x 18; Aransas County
Nearest food, gas, and lodging: Sea Gun Inn in Lamar and the towns of Fulton and Rockport have food, gas, and lodging.
Nearest camping: On-site (250 sites)
Contact: Superintendent, Goose Island State Park (see Appendix C)

99 Rockport-Fulton

Habitats: Bay, estuary, pond, marsh, oak motte, mesquite grassland, coastal prairie, coastal scrub, garden

Key birds: Least Grebe, Brown Pelican, Neotropic Cormorant, White and White-faced Ibis, Roseate Spoonbill, Black-bellied Whistling-Duck, Mottled Duck, **White-tailed Hawk,** Crested Caracara, **Pauraque, Golden-fronted Woodpecker, Great Kiskadee, Green Jay, Long-billed Thrasher, Olive Sparrow,** Seaside Sparrow, and Bronzed Cowbird are present year-round. Anhinga, Magnificent Frigatebird, Least Bittern, Wood Stork, Fulvous Whistling-Duck, Wilson's Plover, Least Tern, **Buff-bellied Hummingbird,** Brown-crested and Scissor-tailed Flycatchers, Painted Bunting, Dickcissel, and Cassin's Sparrow occur in summer. American White Pelican, American Bittern, Hooded Merganser, Merlin, Peregrine Falcon, Sandhill Crane, and Nelson's Sharp-tailed Sparrows can usually be found in winter.

Best times to bird: April and early May for spring migrants and nesting activities; September for hummingbirds

Birding strategies: Spring migration can produce an amazing number of birds, especially during a fallout of neotropical migrants when flycatchers, thrushes, vireos, warblers, and many other birds can be found almost anywhere there are insects. Birding is most productive behind the Best Western Motel (**A**) (along SH 35 in Fulton), the 19-acre preserve at Hummingbird Lodge (**B**) (along FM 1781), and the Connie Hagar Sanctuary woods (**C**) at Church and Third streets.

Look for migrating shorebirds along Fulton Beach Road (**D**), on the east side of town, and Cape Valero (**E**) and Port Bay (**F**) roads to the west. All three routes offer good viewing from the roadside. Waterfowl are more easily observed from Fulton Beach Road and along Copano Bay at the tip of Live Oak Peninsula (**G**) (pullouts and paths to the bay are available). Cape Valero and Port Bay roads terminate at Port Bay, an area that can be particularly rich in waders and shorebirds. The saltwater marsh harbors White and White-faced Ibis, Roseate Spoonbill, Black-bellied Whistling-Duck, Mottled Duck, and Seaside Sparrow year-round and Nelson's Sharp-tailed Sparrow in winter. American White and Brown Pelicans can be found over the bay. Watch for soaring Magnificent Frigatebird in summer.

The patches of mesquite near the end of the Port Bay Road and the adjacent cattail ponds can be teeming with songbirds. The mesquite thickets provide nesting sites for a variety of South Texas species. Most common are Mourning and Inca Doves, Yellow-billed Cuckoo, Greater Roadrunner, **Golden-fronted Wood-pecker,** Ladder-backed Woodpecker, Vermilion Flycatcher, **Green Jay,** Bewick's Wren, Northern Mockingbird, White-eyed Vireo, Painted Bunting, **Olive Sparrow,** and Cassin's Sparrow. Watch also for White-tailed Kite, **White-tailed Hawk,** Crested Caracara, Common Ground-Dove, Groove-billed Ani, Brown-crested Flycatcher, Cactus Wren, **Long-billed Thrasher,** and Pyrrhuloxia. **Pauraque** is present at all the wooded areas, and can best be found after dusk and before dawn.

99 Rockport-Fulton

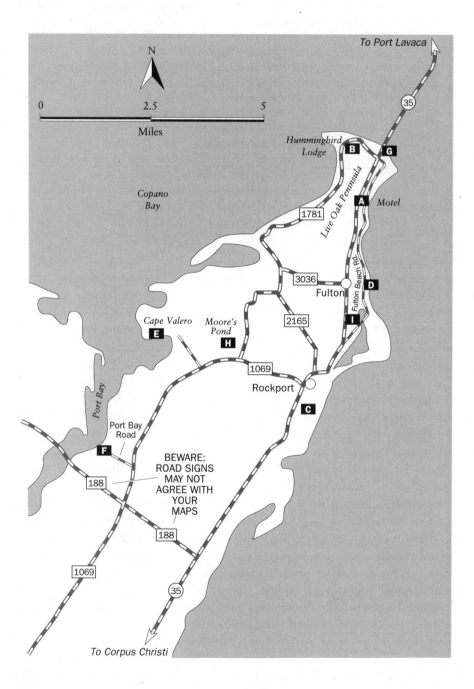

To Port Lavaca

35

N

0   2.5   5
Miles

Hummingbird
Lodge   B   G

Copano
Bay   A   Motel

Live Oak Peninsula

1781

3036   Fulton   D

Fulton Beach Rd.

Cape Valero   Moore's
E   Pond   2165   I
          H

Port Bay   1069
          Rockport

Port Bay
Road   C

F

BEWARE:
ROAD SIGNS
MAY NOT
188   AGREE WITH
          YOUR
          MAPS

188

1069

35

To Corpus Christi

Moore's Pond (H), as well as the cattail-dominated ponds along the Cape Valero Road, can be teeming with water birds during migration. A few species remain all summer: **Least Grebe**, Pied-billed Grebe, Neotropic Cormorant, Anhinga, Least Bittern, Purple Gallinule, Common Moorhen, and American Coot, as well as Wood Stork and Fulvous Whistling-Duck.

In September, when the Hummingbird Garden (I) is readied for the annual Hummer/Bird Celebration, the mass of flowering plants can be alive with hundreds of hummingbirds, primarily Ruby-throats. But **Buff-bellied Hummingbird** and Black-chinned Hummingbird can be expected as well. The boardwalk can also produce many other neotropical migrants.

Records of Review Species: Surfbird, April 1995. Black-legged Kittiwake, Dec 1980. White-collared Swift, Dec 1974. Gray Kingbird, Aug 1951. Black-whiskered Vireo, May 1988.

Directions: The Rockport-Fulton area lies along SH 35, on Live Oak Peninsula, just south of the Lyndon B. Johnson Causeway across Copano Bay. Choice birding sites exist on both sides of the peninsula (see map for details).

General information: Although this was once one of North America's best-known birding hot spots, much of the natural environment has been degraded by developments and grazing since the days of Connie Hagar, the birder who discovered the area to be a birding bonanza. The peripheral wetlands have generally remained intact, but only remnants of the interior oak mottes and ponds remain.

In spite of environmental changes, the residents of Rockport and Fulton have established one of the country's most successful birding festivals, the annual Hummer/Bird Celebration, held in mid-September. Programs, workshops, field trips, hummingbird banding demonstrations, and booths where vendors display birding equipment, books, art, and crafts are all included. Contact the Rockport-Fulton Chamber of Commerce for more information.

ADDITIONAL HELP

Location: Texas Official Travel Map grid U x 18; Aransas County
Nearest food, gas, and lodging: All are available in Rockport and Fulton.
Nearest camping: On-site at numerous RV sites in Rockport and Fulton
Contact: Rockport-Fulton Chamber of Commerce (see Appendix C)

100 Port Aransas

Habitats: Gulf, bay, estuary, mud flat, beach, dune, freshwater marsh, pond, coastal prairie, coastal scrub

Key birds: Least Grebe, Brown Pelican, Reddish Egret, White and White-faced Ibis, Roseate Spoonbill, Black-bellied Whistling-Duck, Mottled Duck, **White-tailed Hawk, Long-billed Thrasher,** Curve-billed Thrasher, Pyrrhuloxia, and Cassin's and Seaside Sparrows are present year-round. Neotropic Cormorant; Magnificent Frigatebird; Least Bittern; Purple Gallinule; Wilson's Plover; Gull-billed, Sandwich, and Least Terns; and Groove-billed Ani occur in summer. Northern Gannet, American White Pelican, American Bittern, Osprey, Ferruginous Hawk, Crested Caracara, Merlin, Peregrine Falcon, King and Virginia Rails, Sandhill Crane, Burrowing and Short-eared Owls, **Buff-bellied Hummingbird,** American and Sprague's Pipits, Palm Warbler, and LeConte's and Nelson's Sharp-tailed Sparrows can usually be found in winter.

Best times to bird: April and May for spring migrants; September and early October for fall migrants; November to March for winter birds

Birding strategies: The Port Aransas Birding Center (**A**), at the wastewater treatment plant, contains a marvelous boardwalk with a viewing tower for easy access into the extensive freshwater marsh. Common year-round species include Pied-billed Grebe; Neotropic Cormorant; Great Blue, Little Blue, and Tricolored Herons; Great and Snowy Egrets; Black-bellied Whistling-Duck; Mottled Duck; American Coot; Laughing Gull; Forster's Tern; and Red-winged Blackbird. Watch also for Black-crowned Night-Heron. In summer Least Bittern and Purple Gallinule are usually present.

In winter at the Birding Center, expect Eared Grebe, Double-crested Cormorant, American Bittern, a wide variety of ducks, Common Moorhen, various shorebirds and American Pipit on the muddy shoreline, Marsh Wren, possibly a Palm Warbler, Common Yellowthroat, and Swamp Sparrow.

The Gulf and beach (**B**), accessible from a number of roads (north to south: Cotter Avenue, Beach Street, Lantana Drive, Avenue G, and Access Road 1A) can produce an amazing number of shorebirds, gulls, and terns during migration. Walk on the jetty (**C**) to find birds that normally remain beyond the breakers, such as Horned Grebe; Brown Pelican; shearwaters; storm-petrels; Masked Booby; Northern Gannet; various sea ducks, such as Redhead, Greater and Lesser Scaup, and Bufflehead; jaegers; and Common Tern.

Bird Port Aransas, including the 11th Street Pond (**D**), open fields, and oak mottes, during migration for **Least Grebe,** Black-bellied Whistling-Duck, and Mottled Duck. Watch for **Buff-bellied Hummingbird** and Rufous Hummingbird (during fall) at feeders around town. Groove-billed Ani, **Long-billed Thrasher,** and Curve-billed Thrasher frequent the overgrown fields in spring and summer, and Grasshopper and LeConte's Sparrow are there in winter.

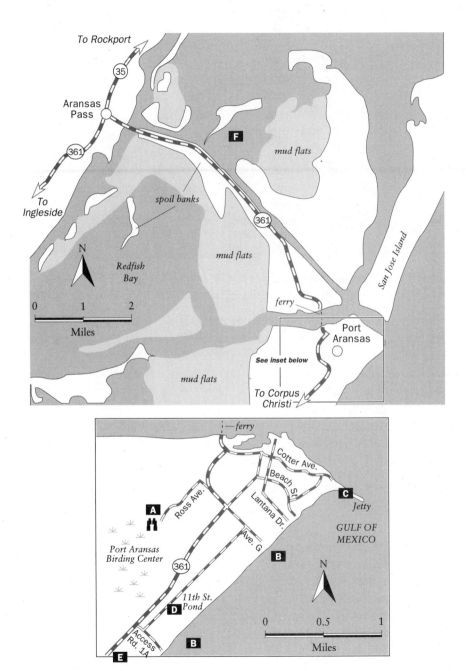

Birders on the boardwalk at the Port Aransas Birding Center.

Drive southwest toward Corpus Christi and bird the coastal prairie habitat (**E**) along SH 361. Expected birds include **White-tailed Hawk,** Northern Bobwhite, Horned Lark, Pyrrhuloxia, and Cassin's Sparrow (sporadic) year-round. White-tailed Kite; Northern Harrier; Red-tailed and Ferruginous Hawks; Crested Caracara; American Kestrel; Merlin; Peregrine Falcon; Sandhill Crane; and Chipping, Field, Vesper, Savannah, Grasshopper, and Lincoln's Sparrows are common here in winter. Fewer numbers of Burrowing and Short-eared Owls, Sedge Wren, Sprague's Pipit, and Song and White-crowned Sparrows can usually be found.

Redfish Bay (**F**) provides a different birding environment, including the highest concentration of wintering Redheads in the world. The majority of the waders, shorebirds, gulls, and terns are the same as can be found along the beach. However, many of these species nest on the spoil banks, including Shamrock Island (Nature Conservancy of Texas preserve, accessible only by boat—see Appendix C). A few of the spoil banks can be visited by tour boats. Nesting birds include Brown Pelican; Neotropic Cormorant; Great Blue, Little Blue, and Tricolored Herons; Great, Snowy, and Reddish Egrets; Black-crowned Night-Heron; White and White-faced Ibis; Roseate Spoonbill; Wilson's Plover; American Oystercatcher; Willet; Laughing Gull; Gull-billed, Caspian, Royal, Sandwich, Forster's, and Least Terns; and Black Skimmer.

Records of Review Species: Sooty Shearwater, June 1952. Audubon's Shearwater, April 1955. Brown Booby, Sept 1971, Aug 1977, Aug 1980. Brant, Jan 1995. Surfbird, April 1975, 1983. Long-tailed Jaeger, June 1987. Thayer's Gull, Feb–March 1976. Great Black-backed Gull, Jan 1986. Sabine's Gull, Oct 1977. Bridled Tern, Sept 1988. Aztec Thrush, Jan 1979.

Directions: Port Aransas, located at the northern end of Mustang Island, is accessible from Corpus Christi (28 miles) via SH 358 to Mustang Island and north on SH 361; or 6.5 miles from Aransas Pass (on SH 35) via SH 361 and the 24-hour, free ferry.

General information: Vegetation has been planted along the parking lot and entrance trail at the Port Aransas Birding Center to attract hummingbirds and butterflies. Plant and bird checklists are available. The birding center is also a good place to see alligators.

The Port Aransas jetty is a popular fishing site, especially on weekends. Fishing boats are available for group birding and deep-sea fishing from Fisherman's Wharf, near the ferry dock in Port Aransas. Birders are welcome aboard these fishing boats at a reduced rate. Bill Gaskins has an agreement with The Nature Conservancy of Texas to provide birding tours of Shamrock Island; for further information, contact Woody's Sport Center, 512-749-6969.

Port Aransas is home to the University of Texas Marine Science Institute, a laboratory and research facility for oceanography studies. The institute houses displays of Gulf marine life and oceanography.

ADDITIONAL HELP

Location: Texas Official Travel Map grid V x 18; San Patricio County
Nearest food, gas, and lodging: All are available in Port Aransas.
Nearest camping: On-site at Port Aransas County Park and Mustang Island State Park (14 miles)
Contact: Port Aransas Convention and Visitors Bureau (see Appendix C)

101 Mustang Island State Park and Packery Channel County Park

Habitats: Gulf, bay, estuary, beach, dune, pond, salt marsh, mud flat, coastal scrub, coastal prairie, oak motte

Key birds: Brown Pelican, Reddish Egret, White and White-faced Ibis, Roseate Spoonbill, Black-bellied Whistling-Duck, Mottled Duck, **White-tailed Hawk,** and Snowy Plover are present year-round. Neotropic Cormorant; Magnificent Frigatebird; Least Bittern; Wilson's Plover; and Gull-billed, Sandwich, and Least Terns occur in summer. Northern Gannet, American White Pelican, Osprey, Ferruginous Hawk, Merlin, Peregrine Falcon, Clapper and King Rails, Sandhill Crane, Piping Plover, Short-eared Owl, American and Sprague's Pipits, Palm Warbler, Pyrrhuloxia, and LeConte's and Nelson's Sharp-tailed Sparrows can usually be found in winter.

Best times to bird: April and May for spring migrants; mid-July to October for fall migration; November to March for winter birds

Birding strategies: Birding is limited to the beach and adjacent waters of the Gulf of Mexico and Corpus Christi Bay, the coastal prairie along SH 361, and a few oak mottes adjacent to the county park.

The beach (**A**) can be filled with shorebirds and the offshore waters can be busy with gulls and terns in both spring and fall. Some of the more interesting migrants include Piping Plover; Hudsonian and Marbled Godwits; Red Knot; Semipalmated, White-rumped, and Stilt Sandpipers; and Black Tern. Migrating Peregrine Falcon can also be numerous along Mustang Island. This same area is worth birding in winter, when sea ducks can be common. Northern Gannets can usually be seen offshore with patience; scoters and jaegers are rare. Brown Pelicans are present year-round, and Magnificent Frigatebird can be expected overhead in summer.

Corpus Christi Bay (**B**) can be even better in winter. Thousands of waders, including Reddish Egret and Roseate Spoonbill, waterfowl, and shorebirds feed in the shallow waters. Scope the bay from the end of the access trail that runs along the north side of Water Exchange Pass. Large populations of Common Loon, grebes, American White Pelican, Double-crested Cormorant, ducks, and shorebirds are normally visible. The area along the water exchange pass is good for all the waders and migrating shorebirds. The open bay also supports wintering Osprey.

Bird the coastal prairie (**C**) from along SH 361 and the unimproved road to Corpus Christi Bay. This habitat can be extremely productive during migration, especially in spring. Thousands of neotropical migrants—flycatchers, vireos, warblers, tanagers, orioles, and numerous other species—can be present, moving from shrub to shrub on their way north in spring and south in fall. **White-tailed Hawk** often perches on the power poles year-round. In winter Osprey, Ferruginous Hawk, American Kestrel, Merlin, and Peregrine Falcon use these poles. Short-eared Owls hunt the prairie at dawn and dusk.

101 Mustang Island State Park and Packery Channel County Park

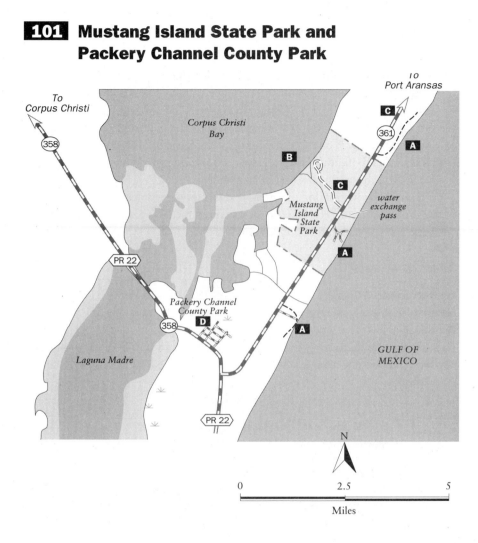

To Corpus Christi

Corpus Christi Bay

I O Port Aransas

water exchange pass

Mustang Island State Park

Packery Channel County Park

Laguna Madre

GULF OF MEXICO

N

0   2.5   5

Miles

The urban neighborhood and oak mottes adjacent to Packery Channel County Park (**D**) often provide a trap for migrating songbirds.

Records of Review Species: Red-throated Loon, Jan 1992. Sooty Shearwater, June 1993, Oct 1993. Manx Shearwater, Aug 1980, Nov 1984, Oct 1987, June 1993. Audubon's Shearwater, Aug 1980, July 1984, Jan 1989. Band-rumped Storm-Petrel, May 1989. Brown Booby, Aug 1980. Barrow's Goldeneye, Dec 1987. Little Gull, Jan 1992. Heermann's Gull, Feb 1983. Great Black-backed Gull, Nov–Jan 1991/92, Dec–March 1992/93, Dec 1993. Sabine's Gull, Nov 1982. Black-whiskered Vireo, April–May 1992, April–May 1993. Varied Bunting, April 1997.

Directions: The state park lies 22 miles east of Corpus Christi, across the John F. Kennedy Causeway (SH 358), then north on SH 361. From Port Aransas, drive 14 miles south on SH 361. Packery Channel County Park is located off SH 358, 1 mile east of the high bridge over Laguna Madre.

General information: Mustang Island, the barrier island just north of Padre Island, is situated between the mainland and the open waters of the Gulf of Mexico. The park receives heavy visitor use, especially on weekends, so birding is best during the early morning hours. Popular recreation activities include fishing, swimming, surfing, camping, picnicking, sunbathing, and beachcombing. Picnic tables with shelters, a beach bathhouse with dressing rooms and restrooms, and a fish-cleaning facility (on the south jetty) are available.

The island is named for the herds of wild horses that once thrived on the island's coastal prairie. The 3,702-acre state park includes 5.5 miles of beach, one of the best in the state, and 10 miles of bay front.

ADDITIONAL HELP

Location: Texas Official Travel Map grid V x 18; Nueces County

Nearest food, gas, and lodging: Food and gas can be found along SH 358. Lodging is available at Port Aransas, 14 miles north.

Nearest camping: On-site (48 sites, plus a number of primitive beach campsites)

Contact: Superintendent, Mustang Island State Park; Nueces County Parks (see Appendix C)

102 Padre Island National Seashore

Habitats: Gulf, estuary, beach, dune, tidal flat, freshwater wetland, saltwater marsh, pond, coastal scrub, coastal prairie

Key birds: Brown Pelican, Reddish Egret, White and White-faced Ibis, Roseate Spoonbill, Mottled Duck, and **White-tailed Hawk** are present year-round. Magnificent Frigatebird; Least Bittern; Wood Stork; Purple Gallinule; Gull-billed, Sandwich, and Least Terns; Black Skimmer; and Painted Bunting occur in summer. Northern Gannet; Surf Scoter; Merlin; Peregrine Falcon; Sandhill Crane; Snowy and Piping Plovers; Red Knot; Burrowing and Short-eared Owls; American and Sprague's Pipits; and LeConte's Sparrow can usually be found in winter.

Best times to bird: April and May for migrants; November to March for winter birds

Birding strategies: Access to the beach is available at Malaquite Beach (**A**); an additional 60 miles of beach is open to four-wheel-drive vehicles to the south (first check on beach conditions with seashore personnel). Typical birds of the beach and surf include Black-bellied Plover; Willet; Ruddy Turnstone; Sanderling; Laughing Gull; and Caspian, Royal, and Forster's Terns. In late spring and summer, also expect Sandwich and Least Terns. Watch overhead for the occasional Magnificent

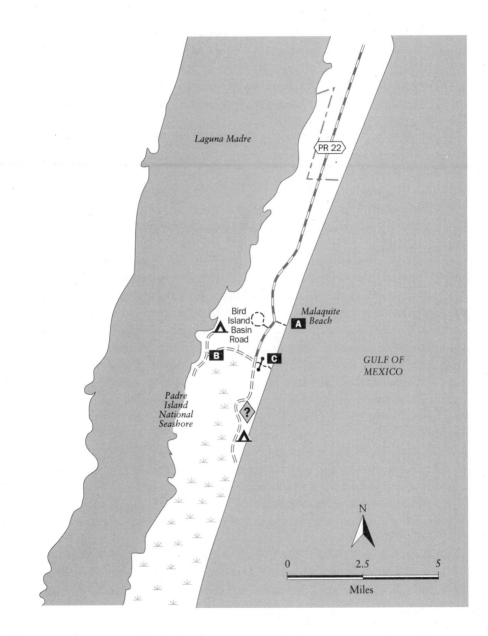

Laguna Madre

PR 22

Bird
Island **A** *Malaquite*
Basin *Beach*
Road

B **C**

*Padre
Island
National
Seashore*

?

GULF OF
MEXICO

N

0 2.5 5

Miles

Frigatebird. Peregrine Falcon can be numerous during migration, and are also present in winter.

Pelagics, such as all three jaegers, occasionally are seen from shore, but don't expect them.

The Gulf waters can be impressive in winter, with thousands of water birds. Common species include Common Loon, Eared Grebe, Brown Pelican, Double-crested Cormorant, Northern Shoveler, Gadwall, Redhead, Lesser Scaup, Red-breasted Merganser, and Ruddy Duck. Fewer numbers of Horned Grebe; Northern Gannet; Canvasback; Ring-necked Duck; Greater Scaup; Black, Surf, and White-winged Scoters; and Common Goldeneye can sometimes be found.

Most of these same water birds can be seen on the back bay (Laguna Madre). View this more protected area and the tidal flats from the south end of PR 22, the Bird Island Basin Road (**B**). The bay and tidal flats support large numbers of American White and Brown Pelicans and all the waders, including Reddish Egret, and White and White-faced Ibis. Roseate Spoonbill is a year-round resident. Wood Stork normally appears in summer and thousands of shorebirds in winter and during migration.

Scope Bird Island for hundreds of egrets, herons, ibis, gulls, terns, and others milling about this long spoil island (island formed by dredging operations) in midbay. Many of these nest on the island. Roseate Spoonbill is almost always present, as are American Oystercatcher and Black Skimmer.

Coastal prairie habitat occurs all along the main paved highway and Bird Island Basin Road, as well as along the gated road (**C**) directly across the highway from Bird Island Basin Road. Typical birds of this habitat include White-tailed Kite, **White-tailed Hawk,** Eastern Meadowlark, and Great-tailed Grackle year-round. When shrubs are present, Loggerhead Shrike and Painted Bunting appear in summer. And in winter, Northern Harrier and American Kestrel are common; Burrowing and Short-eared Owls, Sprague's Pipit, Sedge Wren, and Grasshopper and LeConte's Sparrows are less numerous.

These areas flood after most rains, producing wetlands that support water birds, including all the waders, Black-bellied Whistling-Duck, Mottled Duck, King Rail, Common Moorhen, Black-necked Stilt, Greater and Lesser Yellowlegs, Marsh Wren, Common Yellowthroat, Savannah Sparrow, Eastern Meadowlark, and Red-winged Blackbird. Look also for Fulvous Whistling-Duck, King Rail, and Purple Gallinule. In winter Greater White-fronted and Snow Geese and Sandhill Crane frequent these areas. Check the ponds along the south side of Bird Island Basin Road and a second one along the main road behind the ranger station for waders and ducks.

Records of Review Species: Pacific Loon, Oct 1989. Yellow-nosed Albatross, Oct 1976. Greater Shearwater, Aug 1980. Sooty Shearwater, May 1990, Feb 1996. Audubon's Shearwater, April 1964, Sept 1967, Nov 1968. Leach's Storm-Petrel, June 1975. Band-rumped Storm-Petrel, July 1968, July 1969. Brown Booby, Aug 1967. Greater Flamingo, April 1978. Surfbird, April 1974, April 1994. California Gull, Dec–Jan 1991/92. Great Black-backed Gull, Oct 1975. Black-legged Kittiwake, Feb 1974, Feb 1996. Sabine's Gull, Oct 1976. Brown Noddy, Aug 1979. Black Noddy, June 1975. Mountain Bluebird, Nov 1989. Clay-colored Robin, Jan 1990.

Directions: From Corpus Christi, take SH 358 east (John F. Kennedy Causeway) across Laguna Madre to PR 22, and turn south for 12 miles to Malaquite Beach. From Port Aransas, take SH 361 south. The pavement ends at Malaquite Beach, but beach access for an additional 60 miles to Mansfield Cut is possible with a four-wheel-drive vehicle.

South Padre Island must be accessed from Port Isabel, near Brownsville. One cannot reach Padre Island National Seashore from the south.

General information: Padre Island is one of the longest stretches (70 miles) of undeveloped ocean beach in the United States. Five miles of beach, from the national seashore entrance to Malaquite Beach, are closed to vehicular traffic. Malaquite Beach is the site of the park's visitor center, an observation deck, changing rooms, snack bar, gift shop, and campground. The visitor center has an information desk, a few exhibits, and a sales outlet.

Bird Island Basin contains a boat launch that leads into Laguna Madre and the Intracoastal Waterway. Several additional spoil banks can be visited within the Laguna Madre (26 within the park borders); none of these should be disturbed during the bird nesting season between April 1 and September 30.

ADDITIONAL HELP

Location: Texas Official Travel Map grid W/X/Y x 18; Nueces and Kleberg counties

Nearest food, gas, and lodging: Snacks are available on-site; gas and lodging are 12 miles away in Corpus Christi.

Nearest camping: On-site (50 sites)

Contact: Superintendent, Padre Island National Seashore (see Appendix C)

103 Corpus Christi

Hans A. Suter Wildlife Area, Ocean Drive, Blucher Park, Botanical Gardens, and Elliot Landfill

Habitats: Bay, tidal flat, salt marsh, coastal prairie, coastal scrub, pond, park, landfill

Key birds: Least Grebe, Anhinga, Reddish Egret, White and White-faced Ibis, Roseate Spoonbill, Black-bellied Whistling-Duck, Mottled Duck, Harris's Hawk, Crested Caracara, Black Skimmer, Groove-billed Ani, **Pauraque, Green Kingfisher, Golden-fronted Woodpecker, Long-billed Thrasher,** Pyrrhuloxia, **Olive Sparrow,** and Seaside Sparrow are present year-round. Neotropic Cormorant, Magnificent Frigatebird, Least Bittern, Wood Stork, Purple Gallinule, Gull-billed and Least Terns, Lesser Nighthawk, **Buff-bellied Hummingbird,** Scissor-tailed Flycatcher, **Couch's Kingbird,** Painted Bunting, and Cassin's Sparrow occur in summer. American Bittern, Peregrine Falcon, King and Virginia Rails, and Sandhill Crane can usually be found in winter.

Best times to bird: April and May for spring migrants and nesting activities

Birding strategies: The best saltwater environment can be found at **Hans A. Suter Wildlife Area (A)**, located on the western shore of Oso Bay, off Ennis Joslin Road. A boardwalk provides easy access to good bay views; waders, waterfowl, and shorebirds are common. Typical species include all the herons and egrets and numerous ducks and shorebirds, including Reddish Egret, White and White-faced Ibis, Roseate Spoonbill, Black-bellied Whistling-Duck, Mottled Duck, Black-necked Stilt, Black Skimmer, and Seaside Sparrow. Wood Stork and Gull-billed and Least Terns occur in summer. In winter this area usually contains a wide variety of waterfowl and an occasional Peregrine Falcon.

Many of the same birds can be found along nearby **Ocean Drive (B)**, the entrance to the Texas A&M University at Corpus Christi campus. The shoreline and tidal flats of Oso Bay can be alive with shorebirds, especially during migration. The campus vegetation attracts migrating songbirds, especially in spring fallouts. In summer and fall, watch for Magnificent Frigatebird.

Blucher Park (C), in downtown Corpus Christi adjacent to the central library, is a migrant trap that can produce an amazing assortment of birds in spring. Directly across the street, the front and back yards around the historic Blucher residence are available to birders via an agreement with property owners. Black-chinned Hummingbird nests here; Chuck-will's-widow and Whip-poor-will may be found in spring and fall.

Visit the Corpus Christi **Botanical Gardens (D)** in spring and summer. The abundant flowering plants attract numerous hummingbirds, including **Buff-bellied Hummingbird.** The large pond adjacent to Staples Street attracts waders, waterfowl, and various other water birds, such as **Least Grebe** (irregular), Neotropic

103 Corpus Christi

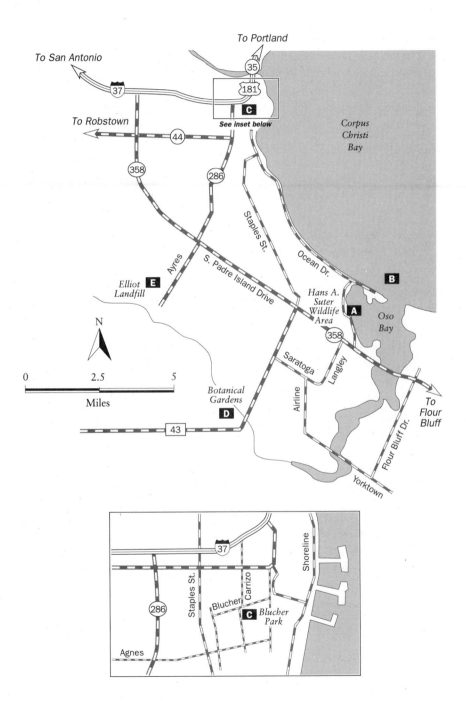

To Portland

To San Antonio

35

37

181

C

See inset below

To Robstown

44

Corpus Christi Bay

358

286

Staples St.

Ocean Dr.

Ayres

S. Padre Island Drive

Elliot Landfill E

Hans A. Suter Wildlife Area

A

B

Oso Bay

358

N

0   2.5   5

Miles

Saratoga

Langley

Botanical Gardens

D

Airline

To Flour Bluff

43

Flour Bluff Dr.

Yorktown

37

Staples St.

Blucher

Carrizo

Shoreline

286

C Blucher Park

Agnes

Cormorant, Anhinga, Least Bittern, Purple Gallinule, and **Green Kingfisher** year-round. The surrounding brush attracts Harris's Hawk, Crested Caracara, Groove-billed Ani, **Pauraque, Golden-fronted Woodpecker,** Brown-crested Flycatcher, **Couch's Kingbird, Long-billed Thrasher,** Curve-billed Thrasher, **Olive Sparrow,** and Pyrrhuloxia. Lesser Nighthawk, Scissor-tailed Flycatcher, Painted Bunting, and Cassin's Sparrow occur here in summer; American Bittern and King and Virginia Rails should be found in winter. Sandhill Cranes can often be seen overhead.

Check the **Elliot Landfill (E)** in winter for thousands of gulls, including an occasional oddity, such as California, Thayer's, or Lesser Black-backed.

Records of Review Species: Jabiru, (Oso Bay) Oct 1979. Masked Duck, Nov–Dec 1968, Dec–Jan 1992/93. Ruff, Oct–Jan 1968/69. California Gull, Feb 1997. Thayer's Gull, Feb 1984, Feb 1997. Great Black-backed Gull, Dec 1991. Green Violet-ear, May–June 1995. Green-breasted Mango, Jan 1992. Clay-colored Robin, Jan–April 1988, March 1995. Aztec Thrush, May 1996. Rufous-capped Warbler, Dec 1992.

Directions: The five key sites occur along the eastern half of the city. Take South Padre Island Drive east to Ennis Joslin Road and north to Hans A. Suter Wildlife Area and Ocean Drive. Blucher Park is located downtown off Carrizo Street, just behind the library. The Botanical Gardens are located at 6000 Staples Street, along Oso Creek, and the Elliot Landfill is located at 7001 Ayres Street. Both are south of South Padre Island Drive.

General information: Corpus Christi, the state's seventh largest city with over 265,000 people, is situated between Corpus Christi and Nueces bays. Much of the Corpus Christi Bay beach is maintained for recreation. Corpus Christi is one of the state's major deep-water ports, and the site of the Texas State Aquarium and the Museum of Science and History. It is also the home port for both the World War II aircraft carrier U.S.S. *Lexington* and the re-created Columbus fleet: *Niña, Pinta,* and *Santa Maria.*

ADDITIONAL HELP

Location: Texas Official Travel Map grid V x 17; Nueces County
Nearest food, gas, and lodging: All are available at numerous locations.
Nearest camping: Several local sites along South Padre Island Drive
Contact: Corpus Christi Area Convention and Visitors Bureau (see Appendix C)

104 West Corpus Christi and Hazel Bazemore County Park

Habitats: Estuary, mud flat, saltwater marsh, pond, creek, riparian, coastal prairie, Tamaulipan scrub

Key birds: Least Grebe, Neotropic Cormorant, Anhinga, White and White-faced Ibis, Roseate Spoonbill, Black-bellied Whistling-Duck, Mottled Duck, Harris's Hawk, **White-tailed Hawk,** Crested Caracara, **White-tipped Dove,** Greater Roadrunner, Groove-billed Ani, **Pauraque, Golden-fronted Woodpecker, Great Kiskadee, Green Jay, Long-billed Thrasher,** and **Olive Sparrow** are present year-round. Least Bittern, Wood Stork, Lesser Nighthawk, **Buff-bellied Hummingbird,** Brown-crested and Scissor-tailed Flycatchers, Cassin's Sparrow, and Painted Bunting occur in summer. American Bittern; Osprey; White-tailed Kite; Merlin; Peregrine Falcon; Short-eared Owl; Vermilion Flycatcher; Sprague's Pipit; Green-tailed Towhee; and Clay-colored, Grasshopper, LeConte's, and Swamp Sparrows can usually be found in winter.

Best times to bird: April and May for spring migrants and nesting activities; mid- to late September for migrating raptors

Birding strategies: Tule Lake (**A**) is a narrow, brackish arm of Corpus Christi Bay. This area is best in winter and during migration when thousands of shorebirds feed on the mud flats. All the waders, including Roseate Spoonbill and Wood Stork (summer), and both Brown and American White Pelicans occur here. Gull-billed Tern is a regular, Least Tern occurs in summer, and five *Charadrius* plovers are occasionally seen together in migration. In winter watch for Osprey, White-tailed Kite, Peregrine Falcon, and, at dawn and dusk, Short-eared Owl.

Hilltop Community Center (**B**), located south of I-37 on higher, drier ground (access off Leopard Street), supports native brush habitat and a number of intermittent creeks, which can be excellent during spring migration. A number of brushland bird species can be expected year-round: Greater Roadrunner, **Great Kiskadee, Green Jay, Long-billed Thrasher,** and **Olive Sparrow.** In winter brushy areas often harbor a variety of seedeaters, such as Green-tailed Towhee and Clay-colored, Field, Vesper, Grasshopper, LeConte's, and Swamp Sparrows. Look in the Hilltop Center for Vermilion Flycatcher.

Pollywog Pond (**C**), on the north side of I-37 near the junction of I-37 and US 77, includes a number of isolated settling ponds with a dike along one edge, dominated by riparian vegetation. Although this area is best in spring, when an array of neotropical migrants are often present, the ponds and dense woodland can be good year-round. Waders and waterfowl, Pied-billed Grebe, Neotropic Cormorant, Anhinga, gulls, terns, rails, Belted Kingfisher, and **Great Kiskadee** can be expected. Nesting birds include **Least Grebe,** Green Heron, Least Bittern, Black-bellied Whistling-Duck, and Mottled Duck.

Hazel Bazemore County Park (**D**), located west of SH 77, is best known for the huge numbers of hawks that pass over during fall migration (peak flights from

104 West Corpus Christi and Hazel Bazemore County Park

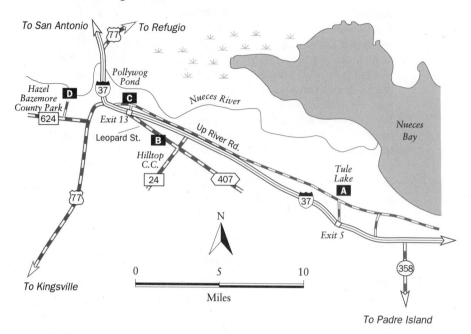

To San Antonio
To Refugio
77

Pollywog Pond

Hazel Bazemore County Park
D
37
C

624
Exit 13
Leopard St.
B

Nueces River
Up River Rd.

Hilltop C.C.
24
407

77
37

Tule Lake
A

Nueces Bay

N

Exit 5

0   5   10
Miles

358

To Kingsville

To Padre Island

September 22 to 25). More than 100,000 can sometimes be found at this chokepoint during a single day. Although Broad-winged Hawk is most numerous, moderate numbers of Swainson's, Red-tailed, Cooper's, and Sharp-shinned Hawks; Mississippi Kite; American Kestrel; Peregrine Falcon; and smaller numbers of Ferruginous, Harris's, Red-shouldered, and Zone-tailed Hawks; Bald and Golden Eagles; Osprey; and White-tailed and Swallow-tailed Kites also move through the area.

The native brush at Bazemore also supports many of the South Texas specialties. These include **White-tipped Dove**, Groove-billed Ani, **Pauraque, Golden-fronted Woodpecker, Great Kiskadee, Long-billed Thrasher,** and Olive Sparrow year-round; and **Buff-bellied Hummingbird,** Brown-crested Flycatcher, and **Couch's Kingbird** in summer. Other summer birds of interest include Lesser Nighthawk, Scissor-tailed Flycatcher, Painted Bunting, and Cassin's Sparrow.

Records of Review Species: Green Violet-ear, May–June 1995.

Directions: Tule Lake, Hilltop Community Center, and Pollywog Pond lie along I-37; Hazel Bazemore County Park is located west of US 77. From Corpus Christi, take I-37 west to Exit 5; take Corn Products Road to Up River Road and turn left (west) for 1.2 miles to a pullout along the bay (Tule Lake). Hilltop is located south of I-37; take the Violet Road exit to Leopard Street; the community center is located 0.3 mile west of Violet Road at 11426 Leopard Street. Pollywog Pond is located farther west on I-37; take Exit 13 onto Callicoate Road, and left on Up River Road for 0.8 mile to a parking area on the right. To find Hazel Bazemore Park, take FM 624 west from SH 77 for about 1 mile to the signed entrance.

General information: Tule Lake is located along Up River Road. There is little room for parking; the area is adjacent to a number of refineries and other businesses. Take care to pull off the road a safe distance. Hilltop Community Center, with its several paths, can be filled with joggers in the mornings. Hazel Bazemore Park can be crowded with picnickers and others on weekends; birding is best during the early mornings.

ADDITIONAL HELP

Location: Texas Official Travel Map grid V x 17; Nueces and San Patricio counties
Nearest food, gas, and lodging: All can be found along I-37 within 5 miles.
Nearest camping: Nueces River Park on US 37, 2 miles north of the junction of I-37 and US 77
Contact: Coastal Bend Audubon Society; Nueces County Parks; Corpus Christi Area Convention and Visitors Bureau (see Appendix C)

105 Kingsville

Dick Kleberg Park, L. E. Ramey County Park, Santa Gertrudis Creek Bird Sanctuary, Texas A&M University Campus, and King Ranch

Habitats: Creek, pond, golf course, Tamaulipan scrub, mesquite savannah, pasture, cropland

Key birds: Least Grebe, Neotropic Cormorant, Anhinga, Black-bellied Whistling-Duck, Mottled Duck, Harris's Hawk, **White-tailed Hawk,** Crested Caracara, Greater Roadrunner, **Pauraque, Golden-fronted Woodpecker, Great Kiskadee, Couch's Kingbird, Green Jay, Long-billed Thrasher,** Curve-billed Thrasher, Pyrrhuloxia, **Olive Sparrow,** and Bronzed Cowbird are present year-round. Roseate Spoonbill; Wood Stork; Fulvous Whistling-Duck; Purple Gallinule; Groove-billed Ani; Lesser Nighthawk; **Buff-bellied Hummingbird;** Ash-throated, Brown-crested, and Scissor-tailed Flycatchers; Cave Swallow; Painted Bunting; Dickcissel; and Hooded Oriole occur in summer. American Bittern; Greater White-fronted, Snow, Ross's, and Canada Geese; King Rail; Sandhill Crane; Rufous Hummingbird; Vermilion Flycatcher; Sprague's Pipit; Clay-colored, Grasshopper, and LeConte's Sparrows; and Lark Bunting can usually be found in winter.

Best times to bird: Year-round for most of the specialty birds; April and May for spring migrants and nesting activities

Birding strategies: Dick Kleberg Park (**A**), on the south side of Kingsville, is a sure place to find Vermilion Flycatcher in winter, and it is one of the few urban parks with its own nesting colony of Cave Swallows. Other resident birds of interest

105 Kingsville

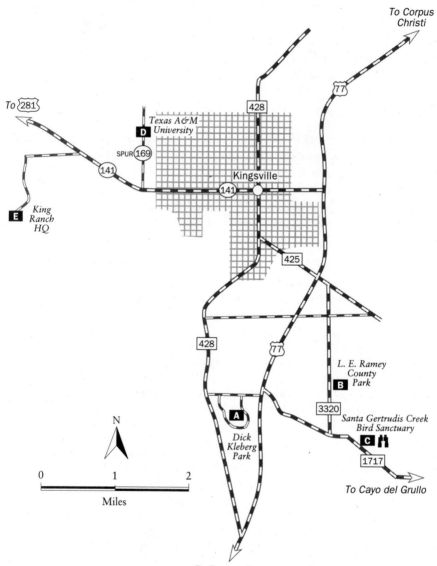

To Corpus Christi

To 281

428

Texas A&M University

D

SPUR 169

141

Kingsville

141

King Ranch HQ

E

425

428

77

L. E. Ramey County Park

B

3320

Dick Kleberg Park

A

Santa Gertrudis Creek Bird Sanctuary

C

1717

To Cayo del Grullo

N

0   1   2

Miles

To Brownsville

include **Golden-fronted Woodpecker,** Ladder-backed Woodpecker, **Great Kiskadee, Long-billed Thrasher,** Pyrrhuloxia, and **Olive Sparrow.** In winter check this area for Sprague's Pipits, and check weedy sites for Clay-colored, Grasshopper, and LeConte's Sparrows and Lark Bunting.

L. E. Ramey County Park (B), east of US 77 off FM 1717 and FM 3320, contains a golf course with several ponds, surrounded by extensive brush and a number of deserted naval base runways. The golf course attracts numerous grassland birds, such as Black-bellied and Mountain (rare) Plovers; American Golden-Plovers; and Upland, Baird's, and Buff-breasted Sandpipers during migration, and numerous geese, Long-billed Curlew, and Sandhill Crane in winter. The ponds in winter support **Least Grebe,** American White Pelican, Double-crested and Neotropic Cormorants, several waders, White and White-faced Ibis, and numerous ducks, including both whistling-ducks, Sora, Common Moorhen, and Common Snipe. Roseate Spoonbill and Wood Stork are common fly-overs. **Golden-fronted Woodpecker,** Vermilion Flycatcher, and **Great Kiskadee** winter in the savannah-like habitat.

The surrounding brush supports Harris's Hawk; Crested Caracara; Groove-billed Ani (spring and summer); **Green Jay;** Carolina, Bewick's, and House Wrens; **Long-billed Thrasher;** Curve-billed Thrasher; White-eyed Vireo; several warblers; Northern Cardinal; Pyrrhuloxia; **Olive Sparrow;** and various other sparrows. **Pauraque** and Lesser Nighthawk (summer) can also be abundant here at dusk and dawn.

Santa Gertrudis Creek Bird Sanctuary (C), southeast of Ramey Park along FM 1717, has a small observation deck that provides good views of the open pond and surrounding cattail marsh. Nesting birds include **Least Grebe** and Pied-billed Grebe, Neotropic Cormorant, Mottled and Ruddy Ducks, Purple Gallinule, Common Moorhen, and American Coot. In winter watch for American Bittern; all the herons and egrets; White and White-faced Ibis; numerous ducks, including Fulvous and Black-bellied Whistling-Ducks; King (rare) and Virginia Rails; Sora; Belted Kingfisher; Marsh Wren; Common Yellowthroat; and Lincoln's and Swamp Sparrows. **Ringed Kingfisher** has appeared here in recent winters.

The campus of **Texas A&M University** at Kingsville **(D),** on the northwest side of town, offers a different group of birds. This is a good place to find nesting White-winged and Inca Doves, Western Kingbird, Cave Swallow, Bronzed Cowbird, and Hooded Oriole.

The **King Ranch (E),** farther west off SH 141, offers both ranching and birding tours for a fee. Some of the more interesting birds to expect along the route include Anhinga, Harris's Hawk, **White-tailed Hawk,** Crested Caracara, Wild Turkey, Common Ground-Dove, Greater Roadrunner, **Golden-fronted Woodpecker, Green Jay, Long-billed Thrasher,** Loggerhead Shrike, Pyrrhuloxia, **Olive Sparrow,** and Bronzed Cowbird year-round. In summer you can expect Ash-throated, Brown-crested, and Scissor-tailed Flycatchers; **Couch's Kingbird;** Western Kingbird; Painted Bunting; Dickcissel; and Lesser Goldfinch. In winter, Snow and Ross's Geese, White-tailed Kite, Ferruginous Hawk, Sandhill Crane, Vermilion Flycatcher, Brown Thrasher, and American and Sprague's Pipits. For information call or visit the King Ranch Tourism Office near the manned gatehouse inside the ranch entrance off SH 141 west of Kingsville, or phone 512-592-8055.

Records of Review Species: Masked Duck, March–April 1993. Double-striped Thick-Knee, Dec 1961. Costa's Hummingbird, Jan 1988. Fork-tailed Flycatcher, Dec 1988. Clay-colored Robin, Jan 1988, Jan–Feb 1990. Black-vented Oriole, June–Oct 1989.

Directions: Kingsville lies along US 77 in Kleberg County. The Texas A&M University campus and the King Ranch entrance are both on the west side of town, and Dick Kleberg Park is located south of town; all are west of US 77. L. E. Ramey Park and Santa Gertrudis Creek Bird Sanctuary are southeast of town, east of US 77 (see map).

General information: Kingsville, named for King Ranch founder Richard King, is a town of about 26,000. It is the home of Naval Air Station Kingsville and Texas A&M University at Kingsville, which houses the Kleberg Hall of Natural History. The King Ranch, the largest ranch in the continental United States at 825,000 acres, has its headquarters and a visitor center just west of Kingsville, where visitors can take a tour of the working cattle ranch.

ADDITIONAL HELP

Location: Texas Official Travel Map grid W x 17; Kleberg County
Nearest food, gas, and lodging: All can be found locally.
Nearest camping: Several on-site locations, including Country Estates, adjacent to Santa Gertrudis Creek Bird Sanctuary
Contact: Kingsville Information Department; King Ranch Visitor Center (see Appendix C)

106 Cayo del Grullo

Habitats: Bay, estuary, mud flat, salt marsh, pond, coastal prairie, coastal scrub, pasture, cropland
Key birds: American White and Brown Pelicans, Neotropic Cormorant, Reddish Egret, White and White-faced Ibis, Roseate Spoonbill, Fulvous and Black-bellied Whistling-Ducks, Mottled Duck, Harris's Hawk, **White-tailed Hawk,** Crested Caracara, **Golden-fronted Woodpecker, Great Kiskadee, Green Jay, Long-billed Thrasher,** and **Olive Sparrow** are present year-round. Magnificent Frigatebird; Least Bittern; Wood Stork; Wilson's Plover; Gull-billed, Sandwich, Least, and Black Terns; Lesser Nighthawk; Brown-crested and Scissor-tailed Flycatchers; Painted Bunting; and Dickcissel occur in summer. American Bittern; Osprey; Peregrine Falcon; Sandhill Crane; Snowy and Piping Plovers; and American and Sprague's Pipits can usually be found in winter.
Best times to bird: April and May for spring migrants and nesting activities; September for fall migrants

Birding strategies: Drum Point (A), off FM 628 on FM 1132 and an unpaved road, offers a wide variety of water birds, including all the waders, shorebirds, and marsh birds, and large numbers of waterfowl in winter. Year-round species of interest include

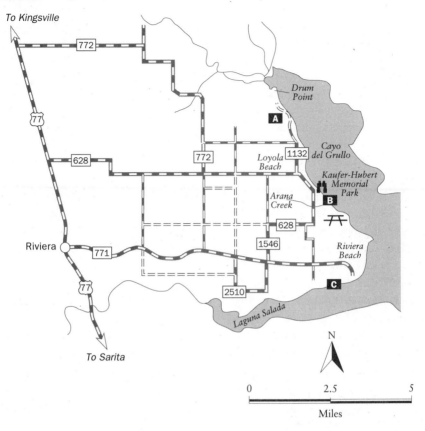

American White and Brown Pelicans, Neotropic Cormorant, Reddish Egret (including the white color phase), White and White-faced Ibis, Roseate Spoonbill, Fulvous and Black-bellied Whistling-Ducks, Clapper Rail, Snowy Plover, American Oystercatcher, Black-necked Stilt, Caspian and Royal Terns, and Seaside Sparrow.

This is an exceptional area during migration, when thousands of waterfowl rest on the bay and numerous shorebirds feed on the mud flats. In winter the bay and marsh can be filled with Lesser Scaup and Bufflehead by the thousands.. The marsh can produce Clapper Rail, Sora, Common Yellowthroat, and Nelson's Sharp-tailed, Seaside, and Swamp Sparrows. Watch also for Osprey and Peregrine Falcon.

Kaufer-Hubert Memorial Park (B) is located off FM 628 to the south, at the mouth of Arana Creek. Birding usually is good along the entire estuary. In summer watch for Magnificent Frigatebird; Wood Stork; Wilson's Plover; and Gull-billed, Sandwich, Least, and Black Terns. In winter expect Snowy and Piping Plovers. The park contains a freshwater pond that can produce some surprising birds, particularly during migration. Typical species include various dabbling ducks, including Mottled Duck, and a huge variety of shorebirds. In winter this pond has produced Greater Scaup, Oldsquaw, and all three scoters.

Bird the trees and surrounding brush year-round for Common Ground-Dove, **Pauraque, Golden-fronted Woodpecker, Great Kiskadee, Green Jay, Long-billed Thrasher,** Curve-billed Thrasher, Cactus Wren, White-eyed Vireo, and **Olive Sparrow.** This same habitat can be filled with neotropical migrants in April and early May.

Riviera Beach (C), at the edge of Laguna Salada, is also worth birding, although the estuary and mud flats normally contain all the same birds. However, because of the adjacent fields, a few additional grassland species are likely during migration: Black-bellied and Mountain Plover; American Golden-Plover; Upland, Baird's, and Buff-breasted Sandpipers; and Long-billed Curlew. These fields can be filled with thousands of Greater White-fronted and Snow Geese. Sandhill Crane and fewer numbers of Ross's and Canada Geese are often present. Watch also for Sprague's Pipit and Mountain Plover.

Bird along the numerous roadways between US 77 and Cayo del Grullo, especially in winter when geese and Sandhill Crane are present. During migration many fields contain shorebirds, the wires are often crowded with swallows and flycatchers, and the roadside vegetation is crowded with feeding songbirds. In summer Harris's Hawk and **White-tailed Hawk,** Crested Caracara, Lesser Nighthawk, Brown-crested and Scissor-tailed Flycatchers, **Couch's Kingbird,** Western Kingbird, Purple Martin, Loggerhead Shrike, Summer Tanager, Blue Grosbeak, Painted Bunting, and Dickcissel can usually be found.

Check the ponds at Riviera (along US 77) and along FM 771. **Least Grebe** and Masked Duck were found here in February and March 1993.

Directions: From US 77, take FM 628 east to Loyola Beach and Kaufer-Hubert Memorial Park. Drum Point is situated to the north via FM 1132 and a secondary unpaved road. From Riviera, take FM 771 east to Riviera Beach.

General information: Riviera (pronounced riv-*air*-ah) Beach is located at the mouth of Laguna Salada on Baffin Bay, a primary bay off Laguna Madre, west of Padre Island. This area can be pleasant in winter but extremely hot and humid in summer. On weekends the area can be busy with fishermen.

The main roads are paved, but the caliche roads, especially the one to Drum Point, beyond the paved FM 1132, should not be driven in rainy weather because it can be extremely slick and muddy.

Kaufer-Hubert Memorial Park includes an RV resort as well as a bird observation tower, picnic shelters, boat ramp, lighted fishing pier, and other recreational facilities. Located at the edge of Cayo del Grullo, this site offers easy access to good birding.

ADDITIONAL HELP

Location: Texas Official Travel Map grid W x 17; Kleberg County
Nearest food, gas, and lodging: Riviera has all three. Gas and snacks are available at Loyola Beach. King's Inn (at Loyola Beach) offers excellent meals.
Nearest camping: Kaufer-Hubert Memorial Park (134 sites)
Contact: Kaufer-Hubert Memorial Park (see Appendix C)

Brush Country Region

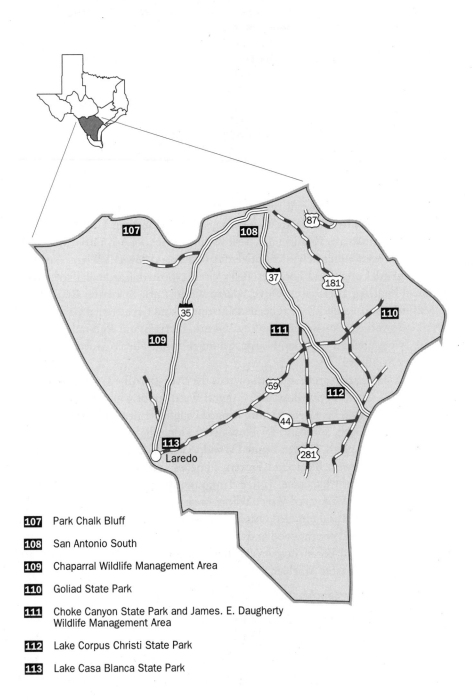

107   Park Chalk Bluff

108   San Antonio South

109   Chaparral Wildlife Management Area

110   Goliad State Park

111   Choke Canyon State Park and James. E. Daugherty
         Wildlife Management Area

112   Lake Corpus Christi State Park

113   Lake Casa Blanca State Park

107 Park Chalk Bluff

Habitats: River, riparian, pecan grove, Tamaulipan scrub, cropland
Key birds: Harris's Hawk, Crested Caracara, Scaled Quail, Greater Roadrunner, **Pauraque, Ringed Kingfisher, Green Kingfisher, Golden-fronted Woodpecker,** Black Phoebe, Vermilion Flycatcher, Cave Swallow, Bushtit, Cactus Wren, Black-tailed Gnatcatcher, **Long-billed Thrasher,** Curve-billed Thrasher, Pyrrhuloxia, and **Olive Sparrow** are present year-round. Zone-tailed Hawk; Lesser and Common Nighthawks; Common Poorwill; Ash-throated, Brown-crested, and Scissor-tailed Flycatchers; **Great Kiskadee;** Painted Bunting; Cassin's Sparrow; Bronzed Cowbird; and Hooded Oriole occur in summer. No key birds are present in winter.
Best times to bird: April and May for spring migrants and nesting activities

Birding strategies: Along the entrance road (**A**), the roadside vegetation, adjacent fields, and Tamaulipan scrub (near the developed complex) offer, in summer, Northern Bobwhite; Killdeer; White-winged and Mourning Doves; Common Ground-Dove; Greater Roadrunner; Yellow-billed Cuckoo; Ash-throated, Brown-crested, and Scissor-tailed Flycatchers; Verdin; Cactus and Bewick's Wrens; Northern Mockingbird; **Long-billed Thrasher;** Bell's Vireo; Northern Cardinal; Pyrrhuloxia; Painted Bunting; Dickcissel; **Olive Sparrow** and Lark Sparrow; Red-winged Blackbird; Bronzed and Brown-headed Cowbirds; and Great-tailed Grackle.

Look overhead for soaring Turkey Vulture, Harris's and Red-tailed Hawks, Lesser Nighthawk at dawn and dusk, Chimney Swift, Purple Martin, and Cliff and Barn Swallows.

The river, riparian area, and cliffs (across the river) (**B**) offer Great Blue Heron, Common Raven, Cliff Swallow, and Canyon Wren, all of which nest on the cliff face. Pied-billed Grebe, Green Heron, **Ringed Kingfisher** (irregular), **Green Kingfisher,** Black Phoebe, and Cave Swallow occur along the river. **Pauraque,** Black-chinned Hummingbird, **Golden-fronted Woodpecker,** Ladder-backed Woodpecker, Eastern Wood-Pewee, Black and Eastern Phoebes, Vermilion Flycatcher, **Great Kiskadee,** Carolina Chickadee, Tufted Titmouse, Bushtit, Carolina Wren, Blue-gray Gnatcatcher, White-eyed Vireo, Yellow-breasted Chat, Summer Tanager, Blue Grosbeak, Orchard and Hooded Orioles, House Finch, and Lesser Goldfinch utilize the riparian and pecan woodlands.

Downriver, bird Pecan Bottom (**C**) for resident Red-shouldered Hawk and nesting Yellow-throated Warbler.

Records of Review Species: Rufous-capped Warbler, April 1995.

Directions: Take SH 55 northwest of Uvalde for 15 miles to the Park Chalk Bluff entrance (signed) and turn left on the entrance road.

General information: Park Chalk Bluff is a 500-acre private park that offers fishing, swimming, tubing, paddle-boating, scuba diving, biking, miniature golf, hay

107 Park Chalk Bluff

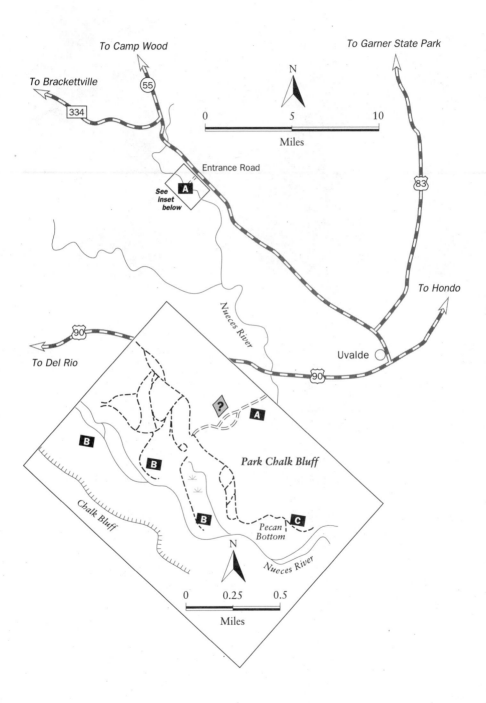

The cliffs of Chalk Bluff across the Nueces River from Park Chalk Bluff.

rides, dancing, picnicking, horseback riding, and birding. There is a $3 per person admission fee. Chalk Bluff is a large hill that rises 300 feet above the surrounding landscape; the northern face (that faces Park Chalk Bluff) has been eroded by the Nueces River.

ADDITIONAL HELP

Location: Texas Official Travel Map grid R x 13; Uvalde County

Nearest food, gas, and lodging: All are available in Uvalde (15 miles); a convenience store and cabins are available on-site.

Nearest camping: On-site, including RV hookups and primitive sites

Contact: Park Chalk Bluff owners Fred and Gwen Wallace (see Appendix C)

108 San Antonio South

Mitchell, Braunig, and Calaveras Lakes

Habitats: Lake, pond, riparian, mesquite grassland, Tamaulipan scrub, field, pasture

Key birds: American White Pelican, Neotropic Cormorant, Black-bellied Whistling-Duck, Harris's Hawk, Crested Caracara, Greater Roadrunner, **Green Kingfisher, Golden-fronted Woodpecker,** Cave Swallow, Verdin, **Long-billed Thrasher,** Curve-billed Thrasher, Pyrrhuloxia, **Olive Sparrow,** and Lesser Goldfinch are present year-round. **Least Grebe;** Least Bittern; Anhinga; Wood Duck; Purple Gallinule; Groove-billed Ani; Lesser and Common Nighthawks; Chuck-will's-widow; Ash-throated, Brown-crested, and Scissor-tailed Flycatchers; Prothonotary Warbler; Painted Bunting; Dickcissel; Cassin's Sparrow; and Bronzed Cowbird occur in summer. Ferruginous Hawk; Long-eared and Short-eared Owls; Say's Phoebe; Vermilion Flycatcher; and Clay-colored, LeConte's, and Harris's Sparrows can usually be found in winter.

Best times to bird: April and May for migrants and nesting activities; late July and August for southbound shorebirds; winter for waterfowl and vagrants

Birding strategies: Mitchell Lake (A) consistently produces the highest numbers of species and vagrants. Although the entrance gate is locked, access can be arranged through a call to the San Antonio Audubon Society (956-733-8306). Likely year-round birds along the entrance road and the various side roads include Black and Turkey Vultures, Harris's and Red-tailed Hawks, Crested Caracara, Northern Bobwhite, White-winged and Mourning Doves, Ladder-backed Woodpecker, Cave Swallow, Carolina Chickadee, Tufted Titmouse, Carolina and Bewick's Wrens, Northern Mockingbird, **Long-billed Thrasher** and Curve-billed Thrasher, Loggerhead Shrike, European Starling, White-eyed Vireo, Northern Cardinal, Pyrrhuloxia, Lark Sparrow, Eastern Meadowlark, Great-tailed Grackle, Brown-headed Cowbird, and House Finch. Less numerous year-round residents include Common Ground-Dove, Verdin, **Olive Sparrow,** Black-throated Sparrow, and Bronzed Cowbird.

During spring and fall, almost any of the neotropical migrants, including flycatchers, thrushes, vireos, warblers, tanagers, and sparrows, are possible. A few remain and nest: Purple Gallinule; Yellow-billed Cuckoo; Groove-billed Ani (along east and south sides of the settling basins); Lesser and Common Nighthawks; Black-chinned Hummingbird; Ash-throated, Brown-crested, and Scissor-tailed Flycatchers; Western Kingbird; Purple Martin; Northern Rough-winged, Cliff, and Barn Swallows; Blue Grosbeak; Painted Bunting; Dickcissel; and Orchard and Bullock's Orioles. In winter weedy sites attract House, Winter, and Sedge Wrens; Common Yellowthroat; Spotted Towhee; Chipping, Clay-colored, Field, Vesper, Savannah, LeConte's, Song, Lincoln's, Swamp, White-throated, White-crowned, and Harris's Sparrows; Lark Bunting; and Lesser and American Goldfinches.

108 San Antonio South

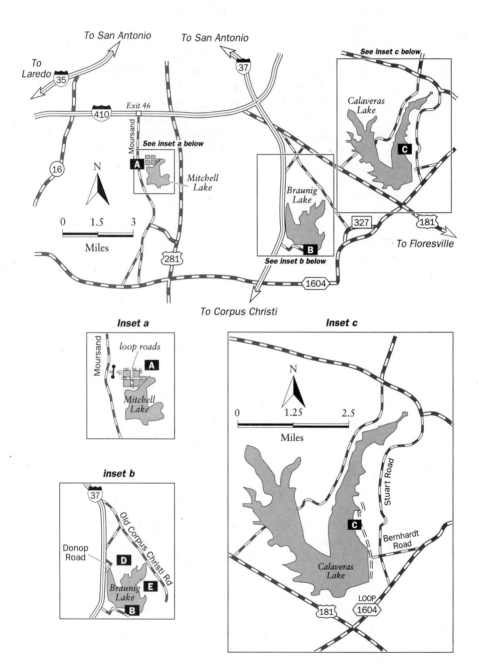

Raptors can be found on the open grasslands in winter; Ferruginous and "Harlan's" Red-tailed Hawks are irregular. Watch also for Peregrine Falcon.

The principal attraction at Mitchell Lake is the water birds. Drive or walk the 5-mile (from entrance) loop route clockwise for the best views. Year-round species include Pied-billed Grebe, American White Pelican, Neotropic Cormorant, Great Blue Heron, Great and Snowy Egrets, Black-crowned Night-Heron, White-faced Ibis, Black-bellied Whistling-Duck, Ruddy Duck, Mallard, Northern Shoveler, Gadwall, Common Moorhen, American Coot, Killdeer, Black-necked Stilt, American Avocet, and Greater Yellowlegs. **Green Kingfisher** is irregular. Water bird populations increase considerably during winter. Large numbers of Eared Grebe; Green-winged and Blue-winged Teal; Northern Pintail; Lesser Scaup; Bufflehead; Spotted, Western, and Least Sandpipers; Long-billed Dowitcher; Common Snipe; Bonaparte's and Ring-billed Gulls; and Forster's Tern can be expected. Fewer numbers of Common Loon, Horned Grebe, Little Blue and Tricolored Herons, Cinnamon Teal, Redhead, Ring-necked Duck, Greater Scaup, Common Goldeneye, Hooded and Red-breasted Mergansers, Lesser Yellowlegs, Solitary and Pectoral Sandpipers, Dunlin, and Laughing and Herring Gulls occur. In summer look for Least Bittern, Green Heron, Yellow-crowned Night-Heron, White Ibis, Roseate Spoonbill, Wood Stork, Purple Gallinule, and Least and Black Terns.

Braunig Lake (B) and **Calaveras Lake (C)** are worthwhile birding, especially if a vagrant has been found. Both lakes include warm-water outlets from power plants and are managed by the San Antonio River Authority, which charges a fee for admission. These areas can be crowded on weekends and holidays. The open mesquite grassland of these two sites offers year-round species such as **Golden-fronted Woodpecker** and Ladder-backed Woodpecker. Flycatchers, Painted Bunting, and orioles are likely in summer.

Both areas are surrounded by good Tamaulipan scrub habitat. At Braunig Lake, the 1-mile Donop Road (D), just outside the northwest edge of the fee area, and the Old Corpus Christi Road and FM 327 (E) offer easy access to neotropical migrants in spring and fall. In summer look for Harris's, Red-shouldered, and Red-tailed Hawks; Crested Caracara; Yellow-billed Cuckoo; Greater Roadrunner; Lesser and Common Nighthawks; Chuck-will's-widow; Ladder-backed Woodpecker; Ash-throated, Brown-crested, and Scissor-tailed Flycatchers; Carolina Chickadee; Tufted Titmouse; Verdin; Bewick's Wren; Northern Mockingbird; **Long-billed Thrasher;** Curve-billed Thrasher; White-eyed Vireo; Summer Tanager; Northern Cardinal; Pyrrhuloxia; Blue Grosbeak; Painted Bunting; Dickcissel; Cassin's and Lark Sparrows; Orchard and Bullock's Orioles; House Finch; and Lesser Goldfinch.

Calaveras Lake (C) offers a 3-mile shoreline with scattered riparian and wetland habitats that are worth birding year-round. In summer a few birds, not always evident elsewhere, can usually be found: **Least Grebe,** Wood Duck, Neotropic Cormorant, Anhinga, **Green Kingfisher,** Great Crested Flycatcher, Eastern Kingbird, Red-eyed Vireo, Northern Parula, Prothonotary Warbler, and Yellow-breasted Chat.

Records of Review Species: *Mitchell Lake*—Band-rumped Storm-Petrel, June 1984. Glossy Ibis, May–June 1991. Sharp-tailed Sandpiper, Sept 1996. Curlew Sandpiper, May 1985. Ruff, Jan–March 1984, Aug–Oct 1985, July–Dec 1986. Red Phalarope, May–June 1983, May 1984, Sept 1987. Mew Gull, Dec–March 1994/95. California Gull, Dec 1989. Black-legged Kittiwake, Dec 1996. Sabine's Gull, Sept 1989, Oct 1993. *Braunig Lake*—Pacific Loon, Dec 1981, Nov 1993. Little Gull, Feb 1993. Sabine's Gull, Nov 1991. *Calaveras Lake*—Red-throated Loon, Dec 1987, 1989. Parasitic Jaeger, Oct 1991. California Gull, March 1991. Black-legged Kittiwake, Oct 1991. Sabine's Gull, Sept 1994.

Directions: To reach Mitchell Lake, take Exit 46 off Loop 410 SE, and turn south onto Moursand for 0.7 mile to the gate on the left. Braunig Lake lies along I-37, between Loops 410 and 1604. Calaveras Lake lies along SH 181, and between Loops 410 and 1604 (see map).

General information: Mitchell Lake includes 660 acres and a number of ponds (called "polders") and extensive grasslands. The area can be well covered by vehicle year-round; a scope is suggested. Once a sewage treatment plant, it has since reverted to a nature preserve managed by the San Antonio Audubon Society. Although there is no fee, visitors must contact the society to make arrangements for entry. Both Braunig and Calaveras lakes are managed by the San Antonio River Authority; entry is $3 per person.

The San Antonio Audubon Society schedules a field trip to Mitchell Lake the fourth Saturday of each month. The gate opens at 7:45 A.M., but is locked at 8:15 A.M. Visitors are welcome.

There are a number of other usually less worthwhile birding sites within the San Antonio area. These include the BFI Landfill (good for gulls in winter) accessible off I-10 on FM 1516 south and right onto Tessman Road; Breckenridge Park, between US 281 and Broadway, and Mulberry and Hilderbrand avenues; Judson Nature Trail in Alamo Heights, along Viesca and Ogden Lane. Friedrich Wilderness Park, northwest of town, off I-10, is good for **Golden-cheeked Warbler** from mid-March to August (see site 37 for details).

ADDITIONAL HELP

Location: Texas Official Travel Map grid R x 15/16; Bexar County.

Nearest food, gas, and lodging: Food and gas are available within or adjacent to each site; lodging can be found in San Antonio.

Nearest camping: Numerous sites in and around San Antonio; none at birding sites

Contact: San Antonio River Authority; San Antonio Audubon Society (see Appendix C)

109 Chaparral Wildlife Management Area

Habitats: Tamaulipan scrub, pond, stock tank

Key birds: Harris's Hawk, Crested Caracara, Wild Turkey, Scaled Quail, Greater Roadrunner, **White-tipped Dove, Pauraque, Golden-fronted Woodpecker,** Vermilion Flycatcher, **Green Jay,** Verdin, Black-tailed Gnatcatcher, Cactus Wren, **Long-billed Thrasher,** Curve-billed Thrasher, Pyrrhuloxia, **Olive Sparrow,** Cassin's and Black-throated Sparrows, and **Audubon's Oriole** are present year-round. Lesser Nighthawk; Common Poorwill; Ash-throated, Brown-crested, and Scissor-tailed Flycatchers; Cave Swallow; Bell's Vireo; Painted Bunting; Dickcissel; Bronzed Cowbird; and Lesser Goldfinch occur in summer. Say's Phoebe, Sage Thrasher, Green-tailed Towhee, and Clay-colored Sparrow can usually be found in winter.

Best times to bird: April and May for spring migrants and nesting activities

Birding strategies: Birders have access to 12,000 acres of quality Tamaulipan scrub habitat along the 8.5-mile Paisano Driving Trail (**A**), which is accessible from either area headquarters (**B**) or the campground (**C**). Typical year-round birds include Black and Turkey Vultures, Harris's and Red-tailed Hawks, Crested Caracara, Wild Turkey, Northern Bobwhite, Scaled Quail, Mourning Dove, Common Ground-Dove, Greater Roadrunner, Great Horned Owl, **Pauraque, Golden-fronted Woodpecker,** Ladder-backed Woodpecker, **Green Jay,** Chihuahuan Raven, Tufted Titmouse, Verdin, Cactus and Bewick's Wrens, Black-tailed Gnatcatcher, Northern Mockingbird, **Long-billed Thrasher,** Curve-billed Thrasher, White-eyed Vireo, Northern Cardinal, Pyrrhuloxia, **Olive Sparrow,** Black-throated and Lark Sparrows, **Audubon's Oriole,** Bronzed and Brown-headed Cowbirds, House Finch, and Lesser Goldfinch. Less numerous are **White-tipped Dove,** Groove-billed Ani, Eastern Screech-Owl, and Hooded Oriole. Vermilion Flycatcher and Great-tailed Grackle are more numerous at headquarters.

In summer look for White-winged Dove; Yellow-billed Cuckoo; Lesser and Common Nighthawks; Common Poorwill; Ash-throated, Brown-crested, and Scissor-tailed Flycatchers; Eastern and Western Kingbirds; Cave and Barn Swallows; Blue Grosbeak; Painted Bunting; Dickcissel; Cassin's Sparrow; and Orchard Oriole. Sage Thrasher, Green-tailed Towhee, Clay-colored Sparrow, and Western Meadowlark are present in winter.

Rosindo Laguna (**D**), a small pond along the driving trail near the campground, attracts birds throughout the year. This is the best location for finding waterfowl during migration and in winter. It's an oasis in this semi-arid habitat for birds to drink and bathe.

Directions: Chaparral Wildlife Management Area is located along FM 133, 8 miles west of Artesia Wells. The 4 birding sites are all located just north of FM 133.

109 Chaparral Wildlife Management Area

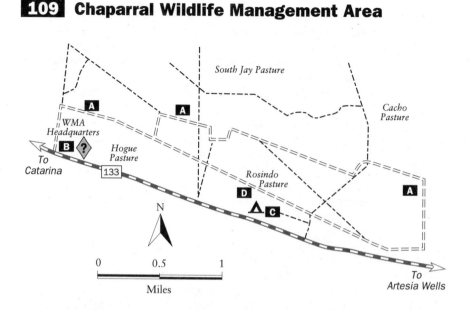

General information: This area, encompassing 15,200 acres of quality South Texas brush country (Tamaulipan scrub), is managed primarily for wildlife research and management; it is enclosed by a deer-proof fence. Principal game species under study include white-tailed deer, javelina, feral hogs, Northern Bobwhite, and Scaled Quail. Nongame animals include South Texas gopher tortoise, Texas horned lizard, and western diamondback rattlesnake.

Birders are welcome from April 1 through August 31, but need to report to area headquarters upon arrival. A limited use permit or silver ($20) or gold ($50) Texas Conservation Passport (available here or at any other state-run facility) is required. Two nature trails—Camino de Fiero and Arena Roja—with numbered brochures begin at area headquarters.

ADDITIONAL HELP

Location: Texas Official Travel Map grid U x 14; Dimmit and LaSalle counties
Nearest food, gas, and lodging: Artesia Wells, 8 miles, has all three.
Nearest camping: Primitive camping on-site; RV hookups in Artesia Wells
Contact: Manager, Chaparral Wildlife Management Area (see Appendix C)

110 Goliad State Park

Habitats: River, riparian, oak motte, coastal prairie, Tamaulipan scrub, mesquite grassland, field, pasture, cropland

Key birds: Anhinga, **White-tailed Hawk,** Harris's Hawk, Crested Caracara, Wild Turkey, Greater Roadrunner, Groove-billed Ani, **Green Kingfisher, Golden-fronted Woodpecker,** Cactus Wren, **Long-billed Thrasher,** Curve-billed Thrasher, **Olive Sparrow,** and Pyrrhuloxia are present year-round. Black-bellied Whistling-Duck, Lesser and Common Nighthawks, **Pauraque, Buff-bellied Hummingbird,** Brown-crested and Scissor-tailed Flycatchers, **Couch's Kingbird,** Cave Swallow, Painted Bunting, Dickcissel, Grasshopper Sparrow, and Bronzed Cowbird occur in summer. Osprey, Sandhill Crane, Burrowing Owl, and American and Sprague's Pipits can usually be found in winter.

Best times to bird: April and May for spring migrants and nesting activities

Birding strategies: The River Trail (**A**), which skirts the San Antonio River, offers the greatest diversity of bird life year-round, although most of the resident birds usually can be found within and along the edge of the campground. These include **Golden-fronted Woodpecker,** Ladder-backed Woodpecker, Carolina Wren, Tufted Titmouse, Carolina and Bewick's Wrens, **Long-billed Thrasher,** Curve-billed Thrasher, White-eyed Vireo, Northern Cardinal, **Olive Sparrow,** and Great-tailed Grackle year-round. In summer watch for Yellow-billed Cuckoo, **Buff-bellied Hummingbird,** Ruby-throated and Black-chinned Hummingbirds, Brown-crested and Scissor-tailed Flycatchers, Cliff Swallow, Blue Grosbeak, Painted Bunting, and Dickcissel. Bell's Vireo, Northern Parula, and Yellow-breasted Chat are most likely along the river. Walk the roads at dusk and dawn in spring and early summer to find owls and nightjars: Eastern Screech-Owl, Great Horned and Barred Owls, Lesser and Common Nighthawks, **Pauraque,** and, occasionally, Chuck-will's-widow.

Bird the open fields (**B**) within and adjacent to the park in spring and summer for Cattle Egret, Wild Turkey, Northern Bobwhite, Greater Roadrunner, Cactus Wren, Eastern Bluebird, Lark and Grasshopper Sparrows, Red-winged Blackbird, and Eastern Meadowlark. Groove-billed Ani (rare), **Couch's Kingbird,** Northern Mockingbird, Pyrrhuloxia, Bronzed Cowbird, and Lesser Goldfinch frequent the brushy edges and fence rows. Overhead one can often find Black and Turkey Vultures, **White-tailed Hawk,** Red-tailed Hawk, Crested Caracara, Common Nighthawk, and Cliff and Barn Swallows. White-tailed Kite, Harris's Hawk, Lesser Nighthawk, and Cave Swallow are less numerous. In winter Sandhill Crane, Burrowing Owl (irregular), and American and Sprague's Pipits utilize the open fields. Osprey utilize the river.

Neotropical migrants are best found along the River Trail—more than 150 species pass through the area in migration. These include 18 species of flycatchers,

110 Goliad State Park

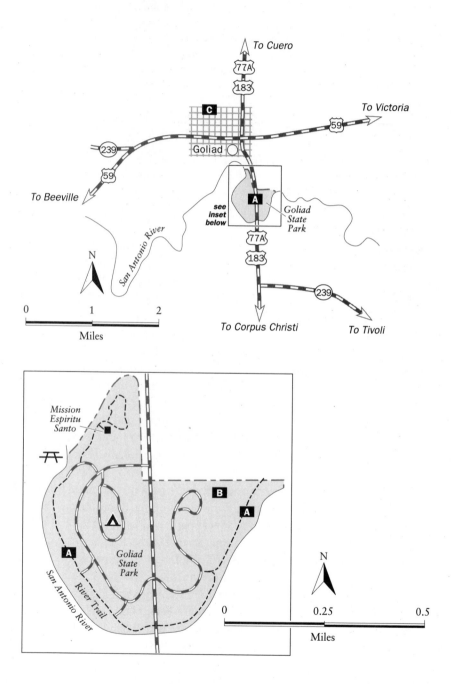

7 thrushes, 6 vireos, 36 warblers, 3 tanagers, and 27 grosbeaks, buntings, and sparrows. Mid-April to early May is best. September to mid-November can produce a good assortment of southbound migrants.

Some urban yards in downtown Goliad (C) provide feeders that attract **Buff-bellied Hummingbird.**

Directions: Take US 183 south from Goliad (on US 59) for 0.3 mile to the park entrance on the right.

General information: This site lies along the San Antonio River, which is the dividing line between the Tamaulipan scrub and the eastern deciduous forests. Several eastern birds, including Ruby-throated Hummingbird, Red-bellied Woodpecker, Great Crested Flycatcher, American Crow, Blue Jay, and Carolina Chickadee, reach the southern limits of their breeding grounds in the area. **Buff-bellied Hummingbird, Golden-fronted Woodpecker, Brown-crested Flycatcher, Long-billed Thrasher,** and **Olive Sparrow** reach the northern limits of their breeding grounds here.

This 2,208-acre state historical park was established to preserve Mission Espiritu Santo (relocated here from near Matagorda Bay in 1724). Other historical features include the Fannin Battlefield (9 miles east of Goliad), site of the 1836 Battle of Coleto Creek; restored Presidio la Bahia, where the Texas troops were executed on orders from the Mexican general Santa Anna; and the Goliad County Courthouse, built in 1894. A huge oak tree on the north courthouse lawn became known as the "hanging tree."

Recreational facilities include playgrounds, two hiking trails, and a nearby swimming pool. The 1.5-mile River Trail follows the river between the picnic area and the primitive campsites. The 0.3-mile Nature Trail, beginning at the Mission Espiritu Santo parking area, follows a loop route through Tamaulipan scrub and bottomland forest.

ADDITIONAL HELP

Location: Texas Official Travel Map grid T x 18; Goliad County
Nearest food, gas, and lodging: Goliad has facilities for all three.
Nearest camping: On-site (24 sites)
Contact: Superintendent, Goliad State Park (see Appendix C)

▐111▌ Choke Canyon State Park and James E. Daugherty Wildlife Management Area

Habitats: Lake, wetland, riparian, mesquite grassland, Tamaulipan scrub, field

Key birds: Neotropic Cormorant, Anhinga, Black-bellied Whistling-Duck, Mottled Duck, Harris's Hawk, Crested Caracara, Scaled Quail, Greater Roadrunner, Groove-billed Ani, **Pauraque, Golden-fronted Woodpecker,** Vermilion Flycatcher, Cave Swallow, Cactus Wren, **Long-billed Thrasher,** Curve-billed Thrasher, **Olive Sparrow,** Pyrrhuloxia, and Bronzed Cowbird are present year-round. Roseate Spoonbill; Wood Stork; **White-tailed Hawk;** Lesser and Common Nighthawks; Black-chinned Hummingbird; **Green Kingfisher;** Ash-throated, Brown-crested, and Scissor-tailed Flycatchers; **Couch's Kingbird;** Prothonotary Warbler; Painted Bunting; Dickcissel; and Hooded Oriole occur in summer. American White Pelican; Osprey; Bald Eagle; Ferruginous Hawk; Sandhill Crane; Say's Phoebe; Sage Thrasher; Sprague's Pipit; Clay-colored, Brewer's, LeConte's, and Harris's Sparrows; Lark Bunting; and McCown's Longspur can usually be found in winter.

Best times to bird: April to mid-May for spring migrants and nesting activities; November to March for winter birds

Birding strategies: Look for unusual spring migrants below the dam in the riparian habitat along the Frio River in the South Shore Unit (**A**) of Choke Canyon State Park. The majority of the more than 65 neotropical migrants that pass through the area, including 15 vireo and warbler species, have been recorded here. A few remain and nest in this area: Black-chinned Hummingbird, **Green Kingfisher, Couch's Kingbird,** and Prothonotary Warbler. Cliff, Cave, and Barn Swallows nest on the shelters in the picnic area below the dam.

You can find resident Harris's Hawk, Crested Caracara, Scaled Quail, Groove-billed Ani, Bewick's Wren, Tufted Titmouse, Northern Mockingbird, **Long-billed Thrasher,** Curve-billed Thrasher, Pyrrhuloxia, and **Olive Sparrow** in the brush adjacent to the Calliham Unit (**B**) of the park. Mesquite grassland birds, such as Common Ground-Dove; Greater Roadrunner; Vermilion, Ash-throated, and Scissor-tailed Flycatchers; Loggerhead Shrike; Lark Sparrow; Painted Bunting; and Dickcissel, can be expected in summer within the campgrounds and surrounding areas in both the Calliham and South Shore units, as well as within the James E. Daugherty Wildlife Management Area (**C**). Less numerous/obvious birds in these areas include Barn, Great Horned, and Barred Owls; Eastern Screech-Owl; Lesser and Common Nighthawk; **Pauraque;** and Hooded Oriole.

Bird along the Frio River in the South Shore Unit for riparian species such as Black-chinned Hummingbird, Brown-crested Flycatcher, **Couch's Kingbird,** White-eyed Vireo, Prothonotary Warbler, Blue Grosbeak, and Painted Bunting. A few water birds, including Neotropic Cormorant, Anhinga, Green Heron, Black-bellied

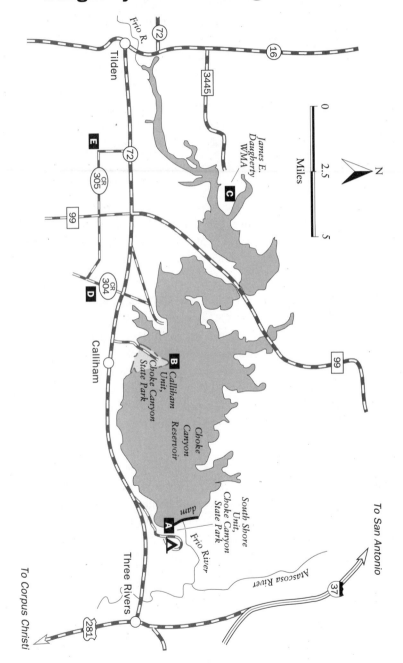

Whistling-Duck, and Mottled Duck frequent the river. Waders, gulls, and terns are most common along the reservoir. In winter American White Pelican, Osprey, Bald Eagle, and a wide variety of waterfowl can be found.

Check the county roads south of SH 72 in all seasons. In winter a stock tank east of CR 304 (D) supports a variety of waterfowl, including Black-bellied Whistling-Duck and Mottled Duck; the dense Tamaulipan scrub along CR 305 (E) harbors Verdin, Cactus Wren, **Long-billed Thrasher,** Curve-billed Thrasher, and Black-throated Sparrow. In winter check the open fields for geese; various raptors, including Ferruginous Hawk; Sandhill Crane; American and Sprague's Pipits; Lark Bunting; and McCown's Longspur. Weedy areas harbor Sage Thrasher; Green-tailed Towhee; and Clay-colored, Brewer's, LeConte's, and Harris's Sparrows.

Records of Review Species: Anna's Hummingbird, Dec 1994, Nov–Dec 1995. Red-headed Woodpecker, Oct 1994. Yellow-bellied Flycatcher, May 1996. Tropical Parula, May 1996.

Directions: Take SH 72 for 4.2 miles west of Three Rivers (on US 281) to the South Shore Unit entrance, or an additional 10.2 miles west on SH 72 to the Calliham Unit. The James E. Daugherty Wildlife Management Area is northeast of Tilden. Take SH 16 north from Tilden to FM 3445, turn right, and drive to the end of the road.

General information: This state park was opened in 1986, and features fishing and boating on the 26,000-surface-acre Choke Canyon Reservoir, created to supply water to Corpus Christi. The Calliham Unit has a recreational complex that includes an auditorium with a gymnasium; an Olympic-size swimming pool and bathhouse; tennis, shuffleboard, and basketball courts; and a baseball diamond.

The area was named for the steep banks near the dam site that choked the Frio River during floods. The James A. Daugherty Wildlife Management Area is primarily a hunting area, but it also contains a birding trail through brush.

ADDITIONAL HELP

Location: Texas Official Travel Map grid T x 16; McMullen and Live Oak counties
Nearest food, gas, and lodging: Food, gas, and lodging are available in Calliham (entrance to Calliham Unit). Lodging is also available at Nolan Ryan's Bass Inn (discount to birders) in Three Rivers.
Nearest camping: On-site at Calliham (60 sites) and South Shore (45 sites)
Contact: Superintendent, Choke Canyon State Park (see Appendix C)

112 Lake Corpus Christi State Park

Habitats: Lake, river, riparian, oak-hackberry savannah, Tamaulipan scrub

Key birds: Least Grebe, Neotropic Cormorant, Anhinga, **White-tailed Hawk,** Harris's Hawk, Crested Caracara, Wild Turkey, Scaled Quail, **White-tipped Dove,** Greater Roadrunner, **Pauraque, Green Kingfisher, Golden-fronted Woodpecker, Great Kiskadee, Green Jay,** Cactus Wren, **Long-billed Thrasher,** Pyrrhuloxia, **Olive Sparrow,** Cassin's and Black-throated Sparrows, and **Audubon's Oriole** are present year-round. Least Bittern; Wood Stork; Fulvous and Black-bellied Whistling-Ducks; Purple Gallinule; Least Tern; Black Skimmer; Groove-billed Ani; Lesser and Common Nighthawks; **Buff-bellied Hummingbird;** Vermilion, Ash-throated, Brown-crested, and Scissor-tailed Flycatchers; **Couch's Kingbird;** Cliff and Cave Swallows; Painted Bunting; Dickcissel; and Grasshopper Sparrow occur in summer. American Bittern, Virginia Rail, Sora, Sandhill Crane, Burrowing and Short-eared Owls, Sprague's Pipit, and Lark Bunting can usually be found in winter.

Best times to bird: April and May for spring migrants and nesting activities; September for migrating raptors

Birding strategies: Look for water birds, waders, waterfowl, gulls, and terns from a boat or points of land near the camping areas (A). In winter the more common waterfowl include Green-winged and Blue-winged Teal, Mallard, Northern Shoveler, Gadwall, American Wigeon, Canvasback, Redhead, Ring-necked Duck, Lesser Scaup, and Hooded Merganser. Fewer numbers of Wood Duck, Cinnamon Teal, Bufflehead, and Red-breasted Merganser can be expected. In summer Wood Stork, Fulvous and Black-bellied Whistling-Ducks, Least Tern, and Black Skimmer are possible.

The various sheltered coves, such as the one near Camping Area 1 (B), as well as the area below the dam (C), support wetlands where the more secretive birds can be found. Look for **Least Grebe,** Pied-billed Grebe, Neotropic Cormorant, Anhinga, Least Bittern, Black-crowned Night-Heron, Purple Gallinule, and **Green Kingfisher** in summer. The adjacent riparian habitats support **White-tipped Dove,** White-winged Dove, Yellow-billed Cuckoo, Barred Owl, **Pauraque,** Black-chinned Hummingbird, **Great Kiskadee, Couch's Kingbird,** Western Kingbird, **Green Jay,** White-eyed and Bell's Vireos, Summer Tanager, Blue Grosbeak, Painted Bunting, and Orchard and Bullock's Orioles.

Nesting birds of the Tamaulipan scrub habitat, such as that within and adjacent to the campground (A), along PR 25 (D) and in the Girl Scout Area (E), include Wild Turkey; Scaled Quail; Common Ground-Dove; Greater Roadrunner; Groove-billed Ani; Common Poorwill; **Buff-bellied Hummingbird; Golden-fronted Woodpecker;** Vermilion, Ash-throated, Brown-crested, and Scissor-tailed Flycatchers; **Couch's Kingbird; Green Jay;** Cactus Wren; Eastern Bluebird; **Long-billed Thrasher;** Curve-billed Thrasher; Pyrrhuloxia; **Olive Sparrow,** Cassin's and

112 Lake Corpus Christi State Park

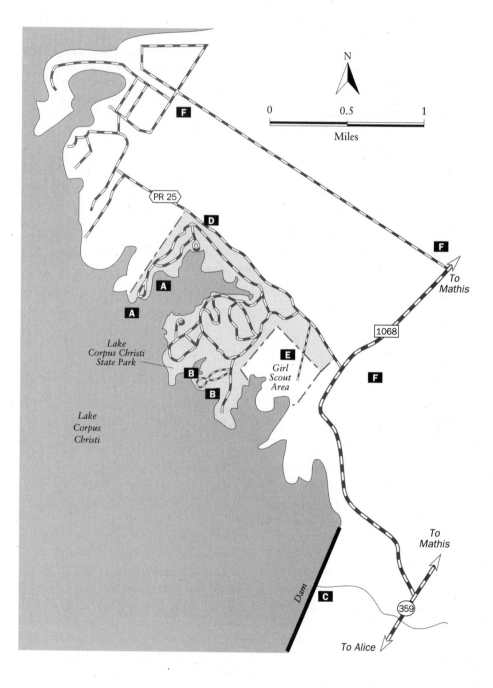

Betty Wauer searching for waterfowl at Lake Corpus Christi State Park.

Black-throated Sparrows; and **Audubon's Oriole**. Watch overhead or on utility poles for Harris's Hawk, Crested Caracara, Common and Lesser Nighthawks, and Cliff and Cave Swallows.

Look in the open pastures and fields adjacent to the state park (**F**) for **White-tailed Hawk**, Common and Lesser Nighthawks, Scissor-tailed Flycatcher, Dickcissel, and Grasshopper Sparrow in summer. In winter Greater White-fronted, Snow, and Canada Geese; Northern Harrier; Sandhill Crane; Burrowing and Short-eared Owls; American and Sprague's Pipits; Loggerhead Shrike; various sparrows; Lark Bunting; Western Meadowlark; and Brewer's Blackbird can be found here.

This area is near enough to the Gulf of Mexico for occasional spring fallouts when neotropical migrants can be abundant in almost every habitat; a total of 35 species of warblers has been recorded in the state park. The area just below the Wesley Seale Dam can be very good in spring, and the wetlands below the south end of the dam usually produce the most water birds.

Directions: The park is 35 miles northwest of Corpus Christi. From I-37 at Mathis, take FM 1068 south for 6 miles to PR 25, the park entrance road.

General information: This 365-acre state park is situated at the southeastern corner of Lake Corpus Christi, which is 24 miles long, has more than 200 miles of shoreline, and covers 15,500 acres. The lake serves as a principal source of water for Corpus Christi. It also provides a popular boating (two ramps), fishing (two lighted piers), picnicking, and swimming area. Weekends and holidays can be extremely crowded, so birding is best in the early morning hours.

Lake Corpus Christi covers the old channel of the Nueces River, which was once a disputed boundary between the United States and Mexico. Some of the land was once inhabited by Karankawa and Lipan Apache Indians. The eighteenth- and nineteenth-century settlements that were once here are now either covered by the lake or deserted.

ADDITIONAL HELP

Location: Texas Official Travel Map grid U x 16; San Patricio County
Nearest food, gas, lodging: Food and gas are available in the park at the concession building. Lodging can be found at Mathis (6 miles).
Nearest camping: On-site (48 sites)
Contact: Superintendent, Lake Corpus Christi State Park (see Appendix C)

113 Lake Casa Blanca State Park

Habitats: Lake, creek, marsh, Tamaulipan scrub, mesquite grassland, field
Key birds: Neotropic Cormorant, Black-bellied Whistling-Duck, Harris's Hawk, Crested Caracara, Scaled Quail, Greater Roadrunner, **Ringed Kingfisher, Green Kingfisher, Golden-fronted Woodpecker,** Vermilion Flycatcher, **Great Kiskadee,** Cave Swallow, **Green Jay,** Chihuahuan Raven, Verdin, Cactus Wren, Black-tailed Gnatcatcher, **Long-billed Thrasher,** Pyrrhuloxia, **Olive Sparrow,** and Black-throated Sparrow are present year-round. Least Tern, Lesser Nighthawk, Common Poorwill, Brown-crested and Scissor-tailed Flycatchers, **Couch's Kingbird,** Summer Tanager, Painted Bunting, and Hooded Oriole occur in summer. American White Pelican, Osprey, Ferruginous Hawk, and Clay-colored Sparrow can usually be found in winter.
Best times to bird: April and May for migrants and nesting activities

Birding strategies: The most productive area is the north shore road (**A**) that passes two fingers of the lake, where open water and cattail marsh habitats are readily available. Expected year-round wetland species include Pied-billed Grebe; Neotropic Cormorant; Great Blue and Tricolored Herons; Great, Snowy, and Cattle Egrets; Black-bellied Whistling-Duck; Common Moorhen; American Coot; Killdeer; **Ringed Kingfisher; Green Kingfisher;** Common Yellowthroat; and Red-winged Blackbird. In summer watch for Green Heron and Least Tern. In winter Green-winged and Blue-winged Teal, Mallard, Northern Pintail, Northern Shoveler, Gadwall, American Wigeon, Lesser Scaup, Ruddy Duck, Spotted and Least Sandpipers, Belted Kingfisher, and Marsh Wren can be expected. The open shoreline, especially at the end of the north shore road, in the Ranchito/Group Facility (**B**), offers good habitat for migratory shorebirds in March and April and again in late August to October.

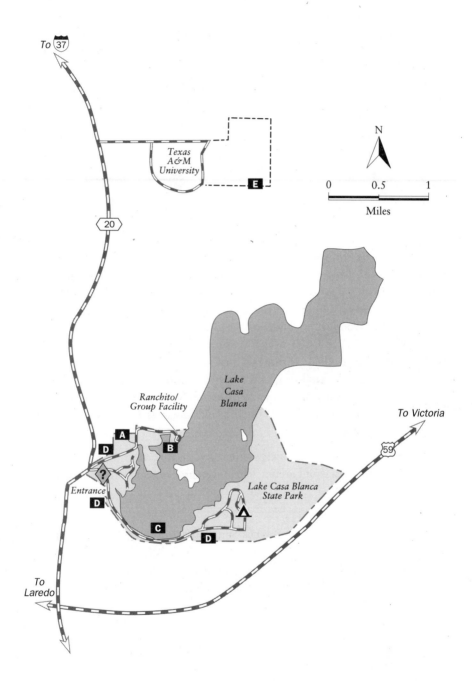

Scan the lake (**C**) for Ring-billed Gull and Forster's Tern year-round. In summer expect Least Tern; winter birds include Eared Grebe, American White Pelican, Double-crested Cormorant, and Osprey. The large island in the center of the lake provides protected roosting sites for numerous waders and other birds throughout the year. Cave Swallow can usually be found overhead year-round, and Cliff and Barn Swallows in summer.

The mesquite grasslands (**D**) near the park entrance and along the southeast lakeshore provide habitat for a variety of year-round species: Cattle Egret, **Golden-fronted Woodpecker**, Ladder-backed Woodpecker, Vermilion Flycatcher, **Great Kiskadee,** Northern Mockingbird, European Starling, Pyrrhuloxia, Great-tailed Grackle, and Brown-headed Cowbird. Summer birds include Brown-crested and Scissor-tailed Flycatchers, **Couch's Kingbird,** Summer Tanager, and Bullock's Oriole. In winter these areas are utilized by Northern Flicker, Eastern Phoebe, American Robin, American Pipit, Loggerhead Shrike, Yellow-rumped Warbler, Chipping and Savannah Sparrows, Eastern Meadowlark, and American Goldfinch.

The area's only native habitat, Tamaulipan scrub, occurs along the outer edge of the park (the northwest corner and north of the county road), between the park and Texas A&M University (**E**). Year-round residents here include Harris's and Red-tailed Hawks, Crested Caracara, Northern Bobwhite, Scaled Quail, Mourning Dove, Common Ground-Dove, Greater Roadrunner, Great Horned Owl, **Golden-fronted Woodpecker,** Ladder-backed Woodpecker, **Green Jay,** Chihuahuan Raven, Verdin, Cactus and Bewick's Wrens, Black-tailed Gnatcatcher, Northern Mockingbird, **Long-billed Thrasher,** Curve-billed Thrasher, White-eyed Vireo, Northern Cardinal, Pyrrhuloxia, **Olive Sparrow,** and Black-throated Sparrow. In summer White-winged Dove; Lesser and Common Nighthawks; Common Poorwill; Say's Phoebe; Ash-throated, Brown-crested, and Scissor-tailed Flycatchers; Painted Bunting; and Hooded Oriole can be found here.

Directions: The state park entrance is situated at the junction of US 59 and PR 20, on the northeastern edge of Laredo. The university lies just north of the state park along Industrial Road. The area of native vegetation (located south of campus and north of the lake) must be reached from the university grounds.

General information: Lake Casa Blanca State Park (formerly Laredo City Park) is in a developmental stage and is without a bird checklist. All observations should be submitted to the park. The park contains a 1,656-acre lake that is among the state's best for black bass fishing. It is located adjacent to a golf course and airport.

ADDITIONAL HELP

Location: Texas Official Travel Map grid W x 14; Webb County
Nearest food, gas, and lodging: Laredo has facilities for all three.
Nearest camping: On-site (partial hookups and primitive sites)
Contact: Superintendent, Lake Casa Blanca State Park (see Appendix C)

Rio Grande Valley Region

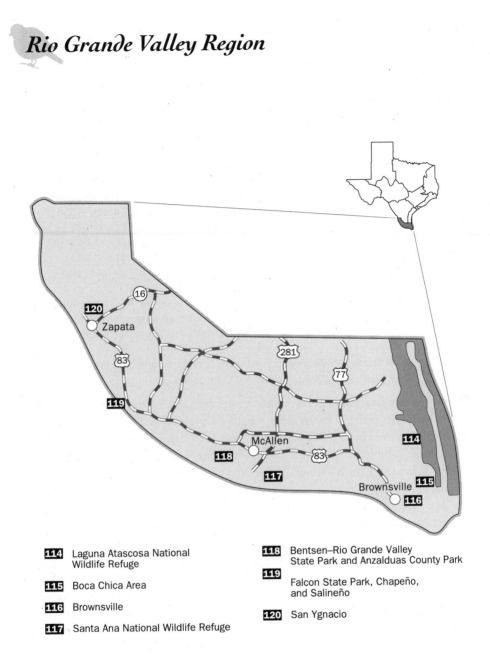

114 Laguna Atascosa National Wildlife Refuge

115 Boca Chica Area

116 Brownsville

117 Santa Ana National Wildlife Refuge

118 Bentsen–Rio Grande Valley State Park and Anzalduas County Park

119 Falcon State Park, Chapeño, and Salineño

120 San Ygnacio

114 Laguna Atascosa National Wildlife Refuge

Habitats: Bay, estuary, lake, mud flat, marsh, coastal prairie, coastal scrub, mesquite grassland, field, cropland

Key birds: Least Grebe, Neotropic Cormorant, Reddish Egret, White and White-faced Ibis, Roseate Spoonbill, Black-bellied Whistling-Duck, Mottled Duck, Harris's Hawk, **White-tailed Hawk,** Crested Caracara, Aplomado Falcon (reintroduced), **Plain Chachalaca,** Gull-billed Tern, **White-tipped Dove,** Greater Roadrunner, **Pauraque, Ringed Kingfisher, Green Kingfisher, Golden-fronted Woodpecker,** Northern Beardless-Tyrannulet, **Great Kiskadee, Couch's Kingbird, Green Jay,** Cactus Wren, **Long-billed Thrasher,** and **Olive Sparrow** are present year-round. Magnificent Frigatebird, Least Bittern, Wood Stork, Purple Gallinule, Groove-billed Ani, Lesser and Common Nighthawks, **Buff-bellied Hummingbird,** Brown-crested and Scissor-tailed Flycatchers, Chihuahuan Raven, Tropical Parula, Varied and Painted Buntings, Dickcissel, Botteri's and Cassin's Sparrows, and Hooded Oriole occur in summer. Osprey, Peregrine and Prairie Falcons, Sandhill Crane, Burrowing and Short-eared Owls, Vermilion Flycatcher, Sage Thrasher, Green-tailed Towhee, Clay-colored and LeConte's Sparrows, and **Altamira Oriole** can usually be found in winter.

Best times to bird: April and May for spring migrants and breeding activities; November to March for winter birds

Birding strategies: Start at the visitor center by walking the short (one-eighth mile) Kiskadee Trail (**A**) for migrant songbirds in spring and fall and a variety of breeding birds, including the irregular Yellow-green Vireo. Expected full-time residents here include **White-tipped Dove, Pauraque, Golden-fronted Woodpecker, Great Kiskadee, Couch's Kingbird, Green Jay,** Tufted (Black-crested) Titmouse, White-eyed Vireo, Northern Cardinal, Great-tailed Grackle, and Bronzed and Brown-headed Cowbirds. Yellow-billed Cuckoo, **Buff-bellied Hummingbird,** Barn Swallow, and Hooded Oriole occur in summer.

Walk the 1.5-mile Mesquite Trail (**B**) through mesquite grasslands and past two small ponds (wet years only). In summer expect Northern Bobwhite; Mourning Dove; Common Ground-Dove; Greater Roadrunner; Brown-crested and Scissor-tailed Flycatchers; Verdin; Cactus and Bewick's Wrens; Northern Mockingbird; **Long-billed Thrasher;** Curve-billed Thrasher; **Olive Sparrow;** Botteri's, Cassin's, and Lark Sparrows; and Eastern Meadowlark. Less numerous are Northern Beardless-Tyrannulet, Chihuahuan Raven, **Tropical Parula,** Summer Tanager, Varied and Painted Buntings, and Orchard Oriole. Overhead one often can find White-tailed Kite, Harris's Hawk, **White-tailed Hawk,** Crested Caracara, Common Nighthawk at dawn and dusk, and Chihuahuan Raven.

In winter the Kiskadee Trail and Mesquite Trail areas consistently harbor Eastern Phoebe, Ash-throated Flycatcher, House and Sedge Wrens, Ruby-crowned Kinglet, Blue-gray Gnatcatcher, Hermit Thrush, American Robin, Loggerhead Shrike, Orange-crowned and Yellow-rumped Warblers, and numerous sparrows, including

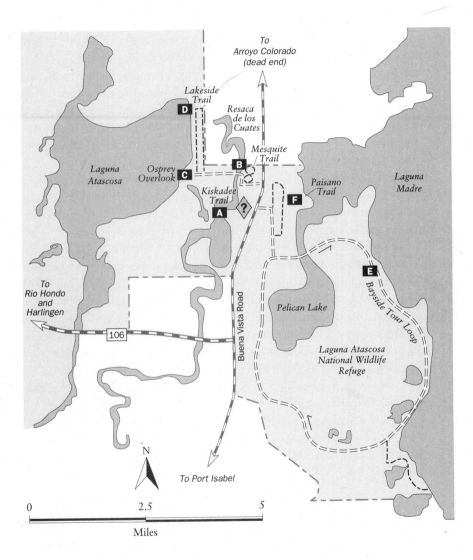

To
Arroyo Colorado
(dead end)

Lakeside
Trail

Resaca
de los
Cuates

Mesquite
Trail

D

Laguna
Atascosa

Osprey
Overlook

C

B

Paisano
Trail

Laguna
Madre

Kiskadee
Trail

A ?

F

E

To
Rio Hondo
and
Harlingen

Buena Vista Road

Pelican Lake

Bayside Tour Loop

Laguna Atascosa
National Wildlife
Refuge

106

N

To Port Isabel

0   2.5   5

Miles

Vesper, Savannah, and Lincoln's. Black and Say's Phoebes; Vermilion Flycatcher; Eastern and Mountain Bluebirds; Sage Thrasher; various other warblers; Western Tanager; Black-headed Grosbeak; Indigo Bunting; Green-tailed and Eastern Towhees; Clay-colored, Field, Grasshopper, LeConte's, Swamp, and White-throated Sparrows; Lark Bunting and Western Meadowlark are less dependable.

Drive to Osprey Overlook (**C**), stopping at the Resaca de los Cuates for Neotropic Cormorant; waders, including White and White-faced Ibis and Roseate Spoonbill; waterfowl, such as Black-bellied Whistling-Duck and Mottled Duck; and various shorebirds year-round. Expect Wood Stork in summer. At Osprey Overlook, scope Laguna Atascosa. In winter watch for vagrant water birds, such as Eurasian Wigeon, Oldsquaw, and scoters, among the multitudes of American Coot and more common ducks, such as Green-winged and Blue-winged Teal, Mottled Duck, Northern Pintail, Northern Shoveler, American Wigeon, Canvasback, Redhead, and Ruddy Duck. Greater White-fronted and Snow Geese, Osprey, Peregrine Falcon and Sandhill Crane are seen regularly.

The Lakeside Trail (**D**) makes a 1.5-mile loop north from the Osprey Overlook parking area, and is productive during migration and in early summer. Besides the water birds mentioned above, many of the same birds listed for the Mesquite Trail can be expected. It is a good place to find winter warblers and sparrows.

The highlight of a refuge visit is often the one-way, 15-mile Bayside Tour Loop (**E**), which contains a diversity of habitats. Watch along the entrance and exit for **Plain Chachalaca** and Groove-billed Ani. The paved 1-mile Paisano Trail (**F**) offers brush where Greater Roadrunner, Verdin, **Long-billed Thrasher,** and **Olive Sparrow** reside. Pelican Lake is a good place to look for waders and shorebirds; a Greater Flamingo spent considerable time here during the mid-1990s.

Scope the shoreline and bay from the numerous pullouts along the bayfront. All the waders, including Reddish Egret; a few resident shorebirds, such as Black-bellied Plover, Killdeer, Black-necked Stilt, American Avocet, Greater and Lesser Yellowlegs, Willet, and Long-billed Curlew; Laughing and Ring-billed Gulls; Gull-billed, Caspian, Royal, and Forster's Terns; and Black Skimmer occur year-round. In winter look for Semipalmated and Piping Plovers; Marbled Godwit; Sanderling; Western, Least, and Stilt Sandpipers; Dunlin; and Long-billed Dowitcher. And in summer, watch for Magnificent Frigatebird and Sandwich, Least, and Black Terns.

The Bayside Tour Loop is a good place to find Osprey in winter and **White-tailed Hawk** and Aplomado Falcon year-round (110 falcons were reintroduced on the refuge during the mid- to late 1990s). A hacking platform, used to reintroduce Aplomados to the refuge, may be seen from near the end of the tour loop, to the east just south of Pelican Lake. If you see one of the falcons, try to see which leg is banded. This will help determine if the bird was released from captivity or raised in the wild.

Coastal prairie habitat, utilized by Aplomado Falcons, along the Bayside Tour Loop at Laguna Atascosa National Wildlife Refuge.

Records of Review Species: White-cheeked Pintail, Nov–April 1978/79. Eurasian Wigeon, Nov–Jan 1994/95. Masked Duck, Jan 1968, April–July 1993/94. Red Phalarope, July 1978. Lesser Black-backed Gull, March 1988, Jan 1995. Mangrove Cuckoo, June 1991, April–July 1992. Northern Wheatear, Nov 1994. Orange-billed Nightingale-Thrush, April 1996. Gray Silky-flycatcher, Oct–Nov 1985.

Directions: From Harlingen (on US 77), take FM 106 east to Rio Hondo, and then 15 miles beyond, to the dead end with Buena Vista Road. From there, go 3 miles north to refuge headquarters. From Brownsville, go north on Paredes Line Road (FM 1847) through Los Fresnos to FM 106, then east to Buena Vista Road.

General information: This 45,000-acre national wildlife refuge (NWR) is a must-visit for birders in South Texas; more than 400 species have been reported, representing the highest number in the NWR system. Laguna Atascosa, the 3,100-acre shallow brackish lake, is part of the greater Laguna Madre of Texas and Mexico, which supports 80 percent of North America's wintering Redhead. The refuge also harbors 30 to 35 ocelots (one-third of the entire Texas population). Jaguarundi also is a resident.

Numerous gunnery ranges and related structures, left over from World War I, are often visible within the refuge, especially in the area of the Bayside Tour Loop.

ADDITIONAL HELP

Location: Texas Official Travel Map grid Y/Z x 17/18; Cameron County

Nearest food, gas, and lodging: Food is available at Shooting Center (4 miles). Gas is at Laguna Vista (12 miles). Lodging can be found in Port Isabel (17 miles) and Harlingen (25 miles).

Nearest camping: Adolph Thomae, Jr., County Park, north end of refuge at end of FM 1847, 20 miles from refuge headquarters; 35 full-service sites

Contact: Manager, Laguna Atascosa National Wildlife Refuge (see Appendix C)

115 Boca Chica Area

Habitats: Gulf, beach, dunes, estuary, tidal salt flat, saltwater pond, river, freshwater pond, thorn forest, Tamaulipan scrub, coastal prairie, pasture

Key birds: Least Grebe, American White and Brown Pelicans, Neotropic Cormorant, Reddish Egret, White and White-faced Ibis, Roseate Spoonbill, Black-bellied Whistling-Duck, Mottled Duck, Harris's Hawk, **White-tailed Hawk,** Crested Caracara, **Plain Chachalaca, White-tipped Dove,** Greater Roadrunner, Groove-billed Ani, **Pauraque, Buff-bellied Hummingbird, Ringed Kingfisher, Green Kingfisher, Golden-fronted Woodpecker,** Northern Beardless-Tyrannulet, **Great Kiskadee, Couch's Kingbird, Green Jay, Long-billed Thrasher, Tropical Parula, Olive Sparrow,** and **Altamira Oriole** occur year-round. Anhinga, Magnificent Frigatebird, Least Bittern, Wood Stork, Fulvous Whistling-Duck, Purple Gallinule, Wilson's Plover, Least Tern, Brown-crested Flycatcher, Blue Grosbeak, and Botteri's Sparrow are present in summer. Northern Gannet, Osprey, **White-tailed Hawk,** Merlin, Peregrine Falcon, Snowy and Piping Plovers, and Vermilion Flycatcher can usually be found in winter.

Best times to bird: Mid-March to May for spring migrants and nesting activities; November to March for winter birds

Birding strategies: All of SH 4, beyond the urban environment of Brownsville to the end of the road, is worth birding year-round. Tamaulipan scrub and thorn forest habitats (**A**) dominate the western portion of the area, where most of the arid-land residents can be found. Expect year-round Black and Turkey Vultures; Harris's Hawk; Crested Caracara; **Plain Chachalaca;** White-winged, Mourning, and Inca Doves; Common Ground-Dove; Greater Roadrunner; **Golden-fronted Woodpecker;** Ladder-backed Woodpecker; **Green Jay;** Tufted Titmouse; Verdin; Cactus, Carolina, and Bewick's Wrens; Northern Mockingbird; **Long-billed Thrasher;** White-eyed Vireo; Northern Cardinal; **Olive Sparrow;** and Great-tailed Grackle. Less numerous are **White-tipped Dove,** Groove-billed Ani (irregular), Eastern Screech-Owl, **Pauraque, Buff-bellied Hummingbird,** Northern Beardless-Tyrannulet (irregular), **Tropical Parula** (irregular), Botteri's Sparrow, and **Altamira Oriole.**

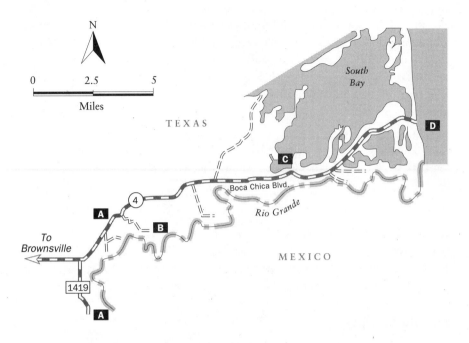

These habitats can be filled with migrants—flycatchers, vireos, warblers, tanagers, orioles, and others—in spring and fall. Brown-crested Flycatcher, **Couch's Kingbird,** Cliff and Barn Swallows, and Blue Grosbeak remain and nest.

To the south of the roadway are numerous ponds (**B**), resacas from the meandering Rio Grande, that offer a different habitat and associated birds, including **Least Grebe** (irregular), Pied-billed Grebe, Neotropic Cormorant, Great Blue and Little Blue Herons, Great and Snowy Egrets, Black-crowned and Yellow-crowned Night-Herons, Black-bellied Whistling-Duck, Mottled Duck, Common Moorhen, American Coot, **Ringed Kingfisher,** and **Green Kingfisher.** Anhinga, Green Heron, Fulvous Whistling-Duck, and Purple Gallinule also occur here in summer. In winter these ponds support Double-crested Cormorant, a wide array of ducks, and occasional rails.

Closer to the coast are extensive tidal flats (**C**) that can be alive with waders and shorebirds during migration. Year-round species here include Tricolored Heron, Reddish Egret, White and White-faced Ibis, Roseate Spoonbill, Killdeer, Black-necked Stilt, Greater and Lesser Yellowlegs, Willet, Long-billed Curlew, Sanderling, Laughing Gull, and Gull-billed and Forster's Terns. Wood Stork can often be found in summer. In winter many more water birds are present. Watch then for Osprey, White-tailed Kite, Northern Harrier, **White-tailed Hawk,** American Kestrel, Merlin, and Peregrine Falcon.

The open estuary, bay, dunes, and beach area at the end of the road (**D**) offer a few additional birds such as American White and Brown Pelicans; American Oystercatcher; and Caspian, Royal, and Black Terns year-round. Magnificent Frigatebird, Wilson's Plover, and Sandwich and Least Terns are here in summer. Common Loon; Eared Grebe; Black-bellied, Snowy, and Piping Plovers; Ruddy Turnstone; and Bonaparte's, Ring-billed, and Herring Gulls can be found in winter. Occasionally wintering Northern Gannet and scoters can be found offshore. The area can be especially productive during migration, when millions of birds pass by.

Records of Review Species: Sooty Shearwater, Jan 1992. Brown Booby, Dec 1987. Purple Sandpiper, Feb–March 1991. Iceland Gull, Jan–Feb 1977. Black-legged Kittiwake, Jan 1991, Jan 1992. Bridled Tern, Sept 1988. Yellow-green Vireo, July 1972.

Directions: From Brownsville, take SH 4 (Boca Chica Boulevard) east from US 77 for 16 miles to the Gulf.

General information: The Boca Chica area does not get the attention from birders that it deserves, so year-round reports are lacking. The area is 1 of 23 units of the Las Palomas Wildlife Management Area, which runs for 120 miles from the mouth of the Rio Grande to the Prieta Unit in Starr County.

ADDITIONAL HELP

Location: Texas Official Travel Map grid Z x 18; Cameron County
Nearest food, gas, and lodging: All are available in Brownsville (16 miles).
Nearest camping: Brownsville; primitive camping allowed on beach at Boca Chica
Contact: Considerable private lands along highway; wetlands and coastal areas are managed under the Las Palomas Wildlife Management Area (see Appendix C)

116 Brownsville

Sabal Palm Grove Audubon Center and Sanctuary and Tamaulipas Crow Sanctuary

Habitats: River, pond, riparian, garden, palm grove, field, pasture, cropland

Key birds: Least Grebe, Neotropic Cormorant, Anhinga, Black-bellied Whistling-Duck, Masked Duck, White-tailed Kite, Harris' Hawk, **White-tailed Hawk,** Crested Caracara, **Plain Chachalaca, White-tipped Dove, Green Parakeet, Red-crowned Parrot, Pauraque, Buff-bellied Hummingbird, Ringed Kingfisher, Green Kingfisher, Golden-fronted Woodpecker,** Brown-crested Flycatcher, **Great Kiskadee,** Tropical Kingbird, **Couch's Kingbird, Green Jay,** Chihuahuan Raven, **Long-billed Thrasher, Olive Sparrow,** Pyrrhuloxia, Bronzed Cowbird, and **Altamira Oriole** are present year-round. Least Bittern, Purple Gallinule, Groove-billed Ani, Elf Owl, Lesser Nighthawk, **Tropical Parula,** Painted Bunting, Dickcissel, and Hooded Oriole occur in summer. Vermilion Flycatcher, **Tamaulipas (Mexican) Crow,** Curve-billed Thrasher, and Lark Bunting can usually be found in winter.

Best times to bird: November to March for winter residents; February to mid-April for unexpected winter visitors; April and May for spring migrants and nesting activities

Birding strategies: Sabal Palm Grove Audubon Center and Sanctuary (A) is the surest place in the valley to see **Buff-bellied Hummingbird;** these come to feeders at the entrance year-round. **Plain Chachalaca, White-tipped Dove, Green Jay, Olive Sparrow,** and **Altamira Oriole** frequent the same feeding station. Check the birder's log inside the headquarters building for any special vagrants that might be present. Then walk the short loop trail, stopping at the blind (overlooking the resaca [pond], which is dry in summer). **Least Grebe;** Neotropic Cormorant; Anhinga; various ducks, including Black-bellied Whistling-Duck and Masked Duck (irregular); **Ringed Kingfisher, Green Kingfisher,** and Belted Kingfisher; **Great Kiskadee;** and Common Yellowthroat occur here in winter. Least Bittern and Purple Gallinule may be present in spring. Golden-crowned Warbler, Gray-crowned Yellowthroat, Crimson-collared Grosbeak, and Blue Bunting have been seen along the trail in recent years. Yellow-throated, Nashville, Black-throated Gray, and Black-throated Green Warblers, and American Redstart are more frequent.

Year-round birds at the sanctuary include Great Horned Owl, **Pauraque, Golden-fronted Woodpecker,** Tufted Titmouse, and **Long-billed Thrasher.** Yellow-billed Cuckoo, Elf Owl, and **Tropical Parula** (irregular) occur in summer.

The adjacent fields and edges near the entrance often contain White-tailed Kite, Harris's Hawk, **White-tailed Hawk,** Crested Caracara, **Couch's Kingbird,** Pyrrhuloxia, and Bronzed Cowbird year-round; Vermilion Flycatcher, Curve-billed Thrasher, a variety of sparrows, and Lark Bunting can often be found in winter; and in summer, watch for Groove-billed Ani, Lesser Nighthawk at dusk and dawn,

Chimney Swift, Brown-crested and Scissor-tailed Flycatchers, Painted Bunting, and Dickcissel.

The Tamaulipas (Mexican) Crow Sanctuary (**B**), also known as the Brownsville Sanitary Landfill, is nearby (north on FM 511), and is the only sure place north of the border to see **Tamaulipas (Mexican) Crow;** these are usually present only during the winter months, but a careful search of the general area may turn up one at almost any time of year. The landfill is open daily except Sundays and closes at 3 P.M. on weekdays. Drive through the gate, using your binoculars as your passport, and continue to the active dumping area. Other expected birds include numerous gulls (primarily Laughing and Ring-billed, but also California, Thayer's, Lesser Black-backed, Slaty-backed, and Glaucous), Chihuahuan Raven, and Great-tailed Grackle. Aplomado Falcon (hacked birds with bands) occasionally are seen here. Continue north on FM 511, a shortcut to Laguna Atascosa National Wildlife Refuge (site 114).

The city of Brownsville offers numerous birding opportunities, but only a few birds that cannot be found more easily elsewhere in the valley. **Green Parakeet** and **Red-crowned Parrot** have taken up residence, and are most likely found in the evening at or en route to their roosts. Their roosting sites change; for current locations, call the local birding hotline: 210-969-2731. The parakeets roost consistently on palms at Fort Brown Hotel (**C**), adjacent to International Crossing. Tropical Kingbird has also taken up residence, and can usually be found at the Saint Joseph Academy (**D**) and in the private community of Rancho Viejo (**E**); park at Casa Grande Clubhouse and walk the neighborhood.

Records of Review Species: Thayer's Gull, Feb 1980, March 1983, Jan 1991, Feb 1992, Feb–March 1997. Slaty-backed Gull, Feb 1992. Ruddy Ground-Dove, Jan 1989. Green-breasted Mango, Sept 1988, June 1989. Cassin's Kingbird, winter 1994. White-throated Robin, Feb 1990. Yellow-green Vireo, June–July 1989. Black-whiskered Vireo, May 1991. Gray-crowned Yellowthroat, Feb–April 1988, March 1989, May–July 1989. Golden-crowned Warbler, Dec–March 1979/80, Jan 1984, Feb–March 1987, Oct–Jan 1989/90. Crimson-collared Grosbeak, Dec–April 1987/88. Blue Bunting, Feb 1988.

Directions: Brownsville lies at the southern end of US 77 and US 83. To reach Sabal Palm Grove Audubon Center and Sanctuary, take Southmost Road (FM 1419) southeast of US 77 for 5.6 miles and turn right on the graveled entrance road. The Brownsville Sanitary Landfill (Tamaulipas Crow Sanctuary) is on FM 511 at the intersection of FM 802. Take SH 48 east from US 77 for 2.9 miles to the signed Y intersection, and proceed to the signed entrance.

General information: Brownsville and its Mexican sister city of Matamoros make up a huge, busy urban area with extensive plantings of tropical trees and shrubs, which attract significant numbers of birds. The landscape south of Matamoros is dominated by vast croplands with very few corridors connecting natural habitats to the south. At least three parrots are now resident in the Greater Brownsville

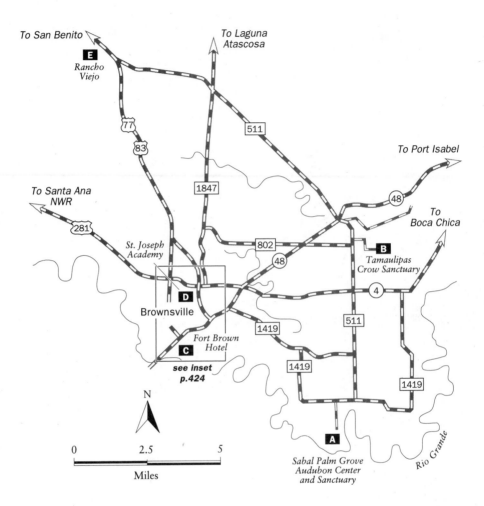

To San Benito

E
Rancho
Viejo

To Laguna
Atascosa

77

83

511

To Port Isabel

To Santa Ana
NWR

281

1847

48

To
Boca Chica

St. Joseph
Academy

802

48

B
Tamaulipas
Crow Sanctuary

D

4

Brownsville

511

Fort Brown
Hotel

C

1419

*see inset
p.424*

1419

1419

N

A

0   2.5   5

Sabal Palm Grove
Audubon Center
and Sanctuary

Rio Grande

Miles

area: Green Parakeet and Red-crowned and Yellow-headed (not yet accepted by the Texas Bird Records Committee) Parrots. Almost every year additional tropical species are found.

Brownsville began in 1846 when Fort Brown was established to defend the Rio Grande as the international boundary, after the republic of Texas became a state. The Brownsville Visitor Information Center, located on US 77 and US 83 (FM 802 exit), contains an information desk and literature about local attractions.

The nearby city of Harlingen is the site for the annual Rio Grande Valley Birding Festival, held each November. Additional information can be obtained from the Harlingen Area Chamber of Commerce (see Appendix C).

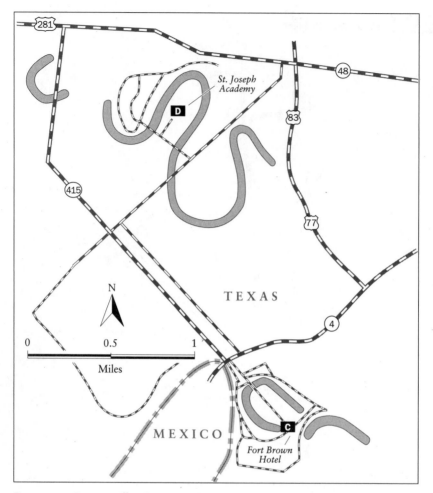

Downtown Brownsville. (See map, page 423)

ADDITIONAL HELP

Location: Texas Official Travel Map grid Z x 17; Cameron County
Nearest food, gas, and lodging: Brownsville has facilities for all three.
Nearest camping: Brownsville
Contact: Manager, Sabal Palm Grove Audubon Center and Sanctuary; Brownsville Sanitary Landfill (Tamaulipas Crow Sanctuary) is owned by the city of Brownsville (see Appendix C)

117 Santa Ana National Wildlife Refuge

Habitats: River, pond, wetland, riparian, thorn forest, Tamaulipan scrub, field, cropland

Key birds: Least Grebe, Neotropic Cormorant, Anhinga, Fulvous and Black-bellied Whistling-Ducks, Mottled Duck, **Hook-billed Kite,** Harris's and Gray Hawks, **White-tailed Hawk, Plain Chachalaca, White-tipped Dove, Pauraque, Buff-bellied Hummingbird, Ringed Kingfisher, Green Kingfisher, Golden-fronted Woodpecker,** Northern Beardless-Tyrannulet, **Great Kiskadee, Green Jay, Clay-colored Robin, Long-billed Thrasher, Tropical Parula, Olive Sparrow,** Pyrrhuloxia, Bronzed Cowbird, **Altamira Oriole,** and **Audubon's Oriole** are present year-round. Least Bittern, White Ibis, Roseate Spoonbill, Purple Gallinule, Groove-billed Ani, Elf Owl, Brown-crested Flycatcher, **Couch's Kingbird,** Painted Bunting, and Dickcissel occur in summer. Crested Caracara, Brown Thrasher, Green-tailed Towhee, Lark Bunting, and Yellow-headed Blackbird can usually be found in winter.

Best times to bird: November to March for winter residents; April and May for spring migrants and nesting activities

Birding strategies: Start your birding day at the levee (**A**) just behind the visitor center. Perched or flying raptors—Hook-billed Kite; White-tailed Kite; Harris's, Gray, and Red-shouldered Hawks; and **White-tailed Hawk**—and even **Red-billed Pigeon** in summer are often visible. Mississippi Kite; Northern Harrier; Sharp-shinned, Cooper's, Broad-winged, Swainson's, Zone-tailed, and Red-tailed Hawks; Crested Caracara; and Common Black-Hawk may be seen in spring, fall, and winter. The wetlands along the levee road are a good place to find Green Kingfisher, Neotropic Cormorant, Sora, Common Moorhen, and American Coot. If the fields north of the levee are flooded, look for White Ibis, Roseate Spoonbill, Wood Stork, and Fulvous and Black-bellied Whistling-Ducks. In winter these fields may also contain Lark Bunting and Yellow-headed Blackbird. Willow and Pintail lakes and the surrounding woodlands can be birded by trails from the refuge visitor center. Willow Lake (**B**) (accessible by Trail A or Trail B) is a good place to find **Least Grebe,** Neotropic Cormorant, Mottled and Masked (irregular) Ducks, **Ringed Kingfisher, Green Kingfisher, Great Kiskadee,** and Red-winged Blackbird year-round. Two observation points, one with a blind, provide good views of the lake and cattails. Woodland birds along the trail include **Plain Chachalaca, White-tipped Dove, Golden-fronted Woodpecker, Green Jay, Long-billed Thrasher, Olive Sparrow,** and **Altamira Oriole. Pauraques,** present year-round, are best detected before dawn and after dusk by their distinct song *("go-weeeeer").*

Pintail Lake (**C**) (accessible by Trail C) is an open environment, offering a slightly different assortment of birds. Waders, waterfowl, and shorebirds are especially common in winter. In spring and summer, look for Anhinga, Least Bittern, and Purple Gallinule. The weedy fields and edges sometimes harbor Groove-billed Ani, Brown-crested and Scissor-tailed Flycatchers, **Couch's Kingbird,** Pyrrhuloxia,

117 Santa Ana National Wildlife Refuge

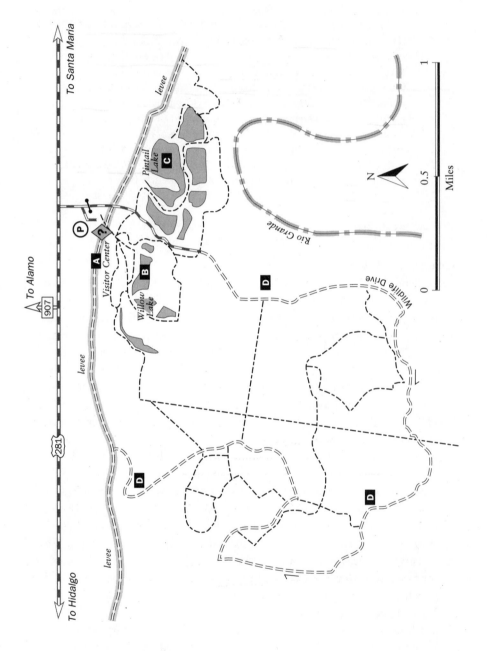

Trailhead at Santa Ana National Wildlife Refuge.

Painted Bunting, Dickcissel, and Bronzed Cowbird. In winter Brown Thrasher, Green-tailed Towhee, and various sparrows can be found here.

En route to Pintail Lake, check the blind behind the lot that was once the site of the manager's house, located along the tour road. The red-flowering shrimp plants here attract **Buff-bellied Hummingbird**. The immediate area also seems to appeal to Northern Beardless-Tyrannulet, **Tropical Parula**, and **Clay-colored Robin**. These birds are not dependable; it is wise to check the birder's log at the visitor's center for the most recent sightings.

Also take the 7-mile, one-way Wildlife Drive (**D**), on your own if possible. From mid-January to mid-April it is accessible only by tram. The tram runs every two hours, and a fee is charged. Birders can get off and on at various stops: High-land Trail, Old Cemetery, Owl and Resaca trails, Vireo Trail, Jaguarundi Trail, Mesquite Trail, Cattail Lake, and Terrace Trail. The best birding stops should depend on your review of the birding log.

Records of Review Species: Crane Hawk, Dec–April 1987/88. Roadside Hawk, Oct–Feb 1982/83. Short-tailed Hawk, Oct 1994. Northern Jacana, Nov 1982, Feb–March 1993, Sept–Oct 1993, April–May 1994. Curlew Sandpiper, May 1994, May 1996. Ruddy Ground-Dove, Oct 1984. Mangrove Cuckoo, Aug 1982. Green-breasted Mango, Aug 1993. Broad-billed Hum-mingbird, Dec–Feb 1985/86. Rose-throated Becard, Dec 1987, Dec 1988, Feb 1990, Jan–March 1993, Feb–Mar 1996, Aug 1997. Gray-crowned Yellowthroat, March 1989. Golden-crowned Warbler, Jan 1984, Dec–March 1987/88, Jan–Feb 1990. Crimson-collared Grosbeak, Dec 1987. Blue Bunting, Oct 1985, Dec–Jan 1987/88. Yellow-faced Grassquit, Jan 1990.

Directions: The refuge is 7.5 miles south of Alamo (on US 83), via FM 907 and a slight jog east on US 281 to the entrance.

General information: Considered one of the gems of the national wildlife refuge system, the 2,000-acre Santa Ana National Wildlife Refuge is the heart of the Rio Grande Valley Wildlife Corridor, a multi-agency project to protect tracts of native landscape between Falcon Dam and the mouth of the Rio Grande. For birders it is one of the must-visit sites in the lower valley. Although the tour route gate does not open until 9 A.M. and closes at 4 P.M., the main gate off Highway 281 is open from sunrise to sunset, permitting foot access.

The 7-mile Wildlife Drive, 12 miles of foot trails, and 3 photo blinds provide excellent birding. The visitor center has exhibits and a good bookstore. Bird walks are available throughout the winter and early spring; see the posted schedule at the visitor center for details.

ADDITIONAL HELP

Location: Texas Official Travel Map grid Z x 16; Hidalgo County
Nearest food, gas, and lodging: All can be found along US 83 (7 miles to the north).
Nearest camping: Bentsen–Rio Grande Valley State Park (25 miles)
Contact: Manager, Santa Ana National Wildlife Refuge (see Appendix C)

118 Bentsen–Rio Grande Valley State Park and Anzalduas County Park

Habitats: River, pond, marsh, riparian, thorn forest, Tamaulipan scrub, mesquite grassland, field, cropland

Key birds: Least Grebe, Neotropic Cormorant, Anhinga, Fulvous and Black-bellied Whistling-Ducks, **Masked Duck, Hook-billed Kite,** White-tailed Kite, Harris's and Gray Hawks, **White-tailed Hawk, Plain Chachalaca, Red-billed Pigeon, White-tipped Dove,** Groove-billed Ani, **Pauraque, Buff-bellied Hummingbird, Ringed Kingfisher, Green Kingfisher, Golden-fronted Woodpecker,** Northern Beardless-Tyrannulet, **Great Kiskadee, Green Jay, Clay-colored Robin** (irregular), **Long-billed Thrasher, Olive Sparrow,** Pyrrhuloxia, Bronzed Cowbird, **Altamira Oriole,** and **Audubon's Oriole** are present year-round. Roseate Spoonbill, Wood Stork, Purple Gallinule, Elf Owl, Brown-crested Flycatcher, Western Kingbird, **Tropical Parula,** Varied and Painted Buntings, and Dickcissel occur in summer. Merlin and Peregrine Falcon can usually be found in winter.

Best times to bird: November to March for year-round and winter residents; April and May for spring migrants and nesting activities

Birding strategies: The campground trailer loop (**A**), especially between sites 1 to 35 where campers put out all types of bird feed, offers the best birding. A stroll

118 Bentsen–Rio Grande Valley State Park

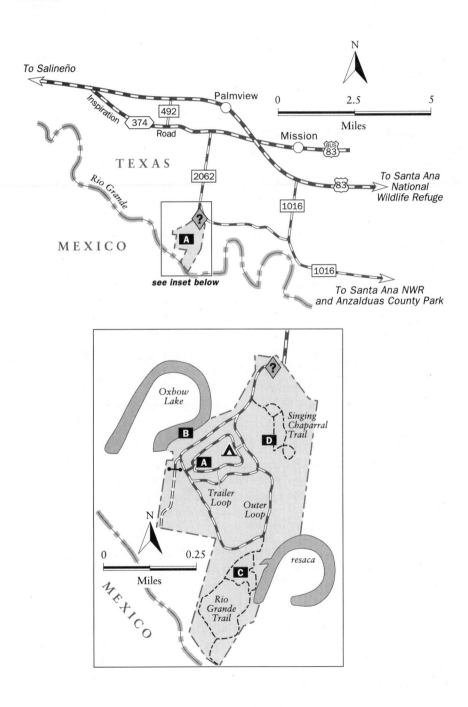

through this area is likely to produce **Plain Chachalaca, Golden-fronted Wood-pecker, Great Kiskadee, Green Jay, Long-billed Thrasher, Olive Sparrow, Altamira Oriole,** and **Audubon's Oriole.** Other less obvious birds of interest are Harris's and Gray Hawks, White-winged Dove, Brown-crested Flycatcher, Curve-billed Thrasher, White-eyed Vireo, Pyrrhuloxia, Painted and Blue (irregular) Buntings, and Bronzed Cowbird.

Walk the outer loop after dark and listen for Barn, Great Horned, and Elf (summer) Owls; Eastern Screech-Owl; Lesser (irregular) and Common Nighthawks; and **Pauraque.** Common Poorwill, Chuck-will's-widow, and Whip-poor-will are also possible in migration.

Oxbow Lake (**B**), a resaca along the western edge of the park, is a great place to look for water birds and other visitors. Watch for Neotropic Cormorant, Anhinga, Roseate Spoonbill and Wood Stork in summer, gulls, terns, Fulvous and Black-bellied Whistling-Ducks, White-tailed Kite, Gray Hawk, Merlin, Peregrine Falcon, **Ringed Kingfisher, Green Kingfisher, Couch's Kingbird, Great Kiskadee,** Great-tailed Grackle, and **Altamira Oriole.** In spring and summer, Elf Owl may nest in utility poles near the boat ramp or group shelter.

Thorn forest and Tamaulipan scrub birds, including **Hook-billed Kite,** can sometimes be found along the Rio Grande (**C**) or Singing Chaparral (**D**) trails. However, this Mexican raptor can be elusive, and one should check at park headquarters about the most recent reports. Other specialty birds possible along these trails include Red-billed Pigeon, usually along the river; Groove-billed Ani; Northern Beardless-Tyrannulet; **Clay-colored Robin;** and Tropical Parula.

Bird Anzalduas County Park, only 5 miles east, for year-round residents. Although about the same birds can be expected, Anzalduas contains slightly different habitat, including better views of the Rio Grande and more extensive weedy fields. In winter a variety of sparrows and allies can be expected.

Records of Review Species: Jabiru, Aug 1985. Roadside Hawk, Oct–Feb 1982/83. Short-tailed Hawk, March 1994. Collared Forest-Falcon, Jan–Feb 1994. Northern Jacana, Nov–Dec 1985. Ruddy Ground-Dove, March 1984. Ruddy Quail-Dove, March 1996. Mottled Owl, Feb 1983. Elegant Trogon, Sept 1977. Masked Tityra, Feb–March 1990. Varied Thrush, Dec 1990. Crimson-collared Grosbeak, June–July 1974.

Directions: The state park is located 2.6 miles south of Business 83. Take the Inspiration Road exit off US 83, just west of Mission, or FM 492 to Loop 374; then drive south 3 miles on FM 2062 to the park entrance. Anzalduas County Park is 5 miles to the east off FM 494.

General information: The 588-acre state park as well as lands below Anzalduas County Park are part of the extensive Rio Grande Valley Wildlife Corridor, a multiagency project to protect tracts of native landscape between Falcon Dam and the mouth of the Rio Grande. Ten habitat types and more than 115 unique vertebrate species occur within this corridor.

The campground trailer loop at Bentsen–Rio Grande Valley State Park, especially between sites 1 to 35, offers excellent birding.

Bentsen is one of two key birding sites in the lower Rio Grande Valley (along with Santa Ana National Wildlife Refuge), but is preferred by campers and night-time birders. Santa Ana is open only during the daylight hours.

The state park is primarily a nature park, although fishing is available on Ox-bow Lake. Two self-guided hiking trails are available: the 1.9-mile Rio Grande Trail begins on the outer loop of the park, and the 1-mile Singing Chaparral Trail begins along the entrance road, just beyond park headquarters. Anzalduas County Park can be extremely busy on weekends.

ADDITIONAL HELP

Location: Texas Official Travel Map grid Z x 16; Hidalgo County
Nearest food, gas, and lodging: All are available in Mission.
Nearest camping: On-site (141 sites)
Contact: Superintendent, Bentsen–Rio Grande Valley State Park; Manager, Anzalduas County Park (see Appendix C)

119 Falcon State Park, Chapeño, and Salineño

Habitats: Reservoir, dam and spillway, river, riparian, thorn forest, Tamaulipan scrub

Key birds: Least Grebe, Neotropic Cormorant, Anhinga, Roseate Spoonbill, Black-bellied Whistling-Duck, "Mexican Duck" (Mallard), **Hook-billed Kite,** White-tailed Kite, Harris's and Gray Hawks, Crested Caracara, **Plain Chachalaca,** Scaled Quail, **White-tipped Dove,** Greater Roadrunner, **Pauraque, Ringed Kingfisher, Green Kingfisher, Golden-fronted Woodpecker, Great Kiskadee, Green Jay,** Chihuahuan Raven, Verdin, Cactus Wren, **Long-billed Thrasher,** Pyrrhuloxia, **Olive Sparrow,** Bronzed Cowbird, **Altamira Oriole,** and **Audubon's Oriole** are present year-round. Least Bittern, **Muscovy Duck,** Least and Gull-billed Terns, **Red-billed Pigeon,** Groove-billed Ani, **Ferruginous Pygmy-Owl,** Elf Owl, Lesser Nighthawk, Common Poorwill, Brown-crested and Scissor-tailed Flycatchers, **Couch's Kingbird,** Cave Swallow, Painted Bunting, Cassin's Sparrow, and Hooded Oriole occur in summer. American White Pelican, Hooded Merganser, Osprey, **White-tailed Hawk,** Black and Say's Phoebes, Vermilion Flycatcher, **Brown Jay,** and Sage Thrasher can usually be found in winter.

Best times to bird: January to April for the greatest majority of Texas specialties; April and May for spring migrants and nesting activities

Birding strategies: Falcon State Park (**A**), located on the southeastern shore of Falcon Lake, is dominated by Tamaulipan scrub. Resident birds include Harris's Hawk, Northern Bobwhite, Scaled Quail, White-winged and Inca Doves, Common Ground-Dove, Greater Roadrunner, **Golden-fronted Woodpecker,** Chihuahuan Raven, Verdin, **Long-billed Thrasher,** Curve-billed Thrasher, Cactus and Bewick's Wrens, Pyrrhuloxia, Lark and Black-throated Sparrows, and **Altamira Oriole.** In summer look for Elf Owl, Lesser Nighthawk, Ash-throated Flycatcher, Cave Swallow, Painted Bunting, Cassin's Sparrow, and Hooded Oriole. During migration, other birds, such as Varied Bunting, can be expected. In winter watch for Vermilion Flycatcher throughout the park. The brushy areas attract a host of sparrows and other species, including Say's Phoebe and Sage Thrasher (both irregular).

The adjacent reservoir attracts numerous water birds year-round, including a nesting colony of Least Tern in summer. Winter birds can include Common Loon, Eared Grebe, American White Pelican, Double-crested Cormorant, all the waders, many ducks, a variety of shorebirds, and Gull-billed Tern.

View the Falcon Dam spillway (**B**) from the overlook below the dam for numerous water birds year-round. All the waders, including night-herons and shorebirds, can usually be found here. **Ringed Kingfisher, Green Kingfisher,** and Belted Kingfisher occur in winter, and Black and Say's Phoebes, Scissor-tailed Flycatcher, and **Couch's Kingbird** perch on posts and wires overhead. Various swallows, gulls, and terns are often present as well. Look for "Mexican Duck" (Mallard) in summer. Shorebirds and rails often are present in or along the river below the spillway.

119 Falcon State Park, Chapeño, and Salineño

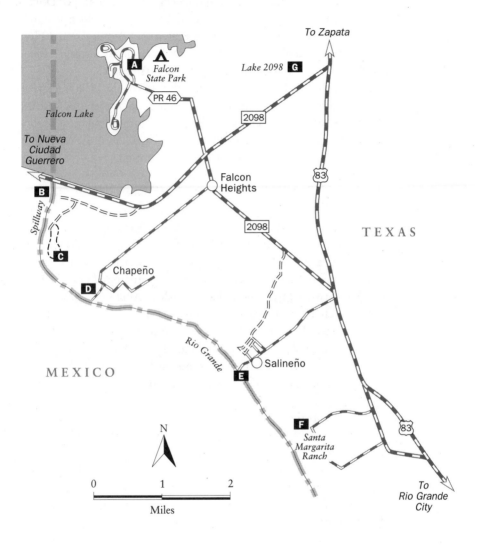

Osprey is common in winter and rare in summer; Rock Wren can sometimes be found by the spillway.

The old, gated road (**C**) that continues downriver from the overlook, passing through dense brush and thorn forest habitats, also offers excellent birding. Occasionally, a **Ferruginous Pygmy-Owl** (best located by its distinct song, a series of *"poik"* notes) can be found in this area, especially below the hobo camp, marked by an old clothesline pole, in late spring. **Note:** *Please read the Birding Ethics on pages 7–9—taped owl calls can severely threaten these rare birds!*

Other spring and summer birds along this route include **Hook-billed Kite** (irregular), Harris's Hawk, **Plain Chachalaca, Red-billed Pigeon, White-tipped Dove,** Yellow-billed Cuckoo, Groove-billed Ani, Elf Owl, **Pauraque, Golden-fronted Woodpecker,** Ladder-backed Woodpecker, Ash-throated and Brown-crested Flycatchers, **Great Kiskadee, Couch's Kingbird, Green Jay, Long-billed Thrasher,** Blue Grosbeak, **Olive Sparrow, Altamira Oriole,** and **Audubon's Oriole.**

Chapeño (**D**), accessible off FM 2098, has recently (starting in 1996) received attention from birders because **Brown Jay** has been seen more consistently here in winter than anywhere else in Texas. This area also is good for finding most of the other valley specialties, including **Muscovy Duck.** Pay a small admission fee and visit the picnic and camping area upstream from the boat ramp.

Salineño (**E**), including the Birder's Colony, a group of mobile homes just above the Rio Grande, is a must for birders. The river offers another chance to find **Muscovy Duck,** especially in spring and summer if the water is low, as well as other ducks that winter here. Watch also for **Red-billed Pigeon** flying along the waterway and perched in the middle branches of the big trees. The bird feeders and flowering vegetation at the Birder's Colony (active from early December until mid-March) attract numerous South Texas specialties: **White-tipped Dove, Great Kiskadee, Green Jay, Brown Jay, Long-billed Thrasher, Altamira Oriole,** and **Audubon's Oriole.** Watch also in this area for Gray Hawk.

Santa Margarita Ranch (**F**), south of Salineño off US 83 (see map), can also be worthwhile, although there is a small fee for birding. The ranch includes access to the river and a number of roads. Most of the same birds mentioned above can usually be found here. Common Poorwill can sometimes be heard calling in spring and summer.

Bird Lake 2098 (**G**), northeast from Falcon Dam along FM 2098, in winter and early spring; it is usually dry in summer. **Least Grebe;** Pied-billed Grebe; American White Pelican; Double-crested and Neotropic Cormorants; Anhinga; various waders, including White Ibis and Roseate Spoonbill; Black-bellied Whistling-Duck, Hooded Merganser; a variety of dabbling ducks; Harris's Hawk; **Golden-fronted Woodpecker;** Ladder-backed Woodpecker; Say's Phoebe; Vermilion Flycatcher; and **Great Kiskadee** occur here.

Watch also for Greater White-fronted and Snow Geese, Crested Caracara, Sandhill Crane, and Cave Swallow flying by in winter and spring; Western Kingbird, Cliff Swallow, Verdin, Cactus Wren, Black-tailed Gnatcatcher, Cassin's Sparrow, and Bronzed Cowbird at Tamaulipan scrub sites in summer; and **Buff-bellied Hummingbird** at flowering plants year-round.

Records of Review Species: Trumpeter Swan, Dec–Jan 1989/90. Eurasian Wigeon, Dec–Jan 1989/90. Roadside Hawk, Jan 1979. Short-tailed Hawk, July 1989. Black-legged Kittiwake, Dec–Feb 1971/72, Jan–Feb 1975. Sulphur-bellied Flycatcher, May–Aug 1975, May–July 1976, July 1977. Tropical Kingbird, June 1991. Rose-throated Becard, Dec–Jan 1987/88. Rufous-capped Warbler, Feb 1973. Blue Bunting, Jan 1988.

Direction: Santa Margarita Ranch, Salineño, Chapeño, and Falcon Dam are located (south to north) along US 83, starting approximately 65 miles above McAllen. Lake 2098 lies along FM 2098, between the junction of PR 46 (road to state park) and US 83 (see map).

General information: The 573-acre Falcon State Park marks the western edge of a wildlife corridor that extends, albeit in more than 100 scattered patches, along the Rio Grande southeast to the Gulf of Mexico. Falcon Lake, a 87,120-acre impoundment owned jointly by the United States and Mexico, extends north for 60 miles and forms part of the border between the two countries.

The Salineño Birder's Colony (deserted in summer), only about 100 yards above the Rio Grande, welcomes birders to visit the feeders; this is usually the best bet for finding **Brown Jay** and **Audubon's Oriole.** The residents are well informed about out-of-the-ordinary birds that might be present throughout the valley.

ADDITIONAL HELP

Location: Texas Official Travel Map grid Y x 14; Starr County

Nearest food, gas, and lodging: Food and gas are at Falcon Heights, between Falcon State Park and Salineño. Lodging can be found at Falcon Heights, Roma (14 miles east), and Zapata (28 miles north).

Nearest camping: On-site at Falcon State Park (62 sites)

Contact: Superintendent, Falcon State Park (see Appendix C)

120 San Ygnacio

Habitats: River, pond, riparian, field, garden, Tamaulipan scrub
Key birds: Neotropic Cormorant, Harris's Hawk, Crested Caracara, Scaled Quail, Greater Roadrunner, Groove-billed Ani, **Pauraque, Ringed Kingfisher, Green Kingfisher, Golden-fronted Woodpecker, Great Kiskadee, Green Jay,** Chihuahuan Raven, Verdin, Cactus Wren, **Long-billed Thrasher,** Curve-billed Thrasher, Pyrrhuloxia, **White-collared Seedeater,** and **Altamira Oriole** are present year-round. **Red-billed Pigeon;** Lesser Nighthawk; Ash-throated, Brown-crested, and Scissor-tailed Flycatchers; Painted Bunting; and Hooded Oriole can be found in summer. Black Phoebe and Vermilion Flycatcher occur in winter.
Best times to bird: Seedeaters occur year-round; other Texas specialties can best be found from mid-March to mid-May

Birding strategies: Downtown San Ygnacio (**A**) contains a number of weedy yards that usually harbor **White-collared Seedeaters.** Drive to the end of Washington Street, park, and walk the streets. These little tropical birds may occur in almost any weedy site; the Rio Grande Valley Rare Bird Alert usually provides an up-to-date location. Seedeaters also have been found at Zapata (14 miles south) in recent years; the best bet there is at the cattail pond south of the library.

Other likely year-round birds at San Ygnacio include Black Vulture, Mourning and Inca Doves, Common Ground-Dove, **Golden-fronted Woodpecker,** Ladder-backed Woodpecker, **Great Kiskadee, Green Jay,** Bewick's Wren, Northern Mockingbird, Northern Cardinal, Great-tailed Grackle, and House Sparrow. In summer White-winged Dove, Lesser Nighthawk, **Couch's Kingbird,** Scissor-tailed Flycatcher, and Bronzed Cowbird also are usually present.

The resaca (**B**) at the west end of Juarez and Uribe avenues is good only during wet years, when various water birds can be present, especially during migration. Waders, ducks, and Neotropic Cormorant, Common Moorhen, and American Coot can be found here. The surrounding Tamaulipan scrub habitat, however, harbors numerous terrestrial species of interest: Harris's Hawk, Crested Caracara, Scaled Quail, Greater Roadrunner, Groove-billed Ani (irregular), Ash-throated and Brown-crested Flycatchers, Chihuahuan Raven, Verdin, Cactus Wren, Black-tailed Gnatcatcher, **Long-billed Thrasher,** Curve-billed Thrasher, Pyrrhuloxia, and Lark and Black-throated Sparrows.

The riparian habitat and river (**C**), accessible by trails from the end of Washington and Trevino streets, offer year-round Neotropic Cormorant, Great Blue Heron, Great Egret, Black-crowned Night-Heron, Red-shouldered Hawk, Killdeer, **Pauraque, Ringed Kingfisher, Green Kingfisher,** Tufted Titmouse, White-eyed Vireo, Pyrrhuloxia, and Red-winged Blackbird. Few ducks utilize this portion of the river, although spring migrants, including shorebirds, can be numerous at times. In summer **Muscovy Duck** and **Red-billed Pigeon** are found here occasionally.

120 San Ygnacio

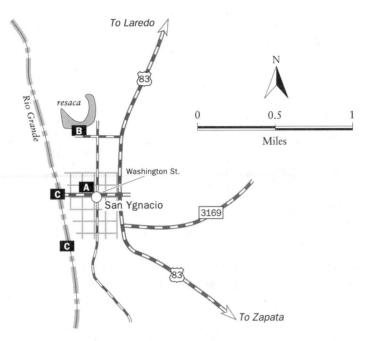

Directions: San Ygnacio is located off US 83, 14 miles north of Zapata. Drive into town to the end of Washington Street and park.

General information: White-collared Seedeater has been reported consistently at San Ygnacio for more than 15 years, making this the only reliable U.S. site. Usually in a flock of a few to 25 birds, they frequent weedy patches almost anywhere in town. However, all the area is private property, so it is essential that birders respect property rights.

ADDITIONAL HELP

Location: Texas Official Travel Map grid X x 14; Zapata County
Nearest food, gas, and lodging: Food and gas are available on-site at the highway junction. Lodging is available at Zapata (14 miles).
Nearest camping: On-site in winter at Cord's RV Park; 210-765-4176
Contact: None

Texas's Nonpublic Birding Sites

All of the sites previously listed are generally open to the public with no preliminary arrangements necessary, although an entry or user fee is assessed at some of them, such as the state and national parks. However, there are other good birding sites in the state that are available to birders who call ahead. Some of these sites contain birds that are difficult to find elsewhere, such as **Ferruginous Pygmy-Owl** on the King, Kenedy, and El Canelo ranches, or they may offer the birder a different experience than public sites can provide. For example, The Nature Conservancy of Texas manages reserves where the birder can either tour choice areas or explore unique habitats without the normal constraints great numbers of people and limited hours of access impose. Access to most Nature Conservancy preserves is restricted and must be arranged well in advance.

TRANS-PECOS

Chandler Independence Creek Preserve. Located on the Stockton Plateau, this 701-acre preserve contains the last mile of the clear spring-fed Independence Creek and its confluence with the Pecos River. The area preserves two rare fishes—small proserpine shiner and Rio Grande darter—as well as nesting habitat for several pairs of **Black-capped Vireos.** Other birds of interest include Zone-tailed Hawk, Golden Eagle, Prairie Falcon, Lesser Nighthawk, Brown-crested Flycatcher, Phainopepla, Gray Vireo, Pyrrhuloxia, and Varied Bunting. Contact: West Texas Land Steward, The Nature Conservancy of Texas, P.O. Box 1619, Alpine, TX 79831; 915-837-1778.

Cibola Creek Ranch. This 25,000-acre working cattle ranch is located in the rugged Chinati Mountains of West Texas. Ranging in elevation from 4,000 to 6,000 feet, the ranch supports a wide variety of birds year-round, including Scaled Quail, Greater Roadrunner, Verdin, Cactus Wren, Pyrrhuloxia, Canyon Towhee, and Black-throated Sparrow. In spring and summer, Zone-tailed Hawk and **Lucifer Hummingbird** are present. The ranch also contains a number of significant historic structures. Exclusive accommodations and bird tours are available. Contact: Cibola Creek Ranch, P.O. Box 44, Shafter, TX 79850; 915-229-3737; fax, 915-837-5300.

EDWARDS PLATEAU

Barton Creek Habitat Preserve. This 4,084-acre Nature Conservancy area contains natural and modified habitat along 4 linear miles of Barton Creek. It includes 1,800 acres for **Golden-cheeked Warbler** and 2,184 acres that will regrow or be restored for habitat for Golden-cheeks over a 30-year period. The area also has a small population of **Black-capped Vireos** as well as a number of other Texas specialties. Contact: Hill Country Land Steward, The Nature Conservancy of Texas, P.O. Box 164255, Austin, TX 78716-4255; 512-327-9472.

Fort Clark Springs. The grounds of Fort Clark (historic home of the U.S. Fifth Cavalry regiment) support a rich diversity of bird habitats, including streams, ponds, oak mottes, Tamaulipan scrub, and grasslands. Expected key bird species include Harris's Hawk, Crested Caracara, **Green Kingfisher, Golden-fronted Woodpecker,** Vermilion Flycatcher, **Great Kiskadee, Long-billed Thrasher,** Pyrrhuloxia, and **Olive Sparrow** year-round. Roads and hiking provide easy access throughout the 2,700-acre private recreation community. Additional facilities include a military museum, golf courses, tennis courts, a swimming pool, a restaurant, a barracks motel, and an RV park. Contact: Fort Clark Springs Association, Inc., P.O. Box 345, Brackettville, TX 78832; 210-563-2493; fax, 210-563-2254.

Kickapoo Cavern State Park. Although this 6,400-acre area is administered by the Texas Parks and Wildlife Department, it is accessible only through prior arrangement. It is well worth the necessary effort and time, however, as the park contains one of the largest populations of breeding **Black-capped Vireo**—more than 125 pairs—anywhere in the state. Other key birds include Zone-tailed Hawk, Elf Owl, Brown-crested Flycatcher, Western Scrub-Jay, Cave Swallow, **Long-billed Thrasher,** Gray Vireo, Varied Bunting, and **Olive Sparrow.** Located off FM 674, 22 miles north of Brackettville, the park is worth birding year-round. A daily entrance fee of $2 is charged. Contact: Kickapoo Cavern State Park, P.O. Box 705, Brackettville, TX 78832; 210-563-2342.

National Wildflower Research Center. Located in southwest Austin, this 42-acre preserve contains a marvelous display of wildflowers that attracts hummingbirds throughout the spring, summer, and fall. The area also harbors a number of Hill Country birds, including Wild Turkey, Greater Roadrunner, **Golden-fronted Woodpecker,** Scissor-tailed Flycatcher, Painted Bunting, and Rufous-crowned Sparrow. The Center, founded in 1982 by Lady Bird Johnson, the former first lady, features 23 display gardens and contains a research library, greenhouses, an exhibition gallery, and a children's education center. A daily fee is required. Contact: National Wildflower Research Center, 4801 La Crosse Avenue, Austin, TX 78739; 512-292-4200; fax, 512-292-4627; web page, http://www.wildflower.org.

NORTHERN PLAINS

Fossil Rim Wildlife Center. This 2,700-acre wildlife preserve is unique because it is dedicated to the preservation of endangered and rare species with the ultimate goal of returning them to the wild. Sixty animal species, including Attwater's Prairie-Chicken, red and mexican wolves, and ocelot, are maintained here. Most of the 1,100 individual animals roam free in expansive pastures that can be visited through safari-type tours. Such a tour in spring and summer is likely to include a variety of native birds, including Wild Turkey, Northern Bobwhite, Greater Roadrunner, Belted Kingfisher, Scissor-tailed Flycatcher, and Eastern Bluebird. **Golden-cheeked Warbler** also occurs on the preserve.

Fossil Rim is located 6 miles west of Glen Rose, via US 67 and FM 2008. There is a $12.95 entry fee to the preserve. Safari ($25) or private ($60) tours are available. Contact: Fossil Rim Wildlife Center, P.O. Box 2189, Route 1, Box 210, Glen Rose, TX 76043; 254-897-2960; fax, 254-897-3785.

Heard Natural Science Museum and Wildlife Sanctuary. Located south of McKinney along US 75, 30 miles north of Dallas, the 187-acre preserve features riparian woodlands, a 50-acre wetland, and upland prairies. Wood Duck, Hooded Merganser, and Prothonotary Warbler nest in the wetland, and 15 species of waterfowl utilize the area in fall and winter. Blue Grosbeak, Indigo and Painted Buntings, and Dickcissel nest in the prairie habitat. Museum personnel operate the oldest continuously run bird banding station in Texas. Most of the banding is done during the spring and fall migration. Museum personnel also monitor a bluebird trail of nearly 30 nesting boxes and operate a raptor rehabilitation center and raptor education outreach program, which uses live birds.

Most of the sanctuary is undisturbed and is available for ecological research. There are over 5 miles of trails, and guided tours are offered on Saturdays and Sundays; reservations are required for group tours. Natural history exhibits, a nature gift store, and classrooms are housed in the museum building. The Heard Museum and Sanctuary is open Monday through Saturday, 9 A.M. to 5 P.M., and Sunday from 1 P.M. to 5 P.M. Admission is $3 for adults and $2 for children. Contact: Heard Natural Science Museum and Wildlife Sanctuary, One Nature Place, McKinney, TX 75069; 972-562-5566; fax, 972-548-9119; or visit the Heard's home page at http://www.heardmuseum.org.

Lennox Woods. This 366-acre preserve, located in Red River County, 10 miles north of Clarksville, contains an excellent old-growth woodland, including a post oak nearly 300 years old and a loblolly pine 140 years old. Bird life of interest includes eight nesting warbler species: Northern Parula; Yellow-throated, Pine, Black-and-white, Prothonotary, Kentucky, and Hooded Warblers; and Louisiana Waterthrush. Daily access, with no appointment, is allowed for research, field trips, or volunteer work. A self-guided nature trail explores key habitats. Contact: North Texas Land Steward, The Nature Conservancy of Texas, County Road 1140, Celeste, TX 75423-0463; 903-568-4139.

UPPER COAST

Big Boggy National Wildlife Refuge. This 4,127-acre refuge is located in Matagorda County, 20 miles south of Bay City. The refuge is dominated by coastal prairie and marsh and includes Dressing Point Island, site of a significant colonial waterbird rookery in season. The area contains about the same species, including **White-tailed Hawk,** as are found at Brazoria and San Bernard national wildlife refuges (sites 90 and 91). The three areas are designated as a joint Internationally Significant Shorebird Site by the Western Hemisphere Shorebird Reserve Network. Access is limited to a designated waterfowl hunting area during the state season or by special arrangement with the refuge manager. Contact: U.S. Fish and Wildlife Service, 1212 North Velasco, Suite 200, Angelton, TX 77512; 409-849-6062; fax, 409-849-5118.

Mad Island Marsh. Located in Matagorda County, the 7,048-acre Clive Runnels Family Mad Island Marsh Preserve contains 1,800 acres of tidal lakes and marsh, coastal prairie and scrub, and rice fields. The area is the hub of the annual Mad Island Marsh Christmas Bird Count, which has tallied more than 200 species each year. Almost 300 bird species have been recorded since 1990, including Reddish Egret, Fulvous and Black-bellied Whistling-Ducks, White-tailed Kite, **White-tailed Hawk,** Crested Caracara, Black Rail, and Vermilion Flycatcher. The preserve headquarters and visitor center are available for use by volunteers, visitors, researchers, and school groups. Contact: Coastal Texas Land Steward, The Nature Conservancy of Texas, P.O. Box 163, Collegeport, TX 77428-0163; 512-972-2559. The Texas Parks and Wildlife Department owns the adjacent Mad Island Wildlife Management Area and conducts a tour during spring and fall. More information can be obtained from the Texas Parks and Wildlife Department, Matagorda County Courthouse, Bay City, TX 77414; 409-244-7636.

Peach Point Wildlife Management Area. This 10,300-acre tract, located 5 miles west of Freeport, was purchased with duck stamp funds and contains coastal woodlands, prairies, and marshes. This area is part of two of the top Christmas Bird Counts: Freeport and San Bernard. The area is most productive during migration when both eastern and western birds may occur. One 40-acre oak woodland tract, located southwest of Jones Creek off SH 36, is available to birders year-round. A tour of the entire wildlife management area is scheduled during spring and fall. Contact: Texas Parks and Wildlife Department, Matagorda County Courthouse, Bay City, TX 77414; 409-244-7636.

COASTAL BEND

Welder Flats. Part of the Cliburn Ranch, this 10,000-acre area offers the birder an option for good looks at **Whooping Crane** in winter. Located just east of Seadrift in Calhoun County, Cliburn Ranch contains a diversity of habitats, including bay, extensive mud flats, ponds, coastal prairie, and scattered oak mottes. This area can be exceptional for waterfowl and shorebirds during migration. A fee is charged for admission. Contact: John Cliburn, P.O. Box 2370, Victoria, TX 77902; 512-576-3517.

Fennessey Ranch. Several thousand acres along the Mission River, 6 miles southeast of Refugio, have been established as a "nature preserve" for birding, hunting, hiking, and educational tours. The ranch boasts more than 400 species of birds, including Wood Stork, Masked Duck (irregular), **White-tailed Hawk,** and **Green Jay.** Tours are available during specific times of the year such as spring and fall migration. Reservations are necessary and admission is charged. Contact: Fennessey Ranch, P.O. Box 99, Bayside, TX 78340; 512-529-6600.

Guadalupe Delta Wildlife Management Area. This 7,200-acre tract, purchased with duck stamp funds, is dominated by coastal wetlands and riparian woodlands. Two sites are available to birders: (1) Buffalo Lake observation platform is located on US 35, 6 miles northeast of Tivoli, and features an overview of a managed freshwater lake. Expect concentrations of waterfowl in winter and shorebirds and waders in spring and fall. At times, hundreds of Wood Storks forage and roost on the lake. (2) Guadalupe River woodland corridor is located 2 miles north of Tivoli on US 35, and 1 mile south on River Road. This site is a narrow, 2-mile woodland bordering the Guadalupe River, and is open year-round. Key birds include **White-tailed Hawk,** Crested Caracara, **Golden-fronted Woodpecker, Couch's Kingbird,** and Vermilion Flycatcher. A guided tour of the area is usually scheduled each spring and fall. Contact: Texas Parks and Wildlife Department, 2601 North Azalea, Suite 31, Victoria, TX 77901; 512-576-0022.

El Canelo Ranch. This private ranch offers birding to individuals and small groups on 11,000 acres of pristine Texas brushlands. The ranch contains the majority of the Rio Grande Valley specialties, including **Ferruginous Pygmy-Owl.** Other key birds include **White-tailed Hawk, White-tipped Dove,** Groove-billed Ani, **Pauraque, Golden-fronted Woodpecker,** Vermilion Flycatcher, **Couch's Kingbird, Great Kiskadee, Green Jay, Long-billed Thrasher, Olive Sparrow,** Hooded Oriole, and **Audubon's Oriole.** The ranch is 10 miles north of Raymondville or 90 miles south of Corpus Christi, just 5 miles west of US 77. Deluxe overnight accommodations with gourmet meals and unrestricted birding or birding tours are available, all by reservation only. Contact: El Canelo Ranch, P.O. Box 487, Raymondville, TX 78580; 210-689-5042 (e-mail: elcanel@vsta.com); or for tours only: Fr. Tom Pincelli, 209 South 10th Street, Harlingen, TX 78550; 956-428-6111.

Kenedy Ranch. Approximately 235,000 acres of coastal prairie, marshes, and Tamaulipan scrub are available to organized tours. Located south of Kingsville near Sarita, this is one of the few sites where birders are likely to find **Ferruginous Pygmy-Owl.** Other specialty birds include **Least Grebe, White-tailed Hawk, White-tipped Dove, Pauraque, Buff-bellied Hummingbird, Ringed Kingfisher, Golden-fronted Woodpecker, Great Kiskadee, Green Jay, Tropical Parula, Olive Sparrow,** and **Audubon's Oriole.** Contact: Kenedy Memorial Foundation, Field Office, P.O. Box 70, Sarita, TX 78385; 512-294-5227.

King Ranch. Covering 825,000 acres, the King Ranch is divided into 4 divisions, 3 of which are accessible to birders through guided tours. The largest known population of **Ferruginous Pygmy-Owl** in the United States is found on the Norias Division. The ranch also contains many of the other specialty birds South Texas is known for, including **Least Grebe, White-tailed Hawk, White-tipped Dove,** Groove-billed Ani, **Pauraque, Buff-bellied Hummingbird, Golden-fronted Woodpecker, Ringed Kingfisher, Green Kingfisher, Great Kiskadee, Couch's Kingbird, Green Jay, Long-billed Thrasher, Tropical Parula, Olive Sparrow,** and **Audubon's Oriole.** A variety of tours is available. Contact: King Ranch Visitor Center, P.O. Box 1090, Kingsville, TX 78364-1090; 512-592-8055; fax, 512-595-1344; or Victor Emanuel Nature Tours, P.O. Box 33008, Austin, TX 78764; 800-328-8368; fax, 512-328-2919.

Welder Wildlife Refuge. Managed for native wildlife, the 7,800-acre preserve is utilized primarily for research and environmental education. Located 7 miles north of Sinton along US 77, the refuge boasts a total of 380 bird species. Birding groups are accommodated by appointment only. A general refuge tour is scheduled each Thursday (holidays excepted) from 3 P.M. to 5 P.M.; interested parties should meet at the entrance. Contact: Welder Wildlife Foundation, P.O. Drawer 1400, Sinton, TX 78387; 512-364-2643.

5. The Great Texas Coastal Birding Trail

When Roger Tory Peterson, the high priest of bird identification, dedicated the Great Texas Coastal Birding Trail in September 1995, it became the nation's first multisite birding trail. Other states will surely follow. This superb idea is one that will attract birders to the Texas Coast year-round.

The 500-mile-long Great Texas Coastal Birding Trail includes more than 200 birding sites from the Texas/Louisiana border to the Rio Grande Valley, many of them known by only a handful of active birders. The varied sites offer a kaleidoscope of Texas birding habitats and bird life. More than 75 percent of the more than 600 birds recorded in Texas have been recorded along this route. Several loop routes, some that include key birding sites more than 100 miles inland, contain different habitats and birds that might not be found along the immediate coast.

The sites include national, state, and county parks; wildlife refuges; wildlife management areas; and a host of private holdings. None of the sites is more than a 30-minute drive from the next. And all are marked, on-site, by an attractive brown sign, depicting a Black Skimmer against the rising sun.

Selected sites along the Great Texas Coastal Birding Trail.

The state Department of Transportation and Texas Parks and Wildlife Commission have collaborated to develop the trail, with support from numerous coastal communities. The project, under the direction of Madge Lindsay of the Parks and Wildlife Commission and consultant Ted Eubanks, is expected to prolong visits by birders along the entire route. The aim is twofold: to increase ecotourism dollars within the various communities as well as to create added interest in birds and bird habitats. These are likely to lead to a greater level of bird protection and conservation.

Three maps, each depicting one of the three sections of trail, are published to guide visitors to the sites. The maps show each site and include a few of the key birds to be found there, directions, the best season for birding, and, occasionally, additional points of interest. The maps—Central Texas Coast (1996), Upper Texas Coast (1997), and Lower Texas Coast (1998)—can be acquired at any one of the 12 Texas Travel Information Centers, at numerous participating convention and visitors bureaus, or from the Texas Department of Transportation, Travel and Information Division, P.O. Box 5064, Austin, TX 78763; 800-452-9292.

The map in this chapter illustrates the general area covered by the Great Texas Coastal Birding Trail and shows a few of the sites you'll find along it. *Birding Texas* includes chapters on many of the GTCBT sites, but size considerations allow our chapters to be far more expansive than the information included on the GTCBT maps. At the same time, the GTCBT map will help you locate and bird an array of choice birding links not listed in the book. For example, between Lake Texana and Port Lavaca, which are treated in this book, the GTCBT Central Texas Coast map includes three other sites: Lavaca/Navidad Estuary, Bennett Park, and Garcitas Creek Boat Ramp. Between Rockport and Corpus Christi, both of which are covered in this book, the map shows the Texas State Aquarium, Indian Point/Sunset Lake, and Fred Jones Nature Sanctuary, all worth a visit.

The Texas birder can benefit considerably from using both this book and the GTCBT maps.

6. Status and Distribution Checklist

Approximately 28 percent (168) of the more than 600 birds recorded in Texas are year-round residents; 18 percent (108) normally reside in the state only during the nesting season; 27 percent (162) are usually present only in winter; about 5 percent (29) are not expected to recur (accidental); the remaining 23 percent (138) usually occur in the state only as migrants or vagrants in spring or fall.

All 605 of the accepted Texas species are listed in the following pages, and the status of each is included for each of the 10 regions of the state.

STATUS

R = Resident: full-time; present year-round in this region
S = Summer: present at least from early May through July; usually nests
W = Winter: may arrive as early as mid-October and remain as late as mid-May
M = Migrant: passing through in spring and/or fall
D = Post-nesting Dispersal: visitor/resident only after nesting elsewhere

ABUNDANCE

◆◆◆◆ = Common: always present in significant numbers in the proper habitat(s)
◆◆◆ = Fairly Common: a few are always present in the proper habitat(s)
◆◆ = Uncommon: sometimes present in small numbers in the proper habitat(s)
◆ = Rare: Occur regularly in small numbers in the proper habitat(s); a good search can usually find one
Irr = Irregular: definitely not expected; but one or a few occur occasionally in the proper habitat(s)
Spor = Sporadic: not expected every year, but may occur occasionally in significant numbers
Vag = Vagrant: scattered records; well out of the bird's normal range (extralimital)

FOOTNOTES

Footnotes (marked with a numeral) indicate miscellaneous facts of distribution.
1 = more numerous in spring
2 = more numerous in fall
3 = more numerous in west
4 = more numerous in east
5 = deep-water pelagic
6 = local
7 = extirpated from this range or believed extinct

Texas Birds

Status and Distribution

Bird Species	Trans-Pecos	Panhandle and Western Plains	Edwards Plateau
❑ LOON, *Red-throated*	W vag	W vag	W vag
❑ *Pacific*	W vag	W vag	W vag
❑ Common	W ♦	S vag M, W irr	M ♦ W ♦♦
❑ *Yellow-billed*	vag	W vag	
❑ GREBE, Least	irr		R* ♦
❑ Pied-billed	S* ♦♦♦ M, W ♦♦	R* ♦♦ M ♦♦♦	S* ♦♦ M, W ♦♦♦♦
❑ Horned	W irr	M, W irr	W irr
❑ *Red-necked*		M, W vag	
❑ Eared	M, W ♦	S* irr M ♦♦♦♦ W irr	M, W ♦♦♦
❑ Western	S irr W ♦	S vag M, W irr	M, W vag
❑ Clark's	S irr, W ♦		
❑ ALBATROSS, *Yellow-nosed*			
❑ PETREL, *White-chinned*			
❑ SHEARWATER, Cory's			
❑ *Greater*			
❑ *Sooty*			
❑ *Manx*			
❑ Audubon's			
❑ STORM-PETREL, *Wilson's*			
❑ *Leach's*			
❑ Band-rumped			
❑ TROPICBIRD, *Red-billed*			
❑ BOOBY, Masked			
❑ *Blue-footed*			vag
❑ Brown			
❑ *Red-footed*			
❑ GANNET, Northern			
❑ PELICAN, American White	M irr W ♦	S irr M ♦♦ W vag	M ♦♦ W ♦

S = Summer

M = Migrant

W = Winter

R = Resident

D = Post-nesting Dispersal

♦ ♦ ♦ ♦ = **Common.** Always present in significant numbers in the proper habitat.

♦ ♦ ♦ = **Fairly Common.** A few are always present in the proper habitat.

♦ ♦ = **Uncommon.** Sometimes present in the proper habitat.

♦ = **Rare.** Occur regularly, but in small numbers; a good search can usually find one.

irr = **Irregular.** Definitely not expected, but a few occur occasionally.

spor = **Sporadic.** Not expected every year, but may occur in significant numbers.

vag = **Vagrant.** Well out of the species' normal range (extralimital).

Northern Plains	Pineywoods	Central Plains	Upper Coast	Coastal Bend	Brush Country	Rio Grande Valley
W irr⁴	W vag		M, W vag			
W irr⁴	W vag	W vag	M, W ♦	W irr		
M, W ♦♦♦⁴	M, W ♦♦♦	M, W ♦♦	M, W ♦♦♦	M ♦♦ W ♦♦♦♦	M, W ♦♦	W ♦
	W vag					
	W vag	R* ♦	M, W irr	R* ♦♦♦	R* ♦♦	R* ♦♦
S* irr M, W ♦♦♦	S* ♦♦ M, W ♦♦♦	S* ♦♦ M, W ♦♦♦	S* ♦♦ M, W ♦♦♦♦	S* ♦♦ M, W ♦♦♦♦	S* ♦♦ M, W ♦♦♦	S* ♦ M, W ♦♦♦
M, W ♦♦♦⁴	M, W ♦♦	W irr	M, W ♦♦	W ♦♦	W irr	W vag
W vag	W vag		M, W vag			
M ♦♦ W irr	M ♦♦♦ W ♦♦	M ♦♦♦♦ W ♦♦♦	M ♦♦♦ W ♦♦♦♦	M, W ♦♦♦♦	M ♦♦♦ W ♦♦	M, W ♦♦
M, W irr	M, W ♦	M, W vag	W irr	W vag	W vag	W vag
						vag⁵
			vag⁵			
			S irr⁵	S ♦♦⁵		S, M ♦♦⁵
			vag⁵	vag⁵		
			vag⁵	vag⁵		vag⁵
				vag⁵		
			S ♦⁵	S ♦♦⁵		S, M ♦♦⁵
				vag⁵		
				S ♦♦⁵		S ♦⁵
				S ♦♦♦⁵		S, M ♦♦⁵
			vag⁵	vag⁵		vag⁵
			S ♦⁵	S ♦⁵		S, M ♦♦⁵
		vag				vag
			S ♦⁵	S ♦⁵		S ♦⁵
			vag⁵			
			M, W ♦♦	M, W ♦♦		M, W ♦♦
S irr M ♦♦♦♦ W ♦♦♦⁴	S, W ♦ M ♦♦	M, W ♦♦♦	S ♦♦ M, W ♦♦♦♦	R* ♦♦♦ M, W ♦♦♦♦	M, W ♦♦	M ♦♦♦ W ♦♦♦♦

Italic type denotes "review" species.
Please report any sightings to Texas Bird Records Committee (see Appendix B).

* = Breeding
1 = More numerous in spring
2 = More numerous in fall
3 = More numerous in west
4 = More numerous in east

5 = Deep-water pelagic
6 = Local
7 = Extirpated from this range or believed extinct

Bird Species	Trans-Pecos	Panhandle and Western Plains	Edwards Plateau
❑ PELICAN, Brown	vag	vag	vag
❑ CORMORANT, Double-crested	S ◆ M, W ◆◆	S* irr M ◆◆◆ W irr	S ◆ M ◆◆◆◆ W ◆◆◆
❑ Neotropic	S, M, W irr		S, M ◆◆ W irr
❑ ANHINGA			S ◆ M ◆◆◆⁴
❑ FRIGATEBIRD, Magnificent			S vag
❑ BITTERN, American	M ◆	S irr M ◆ W irr	M ◆◆ W irr
❑ Least	S irr M ◆	S* irr M ◆	S* ◆⁴
❑ HERON, Great Blue	R ◆◆	S*, M ◆◆◆ W ◆◆	R* ◆◆◆
❑ EGRET, Great	R ◆	S, M ◆	R* ◆◆
❑ Snowy	S* ◆◆ W ◆◆	S, M irr	S, M, W ◆ D ◆◆
❑ HERON, Little Blue	D irr	S, M irr	S* ◆◆ M ◆◆◆⁴ W vag
❑ Tricolored	D irr	D vag	D ◆◆
❑ EGRET, Reddish	D vag		D vag
❑ Cattle	S* ◆◆ M ◆◆◆ W ◆◆	S*, M ◆◆◆ W vag	S, M ◆◆◆◆ W vag
❑ HERON, Green	S* ◆◆◆ W irr	S*, M ◆◆ W ◆	S* ◆◆◆ W irr
❑ NIGHT-HERON, Black-crowned	S* ◆◆ W irr	S*, M ◆◆◆◆ W vag	S ◆ M, W ◆◆
❑ Yellow-crowned	D irr	S*, M, W ◆	S*, M ◆◆ W ◆
❑ IBIS, White	vag		S, D ◆◆⁴
❑ Glossy	vag		
❑ White-faced	M ◆	S* irr M ◆◆◆	M, D ◆◆ W irr

S = Summer	◆ ◆ ◆ ◆ = **Common.** Always present in significant numbers in the proper habitat.
M = Migrant	◆ ◆ ◆ = **Fairly Common.** A few are always present in the proper habitat.
W = Winter	◆ ◆ = **Uncommon.** Sometimes present in the proper habitat.
R = Resident	◆ = **Rare.** Occur regularly, but in small numbers; a good search can usually find one.
	irr = **Irregular.** Definitely not expected, but a few occur occasionally.
	spor = **Sporadic.** Not expected every year, but may occur in significant numbers.
D = Post-nesting Dispersal	vag = **Vagrant.** Well out of the species' normal range (extralimital).

Northern Plains	Pineywoods	Central Plains	Upper Coast	Coastal Bend	Brush Country	Rio Grande Valley
vag	vag	vag	R* ♦♦♦♦	R* ♦♦	vag	R* ♦♦♦
M, W ♦♦♦♦	S ♦ M ♦♦♦♦ W ♦♦♦	S ♦ M, W ♦♦♦♦	S ♦♦ M, W ♦♦♦♦	S ♦[5] M, W ♦♦♦♦	M, W ♦♦♦	M, W ♦♦♦♦
S* ♦♦[4] W irr[4]	S ♦	R* ♦♦	R* ♦♦♦	R* ♦♦♦	R* ♦♦	S* ♦♦♦♦ M ♦♦♦ W ♦♦
S* irr[6] M irr[4]	S*, M ♦♦ W irr	S*, M ♦♦	S*, M ♦♦♦ W ♦♦	R* ♦♦ M ♦♦	M ♦♦	S ♦ M, W ♦♦
			D ♦♦	D ♦♦[4]	vag	D ♦♦
M ♦♦ W irr	M irr W ♦	S ♦ M, W ♦♦	S ♦ M, W ♦♦♦	M, W ♦♦	M, W ♦	M, W irr
S*, M ♦♦	S*, M ♦♦	S*, M ♦♦	S* ♦♦ M ♦♦♦ W irr	S*, M ♦♦♦ W irr	S, M ♦♦	R* ♦♦
S*, M, W ♦♦♦	R* ♦♦♦ W ♦♦♦♦	R* ♦♦♦♦	R* ♦♦♦♦	R* ♦♦♦♦	R* ♦♦♦	R* ♦♦♦ M, W ♦♦♦♦
S* ♦♦♦ W ♦♦	S*, M ♦♦♦[1] W irr	R* ♦♦	R* ♦♦♦♦	R* ♦♦♦♦	R* ♦♦	R* ♦♦♦ M, W ♦♦♦♦
S* ♦♦♦ W irr	S*, M ♦♦[2] W irr	S* ♦♦♦♦ D, W ♦♦	R* ♦♦♦♦	R* ♦♦♦♦	S*, M ♦♦♦ W irr	R* ♦♦♦♦ D ♦♦
S* ♦♦♦♦[3] M, D ♦♦♦	S*, M ♦♦♦♦[2] W ♦	S* ♦♦♦♦ W ♦♦	R* ♦♦♦ M ♦♦♦♦	R* ♦♦♦ M ♦♦♦♦	R* ♦♦	S*, D ♦♦♦ W ♦♦
S, D irr	S*, M ♦	R* ♦♦	R* ♦♦♦♦	R* ♦♦♦♦	R* ♦♦	R* ♦♦♦♦
S vag	vag	D ♦	R* ♦♦♦	R* ♦♦♦	D ♦	R* ♦♦♦♦
S*, M, D ♦♦♦♦ W irr	S*, M ♦♦♦♦[2] W irr	S*, M ♦♦♦♦ W ♦	S* ♦♦♦♦ W ♦♦	S* ♦♦♦♦ W ♦♦	S*, M ♦♦♦♦ W ♦♦	S*, M ♦♦♦♦ W ♦♦
S* ♦♦♦ W irr	S* ♦♦♦♦ M ♦♦♦[1] W ♦	S*, M ♦♦♦♦ W ♦	S* ♦♦♦ M ♦♦♦♦ W irr	S*, M ♦♦♦♦ W ♦	S* ♦♦♦♦ W irr	S*, M ♦♦♦♦ W ♦♦
S*, M ♦♦ W irr	S*, M ♦♦[2] W ♦♦	S*, M ♦♦ W irr	R* ♦♦♦	R* ♦♦♦	S*, M ♦♦ W ♦	S*, W ♦♦♦ M ♦♦♦♦
S*, M ♦♦ W irr	S*, M ♦♦[2] W ♦	S*, M ♦♦ W ♦	S*, M ♦♦♦ W ♦♦	S*, W ♦♦ M ♦♦♦	R* ♦♦	S*, M, W ♦♦
D irr[4]	S*, M ♦♦	R* ♦♦	S* ♦♦♦♦ M, D ♦♦♦ W ♦♦	S* ♦♦♦ M ♦♦♦♦ W ♦♦	R* ♦♦	R*, M ♦♦
irr		vag	R* ♦	R ♦		vag
S, M, D ♦♦	D irr	S* ♦♦♦♦	S* ♦♦♦♦ M, D ♦♦♦ W ♦♦	S*, W ♦♦♦ M ♦♦♦♦	R* ♦♦	R* ♦♦♦♦

Italic type denotes "review" species.
Please report any sightings to Texas Bird Records Committee *(see Appendix B)*.

* = Breeding
1 = More numerous in spring
2 = More numerous in fall
3 = More numerous in west
4 = More numerous in east

5 = Deep-water pelagic
6 = Local
7 = Extirpated from this range or believed extinct

Bird Species	Trans-Pecos	Panhandle and Western Plains	Edwards Plateau
❑ SPOONBILL, Roseate	vag		S, M vag D irr
❑ *JABIRU*			
❑ STORK, Wood			D irr
❑ *FLAMINGO, Greater*			
❑ WHISTLING-DUCK, Fulvous	vag	vag	
❑ Black-bellied		W vag	S*, D ♦♦
❑ SWAN, Tundra	W irr	S vag M, W ♦	W irr
❑ *Trumpeter*		M vag	
❑ GOOSE, Greater White-fronted	M, W irr	S vag M ♦♦ W irr	M, W ♦♦
❑ Snow	M, W ♦	S vag M, W ♦♦♦♦	M ♦♦
❑ Ross's	M, W irr	M ♦♦ W ♦♦♦♦	M, W ♦
❑ *BRANT*		M, W vag	
❑ GOOSE, Canada	M, W irr	S* ♦♦ M, W ♦♦♦♦	M, W ♦♦
❑ DUCK, Muscovy			
❑ Wood	S* ♦ M, W ♦♦	S*, M ♦♦ W irr	S*, W ♦♦
❑ TEAL, Green-winged	M, W ♦♦♦♦	S* ♦ M, W ♦♦♦♦	M ♦♦♦♦ W ♦♦♦
❑ DUCK, *American Black*			
❑ Mottled			irr
❑ MALLARD, ... "Common"	M, W ♦♦♦	S* ♦♦♦ M, W ♦♦♦♦	S* irr M, W ♦♦
❑ ... "Mexican Duck"	R* ♦♦		
❑ PINTAIL, *White-cheeked*			
❑ Northern	M, W ♦♦	S* ♦♦ M, W ♦♦♦♦	M, W ♦♦♦♦
❑ *GARGANEY*	M, W vag	M, W vag	
❑ TEAL, Blue-winged	M ♦♦♦ W irr[4]	S* ♦♦♦ M ♦♦♦♦ W vag	S* irr M ♦♦♦♦ W irr

S = Summer

M = Migrant

W = Winter

R = Resident

D = Post-nesting Dispersal

♦ ♦ ♦ ♦ = **Common.** Always present in significant numbers in the proper habitat.
♦ ♦ ♦ = **Fairly Common.** A few are always present in the proper habitat.
♦ ♦ = **Uncommon.** Sometimes present in the proper habitat.
♦ = **Rare.** Occur regularly, but in small numbers; a good search can usually find one.
irr = **Irregular.** Definitely not expected, but a few occur occasionally.
spor = **Sporadic.** Not expected every year, but may occur in significant numbers.
vag = **Vagrant.** Well out of the species' normal range (extralimital).

Northern Plains	Pineywoods	Central Plains	Upper Coast	Coastal Bend	Brush Country	Rio Grande Valley
D ♦4	D irr	R* ♦♦	R* ♦♦♦	S*, M ♦♦♦ W ♦♦	D ♦♦	R* ♦♦
			D vag	D vag		D vag
D spor	D ♦♦	D ♦♦	S ♦♦	D ♦♦	D ♦♦	D irr
				vag		
S vag	S ♦	S* ♦♦	S* ♦♦♦♦ M ♦♦♦ W ♦	S* ♦♦ M ♦♦♦ W irr	S* ♦♦	S*, W irr M ♦♦
S* ♦♦6	S irr	S* ♦♦♦ W ♦♦	S* ♦♦♦♦ M ♦♦♦ W ♦	S* ♦♦♦♦ M, W ♦♦♦	S*, M ♦♦♦♦ W ♦♦	S*, M ♦♦♦♦ W ♦♦♦
M irr	W ♦	W vag	W irr	W irr	W irr	W vag
						W vag
M ♦♦♦ W ♦♦	M, W ♦♦	M, W ♦♦♦	M, W ♦♦♦♦	M, W ♦♦♦♦	M, W ♦♦♦4	W ♦♦♦♦
M, W ♦♦♦♦6	M ♦♦♦ W ♦♦	M, W ♦♦♦♦	W ♦♦♦♦	M, W ♦♦♦♦	M, W ♦♦♦♦	W ♦♦♦
M, W ♦♦♦	W irr	W ♦♦	W ♦♦♦	W ♦♦	W ♦♦	W ♦
W vag			M, W vag	W irr	W vag	
M ♦♦♦♦ W ♦♦♦	M ♦♦ W ♦	M, W ♦♦♦	W ♦♦♦♦	W ♦♦	W ♦♦4	W ♦♦
						R ♦
S*, M ♦♦ W ♦♦♦4	R* ♦♦♦	S, M, W ♦♦	S, W ♦♦	M ♦♦ W ♦	S*, M, W irr	S*, M, W ♦♦
M ♦♦♦♦ W ♦♦♦	M ♦♦♦♦ W ♦♦♦	M, W ♦♦♦♦	M ♦♦♦ W ♦♦♦♦	M, W ♦♦♦♦	M ♦♦♦♦ W ♦♦♦4	M, W ♦♦♦♦
W vag	W vag		W vag	W vag		
S ♦♦6	S ♦	R* ♦♦	R* ♦♦♦♦	R* ♦♦♦♦	R irr	R* ♦♦♦♦
S* irr M ♦♦♦♦ W ♦♦♦	S ♦ M, W ♦♦♦♦	S* 6 M, W ♦♦♦	M, W ♦♦	M, W ♦♦	M, W irr	M, W irr
						M, W irr
						W vag
M, W ♦♦♦	M ♦♦♦♦ W ♦♦♦	M, W ♦♦♦♦	M ♦♦♦ W ♦♦♦♦	M, W ♦♦♦♦	M, W ♦♦♦♦	M, W ♦♦♦♦
				M, W vag		
S* ♦ M ♦♦♦♦ W irr	S* irr M ♦♦♦♦ W ♦	S ♦ M ♦♦♦♦ W ♦♦	M ♦♦♦♦ W ♦♦♦	S* irr M ♦♦♦♦ W ♦♦♦	M, W ♦♦♦♦	M ♦♦♦♦ W ♦♦♦

Italic type denotes "review" species.
Please report any sightings to Texas Bird Records Committee *(see Appendix B)*.

* = Breeding
1 = More numerous in spring
2 = More numerous in fall
3 = More numerous in west
4 = More numerous in east

5 = Deep-water pelagic
6 = Local
7 = Extirpated from this range or believed extinct

Bird Species	Trans-Pecos	Panhandle and Western Plains	Edwards Plateau
❑ TEAL, Cinnamon	S* W ♦ M ♦♦	S* ♦♦ M ♦♦♦ W vag	M, W ♦♦
❑ SHOVELER, Northern	S* ♦ M, W ♦♦	S* ♦♦ M, W ♦♦♦♦	M, W ♦♦♦♦
❑ GADWALL	M, W ♦♦♦♦	S* ♦ M, W ♦♦♦♦	M, W ♦♦♦♦
❑ WIGEON, *Eurasian*	M, W vag	M, W vag	
❑　 American	M, W ♦♦♦♦	S [6] M, W ♦♦♦♦	M, W ♦♦♦♦
❑ CANVASBACK	M, W ♦♦	S vag M, W ♦♦	M, W ♦♦
❑ REDHEAD	S* ♦ M ♦♦	S* ♦♦♦ M, W ♦♦♦♦	M, W ♦♦
❑ DUCK, Ring-necked	S irr M, W ♦♦	M ♦♦♦ W ♦♦	M, W ♦♦♦
❑ SCAUP, Greater	M vag	M, W vag	W ♦
❑　 Lesser	S irr M, W ♦♦♦	S vag M, W ♦♦♦♦	S irr M, W ♦♦♦♦
❑ DUCK, *Harlequin*			
❑ OLDSQUAW	vag	M, W vag	W irr
❑ SCOTER, Black	W vag		W vag
❑　 Surf	W vag	M, W vag	M, W ♦
❑　 White-winged	W vag	M, W vag	M, W ♦
❑ GOLDENEYE, Common	W irr	M, W ♦♦♦	W ♦
❑　 *Barrow's*	W vag		
❑ BUFFLEHEAD	W ♦♦♦	M, W ♦♦♦	W ♦♦♦♦
❑ MERGANSER, Hooded	M, W ♦	S vag M, W ♦♦	M, W ♦
❑　 Common	W ♦♦	S vag M, W ♦♦♦	W ♦♦
❑　 Red-breasted	W ♦	S vag W irr	W ♦♦
❑ DUCK, Ruddy	S* ♦ M, W ♦♦♦	S* ♦♦ M, W ♦♦♦♦	M, W ♦♦
❑　 *Masked*			
❑ VULTURE, Black	R* ♦♦		R* ♦♦♦
❑　 Turkey	S* ♦♦♦♦ W irr	S*, M ♦♦♦♦ W vag	S* ♦♦♦ M ♦♦♦♦ W ♦♦[4]

S = Summer	♦ ♦ ♦ ♦ = **Common.** Always present in significant numbers in the proper habitat.
M = Migrant	♦ ♦ ♦ = **Fairly Common.** A few are always present in the proper habitat.
W = Winter	♦ ♦ = **Uncommon.** Sometimes present in the proper habitat.
R = Resident	♦ = **Rare.** Occur regularly, but in small numbers; a good search can usually find one. irr = **Irregular.** Definitely not expected, but a few occur occasionally.
D = Post-nesting Dispersal	spor = **Sporadic.** Not expected every year, but may occur in significant numbers. vag = **Vagrant.** Well out of the species' normal range (extralimital).

Northern Plains	Pineywoods	Central Plains	Upper Coast	Coastal Bend	Brush Country	Rio Grande Valley
M ♦♦[1] W irr	M, W irr	M irr W ♦♦	W ♦♦	M, W ♦♦	M, W ♦♦	M irr W ♦♦
M ♦♦♦♦ W ♦♦♦	M ♦♦♦♦ W ♦♦♦	M, W ♦♦♦♦	S ♦ M, W ♦♦♦♦	S* ♦ M, W ♦♦♦♦	M, W ♦♦♦♦	M, W ♦♦♦♦
M ♦♦♦♦ W ♦♦♦	M ♦♦♦♦ W ♦♦♦	M, W ♦♦♦♦	M ♦♦♦ W ♦♦♦♦	M, W ♦♦♦♦	M, W ♦♦♦♦	M, W ♦♦♦♦
W vag	M, W vag	Vag	M, W vag	M, W vag		W vag
M ♦♦♦♦ W ♦♦	M ♦♦♦♦ W ♦♦♦	M, W ♦♦♦♦	M ♦♦♦ W ♦♦♦♦	M, W ♦♦♦♦	M, W ♦♦♦♦	M, W ♦♦♦♦
M ♦♦♦ W ♦♦	M, W ♦♦[2]	M, W ♦♦♦	M, W ♦♦♦	M, W ♦♦♦	M, W ♦♦	M ♦♦♦ W ♦♦♦♦
M ♦♦♦ W ♦♦	M, W ♦[2]	M ♦♦♦	M, W ♦♦♦	S ♦ M, W ♦♦♦♦	M, W ♦♦	M ♦♦♦ W ♦♦♦♦
M, W ♦♦♦	M ♦♦♦♦ W ♦♦♦	M, W ♦♦♦	M, W ♦♦♦	M, W ♦♦♦	M, W ♦♦	M, W ♦♦
M, W ♦♦	M, W irr	M, W ♦	M, W ♦	M, W ♦	M ♦	W ♦
M, W ♦♦♦	S ♦ M, W ♦♦♦♦	S ♦ M, W ♦♦♦♦	S ♦ M, W ♦♦♦♦	S irr M, W ♦♦♦♦	S irr M, W ♦♦♦♦	M, W ♦♦♦♦
W vag	W vag					W vag
M, W irr	M, W ♦	M, W irr	W ♦	M, W ♦	W irr	
W vag[4,2]	M, W ♦		W ♦	W ♦		
M irr[2]		M, W ♦	M, W ♦♦	M, W ♦		W vag
M irr[2]	M, W ♦	M, W ♦	M, W ♦♦	M, W ♦		W vag
W ♦	M, W ♦♦	W ♦♦	W ♦♦	W ♦♦	W ♦	W ♦
W vag	vag		vag			
W ♦♦♦	M, W ♦♦♦	W ♦♦♦	M, W ♦♦♦	M, W ♦♦♦♦	M, W ♦♦♦	M irr W ♦♦
M, W ♦♦	M, W ♦♦	M, W ♦♦	M, W ♦♦	M, W ♦♦♦	M, W ♦♦	W ♦
W irr[4]	W vag	W vag	W ♦	W ♦		W vag
W ♦♦ W ♦♦♦♦[6]	M, W ♦♦	W ♦♦	M, W ♦♦♦	M, W ♦♦♦	W ♦♦	M ♦♦ W ♦♦♦
M, W ♦♦♦	S ♦ M, W ♦♦♦♦	M, W ♦♦♦♦	M, W ♦♦♦	S* irr M, W ♦♦♦♦	M, W ♦♦♦♦	S ♦ M, W ♦♦♦♦
		R* irr	R* ♦	R* ♦	irr	R* ♦
R*, M ♦♦♦♦[4]	R* ♦♦♦	R* ♦♦♦♦	R* ♦♦♦	R ♦♦♦♦	R* ♦♦♦♦	R* ♦♦♦♦
S* ♦♦♦♦ W ♦♦♦[4]	R* ♦♦♦♦	R* ♦♦♦♦	R* ♦♦♦♦	R* ♦♦♦ W ♦♦♦♦	R*, W ♦♦♦♦	R*, W ♦♦♦♦

Italic type denotes "review" species.
Please report any sightings to Texas Bird Records Committee *(see Appendix B)*.

* = Breeding
1 = More numerous in spring
2 = More numerous in fall
3 = More numerous in west
4 = More numerous in east

5 = Deep-water pelagic
6 = Local
7 = Extirpated from this range or believed extinct

Bird Species	Trans-Pecos	Panhandle and Western Plains	Edwards Plateau
❑ OSPREY	M ♦	S vag M ♦♦ W vag	M ♦♦ W irr
❑ KITE, Hook-billed			
❑ American Swallow-tailed	vag	M vag[2]	
❑ White-tailed	vag		W irr
❑ *Snail*			
❑ Mississippi	S*, D ♦ M ♦♦	S*, M ♦♦♦	S* ♦♦♦ M ♦♦
❑ EAGLE, Bald	W irr	M, W ♦♦	M, W ♦♦
❑ HARRIER, Northern	M, W ♦♦	S* ♦ M, W ♦♦♦	M, W ♦♦♦
❑ HAWK, Sharp-shinned	S* ♦ M, W ♦♦	S vag M, W ♦♦	M, W ♦♦
❑ Cooper's	S* ♦♦ M, W ♦♦	S* irr M, W ♦	S* ♦ M, W ♦♦
❑ GOSHAWK, *Northern*	irr	M, W vag	
❑ HAWK, *Crane*			
❑ BLACK-HAWK, Common	S* ♦ M irr	S* ♦	S*, M ♦
❑ HAWK, Harris's	R* ♦	S*, D vag	S*, M ♦
❑ Gray	S* ♦		
❑ *Roadside*			
❑ Red-shouldered	vag	M, W vag	R* irr
❑ Broad-winged	M ♦	S vag M ♦	M irr
❑ *Short-tailed*			vag
❑ Swainson's	S* ♦♦ M ♦♦♦	S*, M ♦♦♦♦	S* ♦♦ M ♦♦♦♦
❑ White-tailed			M ♦[4]
❑ Zone-tailed	S* ♦♦		R* ♦
❑ Red-tailed	R* ♦♦♦ W ♦♦♦♦	R* ♦♦♦	R* ♦♦♦ W ♦♦♦♦
❑ Ferruginous	M, W ♦[3]	S* ♦ M, W ♦♦♦	W ♦♦
❑ Rough-legged	W spor	M, W ♦♦	W irr
❑ EAGLE, Golden	R* ♦♦ W* ♦♦♦	R* [6]	W irr
❑ CARACARA, Crested	vag	vag	R* ♦♦[4]
❑ FOREST-FALCON, *Collared*			

S = Summer	♦ ♦ ♦ ♦ = **Common.** Always present in significant numbers in the proper habitat.
M = Migrant	♦ ♦ ♦ = **Fairly Common.** A few are always present in the proper habitat.
W = Winter	♦ ♦ = **Uncommon.** Sometimes present in the proper habitat.
R = Resident	♦ = **Rare.** Occur regularly, but in small numbers; a good search can usually find one.
D = Post-nesting Dispersal	irr = **Irregular.** Definitely not expected, but a few occur occasionally.
	spor = **Sporadic.** Not expected every year, but may occur in significant numbers.
	vag = **Vagrant.** Well out of the species' normal range (extralimital).

Northern Plains	Pineywoods	Central Plains	Upper Coast	Coastal Bend	Brush Country	Rio Grande Valley
M ♦♦♦ W ♦♦	S irr M ♦♦ W ♦	S ♦ M ♦♦	S ♦ M, W ♦♦	M ♦♦ W ♦♦♦	M, W ♦♦	S ♦ M, W ♦♦♦
						R* ♦♦
S vag	S*, M ♦	M ♦	M ♦	M irr	M irr⁴	M ♦⁴
irr	irr	R* ♦♦	R* ♦♦	R*, W ♦♦	R*, W ♦♦	R* ♦♦♦
					vag	
S* ♦ M ♦♦	M ♦♦	S* ♦ M ♦♦♦	S* ♦♦♦ M ♦♦♦♦	M ♦♦♦♦	M ♦♦♦	M ♦♦
M, W ♦♦	M, W ♦♦	M, W* ♦♦	M, W ♦♦	M, W* ♦		W vag
M, W ♦♦♦	M, W ♦♦	M, W ♦♦♦	M, W ♦♦♦	M, W ♦♦♦	M, W ♦♦♦	M, W ♦♦♦
M ♦♦♦⁴ W ♦♦	M ♦♦♦ W ♦♦	S ♦ M, W ♦♦	M ♦♦♦ W ♦♦	M ♦♦♦ W ♦♦	M, W ♦♦	M, W ♦♦
M, W ♦⁴	S* ♦ M, W ♦♦	S* ♦ M, W ♦♦	S ♦ M ♦♦♦ W ♦♦	S ♦ M ♦♦♦ W ♦♦	S* ♦ M, W ♦♦	M, W ♦♦
W vag		W vag				
						vag
					vag	W irr
W irr		S* irr	irr	R* ♦♦♦	R* ♦♦♦♦	R* ♦♦♦
				irr		R* irr
						vag
R* ♦♦♦	R* ♦♦♦	R* ♦♦♦	R* ♦♦♦	R* ♦♦♦	R* ♦♦	M, W ♦♦
S* ♦⁴ M ♦♦♦♦⁴	S* ♦♦ M ♦♦♦♦	S ♦ M ♦♦♦	M ♦♦♦♦	M ♦♦♦♦	M ♦♦♦⁴	M ♦♦⁴
						vag
S* ♦ M ♦♦³	S, M ♦	S* ♦ M ♦♦♦	S* irr M ♦♦♦	S* ♦♦ M ♦♦♦	S*, M ♦♦♦	S*, W ♦³ M ♦♦♦³
		R* ♦	R* ♦♦	R* ♦♦♦	R* ♦♦⁴	R* ♦♦⁴
		vag		M, W vag	M irr	irr
R* ♦♦♦ W ♦♦♦♦	R* ♦♦ M, W ♦♦♦	R* ♦♦♦ W ♦♦♦♦	R* ♦♦♦ W ♦♦♦♦	R* ♦♦♦ W ♦♦♦♦	R* ♦♦ W ♦♦♦♦	M ♦♦♦ W ♦♦♦♦
M, W irr³	W ♦	W ♦	W ♦	W ♦	W ♦	W irr
W irr	M, W irr	W vag	W ♦	W vag	W vag	
M, W irr	M, W ♦	W vag	W ♦	W ♦	W ♦	W vag
R* ♦⁴,⁶	R* ♦	R* ♦♦♦	R* ♦♦	R* ♦♦♦♦	R* ♦♦♦♦	R* ♦♦♦
						W vag

Italic type denotes "review" species.
Please report any sightings to Texas Bird Records Committee *(see Appendix B)*.

* = Breeding
1 = More numerous in spring
2 = More numerous in fall
3 = More numerous in west
4 = More numerous in east
5 = Deep-water pelagic
6 = Local
7 = Extirpated from this range or believed extinct

Bird Species	Trans-Pecos	Panhandle and Western Plains	Edwards Plateau
❏ KESTREL, American	S* ♦♦ M, W ♦♦♦♦	S*, M, W ♦♦♦	S* irr M, W ♦♦♦♦
❏ MERLIN	W irr	M, W ♦	M, W irr
❏ FALCON, *Aplomado*	vag		
❏ Prairie	S* ♦ M, W ♦♦3	S* irr M, W ♦♦♦	M, W irr
❏ Peregrine	S* ♦♦ M, W irr	S* irr W irr	M, W irr
❏ CHACHALACA, Plain			
❏ PHEASANT, Ring-necked		R* ♦♦♦	
❏ PRAIRIE-CHICKEN, Greater			
❏ Lesser		R* 6	
❏ TURKEY, Wild	R* ♦4	R* ♦♦♦	R* ♦♦♦
❏ QUAIL, Montezuma	R* ♦♦		R* ♦6
❏ BOBWHITE, Northern	R* ♦6	R* ♦♦♦	R* ♦♦♦
❏ QUAIL, Scaled	R* ♦♦♦	R* ♦♦♦	R* ♦♦♦3
❏ Gambel's	R* ♦♦		
❏ RAIL, Yellow		S vag	
❏ Black		S vag	
❏ Clapper			
☒ King	S* irr6 M irr	S*, M irr	R* ♦
❏ Virginia	S* irr6 W ♦	R* ♦♦	S* ♦ M ♦♦ W irr
❏ SORA	S irr6 W ♦	S ♦ M ♦♦ W irr	M ♦♦♦ W irr
❏ CRAKE, *Paint-billed*			
❏ RAIL, *Spotted*			
❏ GALLINULE, Purple	M irr	M vag	M ♦
❏ MOORHEN, Common	R* irr	R* ♦♦	R* ♦♦
❏ COOT, American	S* ♦♦ W ♦♦♦♦	S*, W ♦♦♦ M ♦♦♦♦	S* ♦♦ M, W ♦♦♦♦
❏ CRANE, Sandhill	M ♦	M, W ♦♦♦♦	M ♦♦♦ W irr
❏ Whooping		M, W vag	
❏ THICK-KNEE, *Double-striped*			
❏ PLOVER, Black-bellied	M ♦	S, M ♦	M ♦♦ W irr

S = Summer

M = Migrant

W = Winter

R = Resident

D = Post-nesting Dispersal

♦ ♦ ♦ ♦ = **Common.** Always present in significant numbers in the proper habitat.

♦ ♦ ♦ = **Fairly Common.** A few are always present in the proper habitat.

♦ ♦ = **Uncommon.** Sometimes present in the proper habitat.

♦ = **Rare.** Occur regularly, but in small numbers; a good search can usually find one.

irr = **Irregular.** Definitely not expected, but a few occur occasionally.

spor = **Sporadic.** Not expected every year, but may occur in significant numbers.

vag = **Vagrant.** Well out of the species' normal range (extralimital).

Northern Plains	Pineywoods	Central Plains	Upper Coast	Coastal Bend	Brush Country	Rio Grande Valley
S* irr M, W ◆◆◆◆	S* irr M, W ◆◆◆²	S ◆ M, W ◆◆◆◆	M, W ◆◆◆◆	M, W ◆◆◆◆	S* ◆ M, W ◆◆◆◆	S ◆ M, W ◆◆◆◆
M, W ◆◆²	M irr²	M ◆◆	M, W ◆◆	M, W ◆◆	M, W ◆◆	M irr W ◆◆
				reintroduced		reintroduced
W ◆◆³		vag	M, W vag	W irr	M, W irr	W vag
M, W irr	M irr²	M, W ◆◆	M ◆◆ W ◆	M, W ◆◆	M ◆◆ W ◆	M, W ◆◆
						R* ◆◆◆
R* ◆◆◆			R* ◆			
		R* ◆	R* ◆	R* ◆		
R* ◆◆	R* ◆	R* ◆◆	R* ◆	R* ◆◆◆	R* ◆◆◆	R* ◆◆³
R* ◆◆◆◆	R* ◆◆◆	R* ◆◆◆	R* ◆◆◆	R* ◆◆◆	R* ◆◆◆◆	R* ◆◆
R* irr⁶, ³					R* ◆◆◆³	R* ◆◆³
M ◆	M ◆	M ◆	M ◆◆ W ◆	W ◆◆		W vag
M ◆	M ◆	M ◆	R* ◆◆	R* ◆		R* ◆
		R* ◆◆◆◆	R* ◆◆◆◆			R* ◆◆◆◆
M irr	R* ◆◆	R* ◆	R* ◆◆◆	S* ◆ M, W ◆◆	R* ◆◆	R* ◆◆
M, W irr	M ◆◆²	M irr	M, W ◆	M, W ◆◆	M, W ◆	M, W ◆◆
M ◆◆◆ W ◆◆	S ◆ M ◆◆◆² W ◆	S* ◆ M, W ◆◆	M ◆◆◆ M ◆◆	M ◆◆ W ◆◆◆	M, W ◆◆◆	M, W ◆◆◆⁴
	vag					
vag						
S* irr	S*, M ◆	S, M ◆◆	S*, M ◆◆◆	S*, M ◆◆◆	M ◆	S*, M irr
R* ◆⁶	S*, M ◆◆	R* ◆◆	R* ◆◆◆◆	R* ◆◆◆◆	R* ◆◆	R* ◆◆◆⁴
S* irr M, W ◆◆◆◆	S* ◆ M, W ◆◆◆◆	R* ◆◆◆◆	R* ◆◆◆◆	R* ◆◆◆◆	R* ◆◆◆◆	R* ◆◆ M, W ◆◆◆◆
M ◆◆◆³ W ◆◆³	M irr²	M, W ◆◆◆	M, W ◆◆◆◆	M, W ◆◆◆◆	M ◆◆◆◆ W ◆◆	W ◆◆◆⁴
M irr		M ◆	W ◆³	W ◆◆⁶		
				vag		
M ◆◆	M ◆◆² W ◆	M, W ◆◆	S ◆ M, W ◆◆◆◆	S ◆◆ M, W ◆◆◆◆	M ◆◆◆◆ W ◆◆◆	S ◆ M, W ◆◆◆◆

Italic type denotes "review" species.
Please report any sightings to Texas Bird
Records Committee *(see Appendix B)*.

* = Breeding
1 = More numerous in spring
2 = More numerous in fall
3 = More numerous in west
4 = More numerous in east

5 = Deep-water pelagic
6 = Local
7 = Extirpated from this range
   or believed extinct

Bird Species	Trans-Pecos	Panhandle and Western Plains	Edwards Plateau
❏ GOLDEN-PLOVER, American	M irr	S, M irr W vag	M ♦♦
❏ PLOVER, *Collared*			
❏ Snowy	S ♦[6] M irr	S*, M ♦	S* irr M ♦♦
❏ Wilson's			M vag
❏ Semipalmated	M irr	S vag M ♦♦	M ♦♦
❏ Piping	M vag	M vag	M ♦
❏ KILLDEER	R* ♦♦♦♦	S*, M ♦♦♦♦ W ♦	R* ♦♦♦♦
❏ PLOVER, Mountain	S* ♦ M ♦♦	S irr M ♦	W ♦
❏ OYSTERCATCHER, American			
❏ STILT, Black-necked	S* irr[6] M ♦♦	S*, M ♦♦	S*, M ♦♦
❏ AVOCET, American	S* irr M ♦♦	S* ♦♦♦ M ♦♦♦♦	M ♦♦♦
❏ JACANA, *Northern*	vag		vag
❏ YELLOWLEGS, Greater	M ♦♦♦ W ♦	S ♦♦ M ♦♦♦	M ♦♦♦♦ W ♦♦
❏ Lesser	M ♦♦	M ♦♦♦♦	M ♦♦ W ♦
❏ SANDPIPER, Solitary	M ♦	S, M ♦♦	M ♦♦
❏ WILLET	M ♦	S irr M ♦	M ♦
❏ TATTLER, *Wandering*			
❏ SANDPIPER, Spotted	M ♦♦♦ W ♦[4]	S* ♦♦ M ♦♦♦	M ♦♦♦ W ♦♦
❏ Upland	M ♦♦	S, M ♦♦♦	M ♦♦♦♦[2]
❏ CURLEW, *Eskimo*			7
❏ WHIMBREL	M irr	S vag M irr	M irr

S = Summer
M = Migrant
W = Winter
R = Resident
D = Post-nesting Dispersal

♦ ♦ ♦ ♦ = **Common.** Always present in significant numbers in the proper habitat.
♦ ♦ ♦ = **Fairly Common.** A few are always present in the proper habitat.
♦ ♦ = **Uncommon.** Sometimes present in the proper habitat.
♦ = **Rare.** Occur regularly, but in small numbers; a good search can usually find one.
irr = **Irregular.** Definitely not expected, but a few occur occasionally.
spor = **Sporadic.** Not expected every year, but may occur in significant numbers.
vag = **Vagrant.** Well out of the species' normal range (extralimital).

Northern Plains	Pineywoods	Central Plains	Upper Coast	Coastal Bend	Brush Country	Rio Grande Valley
M ♦♦♦[1]	M ♦♦[1]	M ♦♦♦[1]	M ♦♦♦♦[1] W ♦	M ♦♦♦♦[1]	M ♦♦♦[1]	M ♦♦[1]
					vag	
M irr	M irr	M ♦	M ♦♦ W ♦	S* ♦ M ♦♦♦ W ♦♦	M ♦	S*, M ♦♦ W ♦
	vag	vag	S* ♦♦♦♦ W irr	S* ♦♦♦ W irr		S*, M ♦♦ W ♦
M ♦♦♦	M ♦♦♦[2] W irr	M ♦♦♦	S ♦ M ♦♦♦♦ W ♦♦♦	S ♦ M ♦♦♦♦[1] W ♦♦♦	M ♦♦ W ♦	S ♦ M ♦♦ W ♦♦♦
M irr	M irr[2] W vag	M ♦	M ♦♦♦♦ W ♦♦♦	S ♦ M ♦♦♦ W ♦♦	M ♦	S ♦ M, W ♦♦
R* ♦♦♦ M ♦♦♦♦	R* ♦♦♦♦	R* ♦♦♦♦	R* ♦♦♦♦	R* ♦♦♦♦	R* ♦♦♦♦	R* ♦♦♦♦
M irr		W ♦♦		M, W ♦	M, W ♦	M, W ♦
			R* ♦♦	R* ♦♦[4]		R* ♦♦
M ♦♦[6]	S, M irr	S*, M ♦♦♦ W ♦	S* ♦♦♦♦ W ♦♦	S*, M ♦♦♦♦ W ♦♦♦	S*, M ♦♦ W ♦	S*, M ♦♦♦♦ W ♦♦
M ♦♦♦	S, M ♦♦[2]	S, M ♦♦♦	S irr M, W ♦♦♦	S ♦♦♦ M, W ♦♦♦♦	S, M ♦♦	S* ♦ M ♦♦ W ♦♦♦
		vag	vag[7]	irr*	irr	irr
M ♦♦♦♦ W ♦♦	M ♦♦♦[2] W irr	M ♦♦♦♦ W ♦♦	S ♦♦ M ♦♦♦ W ♦♦♦♦	S ♦ M ♦♦♦♦ W ♦♦♦	M ♦♦♦ W ♦♦	S ♦ M, W ♦♦♦♦
M ♦♦♦♦ W irr	M ♦♦♦♦[2] W ♦	M ♦♦♦♦ W ♦♦	S ♦♦ M ♦♦♦♦ W ♦♦♦	S ♦ M ♦♦♦♦ W ♦♦♦	M ♦♦♦ W ♦♦	S ♦ M, W ♦♦♦♦
M ♦♦♦	M ♦♦♦ W irr	M ♦♦ W irr	M ♦♦ W ♦	M ♦♦ S, W ♦	M ♦♦ W ♦	M ♦♦ W ♦
M ♦♦[4]	M ♦♦[2]	M ♦♦	R* ♦♦♦♦	R* ♦♦♦♦	M ♦♦	R* ♦♦♦♦
			vag			
M ♦♦♦ W irr	S, W ♦ M ♦♦♦	S irr M, W ♦♦♦♦	S ♦ M ♦♦♦♦ W ♦♦♦	S ♦ M ♦♦♦♦ W ♦♦♦	M ♦♦♦ W ♦♦	S ♦ M, W ♦♦
M ♦♦♦♦	M ♦♦[1]	M ♦♦♦	M ♦♦[1]	M ♦♦♦	M ♦♦♦[1]	M ♦♦[1]
		7	vag[7]	7		7
M irr	M irr[1]	M irr	M ♦♦ S, W ♦	M ♦♦[1] S, W ♦	M ♦	M ♦♦ W ♦

Italic type denotes "review" species.
Please report any sightings to Texas Bird Records Committee (see Appendix B).

* = Breeding
1 = More numerous in spring
2 = More numerous in fall
3 = More numerous in west
4 = More numerous in east

5 = Deep-water pelagic
6 = Local
7 = Extirpated from this range or believed extinct

Bird Species	Trans-Pecos	Panhandle and Western Plains	Edwards Plateau
☐ CURLEW, Long-billed	M irr	S*[6] M ◆◆◆◆ W irr	M ◆◆◆ W ◆◆
☐ GODWIT, Hudsonian	vag		M irr[1a]
☐ Marbled	M irr	S, M ◆	M ◆◆
☐ TURNSTONE, Ruddy	vag		M ◆[2]
☐ SURFBIRD			
☐ KNOT, Red	vag	M vag	M vag
☐ SANDERLING	M irr	S vag M ◆	M ◆
☐ SANDPIPER, Semipalmated	M irr	S, M ◆◆◆	M ◆◆[1a]
☐ Western	M ◆ W irr	S ◆◆ M ◆◆◆◆ W vag	M ◆◆◆◆ W ◆
☐ STINT, *Red-necked*	vag		
☐ SANDPIPER, Least	M ◆◆◆◆ W ◆	S ◆◆ M ◆◆◆◆ W vag	M ◆◆◆◆ W ◆◆◆
☐ White-rumped	M irr	M ◆[1]	M ◆
☐ Baird's	M ◆◆	S ◆◆ M ◆◆◆◆	M ◆◆◆
☐ Pectoral	M irr	M ◆◆	M ◆◆
☐ *Sharp-tailed*			
☐ *Purple*			M vag
☐ DUNLIN	M irr W irr	M vag	M ◆◆
☐ SANDPIPER, *Curlew*			
☐ Stilt	M ◆[3]	M ◆◆◆ W vag	M ◆
☐ Buff-breasted		M vag	M irr[2]
☐ *RUFF*	vag	vag	vag
☐ DOWITCHER, Short-billed	M irr	S, M vag	M irr[2]
☐ Long-billed	M ◆◆ W ◆	M ◆◆◆◆ W vag	M, W ◆◆
☐ SNIPE, Common	M, W ◆◆	M ◆◆ W irr	M, W ◆◆◆

S = Summer

M = Migrant

W = Winter

R = Resident

D = Post-nesting Dispersal

◆ ◆ ◆ ◆ = **Common.** Always present in significant numbers in the proper habitat.

◆ ◆ ◆ = **Fairly Common.** A few are always present in the proper habitat.

◆ ◆ = **Uncommon.** Sometimes present in the proper habitat.

◆ = **Rare.** Occur regularly, but in small numbers; a good search can usually find one.

irr = **Irregular.** Definitely not expected, but a few occur occasionally.

spor = **Sporadic.** Not expected every year, but may occur in significant numbers.

vag = **Vagrant.** Well out of the species' normal range (extralimital).

Northern Plains	Pineywoods	Central Plains	Upper Coast	Coastal Bend	Brush Country	Rio Grande Valley
M ♦♦³	S irr M ♦♦	M ♦♦♦	S ♦ M, W ♦♦♦	S ♦ M, W ♦♦♦♦	M ♦♦	S ♦♦ M, W ♦♦♦
M ♦♦¹	M irr¹	M ♦	M ♦♦♦¹	M ♦♦¹	M ♦¹	M ♦¹
M irr	M irr	M ♦	S ♦ M ♦♦♦♦ W ♦♦♦	S ♦ M, W ♦♦♦	M ♦	M, W ♦♦
M irr²	M, W irr	M, W ♦♦	S ♦ M ♦♦♦♦ W ♦♦♦	S ♦♦ M, W ♦♦♦♦	M, W ♦♦♦	M, W ♦♦♦♦
			M vag	M vag		
M irr²	M irr²	M vag	S, W irr M ♦♦	S ♦ M, W ♦♦♦		M ♦♦♦ W ♦
M ♦♦	M ♦♦²	M ♦♦	S ♦♦ M, W ♦♦♦♦	S ♦♦ M, W ♦♦♦♦	M, W ♦♦♦	S ♦ M, W ♦♦♦♦
M ♦♦♦	M ♦♦♦²	M ♦♦♦	M ♦♦♦	S ♦ M ♦♦♦	M ♦♦	S, M ♦♦
M ♦♦♦ W irr	M ♦♦♦²	M, W ♦♦♦♦	M ♦♦♦ W ♦♦♦♦	S ♦♦ M, W ♦♦♦♦	M, W ♦♦	S ♦♦ M, W ♦♦♦♦
M ♦♦♦♦ W ♦♦♦	M ♦♦♦♦² W ♦♦♦	M ♦♦♦♦ W ♦♦♦	M ♦♦♦ W ♦♦♦♦	S ♦♦ M, W ♦♦♦♦	M ♦♦♦ W ♦♦	M, W ♦♦♦♦
M ♦♦♦♦¹	M ♦♦♦¹	M ♦♦¹	M ♦♦♦♦¹	M ♦♦♦¹	M ♦¹	M ♦♦
M ♦♦♦	M ♦♦	M ♦♦¹	M ♦♦♦♦¹	M ♦♦♦¹	M ♦¹	M ♦♦
M ♦♦♦♦	M ♦♦♦♦²	M ♦♦♦	M ♦♦♦♦	M ♦♦	M ♦¹	M ♦♦♦
M vag						
			W vag	M vag		W vag
M ♦♦² W irr	M ♦♦² W irr	M ♦♦ W ♦	M, W ♦♦♦	M, W ♦♦♦♦	M ♦♦ W ♦	M, W ♦♦♦
		M vag	M vag			M vag
M ♦♦♦	M ♦♦² W ♦	M ♦♦ W irr	M ♦♦♦ W ♦	S, W ♦♦ M ♦♦♦♦	M ♦♦ W ♦	M ♦♦♦ W ♦♦
M ♦♦	M ♦♦²	M ♦♦	M ♦♦	M ♦♦	M ♦¹	M ♦♦²
vag	vag²	vag	vag	vag		W vag
M irr²	M ♦♦²	M ♦♦♦ W ♦♦	M, W ♦♦	M, W ♦♦♦♦	M ♦♦	M ♦♦♦♦ W ♦♦
M ♦♦♦ W irr	M ♦♦♦² W ♦	M ♦♦♦♦ W ♦♦♦	M ♦♦♦ W ♦♦♦♦	S ♦♦ M, W ♦♦♦♦	M ♦♦♦ W ♦♦	M, W ♦♦♦♦
M, W ♦♦♦	M, W ♦♦♦♦	M, W ♦♦♦	M, W ♦♦♦	M, W ♦♦♦	M, W ♦♦	M, W ♦♦

Italic type denotes "review" species.
Please report any sightings to Texas Bird Records Committee (see Appendix B).

* = Breeding
1 = More numerous in spring
2 = More numerous in fall
3 = More numerous in west
4 = More numerous in east

5 = Deep-water pelagic
6 = Local
7 = Extirpated from this range or believed extinct

Bird Species	Trans-Pecos	Panhandle and Western Plains	Edwards Plateau
❑ WOODCOCK, American	W vag	W vag	W irr
☒ PHALAROPE, Wilson's	M ♦♦	S*, M ♦♦♦♦ W vag	M ♦♦♦♦[1]
❑ Red-necked	M ♦	M vag	M, W irr
❑ Red	vag	M vag	vag
❑ JAEGER, Pomarine			
❑ Parasitic			
❑ Long-tailed	M vag	M vag	
❑ GULL, Laughing	vag		vag
❑ Franklin's	M ♦♦	S irr M ♦♦♦ W vag	M ♦♦
❑ Little		M, W vag	
❑ Common Black-headed			
❑ Bonaparte's	M irr W ♦[4]	M ♦ W irr	M, W ♦♦
❑ Heermann's	vag	W vag	W vag
❑ Mew	W vag		
❑ Ring-billed	M, W ♦♦♦♦	S ♦♦ M, W ♦♦♦♦	M, W ♦♦♦♦
❑ California	W vag	W vag	
❑ Herring	M, W irr	M, W ♦	M, W ♦♦
❑ Thayer's			
❑ Iceland			
❑ Lesser Black-backed	W vag		
❑ Slaty-backed			
❑ Western	M vag		
❑ Glaucous	M, W vag	M, W vag	
❑ Great Black-backed	W vag		
❑ Kelp			
❑ KITTIWAKE, Black-legged	M, W vag	M, W vag	W vag
❑ GULL, Sabine's	M vag	M vag	
❑ TERN, Gull-billed			S irr
❑ Caspian	S, M irr		M, W ♦
❑ Royal			
❑ Elegant	vag		
❑ Sandwich			

S = Summer

M = Migrant

W = Winter

R = Resident

D = Post-nesting Dispersal

♦ ♦ ♦ ♦ = **Common.** Always present in significant numbers in the proper habitat.
♦ ♦ ♦ = **Fairly Common.** A few are always present in the proper habitat.
♦ ♦ = **Uncommon.** Sometimes present in the proper habitat.
♦ = **Rare.** Occur regularly, but in small numbers; a good search can usually find one.
irr = **Irregular.** Definitely not expected, but a few occur occasionally.
spor = **Sporadic.** Not expected every year, but may occur in significant numbers.
vag = **Vagrant.** Well out of the species' normal range (extralimital).

Northern Plains	Pineywoods	Central Plains	Upper Coast	Coastal Bend	Brush Country	Rio Grande Valley
W irr[4]	M* irr W ♦♦	W ♦♦	W ♦♦	W ♦	W ♦	M, W ♦
M ♦♦♦[1]	M ♦♦	M ♦♦♦	M ♦♦♦[1]	M ♦♦♦	M ♦	M ♦♦♦
M irr[2]	M ♦[2]	M vag	♦	M irr	M irr	M ♦
M vag[2]	vag	M vag[2]	vag		vag	M vag
	vag		M, W ♦[5]	M ♦♦		M, W ♦
M vag			M, W ♦[5]	M, W irr		M, W ♦
M vag	M vag		vag	vag		vag
irr[4]	irr	D ♦	R* ♦♦♦♦	R* ♦♦♦♦	R ♦♦[4]	R* ♦♦♦♦
M ♦♦♦ W irr	M ♦♦[1] W irr	M ♦♦♦ W ♦	M ♦♦♦ W ♦	M ♦♦♦♦ W ♦	M ♦♦♦	M ♦♦♦♦[1] W ♦
M, W ♦	vag	W vag	W vag			
W vag	W vag	W vag		W vag		
M, W ♦♦♦	M, W ♦♦♦	M, W ♦♦♦	M irr W ♦♦	M irr W ♦♦	M irr W ♦	M, W ♦♦
				W vag		
W vag		W vag				
M, W ♦♦♦♦	M, W ♦♦♦♦	M, W ♦♦♦♦	S irr M, W ♦♦♦♦	S ♦ M, W ♦♦♦♦	M, W ♦♦♦	M, W ♦♦♦♦
W vag		W vag	W vag	W vag		W vag
M, W ♦♦♦	M, W ♦♦[1]	M, W ♦♦	M, W ♦♦♦	M, W ♦♦♦♦	M, W ♦♦	M, W ♦♦♦♦
M, W vag		M, W vag	M, W vag	M, W vag		M, W vag
						W vag
W vag			W ♦	W ♦	W vag	M, W ♦
				W vag		W vag
						M vag
M, W vag		W vag	W vag	W vag	M, W vag	W ♦
	W vag		W vag	W vag		W vag
			vag			
W irr	W vag	W vag	W irr	W vag	W vag	W vag
M vag[2]	M vag	M vag	M vag	M vag	M vag	
		S ♦	S* ♦♦♦ W ♦	S* ♦♦♦♦ W ♦♦	S* ♦	S*, M ♦♦♦♦ W ♦♦
M ♦[4]	M ♦♦[2]	M, W ♦♦	R* ♦♦♦	R* ♦♦♦♦	M, W ♦	R* ♦♦♦
S vag	vag		R* ♦♦♦♦	R* ♦♦♦♦	vag	R* ♦♦♦♦
				vag		
	vag	vag	S* ♦♦♦♦ W ♦	S* ♦♦♦♦ W ♦♦	vag	S* ♦♦♦ W ♦♦

Italic type denotes "review" species.
Please report any sightings to Texas Bird Records Committee (see Appendix B).

* = Breeding
1 = More numerous in spring
2 = More numerous in fall
3 = More numerous in west
4 = More numerous in east
5 = Deep-water pelagic
6 = Local
7 = Extirpated from this range or believed extinct

Bird Species	Trans-Pecos	Panhandle and Western Plains	Edwards Plateau
❑ TERN, Common	M irr	M irr	vag
❑ Forster's	M ♦♦	M ♦♦	M ♦♦ W ♦
❑ Least	S*⁶, M irr	S*, M ♦	S ♦ M irr
❑ Bridled			
❑ Sooty	vag		
❑ Black	M ♦♦	S irr M ♦♦♦	M ♦♦♦♦
❑ NODDY, *Brown*			
❑ *Black*			
❑ SKIMMER, Black			vag
❑ DOVE, Rock	R* ♦♦♦♦	R* ♦♦♦♦	R* ♦♦♦♦
❑ PIGEON, Red-billed			
❑ Band-tailed	S* ♦♦♦ W irr	vag	vag
❑ DOVE, White-winged	R* ♦♦♦	S* ♦♦	R* ♦♦♦♦⁴
❑ Mourning	R* ♦♦♦♦	R* ♦♦♦♦	R* ♦♦♦♦
❑ Inca	R* ♦♦♦♦³	R* ♦♦	R* ♦♦♦♦
❑ GROUND-DOVE, Common	R* ♦♦	M vag	R* ♦♦♦♦
❑ *Ruddy*	vag		
❑ DOVE, White-tipped			
❑ QUAIL-DOVE, *Ruddy*			
❑ PARAKEET, Monk	R* ⁶		R* ♦⁶
❑ *Green*			
❑ PARROT, Red-crowned			
❑ CUCKOO, Black-billed	M vag	M vag	M ♦
❑ Yellow-billed	S*, M ♦♦	S*, M ♦♦	S*, M ♦♦♦♦
❑ *Mangrove*			
❑ ROADRUNNER, Greater	R* ♦♦♦♦	R* ♦♦	R* ♦♦
❑ ANI, Groove-billed	S irr⁴		S* irr
❑ OWL, Barn	R* ♦	R* ♦♦	R* ♦♦
❑ Flammulated	S* ♦♦		vag
❑ SCREECH-OWL, Eastern	R* ♦♦	R* ♦♦♦	R* ♦♦♦
❑ Western	R* ♦♦		R* ♦♦
❑ OWL, Great Horned	R* ♦♦♦♦	R* ♦♦♦	R* ♦♦♦

S = Summer

M = Migrant

W = Winter

R = Resident

D = Post-nesting Dispersal

♦ ♦ ♦ ♦ = **Common.** Always present in significant numbers in the proper habitat.
♦ ♦ ♦ = **Fairly Common.** A few are always present in the proper habitat.
♦ ♦ = **Uncommon.** Sometimes present in the proper habitat.
♦ = **Rare.** Occur regularly, but in small numbers; a good search can usually find one.
irr = **Irregular.** Definitely not expected, but a few occur occasionally.
spor = **Sporadic.** Not expected every year, but may occur in significant numbers.
vag = **Vagrant.** Well out of the species' normal range (extralimital).

Northern Plains	Pineywoods	Central Plains	Upper Coast	Coastal Bend	Brush Country	Rio Grande Valley
M irr	M irr²		S ◆◆ M ◆◆²	S ◆◆ M ◆◆◆		M ◆◆
M, W ◆◆◆	M ◆◆◆◆² W ◆◆◆	M, W ◆◆	R* ◆◆◆◆	R* ◆◆◆◆	M, W ◆◆	R* ◆◆◆◆
S* ◆ M ◆◆	S irr M ◆◆²	S, M ◆	S* ◆◆◆	S*, M ◆◆◆◆ W irr	S ◆ M irr	S*, M ◆◆◆
			S ◆◆⁵	S ◆◆⁵		S ◆◆⁵
			S ◆⁵	S*, M ⁵		S, M irr⁵
M ◆◆◆	M ◆◆◆◆	M ◆◆◆	S ◆◆ M ◆◆◆◆	S, M ◆◆◆◆	M ◆◆◆	S ◆◆ M ◆◆◆◆
				D vag vag		D vag
S vag²	vag	vag	S* ◆◆◆◆	R* ◆◆◆	vag	R* ◆◆◆
R* ◆◆◆◆	R* ◆◆◆	R* ◆◆◆◆	R* ◆◆◆◆	R* ◆◆◆◆	R* ◆◆◆◆	R* ◆◆◆◆
				7	S* irr	S* ◆◆ W ◆
			vag	vag		
R* ◆◆⁶, ³		R* ⁶	R* ◆◆³	S* ◆◆◆◆ W ◆◆	R* ◆◆◆◆	S* ◆◆◆◆ W ◆◆
R* ◆◆◆◆	R* ◆◆◆◆²	R* ◆◆◆◆	R* ◆◆◆◆	R* ◆◆◆◆	R* ◆◆◆◆	R* ◆◆◆◆
R* ◆◆	R* ◆◆	R* ◆◆◆◆	R* ◆◆◆◆	R* ◆◆◆◆	R* ◆◆◆◆	R* ◆◆◆◆
irr	R* ◆	R* ◆◆	R* ◆◆	R* ◆◆◆	R* ◆◆◆◆	R* ◆◆
						vag
				R* ◆◆	R* ◆◆	R* ◆◆
						vag
irr*	R* ⁶	R* ⁶	R* ◆⁶			
						R* ◆◆
						R* ◆◆
M irr	M ◆◆¹	M ◆◆	M ◆◆	M ◆	M irr	M ◆◆
S*, M ◆◆◆◆	S*, M ◆◆◆◆	S*, M ◆◆◆◆	S*, M ◆◆◆◆	S*, M ◆◆◆◆	S*, M ◆◆◆◆	S*, M ◆◆◆◆
			vag			vag
R* ◆◆◆³	R* ◆◆	R* ◆◆	R* ◆◆	R* ◆◆	R* ◆◆◆	R* ◆◆◆³
M vag	M irr	M ◆	M, W spor	S*, M ◆◆	S*, M ◆◆	S* ◆◆◆ W ◆
R* ◆◆	R* ◆	R* ◆◆	R* ◆◆	R* ◆◆◆	R* ◆◆◆	R* ◆◆
				vag		
R* ◆◆◆	R* ◆◆◆◆	R* ◆◆	R* ◆◆◆	R* ◆◆◆	R* ◆◆◆	R* ◆◆◆
R* ◆◆◆	R* ◆◆	R* ◆◆◆	R* ◆◆◆	R* ◆◆◆	R* ◆◆◆	R* ◆◆◆

Italic type denotes "review" species.
Please report any sightings to Texas Bird Records Committee (see Appendix B).

* = Breeding
1 = More numerous in spring
2 = More numerous in fall
3 = More numerous in west
4 = More numerous in east

5 = Deep-water pelagic
6 = Local
7 = Extirpated from this range or believed extinct

Bird Species	Trans-Pecos	Panhandle and Western Plains	Edwards Plateau
☐ OWL, *Snowy*			
☐ PYGMY-OWL, *Northern*	vag		
☐ *Ferruginous*			
☐ OWL, Elf	S* ♦♦♦		S ♦
☐ Burrowing	R* ♦♦[6] W ♦	S*, M ♦♦♦ W ♦	W, M ♦♦♦
☐ *Mottled*			
☐ Spotted	R* ♦[6]		
☐ Barred		R* ♦[2]	vag
☐ Long-eared	S* [6] M, W irr	S* irr M, W ♦♦	M, W ♦
☐ Short-eared	M, W irr	M, W ♦	M, W ♦
☐ *Northern Saw-whet*	S, M, W irr	vag	
☐ NIGHTHAWK, Lesser	S*, M ♦♦♦♦		S*, M ♦♦
☐ Common	S*, M ♦♦	S*, M ♦♦♦	S* ♦♦♦ M ♦♦♦♦
☐ PAURAQUE			
☐ POORWILL, Common	S*, M ♦♦♦ W irr	S*, M ♦♦	S*, M ♦♦♦[3] W irr
☐ CHUCK-WILL'S-WIDOW		S, M ♦	S*, M ♦♦
☐ WHIP-POOR-WILL			
☐ ... "Eastern"		M vag	M irr
☐ ... "Stephen's"	S* ♦♦	M vag	
☐ SWIFT, *White-collared*			
☐ Chimney	S*, M irr[6]	S*, M ♦♦♦♦	S*, M ♦♦♦♦
☐ White-throated	S* ♦♦♦♦ W ♦♦	M, W irr	M irr
☐ *VIOLET-EAR, Green*			S vag
☐ *MANGO, Green-breasted*			
☐ HUMMINGBIRD, *Broad-billed*	vag		M vag
☐ *White-eared*	D vag		
☐ *Buff-bellied*			
☐ *Berylline*	vag		
☐ *Violet-crowned*	vag		
☐ Blue-throated	S* ♦♦		vag

S = Summer

M = Migrant

W = Winter

R = Resident

D = Post-nesting Dispersal

♦ ♦ ♦ ♦ = **Common.** Always present in significant numbers in the proper habitat.

♦ ♦ ♦ = **Fairly Common.** A few are always present in the proper habitat.

♦ ♦ = **Uncommon.** Sometimes present in the proper habitat.

♦ = **Rare.** Occur regularly, but in small numbers; a good search can usually find one.

irr = **Irregular.** Definitely not expected, but a few occur occasionally.

spor = **Sporadic.** Not expected every year, but may occur in significant numbers.

vag = **Vagrant.** Well out of the species' normal range (extralimital).

Northern Plains	Pineywoods	Central Plains	Upper Coast	Coastal Bend	Brush Country	Rio Grande Valley
W vag						
				R* ♦6	R* ♦4	R* ♦
					S* irr	S* ♦♦ W ♦
S*, M ♦6, 3 W irr		W ♦	M, W ♦	M, W ♦	M, W ♦	W ♦
						vag
R* ♦♦♦	R* ♦♦♦	R* ♦♦♦♦	R* ♦♦♦	R* ♦♦6	R* ♦♦6	vag
M, W irr		M, W ♦	W ♦		M, W ♦	W irr
W ♦	W irr	M, W 6	M, W ♦♦	M, W ♦♦	M, W ♦	W ♦
vag						
		S* 6	M ♦	S, M vag	S*, M ♦♦♦	S* ♦♦♦3 M irr
S*, M ♦♦♦♦	S* irr M ♦♦♦1 W ♦	S*, M ♦♦♦♦	S*, M ♦♦♦♦	S*, M ♦♦♦♦	S*, M ♦♦♦♦	S* ♦♦♦♦ M ♦♦ W irr
		R6	R ♦6	R* ♦♦♦	R* ♦♦	R* ♦♦♦
S*, M ♦♦3		S6		M vag	S*, M ♦♦	R* ♦♦3
S*, M ♦♦♦	S*, M ♦♦♦♦1	S, M ♦♦♦♦	M ♦♦	M ♦♦ W vag	M ♦♦	M ♦♦
M irr	M ♦♦	M ♦♦♦	M ♦♦♦	M ♦♦ W vag	M irr	M vag
			vag	vag		
S*, M ♦♦♦♦	S*, M ♦♦♦♦	S*, M ♦♦♦♦	S*, M ♦♦♦♦	S*, M ♦♦♦♦	S*, M ♦♦♦♦	S ♦ M ♦♦♦♦
				vag		
	S vag	S vag		vag		vag
				vag		vag
		M vag		M vag	M vag	M vag
					vag	vag
		S6	W ♦	R* ♦♦	R* ♦♦4	S* ♦♦ M, W irr
				M ♦	vag	vag

Italic type denotes "review" species.
Please report any sightings to Texas Bird
Records Committee *(see Appendix B).*

* = Breeding
1 = More numerous in spring
2 = More numerous in fall
3 = More numerous in west
4 = More numerous in east

5 = Deep-water pelagic
6 = Local
7 = Extirpated from this range
    or believed extinct

Bird Species	Trans-Pecos	Panhandle and Western Plains	Edwards Plateau
❑ HUMMINGBIRD, Magnificent	S* ♦[6]		
❑ Lucifer	S* ♦♦		vag
❑ Ruby-throated	M ♦[4]	S*, M irr	M ♦♦
❑ Black-chinned	S* ♦♦♦♦	S*, M ♦♦	S* ♦♦♦♦
❑ Anna's	D, W irr	W vag	M, W irr
❑ *Costa's*	vag		vag
❑ Calliope	M irr[2]	S, M ♦[2]	M ♦
❑ Broad-tailed	S* ♦♦♦ M ♦♦	S, M ♦♦	M ♦♦
❑ Rufous	M ♦♦♦♦[2]	S, M ♦♦[2]	M ♦♦
❑ *Allen's*	vag		vag
❑ TROGON, *Elegant*	vag		
❑ KINGFISHER, Ringed			vag
❑ Belted	W ♦♦	S*, M, W ♦♦	S* ♦ W ♦♦
❑ Green	irr	M vag[2]	R* ♦♦
❑ WOODPECKER, *Lewis's*	W vag	M irr	vag
❑ Red-headed	vag	S*, M ♦♦♦ W ♦	W vag
❑ Acorn	R* ♦♦♦	M vag	irr
❑ Golden-fronted	R* ♦♦♦	R* ♦♦♦	R* ♦♦♦♦
❑ Red-bellied		R* ♦♦	vag
❑ SAPSUCKER, Yellow-bellied	M, W ♦♦	M, W ♦♦	M, W ♦♦
❑ Red-naped	W ♦	M, W ♦	M, W ♦[3]
❑ *Williamson's*	spor	M, W irr	M, W irr
❑ WOODPECKER, Ladder-backed	R* ♦♦♦♦	R* ♦♦♦	R* ♦♦♦♦
❑ Downy	M, W irr	R* ♦♦	M, W ♦
❑ Hairy	R* ♦[6] W irr	R* ♦♦	M, W irr
❑ Red-cockaded			
❑ FLICKER, Northern, ..."Red shafted"	R* ♦[3] M, W ♦♦♦	M, W ♦♦♦[3]	M, W ♦♦
❑ ..."Yellow-shafted"	M, W irr[4]	S* ♦♦ M, W ♦♦♦[4]	M, W ♦♦♦♦
❑ WOODPECKER, Pileated			
❑ *Ivory-billed*			
❑ BEARDLESS-TYRANNULET, Northern			

S = Summer	♦ ♦ ♦ ♦ = **Common.** Always present in significant numbers in the proper habitat.
M = Migrant	♦ ♦ ♦ = **Fairly Common.** A few are always present in the proper habitat.
W = Winter	♦ ♦ = **Uncommon.** Sometimes present in the proper habitat.
R = Resident	♦ = **Rare.** Occur regularly, but in small numbers; a good search can usually find one.
	irr = **Irregular.** Definitely not expected, but a few occur occasionally.
D = Post-nesting Dispersal	spor = **Sporadic.** Not expected every year, but may occur in significant numbers.
	vag = **Vagrant.** Well out of the species' normal range (extralimital).

Northern Plains	Pineywoods	Central Plains	Upper Coast	Coastal Bend	Brush Country	Rio Grande Valley
					vag	
S* ♦♦4 M ♦♦♦4	S* ♦♦♦ M ♦♦♦♦ W ♦	S*, M ♦♦♦♦	S, M ♦♦♦♦ W ♦	M ♦♦♦♦ S, W ♦	M ♦♦4	M ♦♦♦ W ♦
S* ♦♦ M ♦	M ♦1	S*, M ♦♦♦3	W ♦	S* ♦♦	S*, M ♦♦♦ W ♦	S* irr M ♦♦
M, W irr		W ♦	M, W irr	W ♦♦	vag	M irr2
			vag			
			M ♦	M ♦		
	W ♦	W ♦	W ♦	M ♦ W ♦♦	M ♦ W ♦♦	W ♦
M irr	M, W ♦	M irr	M, W irr	M2, W ♦♦♦	M2, W ♦♦♦	M, W ♦♦
	vag		vag	W vag		
						vag
		♦	vag	R irr	R irr	R* ♦♦
R* ♦♦♦	S* ♦♦ M, W ♦♦♦	S* ♦♦ W ♦♦♦♦	S6	S irr M, W ♦♦♦♦	S ♦ M, W ♦♦♦♦	M, W ♦♦
vag		R* ♦		R ♦	R* ♦♦	R* ♦♦
vag						
R* ♦♦4	R* ♦♦	R* 6	R* ♦	M, W spor	M, W spor	vag
R* ♦♦4			vag	R* ♦♦♦♦	R* ♦♦♦♦	R* ♦♦♦♦
R* ♦♦♦♦4	R* ♦♦♦♦	R* ♦♦♦♦	R* ♦♦♦♦	R* ♦♦6		W vag
M, W ♦♦♦	M, W ♦♦♦♦	M, W ♦♦	M, W ♦♦♦	M, W ♦♦♦	M, W ♦♦	M, W irr
					vag	vag
	W vag					
R* ♦♦♦3	R irr	R* ♦♦♦♦	R* ♦	R* ♦♦♦♦	R* ♦♦♦♦	R* ♦♦♦♦
R* ♦♦♦4	R* ♦♦♦	R*, S ♦♦ W ♦♦♦♦	R* ♦♦♦	W ♦		W vag
R* irr4	R* ♦♦	W ♦♦	M, W ♦♦	W vag		
	R* ♦					
M, W ♦♦	M, W ♦	M, W 6	M, W ♦	M, W irr	M, W irr	
S* ♦4 M, W ♦♦♦	S* ♦♦ M, W ♦♦♦	M, W ♦♦♦♦	M, W ♦♦♦	M, W ♦♦♦	M, W ♦♦	M, W ♦
R* ♦4	R* ♦♦♦	R* ♦♦	R* ♦♦♦	R* ♦4		
	7					
				R* ♦	vag	R* ♦

Italic type denotes "review" species.
Please report any sightings to Texas Bird Records Committee (see Appendix B).

* = Breeding
1 = More numerous in spring
2 = More numerous in fall
3 = More numerous in west
4 = More numerous in east

5 = Deep-water pelagic
6 = Local
7 = Extirpated from this range or believed extinct

Bird Species	Trans-Pecos	Panhandle and Western Plains	Edwards Plateau
❏ ELAENIA, *Greenish*			
❏ FLYCATCHER, *Tufted*	vag		
❏ Olive-sided	S* irr M ♦♦♦	M ♦♦	M irr
❏ *PEWEE, Greater*	vag	vag	vag
❏ WOOD-PEWEE, Western	S* ♦ M ♦♦♦♦	S ♦ M ♦♦	S, M irr
❏ Eastern	vag	S irr M irr	S*, M ♦♦
❏ FLYCATCHER, Yellow-bellied	M irr		M ♦
❏ Acadian			S* ♦
❏ Alder			M irr
❏ Willow	M ♦	S ♦ M ♦♦♦	S*, M ♦
❏ Least	M ♦♦²	S, M ♦♦♦	M ♦♦♦
❏ Hammond's	M ♦	S, M ♦	W vag
❏ Dusky	M ♦♦♦¹, W irr	S, M ♦♦	M irr
❏ Gray	S*, W irr M ♦♦¹	M vag	M, W irr
❏ Cordilleran	S* ♦♦ M irr²	S, M irr	M irr
❏ PHOEBE, Black	R* ♦♦♦	M vag	R* irr³
❏ Eastern	M, W ♦♦	S* ♦ M ♦♦ W vag	S* ♦♦ W ♦
❏ Say's	R* ♦♦♦	S* ♦ M ♦♦♦	W ♦♦
❏ FLYCATCHER, Vermilion	S* ♦♦♦⁴ W ♦♦♦	S*, M vag	S* ♦♦♦ W ♦♦
❏ *Dusky-capped*	S* vag⁶		
❏ Ash-throated	S* ♦♦♦♦ W irr	S* ♦♦♦	S* ♦♦♦³
❏ Great Crested	M ♦	S* ♦♦♦⁴ M ♦♦	S* ♦⁴
❏ Brown-crested	S* irr		S* ♦
❏ KISKADEE, Great			R* ♦⁶
❏ FLYCATCHER, *Sulphur-bellied*	vag		
❏ KINGBIRD, *Tropical*	S vag		

S = Summer	♦ ♦ ♦ ♦ = **Common.** Always present in significant numbers in the proper habitat.
M = Migrant	♦ ♦ ♦ = **Fairly Common.** A few are always present in the proper habitat.
W = Winter	♦ ♦ = **Uncommon.** Sometimes present in the proper habitat.
R = Resident	♦ = **Rare.** Occur regularly, but in small numbers; a good search can usually find one.
	irr = **Irregular.** Definitely not expected, but a few occur occasionally.
D = Post-nesting Dispersal	spor = **Sporadic.** Not expected every year, but may occur in significant numbers.
	vag = **Vagrant.** Well out of the species' normal range (extralimital).

Northern Plains	Pineywoods	Central Plains	Upper Coast	Coastal Bend	Brush Country	Rio Grande Valley
			M vag			
M ♦♦	M irr	M ♦♦♦	M ♦♦	M ♦♦♦	M ♦♦	S ♦ M ♦♦
vag			M vag	M vag	M irr	vag
S* ♦[4] M ♦♦♦[4]	S*, M ♦♦♦	S* ♦♦ M ♦♦♦♦	S* ♦♦ M ♦♦♦♦	M ♦♦♦♦	M ♦♦♦	M ♦♦♦
M ♦♦	M ♦♦[1]	M ♦♦	M ♦♦♦	M ♦♦	M ♦♦	M irr
S* ♦[4] M irr[4]	S*, M ♦♦♦♦[1]	S* ♦♦♦ M ♦♦[1]	S* ♦♦ M ♦♦♦♦	M ♦♦♦[1]	M ♦♦	M irr
M ♦[4]	M ♦♦[1]	M ♦	M ♦♦	M ♦♦[2]	M ♦	M irr
M ♦[4]	M ♦♦[1]	M ♦♦[2]	M ♦♦	M ♦♦[2]	M ♦♦	M irr
M ♦♦♦	M ♦♦♦	M ♦♦♦	M ♦♦♦	M ♦♦♦ W irr	M ♦♦	M ♦♦♦ W irr
					W vag	
						S, M vag
					W vag	
				vag		
vag			M, W vag	W irr	W ♦	W ♦
S*, M ♦♦♦ W ♦♦	S* irr M[2], W ♦♦♦	S* [6] M, W ♦♦♦♦	W ♦♦♦♦	M, W ♦♦♦♦	M, W ♦♦♦♦	M, W ♦♦
M, W irr	M, W vag	M, W [6]	M, W ♦	M, W ♦	M, W ♦♦	M, W ♦
M irr	M irr W ♦	M, W irr	S ♦ M, W ♦♦	M, W ♦♦	R* ♦♦ W ♦♦♦	M, W ♦♦
S* ♦♦[3] M, W irr		S*, M ♦♦	M, W ♦♦	S*, M ♦♦♦	S* irr W ♦	S*, W irr M ♦♦
S*, M ♦♦♦♦	S*, M ♦♦♦[1]	S*, M ♦♦♦♦	S* ♦♦♦ M ♦♦♦♦ W irr	M ♦♦♦♦	S*, M ♦♦	M ♦♦[1]
		S* ♦♦[3]	vag	S* ♦♦♦♦	S*, M ♦♦♦♦	S*, M ♦♦♦ W vag
vag		D vag	vag	R* ♦♦♦	R* ♦♦♦[4]	R* ♦♦♦
			vag	vag		vag
						R* ♦

Bird Species	Trans-Pecos	Panhandle and Western Plains	Edwards Plateau
KINGBIRD, Couch's	S* ♦		S* ♦⁶
Cassin's	S* ♦♦	S* vag M ♦	M irr
Thick-billed	S* irr, W vag		
Western	S*, M ♦♦♦♦	S*, M ♦♦♦♦	S*, M ♦♦♦
Eastern	M ♦	S*, M ♦♦♦	S*, M ♦♦
Gray			
FLYCATCHER, Scissor-tailed	S* irr⁴ M ♦♦	S*, M ♦♦♦♦	S*, M ♦♦♦♦
Fork-tailed			
BECARD, *Rose-throated*	S vag		
TITYRA, *Masked*			
LARK, Horned	R* ♦♦♦	S*, M ♦♦♦ W ♦♦♦♦	R* ♦♦♦ M, W ♦♦♦♦
MARTIN, Purple	M ♦⁴	S*, M ♦♦♦	S*, M ♦♦♦♦
Gray-breasted			
SWALLOW, Tree	M ♦♦	M ♦♦♦♦	M ♦♦♦ W ♦³
Violet-green	S* ♦♦♦ M ♦♦	M irr	vag
Northern Rough-winged	S* ♦ M ♦♦♦ W ♦	S* ♦ M ♦♦♦	S* ♦ M ♦♦♦ W irr
Bank	M ♦♦	M ♦♦	S irr M ♦♦
Cliff	S* ♦♦♦ M ♦♦♦♦	S*, M ♦♦♦♦	S* ♦♦♦ M ♦♦♦♦
Cave	S* ♦ M ♦♦♦		S* ♦♦
Barn	S* ♦♦♦♦ M ♦♦♦♦	S* ♦♦♦ M ♦♦♦♦	S*, M ♦♦♦♦
JAY, Steller's	R*⁶ W spor	W vag	
Blue	W vag	R* ♦♦♦	R* ♦♦
Green			vag
Brown			
SCRUB-JAY, Western	R*, W ♦♦♦	R* ♦♦♦⁶	R* ♦♦

S = Summer

M = Migrant

W = Winter

R = Resident

D = Post-nesting Dispersal

♦ ♦ ♦ ♦ = **Common.** Always present in significant numbers in the proper habitat.

♦ ♦ ♦ = **Fairly Common.** A few are always present in the proper habitat.

♦ ♦ = **Uncommon.** Sometimes present in the proper habitat.

♦ = **Rare.** Occur regularly, but in small numbers; a good search can usually find one.

irr = **Irregular.** Definitely not expected, but a few occur occasionally.

spor = **Sporadic.** Not expected every year, but may occur in significant numbers.

vag = **Vagrant.** Well out of the species' normal range (extralimital).

Northern Plains	Pineywoods	Central Plains	Upper Coast	Coastal Bend	Brush Country	Rio Grande Valley
		D vag	M, W irr	S*, M ♦♦♦ W ♦	S* ♦♦ M ♦♦♦[2] W ♦	S*, M ♦♦♦ W irr
			vag	W ♦		vag
S*, M ♦♦♦	S, M vag	S*, M ♦♦	S* ♦♦ M, W ♦	S* ♦♦ M ♦♦♦	S* ♦♦♦ M ♦♦♦	S*, M ♦♦
S* ♦♦ M ♦♦♦	S* ♦♦♦ M ♦♦♦♦	S* ♦♦ M ♦♦♦♦	S* ♦♦♦ M ♦♦♦♦	M ♦♦♦♦	M ♦♦♦	M ♦♦♦
			vag	vag		
S*, M ♦♦♦♦	S* ♦♦♦ M ♦♦♦♦	S*, M ♦♦♦♦	S*, M ♦♦♦♦ W irr	S*, M ♦♦♦♦ W irr	S*, M ♦♦♦♦	S*, M ♦♦♦♦ W ♦
			vag	vag		W vag
				vag		W ♦
						W vag
S* ♦[3] M, W ♦♦♦	M, W ♦	M, W [6]	R* ♦♦ M, W ♦♦♦	R* ♦♦	M, W ♦♦	R* ♦♦
S*, M ♦♦♦♦♦[4]	S*, M ♦♦♦♦	S*, M ♦♦♦♦	S*, M ♦♦♦	S*, M ♦♦♦	S*, M ♦♦♦♦	S*, M ♦♦♦
						M vag
M ♦♦♦	M ♦♦♦	M ♦♦♦♦	M ♦♦♦♦ W ♦♦	M ♦♦♦♦ W ♦	M ♦♦♦♦ W ♦	M ♦♦ W irr
		M vag			M vag	M vag
S* ♦♦ M ♦♦♦	S* ♦♦ M ♦♦♦♦	S* [6] M ♦♦♦♦	M ♦♦♦♦ W ♦	M ♦♦♦♦ W ♦	S ♦ M ♦♦♦♦ W ♦	S, W ♦♦ M ♦♦♦♦
M ♦♦	M ♦♦♦	S*, M ♦♦	M ♦♦♦	M ♦♦♦	S*, M ♦♦ W ♦	S*, M ♦♦ W irr
S* ♦♦♦[3] M ♦♦♦♦	S* irr M ♦♦♦	S* ♦♦♦♦	S* ♦♦♦ M ♦♦♦♦	S*, M ♦♦♦♦	S*, M ♦♦♦♦	S*, M ♦♦♦
S irr		S* ♦♦♦	S* ♦[6]	S* ♦♦♦ M ♦♦ W irr	S* ♦♦♦♦ M ♦♦ W irr	S*, M ♦♦♦ W irr
S* ♦♦♦ M ♦♦♦♦	S*, M ♦♦♦♦	S*, M ♦♦♦♦	S* ♦♦♦ M ♦♦♦♦ W irr	S* ♦♦♦ M ♦♦♦♦ W ♦	S*, M ♦♦♦♦ W ♦	S* ♦[3] M ♦♦♦♦ W ♦
R* ♦♦♦♦[4]	R* ♦♦♦♦	R* ♦♦♦♦	R* ♦♦♦♦	W spor		vag
vag				R* ♦♦	R* ♦♦[4]	R* ♦♦♦
						R* irr
W irr						

Italic type denotes "review" species.
Please report any sightings to Texas Bird Records Committee *(see Appendix B)*.

* = Breeding
1 = More numerous in spring
2 = More numerous in fall
3 = More numerous in west
4 = More numerous in east

5 = Deep-water pelagic
6 = Local
7 = Extirpated from this range or believed extinct

Bird Species	Trans-Pecos	Panhandle and Western Plains	Edwards Plateau
☐ JAY, Mexican	R* ◆◆◆[6]		
☐ Pinyon	W irr	W vag	
☐ NUTCRACKER, *Clark's*	W vag	W vag	W vag
☐ MAGPIE, *Black-billed*	M, W vag	W vag	
☐ CROW, American	W irr	R* ◆◆◆◆	irr[4]
☐ Tamaulipas (Mexican)			
☐ Fish			
☐ RAVEN, Chihuahuan	R* ◆◆◆	R* ◆◆◆ W irr	R* irr[3]
☐ Common	R* ◆◆◆	R ◆[6]	R* ◆◆
☐ CHICKADEE, *Black-capped*	vag[7]		
☐ Carolina		R* ◆◆◆	S* ◆◆[4] M, W ◆◆◆
☐ Mountain	R* ◆◆◆[6] W spor	W vag	
☐ TITMOUSE, Juniper (Plain)	R* ◆◆◆[6]		
☐ Tufted, ..."Tufted"			
☐ ..."Black-crested"	R* ◆◆◆◆	R* ◆◆	R* ◆◆◆
☐ VERDIN	R* ◆◆◆	R* irr	R* ◆◆[3]
☐ BUSHTIT	R* ◆◆◆	R* ◆◆	R* ◆◆[3]
☐ NUTHATCH, Red-breasted	S* [6] W spor	M ◆◆ W spor	W spor
☐ White-breasted	R* ◆[6], W spor	S*, W irr	W spor
☐ Pygmy	R* ◆◆[6] D irr	W vag	
☐ Brown-headed			
☐ CREEPER, Brown	R* ◆[6] W spor	M, W ◆	W ◆
☐ WREN, Cactus	R* ◆◆◆◆	R* irr	R* ◆◆◆
☐ Rock	R* ◆◆◆	R*, M ◆◆◆ W ◆◆	S* ◆[3] W ◆◆◆◆
☐ Canyon	R* ◆◆◆	R* ◆◆	R* ◆
☐ Carolina	R* ◆	R* ◆◆	R* ◆◆[4]
☐ Bewick's	S* ◆◆◆◆ M, W ◆◆	R* ◆◆◆	R* ◆◆◆
☐ House	M, W ◆◆	S*, M ◆◆◆ W vag	M, W ◆◆
☐ Winter	M, W ◆	M, W ◆	W irr

S = Summer

M = Migrant

W = Winter

R = Resident

D = Post-nesting Dispersal

◆ ◆ ◆ ◆ = **Common.** Always present in significant numbers in the proper habitat.
◆ ◆ ◆ = **Fairly Common.** A few are always present in the proper habitat.
◆ ◆ = **Uncommon.** Sometimes present in the proper habitat.
◆ = **Rare.** Occur regularly, but in small numbers; a good search can usually find one.
irr = **Irregular.** Definitely not expected, but a few occur occasionally.
spor = **Sporadic.** Not expected every year, but may occur in significant numbers.
vag = **Vagrant.** Well out of the species' normal range (extralimital).

Northern Plains	Pineywoods	Central Plains	Upper Coast	Coastal Bend	Brush Country	Rio Grande Valley
vag						
R* ♦♦♦♦	R* ♦♦♦♦	R* ♦♦♦♦	R* ♦♦♦♦	R* ♦♦♦6	R* ♦♦♦6	
						S ♦ W ♦♦
R ♦♦6	R*6		R* ♦♦			
S ♦3			M vag	irr	R* ♦♦♦	R* ♦♦♦
		W ♦				
vag						
R* ♦♦♦	R* ♦♦♦♦	R* ♦♦♦♦	R* ♦♦♦♦	R* ♦♦♦6	vag	W vag
R* ♦♦♦4	R* ♦♦♦♦	R* ♦♦♦♦4	R* ♦♦♦♦			
R* ♦♦♦3		R* ♦♦♦3	R* ♦3	R* ♦♦♦♦	R* ♦♦♦♦	R* ♦♦♦♦
R* ♦♦6		W ♦		R* ♦♦	R* ♦♦	R* ♦♦3
R* ♦3						
M, W spor	M, W ♦♦2	M, W spor	W irr	W irr	W vag	W vag
R* ♦♦♦4	R* irr	W ♦	vag			
R* ♦♦♦4, 6	R* ♦♦♦		R* ♦			
W ♦♦♦	M, W ♦♦♦2	M, W ♦♦	W ♦♦	W irr	W vag	W ♦
S* irr3		R* 6, 3		R* ♦♦	R* ♦♦♦	R* ♦♦♦3
W ♦		W vag	W vag	W vag	W vag	R* ♦
R* ♦♦6, 3						
R* ♦♦♦4	R* ♦♦♦♦	R* ♦♦♦♦	R* ♦♦♦♦	R* ♦♦	R* ♦♦	R* ♦♦♦
R* ♦♦♦3	M, W irr2	R* ♦♦	S* ♦3 W ♦♦	R* ♦♦♦♦	R* ♦♦♦♦	R* ♦♦♦♦3
M ♦♦♦ W ♦♦	M ♦♦♦ W ♦♦	M, W ♦♦♦♦	W ♦♦♦♦	M, W ♦♦♦♦	M, W ♦♦♦♦	M, W ♦♦
W ♦	M, W ♦♦2	M, W ♦♦	W ♦♦	W ♦♦	W ♦	W ♦

Italic type denotes "review" species.
Please report any sightings to Texas Bird
Records Committee (see Appendix B).

* = Breeding
1 = More numerous in spring
2 = More numerous in fall
3 = More numerous in west
4 = More numerous in east

5 = Deep-water pelagic
6 = Local
7 = Extirpated from this range
    or believed extinct

Bird Species	Trans-Pecos	Panhandle and Western Plains	Edwards Plateau
❏ WREN, Sedge	vag		M irr
❏ Marsh	S* irr M, W ♦♦	M, W ♦♦	W ♦♦♦
❏ DIPPER, *American*	vag	vag	vag
❏ KINGLET, Golden-crowned	W spor	M, W ♦♦	M, W irr
❏ Ruby-crowned	M, W ♦♦♦	M ♦♦♦ W ♦♦	M, W ♦♦♦
❏ GNATCATCHER, Blue-gray	S*, M ♦♦♦ W ♦	S*, M ♦♦	S*, M ♦♦ W ♦
❏ Black-tailed	R* ♦♦♦		R* ♦♦³
❏ *WHEATEAR, Northern*			
❏ BLUEBIRD, Eastern	S* irr M, W ♦	S*, M ♦♦♦ W ♦♦	R* ♦♦
❏ Western	S* ♦♦♦ M, W ♦♦♦	W vag	W irr
❏ Mountain	S* ⁶, W irr	M, W ♦♦♦	W ♦♦³
❏ SOLITAIRE, Townsend's	W ♦♦♦	M, W ♦♦	vag³
❏ *NIGHTINGALE-THRUSH, Orange-billed*			
❏ VEERY	M vag	M vag	M irr
❏ THRUSH, Gray-cheeked	M vag	M vag	M irr
❏ Swainson's	M irr	M ♦♦	M ♦
❏ Hermit	S* ♦⁶ M, W ♦♦♦	M ♦♦♦ W ♦	M, W ♦♦
❏ Wood	M irr	M vag	M irr
❏ ROBIN, *Clay-colored*			
❏ *White-throated*			
❏ *Rufous-backed*	W vag		
❏ American	S* ♦♦³ M, W ♦♦♦	S* ♦♦♦ M, W ♦♦♦♦	S* ♦♦ M, W ♦♦♦♦
❏ THRUSH, *Varied*	W vag	W vag	
❏ *Aztec*	vag		
❏ CATBIRD, Gray	M irr	S irr M ♦ W vag	M irr
❏ *Black*			
❏ MOCKINGBIRD, Northern	R* ♦♦♦♦	S*, M ♦♦♦ W ♦♦	R* ♦♦♦♦

S = Summer

M = Migrant

W = Winter

R = Resident

D = Post-nesting Dispersal

♦ ♦ ♦ ♦ = **Common.** Always present in significant numbers in the proper habitat.
♦ ♦ ♦ = **Fairly Common.** A few are always present in the proper habitat.
♦ ♦ = **Uncommon.** Sometimes present in the proper habitat.
♦ = **Rare.** Occur regularly, but in small numbers; a good search can usually find one.
irr = **Irregular.** Definitely not expected, but a few occur occasionally.
spor = **Sporadic.** Not expected every year, but may occur in significant numbers.
vag = **Vagrant.** Well out of the species' normal range (extralimital).

Northern Plains	Pineywoods	Central Plains	Upper Coast	Coastal Bend	Brush Country	Rio Grande Valley
M, W ♦	M, W ♦♦	M, W ♦♦	M, W ♦♦♦♦	M, W ♦♦♦♦	M, W ♦♦	M irr W ♦♦
M ♦♦ W ♦	M, W irr[2]	M, W ♦♦	S* ♦♦ M, W ♦♦♦	M, W ♦♦♦	M, W ♦♦	M, W ♦♦♦
W spor	M, W ♦♦♦[2]	M, W ♦♦	W spor	W spor	W spor	W spor
M, W ♦♦♦♦	M, W ♦♦♦♦	M, W ♦♦♦♦	M, W ♦♦♦♦	M, W ♦♦♦♦	M, W ♦♦♦	M, W ♦♦♦♦
S* ♦♦ M ♦♦♦ W irr	S*, M ♦♦♦♦ W irr	S* ♦♦ M ♦♦♦♦ W ♦♦	S* ♦ M, W ♦♦♦♦	S* ♦ M, W ♦♦♦♦	S*, M, W ♦♦♦	M ♦♦♦♦ W ♦♦♦
					R* ♦♦[3]	R* ♦♦[3]
						vag
R* ♦♦♦	S* ♦♦♦	S*, W ♦♦♦	R* ♦♦ W ♦♦♦	R* ♦♦ W ♦♦♦	R* ♦♦ W ♦♦	M, W irr
W irr						W irr
W spor	W vag	W vag		W vag	W vag	W vag
W irr		W vag		W vag		W vag
						vag
M ♦	M ♦♦[1]	M ♦♦	M ♦♦	M ♦♦[1]	M ♦	M ♦♦[1]
M ♦	M ♦♦[1]	M ♦♦	M ♦♦	M ♦♦[1]	M ♦♦	M ♦♦[1]
M ♦♦♦	M ♦♦♦[1]	M ♦♦	M ♦♦	M ♦♦[1]	M ♦♦	M ♦♦[1]
M, W ♦♦	M, W ♦♦♦	M, W ♦♦♦	M, W ♦♦♦	M ♦♦ W ♦♦♦	M, W ♦♦	M irr W ♦♦
M irr[4, 1]	S*, M ♦♦♦[1]	S* ♦♦[4] M ♦♦	S ♦ M ♦♦♦	M ♦♦[1]	M ♦♦	M ♦♦[1]
		vag		W vag		irr*
						W vag
						W vag
S* ♦♦ M ♦♦♦ W ♦♦♦♦	S* ♦♦♦ M, W ♦♦♦♦	S* ♦♦ M, W ♦♦♦♦	S* ♦♦ M, W ♦♦♦♦[1]	S* ♦ M, W ♦♦♦	M ♦♦ W ♦♦♦	M ♦♦ W ♦♦♦
vag			vag			W vag
				vag		
S* ♦ M ♦♦ W irr	S* ♦♦ M ♦♦♦♦[1] W ♦	S ♦[4] M ♦♦♦ W ♦	S ♦ M ♦♦♦ W ♦♦	M ♦♦♦ W ♦♦	M ♦♦♦ W ♦	M ♦♦♦ W ♦
						vag[7]
R* ♦♦♦♦	R* ♦♦♦♦	R* ♦♦♦♦	R* ♦♦♦♦	R* ♦♦♦♦	R* ♦♦♦♦	R* ♦♦♦♦

Italic type denotes "review" species.
Please report any sightings to Texas Bird Records Committee (see Appendix B).

* = Breeding
1 = More numerous in spring
2 = More numerous in fall
3 = More numerous in west
4 = More numerous in east

5 = Deep-water pelagic
6 = Local
7 = Extirpated from this range or believed extinct

Bird Species	Trans-Pecos	Panhandle and Western Plains	Edwards Plateau
❑ THRASHER, Sage	M ♦♦♦ W ♦♦	M, W ♦	W spor
❑ Brown	M ♦	R* ♦♦	W ♦
❑ Long-billed	vag		vag
❑ Curve-billed	R* ♦♦♦	R* ♦♦	R* ♦♦
❑ Crissal	S*, W ♦♦		vag[3]
❑ PIPIT, American	M, W ♦♦♦	M ♦♦♦ W irr	M, W ♦♦♦
❑ Sprague's	W irr	M irr	M, W ♦♦
❑ WAXWING, *Bohemian*		W irr	
❑ Cedar	M, W irr	M ♦♦♦ W ♦♦♦♦	M, W ♦♦♦♦
❑ *SILKY-FLYCATCHER, Gray*	vag		
❑ PHAINOPEPLA	R* ♦♦	vag	vag[3]
❑ SHRIKE, Northern	vag	M, W ♦	vag
❑ Loggerhead	R* ♦♦ W ♦♦♦	S*, W ♦♦ M ♦♦♦	S* ♦ M, W ♦♦♦
❑ STARLING, European	R* ♦♦♦	R* ♦♦♦♦	R* ♦♦♦♦
❑ VIREO, White-eyed	R ♦[4] M ♦	M vag	S*, M ♦♦
❑ Bell's	S* ♦♦♦♦	S*, M irr	S* ♦♦♦
❑ Black-capped	S* ♦[4]		S* ♦♦
❑ Gray	S* ♦♦♦ W irr		S* irr
❑ Blue-headed		M ♦♦	M, W irr[4]
❑ Plumbeous (Solitary)	S* ♦♦ W ♦ M ♦♦♦		
❑ Cassin's	M ♦♦ W ♦	M irr	
❑ Yellow-throated	S* [6] M irr	S, M vag	S* ♦♦
❑ Hutton's	R* ♦♦♦		S* [6]
❑ Warbling	S* irr M ♦♦	S* ♦♦♦ M ♦♦	S irr
❑ Philadelphia	M vag	M vag	M vag[4]
❑ Red-eyed	M vag	S vag M ♦	S*, M ♦♦[4]

S = Summer
M = Migrant
W = Winter
R = Resident
D = Post-nesting Dispersal

♦ ♦ ♦ ♦ = **Common.** Always present in significant numbers in the proper habitat.
♦ ♦ ♦ = **Fairly Common.** A few are always present in the proper habitat.
♦ ♦ = **Uncommon.** Sometimes present in the proper habitat.
♦ = **Rare.** Occur regularly, but in small numbers; a good search can usually find one.
irr = **Irregular.** Definitely not expected, but a few occur occasionally.
spor = **Sporadic.** Not expected every year, but may occur in significant numbers.
vag = **Vagrant.** Well out of the species' normal range (extralimital).

Northern Plains	Pineywoods	Central Plains	Upper Coast	Coastal Bend	Brush Country	Rio Grande Valley
W irr		W ♦	W vag	W irr	W spor	W irr
S*, M ♦♦♦[4] W ♦♦	S* ♦♦ M, W ♦♦♦♦	R* ♦♦ M, W ♦♦♦	S ♦ M, W ♦♦♦♦	M, W ♦♦♦	W ♦♦	M, W ♦
		R* ♦[6,3]	R* ♦[3]	R* ♦♦♦♦	R* ♦♦♦	R* ♦♦♦
R* ♦[3]		R* ♦[6,3]	R* ♦[3]	R* ♦♦♦	R* ♦♦♦♦	R* ♦♦
M, W ♦♦♦	M, W ♦♦♦[2]	M, W ♦♦♦	M, W ♦♦♦	M, W ♦♦♦♦	M, W ♦♦♦♦	M, W ♦♦
W ♦	M ♦♦ W irr	M, W ♦♦	M, W ♦♦	M, W ♦♦	W ♦♦	M, W ♦♦
W vag					W vag	
M, W ♦♦♦♦	M, W ♦♦♦♦[1]	M, W ♦♦♦♦	M, W ♦♦♦♦	M, W ♦♦♦♦[1]	M, W ♦♦♦	M, W ♦♦
						vag
						W vag
W irr						
S*, M, W ♦♦♦	S*, M ♦♦♦ W ♦♦♦♦	R* ♦♦♦ W ♦♦♦♦	R* ♦♦♦ W ♦♦♦♦	S* ♦♦ M, W ♦♦♦♦	S* ♦♦ M, W ♦♦♦♦	S* ♦ M, W ♦♦♦
R* ♦♦♦♦	R* ♦♦♦♦	R* ♦♦♦♦	R* ♦♦♦♦	R* ♦♦♦♦	R* ♦♦♦♦	R* ♦♦♦♦
S* ♦♦♦ M ♦♦	S*, M ♦♦♦♦ W irr	S*, M ♦♦♦ W ♦♦	S*, M ♦♦♦♦ W ♦♦	R* ♦♦♦♦	R* ♦♦♦	R* ♦♦ M ♦♦♦
S* ♦♦[3] M irr	S*, M irr	S*, M ♦[3]	M ♦	R* ♦	R* ♦	S*, M ♦
S* irr				M irr		M vag
M ♦♦ W irr	M, W ♦♦	M ♦♦♦ W ♦♦	M, W ♦♦♦	M, W ♦♦♦	M ♦♦♦ W ♦♦	M, W ♦♦♦
				vag		
S*, M irr	S*, M ♦♦♦[1]	S*, M ♦♦	S* ♦♦ M ♦♦♦[2]	M ♦♦ W ♦	M ♦♦ W ♦	M irr
S* ♦♦ M ♦♦♦	M ♦♦	M ♦♦	M ♦♦	M ♦♦[1]	M ♦♦♦	M ♦♦
M ♦[1]	M ♦♦[1]	M ♦♦[1]	M ♦♦	M ♦♦[1]	M ♦♦	M irr
S* ♦♦[4] M ♦♦♦	S*, M ♦♦♦♦	S*, M ♦♦♦	S* ♦♦♦ M ♦♦♦♦	S* ♦[4,6] M ♦♦♦[1]	S* ♦[4,6] M ♦♦♦[1]	M ♦♦

Bird Species	Trans-Pecos	Panhandle and Western Plains	Edwards Plateau
❏ VIREO, *Yellow-green*	vag		
❏ *Black-whiskered*			
❏ *Yucatan*			
❏ WARBLER, Blue-winged	M vag	S, M vag	
❏ Golden-winged	M vag	S, M vag	
❏ Tennessee	M vag	S, M irr	M vag
❏ Orange-crowned	S* irr[6] M, W ♦♦♦	S ♦♦ M ♦♦♦	M ♦♦♦ W ♦♦
❏ Nashville	M ♦♦	M ♦♦	M ♦♦♦
❏ Virginia's	S* ♦♦[6] M ♦♦	M irr	
❏ Colima	S* ♦♦♦[6]		
❏ Lucy's	S* ♦, W ♦		
❏ PARULA, Northern	M ♦ W irr	M irr	M vag[4]
❏ Tropical	vag		vag
❏ WARBLER, Yellow	S* [7] M ♦♦	S ♦♦ M ♦♦♦	M ♦♦
❏ Chestnut-sided	M vag	M irr	M vag[4]
❏ Magnolia	M vag	M irr	M vag[4]
❏ Cape May	M vag	M vag	
❏ Black-throated Blue	M vag	M irr	
❏ Yellow-rumped, ..."Myrtle"	M, W ♦[3]	M ♦♦♦ W ♦♦	M, W ♦♦♦
❏ ..."Audubon's"	S* ♦[6] M, W ♦♦♦♦	M ♦♦♦ W ♦♦	M, W ♦♦♦
❏ Black-throated Gray	M, W ♦	M irr	
❏ Townsend's	M ♦	M ♦	vag
❏ Hermit	M irr	M vag	
❏ Black-throated Green	M irr[3]	M ♦	M vag[4]
❏ Golden-cheeked			S* ♦
❏ Blackburnian	M vag	M irr	M vag[4]
❏ Yellow-throated	M vag	M vag	S ♦♦
❏ Grace's	S*, M ♦		
❏ Pine	vag	M vag	W vag
❏ Prairie	M vag	M vag	M vag

S = Summer
M = Migrant
W = Winter
R = Resident
D = Post-nesting Dispersal

♦ ♦ ♦ ♦ = **Common.** Always present in significant numbers in the proper habitat.
♦ ♦ ♦ = **Fairly Common.** A few are always present in the proper habitat.
♦ ♦ = **Uncommon.** Sometimes present in the proper habitat.
♦ = **Rare.** Occur regularly, but in small numbers; a good search can usually find one.
irr = **Irregular.** Definitely not expected, but a few occur occasionally.
spor = **Sporadic.** Not expected every year, but may occur in significant numbers.
vag = **Vagrant.** Well out of the species' normal range (extralimital).

Northern Plains	Pineywoods	Central Plains	Upper Coast	Coastal Bend	Brush Country	Rio Grande Valley
		vag	vag	R ♦		S vag
			M vag	M vag		M vag
			vag			
M irr	M irr	M ♦	M ♦♦♦	M ♦♦[1]	M ♦♦[1]	M ♦♦[4,1]
M irr	M irr[1]	M ♦	M ♦♦	M ♦♦[1]	M ♦♦[1]	M irr[4,1]
M ♦[4,1]	M ♦♦♦♦[1]	M ♦♦	M ♦♦♦♦	M ♦♦♦♦[1]	M ♦♦♦[1]	M ♦♦♦[4,1]
M ♦♦♦ W ♦♦	M ♦♦♦ W ♦♦	M, W ♦♦♦	M, W ♦♦♦♦	M, W ♦♦♦♦	M, W ♦♦♦♦	M, W ♦♦♦
M ♦♦♦♦	M ♦♦♦♦	M ♦♦♦	M ♦♦♦ W ♦	M ♦♦♦ W ♦	M ♦♦	M ♦♦ W irr
			W vag			W vag
						vag
S* ♦♦ M ♦	S*, M ♦♦♦♦[1]	S*, M ♦♦♦	S*, M ♦♦♦♦ W ♦	S* ♦[6] M ♦♦♦	S* ♦[4,6] M ♦♦	S, W ♦ M ♦♦[1]
			vag	S* ♦[6]		R* irr
M ♦♦♦♦	M ♦♦♦	M ♦♦♦♦	M ♦♦♦	M ♦♦♦♦ W ♦	M ♦♦♦	M ♦♦♦♦ W ♦
M irr[1]	M ♦♦♦[1]	M ♦♦♦	M ♦♦♦♦	M ♦♦♦[1]	M ♦♦[1]	M ♦♦♦[4]
M ♦♦♦[1]	M ♦♦♦♦[1]	M ♦♦♦	M ♦♦♦♦	M ♦♦♦[1]	M ♦♦[1]	M ♦♦♦[4]
M vag		M vag	M ♦	M irr		M, W ♦
M irr[2]	M vag[2]	M ♦	M, W ♦	M irr		M, W ♦
M, W ♦♦♦♦	M, W ♦♦♦♦[1]	M, W ♦♦♦♦	M, W ♦♦♦♦	M, W ♦♦♦♦	M, W ♦♦♦♦	M ♦♦ W ♦♦♦
M, W irr	M, W irr	M, W ♦♦	M, W ♦	M, W ♦♦	M, W ♦♦[3]	W irr[3]
M vag		M vag	M, W ♦	M, W irr	M irr	M, W irr
M vag		M vag	M vag	M vag		M ♦
		M vag				vag
M ♦♦♦	M ♦♦♦[1]	M ♦♦♦	M ♦♦♦♦ W ♦	M ♦♦♦♦[1] W ♦	M ♦♦♦[1]	M ♦♦ W irr
S* ♦[6]		M vag				S, M vag
M irr	M ♦♦[1]	M ♦♦	M ♦♦♦	M ♦♦♦[1]	M ♦♦[1]	M ♦♦[4,1]
S*, M ♦♦♦[6] W vag	S*, M ♦♦♦ W ♦	S* ♦♦ W ♦	S*, M ♦♦ W ♦	M ♦♦♦[1] W ♦	M ♦♦ W ♦	M, W ♦♦
R* ♦♦[4]	R* ♦♦♦♦	S* ♦♦♦[6] W ♦♦♦♦	R* ♦♦♦	W spor	W irr	M, W ♦
M irr[4,2]	S*, M ♦♦[1]	M ♦	M, W ♦	M, W ♦ W irr		M ♦[4]

Bird Species	Trans-Pecos	Panhandle and Western Plains	Edwards Plateau
❏ WARBLER, Palm	M vag	M irr	M vag[4]
❏ Bay-breasted	M irr[1]	M irr	M vag[4]
❏ Blackpoll	M vag	M irr	
❏ Cerulean	M vag		
❏ Black-and-white	M ♦	M ♦♦	S*, M ♦♦[4]
❏ REDSTART, American	M ♦	M ♦♦	M ♦[4]
❏ WARBLER, Prothonotary	M vag	M vag	M vag[4]
❏ Worm-eating	M ♦	M vag	M vag[4]
❏ Swainson's	M vag		
❏ OVENBIRD	M ♦	M ♦♦	M vag[4]
❏ WATERTHRUSH, Northern	M ♦♦	M ♦♦	M ♦[4]
❏ Louisiana	M vag	M vag	M vag[4]
❏ WARBLER, Kentucky	M ♦	M irr	
❏ Connecticut		M vag	
❏ Mourning	M vag	M vag	M vag[4]
❏ MacGillivray's	M ♦♦♦	M ♦♦	M ♦[3]
❏ YELLOWTHROAT, Common	S*, M, W ♦♦	S*, M ♦♦	S* ♦ M, W ♦♦♦
❏ *Gray-crowned*			
❏ WARBLER, Hooded	M vag	M irr	M vag[4]
❏ Wilson's	M ♦♦♦♦	M ♦♦♦	M ♦♦♦
❏ Canada	M vag	M vag	
❏ *Red-faced*	S vag		
❏ REDSTART, Painted	S* irr		vag
❏ *Slate-throated*	vag		
❏ WARBLER, *Golden-crowned*			
❏ *Rufous-capped*	vag		vag

S = Summer

M = Migrant

W = Winter

R = Resident

D = Post-nesting Dispersal

♦ ♦ ♦ ♦ = **Common.** Always present in significant numbers in the proper habitat.

♦ ♦ ♦ = **Fairly Common.** A few are always present in the proper habitat.

♦ ♦ = **Uncommon.** Sometimes present in the proper habitat.

♦ = **Rare.** Occur regularly, but in small numbers; a good search can usually find one.

irr = **Irregular.** Definitely not expected, but a few occur occasionally.

spor = **Sporadic.** Not expected every year, but may occur in significant numbers.

vag = **Vagrant.** Well out of the species' normal range (extralimital).

Northern Plains	Pineywoods	Central Plains	Upper Coast	Coastal Bend	Brush Country	Rio Grande Valley
M irr[4,2]	M, W ♦	M ♦	M ♦ W ♦♦	M irr W ♦		M, W ♦
M irr[1]	M ♦♦[1]	M ♦♦♦	M ♦♦♦ W ♦	M ♦♦♦[1]	M ♦♦[1]	M ♦♦[1]
M irr[4,1]	M ♦[1]	M ♦♦[4]	M ♦♦	M ♦♦[1]		M ♦♦[4,1]
M irr[4,1]	M irr[1]	M ♦♦[4]	M ♦♦	M ♦♦[1]		M irr[4,1]
S* ♦♦ M ♦♦♦	S*, M ♦♦♦[1] W vag	S* ♦♦ M ♦♦♦	M ♦♦♦♦ W ♦	M ♦♦♦♦ W ♦	M ♦♦♦ W ♦	S ♦ M ♦♦♦ W ♦♦
M ♦♦♦	S* ♦♦ M ♦♦♦[1]	M ♦♦♦	M ♦♦♦♦ S, W irr	M ♦♦♦♦[1] W irr	M ♦♦♦[1]	M ♦♦♦[4] W ♦
S* ♦♦♦[6] M ♦	S*, M ♦♦♦[1]	S*[4], M ♦♦	S* ♦♦♦ M ♦♦♦♦[1]	M ♦♦[1]	M ♦♦[1]	M ♦♦[4]
M irr	S*, M irr[1]	M ♦♦	M ♦♦♦[1]	M ♦♦♦[1]	M ♦♦[1]	M ♦♦[4]
M irr	S*, M ♦♦[1]	S*[6], M ♦	S* ♦♦♦ M ♦♦♦♦[1]	M ♦♦		M ♦[4,1]
M ♦♦	M ♦♦[1]	M ♦♦♦	M ♦♦♦♦[1] W irr	M ♦♦♦[1] W irr	M ♦♦[1]	M ♦♦[4] W ♦[4]
M irr	M ♦♦♦[1]	M ♦♦	M ♦♦♦♦[1] W irr	M ♦♦♦[1] W irr	M ♦♦[1]	M ♦♦[4,1] W ♦[4]
M ♦♦[4,1]	S*, M ♦♦[1]	S*, M ♦♦	M ♦♦♦[1]	M ♦♦♦[1] W irr	M ♦♦[1]	M ♦♦[4,1]
S*, M ♦♦[4,1]	S*, M ♦♦♦[1]	S* ♦ M ♦♦	S* ♦♦♦ M ♦♦♦♦	M ♦♦♦[1]	M ♦♦[1]	M ♦♦[4]
M vag[1]			M vag	M vag		
M ♦♦	M ♦♦	M ♦♦	M ♦♦[2]	M ♦♦♦[1]	M ♦♦[1]	M irr W ♦
M vag[1]		M vag	W irr	M vag	vag	M ♦
S* ♦♦ M ♦♦♦ W irr	S* ♦♦♦ M ♦♦♦♦[1] W ♦	S* ♦♦ M ♦♦♦♦ W ♦♦♦	R* ♦♦♦♦ M, W ♦♦♦♦	S* ♦♦ M, W ♦♦♦♦	S* ♦♦ M, W ♦♦♦	S* ♦♦ M, W ♦♦♦♦
						S vag
M irr[4]	S*, M ♦♦♦[1]	S*, M ♦♦	S* ♦♦♦ M ♦♦♦♦	M ♦♦♦[1]	M ♦♦[1]	M ♦♦♦[4,1]
M ♦♦♦	M ♦♦♦[2]	M ♦♦♦ W ♦	M, W ♦♦[2]	M ♦♦♦ W irr	M ♦♦	M ♦♦♦[4] W ♦♦[4]
M ♦♦[1]	M ♦♦	M ♦♦♦	M ♦♦	M ♦♦♦	M ♦♦	M ♦♦[4]
		vag				M vag
			M vag		vag	M vag
						W vag
				vag	vag	vag

Italic type denotes "review" species.
Please report any sightings to Texas Bird Records Committee *(see Appendix B)*.

* = Breeding
1 = More numerous in spring
2 = More numerous in fall
3 = More numerous in west
4 = More numerous in east

5 = Deep-water pelagic
6 = Local
7 = Extirpated from this range or believed extinct

Bird Species	Trans-Pecos	Panhandle and Western Plains	Edwards Plateau
❑ CHAT, Yellow-breasted	S* ♦♦♦♦ M ♦♦	S, M ♦♦	S*, M ♦♦♦
❑ WARBLER, *Olive*	vag[1]		
❑ TANAGER, Hepatic	S* ♦♦♦ M ♦	M vag	
❑ Summer	S* ♦♦♦ M ♦♦	M ♦	S*, M ♦♦
❑ Scarlet	M vag	M irr	
❑ Western	S* ♦ M ♦♦♦	M ♦♦	M vag[2]
❑ *Flame-colored*	M vag		
❑ GROSBEAK, *Crimson-collared*			
❑ CARDINAL, Northern	R* ♦♦♦♦	R* ♦♦♦	R* ♦♦♦
❑ PYRRHULOXIA	R* ♦♦♦♦	R* irr	R* ♦♦♦
❑ GROSBEAK, Rose-breasted	M ♦	M ♦♦	M vag[4]
❑ Black-headed	S* ♦♦♦ M ♦♦♦	M ♦♦	M ♦
❑ BUNTING, *Blue*			
❑ GROSBEAK, Blue	S* ♦♦♦ M ♦♦♦	S*, M ♦♦♦	S*, M ♦♦♦
❑ BUNTING, Lazuli	M ♦♦	S, M ♦♦	M irr[3]
❑ Indigo	S irr[6] M ♦♦	S*, M ♦♦	S, M irr[4]
❑ Varied	S* ♦♦♦ W spor	M vag	vag
❑ Painted	S* ♦♦♦ M ♦♦	S*, M ♦♦♦	S*, M ♦♦♦
❑ DICKCISSEL	M ♦♦	S*, M ♦♦♦	S*, M ♦♦
❑ SPARROW, Olive			R* [6]
❑ TOWHEE, Green-tailed	S*[6], M, W ♦♦	M ♦♦	M, W ♦
❑ Spotted	R* ♦♦♦[3] M ♦♦	M, W ♦♦♦	M, W ♦♦♦
❑ Eastern		W irr	M, W ♦♦
❑ Canyon	R* ♦♦♦	R* ♦[6]	R* ♦♦♦
❑ SEEDEATER, White-collared			
❑ GRASSQUIT, *Yellow-faced*			

S = Summer
M = Migrant
W = Winter
R = Resident
D = Post-nesting Dispersal

♦♦♦♦ = **Common.** Always present in significant numbers in the proper habitat.
♦♦♦ = **Fairly Common.** A few are always present in the proper habitat.
♦♦ = **Uncommon.** Sometimes present in the proper habitat.
♦ = **Rare.** Occur regularly, but in small numbers; a good search can usually find one.
irr = **Irregular.** Definitely not expected, but a few occur occasionally.
spor = **Sporadic.** Not expected every year, but may occur in significant numbers.
vag = **Vagrant.** Well out of the species' normal range (extralimital).

Northern Plains	Pineywoods	Central Plains	Upper Coast	Coastal Bend	Brush Country	Rio Grande Valley
S irr M ♦♦[4,1]	S* ♦♦♦ M ♦♦♦♦[1]	S* ♦♦ M ♦♦♦	S* ♦♦ M ♦♦♦ W irr	S, W irr M ♦♦♦♦	M ♦♦♦	S, W ♦ M ♦♦[1,3]
		W vag		M vag	M vag	vag
S* ♦♦♦[4]	S*, M ♦♦♦♦ W ♦	S* ♦♦♦	S* ♦♦♦ M ♦♦♦♦[1] W irr	S* ♦♦[6] M ♦♦♦[1]	S* ♦♦[4] M ♦♦♦	M ♦♦♦[4,1] W ♦
M irr[1]	M ♦♦[1]	M ♦♦[4]	M ♦♦[1]	M ♦♦	M ♦	M ♦♦[4]
vag		M ♦	M, W irr	M ♦ W irr	M ♦	M, W ♦
				vag	vag	M, W vag
R* ♦♦♦♦	R* ♦♦♦♦	R* ♦♦♦♦	R* ♦♦♦♦	R* ♦♦♦♦	R* ♦♦♦♦	R* ♦♦♦♦
irr[3]		W ♦♦	W irr	R* ♦♦♦	R* ♦♦♦♦	R* ♦♦♦[3]
M ♦♦[4,1]	M ♦♦♦[1]	M ♦♦♦	M ♦♦♦[1] W irr	M ♦♦♦[1] W irr	M ♦♦[1]	M ♦♦♦[4,1]
M irr	M vag[2]	M ♦	W irr	M, W irr	M, W irr	M, W ♦
			W vag			W ♦
S* ♦♦ M ♦♦♦	S*, M ♦♦♦	S* ♦♦ M ♦♦♦	S* ♦♦ M ♦♦♦	S*, M ♦♦♦	S*, M ♦♦♦	S* irr M ♦♦[4]
M ♦[1]		M ♦♦	S vag	M ♦[1]	M ♦	M, W ♦
S*, M ♦♦♦	S*, M ♦♦♦♦	S* ♦♦ M ♦♦♦♦	S* ♦♦ M ♦♦♦♦ W irr	M ♦♦♦♦ W ♦	M ♦♦♦♦	M ♦♦♦[4] W irr
	vag			vag	vag	S, M ♦
S* ♦♦♦	S*, M ♦♦♦[1]	S*, M ♦♦♦♦	S* ♦♦♦ W vag	S*, M ♦♦♦♦	S*, M ♦♦♦	S*, M ♦♦♦[3] W ♦
S*, M ♦♦♦♦	S* ♦♦♦ M ♦♦♦♦[1] W vag	S*, M ♦♦♦♦	S* ♦♦♦♦ W vag	S*, M ♦♦♦♦ W ♦	S* ♦♦ M ♦♦♦♦	S* ♦♦ M ♦♦♦
				R* ♦♦♦	R* ♦♦♦	R* ♦♦♦[4]
M, W irr	M vag[2]	W irr	W vag	M, W ♦	M, W ♦♦	M, W irr[3]
M, W ♦♦♦[3]		W ♦♦	W ♦	M, W ♦♦	M, W ♦♦	M, W irr
M, W ♦♦♦[4]	M, W ♦♦♦[2]	W ♦♦	M, W ♦♦	M, W ♦	M, W ♦	W ♦
irr[6,3]		W ♦				
						R* ♦[3]
						vag

Italic type denotes "review" species.
Please report any sightings to Texas Bird
Records Committee (see Appendix B).

* = Breeding	5 = Deep-water pelagic
1 = More numerous in spring	6 = Local
2 = More numerous in fall	7 = Extirpated from this range
3 = More numerous in west	or believed extinct
4 = More numerous in east	

Bird Species	Trans-Pecos	Panhandle and Western Plains	Edwards Plateau
❑ SPARROW, Bachman's			
❑ Botteri's	S* vag		
❑ Cassin's	S* spor W spor	S* ◆◆◆ M ◆◆	S*, M ◆◆◆ W irr
❑ Rufous-crowned	R* ◆◆◆	R* ◆◆	R* ◆◆◆
❑ American Tree	vag	M, W ◆◆	vag
❑ Chipping	S* irr M, W ◆◆◆	M ◆◆◆◆ W irr	S* ◆ M, W ◆◆◆
❑ Clay-colored	M ◆◆ W spor	M ◆◆◆◆	M ◆◆◆ W irr
❑ Brewer's	M, W ◆◆	M ◆◆ W vag	M, W ◆
❑ Field	M, W irr⁴	S*, M, W ◆◆◆	S* ◆ M, W ◆◆
❑ Black-chinned	R* ◆◆◆		
❑ Vesper	M, W ◆◆	M ◆◆◆	M, W ◆◆◆
❑ Lark	S* ◆◆ W spor	S*, M ◆◆◆	S*, M ◆◆◆ W ◆◆
❑ Black-throated	R* ◆◆◆◆	S*, M ◆ W irr	R* ◆◆
❑ Sage	W ◆◆◆⁶		
❑ BUNTING, Lark	M, W ◆◆◆	S*, W ◆◆ M ◆◆◆◆	S* ◆ M, W ◆◆◆◆
❑ SPARROW, Savannah	M, W ◆◆	M ◆◆◆ W ◆◆	M, W ◆◆◆
❑ *Baird's*	M irr	M irr	M, W irr
❑ Grasshopper	S* spor, M ◆ W spor	S*, M ◆◆◆	S*, M ◆◆◆ W ◆
❑ Henslow's			
❑ LeConte's	M irr	M, W irr	W ◆
❑ *Saltmarsh Sharp-tailed*			
❑ Nelson's Sharp-tailed	vag		
❑ Seaside			
❑ Fox	M, W ◆	M, W ◆	M, W ◆◆
❑ Song	M, W ◆◆	M, W ◆◆◆	M, W ◆◆◆
❑ Lincoln's	M, W ◆◆	M, W ◆◆	M, W ◆◆◆
❑ Swamp	M, W ◆◆⁴	M, W ◆	M, W ◆◆

S = Summer
M = Migrant
W = Winter
R = Resident
D = Post-nesting Dispersal

◆ ◆ ◆ ◆ = **Common.** Always present in significant numbers in the proper habitat.
◆ ◆ ◆ = **Fairly Common.** A few are always present in the proper habitat.
◆ ◆ = **Uncommon.** Sometimes present in the proper habitat.
◆ = **Rare.** Occur regularly, but in small numbers; a good search can usually find one.
irr = **Irregular.** Definitely not expected, but a few occur occasionally.
spor = **Sporadic.** Not expected every year, but may occur in significant numbers.
vag = **Vagrant.** Well out of the species' normal range (extralimital).

Northern Plains	Pineywoods	Central Plains	Upper Coast	Coastal Bend	Brush Country	Rio Grande Valley
	S* irr		vag			
				S* ♦		S*, M ♦♦[4]
S* spor[3]	M vag	S* ♦♦[3]	S* ♦[3]	R* ♦♦♦	R* ♦♦♦	S*, M ♦♦[3] W irr
R* ♦♦[3] W irr				vag	R* ♦♦[3]	R* ♦[3]
M ♦♦♦ W irr	S* ♦♦ M, W ♦♦♦♦	M, W ♦♦♦♦	M, W ♦♦♦♦	M, W ♦♦♦♦	M, W ♦♦♦	M, W ♦♦♦[2,4]
M ♦♦	M ♦[1]	M ♦♦	M ♦[3] W irr	M ♦♦♦[1] W ♦♦	M ♦♦[1] W ♦	M ♦♦ W irr[3]
						W ♦[3]
S* ♦ M, W ♦♦♦	S*, M ♦♦♦ W ♦♦♦♦	S* ♦♦ M, W ♦♦♦	W ♦♦♦	R*, M ♦♦♦	R*, M ♦♦♦	M, W ♦♦
M ♦♦♦ W ♦♦	M ♦♦ W ♦♦♦	M ♦♦♦	W ♦♦♦♦	M, W ♦♦♦♦	M, W ♦♦♦♦	M, W ♦♦
S* ♦♦♦ W ♦♦	S* ♦♦♦ M, W ♦♦	R* ♦♦♦	R* irr	R* ♦♦♦♦	R* ♦♦♦♦	R* ♦♦♦♦[3]
irr[3]		vag	vag[3]	R* ♦♦	R* ♦♦♦[3]	R* ♦♦♦[3]
M spor W irr	M vag[1]	W spor	W irr	M, W ♦♦	M, W ♦♦♦[3]	M, W ♦♦[3]
M, W ♦♦♦♦	M, W ♦♦♦♦	M, W ♦♦♦♦	M, W ♦♦♦♦	M, W ♦♦♦♦	M, W ♦♦♦♦	M, W ♦♦♦♦
W irr					vag	W vag
S* ♦♦♦ W ♦	S*, W ♦ M irr	S* ♦♦ M, W ♦♦♦	S irr M, W ♦♦	S* ♦ M, W ♦♦♦	S* ♦♦ M, W ♦♦♦	M, W irr[4]
W irr	M, W irr[2]	M ♦	M, W ♦	W vag		
W ♦♦♦	M, W ♦♦♦[2]	M, W ♦♦	W ♦♦♦	M, W ♦♦♦	W ♦	W ♦
				W vag		
M irr	M irr[2]	M ♦	W ♦♦♦	M, W ♦♦		W ♦
		W vag	R* ♦♦♦♦	R* ♦♦		R irr
W ♦♦♦	M ♦♦[2] W ♦♦♦	M, W ♦♦	W irr	W ♦	W ♦	
W ♦♦♦♦	M, W ♦♦♦♦[2]	M, W ♦♦♦	W ♦♦♦	M, W ♦♦	M, W ♦♦	M irr W ♦
M ♦♦♦♦ W ♦♦♦	M ♦♦♦♦ W ♦♦	M, W ♦♦♦♦	M, W ♦♦♦♦	M, W ♦♦♦♦	M, W ♦♦♦♦	M, W ♦♦♦♦
M, W ♦♦	M, W ♦♦♦♦	M, W ♦♦♦	M, W ♦♦♦♦	M, W ♦♦♦	W ♦♦	M irr W ♦♦[4]

Italic type denotes "review" species.
Please report any sightings to Texas Bird Records Committee (see Appendix B).

* = Breeding
1 = More numerous in spring
2 = More numerous in fall
3 = More numerous in west
4 = More numerous in east

5 = Deep-water pelagic
6 = Local
7 = Extirpated from this range or believed extinct

Bird Species	Trans-Pecos	Panhandle and Western Plains	Edwards Plateau
❏ SPARROW, White-throated	M, W ♦	M, W ♦♦	M, W ♦♦4
❏ Golden-crowned	M, W vag	M, W vag	W vag
❏ White-crowned	M, W ♦♦♦♦	M, W ♦♦♦♦	M, W ♦♦♦♦
❏ Harris's	W vag	M, W ♦	W ♦♦4
❏ JUNCO, Dark-eyed, ... "Slate-colored"	M, W ♦	M, W ♦♦♦	M, W ♦♦
❏ ... "Oregon"	M, W ♦♦	M, W ♦♦♦	M, W spor
❏ ... "Pink-sided"	M, W ♦♦♦	M, W ♦♦♦	M, W ♦
❏ ... "Gray-headed"	S*, M, W ♦♦♦	M, W ♦	W ♦♦
❏ ... "Red-backed"	R* ♦♦♦6		
❏ Yellow-eyed	vag		
❏ LONGSPUR, McCown's	M irr	M, W ♦♦♦♦	W ♦♦♦♦
❏ Lapland	W vag	M ♦♦♦ W ♦♦♦♦	
❏ Smith's	W vag	M, W vag	W vag
❏ Chestnut-collared	M ♦♦	M, W ♦♦♦♦	W ♦♦♦♦
❏ BUNTING, Snow	W vag	W vag	
❏ BOBOLINK		M vag	M vag
❏ BLACKBIRD, Red-winged	S* ♦♦♦ M, W ♦♦	R* ♦♦♦♦	S* ♦♦♦ W ♦♦♦♦
❏ MEADOWLARK, Eastern ❏ ... "Lillian's"	R* ♦♦♦ M, W ♦♦	R* ♦♦♦♦	R* ♦♦4
❏ Western	R* ♦♦ W ♦♦♦	R* ♦♦♦♦	R* ♦♦♦ W ♦♦♦♦
❏ BLACKBIRD, Yellow-headed	M ♦♦♦ W ♦	S* ♦♦♦ M ♦♦♦♦	S irr M ♦
❏ Rusty	W vag	W irr	W vag
❏ Brewer's	M, W ♦♦♦	M, W ♦♦♦♦	M, W ♦♦♦♦
❏ GRACKLE, Great-tailed	R* ♦♦	S*, M ♦♦♦ W ♦♦♦♦	R* ♦♦♦
❏ Boat-tailed			
❏ Common ❏ ... "Bronzed"	W irr	S*, M ♦♦♦♦ W irr	R* ♦♦♦
❏ ... "Purple"			
❏ COWBIRD, Shiny			
❏ Bronzed	S* ♦♦ M ♦	M vag	S* ♦
❏ Brown-headed	S* ♦♦♦♦ M, W ♦♦♦	S*, W ♦♦♦ M ♦♦♦♦	S* ♦♦♦ W ♦♦♦♦
❏ ORIOLE, Black-vented	vag		

S = Summer
M = Migrant
W = Winter
R = Resident
D = Post-nesting Dispersal

♦ ♦ ♦ ♦ = **Common.** Always present in significant numbers in the proper habitat.
♦ ♦ ♦ = **Fairly Common.** A few are always present in the proper habitat.
♦ ♦ = **Uncommon.** Sometimes present in the proper habitat.
♦ = **Rare.** Occur regularly, but in small numbers; a good search can usually find one.
irr = **Irregular.** Definitely not expected, but a few occur occasionally.
spor = **Sporadic.** Not expected every year, but may occur in significant numbers.
vag = **Vagrant.** Well out of the species' normal range (extralimital).

Northern Plains	Pineywoods	Central Plains	Upper Coast	Coastal Bend	Brush Country	Rio Grande Valley
M, W ♦♦♦♦	M, W ♦♦♦♦	M, W ♦♦♦♦	M, W ♦♦♦♦	M, W ♦♦♦♦	M, W ♦♦♦	M, W irr[3]
		vag				W vag
M ♦♦♦♦ W ♦♦♦	M, W ♦♦	M, W ♦♦♦♦	M, W ♦♦♦	M, W ♦♦♦♦	M, W ♦♦♦♦	M, W ♦♦[3]
W ♦♦♦[3]	M, W ♦♦	M, W ♦♦	W irr	W ♦	W ♦	
M, W ♦♦♦♦ W ♦♦♦[3] W ♦ W irr	M, W ♦♦♦ W irr W vag	W spor W irr W irr W vag	W irr W irr W irr	W irr W irr W vag	W ♦♦ W ♦♦ W vag	W vag
W spor[3]		W ♦		W vag[7]		
W ♦♦♦	M, W irr[2]	W irr	W irr			
W ♦♦♦♦[4, 6]	W vag					
W ♦♦	M ♦[1]	W ♦♦	vag	W vag		W ♦
	W vag					
M irr	M ♦♦[1]	M irr	M ♦♦[1]	M ♦[4]		M ♦[4]
S*, W ♦♦♦♦	R* ♦♦♦♦	R* ♦♦♦♦	R* ♦♦♦♦	R* ♦♦♦♦	R* ♦♦♦♦	R* ♦♦♦♦
S* ♦♦♦	R* ♦♦♦♦	R* ♦♦♦♦	R* ♦♦♦♦	R* ♦♦♦♦	R* ♦♦♦♦	R* ♦♦♦♦[4]
S* ♦[3] W ♦♦♦	M, W irr[1]	W ♦♦♦♦	W ♦♦	S ♦ W ♦♦	M, W ♦♦♦♦	M, W ♦♦[3]
M ♦♦♦[1] W ♦	M ♦[1]	M ♦♦	M ♦ W irr	M ♦♦	M ♦♦	M irr
W ♦	M, W ♦♦[2]	W ♦	W ♦	W irr		W vag
W ♦♦[3]	M, W irr	W ♦♦♦	W ♦♦♦	W ♦♦♦♦	M, W ♦♦♦♦	M, W ♦♦[3]
R* ♦♦♦♦[4]		R* ♦♦♦♦	R* ♦♦♦♦	R* ♦♦♦♦	R* ♦♦♦♦	R* ♦♦♦♦
			R* ♦♦♦♦	S* ♦♦♦[6]		W vag
R* ♦♦♦♦ S* ♦♦♦ M, W ♦♦♦♦	R* ♦♦♦♦	R*, M, W ♦♦♦♦	R* ♦♦♦♦	S* ♦♦[6] M, W ♦♦♦♦	M, W ♦♦♦	vag
	vag		vag			
vag			vag		vag	
		S*, M, W ♦♦	vag[3]	R*, M, W ♦♦♦♦[6]	R*, M, W ♦♦♦♦[6]	S* ♦♦♦♦ R* ♦♦[4]
S*, M, W ♦♦♦♦	R* ♦♦♦♦	R* ♦♦♦♦	R* ♦♦♦♦	R* ♦♦♦♦	R* ♦♦♦♦	S* ♦♦ M, W ♦♦♦♦
				vag		

Italic type denotes "review" species.
Please report any sightings to Texas Bird Records Committee (see Appendix B).

* = Breeding
1 = More numerous in spring
2 = More numerous in fall
3 = More numerous in west
4 = More numerous in east
5 = Deep-water pelagic
6 = Local
7 = Extirpated from this range or believed extinct

Bird Species	Trans-Pecos	Panhandle and Western Plains	Edwards Plateau
❑ ORIOLE, Orchard	S* ♦♦♦	S*, M ♦♦	S* ♦♦
❑ Hooded	S* ♦♦	M vag	S* ♦♦
❑ Altamira			
❑ Audubon's			vag
❑ Baltimore	M ♦	S*, M ♦♦	M ♦♦
❑ Bullock's	S*, M ♦♦♦	S*, M ♦♦♦	S*, M ♦♦♦
❑ Scott's	S* ♦♦♦	M vag	S* ♦♦♦[3]
❑ GROSBEAK, *Pine*		W vag	
❑ FINCH, Purple	vag	W irr	M, W ♦
❑ Cassin's	W spor	W vag	vag[3]
❑ House	R* ♦♦♦♦	R* ♦♦♦	R* ♦♦♦
❑ CROSSBILL, Red	S, M, W irr	M, W irr	W irr
❑ *White-winged*		M, W vag	
❑ REDPOLL, *Common*		W vag	
❑ SISKIN, Pine	S*[6], M ♦♦ W spor	S* irr M, W ♦♦♦	M, W spor
❑ GOLDFINCH, Lesser	R* ♦♦♦	S*, M ♦♦ W vag	R* ♦♦♦
❑ *Lawrence's*	W vag		
❑ American	M, W ♦♦	S* ♦ M, W ♦♦♦	M, W ♦♦
❑ GROSBEAK, Evening	W irr	M, W spor	vag
❑ SPARROW, House	R* ♦♦♦♦	R* ♦♦♦♦	R* ♦♦♦♦

S = Summer	♦ ♦ ♦ ♦ = **Common.** Always present in significant numbers in the proper habitat.
M = Migrant	♦ ♦ ♦ = **Fairly Common.** A few are always present in the proper habitat.
W = Winter	♦ ♦ = **Uncommon.** Sometimes present in the proper habitat.
R = Resident	♦ = **Rare.** Occur regularly, but in small numbers; a good search can usually find one.
	irr = **Irregular.** Definitely not expected, but a few occur occasionally.
	spor = **Sporadic.** Not expected every year, but may occur in significant numbers.
D = Post-nesting Dispersal	vag = **Vagrant.** Well out of the species' normal range (extralimital).

Northern Plains	Pineywoods	Central Plains	Upper Coast	Coastal Bend	Brush Country	Rio Grande Valley
S* ♦♦ M ♦♦♦	S* ♦♦♦ M ♦♦♦♦[1]	S*, M ♦♦	S* ♦♦♦ M ♦♦♦♦	S* ♦ M ♦♦♦	S* ♦ M ♦♦♦	S* irr M ♦♦♦
		S ♦		S, M ♦	S* ♦♦	S*, M ♦♦[3] W ♦
				S* irr		R* ♦♦
				R* ♦♦	R* ♦♦	R* ♦♦
S* ♦♦[4] M ♦♦♦ W irr	S* irr M ♦♦♦♦[1] W irr	M ♦♦♦	M ♦♦♦♦ W irr	M ♦♦♦♦ W irr	M ♦♦♦	M ♦♦♦
S* ♦♦[3] M ♦♦♦ W irr		M ♦	W irr	S* ♦♦ M ♦♦♦	S* ♦♦ M ♦♦♦	S*, M ♦♦[3] W ♦
vag	vag				vag	W vag
W vag						
W spor	M, W ♦♦♦	W irr	W irr	W irr		W vag
W vag						
R* ♦♦♦		R* [6]	irr	R* ♦♦	R* ♦♦[3]	M, W vag
W irr		W spor	W vag			W vag
W vag						
W vag						
W spor	M, W ♦♦[1]	W spor	W spor	M, W spor	M, W spor	W spor
irr[3]		S ♦[3]	W vag	S*, M ♦♦ W irr	S*, M ♦♦ W irr	irr[3]
M, W ♦♦♦♦	S* irr M, W ♦♦♦♦	M, W ♦♦♦♦	M, W ♦♦♦♦	M ♦♦ W ♦♦♦♦	M ♦♦ W ♦♦♦	M, W ♦♦♦[3]
irr	M, W irr	vag	W irr			
R* ♦♦♦♦	R* ♦♦♦♦	R* ♦♦♦♦	R* ♦♦♦♦	R* ♦♦♦♦	R* ♦♦♦♦	R* ♦♦♦♦

Italic type denotes "review" species.
Please report any sightings to Texas Bird Records Committee (see Appendix B).

* = Breeding
1 = More numerous in spring
2 = More numerous in fall
3 = More numerous in west
4 = More numerous in east

5 = Deep-water pelagic
6 = Local
7 = Extirpated from this range or believed extinct

Selected References

GENERAL

American Ornithologists' Union. 1983. *The A.O.U. Check-list of North American Birds, 6th Ed.* Lawrence, Kans.: American Ornithologists' Union.

Graham, Gary L. 1992. *Texas Wildlife Viewing Guide.* Helena, Mont.: Falcon Publishing Co.

Kutac, Edward A. 1989. *Birder's Guide to Texas.* Houston: Gulf Publishing Co.

Lasley, Greg W., and Chuck Sexton. 1997. *Rare Birds of Texas Master List of Review Species.* Photocopy.

Mlodinow, Steven G., and Michael O'Brien. 1996. *America's 100 Most Wanted Birds.* Helena, Mont.: Falcon Publishing Co.

Oberholser, Harry C. 1974. *The Bird Life of Texas.* 2 vols. Austin: University of Texas Press.

Texas Ornithological Society. 1995. *Checklist of the Birds of Texas.* Austin: Texas Ornithological Society.

Tveten, John L. 1993. *The Birds of Texas.* Fredericksburg, Tex.: Shearer Publishing.

Wauer, Ro[land H.]. 1991. Profile of an ABA birder. *Birding,* June, 146–154.

NORTHERN PLAINS

Pulich, Warren M. 1988. *The Birds of North Central Texas.* College Station: Texas A&M University Press.

COASTAL TEXAS

Elwonger, Mark. 1995. *Finding Birds on the Central Texas Coast.* Victoria, Tex.: Mark Elwonger.

Holt, Harold R. 1993. *A Birder's Guide to the Texas Coast.* Colorado Springs, Colo.: American Birding Association.

Peake, Dwight E., and Mark Elwonger. 1996. A new frontier: pelagic birding in the Gulf of Mexico. *Winging It,* January, 1, 4–9.

Rappole, John H., and Gene W. Blacklock. 1985. *Birds of the Texas Coastal Bend: Abundance and Distribution.* College Station: Texas A&M University Press.

Texas Parks and Wildlife Department and Department of Transportation. 1996. *The Great Texas Coastal Birding Trail, Central Texas Coast* (map). Austin: Texas Parks and Wildlife Department.

RIO GRANDE VALLEY

Holt, Harold R. 1992. *A Birder's Guide to the Rio Grande Valley of Texas.* Colorado Springs, Colo.: American Birding Association.

SPECIFIC AREAS

Aransas National Wildlife Refuge

Jones, Barry. 1992. *A Birder's Guide to Aransas National Wildlife Refuge*. Albuquerque: Southwest Natural and Cultural Heritage Association.

Big Bend National Park

Wauer, Roland H. 1996. *A Field Guide to Birds of the Big Bend*. Houston: Gulf Publishers.

Wauer, Roland H. 1993. *The Visitor's Guide to the Birds of the Rocky Mountain National Parks, United States and Canada*. Santa Fe: John Muir Publications.

Wauer, Roland H. 1973. *Naturalist's Big Bend*. College Station: Texas A&M University Press.

Big Thicket

Ajilvsgi, Geyata. 1979. *Wild Flowers of the Big Thicket*. College Station: Texas A&M University Press.

Wauer, Roland H. 1994. *The Visitor's Guide to the Birds of the Central National Parks, United States and Canada*. Santa Fe: John Muir Publications.

El Paso Area

Paton, James N., and Barry R. Zimmer. 1996. *Birds and Birdfinding in the El Paso Area*. El Paso, Tex.: Paton and Zimmer.

Guadalupe Mountains

Wauer, Roland H. 1993. *The Visitor's Guide to the Birds of the Rocky Mountain National Parks, United States and Canada*. Santa Fe: John Muir Publications.

Lost Maples State Park

Osborne, June. 1994. *Birder's Guide to Concan*. Waco, Tex.: June Osborne.

Padre Island

Wauer, Roland H. 1994. *The Visitor's Guide to the Birds of the Central National Parks, United States and Canada*. Santa Fe: John Muir Publications.

Appendix A

PELAGIC BIRDING IN TEXAS WATERS

When Texas birders want to build their lists, they visit places like Boot Springs in Big Bend's Chisos Mountains, The Bowl in the Guadalupe Mountains, or Lake Tawakoni near Dallas in January. But just 70 miles off the coast is a rarely birded area that has greater potential for producing new and interesting sightings than the coastal and inland locations—the deep waters of the Gulf of Mexico.

Pelagic birding in Texas once was limited to documentation of dead or dying birds that washed or were blown ashore. While these strandings suggested more interesting birds beyond the Gulf horizon, few birders had the time, energy, funds, or inclination to search offshore in earnest.

Pelagic birding efforts in California waters helped that state close the gap between its bird list and that of Texas, which leads the United States in species recorded. But in Texas, birders have only recently made regular efforts to investigate what birds might occur over the deep Gulf waters.

Early excursions to explore the near-shore snapper banks and oil rigs produced new records of Cory's Shearwater, Masked Booby, and Pomarine Jaeger. But longer trips, begun in 1994, beyond the 100-fathom line, began to flood the Texas Bird Records Committee (TBRC) with records of Band-rumped Storm-Petrel, Audubon's Shearwater, and Bridled Tern.

Getting to deep water in Texas is a tedious and expensive process. The continental shelf is anywhere from 130 miles wide in the east to 45 miles wide in the south, so an affordable 15-knot crew boat from the central coast site of Port O'Connor might take four hours to get to deep water.

Pelagic birding is not for everyone. There are long periods of boredom. You and your binoculars can get soaked in salt spray and seas can be rough. Some folks lose their equilibrium and become seasick. Some lose their balance and fall down hard. It can be hours before you can get treatment if there is a medical emergency.

But many discoveries await the birder willing to make the trip. The northwestern Gulf of Mexico is often sprinkled with long weedlines and mats of sargassum, evidence that an eddy has been shed from the nearby Loop Current. Eddies and current rips carry food that attracts schools of tuna, whale sharks, whales, several species of dolphins, and sea turtles. Even sperm whales are occasionally sighted. Pelagic birds are also present, presumably feeding on tiny marine organisms.

In spring and fall, tired passerines making the trip across the Gulf often drop down to the boat, tempted to land and rest. But the attractions offshore to birders are the "regulars," including Band-rumped and Leach's Storm-Petrels, Cory's and Audubon's Shearwaters, and Bridled and Sooty Terns. Adding spice to the trip is the possibility of seeing an unusual wanderer, such as Black-capped Petrel; Greater, Sooty, or Manx Shearwater; Red-Billed Tropicbird; or Arctic Tern.

The following pelagic bird species have been reported or recorded in recent years:

Yellow-nosed Albatross*, vagrant
Black-capped Petrel*, vagrant

White-chinned Petrel*, vagrant
Cory's Shearwater, fairly common; May to Nov, vagrant in winter
Greater Shearwater*, rare
Sooty Shearwater*, rare
Manx Shearwater*, vagrant
Audubon's Shearwater, fairly common May to Sept
Wilson's Storm-Petrel*, vagrant April to June
Leach's Storm-Petrel*, uncommon May to Sept
Band-rumped Storm-Petrel, fairly common, May to early Sept
Red-billed Tropic-bird*, vagrant
Masked Booby, uncommon in summer and fall; rare in winter
Brown Booby*, vagrant
Red-footed Booby*, vagrant
Red Phalarope*, rare in migration
Pomarine Jaeger, common late Oct to May; rare June to Sept
Parasitic Jaeger, rare to uncommon migrant and winter visitor; rare in summer
Long-tailed Jaeger*, irregular fall migrant
Black-legged Kittiwake*, rare migrant, winter visitor
Sabine's Gull, irregular fall migrant
Arctic Tern*, vagrant
Bridled Tern, uncommon to rare in fall, winter, and spring
Sooty Tern, common summer; uncommon to rare in fall, winter, and spring
Brown Noddy*, vagrant
Black Noddy*, vagrant

* = Review species (see Appendix B)

DEEP-WATER TRIPS

Begun in 1994, the Texas Gulf Seabird Study Association has expanded the horizon of pelagic birding in Texas beyond the continental shelf. Future plans provide for at least one trip per month from June through September. Rough seas from October through May make trips impractical then. Charters currently depart from Port O'Connor, but the association is also considering departures from Freeport and Port Isabel. An annual newsletter, published in March, is available by writing Mark Elwonger at 405 W. Brazos, Victoria, TX 77901.

NEAR-SHORE TRIPS

As an alternative to the somewhat "punishing" deep-water trips, one might consider sharing passage with fishermen aboard a catamaran to the near-shore snapper banks approximately 20 miles offshore on the continental shelf. Sightings of Northern Gannets (winter), Masked Boobies, Magnificent Frigatebirds (summer and fall), Cory's Shearwaters, and Jaegers are possible. Charter information is available from The Fisherman's Wharf in Port Aransas, 800-605-5448. Additional offshore trips are available by special arrangement with Ray Little, HC 1, Box 347J12, Rockport, TX 78382; 512-729-8816.

Appendix B

TEXAS BIRD RECORDS COMMITTEE

The Texas Bird Records Committee (TBRC), a standing committee of the Texas Ornithological Society, is responsible for maintaining the official *Checklist of the Birds of Texas*. As of December 15, 1997, 605 species have been accepted, and another 11 species are pending. The TBRC secretary is Greg W. Lasley, 305 Loganberry Court, Austin, TX 78745-6527. Dr. Keith Arnold, Department of Wildlife and Fisheries Sciences, Texas A&M University, College Station, TX 77843-2258, serves on the committee representing the academic profession of ornithology.

The TBRC asks that all birders report any new or rare birds discovered in Texas. These include the following "review" species, generally those birds that have been recorded in Texas fewer than 5 times per year, over a 10-year average:

Red-throated Loon	Wandering Tattler	White-eared Hummingbird
Pacific Loon	Eskimo Curlew	Berylline Hummingbird
Yellow-billed Loon	Surfbird	Violet-crowned Hummingbird
Red-necked Grebe	Red-necked Stint	Costa's Hummingbird
Yellow-nosed Albatross	Sharp-tailed Sandpiper	Allen's Hummingbird
White-chinned Petrel	Purple Sandpiper	Elegant Trogon
Greater Shearwater	Curlew Sandpiper	Lewis's Woodpecker
Sooty Shearwater	Ruff	Ivory-billed Woodpecker
Manx Shearwater	Red Phalarope	(presumed extirpated in
Wilson's Storm-Petrel	Long-tailed Jaeger	Texas)
Leach's Storm-Petrel	Little Gull	Greenish Elaenia
Red-billed Tropicbird	Common Black-headed Gull	Tufted Flycatcher
Blue-footed Booby	Heermann's Gull	Greater Pewee
Brown Booby	Mew Gull	Dusky-capped Flycatcher
Red-footed Booby	California Gull	Sulphur-bellied Flycatcher
Jabiru	Thayer's Gull	Tropical Kingbird
Greater Flamingo	Iceland Gull	Thick-billed Kingbird
Trumpeter Swan	Slaty-backed Gull	Gray Kingbird
Brant	Western Gull	Fork-tailed Flycatcher
American Black Duck	Great Black-backed Gull	Rose-throated Becard
White-cheeked Pintail	Kelp Gull	Masked Tityra
Garganey	Black-legged Kittiwake	Gray-breasted Martin
Eurasian Wigeon	Sabine's Gull	Clark's Nutcracker
Harlequin Duck	Elegant Tern	Black-billed Magpie
Barrow's Goldeneye	Brown Noddy	Black-capped Chickadee
Masked Duck	Black Noddy	American Dipper
Snail Kite	Ruddy Ground-Dove	Northern Wheatear
Northern Goshawk	Ruddy Quail-Dove	Orange-billed Nightingale-
Crane Hawk	Mangrove Cuckoo	Thrush
Roadside Hawk	Snowy Owl	Clay-colored Robin
Short-tailed Hawk	Northern Pygmy-Owl	White-throated Robin
Collared Forest-Falcon	Mottled Owl	Rufous-backed Robin
Paint-billed Crake	Northern Saw-whet Owl	Varied Thrush
Spotted Rail	White-collared Swift	Aztec Thrush
Double-striped Thick-Knee	Green Violet-ear	Black Catbird
Collared Plover	Green-breasted Mango	Bohemian Waxwing
Northern Jacana	Broad-billed Hummingbird	Gray Silky-flycatcher

Yellow-green Vireo
Black-whiskered Vireo
Yucatan Vireo
Connecticut Warbler
Gray-crowned Yellowthroat
Red-faced Warbler
Slate-throated Redstart
Golden-crowned Warbler
Rufous-capped Warbler

Olive Warbler
Flame-colored Tanager
Crimson-collared Grosbeak
Blue Bunting
Yellow-faced Grassquit
Baird's Sparrow
Saltmarsh Sharp-tailed
 Sparrow
Golden-crowned Sparrow

Yellow-eyed Junco
Snow Bunting
Shiny Cowbird
Black-vented Oriole
Pine Grosbeak
White-winged Crossbill
Common Redpoll
Lawrence's Goldfinch

A second list includes species under special study by a subcommittee of the TBRC concerning their distribution and status in Texas. To assist in these studies, documentation is requested for the following species:

Clark's Grebe
Cory's Shearwater
Glossy Ibis
Muscovy Duck
Common Black-Hawk
Swainson's Hawk (Dec–Jan)

Aplomado Falcon
 (reintroduction program in
 progress)
Semipalmated Sandpiper
 (Dec–Jan)
Pomarine Jaeger

Parasitic Jaeger
Spotted Owl
Williamson's Sapsucker
Northern Shrike

A third list of "presumptive" species includes those that have been accepted by the TBRC but have not yet met the requirements for full acceptance on the Texas checklist (specimen, photo, or tape recording of at least one record). These include Murre species, White-crowned Pigeon, Berylline Hummingbird, Social Flycatcher, Crescent-chested Warbler, and Slate-throated Redstart.

Please prepare a report for any of the above birds found in Texas, using the TBRC report form on the following pages, and mail it to either Greg Lasley or Dr. Keith Arnold of the Texas Bird Records Committee.

Texas Ornithological Society

Texas Bird Records Committee
REPORT FORM

This form is intended as a convenience in reporting observations of rare or unusual birds. It may be used flexibly and need not be used at all except as a guideline. Attach additional sheets as necessary. **Please print in black ink or type.** Attach drawings, photos, etc., if possible. When complete, mail to: Greg W. Lasley, Secretary, Texas Bird Records Committee, 305 Loganberry Ct., Austin, TX 78745-6527 or Dr. Keith Arnold, Dept. of Wildlife and Fisheries Sciences, Texas A&M University, College Station, TX 77843-2258. Thank you!

1. Common and scientific name _____

_____

2. Number of individuals, sexes, ages, general plumage (e.g. two adults in breeding plumage)

_____

_____

3. Location _____ County _____ TX

4. Date and time when observed _____

5. Reporting observer and address _____

_____

_____

6. Other observers _____

_____

7. Light conditions _____

8. Optical equipment _____

9. Distance to bird _____

10. Duration of observation _____

11. Habitat (be specific) _____

_____

12. Description (include only what was actually seen, not what "should have been seen"). Include, if possible, body bulk, shape, bill, eye, plumage pattern, color, and other physical characteristics. Describe voice, behavior, and anything else that might help identify the bird.

_____

_____

_____

_____

_____

_____

_____

_____

13. How were similar species eliminated? _____

_____

_____

_____

14. Was it photographed? By whom? Attached? _____

_____

15. Previous experience with species _____

_____

_____

16. List any books or references used in identification:

(a) at time of observation _____

_____

(b) after observation _____

_____

17. This description written from:

_____ (a) notes made during observation

_____ (b) notes made after observation

_____ (c) memory

18. Are you positive of your observation? _____ If not, explain _____

_____

_____

19. Signature of reporter along with date and time of writing this account

_____

_____

Additional notes (please use extra sheets if necessary) _____

_____

_____

_____

_____

_____

_____

_____

_____

_____

_____

_____

Appendix C

CONTACTS

1. **FRANKLIN MOUNTAINS STATE PARK,** P.O. Box 200, Canutillo, TX 79835; 915-566-6441; fax, 915-566-6468; **FRED HERVEY WATER RECLAMATION PONDS,** City of El Paso, 11700 Railroad Drive, El Paso, TX 79995; 915-594-5720; also: El Paso/Trans-Pecos Audubon Society, P.O. Box 9655, El Paso, TX 79995; 915-532-9645 or 915-757-1876

2. **EL PASO VALLEY,** El Paso/Trans-Pecos Audubon Society, P.O. Box 9655, El Paso, TX 79995; 915-532-9645 or 915-757-1876

3. **HUECO TANKS STATE PARK,** 6900 Hueco Tanks Road, #1, El Paso, TX 79938; 915-857-1135; fax, 915-857-3628

4. **GUADALUPE MOUNTAINS NATIONAL PARK,** HC 60, Box 400, Salt Flat, TX 79847-9400; 915-828-3251; fax, 915-857-3628

5. **BALMORHEA LAKE** and **BALMORHEA STATE PARK,** Box 15, Toyahvale, TX 79786; 915-375-2370; fax, 915-375-2429

6. **DAVIS MOUNTAINS** and **DAVIS MOUNTAINS STATE PARK,** Box 1458, Fort Davis, TX 79734; 915-426-3337; fax, 915-426-2063

7. **MARATHON BASIN,** Marathon Chamber of Commerce, P.O. Box 163, Marathon, TX 79842; 915-386-4516

8. **BIG BEND RANCH STATE PARK,** P.O. Box 1220, Presidio, TX 79845; 915-229-3613; fax, 915-229-4814

9. **BIG BEND NATIONAL PARK,** Big Bend National Park, TX 79834; 915-477-2251; fax, 915-477-2357

10. **BLACK GAP WILDLIFE MANAGEMENT AREA,** HC 65, Box 433, Alpine, TX 79830; 915-376-2216; fax, 915-376-2246

11. **AMISTAD NATIONAL RECREATION AREA,** P.O. Box 420367, Del Rio, TX 78842-0367; 830-775-2491; fax, 830-775-7299; **SEMINOLE CANYON STATE PARK,** Box 820, Comstock, TX 78837; 915-292-4464; fax, 915-292-4596

12. **LAKE RITA BLANCA STATE PARK,** c/o Palo Duro Canyon State Park, Route 2, Box 285, Canyon, TX 79015; 806-488-2227; fax, 806-488-2556; **RITA BLANCA NATIONAL GRASSLAND,** U.S. Forest Service, 714 Main Street, Clayton, NM 88415; 505-374-9652; fax, 505-374-9664

13. **LAKE MEREDITH NATIONAL RECREATION AREA,** P.O. Box 1460, Fritch, TX 79036; 806-857-3151; fax, 806-857-2319

14. **LAKE MARVIN** and **GENE HOWE WILDLIFE MANAGEMENT AREA,** U.S. Forest Service, Black Kettle Ranger District, Route 1, Box 55-B, Cheyenne, OK 73628; 405-497-2143; fax, 405-497-2379

15. **BUFFALO LAKE NATIONAL WILDLIFE REFUGE,** P.O. Box 179, Umbarger, TX 79091; 806-499-3382; fax, 806-499-3254; **CANYON PRAIRIE DOG COLONY,** Canyon Chamber of Commerce, P.O. Box 8, Canyon, TX 79015; 806-655-1183

16. **PALO DURO CANYON STATE PARK,** Route 2, Box 285, Canyon, TX 79015; 806-488-2227; fax, 806-488-2556

17. **CAPROCK CANYONS STATE PARK,** P.O. Box 204, Quitaque, TX 79255; 806-455-1492; fax, 806-455-1254

18. **MULESHOE NATIONAL WILDLIFE REFUGE,** U.S. Fish and Wildlife Service, P.O. Box 549, Muleshoe, TX 79347; 806-946-3341; fax, 806-946-3317

19. **COPPER BREAKS STATE PARK,** Route 2, Box 480, Quanah, TX 79252; 817-839-4331; fax, 817-839-4332

20. **LUBBOCK: Buffalo Springs Lake,** Route 10, Box 400, Lubbock, TX 79409; 806-747-3352; **Lake Ransom, Twin Ponds, Boles Lake, and Mackenzie Park,** City of Lubbock Parks and Recreation Department, 916 Texas, Lubbock, TX 79401; 806-767-2687; also, **Llano Estacado Audubon Society,** P.O. Box 6066, Lubbock, TX 79493; 806-797-6690

21. **RED BLUFF LAKE,** Pecos Chamber of Commerce, P.O. Box 27, Pecos, TX 79772-0027; 915-445-2406; fax, 915-445-4653

22. **MONAHANS SANDHILLS STATE PARK,** Box 1738, Monahans, TX 79756; 915-943-2092; fax, 915-943-2806

23. **BIG SPRING: Big Spring State Park,** 1 Scenic Drive, Big Spring, TX 79720; 915-263-4931; fax, 915-263-3935; **Comanche Trail Park, Perimeter Road,** and **Sandhill Crane Sanctuary,** City of Big Spring, Box 3190, Big Spring, TX 79721; 915-763-8311

24. **LAKE COLORADO CITY STATE PARK,** 4582 FM 2836, Colorado City, TX 79512; 915-728-3931; fax, 915-728-3420

25. **ABILENE: Abilene State Park,** 150 Park Road 32, Tuscola, TX 79562; 915-572-3204; fax, 915-572-3008; **Kirby Lake** and **Abilene Waste Water Treatment Plant,** City of Abilene, Parks Department, 633 Walnut, Abilene, TX 79601; 915-676-6217

26. **SAN ANGELO STATE PARK,** 3900-2 Mercedes, San Angelo, TX 76901; 915-949-4757; fax, 915-949-2963

27. **GARNER STATE PARK,** HCR 70, Box 599, Concan, TX 78838; 830-232-6132; fax, 830-232-6139

28. **LOST MAPLES STATE PARK,** HC 01, Box 156, Vanderpool, TX 78885; 830-966-6213; fax, 830-966-6213

29. **SOUTH LLANO RIVER STATE PARK,** HC 15, Box 224, Junction, TX 76849; 915-446-3994; fax, 915-446-4534

30. **KERRVILLE-SCHREINER STATE PARK,** 2385 Bandera Highway, Kerrville, TX 78028; 830-257-5392; fax, 830-257-7275

31. **ENCHANTED ROCK STATE NATURAL AREA,** 16710 Ranch Road 965, Fredericksburg, TX 78624; 915-247-3903; fax, 915-247-4977

32. **LONGHORN CAVERNS STATE PARK,** Route 2, Box 23, Burnet, TX 78611; 512-756-4680; fax, 512-355-3273; **INKS LAKE STATE PARK,** Route 2, Box 31, Burnet, TX 78611; 512-793-2223; fax, 512-793-2065; **INKS DAM NATIONAL FISH HATCHERY,** U.S. Fish and Wildlife Service, Route 2, Box 320B, Burnet, TX 78611; 512-793-2474

33. **PEDERNALES FALLS STATE PARK,** Route 1, Box 450, Johnson City, TX 78636; 830-868-7304; fax, 830-868-4186

34. **BALCONES CANYONLANDS NATIONAL WILDLIFE REFUGE,** U.S. Fish and Wildlife Service, Hartland Bank Building, Suite 201, 10711 Burnet Road, Austin, TX 78758; 512-339-9432; fax, 512-339-9453

35. **AUSTIN: State Capitol Grounds; Eastwoods, Emma Long,** and **Zilker Metropolitan Parks;** and **Forest Ridge Preserve,** Austin Parks and Recreation, 200 South Lamar Boulevard, Austin, TX 78704; 512-499-6700; **Wild Basin Wilderness Preserve,** 805 North Capitol of Texas Highway, Austin, TX 78746; 512-327-7622; **Town Lake** and **Longhorn Dam,** Lower Colorado River Authority, P.O. Box 220, Austin, TX 78767; 800-776-5272

36. **GUADALUPE RIVER STATE PARK,** 3350 Park Road 31, Spring Branch, TX 78070; 830-438-2656; fax, 830-438-2229

37. **FRIEDRICH WILDERNESS PARK,** City of San Antonio, 21395 Milsa Road, San Antonio, TX 78256; 830-698-1057; fax, 830-698-4276

38. **LAKE ARROWHEAD STATE PARK,** Route 2, Box 260, Wichita Falls, TX 76301; 940-528-2211; fax, 940-528-2213

39. **HAGERMAN NATIONAL WILDLIFE REFUGE,** U.S. Fish and Wildlife Service, Route 3, Box 123, Sherman, TX 75092; 903-786-2826; fax, 903-786-3327

40. **POSSUM KINGDOM STATE PARK,** P.O. Box 70, Caddo, TX 76429; 940-549-1803; fax, 940-549-0741; **POSSUM KINGDOM DAM,** Brazos River Authority, HC 51, Box 23, Graford, TX 76449; 940-779-2321; fax, 940-779-3440

41. **LAKE MINERAL WELLS STATE PARK,** Route 4, Box 39C, Mineral Wells, TX 76067; 817-328-1171; fax, 817-328-8536

42. **FORT WORTH NATURE CENTER,** Park and Recreation Department, 9601 Fossil Ridge, Fort Worth, TX 76135; 817-237-1111; fax, 817-237-0653

43. **BENBROOK LAKE,** U.S. Army Corps of Engineers, Benbrook Project Office, P.O. Box 26619, Fort Worth, TX 76126-0619; 817-292-2400

44. **VILLAGE CREEK WASTEWATER TREATMENT PLANT,** City of Fort Worth, P.O. Box 870, Fort Worth, TX 76101; 817-265-4643; **RIVER LEGACY PARK,** River Legacy Foundation, 703 NW Green Oaks, Arlington, TX 76006; 817-860-6752; fax, 817-860-1595

45. **LEWISVILLE LAKE PARK,** Lewisville Parks and Leisure Services, 151 West Church Street, Lewisville, TX 75057; 972-219-3550

46. **PLANO OUTDOOR LEARNING CENTER,** also known as Holifield Science Learning Center, 3100 Shiloh Road, Plano, TX 75074-3145; 972-519-8761

47. **WHITE ROCK LAKE PARK,** Dallas Park and Recreation Department, 1500 Marilla, Room 6FN, Dallas, TX 75201; 214-670-4071; fax, 214-670-4078

48. **CEDAR HILL STATE PARK,** P.O. Box 2649, Cedar Hill, TX 75104; 972-291-3900; fax, 972-291-3900; **DALLAS NATURE CENTER,** 7171 Mountain Creek Parkway, Dallas, TX 75249; 972-296-1955

49. **SOUTHSIDE WATER TREATMENT PLANT,** City of Dallas, Southside Water Treatment Plant, 10011 Log Cabin Road, Dallas, TX 75253; 972-670-0408

50. **COOPER LAKE,** U.S. Army Corps of Engineers, P.O. Box 461, Cooper, TX 75432; 903-945-2108; **COOPER LAKE STATE PARK,** R.R. 3, Box 741, Sulphur, TX 75482; 903-945-5256; fax, 903-945-3059

51. **LAKE TAWAKONI,** Sabine River Authority, P.O. Box 310, Point, TX 75472-9998; 903-598-2216; fax, 903-598-2992

52. **LAKE BROWNWOOD STATE PARK,** R.R. 5, Box 160, Brownwood, TX 76801; 915-784-5223; fax, 915-784-6203

53. **DINOSAUR VALLEY STATE PARK,** Box 396, Glen Rose, TX 76043; 254-897-4588; fax, 254-897-3409

54. **CLEBURNE STATE PARK,** 5800 Park Road 21, Cleburne, TX 76031; 817-645-4215; fax, 817-641-6013

55. **MERIDIAN STATE PARK,** Box 188, Meridian, TX 76665; 254-435-2536; fax, 254-435-2076

56. **LAKE WHITNEY STATE PARK,** P.O. Box 1175, Whitney, TX 76692; 817-694-3793; fax, 817-694-6934; **WHITNEY LAKE,** Whitney Project Office, U.S. Army Corps of Engineers, P.O. Box 5038, Laguna Park, TX 76634; 816-624-3189

57. **WACO: Cameron Park,** Waco Parks and Recreation Department, P.O. Box 2570, Waco, TX 67602; 800-922-6386; **Waco Lake,** U.S. Army Corps of Engineers, Lake Waco, Route 10, Box 173-G, Waco, TX 76708-9602; 254-756-5359; **Water Treatment Plant** and **Tradinghouse Creek Reservoir,** Brazos River Authority, 4525 Lake Shore Drive, Waco, TX 76710; 254-776-1441

58. **MOTHER NEFF STATE PARK,** 1680 Texas 236 Highway, Moody, TX 76557; 817-853-2388; fax, 817-853-3903

59. **FORT PARKER STATE PARK,** Route 2, Box 95, Mexia, TX 76667; 254-562-5751; fax, 254-562-9787

60. **FAIRFIELD LAKE STATE PARK,** Route 2, Box 912, Fairfield, TX 75840; 903-389-4515; fax, 903-389-2130

61. **ATLANTA STATE PARK,** Route 1, Box 116, Atlanta, TX 75551; 903-796-6476; fax, 903-796-7609; **WRIGHT PATMAN LAKE,** U.S. Army Corps of Engineers, P.O. Box 1817, Texarkana, TX 75504-1817; 903-838-6396; fax, 903-826-0935

62. **DAINGERFIELD STATE PARK,** Route 1, Box 186B, Daingerfield, TX 75638; 903-645-2931; fax, 903-645-2921

63. **LAKE O' THE PINES,** U.S. Army Corps of Engineeers, P.O. Drawer W, Jefferson, TX 75657-0660; 903-665-2336; fax, 903-665-8441

64. **CADDO LAKE STATE PARK and WILDLIFE MANAGEMENT AREA,** Route 2, Box 15, Karnack, TX 75661; 903-679-3351; fax, 903-679-4006

65. **TYLER STATE PARK,** 789 Park Road 16, Tyler, TX 75706-9141; 903-597-5338; fax, 903-533-0818

66. **DAVY CROCKETT NATIONAL FOREST,** U.S. Forest Service, 1240 East Loop #304, Crockett, TX 75835; 409-544-2046; fax, 409-544-7806

67. **ANGELINA NATIONAL FOREST,** U.S. Forest Service, P.O. Box 756, Lufkin, TX 75901; 409-634-7709; fax, 409-634-8620; **SAM RAYBURN RESERVOIR,** U.S. Army Corps of Engineers, Route 3, Box 486, Jasper, TX 75951; 409-384-5716

68. **SABINE NATIONAL FOREST,** U.S. Forest Service, 201 South Palm, P.O. Box 227, Hemphill, TX 75948; 409-787-3870; fax, 409-787-3878; **TOLEDO BEND RESERVOIR,** Sabine River Authority of Texas, Route 1, Box 270, Burkeville, TX 75932; 409-787-3870

69. **SAM HOUSTON NATIONAL FOREST,** U.S. Forest Service, FM 1375, P.O. Drawer 1000, New Waverly, TX 77358; 409-344-6205; fax, 409-344-2123; **HUNTSVILLE STATE PARK,** P.O. Box 508, Huntsville, TX 77342-0508; 409-295-5644; fax, 409-295-9426

70. **LAKE LIVINGSTON STATE PARK,** Route 9, Box 1300, Livingston, TX 77351; 409-365-2201; fax, 409-365-3681

71. **MARTIN DIES, JR., STATE PARK,** Route 4, Box 174, Jasper, TX 75951; 409-384-5231; fax, 409-384-1437; **B. A. STEINHAGEN LAKE,** U.S. Army Corps of Engineers, 890 FM 92, Woodville, TX 77979-9631; 409-429-3491

72. **W. G. JONES STATE FOREST,** Texas Forest Service, Route 7, Box 151, Conroe, TX 77384; 409-273-2261; fax, 409-273-2282

73. **BIG THICKET: Big Thicket National Preserve,** 3785 Milam, Beaumont, TX 77701; 409-839-2689; fax, 409-839-2599; **Village Creek State Park,** P.O. Box 8575, Lumberton, TX 77711; 409-755-7322; fax, 409-755-3183; **Roy E. Larsen Sandyland Sanctuary,** The Nature Conservancy of Texas, P.O. Box 909, Silsbee, TX 77656-0909; 409-385-0445; fax, 409-385-4745; **Tyrrell Park,** City of Beaumont, P.O. Box 3827, Beaumont, TX 77704; 409-866-0023

74. **AUSTIN EAST: Hornsby Bend and Walnut Creek Wastewater Treatment Plants,** 2210 South FM 973, Austin, TX 78725; 512-929-1000; fax, 512-929-1004; **McKinney Falls State Park,** 5808 McKinney Falls Parkway, Austin, TX 78744; 512-389-8926; fax, 512-389-8998

75. **BASTROP** and **LAKE BASTROP STATE PARKS,** Box 512, Bastrop, TX 78602; 512-321-2102; fax, 512-321-3300; **BUESCHER STATE PARK,** P.O. Box 75, Smithville, TX 78957; 512-237-2241; fax, 512-237-2580

76. **ALCOA LAKE,** Aluminum Company of America, P.O. Box 472, Rockdale, TX 76567; 817-446-5811; **GRANGER LAKE,** U.S. Army Corps of Engineers Project Office, Route 1, Box 172, Granger, TX 76530-9801; 512-859-2668; fax, 512-859-2934.

77. **LAKE SOMERVILLE STATE PARK,** Route 1, Box 499, Somerville, TX 77879; 409-535-7763; fax, 409-535-7718; **SOMERVILLE LAKE,** U.S. Army Corps of Engineers, P.O. Box 549, Somerville, TX 77879; 409-596-1622

78. **PALMETTO STATE PARK,** Route 5, Box 201, Gonzales, TX 78629; 830-672-3266; fax, 830-672-2382

79. **FAYETTE LAKE,** Lower Colorado River Authority, P.O. Box 178, LaGrange, TX 78945; 409-968-6071; Park Concessionaires: for Oak Thicket, 409-249-3504; for Park Prairie, 409-249-3344

80. **ATTWATER PRAIRIE CHICKEN NATIONAL WILDLIFE REFUGE,** U.S. Fish and Wildlife Service, P.O. Box 519, Eagle Lake, TX 77434; 409-234-3021; fax, 409-234-3278

81. **HOUSTON WEST: Bear Creek Park,** Harris County Parks, 3535 War Memorial Drive, Houston, TX 77084; 281-496-2177; **Addicks Reservoir,** U.S. Army Corps of Engineers, 1042 Highway 6 South, Houston, TX 77077; 281-497-0740; **Spring Creek Park,** City of Tomball, 401 Market, Tomball, TX 77375; 281-351-5484

82. **LAKE TEXANA,** Lavaca-Navidad River Authority, Farm Road 3131, Edna, TX 77957; 512-782-2842; **LAKE TEXANA STATE PARK,** P.O. Box 760, Edna, TX 77957-0760; 512-782-5718; fax, 512-782-3625

83. **SEA RIM STATE PARK,** P.O. Box 1066, Sabine Pass, TX 77955; 409-971-2559; fax, 409-971-2917; **McFADDIN** and **TEXAS POINT NATIONAL WILDLIFE REFUGES,** c/o Anahuac National Wildlife Refuge, U.S. Fish and Wildlife Service, P.O. Box 278, Anahuac, TX 77514; 409-267-3337; fax, 409-267-4314; **SABINE WOODS,** Golden Triangle Audubon Society, P.O. Box 1292, Nederland, TX 77627; 409-768-1340

84. **ANAHUAC NATIONAL WILDLIFE REFUGE,** U.S. Fish and Wildlife Service, P.O. Box 278, Anahuac, TX 77514; 409-267-3337; fax, 409-267-4314

85. **HIGH ISLAND** and **BOLIVAR PENINSULA: Boy Scout Woods, Smith Oaks Sanctuary, and Bolivar Flats Shorebird Sanctuary,** Houston Audubon Society, 440 Wilchester, Houston, TX 77079; 713-932-1639; **Fort Travis Seashore Park,** 601 Tremont, Suite 100, Galveston, TX 77550; 409-766-2411; fax, 409-766-5412; also, Bolivar Peninsula Chamber of Commerce, P.O. Box 1170, Crystal Beach, TX; 800-386-8763

86. **GALVESTON ISLAND,** Galveston Island Convention and Visitors Bureau, 2106 Seawall Boulevard, Galveston Island, TX 77550; 409-763-4311; 800-351-4237; **GALVESTON ISLAND STATE PARK,** 14901 FM 3005, Galveston, TX 77554; 409-737-1222; fax, 409-737-5496

87. **ARMAND BAYOU: Armand Bayou Nature Center,** 8500 Bay Area Boulevard, Houston, TX 77258; 281-474-2551; **Bay Area Park,** 7500 Bay Area Boulevard, Houston, TX 77258; 281-326-6539

88. **HOUSTON EAST: Jesse H. Jones Park,** 20634 Kenswick Drive, Humble, TX 77338; 281-446-8588; fax, 281-446-5108; **Alexander Deussen Park,** Harris County Parks, 12303 Sonnier Drive, Houston, TX 77044; 281-591-6951; fax, 281-591-6961; **Sheldon Lake State Park,** 14320 Garrett Road, Houston, TX 77044; 281-456-9350; fax, 281-456-8216; **San Jacinto State Park,** 3527 Highway 134, LaPorte, TX 77571; 281-479-2431; fax, 281-479-5618; **Baytown Nature Center,** Baytown Parks and Recreation Department, 2407 Market Street, Baytown, TX 77520; 281-420-6597; fax, 281-420-5847

89. **BRAZOS BEND STATE PARK,** 21901 FM 762, Needville, TX 77461; 409-553-5101; fax, 409-553-5108

90. **BRAZORIA NATIONAL WILDLIFE REFUGE,** U.S. Fish and Wildlife Service, 1212 North Velasco, Suite 200, Angelton, TX 77512; 409-849-6062; fax, 409-849-5118

91. **SAN BERNARD NATIONAL WILDLIFE REFUGE,** U.S. Fish and Wildlife Service, 1212 North Velasco, Suite 200, Angelton, TX 77512; 409-849-6062; fax, 409-849-5118

92. **COLORADO RIVER DELTA,** Bay City Chamber of Commerce, P.O. Box 768, Bay City, TX 77404-0768; 409-245-8333

93. **PALACIOS,** Palacios Chamber of Commerce, 312 Main Street, Palacios, TX 77465; 512-972-2615

94. **PORT LAVACA** and **INDIANOLA,** Port Lavaca/Calhoun County Chamber of Commerce, P.O. Box 528, Port Lavaca, TX 77979; 512-552-2959 or 800-556-7678

95. **MATAGORDA ISLAND STATE PARK,** P.O. Box 117, Port O'Connor, TX 77982; 512-983-2215; fax, 512-983-4933

96. **PORT O'CONNOR** and **SEADRIFT,** Port Lavaca/Calhoun County Chamber of Commerce, P.O. Box 528, Port Lavaca, TX 77979; 512-552-2959 or 800-556-7678

97. **ARANSAS NATIONAL WILDLIFE REFUGE,** P.O. Box 100, Austwell, TX 77950-0100; 512-286-3559; fax, 512-286-3722

98. **GOOSE ISLAND STATE PARK,** HC 01, Box 105, Rockport, TX 78382; 512-729-2858; fax, 512-729-1041

99. **ROCKPORT-FULTON,** Rockport-Fulton Chamber of Commerce, 404 Broadway, Rockport, TX 78382; 800-242-0071

100. **PORT ARANSAS,** Port Aransas Convention and Visitors Bureau, 421 West Cotter, Port Aransas, TX 78375; 800-452-6278; Shamrock Islands Tour, Bill Gaskins, Woody's Sport Center; 512-749-6969

101. **MUSTANG ISLAND STATE PARK,** P.O. Box 326, Port Aransas, TX 78373; 512-749-5246; fax, 512-749-6455; **PACKERY CHANNEL COUNTY PARK,** Nueces County Parks and Recreation Department, 415 Mainer Road, Robstown, TX 78380; 512-387-5904

102. **PADRE ISLAND NATIONAL SEASHORE,** 9405 South Padre Island Drive, Corpus Christi, TX 78418-5597; 512-949-8173; fax, 512-937-9247

103. **CORPUS CHRISTI: Hans A. Suter Wildlife Area, Ocean Drive, Blucher Park, Botanical Gardens,** and **Elliot Landfill:** Corpus Christi Area Convention and Visitors Bureau, P.O. Box 2664, Corpus Christi, TX 78403; 800-678-6232; also, Coastal Bend Audubon Society, P.O. Box 3352, Corpus Christi, TX 78463 (no telephone number)

104. **WEST CORPUS CHRISTI,** Corpus Christi Area Convention and Visitors Bureau, P.O. Box 2664, Corpus Christi, TX 78403; 800-678-6232; **HAZEL BAZEMORE COUNTY PARK,** Nueces County Parks and Recreation Department, 415 Mainer Road, Robstown, TX 78380; 512-387-5904; also, Coastal Bend Audubon Society, P.O. Box 3352, Corpus Christi, TX 78463 (no telephone number)

105. **KINGSVILLE: Dick Kleberg Park, Santa Gertrudis Creek Bird Sanctuary,** and **L. E. Ramey County Park,** Dick Kleberg Park, Kingsville, TX 78364; 512-595-8591; also Kingsville Information Department, 1501 South Highway 77, Kingsville, TX 78364; 512-592-4121; **King Ranch,** King Ranch Visitor Center, P.O. Box 1090, Kingsville, TX 78364-1090; 512-592-8055; fax, 512-595-1344

106. **CAYO DEL GRULLO,** Kaufer-Hubert Memorial Park, Route 1, Box 67-D, Riviera, TX 78379; 512-297-5738

107. **PARK CHALK BLUFF,** Fred and Gwen Wallace, HCR 33, Box 566, Uvalde, TX 78801; 830-278-5515

108. **SAN ANTONIO SOUTH: Mitchell Lake,** San Antonio Audubon Society; 956-733-8306; **Braunig Lake,** 17500 Donop Road, San Antonio, TX 78112; 956-635-8289; and **Calaveras Lake,** 12991 Bernhardt Road, San Antonio, TX 78263; 956-635-8359

109. **CHAPARRAL WILDLIFE MANAGEMENT AREA,** P.O. Box 115, Artesia Wells, TX 78001; 830-676-3413; fax, 830-676-3413

110. **GOLIAD STATE PARK,** P.O. Box 727, Goliad, TX 77963; 512-645-3405; fax, 512-645-8538

111. **CHOKE CANYON STATE PARK,** P.O. Box 2, Calliham, TX 78007; 512-786-3868; fax, 512-786-3414

112. **LAKE CORPUS CHRISTI STATE PARK,** P.O. Box 1167, Mathis, TX 78367; 512-547-2635; fax, 512-547-7084

113. **LAKE CASA BLANCA STATE PARK,** P.O. Box 1844, Laredo, TX 78044; 956-725-3826; fax, 956-725-9987

114. **LAGUNA ATASCOSA NATIONAL WILDLIFE REFUGE,** U.S. Fish and Wildlife Service, Box 450, Rio Hondo, TX 70583; 956-748-3607; fax, 956-748-3609

115. **BOCA CHICA,** Las Palomas Wildlife Management Area, 410 North 13th, Edinburg, TX 78539; 956-383-8982; also Brownsville Chamber of Commerce, P.O. Box 752, Brownsville, TX 78522; 956-542-4341 or 800-626-2639; fax, 956-504-3348

116. **BROWNSVILLE: Sabal Palm Grove Audubon Center and Sanctuary,** P.O. Box 5052, Brownsville, TX 78523; 956-541-8034; **Tamaulipas Crow Sanctuary,** City of Brownsville Convention and Visitors Bureau, P.O. Box 4697, Brownsville, TX 78523; 956-546-3721 or 800-626-2639

117. **SANTA ANA NATIONAL WILDLIFE REFUGE,** U.S. Fish and Wildlife Service, Route 2, Box 202A, Alamo, TX 78516; 956-787-3079; fax, 956-787-8338

118. **BENTSEN–RIO GRANDE VALLEY STATE PARK,** P.O. Box 988, Mission, TX 78573-0988; 956-585-1107; fax, 956-585-3448; **ANZALDUAS COUNTY PARK,** Hidalgo County Parks, South Conway, Mission, TX 78572; 956-585-5311

119. **FALCON STATE PARK,** P.O. Box 2, Falcon Heights, TX 78545; 956-848-5327; fax, 956-848-5303

120. **SAN YGNACIO:** none

Internet address for changing area codes:

http://www.BELLCORE.com/NANP/

Index

Numbers in roman type refer to site descriptions.
Numbers in italic type refer to page numbers.

About the Authors

Ro Wauer (left) and Mark Elwonger (right) in the field on a winter day.

Ro WAUER is a retired naturalist and biologist for the National Park Service. He worked for six years at Big Bend National Park and at Crater Lake, Death Valley, Pinnacles, Zion, Great Smoky Mountains, and Virgin Islands national parks. During his 32-year career with the NPS, he also served as Chief of Natural Resources Management and Regional Chief Scientist. He is the author of 15 books, including *A Field Guide to Birds of the Big Bend, Naturalist's Big Bend, For All Seasons: A Big Bend Journal, Naturalist's Mexico, Birder's West Indies,* and a series of guides to the national parks of the U.S. and Canada. *Birding Texas* is Wauer's first book for Falcon. He lives in Victoria, Texas.

MARK ELWONGER is a professional engineer and the owner of a consulting firm in Victoria. He has been observing birds in Texas since 1970 and has helped compile a database of thousands of bird sightings made along the central Texas coast. He has helped organize and lead birding trips to Central and South America, Australia, and Asia, as well as pelagic trips off the Texas coast.

More Birding Guides From FALCON

FALCON will soon be releasing **FALCON** GUIDES for all major birding states. The following titles are available now, and others will be coming soon.

AVAILABLE NOW:
Birding Arizona
Birding Minnesota
Birding Montana
Birding Texas
Birding Utah

Also Available. . .

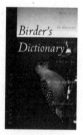

Birder's Dictionary
By Randall T. Cox, Illustrated by Todd Telander
A unique pocket reference for birders of all levels, or for anyone who needs quick reference to ornithological terms, such as editors, writers, and students.

Softcover, 4 ¹/₂ x 7 ¹/₂", illustrated.
Only $8.95 plus shipping.

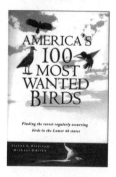

America's 100 Most Wanted Birds
By Stephen G. Mlodinow and Michael O'Brien
A guide to finding and seeing 100 of the rarest regularly occurring birds in the continental United States.

Softcover, 6 x 9", 40-page color section.
Only $24.95 plus shipping.

■ *To order any of these books, check with your local bookseller or call FALCON at* **1-800-582-2665**.

Visit us on the world wide web at:
www.falconguide.com

 **FALCON** GUIDES® are available for where-to-go hiking, mountain biking, rock climbing, walking, scenic driving, fishing, rockhounding, paddling, birding, wildlife viewing, and camping. We also have FalconGuides on essential outdoor skills and subjects and field identification. The following titles are currently available, but this list grows every year. For a free catalog with a complete list of titles, call FALCON toll-free at 1-800-582-2665.

SCENIC DRIVING GUIDES

Scenic Driving Alaska and the Yukon
Scenic Driving Arizona
Scenic Driving the Beartooth Highway
Scenic Driving California
Scenic Driving Colorado
Scenic Driving Florida
Scenic Driving Georgia
Scenic Driving Hawaii
Scenic Driving Idaho
Scenic Driving Michigan
Scenic Driving Minnesota
Scenic Driving Montana
Scenic Driving New England
Scenic Driving New Mexico
Scenic Driving North Carolina
Scenic Driving Oregon
Scenic Driving the Ozarks including the
    Ouchita Mountains
Scenic Driving Texas
Scenic Driving Utah
Scenic Driving Washington
Scenic Driving Wisconsin
Scenic Driving Wyoming
Back Country Byways
National Forest Scenic Byways
National Forest Scenic Byways II

HISTORIC TRAIL GUIDES

Traveling California's Gold Rush Country
Traveler's Guide to the Lewis & Clark Trail
Traveling the Oregon Trail
Traveler's Guide to the Pony Express Trail

WILDLIFE VIEWING GUIDES

Alaska Wildlife Viewing Guide
Arizona Wildlife Viewing Guide
California Wildlife Viewing Guide
Colorado Wildlife Viewing Guide
Florida Wildlife Viewing Guide
Idaho Wildlife Viewing Guide
Indiana Wildlife Vewing Guide
Iowa Wildlife Viewing Guide
Kentucky Wildlife Viewing Guide
Massachusetts Wildlife Viewing Guide
Montana Wildlife Viewing Guide
Nebraska Wildlife Viewing Guide
Nevada Wildlife Viewing Guide
New Hampshire Wildlife Viewing Guide
New Jersey Wildlife Viewing Guide
New Mexico Wildlife Viewing Guide
New York Wildlife Viewing Guide
North Carolina Wildlife Viewing Guide
North Dakota Wildlife Viewing Guide
Ohio Wildlife Viewing Guide
Oregon Wildlife Viewing Guide
Tennessee Wildlife Viewing Guide
Texas Wildlife Viewing Guide
Utah Wildlife Viewing Guide
Vermont Wildlife Viewing Guide
Virginia Wildlife Viewing Guide
Washington Wildlife Viewing Guide
West Virginia Wildlife Viewing Guide
Wisconsin Wildlife Viewing Guide

■ *To order any of these books, check with your local bookseller or call FALCON® at **1-800-582-2665***.

Visit us on the world wide web at:
www.falconguide.com

FALCON®

get

FALCON GUIDED

FALCON®

■ *To order any of these books, check with your local bookseller
or call FALCON® at **1-800-582-2665**.*

Visit us on the world wide web at:
www.falconguide.com